THE HUMAN ENCOUNTER

THE HUMAN ENCOUNTER

Readings in Education

SHELDON STOFF **HERBERT SCHWARTZBERG**

Queens College of the City University of New York

HARPER & ROW, PUBLISHERS

New York, Evanston, and London

THE HUMAN ENCOUNTER: *Readings in Education*

Library of Congress Catalog Card Number: 70-85972

To Matthew, Jesse, and Joshua.
May theirs be an education in balance.

Contents

Preface

One of the primary functions of the education of teachers today is to challenge students to develop the rationale and the insights necessary for making significant decisions. Beyond mere thinking and acting, students must be brought to a deep-seated sense of responsibility for their actions. They must become sensitive to the relationships among people, and to the complex of interactions that make community living possible. They must become aware of what is truly human and richly rewarding, in a world that too often is fearful, sterile, and mechanical. They must commit themselves to the most important career in our social order, one that is exciting, demanding, and dangerous. They must look forward to a lifetime of change and growth, in a revolutionary era that they will help to shape.

With these considerations in mind, we have attempted to vitalize teacher education through a series of informative and provocative positions and papers. Some are classical and historical, by way of background; others deal with the realities of the contemporary scene. Their analysis in the college classroom will help the teacher-to-be to visualize the relationship of theory to practice, in an atmosphere of immediacy and directness.

Two main goals are sought here: one, an awareness of those values that make for rich, warm, human living and learning; and, two, the development of the powers and the skills necessary to react positively and wholeheartedly to the management of the tasks of education. There are no "right" or "wrong" answers to the issues and the problems posed here; rather, there are fundamental questions to which the learner may consider relevant alternatives. Out of the resolution of these alternatives, decision will come.

Confrontation of the problem itself may call for exploration and information-gathering beyond the scope of this volume. Almost certainly, it will demand intense self-scrutiny. In time, there will be a response marked by wholeness and spontaneity. The learner's feelings of commitment and responsibility are free to take shape and direction. The end product is a consistent and characteristic way of acting and of being, a "life style." There is no longer need to vacillate, to "flounder."

The book has been divided into eight areas. Each affects the other and carries implications for the other. However, all of the chapters are manageable in terms of a concept of man as uniquely individual and completely human.

SHELDON STOFF
HERBERT SCHWARTZBERG

April 1969

PART ONE | *Basis for Action*

CHAPTER 1 Goals of Education

Education in any social order arises out of the need to perpetuate that society, to provide continuity in its ways of thinking, doing, and behaving, to reinforce its value structure, and to establish conformity to those norms that it sees as consequential and sustaining. At the same time, to insure its viability in a changing, demanding, and challenging modern world setting, it must seek to redirect and reconstruct the social order to meet the needs of the future.

Education in a democratic society is of a particular hue and tone. It is infused with a certain vision of man, of what he is and what he may become. It subscribes to ends that are describable in words such as *freedom, justice,* and *equality*. It is charged with the responsibility for translating these words and the concepts for which they stand into reality. It must determine the means by which this will be achieved. In its mind's eye, it must picture clearly the person who is the tangible embodiment of the democratic concepts and ideals. Education has meaning only in terms of human flesh and blood. Individuality is clearly the focus of concern.

No teacher can operate without a philosophy of education. To have a philosophy, one must be a philosopher, a "lover of wisdom," as Sawyer has pointed out. The two key words, *love* and *wisdom,* are particularly applicable to education at this point in its history; they seem seldom to have been heard less frequently.

Quite deliberately, to encourage the adoption of a stance, the positions offered in this chapter demand scrutiny of a variety of goals for education, some broad, some narrow; some pragmatic, some poetic. Working through to a philosophy of education means to see education whole, to have the insights, the sentiments and the convictions that enable one to react unhesitatingly and truthfully to all situations in a manner in tune with one's being.

Having clearly in mind the goals of education places what follows in subsequent chapters in clearer perspective. This perspective makes the history of education the bearer of insights and the source of object lessons. It causes contemporary problems to become alive and challenging and, out of breadth of vision, capable of resolution.

The informed and militant educator of today no longer simply follows the lead of others; he accepts the responsibility for speaking out in a strong, clear voice in educational decision-making. He is deeply committed to a posture that challenges the past. He insists upon the purposes of education and the role of the educator. He is an activist who is willing to pay the price for being "'where the action is." He is determined to help channel the direction in which the action goes.

JAMES B. CONANT | *The American High School Today*

In the half-century that has elapsed, there have been no drastic changes in the basic pattern of education in either Europe or the United States. But in two respects the American pattern has diverged even more from that to be found in other countries; certain unique characteristics have been emphasized, so to speak. The percentage of youth attending a college or university has jumped from 4 to 35, and, at the same time, the percentage enrolled in grades eleven to twelve of the high school has about doubled. In 1910, only 35 per cent of the seventeen-year-olds were in school; today, the corresponding figure is over 70 per cent. These changes could easily have been predicted in 1900 by a student of American Education. He would already have seen how enormous was the power of the twin ideals of equality of opportunity and equality of status; it was evident that the American people had come to believe that more education provided the means by which these ideals were to be realized. But two other factors also played a role. First, there was the urge for institutional expansion—the drive for larger faculties and student bodies in the colleges and universities; fifty years ago expansion was more than welcomed. Second, there was a radical change in the picture regarding the employment of youth. When this century began, approximately half of the boys and girls fifteen years of age were not attending school; many were at work. Thirty years later the percentage of this group attending school had reached 85. This alteration was not a consequence of state laws raising the school-leaving age; the laws were rather a consequence of profound economic and social changes. To explore adequately the background of this shift in the American scene would require many pages; suffice it to remind the reader that in the second decade of this century the campaign against child labor was being pushed vigorously at the state and national levels. Today, as a result of laws affecting employment, as well as the attitude of management and labor, it is difficult for boys even at the age of seventeen to obtain many types of jobs. In European countries three quarters or more of the youth go to work at fourteen or fifteen years of age. (pp. 6–7)

Thousands of comprehensive high schools of considerable size exist throughout the United States. Though generalization about American public education is highly dangerous (and I shall avoid it as far as possible

---

Reprinted from James B. Conant, *The American High School Today* (New York: McGraw-Hill Book Co., 1959), pp. 6–77 *passim,* with permission of the author and the Educational Testing Service.

in this report), I believe it accurate to state that a high school accommodating all the youth of a community is typical of American public education. I think it safe to say that the comprehensive high school is characteristic of our society and further that it has come into being because of our economic history and our devotion to the ideals of equality of opportunity and equality of status.

THE QUESTION TO BE ANSWERED

As I indicated in Section I of this report, the comprehensive high school is an American development of this century. It has no equivalent, so far as I am aware, in any European country. If the high school is of sufficient size and located in a community where parental pressure for preparing for college is not overriding, those boys and girls who desire to pursue education beyond the high school level will be in a minority. The question arises whether, being in a minority, such students can obtain an adequate education. Stating it another way, one can raise the question whether, under one roof and under the same management, it is possible for a school to fulfill satisfactorily three functions: Can a school at one and the same time provide a good general education for all the pupils as future citizens of a democracy, provide effective programs for the majority to develop useful skills, and educate adequately those with a talent for handling advanced academic subjects—particularly foreign languages and advanced mathematics? The answer to this question would seem to be of considerable importance for the future of American education. If the answer were clearly in the negative, then a radical change in the structure of American public secondary education would be in order. If the students in a given geographic area who have the ability to profit from the study of foreign languages and advanced mathematics on the high school level cannot obtain an adequate education in a comprehensive high school, then one can argue that separate high schools for these students should be maintained, as is now the case in some of the large eastern cities. On the other hand, if the answer is in the affirmative, then no radical change in the basic pattern of American education would seem to be required. (pp. 14–15)

AN EXAMINATION OF COMPREHENSIVE HIGH SCHOOLS IN EIGHTEEN STATES

To repeat, the three main objectives of a comprehensive high school are: *first,* to provide a general education for all the future citizens; *second,* to provide good elective programs for those who wish to use their acquired skills immediately on graduation; *third,* to provide satisfactory programs for those whose vocations will depend on their subsequent education in a college or university. If one could find a single comprehensive high school in the United States in which all three objectives were reached in a highly satisfactory manner, such a school might be taken as a model or pattern. Furthermore, unless there were some especially favorable local features which enabled such a school to attain these three objectives, the characteristics found might be developed in all the other schools of sufficient size in the United States. (p. 17)

ELIMINATION OF THE SMALL HIGH SCHOOL—A TOP PRIORITY

Most of the schools visited by me and my staff during this past year have had graduating classes of one hundred or more. From what I observed in these schools, in the two schools noted with graduating classes of less than one hundred, and in a much smaller school I visited, I am convinced small high schools can be satisfactory only at an exorbitant expense. The truth of this statement is evident if one considers the distribution of academic talent in the school which serves all the youth of a community. It will be a rare district where more than 25 per cent of a high school class can study with profit twelfth-grade mathematics, physics, and a foreign language for four years (assuming that standards are maintained). If a school has a twelfth grade of only forty and if indeed only a quarter of the group can handle the advanced subjects effectively, instruction in mathematics, science, and foreign languages would have to be provided for a maximum of ten students. If the girls shy away from the mathematics and science as they do in most of the schools I visited, the twelfth-grade mathematics classes may be as small as six or seven. To provide adequate teachers for specialized subjects is extremely expensive. Furthermore, to maintain an interest in academic subjects among a small number is not always easy. (p. 37)

There are three requisites for the successful operation of a high school: *first,* a school board composed of intelligent, honest, devoted citizens who understand that their function is policy-making and not administration; *second,* a first-rate superintendent; *third,* a good principal. Without a good school board the situation is almost hopeless. If members of a school board become involved in the appointment of teachers and in other matters of patronage, the maintenance of good morale in the teaching staff becomes almost impossible, however excellent may be the superintendent and the principal. Given a good school board and strong leadership by the superintendent and principal, an excellent group of teachers will be recruited, and it is hardly necessary to emphasize that on the quality of the teachers (assuming wise leadership) the quality of the education must ultimately depend.

Probably one of the most important factors in determining whether a high school is providing adequately for the education of the academically talented is the attitude of the community. Too much emphasis on basketball, football, and marching bands may affect the decisions of the school board, the administrators, and the teachers; and, often equally important, community activities may take up too much of the students' time. (pp. 38–39)

RECOMMENDATION 1: THE COUNSELING SYSTEM

There should be one full-time counselor (or guidance officer) for every two hundred fifty to three hundred pupils in the high school. The counselors should have had experience as teachers but should be devoting virtually full time to the counseling work; they should be familiar with the use of tests and measurements of the aptitudes and achievement of pupils. (p. 44)

RECOMMENDATION 2: INDIVIDUALIZED PROGRAMS

It should be the policy of the school that every student has an individualized program; there would be no classification of students according to clearly defined and labeled programs or tracks such as "college-preparatory," "vocational," "commercial." (p. 46)

RECOMMENDATION 3: REQUIRED PROGRAMS FOR ALL

General education

The requirements for graduation for all students should be as follows:

four years of English, three or four years of social studies—including two years of history (one of which should be American history—and a senior course in American problems or American government—one year of mathematics in the ninth grade (algebra or general mathematics), and at least one year of science in the ninth or tenth grade, which might well be biology or general physical science. (p. 47)

RECOMMENDATION 4: ABILITY GROUPING

In the required subjects and those elected by students with a wide range of ability, the students should be grouped according to ability, subject by subject. (p. 49)

RECOMMENDATION 5: A SUPPLEMENT TO A HIGH SCHOOL DIPLOMA

The awarding of a diploma is evidence only that a student has (1) completed the required work in general education to the best of his ability, and (2) had finished satisfactorily a certain sequence of elective courses. In addition to the diploma, each student should be given a durable record of the courses studied in four years and the grades obtained. The existence of such a record should be well publicized. (p. 50)

RECOMMENDATION 6: ENGLISH COMPOSITION

The time devoted to English composition during the four years should occupy about half the total time devoted to the study of English. Each student should be required to write an average of one theme a week. (p. 50)

RECOMMENDATION 7: DIVERSIFIED PROGRAMS FOR THE DEVELOPMENT OF MARKETABLE SKILLS

Programs should be available for girls interested in developing skills in typing, stenography, the use of clerical machines, home economics, or a specialized branch of home economics which through further work in college might lead to the profession of dietitian. Distributive education should be available if the retail shops in the community can be persuaded to provide suitable openings. If the community is rural, vocational agriculture should be included. For boys, depending on the community, trade and industrial programs should be available.

As stated in Recommendation 3, the students enrolled in programs which develop marketable skills should also be enrolled in English, social studies, and other courses required for graduation. Furthermore, efforts should be made to prevent isolation from the other students. (pp. 51–52)

RECOMMENDATION 8: SPECIAL CONSIDERATION FOR THE VERY SLOW READERS

Those in the ninth grade of the school who read at a level of the sixth grade or below should be given special consideration. These pupils should be instructed in English and the required social studies by special teachers who are interested in working with such students and who are sympathetic to their problems. Remedial reading should be part of the work, and special types of textbooks should be provided. The elective programs of these pupils should be directed toward simple vocational work, and they should be kept out of the regular vocational programs for boys, the distributive education program, and the regular commercial program for girls. These students should not be confused with mentally retarded students. The education of the mentally retarded is a special problem which in some states is also handled in the regular high school through special instruction and the use of special state funds. (p. 55)

RECOMMENDATION 9: THE PROGRAMS OF THE ACADEMICALLY TALENTED

Four years of mathematics, four years of one foreign language, three years of science, in addition to the required four years of English and three years of social studies; a total of eighteen courses with homework to be taken in four years. This program will require at least fifteen hours of homework each week. (p. 57)

RECOMMENDATION 10: HIGHLY GIFTED PUPILS

For the highly gifted pupils some type of special arrangement should be made. These pupils of high ability, who constitute on a national basis about 3 per cent of the student population. . . . (p. 62)

RECOMMENDATION 11: THE ACADEMIC INVENTORY

In order to provide meaningful statistics about the education of the academically talented, a school board through the superintendent should ask the principal each year to provide an academic inventory. As explained earlier, the academic inventory summarizes the programs of the academically talented students in the senior class without giving their names. (pp. 63–64)

RECOMMENDATION 12: ORGANIZATION OF THE SCHOOL DAY

The school day should be so organized that there are at least six periods in addition to the required physical education and driver education which in many states occupy at least a period each day. (p. 64)

RECOMMENDATION 13: PREREQUISITES FOR ADVANCED ACADEMIC COURSES

Standards in advanced courses should be such that those who enroll in each successive course of a sequence have demonstrated the ability required to handle that course. (p. 65)

RECOMMENDATION 14: STUDENTS SHOULD NOT BE GIVEN A RANK IN CLASS ACCORDING TO THEIR GRADES IN ALL SUBJECTS

In many schools, it is customary to designate a rank in class on graduation as determined by the marks received; the position of valedictorian is usually held by the student whose rank is number one. The ranking is calculated by averaging the grades in all subjects taken during the four years. I have found that in many schools the desire to rank high has led bright students to elect easy courses in order to obtain high grades. (p. 66)

RECOMMENDATION 15: ACADEMIC HONORS LIST

At the end of each marking period, a list should be published of the students who had elected courses recommended for the academically talented and had made an average grade of B. On graduation a notation might be made on the diploma if a student had placed on the academic honors list in all four years.

In order to provide an incentive for the election of a meaningful nonacademic sequence, those students whose achievement was outstanding in the courses that are usually labeled "commercial" or "vocational" should receive some special recognition. (p. 67)

RECOMMENDATION 16: DEVELOPMENTAL READING PROGRAM

A school should have the equipment for a developmental reading program. (p. 67)

RECOMMENDATION 17: SUMMER SCHOOL

The school board should operate a tuition-free summer school in which courses are available not only for students who have to repeat a subject, but also for the bright and ambitious students who wish to use the summer to broaden the scope of their elective programs. (p. 68)

RECOMMENDATION 18: FOREIGN LANGUAGES

The school board should be ready to offer a third and fourth year of a foreign language, no matter how few students enroll. (p. 69)

RECOMMENDATION 19: SCIENCE COURSES

All students should obtain some understanding of the nature of science and the scientific approach by a required course in physical science or biology. This course should be given in at least three sections grouped by ability. (p. 73)

RECOMMENDATION 20: HOMEROOMS

For the purpose of developing an understanding between students of different levels of academic ability and vocational goals, homerooms should be organized in such a way as to make them significant social units in the school. (p. 74)

RECOMMENDATION 21: TWELFTH-GRADE SOCIAL STUDIES

In the twelfth grade a course on American problems or American government should be required. (p. 75)

THE SMALL HIGH SCHOOL

The enrollment of many American public high schools is too small to allow a diversified curriculum except at exorbitant expense. The prevalence of such high schools—those with graduating classes of less than one hundred students—constitutes one of the serious obstacles to good secondary education throughout most of the United States. I believe such schools are not in a position to provide a satisfactory education for any group of their students—the academically talented, the vocationally oriented, or the slow reader. (p. 77)

DISCUSSION QUESTIONS

1. Do you agree with Conant's objectives for a comprehensive high school, in view of the goals that you would set for our democratic society?
2. Are Conant's objectives stated clearly enough to furnish a workable guide?
3. Would Conant's program fulfill his objectives?
4. Do you believe that Conant's program would promote intergroup understanding and fluidity?

MARTIN BUBER | *The Education of Character*

I

Education worthy of the name is essentially education of character. For the genuine educator does not merely consider individual functions of his pupil, as one intending to teach him only to know or be capable of certain definite things; but his concern is always the person as a whole, both in the

Reprinted from Martin Buber, *Between Man and Man* (New York: The Macmillan Co., 1965), pp. 104–117.

actuality in which he lives before you now and in his possibilities, what he can become. But in this way, as a whole in reality and potentiality, a man can be conceived either as personality, that is, as a unique spiritual-physical form with all the forces dormant in it, or as character, that is, as the link between what this individual is and the sequence of his actions and attitudes. Between these two modes of conceiving the pupil in his wholeness there is a fundamental difference. Personality is something which in its growth remains essentially outside the influence of the educator; but to assist in the moulding of character is his greatest task. Personality is a completion, only character is a task. One may cultivate and enhance personality, but in education one can and one must aim at character.

However—as I would like to point out straightaway—it is advisable not to over-estimate what the educator can even at best do to develop character. In this more than in any other branch of the science of teaching it is important to realize, at the very beginning of the discussion, the fundamental limits to conscious influence, even before asking what character is and how it is to be brought about.

If I have to teach algebra I can expect to succeed in giving my pupils an idea of quadratic equations with two unknown quantities. Even the slowest-witted child will understand it so well that he will amuse himself by solving equations at night when he cannot fall asleep. And even one with the most sluggish memory will not forget, in his old age, how to play with x and y. But if I am concerned with the education of character, everything becomes problematic. I try to explain to my pupils that envy is despicable, and at once I feel the secret resistance of those who are poorer than their comrades. I try to explain that it is wicked to bully the weak, and at once I see a suppressed smile on the lips of the strong. I try to explain that lying destroys life, and something frightful happens: the worst habitual liar of the class produces a brilliant essay on the destructive power of lying. I have made the fatal mistake of giving instruction in ethics, and what I said is accepted as current coin of knowledge; nothing of it is transformed into character-building substance.

But the difficulty lies still deeper. In all teaching of a subject I can announce my intention of teaching as openly as I please, and this does not interfere with the results. After all, pupils do want, for the most part, to learn something, even if not overmuch, so that a tacit agreement becomes possible. But as soon as my pupils notice that I want to educate their characters I am resisted precisely by those who show most signs of genuine independent character: they will not let themselves be educated, or rather, they do not like the idea that somebody wants to educate them. And those, too, who are seriously labouring over the question of good and evil, rebel when one dictates to them, as though it were some long established truth, what is good and what is bad; and they rebel just because they have experienced over and over again how hard it is to find the right way. Does it follow that one should keep silent about one's intention of educating character, and act by ruse and subterfuge? No; I have just said that the difficulty lies deeper. It is not enough to see that education of character is not introduced into a lesson in class; neither may one conceal it in cleverly arranged intervals. Education cannot tolerate such politic action. Even if the pupil does not notice the hidden motive it will have its negative effect on the actions of the teacher himself by depriving him of the directness which is his strength. Only in his whole being, in all his spontaneity can the educator truly affect the whole being of his pupil. For educating characters you do not need a moral genius, but you do need a man who is wholly alive and able to communicate himself directly to his fellow beings. His aliveness streams out to them and affects them most strongly and purely when he has no thought of affecting them.

The Greek word *character* means impression. The special link between man's being and his appearance, the special connexion between the unity of what he is and the sequence of his actions and attitudes is impressed on his still plastic substance. Who does the impressing? Everything does: nature and the social context, the house and the street, language and custom, the world of history and the world of daily news in the form of rumors, of broadcast and newspaper, music and technical science, play and dream—everything together. Many of these factors exert their influence by stimulating agreement, imitation, desire, effort; others by arousing questions, doubts, dislike, resistance. Character is formed by the interpenetration of all those multifarious, opposing influences. And yet, among this infinity of form-giving forces the educator is only one element among innumerable others, but distinct from them all by his will to take part in the stamping of character and by his consciousness that he represents in the eyes of the growing person a certain selection of what is, the selection of what is "right," of what should be. It is in this will and this consciousness that his vocation as an educator finds its fundamental expression. From this the genuine educator gains two things: first, humility, the feeling of being only one element amidst the fullness of life; only one single existence in the midst of all the tremendous inrush of reality on the pupil; but secondly, self-awareness, the feeling of being therein the only existence that wants to affect the whole person, and thus the feeling of responsibility for the selection of reality which he represents to the pupil. And a third thing emerges from all this, the recognition that in this realm of the education of character, of wholeness, there is only one access to the pupil: his confidence. For the adolescent who is frightened and disappointed by an unreliable world, confidence means the liberating insight that there is human truth, the truth of human existence. When the pupil's confidence has been won, his resistance against being educated gives way to a singular happening: he accepts the educator as a person. He feels he may trust this man, that this man is not making a business out of him, but is taking part in his life, accepting him before desiring to influence him. And so he learns to ask.

The teacher who is for the first time approached by a boy with somewhat defiant bearing, but with trembling hands, visibly opened-up and fired by a daring hope, who asks him what is the right thing in a certain situation—for instance, whether in learning that a friend has betrayed a secret entrusted to him one should call him to account or be content with entrusting no more secrets to him—the teacher to whom this happens realizes that this is the moment to make the first conscious step towards education of character; he has to answer, to answer under a responsibility, to give an answer which will probably lead beyond the alternatives of the question by showing a third possibility which is the right one. To dictate what is good and evil in general is not his business. His business is to answer a concrete question, to answer what is right and wrong in a given situation. This, as I have said, can only happen in an atmosphere of confidence. Confidence, of course, is not won by the strenuous endeavour to win it, but by direct and ingenuous participation in the life of the people one is dealing with—in this case in the life of one's pupils—and by assuming the responsibility which arises from such participation. It is not the educational intention but it is the meeting which is educationally fruitful. A soul suffering from the contradictions of the world of human society, and of its own physical existence, approaches me with a question. By trying to answer it to the best of my knowledge and conscience I help it to become a character that actively overcomes the contradictions.

If this is the teacher's standpoint towards his pupil, taking part in his life and conscious of responsibility, then everything that passes between them can, without any deliberate or politic intention, open a way to the education of character: lessons and games, a conversation about quarrels in the class, or about the problems of a world-war. Only, the teacher must not forget the limits of education; even when he enjoys confidence he cannot always expect agreement. Confidence implies a break-through from reserve, the bursting of the bonds which imprison an unquiet heart. But it does not imply unconditional agreement. The teacher must never forget that conflicts too, if only they are decided in a healthy atmosphere, have an educational value. A conflict with a pupil is the supreme test for the educator. He must use his own insight wholeheartedly; he must not blunt the piercing impact of his knowledge, but he must at the same time have in readiness the healing ointment for the heart pierced by it. Not for a moment may he conduct a dialectical manoeuvre instead of the real battle for truth. But if he is the victor he has to help the vanquished to endure defeat; and if he cannot conquer the self-willed soul that faces him (for victories over souls are not so easily won), then he has to find the word of love which alone can help to overcome so difficult a situation.

II

So far I have referred to those personal difficulties in the education of character which arise from the relation between educator and pupil, while for the moment treating character itself, the object of education, as a simple concept of fixed content. But it is by no means that. In order to penetrate to the real difficulties in the education of character we have to examine critically the concept of character itself.

Kerschensteiner in his well-known essay on *The Concept and Education of Character* distinguished between "character in the most general sense," by which he means "a man's attitude to his human surroundings, which is constant and is expressed in his actions," and real "ethical character," which he defines as "a special attitude, and one which in action gives the preference before all others to absolute values." If we begin by accepting this distinction unreservedly—and undeniably there is some truth in it—we are faced with such heavy odds in all education of character in our time that the very possibility of it seems doubtful.

The "absolute values" which Kerschensteiner refers to cannot, of course, be meant to have only subjective validity for the person concerned. Don Juan finds absolute and subjective value in seducing the greatest possible number of women, and the dictator sees it in the greatest possible accumulation of power. "Absolute validity" can only relate to universal values and norms, the existence of which the person concerned recognizes and acknowledges. But to deny the presence of universal values and norms of absolute validity—that is the conspicuous tendency of our age. This tendency is not, as is sometimes supposed, directed merely against the sanctioning of the norms by religion, but against their universal character and absolute validity, against their claim to be of a higher order than man and to govern the whole of mankind. In our age values and norms are not permitted to be anything but expressions of the life of a group which translates its own needs into the language of objective claims, until at last the group itself, for example a nation, is raised to an absolute value—and moreover to the only value. Then this splitting up into groups so pervades the whole of life that it is no longer possible to re-establish a sphere of values common to a mankind, and a commandment to mankind is no longer observed. As this tendency grows the basis for the development of what Kerschensteiner means by moral character steadily diminishes. How, under these circumstances, can the task of educating character be completed?

At the time of the Arab terror in Palestine, when there were single Jewish acts of reprisal, there must have been many discussions between teacher and pupils on the question: Can there be any suspension of the Ten Commandments, i.e. can murder become a good deed if committed in the interest of one's own group? One such discussion was once repeated to me.

The teacher asked: "When the commandment tells you 'Thou shalt not bear false witness against thy neighbour,' are we to interpret it with the condition, 'provided that it does not profit you'?" Thereupon one of the pupils said, "But it is not a question of my profit, but of the profit of my people." The teacher: "And how would you like it, then, if we put our condition this way: 'Provided that it does not profit your family'?" The pupil: "But family—that is still something more or less like myself; but the people—that is something quite different; there all questions of I disappears." The teacher: "Then if you are thinking, 'we want victory,' don't you feel at the same time, 'I want victory'?" The pupil: "But the people, that is something infinitely more than just the people of to-day. It includes all past and future generations." At this point the teacher felt the moment had come to leave the narrow compass of the present and to invoke historical destiny. He said: "Yes, all past generations. But what was it that made those past generations of the Exile live? What made them outlive and overcome all their trials? Wasn't it that the cry 'Thou shalt not' never faded from their hearts and ears?" The pupil grew very pale. He was silent for a while, but it was the silence of one whose words threatened to stifle him. Then he burst out: "And what have we achieved that way? This!" And he banged his fist on the newspaper before him, which contained the report on the British White Paper. And again he burst out with "Live? Outlive? Do you call that life? We want to live!"

I have already said that the test of the educator lies in conflict with his pupil. He has to face this conflict and, whatever turn it may take, he has to find the way through it into life, into a life, I must add, where confidence continues unshaken—more, is even mysteriously strengthened. But the example I have just given shows the extreme difficulty of this task, which seems at times to have reached an impassable frontier. This is no longer merely a conflict between two generations, but between a world which for several millennia has believed in a truth superior to man, and an age which does not believe in it any longer—will not or cannot believe in it any longer.

But if we now ask, "How in this situation can there be any education of character?" something negative is immediately obvious: it is senseless to want to prove by any kind of argument that nevertheless the denied absoluteness of norms exists. That would be to assume that the denial is the result of reflection, and is open to argument, that is, to material for renewed reflection. But the denial is due to the disposition of a dominant human type of our age. We are justified in regarding this disposition as a sickness of the human race. But we must not deceive ourselves by believing that the disease can be cured by formulae which assert that nothing is really as the sick person imagines. It is an idle undertaking to call out, to a mankind that has grown blind to eternity: "Look! the eternal values!" To-day host upon host of men have everywhere sunk into the slavery of collectives, and each collective is the supreme authority for its own slaves; there is no longer, superior to the collectives any universal sovereignty in idea, faith, or spirit. Against the values, decrees and decisions of the collective no appeal is possible. This is true, not only for the totalitarian countries, but also for the parties and party-like groups in the so-called democracies. Men who have so lost themselves to the collective Moloch cannot be rescued from it by any reference, however eloquent, to the absolute whose kingdom the Moloch has usurped. One has to begin by pointing to that sphere where man himself, in the hours of utter solitude, occasionally becomes aware of the disease through sudden pain: by pointing to the relation of the individual to his own self. In order to enter into a personal relation with the absolute, it is first necessary to be a person again, to rescue one's real personal self from the fiery jaws of collectivism which devours all self-hood. The desire to do this is latent in the pain the individual suffers through his distorted relation to his own self. Again and again he dulls the pain with a subtle poison and thus suppresses the desire as well. To keep the pain awake, to waken the desire—that is the first task of everyone who regrets the obscuring of eternity. It is also the first task of the genuine educator in our time.

The man for whom absolute values in a universal sense do not exist cannot be made to adopt "an attitude which in action gives the preference over all others to absolute values." But what one can inculcate in him is the desire to attain once more to a real attitude, and that is, the desire to become a person following the only way that leads to this goal to-day.

But with this the concept of character formulated by Kerschensteiner and deriving, as we know, from Kant is recognized to be useless for the specifically modern task of the education of character. Another concept has to be found if this task is to be more precisely defined.

We cannot conceal from ourselves that we stand to-day on the ruins of the edifice whose towers were raised by Kant. It is not given to us living to-day to sketch the plan for a new building. But we can perhaps begin by laying the first foundation without a plan, with only a dawning image before our mind's eye.

According to Kerschensteiner's final definition character is "fundamentally nothing but voluntary obedience to the maxims which have been moulded in the individual by experience, teaching, and self-reflection, whether they have been adopted and then completely assimilated or have originated in the consciousness through self-legislation." This voluntary obedience "is, however, only a form of self-control." At first, love or fear of other people must have produced in man "the habit of self-conquest." Then, gradually, "this outer obedience must be transformed into inner obedience."

The concept of habit was then enlarged, especially by John Dewey in his book, *Human Nature and Conduct*. According to him character is "the interpenetration of habits." Without "the continued operation of all habits in every act" there would be no unified character, but only "a juxtaposition of disconnected reactions to separated situations."

With this concept of character as an organization of self-control by means of the accumulation of maxims, or as a system of interpenetrating habits, it is very easy to understand how powerless modern educational science is when faced by the sickness of man. But even apart from the special problems of the age, this concept can be no adequate basis for the construction of a genuine education of character. Not that the educator could dispense with employing useful maxims of furthering good habits. But in moments that come perhaps only seldom, a feeling of blessed achievement links him to the explorer, the inventor, the artist, a feeling of sharing in the revelation of what is hidden. In such moments he finds himself in a sphere very different from that of maxims and habits. Only on this, the highest plane of his activity, can he fix his real goal, the real concept of character which is his concern, even though he might not often reach it.

For the first time a young teacher enters a class independently, no longer sent by the training college to prove his efficiency. The class before him is like a mirror of mankind, so multiform, so full of contradictions, so inaccessible. He feels "These boys—I have not sought them out; I have been put here and have to accept them as they are—but not as they now are in this moment, no, as they really are, as they can become. But how can I find out what is in them and what can I do to make it take shape?" And the boys do not make things easy for him. They are noisy, they cause trouble, they stare at him with impudent curiosity. He is at once tempted to check this or that trouble-maker, to issue orders, to make compulsory the rules of decent behaviour, to say No, to say No to everything rising against him from beneath: he is at once tempted to start from beneath. And if one starts from beneath one perhaps never arrives above, but everything comes down. But then his eyes meet a face which strikes him. It is not a beautiful face nor particularly intelligent; but it is a real face, or rather, the chaos preceding the cosmos of a real face. On it he reads a question which is something different from the general curiosity: "Who are you? Do you know something that concerns me? Do you bring me something? What do you bring?"

In some such way he reads the question. And he, the young teacher, addresses this face. He says nothing very ponderous or important, he puts an ordinary introductory question: "What did you talk about last in geography? The Dead Sea? Well, what about the Dead Sea?" But there was obviously something not quite usual in the question, for the answer he gets is not the ordinary schoolboy answer; the boy begins to tell a story. Some months earlier he had stayed for a few hours on the shores of the Dead Sea and it is of this he tells. He adds: "And everything looked to me as if it had been created a day before the rest of creation." Quite unmistakably he had only in this moment made up his mind to talk about it. In the meantime his face has changed. It is no longer quite as chaotic as before. And the class has fallen silent. They all listen. The class, too, is no longer a chaos. Something has happened. The young teacher has started from above.

The educator's task can certainly not consist in educating great characters. He cannot select his pupils, but year by year the world, such as it is, is sent in the form of a school class to meet him on his life's way as his destiny; and in this destiny lies the very meaning of his life's work. He has to introduce discipline and order, he has to establish a law, and he can only strive and hope for the result that discipline and order will become more and more inward and autonomous, and that at last the law will be written in the heart of his pupils. But his real goal which, once he has well recognized it and well remembers it, will influence all his work, is the great character.

The great character can be conceived neither as a system of maxims nor as a system of habits. It is peculiar to him to act from the whole of his substance. That is, it is peculiar to him to react in accordance with the uniqueness of every situation which challenges him as an active person. Of course there are all sorts of similarities in different situations; one can construct types of situations, one can always find to what section the particular situation belongs, and draw what is appropriate from the hoard of established maxims and habits, apply the appropriate maxim, bring into operation the appropriate habit. But what is untypical in the particular situation remains unnoticed and unanswered. To me that seems the same as if, having ascertained the sex of a new-born child, one were immediately to establish its type as well, and put all the children of one type into a common cradle on which not the individual name but the name of the type was inscribed. In spite of all similarities every living situation has, like a new-born child, a new face, that has never been before and will never come again. It demands of you a reaction which cannot be prepared beforehand. It demands nothing of what is past. It demands presence, responsibility; it demands you. I call a great character one who by his actions and attitudes satisfies the claim of situations out of deep readiness to respond with his whole life, and in such a way that the sum of his actions and attitudes expresses at the same time the unity of his being in its willingness to accept responsibility. As his being is unity, the unity of accepted responsibility, his active life, too, coheres into unity. And one might perhaps say that for him there rises a unity out of the situations he has responded to in responsibility, the indefinable unity of a moral destiny.

All this does not mean that the great character is beyond the acceptance of norms. No responsible person remains a stranger to norms. But the command inherent in a genuine norm never becomes a maxim and the fulfilment of it never a habit. Any command that a great character takes to himself in the course of his development does not act in him as part of his consciousness or as material for building up his exercises, but remains latent in a basic layer of his substance until it reveals itself to him in a concrete way. What it has to tell him is revealed whenever a situation arises which demands of him a solution of which till then he had perhaps no idea. Even the most universal norm will at times be recognized only in a very special situation. I know of a man whose heart was struck by the lightning flash of "Thou shalt not steal" in the very moment when he was moved by a very different desire from that of stealing, and whose heart was so struck by it that he not only abandoned doing what he wanted to do, but with the whole force of his passion did the very opposite. Good and evil are not each other's opposites like right and left. The evil approaches us as a whirlwind, the good as a direction. There is a direction, a "yes," a command, hidden even in a prohibition, which is revealed to us in moments like these. In moments like these the command addresses us really in the second person, and the Thou in it is no one else but one's own self. Maxims command only the third person, the each and the none.

One can say that it is the unconditioned nature of the address which distinguishes the command from the maxim. In an age which has become deaf to unconditioned address we cannot overcome the dilemma of the education of character from that angle. But insight into the structure of great character can help us to overcome it.

Of course, it may be asked whether the educator should really start "from above," whether, in fixing his goal, the hope of finding a great character, who is bound to be the exception, should be his starting-point; for in his methods of educating character he will always have to take into consideration the others, the many. To this I reply that the educator would not have the right to do so if a method inapplicable to these others were to result. In fact, however, his very insight into the structure of a great character helps him to find the way by which alone (as I have indicated) he can begin to influence also the victims of the collective Moloch, pointing out to them the sphere in which they themselves suffer—namely, their relation to their own selves. From this sphere he must elicit the values which he can make credible and desirable to his pupils. That is what insight into the structure of a great character helps him to do.

A section of the young is beginning to feel today that, because of their absorption by the collective, something important and irreplaceable is lost to them—personal responsibility for life and the world. These young people, it is true, do not yet realize that their blind devotion to the collective, e.g. to a party, was not a genuine act of their personal life; they do not realize that it sprang, rather, from the fear of being left, in this age of confusion, to rely on themselves, on a self which no longer receives its direction from eternal values. Thus they do not yet realize that their devotion was fed on the unconscious desire to have responsibility removed from them by an authority in which they believe or want to believe. They do not yet realize that this devotion was an escape. I repeat, the young people I am speaking of do not yet realize this. But they are beginning to notice that he who no longer, with his whole being, decides what he does or does not, and assumes responsibility for it, becomes sterile in soul. And a sterile soul soon ceases to be a soul.

This is where the educator can begin and should begin. He can help the feeling that something is lacking to grow into the clarity of consciousness and into the force of desire. He can awaken in young people the courage to shoulder life again. He can bring before his pupils the image of a great character who denies no answer to life and the world, but accepts responsibility for everything essential that he meets. He can show his pupils this image without the fear that those among them who most of all need discipline and order will drift into a craving for aimless freedom: on the contrary, he can teach them in this way to recognize that discipline and order too are starting-points on the way towards self-responsibility. He can show that even the great character is not born perfect, that the unity of his being has first to mature before expressing itself in the sequence of his actions and attitudes. But unity itself, unity of the person, unity of the lived life, has to be emphasized again and again. The confusing contradictions cannot be remedied by the collectives, not one of which knows the taste of genuine unity and which if left to themselves would end up, like the scorpions imprisoned in a box, in the witty fable, by devouring one another. This mass of contradictions can be met and conquered only by the rebirth of personal unity, unity of being, unity of life, unity of action—unity of being, life and action together. This does not mean a static unity of the uniform, but the great dynamic unity of the multiform in which multiformity is formed into unity of character. Today the great characters are still "enemies of the people," they who love their society, yet wish not only to preserve it but to raise it to a higher level. To-morrow they will be the architects of a new unity of mankind. It is the longing for personal unity, from which must be born a unity of mankind, which the educator should lay hold of and strengthen in his pupils. Faith in this unity and the will to achieve it is not a "return" to individualism and collectivism. A great and full relation between man and man can only exist between unified and responsible persons. That is why it is much more rarely found in the totalitarian collective than in any historically earlier form of society; much more rarely also in the authoritarian party than in any earlier form of free association. Genuine education of character is genuine education for community.

In a generation which has had this kind of upbringing the desire will also be kindled to behold again the eternal values, to hear again the language of the eternal norm. He who knows inner unity, the innermost life of which is mystery, learns to honour the mystery in all its forms. In an understandable reaction against the former domination of a false, fictitious mystery, the present generations are obsessed with the desire to rob life of all its mystery.

The fictitious mystery will disappear, the genuine one will rise again. A generation which honours the mystery in all its forms will no longer be deserted by eternity. Its light seems darkened only because the eye suffers from a cataract; the receiver has been turned off, but the resounding ether has not ceased to vibrate. To-day, indeed, in the hour of upheaval, the eternal is sifted from the pseudo-eternal. That which flashed into the primal radiance and blurred the primal sound will be extinguished and silenced, for it has failed before the horror of the new confusion and the questioning soul has unmasked its futility. Nothing remains but what rises above the abyss of today's monstrous problems, as above every abyss of every time: the wing-beat of the spirit and the creative word. But he who can see and hear out of unity will also behold and discern again what can be beheld and discerned eternally. The educator who helps to bring man back to his own unity will help to put him again face to face with God.

DISCUSSION QUESTIONS

1. What is Buber's definition of "character"? How does this differ from the "character" with which the schools are concerned?
2. Does the concept of mass education, with the establishment of norms and the mechanization of learning, make possible the development of character that Buber sees as the main goal of education?
3. Buber speaks of the evils of the collective society, where the collective "is the supreme authority" and "there is no longer, superior to the collective, any universal sovereignty in idea, faith, or spirit." Could the "hippies" of today be considered as rebels against our collective society, seeking universalities of spirit and faith?
4. Where would the draft-card burners fit into Buber's picture?
5. To what "universals of idea, faith, and spirit" do the members of our society subscribe? For which of these are we prepared to die?

JOHN DEWEY | *Education as Growth*

THE CONDITIONS OF GROWTH

In directing the activities of the young, society determines its own future in determining that of the young. Since the young at a given time will at some later date compose the society of that period, the latter's nature will

Reprinted from John Dewey, *Democracy and Education* (New York: The Macmillan Co., 1916), pp. 41–53, with permission of the publisher.

largely turn upon the direction children's activities were given at an earlier period. This cumulative movement of action toward a later result is what is meant by growth.

The primary condition of growth is immaturity. This may seem to be a mere truism—saying that a being can develop only in some point in which he is undeveloped. But the prefix "im" of the word immaturity means something positive, not a mere void or lack. It is noteworthy that the terms "capacity" and "potentiality" have a double meaning, one sense being negative, the other positive. Capacity may denote mere receptivity, like the capacity of a quart measure. We may mean by potentiality a merely dormant or quiescent state—a capacity to become something different under external influences. But we also mean by capacity an ability, a power; and by potentiality potency, force. Now when we say that immaturity means the possibility of growth, we are not referring to absence of powers which may exist at a later time; we express a force positively present—the *ability* to develop.

Our tendency to take immaturity as mere lack, and growth as something which fills up the gap between the immature and the mature is due to regarding childhood *comparatively*, instead of intrinsically. We treat it simply as a privation because we are measuring it by adulthood as a fixed standard. This fixes attention upon what the child has not, and will not have till he becomes a man. This comparative standpoint is legitimate enough for some purposes, but if we make it final, the question arises whether we are not guilty of an overweening presumption. Children, if they could express themselves articulately and sincerely, would tell a different tale; and there is excellent adult authority for the conviction that for certain moral and intellectual purposes adults must become as little children.

The seriousness of the assumption of the negative quality of the possibilities of immaturity is apparent when we reflect that it sets up as an ideal and standard a static end. The fulfillment of growing is taken to mean an *accomplished* growth: that is to say, an Ungrowth, something which is no longer growing. The futility of the assumption is seen in the fact that every adult resents the imputation of having no further possibilities of growth; and so far as he finds that they are closed to him mourns the fact as evidence of loss, instead of falling back on the achieved as adequate manifestation of power. Why an unequal measure for child and man?

Taken absolutely, instead of comparatively, immaturity designates a positive force or ability—the *power* to grow. We do not have to draw out or educe positive activities from a child, as some educational doctrines would have it. Where there is life, there are already eager and impassioned activities. Growth is not something done to them; it is something they do. The positive and constructive aspect of possibility gives the key to understanding the two chief traits of immaturity, dependence and plasticity. (1)

It sounds absurd to hear dependence spoken of as something positive, still more absurd as a power. Yet if helplessness were all there were in dependence, no development could ever take place. A merely impotent being has to be carried, forever, by others. The fact that dependence is accompanied by growth in ability, not by an ever increasing lapse into parasitism, suggests that it is already something constructive. Being merely sheltered by others would not promote growth. For (2) it would only build a wall around impotence. With reference to the physical world, the child is helpless. He lacks at birth and for a long time thereafter power to make his way physically, to make his own living. If he had to do that by himself, he would hardly survive an hour. On this side his helplessness is almost complete. The young of the brutes are immeasurably his superiors. He is physically weak and not able to turn the strength which he possesses to coping with the physical environment.

1. The thoroughgoing character of this helplessness suggests, however, some compensating power. The relative ability of the young of brute animals to adapt themselves fairly well to physical conditions from an early period suggests the fact that their life is not intimately bound up with the life of those about them. They are compelled, so to speak, to have physical gifts because they are lacking in social gifts. Human infants, on the other hand, can get along with physical incapacity just because of their social capacity. We sometimes talk and think as if they simply happened to be *physically* in a social environment; as if social forces exclusively existed in the adults who take care of them, they being passive recipients. If it were said that children are themselves marvelously endowed with *power* to enlist the coöperative attention of others, this would be thought to be a backhanded way of saying that others are marvelously attentive to the needs of children. But observation shows that children are gifted with an equipment of the first order for social intercourse. Few grown-up persons retain all of the flexible and sensitive ability of children to vibrate sympathetically with the attitudes and doings of those about them. Inattention to physical things (going with incapacity to control them) is accompanied by a corresponding intensification of interest and attention as to the doings of people. The native mechanism of the child and his impulses all tend to facile social responsiveness. The statement that children, before adolescence, are egotistically self-centered, even if it were true, would not contradict the truth of this statement. It would simply indicate that their social responsiveness is employed on their own behalf, not that it does not exist. But the statement is not true as matter of fact. The facts which are cited in support of the alleged pure egoism of children really show the intensity and directness with which they go to their mark. If the ends which form the mark seem narrow and selfish to adults, it is only because adults (by means of a similar engrossment in their day) have mastered these ends, which have conse-

quently ceased to interest them. Most of the remainder of children's alleged native egoism is simply an egoism which runs counter to an adult's egoism. To a grown-up person who is too absorbed in his own affairs to take an interest in children's affairs, children doubtless seem unreasonably engrossed in *their* own affairs.

From a social standpoint, dependence denotes a power rather than a weakness; it involves interdependence. There is always a danger that increased personal independence will decrease the social capacity of an individual. In making him more self-reliant, it may make him more self-sufficient; it may lead to aloofness and indifference. It often makes an individual so insensitive in his relations to others as to develop an illusion of being really able to stand and act alone—an unnamed form of insanity which is responsible for a large part of the remediable suffering of the world.

2. The specific adaptability of an immature creature for growth constitutes his *plasticity*. This is something quite different from the plasticity of putty or wax. It is not a capacity to take on change of form in accord with external pressure. It lies near the pliable elasticity by which some persons take on the color of their surroundings while retaining their own bent. But it is something deeper than this. It is essentially the ability to learn from experience; the power to retain from one experience something which is of avail in coping with the difficulties of a later situation. This means power to modify actions on the basis of the results of prior experiences, the power to *develop dispositions*. Without it, the acquisition of habits is impossible.

It is a familiar fact that the young of the higher animals, and especially the human young, have to *learn* to utilize their instinctive reactions. The human being is born with a greater number of instinctive tendencies than other animals. But the instincts of the lower animals perfect themselves for appropriate action at an early period after birth, while most of those of the human infant are of little account just as they stand. An original specialized power of adjustment secures immediate efficiency, but, like a railway ticket, it is good for one route only. A being who, in order to use his eyes, ears, hands, and legs, has to experiment in making varied combinations of their reactions, achieves a control that is flexible and varied. A chick, for example, pecks accurately at a bit of food in a few hours after hatching. This means that definite coördinations of activities of the eyes in seeing and of the body and head in striking are perfected in a few trials. An infant requires about six months to be able to gauge with approximate accuracy the action in reaching which will coordinate with his visual activities; to be able, that is, to tell whether he can reach a seen object and just how to execute the reaching. As a result, the chick is limited by the relative perfection of its original endowment. The infant has the advantage of the *multitude* of instinctive tentative reactions and of the experiences that accompany them, even though he is at a temporary disadvantage because they cross one another. In learning an action, instead of having it given readymade, one of necessity learns to vary its factors, to make varied combinations of them, according to change of circumstances. A possibility of continuing progress is opened up by the fact that in learning one act, methods are developed good for use in other situations. Still more important is the fact that the human being acquires a habit of learning. He learns to learn.

The importance for human life of the two facts of dependence and variable control has been summed up in the doctrine of the significance of prolonged infancy.[1] This prolongation is significant from the standpoint of the adult members of the group as well as from that of the young. The presence of dependent and learning beings is a stimulus to nurture and affection. The need for constant continued care was probably a chief means in transforming temporary cohabitations into permanent unions. It certainly was a chief influence in forming habits of affectionate and sympathetic watchfulness; that constructive interest in the well-being of others which is essential to associated life. Intellectually, this moral development meant the introduction of many new objects of attention; it stimulated foresight and planning for the future. Thus there is a reciprocal influence. Increasing complexity of social life requires a longer period of infancy in which to acquire the needed powers; this prolongation of dependence means prolongation of plasticity, or power of acquiring variable and novel modes of control. Hence it provides a further push to social progress.

HABITS AS EXPRESSIONS OF GROWTH

We have already noted that plasticity is the capacity to retain and carry over from prior experience factors which modify subsequent activities. This signifies the capacity to acquire habits, or develop definite dispositions. We have now to consider the salient features of habits. In the first place, a habit is a form of executive skill, of efficiency in doing. A habit means an ability to use natural conditions as means to ends. It is an active control of the environment through control of the organs of action. We are perhaps apt to emphasize the control of the body at the expense of control of the environment. We think of walking, talking, playing the piano, the specialized skills characteristic of the etcher, the surgeon, the bridge-builder, as if they were simply ease, deftness, and accuracy on the part of the organism. They are that, of course; but the measure of the value of these qualities lies in the economical and effective control of the environment which they secure. To be able to walk is to have certain properties of nature at our disposal—and so with all other habits.

Education is not infrequently defined as consisting in the acquisition of

[1] Intimations of its significance are found in a number of writers, but John Fiske, in his *Excursions of an Evolutionist,* is accredited with its first systematic exposition.

those habits that effect an adjustment of an individual and his environment. The definition expresses an essential phase of growth. But it is essential that adjustment be understood in its active sense of *control* of means for achieving ends. If we think of a habit simply as a change wrought in the organism, ignoring the fact that this change consists in ability to effect subsequent changes in the environment, we shall be led to think of "adjustment" as a conformity to environment as wax conforms to the seal which impresses it. The environment is thought of as something fixed, providing in its fixity the end and standard of changes taking place in the organism; adjustment is just fitting ourselves to this fixity of external conditions.[2] Habit as *habituation* is indeed something *relatively* passive; we get used to our surroundings—to our clothing, our shoes, and gloves; to the atmosphere as long as it is fairly equable; to our daily associates, etc. Conformity to the environment, a change wrought in the organism without reference to ability to modify surroundings, is a marked trait of such habituations. Aside from the fact that we are not entitled to carry over the traits of such adjustments (which might well be called *accommodations,* to mark them off from active adjustments) into habits of active use of our surroundings, two features of habituations are worth notice. In the first place, we get used to things by *first* using them.

Consider getting used to a strange city. At first, there is excessive stimulation and excessive and ill-adapted response. Gradually certain stimuli are selected because of their relevancy, and others are degraded. We can say either that we do not respond to them any longer, or more truly that we have effected a persistent response to them—an equilibrium of adjustment. This means, in the second place, that this enduring adjustment supplies the background upon which are made specific adjustments, as occasion arises. We are never interested in changing the *whole* environment; there is much that we take for granted and accept just as it already is. Upon this background our activities focus at certain points in an endeavor to introduce needed changes. Habituation is thus our adjustment to an environment which at the time we are not concerned with modifying, and which supplies a leverage to our active habits.

Adaptation, in fine, is quite as much adaptation *of* the environment to our own activities as of our activities *to* the environment. A savage tribe manages to live on a desert plain. It adapts itself. But its adaptation involves a maximum of accepting, tolerating, putting up with things as they are, a maximum of passive acquiescence, and a minimum of active control, of subjection to use. A civilized people enters upon the scene. It also adapts itself. It introduces irrigation; it searches the world for plants and animals that will flourish under such conditions; it improves, by careful selection,

2 This conception is, of course, a logical correlate of the conceptions of the external relation of stimulus and response, and of the negative conceptions of immaturity and plasticity noted in this chapter.

those which are growing there. As a consequence, the wilderness blossoms as a rose. The savage is merely habituated; the civilized man has habits which transform the environment.

The significance of habit is not exhausted, however, in its executive and motor phase. It means formation of intellectual and emotional disposition as well as an increase in ease, economy, and efficiency of action. Any habit marks an *inclination*—an active preference and choice for the conditions involved in its exercise. A habit does not wait, Macawber-like, for a stimulus to turn up so that it may get busy; it actively seeks for occasions to pass into full operation. If its expression is unduly blocked, inclination shows itself in uneasiness and intense craving. A habit also marks an intellectual disposition. Where there is a habit, there is acquaintance with the materials and equipment to which action is applied. There is a definite way of understanding the situations in which the habit operates. Modes of thought, of observation and reflection, enter as forms of skill and of desire into the habits that make a man an engineer, an architect, a physician, or a merchant. In unskilled forms of labor, the intellectual factors are at minimum precisely because the habits involved are not of a high grade. But there are habits of judging and reasoning as truly as of handling a tool, painting a picture, or conducting an experiment.

Such statements are, however, understatements. The habits of mind involved in habits of the eye and hand supply the latter with their significance. Above all, the intellectual element in a habit fixes the relation of the habit to varied and elastic use, and hence to continued growth. We speak of *fixed* habits. Well, the phrase may mean powers so well established that their possessor always has them as resources when needed. But the phrase is also used to mean ruts, routine ways, with loss of freshness, openmindedness, and originality. Fixity of habit may mean that something has a fixed hold upon us, instead of our having a free hold upon things. This fact explains two points in a common notion about habits: their identification with mechanical and external modes of action to the neglect of mental and moral attitudes, and the tendency to give them a bad meaning, an identification with "bad habits." Many a person would feel surprised to have his aptitude in his chosen profession called a habit, and would naturally think of his use of tobacco, liquor, or profane language as typical of the meaning of habit. A habit is to him something which has a hold on him, something not easily thrown off even though judgment condemn it.

Habits reduce themselves to routine ways of acting, or degenerate into ways of action to which we are enslaved just in the degree in which intelligence is disconnected from them. Routine habits are unthinking habits: "bad" habits are habits so severed from reason that they are opposed to the conclusions of conscious deliberation and decision. As we have seen, the acquiring of habits is due to an original plasticity of our natures: to our ability to vary responses till we find an appropriate and efficient way of acting. Routine habits, and habits that possess us instead of our possessing them, are habits which put an end to plasticity. They mark the close of power to vary. There can be no doubt of the tendency of organic plasticity, of the physiological basis, to lessen with growing years. The instinctively mobile and eagerly varying action of childhood, the love of new stimuli and new developments, too easily passes into a "settling down," which means aversion to change and a resting on past achievements. Only an environment which secures the full use of intelligence in the process of forming habits can counteract this tendency. Of course, the same hardening of the organic conditions affects the physiological structures which are involved in thinking. But this fact only indicates the need of persistent care to see to it that the function of intelligence is invoked to its maximum possibility. The short-sighted method which falls back on mechanical routine and repetition to secure external efficiency of habit, motor skill without accompanying thought, marks a deliberate closing in of surroundings upon growth.

THE EDUCATIONAL BEARINGS OF THE CONCEPTION OF DEVELOPMENT

We have had so far but little to say in this chapter about education. We have been occupied with the conditions and implications of growth. If our conclusions are justified, they carry with them, however, definite educational consequences. When it is said that education is development, everything depends upon *how* development is conceived. Our net conclusion is that life is development, and that developing, growing, is life. Translated into its educational equivalents, that means (*i*) that the educational process has no end beyond itself; it is its own end; and that (*ii*) the educational process is one of continual reorganizing, reconstructing, transforming.

1. Development when it is interpreted in *comparative* terms, that is, with respect to the special traits of child and adult life, means the direction of power into special channels: the formation of habits involving executive skill, definiteness of interest, and specific objects of observation and thought. But the comparative view is not final. The child has specific powers; to ignore that fact is to stunt or distort the organs upon which his growth depends. The adult uses his powers to transform his environment, thereby occasioning new stimuli which redirect his powers and keep them developing. Ignoring this fact means arrested development, a passive accommodation. Normal child and normal adult alike, in other words, are engaged in growing. The difference between them is not the difference between growth and no growth, but between the modes of growth appropriate to different conditions. With respect to the development of powers devoted to coping with specific scientific and economic problems we may say the child should

be growing in manhood. With respect to sympathetic curiosity, unbiased responsiveness, and openness of mind, we may say that the adult should be growing in childlikeness. One statement is as true as the other.

Three ideas which have been criticized, namely, the merely privative nature of immaturity, static adjustment to a fixed environment, and rigidity of habit, are all connected with a false idea of growth or development—that it is a movement toward a fixed goal. Growth is regarded as *having* an end, instead of *being* an end. The educational counterparts of the three fallacious ideas are first, failure to take account of the instinctive or native powers of the young; secondly, failure to develop initiative in coping with novel situations; thirdly, an undue emphasis upon drill and other devices which secure automatic skill at the expense of personal perception. In all cases, the adult environment is accepted as a standard for the child. He is to be brought up *to* it.

Natural instincts are either disregarded or treated as nuisances—as obnoxious traits to be suppressed, or at all events to be brought into conformity with external standards. Since conformity is the aim, what is distinctively individual in a young person is brushed aside, or regarded as a source of mischief or anarchy. Conformity is made equivalent to uniformity. Consequently, there are induced lack of interest in the novel, aversion to progress, and dread of the uncertain and the unknown. Since the end of growth is outside of and beyond the process of growing, external agents have to be resorted to to induce movement toward it. Whenever a method of education is stigmatized as mechanical, we may be sure that external pressure is brought to bear to reach an external end.

2. Since in reality there is nothing to which growth is relative save more growth, there is nothing to which education is subordinate save more education. It is a commonplace to say that education should not cease when one leaves school. The point of this commonplace is that the purpose of school education is to insure the continuance of education by organizing the powers that insure growth. The inclination to learn from life itself and to make the conditions of life such that all will learn in the process of living is the finest product of schooling.

When we abandon the attempt to define immaturity by means of fixed comparison with adult accomplishments, we are compelled to give up thinking of it as denoting lack of desired traits. Abandoning this notion, we are also forced to surrender our habit of thinking of instruction as a method of supplying this lack by pouring knowledge into a mental and moral hole which awaits filling. Since life means growth, a living creature lives as truly and positively at one stage as at another, with the same intrinsic fullness and the same absolute claims. Hence education means the enterprise of supplying the conditions which insure growth, or adequacy of life, irrespective of age. We first look with impatience upon immaturity, regarding it as something to be got over as rapidly as possible. Then the adult formed by such educative methods looks back with impatient regret upon childhood and youth as a scene of lost opportunities and wasted powers. This ironical situation will endure till it is recognized that living has its own intrinsic quality and that the business of education is with that quality.

Realization that life is growth protects us from that so-called idealizing of childhood which in effect is nothing but lazy indulgence. Life is not to be identified with every superficial act and interest. Even though it is not always easy to tell whether what appears to be mere surface fooling is a sign of some nascent as yet untrained power, we must remember that manifestations are not to be accepted as ends in themselves. They are signs of possible growth. They are to be turned into means of development, of carrying power forward, not indulged or cultivated for their own sake. Excessive attention to surface phenomena (even in the way of rebuke as well as of encouragement) may lead to their fixation and thus to arrested development. What impulses are moving toward, not what they have been, is the important thing for parent and teacher. The true principle of respect for immaturity cannot be better put than in the words of Emerson: "Respect the child. Be not too much his parent. Trespass not on his solitude. But I hear the outcry which replies to this suggestion: Would you verily throw up the reins of public and private discipline; would you leave the young child to the mad career of his own passions and whimsies, and call this anarchy a respect for the child's nature? I answer—Respect the child, respect him to the end, but also respect yourself. . . . The two points in a boy's training are, to keep his *naturel* and train off all but that; to keep his *naturel,* but stop off his uproar, fooling, and horseplay; keep his nature *and arm it with knowledge in the very direction in which it points.*" And as Emerson goes on to show, this reverence for childhood and youth instead of opening up an easy and easy-going path to the instructors, "involves at once, immense claims on the time, the thought, on the life of the teacher. It requires time, use, insight, event, all the great lessons and assistances of God; and only to think of using it implies character and profoundness."

SUMMARY

Power to grow depends upon need for others and plasticity. Both of these conditions are at their height in childhood and youth. Plasticity or the power to learn from experience means the formation of habits. Habits give control over the environment, power to utilize it for human purposes. Habits take the form both of habituation, or a general and persistent balance of organic activities with the surroundings, and of active capacities to readjust activity to meet new conditions. The former furnishes the background of growth; the latter constitute growing. Active habits involve thought, invention, and initiative in applying capacities to new aims. They are opposed to routine which marks an arrest of growth. Since growth is the characteristic of life, education is all one with growing; it has no end beyond itself. The criterion of the value of school education is the extent in which it creates a desire for continued growth and supplies means for making the desire effective in fact.

DISCUSSION QUESTIONS

1. Evaluate your own childhood education against the criterion of Dewey's concept of "growth."
2. Is the concept of "growth" precise enough to furnish workable guidelines for a teacher?
3. Do modern innovations in education, such as programed learning and teaching machines, fit into Dewey's definition of education?
4. Must mass education necessarily result in the kind of conformity that Dewey sees as antithetical to the development of "humanness"?
5. Is education its own end?

FRANZ E. WINKLER | *Information and Education*

The fate of our civilization may well depend on the answers our children receive to their questions. Mastery of the atomic age requires a strong capacity for imaginative and creative thinking, a capacity whose wellspring is the consciousness of childhood. The channels from this "fountain of youth" must be cleared and guarded so that they may flow into adolescence and adulthood; otherwise future generations will be even less capable than ours of mastering their problems. Possibly due to the materialistic climate into which children are born today, their reservoir of youthfulness is shallow enough. In their questions they ask for help, only to receive answers which dim further the light of their intuitive consciousness and thus deprive them of an irreplaceable source of happiness and future strength. For purely intellectual knowledge, when offered too early, will block the child's intuitive lifeline as effectively as lime will clog the narrow shaft of a well.

In the previous chapter we have tried to show how such damage could be averted. Obviously, the individual child is not wiser than the average adult,

---

Reprinted from Franz Winkler, *Man: The Bridge Between Two Worlds* (New York: Harper and Row, Publishers, Inc., 1960), pp. 205–215, with permission of the publisher.

but is fully dependent on his guidance and leadership. Yet the consciousness which sustains the child is richer and far closer to reality than the thinking habits of modern intellectualism. Possibly owing to the fact that so few of them were ever granted the blessings of real childhood, the majority of today's parents and teachers know little about the psychology of the normal child. The clue to his consciousness lies in mythology and folklore, which carry in an indelible script an imprint of the childhood of the human race itself. This is not true of fairy tales invented by clever individuals, but of those which, emerging as archetypal images in the consciousness of generations, have been preserved through the ages. In folklore of this sort, figures and images are similar the world over; and in them the last residues of the "One Language" linger, the language which was confounded when man set out on his material conquest of earth and sky. Modern child psychologists make a tragic error when they frown on fairy tales, and blame them for untoward effects which result, actually, from a wrong emotional attitude on the part of the storyteller himself. For centuries, as we all know, generation after generation has grown up under the influence of fairy tales, to become far less neurotic and desperate than modern youth; and many years of caring for problem children have convinced us of the protection from anxiety and criminal urges that folklore affords.

When we tell a fairy tale to a child, we must never forget that it deals primarily with man's inner life, his soul life. Its characters represent psychological qualities rather than people of flesh and blood. Its kingdoms are not of this world; they symbolize the vast, partly hidden realms of the human soul. In these realms, unselfish will and purified emotion must find their union as prince and princess, to rule their domain with the help of reason grown into wisdom. Such wisdom, according to the fairy tale, is to be found in nature. Her animals, forests, rivers, flowers, and stones can become man's teachers on his quest for inner kingship; and yet if his search for knowledge is selfish and overbearing, the power he acquires may become his undoing. For in the fairy tale, as in reality, everyone can grow up to be king in his own soul only if he learns to respect the dignity and sacredness of his fellow creatures. While most branches of modern psychology merely describe and analyze the psyche, the fairy tale reveals the most intimate secrets of the human soul due to a knowledge which is not analytical but creative, and capable of speaking directly to the child's innate understanding.

If critics of folklore would only accept the obvious—namely, that the evil witch and the magician represent greed and cruelty—they would be less shocked by the punishment dealt out to them. For in the crucial struggle within the human soul there is no room for leniency toward evil. When parents and teachers are too sentimental to expose their children to this truth, they may find themselves fully responsible for criminal careers, for lives ruined by lack of self-control or prematurely ended by guilt and despair. Theirs is the kind of sentimentality so often encountered today in "do-gooders," who try to protect the criminal at the expense of his future victims, and thus take upon themselves the spiritual consequences of his crimes.

In the unavoidable struggle between good and evil, it is the fairy tale which can best aid the cause of good—if it is permitted to speak to the child in its own unique language, the one language which goes straight to the heart. Naturally, it will be necessary to choose the right kind of stories for different temperaments and personalities, and it may be permissible to mitigate some of the modes of punishment taken from medieval justice. Otherwise, no changes should be made, for there is intuitive wisdom in mythology and folklore which by far transcends intellectual psychology, a wisdom which prompted the great philosopher and poet Novalis to see in the true fairy tale "a presentation of prophecy, of ideals, and of absolute inner necessity."

Dr. Mary H. B. Wollner, in an article published in the September 1957 issue of *Todays' Health,* says:

> A miasmic reform has crept upon many of the old fables, fairy tales and nursery lore. Radio and television versions now omit or alter the once satisfyingly drastic punishments meted out to wicked stepmothers or blood-thirsty giants. Jack's Giant . . . no longer meets his death by crashing headlong from the top of the beanstalk . . . but fades out in a huge bubbling giggle. . . . I should think children today might be alarmed by the possibility that such a giant might giggle his way into life again; he obviously isn't quite dead enough.
>
> An inexpensive series of children's books presents further ingenious decontaminations: witches . . . are now delightful, whimsical creatures . . . the Wolf in Red Riding Hood doesn't get to swallow Granny . . . Humpty-Dumpty is carefully mended, and equally absurd liberties are taken with many, many other well-known Mother Goose characters.
>
> . . . .
>
> Grimm's too grim for the modern child, we are told. Children don't like violence and cruelty; besides, if all their reading is purged of baseness, they will grow up noble, kind and gentle. In fact, they might turn out to be such lofty citizens, because of lofty literature, that all society would benefit.
>
> . . . .
>
> There has, indeed, hovered over us in the last two decades a cloudy theory in child development and educational practices. It is a theory ascribed to psychologists who once warned . . . that indulging children in folk-tales, fairy tales and stories of magic and enchantment, would encourage unhealthy wish-fulfillment fantasies and daydreaming, or cause confusion . . . between the real and the fanciful. . . .
>
> . . . .
>
> Now if the psychologists and educators would take a good long look at the adult in these United States . . . , they would see that today he is reading magazine fiction allied to soap operas—that is, written to formula and sparing no pains to arouse false . . . daydreams; that he attends movies, which . . . wallow in suggestiveness

and flaunting self-indulgence; that he is filling his literature- and truth-starved mind with blood and thunder and magic and superstition in radio and television and comics.

. . . .

. . . Children's psyches are not as naïve as some people think, and . . . their tastes, when not distorted and misguided, lead them to enjoy stories which would be judged great by the standards used in judging all great literature. In other words, the nursery lore, folk tales, fairy stories, myths and legends . . . because they are literary expressions of timeless psychological and sociological truths, as these truths have welled up out of the unconscious cumulative wisdom of the human race—persist in their appeal . . . and at the same time yield vital and indispensable nourishment for the growth of children.

. . . To study folklore and mythology is to come into possession of almost more than we can assimilate and use about the development of the human soul. To study the child is to appreciate with what astonishing accuracy literature reflects life.

. . . .

Fortunately, for every insipid story found in the graded readers, some Aesop's fable, myth or folk tale . . . could be found to offset it. . . . Adults need to read aloud and tell stories much more than they are doing. To revive the fainting, doubting spirits of our apparently apathetic school children, we need to revive the children's classics and to inject powerful emergency doses of enlightenment, enjoyment and effortless understanding into library, schoolroom and nursery.

. . . .

. . . We of little faith need to draw upon the wellsprings of faith in the world's literature.[1]

The fairy tale not only offers the child an incentive to be good, but serves as his natural guide to religion. It gives food to his starved intuitive faculties, puts them into their legitimate place, and keeps them from seeking outlets in purely libidinous adventures. Such danger of perverted intuition exists; in the words of the fairy tale, somewhere within the soul lies hidden the cruel sorcerer or the evil witch, waiting to turn human longings into animal instincts and man's heart into unfeeling stone.

The dreariness of our abstract intellectualism, which robs the child of happiness, is responsible for his seeking joy in realms destructive to his mind and body. This futile search will drive him into libido long before he is old enough to purify it through true affection for an individual, or else it will bring him to cruelty and crime as a means of abnormal satisfaction. But the fairy tale, if permitted to bestow its blessing, can deepen and prolong the happiness of childhood, and provide the sense of adventure which the young needs for the preservation of his moral and mental health.

Regularly recurring occasions for joy have been celebrated for ages as the most powerful healers and protectors of the human soul. But what is a great religious festival, like Christmas, without the magic key of the fairy tale? An

[1] Mary H. B. Wollner, "Back to the Classics," in *Today's Health,* Vol. 35, No. 9, September, 1957.

expensive nuisance to the donor, and a source of a strange, subconscious resentment to the recipient of gifts. Or is it true that its mystery is a deception, be it concerned with "Santa Claus," the "Christ Child," or any of the heavenly messengers of other creeds? And is it true that these stories must eventually lead to disappointment and mistrust? We do not believe so. For the fruits they bear are real, so real that years later the memory of them has sustained many a person in hours of trial and grief.

However, we could avoid deception and disillusionment altogether, were we only to abstain from sentimental materialism. It is not necessary to tell a child that Christ or Santa Claus has brought the Christmas presents which, after all, he may have seen in a shop window. Would it not be better to say that these gifts have received a special blessing from such beings? This would add to the gifts an unseen treasure, a breath of the invisible for which every normal child longs with all his heart. Would such a statement be a lie? If so, then every prayer, every blessing, and every religious service is also a lie.

The great religious festivals, if celebrated correctly, are the child's safest guides on his dangerous journey into adulthood. It is they which gently lead his inner perception from the world of the fairy tale into the world of adult religion. It is they which bring purely qualitative faculties, such as joy and gratitude, into proper relation with pleasure derived from material gifts. And it is they which weave magic bands of love around a family, and thus prevent the estrangement between parents and children, so often at the root of juvenile delinquency.

But the bridge between childhood and maturity, between the intuitive and intellectual poles of consciousness, does not end at the completion of preschool age, the age in which the fairy tale should reign supreme. The fostering of factual knowledge and the development of acute intellectual powers, together with a preserving and strengthening of intuitive faculties, should be the goal from the day the child enters elementary school to the end of his studies. The two main principles of upbringing are education and information. The very word "educate," derived from the Latin *educere,* means "to lead outward"—while "inform," coming from *in-formare,* indicates a form-giving process. In Latin *e* expresses an outward motion, while the *in* points to something static or inward bound.

Education thus signifies an effort to bring to healthy manifestation what already exists in a human being as the content of his personality. Information denotes an attempt to impose limits on that personality by molding it according to the strict rules of logical and natural laws.

Traditional pedagogy was predominantly concerned with information and discipline. It functioned under the more or less overt assumption that a human being is evil unless remodeled by puritan discipline, and brutish unless enlightened by knowledge. Today the other extreme prevails. Strangely, it is materialism which considers the human being intrinsically good, and therefore seeks the cause of his shortcomings in suppression and inhibition. Both extremes are harmful. The first has often resulted in the development of repressed, inhibited personalities, prone to be overly docile and hypocritical. The other is likely to promote shapeless individualities dominated by their own unrestrained instincts.

What the child and the adolescent needs from his parents and teachers is a deep understanding of his innate longings. He must be permitted, and even encouraged, to express himself. This is *e-ducation* in the strict sense of the word; it requires leniency, love, kindness, intuitive understanding, and self-effacement on the part of teachers and parents. Yet this is not enough. The child asks of the adult not only encouragement of self-expression, but also the limitations needed to shape and mold his character. And the "kindly" pedagogue who fails to see this is either too foolish or too selfish to recognize his true duty toward the young lives placed in his charge.

The two extremes in educational philosophy may be illustrated by a rather commonplace example. In earlier times a child inclined to be noisy was usually ordered to be quiet, and punished when disobedient. Thus a repression occurred which often caused neurotic tendencies in later life. Today the prevailing trend permits the child to make as much noise as he will, with little or no concern for the comfort of innocent bystanders. For this reason the child fails to learn respect for the undeniable rights of others, a failing which in later life tends to make him lonely because it estranges him from society. From both an educational and a disciplinary viewpoint, the problem might be solved by providing a variety of artistic outlets—one of which might be the playing of a musical instrument—but always with due regard for other people's rights.

This example is anything but original, and known to almost every kindergarten teacher. Yet the application of the principle involved should be by far wider and more scientific than it is today. Experience shows that, while very strict parents and teachers are often remembered with warm affection in later years, too lenient ones become more resented as time goes on. This psychological paradox may be explained by the fact that, whereas worthwhile qualities will generally surmount the severest restrictions, the shapelessness of an undisciplined personality cannot be amended later, except through grievous suffering; hence the pampered child's bitter hatred of parents, whose omissions have doomed him to a life of neurosis and frustration.

What has scholastic information to do with discipline? Knowledge serves as a mold for the volcanic content of the growing individual, whose degree of balance depends on it. Knowledge of a large number of confusing and apparently unrelated facts misshapes the personality into a mental and emotional structure both bizarre and discordant. On the other hand, knowledge imparted with the understanding that every item of information is but a piece in the mosaic of an all-encompassing wisdom, creates a harmonious structure promoting a sense of security as well as a feeling of freedom within the framework of purposeful necessity.

Naturally, this does not mean that the modern teacher should preach a creed, or try to show purpose and meaning in facts when he does not see them. But twentieth-century science has already rendered materialism untenable and therefore unscientific. Today every well-trained teacher has the right to say:

> Underlying the new ideas, including those of modern physics, is a unifying order, but it is not causality; it is purpose. . . . One might even say, as a general "modern" principle, that the elements (for we no longer really talk of "parts") will be found to arrange themselves so as to serve the purpose of the whole.[2]

If the individual is permitted to see facts as building stones, arranged by a higher wisdom to serve "the purpose of the whole," he himself becomes a harmonious being. It is knowledge which gives shape to the character. If this knowledge is a true reflection of a meaningful universe, our minds will reflect the higher purpose underlying the order of the cosmos.

A child brought up in this way is rather easy to discipline. For it is not true that man wants to obey his selfish desires. He does so only when he despairs of a higher meaning in life. It was the search for such a meaning, rather than desire for a comfortable life, that inspired our most significant discoveries in natural science and technology; for one hoped to find the secrets of creation in matter and energy. Now that we have been disillusioned, it has become difficult to attract an adequate number of young people to the study of the sciences. A certain hopelessness as to cognition of truth has invaded all facets of our civilization, and led us to doubt the very existence of true values, of meaning and purpose in life. Strangely enough, it is the adolescent and even the small child who most keenly, if subconsciously, divine the frustration which haunts our age. The grown-up can find moral support in his work, in the hope he bears for his children, in his obligations, and in the satisfactions and pleasures of his daily life. The child understands little of all this. For him, the main source of joy lies in his phantasy which, contrary to general belief, can never be fully content with sports, material gains, or intellectual achievements. His future as foreshadowed in the life of his elders appears unspeakably dreary to him, and not worth fighting and working for. Only if adults see life through the eyes of a child, can they become the friends and leaders of their charges. Actually, schooling is of little use for the foundation of a secure and happy individuality unless it is a truly joint adventure shared by teacher and pupil alike.

This, however, can hardly be achieved by a kind of education which burdens a child with the responsibilities of initiative and leadership he

---

[2] Peter F. Drucker, "The New Philosophy Comes to Life," section entitled "The Purposeful Universe," in *Harper's Magazine,* August, 1957.

rightly expects from his elders. What counts is the teacher's awareness that the unspoiled child intuitively knows more about the meaning of life than the most brilliant intellectual. Such awareness opens an adult's mind to the rejuvenating influence of an intuitive consciousness, and his eyes to the individual needs of his pupil. He will see, for instance, that too much information given too early or too quickly may overwhelm the child's inner life, just as logs thrown too quickly into a fire may extinguish the flame they were meant to sustain. This can result in a warped, narrow-minded, unimaginative character. But he will also recognize that lack of discipline and insufficient knowledge may bring forth a world-estranged, shapeless personality.

There is still another angle that deserves attention. Obviously, it is possible to impart a great deal of information to pupils by mnemotechnical methods or through television. But this is not education. A child watching passively may remember much of what he has seen and heard but, unless he is made to struggle with the subject, the information received will remain a foreign body in his mind. For any kind of knowledge is useful only to the extent to which it enhances inner activity. If merely imposed on the mind, it becomes a heavy weight, paralyzing the forces of will.

What, in the last analysis, is human will? It is man's individual share of the power of creation. This share, feeble in our generation, can be aroused by wrestling with the facts and phenomena of nature, the laws of mathematics, and the major events of history. It is weakened, and often extinguished, when knowledge is channeled into a mind reduced to a mere receptacle. This, however, does not mean that everything a child has to memorize should be "explained" to him intellectually. On the contrary, experience has convinced us that a youngster exposed to too much reasoning before the age of twelve to fourteen years is often likely to become over-argumentative and neurotic.

There is a great capacity for acquiring and retaining knowledge in the age groups of seven to fourteen years. This capacity should be fully utilized, and not allowed to remain passive: every piece of information transmitted by the teacher should be met by an imaginative-artistic activity on the part of the pupil. Geometric figures ought to be traced in games and motion, historical characters interpreted in improvised plays, botanical and zoological facts brought to life through drawing, painting, and sculpturing.

In this manner, the creative in man responds to the created in nature, and knowledge becomes alive through comprehension. The faculty to comprehend, however, differs in degree only from the power to create; it is the gift of man which once made it possible for him to "give names" to all other creatures.

With the externalization of human consciousness, man's instinctive comprehension of nature has become replaced by a vast knowledge of external facts—and, consequently, his creativeness by technological productivity. Today, to re-establish the balance of consciousness, the process of externalization must be reversed. Such reversal does not require abandonment of scientific progress. It does, however, require the teacher's understanding that every piece of information must be imparted in a way that will challenge the student, and stimulate his creative imagination.

DISCUSSION QUESTIONS

1. What faculties of the child do you see as being "starved" in the schools?
2. Do you subscribe to Winkler's belief in a "meaningful universe"?
3. What is your concept of a "higher meaning" in life? If you believe there is such a thing, state your arguments for it.
4. Winkler's position is that the healthy being blends the two worlds of the spirit and science. In terms of today's realities, are the two proving themselves antithetical?
5. To what extent is the public school developing in children an understanding and appreciation of both worlds?

A. S. NEILL

Summerhill Education vs. Standard Education

I hold that the aim of life is to find happiness, which means to find interest. Education should be a preparation for life. Our culture has not been very successful. Our education, politics, and economics lead to war. Our medicines have not done away with disease. Our religion has not abolished usury and robbery. Our boasted humanitarianism still allows public opinion to approve of the barbaric sport of hunting. The advances of the age are advances in mechanism—in radio and television, in electronics, in jet planes. New world wars threaten, for the world's social conscience is still primitive.

If we feel like questioning today, we can pose a few awkward questions. Why does man seem to have many more diseases than animals have? Why does man hate and kill in war when animals do not? Why does cancer increase? Why are there so many suicides? So many insane sex crimes? Why the hate that is anti-Semitism? Why Negro hating and lynching? Why backbiting and spite? Why is sex obscene and a leering joke? Why is being a

Reprinted from A. S. Neill, *Summerhill* (New York: Hart Publishing Co., Inc., 1960), p. 24, with permission of the publisher.

bastard a social disgrace? Why the continuance of religions that have long ago lost their love and hope and charity? Why, a thousand whys about our vaunted state of civilized eminence!

I ask these questions because I am by profession a teacher, one who deals with the young. I ask these questions because those so often asked by teachers are the unimportant ones, the ones about school subjects. I ask what earthly good can come out of discussions about French or ancient history or what not when these subjects don't matter a jot compared to the larger question of life's natural fulfillment—of man's inner happiness.

DISCUSSION QUESTIONS

1. Neill says that "the aim of life is to find happiness." Does this constitute a workable guide for life development?
2. Do you agree with Neill that the prime function of the school is to help children find happiness?
3. Using your own educational experiences as a basis for discussion, which of the school's activities contributed to your wholesome individual development? Which were negative or hurtful?

PAUL GOODMAN | *Compulsory Mis-education*

The immediate future of our country seems to me to have two looming prospects, both gloomy. If the powers-that-be proceed as stupidly, timidly, and "politically" as they have been doing, there will be a bad breakdown and the upsurge of a know-nothing fascism of the right. Incidentally, let me say that I am profoundly unimpressed by our so-called educational system when, as has happened, Governor Wallace comes from the South as a candidate in Northern states and receives his highest number of votes (in some places a majority) in suburbs that have had the *most* years of schooling, more than 16.

The other prospect—which, to be frank, seems to me to be the goal of the school-monks themselves—is a progressive regimentation and brainwashing, on scientific principles, directly toward a fascism-of-the-center, 1984. Certainly this is not anybody's deliberate purpose; but given the maturing of automation, and the present dominance of the automating spirit in school-

Reprinted from Paul Goodman, *Compulsory Mis-education* (New York: Horizon Press, 1964), pp. 10–24; 31–34 with permission of the publisher. Copyright 1964.

ing, so that all of life becomes geared to the automatic system, that is where we will land.

Therefore in this book I do not choose to be "generous" and "fair."

Underlying the present superstition, however, is an objective fact. Major conditions of modern life *are* unprecedented and we do not know how to cope with them. Confused, people inevitably try to ward off anxiety by rigidifying the old methods of dominant economic and intellectual groups. Omitting the changed international conditions, let me just mention some unprecedented domestic developments that are crucial for even primary education.

Within the United States, we have reached a point of productivity when it becomes absurd to use the rate of growth and the Gross National Product as measures of economic health. To be useful, new production must be much more narrowly qualified, e.g. serve the public sector or eliminate grinding poverty. Unqualified growth already does more harm than good. Thus, we must consider concepts like "work" and "leisure" and "unemployment" in a new way, and we must begin to distinguish between economic well-being and mere affluence. Yet only a handful of economists are thinking along these lines, and almost no one escapes the mesmerism of the GNP. We cannot expect educators to be far ahead.

Correspondingly, the social valuation of scientific technology and science must change. Up to now, the emphasis has been on the products, including the research products, the Knowledge Explosion. But these become diminishingly useful, and the more they flood the environment, the less skillful the average man becomes. The problem for general education, rather, is to learn to *live* in a high technology. The emphasis ought to be on the moral virtues of science itself, both austere and liberating; on its humane beauty; on the selectivity and circumspect reasonableness of sciences like ecology and psychosomatic medicine. These are very different values from the present gearing of general education to the processing of Ph.D.'s.

Urbanization is almost total; independent farming, farming as "a way of life," is at the point of extinction. Yet this development is unexamined and uncontrolled. The disastrous pattern of blighted center, suburbs, and conurbation is taken for granted, and highway tax, housing, and schooling policies serve only to intensify it. Then astoundingly, we come to suffer from what looks like a population explosion, even though, in this country, vast and beautiful regions are being depopulated. One weeps to see it, yet nothing is done to find possible principles of rural recovery and better balance. Or, in the dense cities, to find functional equivalents for the lost self-reliance, extended family, and community.

There is anomie and an alarming rate of urban mental illness. My own view is that an important factor in these is powerlessness; it is impossible to become engaged or usefully to identify when one cannot initiate and have a say in deciding. If this is so, we should be studying new patterns of decentralizing while we centralize. But there are no such studies and, in my opinion, the bureaucratic methods of social psychiatry probably worsen the social diseases. Certainly we are in a political crisis, for, though the forms of democracy are intact, the content is vanishing. Such political vitality as there is finds its expression in paralegal ways; but these will eventually either renovate the constitution or degenerate into violence and gross injustice. Meantime, there is a proliferation of media of communication and messages communicated, for people need to be informed and want to be informed; yet, partly just because of the communications, there is brainwashing and conformity.

Such are some of the extraordinary conditions for which our schooling fails to educate. It is essential to find alternative ways of educating.

. . . .

Since schooling undertakes to be compulsory, must it not continually review its claim to be useful? Is it the only means of education? Isn't it unlikely that *any* single type of social institution could fit almost every youngster up to age 16 and beyond? (It is predicted that by 1970, 50% will go to college.)

But conferences on drop-outs are summoned by school professionals, so perhaps we cannot hope that such elementary questions will be raised. Yet neither are they raised by laymen. There is a mass superstition, underwritten by additional billions every year, that adolescents must continue going to school. The middle-class *know* that no professional competence—i.e. status and salary—can be attained without many diplomas; and poor people have allowed themselves to be convinced that the primary remedy for their increasing deprivation is to agitate for better schooling. Nevertheless, I doubt that, *at present or with any reforms that are conceivable under present school administration,* going to school is the best use for the time of life of the majority of youth.

Education is a natural community function and occurs inevitably, since the young grow up on the old, toward their activities, and into (or against) their institutions; and the old foster, teach, train, exploit, and abuse the young. Even neglect of the young, except physical neglect, has an educational effect—not the worst possible.

Formal schooling is a reasonable auxiliary of the inevitable process, whenever an activity is best learned by singling it out for special attention with a special person to teach it. Yet it by no means follows that the complicated artifact of a school system has much to do with education, and certainly not with good education.

Let us bear in mind the way in which a big school system might have nothing to do with education at all. The New York system turns over $700 millions annually, not including capital improvements. There are 750 schools, with perhaps 15 annually being replaced at an extra cost of $2 to $5 millions each. There are 40,000 paid employees. This is a vast vested interest, and it is very probable that—like much of our economy and almost all of our political structure, of which the public schools are a part—it goes on for its own sake, keeping more than a million people busy, wasting wealth, and pre-empting time and space in which something else could be going on. It is a gigantic market for textbook manufacturers, building contractors, and graduate-schools of Education.

The fundamental design of such a system is ancient, yet it has not been altered although the present operation is altogether different in scale from what it was, and therefore it must have a different meaning. For example, in 1900, 6% of the 17-year-olds graduated from high school, and less than ½% went to college; whereas in 1963, 65% graduated from high school and 35% went on to something called college. Likewise, there is a vast difference between schooling intermitted in life on a farm or in a city with plenty of small jobs, and schooling that is a child's only "serious" occupation and often his only adult contact. Thus, a perhaps outmoded institution has become almost the only allowable way of growing up. And with this pre-empting, there is an increasing intensification of the one narrow experience, e.g. in the shaping of the curriculum and testing according to the increasing requirements of graduate schools far off in time and place. Just as our American society as a whole is more and more tightly organized, so its school system is more and more regimented as part of that organization.

In the organizational plan, the schools play a non-educational and an educational role. The non-educational role is very important. In the tender grades, the schools are a baby-sitting service during a period of collapse of the old-type family and during a time of extreme urbanization and urban mobility. In the junior and senior high school grades, they are an arm of the police, providing cops and concentration camps paid for in the budget under the heading "Board of Education." The educational role is, by and large, to provide—at public and parents' expense—apprentice-training for corporations, government, and the teaching professions itself, and also to train the young, as New York's Commissioner of Education has said (in the Worley case), "to handle constructively their problems of adjustment to authority."

The public schools of America have indeed been a powerful, and beneficent, force for the democratizing of a great mixed population. But we must be careful to keep reassessing them when, with changing conditions, they become a universal trap and democracy begins to look like regimentation.

Let me spend a page on the history of the compulsory nature of the school systems. In 1961, in *The Child, the Parent, and the State,* James Conant mentions a possible incompatibility between "individual development" and "national needs"; this, to my mind, is a watershed in American philosophy of education and puts us back to the ideology of Imperial Germany, or on a par with contemporary Russia.

When Jefferson and Madison conceived of compulsory schooling, such an incompatibility would have been unthinkable. They were in the climate of the Enlightenment, were strongly influenced by Congregational (town-meeting) ideas, and were of course makers of a revolution. To them, "citizen" meant society-*maker,* not one "participating in" or "adjusted to" society. It is clear that they regarded themselves and their friends as citizens existentially, so to speak; to make society was their breath of life. But obviously such conceptions are worlds removed from, and diametrically opposed to, our present political reality, where the ground rules and often the score are pre-determined.

For Jefferson, people had to be taught in order to multiply the sources of citizenly initiative and to be vigilant for freedom. Everybody had to become literate and study history, in order to make constitutional innovations and be fired to defend free institutions, which was presumably the moral that history taught. And those of good parts were to study a technological natural philosophy, in order to make inventions and produce useful goods for the new country. By contrast, what are the citizenly reasons for which we compel everybody to be literate, etc.? To keep the economy expanding, to understand the mass-communications, to choose between indistinguishable Democrats and Republicans. Planning and decision-making are lodged in top managers; rarely, and at most, the electorate serves as a pressure-group. There is a new emphasis on teaching science—we will discuss this in another context—but the vast majority will never use this knowledge and will forget it; they are consumers.

Another great impulse for compulsory education came from the new industrialism and urbanism during the three or four decades after the Civil War, a time also of maximum immigration. Here the curricular demands were more mundane: in the grades, literacy and arithmetic; in the colleges, professional skills to man the expanding economy. But again, no one would have spoken of an incompatibility between "individual development" and "national needs," for it was considered to be an open society, abounding in opportunity. Typically, the novels of Horatio Alger, Jr., treat schooling as morally excellent as well as essential for getting ahead; and there is no doubt that the immigrants saw education-for-success as also a human value for their children. Further, the school-system was not a trap. The 94% who in 1900 did not finish high school had other life opportunities, including making a lot of money and rising in politics. But again, by and large this is not our present situation. There is plenty of social mobility, opportunity to rise—except precisely for the ethnic minorities who are our main concern as drop-outs—but the statuses and channels are increasingly stratified, rigidified, cut and dried. Most enterprise is parceled out by feudal corporations, or by the state; and these determine the requirements. Ambition with average talent meets these rules or fails; those without relevant talent, or with unfortunate backgrounds, cannot even survive in decent poverty. The requirements of survival are importantly academic, attainable only in schools and universities; but such schooling is ceasing to have an initiating or moral meaning.

We do not have an open economy; even when jobs are not scarce, the corporations and state dictate the possibilities of enterprise. General Electric swoops down on the high schools, or IBM on the colleges, and skims off the youth who have been pre-trained for them at public or private expense. (Private college tuition runs upward of $6000, and this is estimated as a third or less of the actual cost for "education and educational administration.") Even a department store requires a diploma for its salespeople, not so much because of the skills they have learned as that it guarantees the right character: punctual and with a smooth record. And more generally, since our powers-that-be have opted for an expanding economy with a galloping standard of living, and since the powers of the world are in an arms and space race, there *is* a national need for many graduates specifically trained. Thus, even for those selected, the purpose is irrelevant to citizenly initiative, the progress of an open society, or personal happiness, and the others have spent time and effort in order to be progressively weeded out. Some drop out.

It is said that our schools are geared to "middle-class values," but this is a false and misleading use of terms. The schools less and less represent *any* human values, but simply adjustment to a mechanical system.

Because of the increasing failure of the schools with the poor urban mass, there has developed a line of criticism—e.g. Oscar Lewis, Patricia Sexton, Frank Riessman, and even Edgar Friedenberg—asserting that there is a "culture of poverty" which the "middle-class" schools do not fit, but which has its own virtues of spontaneity, sociality, animality. The implication is that the "middle class," for all its virtues, is obsessional, prejudiced, prudish.

Pedagogically, this insight is indispensable. A teacher must try to reach each child in terms of what he brings, his background, his habits, the language he understands. But if taken to be more than technical, it is a disastrous conception. The philosophic aim of education must be to get each one out of his isolated class and into the one humanity. Prudence and responsibility are not middle-class virtues but human virtues; and spontaneity and sexuality are not powers of the simple but of human health. One has the impression that our social-psychologists are looking not to a human community but to a future in which the obsessionals will take care of the impulsives!

In fact, some of the most important strengths that have historically belonged to the middle class are flouted by the schools: independence, initiative, scrupulous honesty, earnestness, utility, respect for thorough scholarship. Rather than bourgeois, our schools have become petty-bourgeois, bureaucratic, time-serving, gradgrind-practical, timid, and *nouveau riche* climbing. In the upper grades and colleges, they often exude a cynicism that belongs to rotten aristocrats.

Naturally, however, the youth of the poor and of the middle class respond differently to the petty bourgeois atmosphere. For many poor children, school is orderly and has food, compared to chaotic and hungry homes, and it might even be interesting compared to total deprivation of toys and books. Besides, the wish to improve a child's lot, which on the part of a middle-class parent might be frantic status-seeking and pressuring, on the part of a poor parent is a loving aspiration. There is here a gloomy irony. The school that for a poor Negro child might be a great joy and opportunity is likely to be dreadful; whereas the middle-class child might be better off *not* in the "good" suburban school he has.

Other poor youth, herded into a situation that does not fit their disposition, for which they are unprepared by their background, and which does not interest them, simply develop a reactive stupidity very different from their behavior on the street or ball field. They fall behind, play truant, and as soon as possible drop out. If the school situation is immediately useless and damaging to them, their response must be said to be life-preservative. They thereby somewhat diminish their chances of a decent living, but we shall see that the usual propaganda—that schooling is a road to high salaries—is for most poor youth a lie; and the increase in security is arguably not worth the torture involved.

The reasonable social policy would be not to have these youth in school, certainly not in high school, but to educate them otherwise and provide opportunity for a decent future in some other way. How? I shall venture some suggestions later; in my opinion, the wise thing would be to have our conferences on *this* issue, and omit the idea of drop-out altogether. But the brute fact is that our society isn't really interested; the concern for the drop-outs is mainly because they are a nuisance and a threat and can't be socialized by the existing machinery.

Numerically far more important than these overt drop-outs at 16, however, are the children who conform to schooling between the ages of 6 to 16 or 20, but who drop out internally and day-dream, their days wasted, their liberty caged and scheduled. And there are many such in the middle class, from backgrounds with plenty of food and some books and art, where the youth is seduced by the prospect of money and status, but even more where he is terrified to jeopardize the only pattern of life he knows.

It is in the schools and from the mass media, rather than at home or from their friends, that the mass of our citizens in all classes learn that life is inevitably routine, depersonalized, venally graded; that it is best to toe the mark and shut up; that there is no place for spontaneity, open sexuality, free spirit. Trained in the schools, they go on to the same quality of jobs, culture, politics. This *is* education, mis-education, socializing to the national norms and regimenting to the national "needs."

John Dewey used to hope, naïvely, that the schools could be a community somewhat better than society and serve as a lever for social change. In fact, our schools reflect our society closely, except that they *emphasize* many of its worst features, as well as having the characteristic defects of academic institutions of all times and places.

. . . .

What then? The compulsory system has become a universal trap, and it is no good. Very many of the youth, both poor and middle class, might be better off if the system simply did not exist, even if they then had no formal schooling at all. (I am extremely curious for a philosophic study of Prince Edward County in Virginia, where for some years schooling did not exist for Negro children.)

But what would become of these children? For very many, both poor and middle class, their homes are worse than the schools, and the city streets are worse in another way. Our urban and suburban environments are precisely not cities or communities where adults naturally attend to the young and educate to a viable life. Also, perhaps especially in the case of the overt dropouts, the state of their body and soul is such that we must give them refuge and remedy, whether it be called school, settlement house, youth worker, or work camp.

There are thinkable alternatives. Throughout this little book, as occasion arises, I shall offer alternative proposals that I as a single individual have heard of or thought up. Here are half a dozen directly relevant to the subject we have been discussing, the system as compulsory trap. In principle, when a law begins to do more harm than good, the best policy is to alleviate it or try doing without it.

1. Have "no school at all" for a few classes. These children should be selected from tolerable, though not necessarily cultured, homes. They should be neighbors and numerous enough to be a society for one another and so that they do not feel merely "different." Will they learn the rudiments anyway? This experiment cannot do the children any academic harm, since there is good evidence that normal children will make up the first seven years school-work with four to seven months of good teaching.

2. Dispense with the school building for a few classes; provide teachers and use the city itself as the school—its streets, cafeterias, stores, movies, museums, parks, and factories. Where feasible, it certainly makes more sense to teach using the real subject-matter than to bring an abstraction of the subject-matter into the school building as "curriculum." Such a class should probably not exceed 10 children for one pedagogue. The idea—it is the

model of Athenian education—is not dissimilar to Youth gang work, but not applied to delinquents and not playing to the gang ideology.

3. Along the same lines, but both outside and inside the school building, use appropriate *unlicensed* adults of the community—the druggist, the storekeeper, the mechanic—as the proper educators of the young into the grown-up world. By this means we can try to overcome the separation of the young from the grown-up world so characteristic in modern urban life, and to diminish the omnivorous authority of the professional school-people. Certainly it would be a useful and animating experience for the adults. (There is the beginning of such a volunteer program in the New York and some other systems.)

4. Make class attendance not compulsory, in the manner of A. S. Neill's Summerhill. If the teachers are good, absence would tend to be eliminated; if they are bad, let them know it. The compulsory law is useful to get the children away from the parents, but it must not result in trapping the children. A fine modification of this suggestion is the rule used by Frank Brown in Florida: he permits the children to be absent for a week or a month to engage in any worthwhile enterprise or visit any new environment.

5. Decentralize an urban school (or do not build a new big building) into small units, 20 to 50, in available store-fronts or clubhouses. These tiny schools, equipped with record-player and pin-ball machine, could combine play, socializing, discussion, and formal teaching. For special events, the small units can be brought together into a common auditorium or gymnasium, so as to give the sense of the greater community. Correspondingly, I think it would be worthwhile to give the Little Red Schoolhouse a spin under modern urban conditions, and see how it works out: that is, to combine all the ages in a little room for 25 to 30, rather than to grade by age.

6. Use a pro rata part of the school money to send children to economically marginal farms for a couple of months of the year, perhaps 6 children from mixed backgrounds to a farmer. The only requirement is that the farmer feed them and not beat them; best, of course, if they take part in the farm-work. This will give the farmer cash, as part of the generally desirable program to redress the urban-rural ratio to something nearer to 70% to 30%. (At present, less than 8% of families are rural.) Conceivably, some of the urban children will take to the other way of life, and we might generate a new kind of rural culture.

I frequently suggest these and similar proposals at teachers colleges, and I am looked at with an eerie look—do I really mean to *diminish* the state-aid grant for each student-day? But mostly the objective is that such proposals entail intolerable administrative difficulties.

Above all, we must apply these or any other proposals to particular individuals and small groups, without the obligation of uniformity. There is a case for uniform standards of achievement, lodged in the Regents, but they *cannot* be reached by uniform techniques. The claim that standardization of procedure is more efficient, less costly, or alone administratively practical, is often false. Particular inventiveness requires thought, but thought does not cost money.

DISCUSSION QUESTIONS

1. Evaluate Goodman's charges against the schools.
2. In terms of your own education, how valid are Goodman's criticisms?
3. Are public schools necessarily poor schools?
4. What is the future of public education in America?
5. Goodman's charges appear to level public education. How adequate are his suggestions for change?

JOHN F. GARDNER | *The Experience of Knowledge*

To me . . . the real crisis in the life of our society is the crisis of the life of the imagination. Far more than we need an intercontinental missile or a moral rearmament or a religious revival, we need to come alive again, to recover the virility of the imagination on which all earlier civilizations have been based: Coleridge's "synthetic and magical power" by which 'the whole soul of man' may be brought to activity, and knowledge may be known.
Archibald MacLeish, "The Poet and the Press"

One of my chief duties during the last twelve years has been to interview all students applying for admission to the Waldorf School of Adelphi College. There comes a time in every interview when the student leaves my office to be seen by the appropriate teacher, and I am alone with his parents. I generally ask, "Why have you brought your child to *this* school?"

The answers are varied and often vague. I am told that the school is known to have high standards, to provide an enriched curriculum, to work for the all-round development of the child. There is said to be an atmosphere of warmth and idealism in our school; art is much cultivated; French and German are taught through the elementary grades. One hears that our

Reprinted from John F. Gardner, *The Experience of Knowledge* (Garden City, N.Y.: The Myrin Institute, Inc., Adelphi University, 1962), pp. 5–9 and 35–38, with permission of the author and publisher.

teachers give attention to the individual student; gifted students are challenged; the maverick has a chance to find himself . . .

While all of these allegations are actually true, none of them serves clearly to distinguish the Waldorf style of education from others. I feel duty-bound eventually to point this fact out to parents, but as soon as I do so, of course, the tables are turned. Now it is I who must answer questions: "How *does* the Waldorf School differ from other schools? What can I expect my child to receive here that he would not get somewhere else?"

It might seem easy to reply, provided there *is* anything distinctive about Waldorf education, and yet it is not easy. While it does appear sometimes that schools make their reputation with a specialty such as strict discipline, emphasis on creative arts, high academic standards, the international exchange of students, and exceptional athletic program, or a particular religious attitude, Waldorf schools have no specialty of this kind. The emphasis they place upon the arts is well known, yet the stress they lay on science is equally strong and deserves equal attention. They have developed a unique twelve-year curriculum, involving a great number of new methods of teaching the various subjects, yet no subject or particular method can be singled out as most important. Curriculum and methods are, in any case, subject to evolutionary change, and they derive from something more basic than themselves. To answer an inquirer's simple question, therefore, with an equally simple answer—or as the request is usually phrased, 'in a few words'—is very difficult, even impossible, for anyone intimately acquainted with the scope of the educational undertaking known as a Waldorf school.

Perhaps not all Waldorf educators would simplify matters in the same way, but when I face the necessity of choosing according to my own preference from among the possible ways of describing what we are trying to do in The Waldorf School of Adelphi College, I come back invariably to our belief that *knowledge should be fully experienced.*

Ordinarily, the knowledge with which education confronts the child consists of facts that are to be observed and ideas that are to be thought. Such observations and thoughts certainly use a part of the human capacity for experience, but not the larger part. They leave out both the feeling and the active sides of a child's inner nature. Arithmetic, spelling, grammar, science, geography, and history, as these are generally taught in school, make no contribution to a student's desire to be inwardly touched and moved.

What we call natural scientific method has influenced education as it has all of culture, and this method has seemed to demand suppression of the feelings that naturally rise in the scientific observer and thinker. Waldorf education, however, supports Rudolf Steiner's concept of a spiritual science of the future. Such a science calls for the transmutation of feeling and will into thinking, rather than their elimination from it. It would purge irrelevancies from one's psychological reaction, but not psychological reaction from one's objective study of the world.* The special effort of Waldorf education, therefore, is to strengthen, clarify, and articulate the student's capacity to feel, his readiness to unfold inward movement, by letting every percept and concept awaken its appropriate experience.

Waldorf teachers believe that nuances of feeling and inward gestures belong to each perceived fact quite as objectively as does a certain concept. Just as the fact awakens thoughts in an observer and these thoughts reveal something about this fact; so, if we do not arbitrarily prevent it from doing so, this same fact will awaken, with equal necessity, configurations of feeling; it will stir the observer in his will. Such inward stirrings and feelings also reveal something about the fact. They are signs that one is dealing with the whole fact, not just its external body.

We become aware of the higher, deeper, or truer aspects of nature and the world-process at first as obscure stirrings within ourselves. If we encourage the whole man to respond to the complete phenomenon, and if we are patient, we can expect that what starts in subjective obscurity will gradually rise to objective consciousness as surely as bubbles will form at the bottom of a pot of boiling water, out of the water itself, and will rise at last to join the upper air.

Waldorf schools bear ever in mind, besides, that when a student allows facts and events to engage his attention completely, the world not only begins to confide its secret life to him; its effect upon him is also penetrating, and therefore thoroughly educative. The pursuit of knowledge becomes a true *discipline* for him. He is transformed, as well as informed, by the knowledge he acquires.

. . . .

CREATIVE ABILITY OPENS THE DOOR TO PRACTICAL LIFE

The impracticality of minds that pass for practical has thus far contrived a technological civilization in which it seems that the steps forward are matched by steps backward: where those who save most time actually have least; where those who cover more space see less; where creature comforts engender dissatisfaction and restlessness; where crops grow big while nourishment shrinks; where such an all-purpose advance as the use of atomic energy endangers the safety and health of every living thing on earth.

We need a practicality that *is* practical. We need successes that really do succeed. Human society today more than ever before needs creative artists

* "I believe that some of the worst confusions in contemporary thinking and doing arise from the general failure to realize that there is as great an 'objective within' as there is an 'objective without.'" Laurens van der Post, *The Dark Eye in Africa,* William Morrow and Co., Inc., New York, 1955.

in the shaping of economic, political, legal, medical, agricultural, educational affairs.

The main distinction between a theorist and one who actually shapes events, aside from the difference in sheer energy flowing through them, is that the theorist approaches life from outside. He comes as a stranger, seeking to impose his good ideas on wayward reality. The practical artist, however, approaches from within life. He is at one with events. His good ideas rise directly from the ripening of his experience of fact. His ideals are not hatched all too predictably out of abstract logic on the one hand, or personal ambition on the other. Rather, they are learned by him, perhaps unexpectedly and to his surprise, as he follows the metamorphoses of real events. Such ideals gradually emerge from reality itself, albeit with the help of his thought and of his hand.

Why does a theorist so often stumble against reality? Of theoretical minds we feel that they do not learn properly from life. They work from and toward generalities. The theorist thinks out principles, but has difficulty with their application. He does not know precisely where to place his feet, as it were. It is likely that his timing will be off, or his approach will offend. He may well become discouraged in his attempts to improve the world, because "hard facts" seem to fight him. All this is because he tends to draw his original conception from the air, from his own head, from a book, rather than from reality. The difficulty is that, even when facts are straight and his ideas appropriate, reality will have taught only his head. Until his knowing becomes an experience of the whole man, reality will not also give power to his heart, and ability to his hands.

PRACTICALITY OPENS THE DOOR TO PEACE

Nearly everyone wants peace today. But unless schools educate men who are more practical to occupy leading positions in society, there is no telling whether the universal desire for peace will actually succeed in bringing to an end the succession of wars that has thus far characterized our century.

We have mentioned the paradoxical nature of modern technological progress. Starting from the wish to make land more fertile, we continue to reduce its natural fertility and so find ourselves chained to the necessity of ever bigger doses of fertilizer to maintain the status quo. Starting from the idea of destroying bacteria and bugs, we call into being new strains of frightening virulence. Starting from the presumably sincere wish to reduce the farm surplus, or the federal deficit, one administration after another finds itself watching their continued growth. And starting from the desire to do something to uplift the little man, socialistic big government shows signs that it could end by crushing him altogether.

The results of cold-blooded intelligence may seem scientific, but in practical life they will always be paradoxical, which really means, in the end, impractical. For every one-sidedness calls out its opposite. Cold blood calls forth hot; an overdose of rationalism calls forth an upsurge of the irrational—whether revolutionary, criminal, psychotic, mystical, or "beat." As these opposites collide inside the individual, they engender frustration, paralysis, and atrophy; or they break out of him in violence and destruction. Colliding in society, they bring about warfare, cold or hot. Only a whole intelligence, maturing from complete experience, well centered and in harmony with itself, can actually do what it sets out to do. Only such an intelligence can so master the extreme paradoxicality of modern life as to achieve peace.

An intelligence that matures from experience, that shares in the life of nature, that is creative and practical, fulfills itself. It finds satisfaction in properly human pursuits. Not at war with nature or with itself, it does not project war into human society. Waldorf schools aim to develop this kind of intelligence, for in it they see the only prospect for freedom and peace in the world.

DISCUSSION QUESTIONS

1. Do you agree with Gardner that not ". . . facts to be observed and ideas that are to be thought" but ". . . the feeling and active sides of a child's inner nature" are ". . . the larger part of the human capacity for experience"?
2. Should the child be "transformed, as well as informed, by the knowledge he acquires"?
3. Is it possible and practical to build a pedagogy that recognizes that "nuances of feeling and inward gestures belong to each perceived fact quite as objectively as does a certain concept"?
4. Is the Waldorf approach to education applicable to the public schools?
5. Might independent Waldorf schools, available to all who wish to attend, be a reasonable alternative to the public schools? What proportion of the public, do you think, would send its children to such schools? How might they be financed?

CHAPTER 2 *Freedom*

Can we compromise freedom in any of its forms—freedom of thought, of expression, of movement, of choice—the freedom of students, of teachers, of the "deprived" and the "disadvantaged"—and still maintain that "freedom" is a dominant goal of the social organism?

Consideration of the concept of freedom in education raises many questions. Can students at all levels of the educational process live freely so that they can learn the modes and habits of free adults? Do teachers possess the freedom to deal fully and frankly with controversial issues so that students will learn the ways of inquiry and investigation and the habit of using knowledge at the cutting edge of intelligence? Is freedom to change built into the educational structure? Do schools cherish diversity of thought and nonconformity in all of its manifestations? What does it mean to be free? Do we mean to be free?

In the American educational scene today, freedom is too often misunderstood, too often abused and denied. Students doubt their rights, or are unaware that they have any rights. Teachers, perhaps more than any other group, are under tremendous pressure to exchange their freedom for security and advancement. Academic freedom is discovered to be no more or less than the freedom of the community at large.

The concept of freedom is central to all that is said in this chapter. Hopefully, a sharper insight into the complex nature of freedom will evolve out of consideration of the various issues presented here. If man is to be "free," if freedom can command a heartfelt dedication, man must understand what freedom signifies. For teachers, the future of freedom is a charge upon them.

JOHN DEWEY | *What Is Freedom?*

The place of natural fact and law in morals brings us to the problem of freedom. We are told that seriously to import empirical facts into morals is equivalent to an abrogation of freedom. Facts and laws mean necessity we are told. The way to freedom is to turn our back upon them and take flight to a separate ideal realm. Even if the flight could be successfully accomplished, the efficacy of the prescription may be doubted. For we need freedom in and among actual events, not apart from them. It is to be hoped therefore that there remains an alternative; that the road to freedom may be found in that knowledge of facts which enables us to employ them in connection with desires and aims. A physician or engineer is free in his thought and his action in the degree in which he knows what he deals with. Possibly we find here the key to any freedom.

What men have esteemed and fought for in the name of liberty is varied and complex—but certainly it has never been a metaphysical freedom of will. It seems to contain three elements of importance, though on their face not all of them are directly compatible with one another. (1) It includes efficiency in action, ability to carry out plans, the absence of cramping and thwarting obstacles. (2) It also includes capacity to vary plans, to change the course of action, to experience novelties. And again (3) it signifies the power of desire and choice to be factors in events.

Few men would purchase even a high amount of efficient action along definite lines at the price of monotony, or if success in action were bought by all abandonment of personal preference. They would probably feel that a more precious freedom was possessed in a life of ill-assured objective achievement that contained undertaking of risks, adventuring in new fields, a pitting of personal choice against the odds of events, and a mixture of success and failures, provided choice had a career. The slave is a man who executes the wish of others, one doomed to act along lines predetermined to regularity. Those who have defined freedom as ability to act have unconsciously assumed that this ability is exercised in accord with desire, and that its operation introduces the agent into fields previously unexplored. Hence the conception of freedom as involving three factors.

Yet efficiency in execution cannot be ignored. To say that a man is free to choose to walk while the only walk he can take will lead him over a precipice is to strain words as well as facts. Intelligence is the key to freedom

---

Reprinted from John Dewey, *Human Nature and Conduct* (New York: Holt, Rinehart & Winston, Inc., 1922), pp. 303–313, with permission of the publisher.

in act. We are likely to be able to go ahead prosperously in the degree in which we have consulted conditions and formed a plan which enlists their consenting cooperation. The gratuitous help of unforeseen circumstance we cannot afford to despise. Luck, bad if not good, will always be with us. But it has a way of favoring the intelligent and showing its back to the stupid. And the gifts of fortune when they come are fleeting except when they are made taut by intelligent adaptation of conditions. In neutral and adverse circumstances, study and foresight are the only roads to unimpeded action. Insistence upon a metaphysical freedom of will is generally at its most strident pitch with those who despise knowledge of matters-of-fact. They pay for their contempt by halting and confined action. Glorification of freedom in general at the expense of positive abilities in particular has often characterized the official creed of historic liberalism. Its outward sign is the separation of politics and law from economics. Much of what is called the "individualism" of the early nineteenth century has in truth little to do with the nature of individuals. It goes back to a metaphysics which held that harmony between man and nature can be taken for granted, if once certain artificial restrictions upon man are removed. Hence it neglected the necessity of studying and regulating industrial conditions so that a nominal freedom can be made an actuality. Find a man who believes that all men need is freedom *from* oppressive legal and political measures, and you have found a man who, unless he is merely obstinately maintaining his own private privileges, carries at the back of his head some heritage of the metaphysical doctrine of free-will, plus an optimistic confidence in natural harmony. He needs a philosophy that recognizes the objective character of freedom and its dependence upon a congruity of environment with human wants, an agreement which can be obtained only by profound thought and unremitting application. For freedom as a fact depends upon conditions of work which are socially and scientifically buttressed. Since industry covers the most pervasive relations of man with his environment, freedom is unreal which does not have as its basis an economic command of environment.

I have no desire to add another to the cheap and easy solutions which exist of the seeming conflict between freedom and organization. It is reasonably obvious that organization may become a hindrance to freedom; it does not take us far to say that the trouble lies not in organization but in over-organization. At the same time, it must be admitted that there is no effective or objective freedom without organization. It is easy to criticize the contract theory of the state which states that individuals surrender some at least of their natural liberties in order to make secure as civil liberties what they retain. Nevertheless there is some truth in the idea of surrender and exchange. A certain natural freedom is possessed by man. That is to say, in some respects harmony exists between a man's energies and his surroundings such that the latter support and execute his purposes. In so far he is free; without such a basic natural support, conscious contrivances of legislation, administration and deliberate human institution of social arrangements cannot take place. In this sense natural freedom is prior to political freedom and is its condition. But we cannot trust wholly to a freedom thus procured. It is at the mercy of accident. Conscious agreements among men must supplement and in some degree supplant freedom of action which is the gift of nature. In order to arrive at these agreements, individuals have to make concessions. They must consent to curtailment of some natural liberties in order that any of them may be rendered secure and enduring. They must, in short, enter into an organization with other human beings so that the activities of others may be permanently counted upon to assure regularity of action and far-reaching scope of plans and courses of action. The procedure is not, in so far, unlike surrendering a portion of one's income in order to buy insurance against future contingencies, and thus to render the future course of life more equably secure. It would be folly to maintain that there is no sacrifice; we can however contend that the sacrifice is a reasonable one, justified by results.

Viewed in this light, the relation of individual freedom to organization is seen to be an experimental affair. It is not capable of being settled by abstract theory. Take the question of labor unions and the closed or open shop. It is folly to fancy that no restrictions and surrenders of prior freedoms and possibilities of future freedoms are involved in the extension of this particular form of organization. But to condemn such organization on the theoretical ground that a restriction of liberty is entailed is to adopt a position which would have been fatal to every advance step in civilization, and to every net gain in effective freedom. Every such question is to be judged not on the basis of antecedent theory but on the basis of concrete consequences. The question is to the balance of freedom and security achieved, as compared with practicable alternatives. Even the question of the point where membership in an organization ceases to be a voluntary matter and becomes coercive or required, is also an experimental matter, a thing to be decided by scientifically conducted study of consequences, of pros and cons. It is definitely an affair of specific detail, not of wholesale theory. It is equally amusing to see one man denouncing on grounds of pure theory the coercion of workers by a labor union while he avails himself of the increased power due to corporate action in business and praises the coercion of the political state; and to see another man denouncing the latter as pure tyranny, while lauding the power of industrial labor organizations. The position of one or the other may be justified in particular cases, but justification is due to results in practice not to general theory.

Organization tends, however, to become rigid and to limit freedom. In addition to security and energy in action, novelty, risk, change are ingredients of the freedom which men desire. Variety is more than the spice of life; it is largely of its essence, making a difference between the free and the enslaved. Invariant virtue appears to be as mechanical as uninterrupted vice, for true excellence changes with conditions. Unless character rises to overcome some new difficulty or conquer some temptation from an unexpected quarter we suspect its gain is only a veneer. Choice is an element in freedom and there can be no choice without unrealized and precarious possibilities. It is this demand for genuine contingency which is caricatured in the orthodox doctrine of a freedom of indifference, a power to choose this way or that apart from any habit or impulse, without even a desire on the part of will to show off. Such an indetermination of choice is not desired by the lover of either reason or excitement. The theory of arbitrary free choice represents indeterminateness of conditions grasped in a vague and lazy fashion and hardened into a desirable attribute of will. Under the title of freedom men prize such uncertainty of conditions as give deliberation and choice an opportunity. But uncertainty of volition which is more than a reflection of uncertainty of conditions is the mark of a person who has acquired imbecility of character through permanent weakening of his springs of action.

Whether or not indeterminateness, uncertainty, actually exists in the world is a difficult question. It is easier to think of the world as fixed, settled once for all, and man as accumulating all the uncertainty there is in his will and all the doubt there is in his intellect. The rise of natural science has facilitated this dualistic partitioning, making nature wholly fixed and mind wholly open and empty. Fortunately for us we do not have to settle the question. A hypothetical answer is enough. *If* the world is already done and done for, if its character is entirely achieved so that its behavior is like that of a man lost in routine, then the only freedom for which man can hope is one of efficiency in overt action. But *if* change is genuine, if accounts are still in process of making, and if objective uncertainty is the stimulus to reflection, then variation in action, novelty and experiment, have a true meaning. In any case the question is an objective one. It concerns not man in isolation from the world but man in his connection with it. A world that is at points and times indeterminate enough to call out deliberation and to give play to choice to shape its future is a world in which will is free, not because it is inherently vacillating and unstable, but because deliberation and choice are determining and stabilizing factors.

Upon an empirical view, uncertainty, doubt, hesitation, contingency and novelty, genuine change which is not mere disguised repetition, are facts. Only deductive reasoning from certain fixed premises creates a bias in favor of complete determination and finality. To say that these things exist only in human experience not in the world, and exist there only because of our "finitude" is dangerously like paying ourselves with words. Empirically the life of man seems in these respects as in others to express a culmination of facts in nature. To admit ignorance and uncertainty in man while denying them to nature involves a curious dualism. Variability, initiative, innovation, departure from routine, experimentation are empirically the manifestation of a genuine nisus in things. At all events it is these things that are precious to us under the name of freedom. It is their elimination from the life of a slave which makes his life servile, intolerable to the freeman who has once been on his own, no matter what his animal comfort and security. A free man would rather take his chance in an open world than be guaranteed in a closed world.

These considerations give point to the third factor in love of freedom: the desire to have desire count as a factor, a force. Even if will chooses unaccountably, even if it be a capricious impulse, it does not follow that there are real alternatives, genuine possibilities, open in the future. What we want is possibilities open in the *world* not in the will, except as will or deliberate activity reflects the world. To foresee future objective alternatives and to be able by deliberation to choose one of them and thereby weight its chances in the struggle for future existence, measures our freedom. It is assumed sometimes that if it can be shown that deliberation determines choice and deliberation is determined by character and conditions, there is no freedom. This is like saying that because a flower comes from root and stem it cannot bear fruit. The question is not what are the antecedents of deliberation and choice, but what are their consequences. What do they do that is distinctive? The answer is that they give us all the control of future possibilities which is open to us. And this control is the crux of our freedom. Without it, we are pushed from behind. With it we walk in the light.

The doctrine that knowledge, intelligence rather than will, constitutes freedom is not new. It has been preached by moralists of many a school. All rationalists have identified freedom with action emancipated by insight into truth. But insight into necessity has by them been substituted for foresight of possibilities. Tolstoi for example expressed the idea of Spinoza and Hegel when he said that the ox is a slave as long as he refuses to recognize the yoke and chafes under it, while if he identifies himself with its necessity and draws willingly instead of rebelliously, he is free. But as long as the yoke is a yoke it is impossible that voluntary identification with it should occur. Conscious submission is then either fatalistic submissiveness or cowardice. The ox accepts in fact not the yoke but the stall and the hay to which the yoke is a necessary incident. But if the ox foresees the consequences of the use of the yoke, if he anticipates the possibility of harvest, and identifies himself not with the yoke but with the realization of its possibilities, he acts freely, voluntarily. He hasn't accepted a necessity as unavoidable; he has welcomed a possibility as a desirability.

Perception of necessary law plays, indeed, a part. But no amount of insight into necessity brings with it, as such, anything but a consciousness of necessity. Freedom is the "truth of necessity" only when we use one "necessity" to alter another. When we use the law to foresee consequences and to consider how they may be averted or secured, then freedom begins. Employing knowledge of law to enforce desire in execution gives power to the engineer. Employing knowledge of law in order to submit to it without further action constitutes fatalism, no matter how it be dressed up. Thus we recur to our main contention. Morality depends upon events, not upon demands and ideals alien to nature. But intelligence treats events as moving, as fraught with possibilities, not as ended, final. In forecasting their possibilities, the distinction between better and worse arises. Human desire and ability cooperates with this or that natural force according as this or that eventuality is judged better. We do not use the present to control the future. We use the foresight of the future to refine and expand present activity. In this use of desire, deliberation and choice, freedom is actualized.

DISCUSSION QUESTIONS

1. What is the relationship between freedom and education?
2. How does Dewey's view on variety in life fit into his trifold criteria for freedom?
3. Is modern man's freedom inevitably curtailed by the increasing mechanization and stratification of the age of technology?
4. What does Dewey's concept of freedom mean when applied to the current civil rights struggles of minority groups?

A. S. NEILL — *The Free Child*

Freedom is necessary for the child because only under freedom can he grow in his natural way—the good way. I see the results of bondage in new pupils coming from prep schools and convents. They are bundles of insincerity, with an unreal politeness and phony manners.

Their reaction to freedom is rapid and tiresome. For the first week or two, they open doors for the teachers, call me "Sir," and wash carefully. They glance at me with "respect," which is easily recognized as fear. After a few weeks of freedom, they show what they really are. They become impudent, unmannerly, unwashed. They do all the things they have been forbidden to do in the past: they swear, they smoke, they break things. And all the time, they have a polite and insincere expression in their eyes and in their voices.

It takes at least six months for them to lose their insincerity. After that, they also lose their deference to what they regarded as authority. In just about six months, they are natural, healthy kids who say what they think without fluster or hate. When a child comes to freedom young enough, he

Reprinted from A. S. Neill, *Summerhill* (New York: Hart, 1960), pp. 110–111, with permission of the publisher.

does not have to go through this stage of insincerity and acting. The most striking thing about Summerhill is this absolute sincerity among the pupils.

This business of being sincere in life and to life is a vital one. It is really the most vital one in the world. If you have sincerity, all other things will be added to you. Everyone realizes the value of sincerity in, say, acting. We expect sincerity from our politicians (such is the optimism of mankind), from our judges and magistrates, teachers and doctors. Yet we educate our children in such a way that they dare not be sincere.

Possibly the greatest discovery we have made in Summerhill is that a child is born a sincere creature. We set out to let children alone so that we might discover what they were like. It is the only possible way of dealing with children. The pioneer school of the future must pursue this way if it is to contribute to child knowledge and, more important, to child happiness.

DISCUSSION QUESTIONS

1. Should children have freedom? If so, what kind?
2. Is Neill's concept of freedom possible in the public schools? Does any of it apply to the public schools? Should it apply?
3. Given a choice between your past education and education at Summerhill, which would you choose? Defend your choice.

ABRAHAM J. HESCHEL | *The Insecurity of Freedom*

We all share a supreme devotion to the hard-won freedoms of the American people. Yet to be worthy of retaining our freedoms we must not lose our understanding of the essential nature of freedom. Freedom means more than mere emancipation. It is primarily freedom of conscience, bound up with inner allegiance. The danger begins when freedom is thought to consist in the fact that "I can act as I desire." This definition not only overlooks the compulsions which often lie behind our desires; it reveals the tragic truth that freedom may develop within itself the seed of its own destruction. The will is not an ultimate and isolated entity, but determined by motives beyond its own control. *To be* what one wants to be is also not freedom, since the wishes of the ego are largely determined by external factors.

Reprinted from Abraham J. Heschel, *The Insecurity of Freedom* (New York: Farrar, Straus & Giroux, Inc., 1966), pp. 14–21, with permission of the publisher.

Freedom is not a principle of uncertainty, the ability to act without a motive. Such action would be chaotic and subrational, rather than free.

Although political and social freedom must include all this, even the freedom to err—its true essence is in man's ability to surpass himself, even to act against his inclinations and in defiance of his own needs and desires, to sacrifice prejudice even if it *hurts,* to give up superstition even when it claims to be a doctrine.

Freedom is the liberation from the tyranny of the self-centered ego. It comes about in moments of transcending the self as an act of spiritual ecstasy, of stepping out of the confining framework of routine reflexive concern. Freedom presupposes *the capacity for sacrifice.*

Although all men are potentially free, it is our sacred duty to safeguard all those political, social, and intellectual conditions which will enable every man to bring about the concrete actualization of freedom which is the essential prerequisite of creative achievement.

The shock of radical amazement, the humility born in awe and reverence, the austere discipline of unremitting inquiry and self-criticism are acts of liberating man from the routine way of looking only at those features of experience which are similar and regular, and opening his soul to the unique and transcendent. This sensitivity to the novel and the unprecedented is the foundation of God-awareness and of the awareness of the preciousness of all beings. It leads from reflexive concern and the moral and spiritual isolation which is the result of egocentricity to a mode of responding to each new and unique experience in terms of broader considerations, wider interests, deeper appreciation and new, as yet unrealized values.

As the object of divine transitive concern *man is;* knowing himself to be the object of divine concern and responding through acts of his own transitive concern *he is free.*

The meaning of freedom is not exhausted by deliberation, decision, and responsibility, although it must include all this. The meaning of freedom presupposes an openness to transcendence, and man has to be *responsive* before he can become *responsible.*

For freedom is not an empty concept. Man is free to be free; he is not free in choosing to be a slave; he is free in doing good; he is not free in doing evil. To choose evil is to fail to be free. In choosing evil he is not free but determined by forces which are extraneous to the spirit. Free is he who has decided to act in agreement with the spirit that goes beyond all necessities.

Freedom is a challenge and a burden against which man often rebels. He is ready to abandon it, since it is full of contradiction and continually under attack. Freedom can only endure as a vision, and loyalty to it is an act of faith.

There is no freedom without awe. We must cultivate many moments of silence to bring about one moment of expression. We must bear many burdens to have the strength to carry out one act of freedom.

Man's true fulfillment cannot be reached by the isolated individual, and his true good depends on communion with, and participation in, that which transcends him. Each challenge from beyond the person is unique, and each response must be new and creative. Freedom is an act of engagement of the self to the spirit, a spiritual event.

Loyalty to freedom means loyalty to the substance of freedom. But such loyalty must be actualized again and again. Here our way of living must change: it must open the sight of sublime horizons under which we live.

Refusal to delegate the power to make ultimate decisions to any human institution derives its strength either from the awareness of one's mysterious dignity or from the awareness of one's ultimate responsibility. But that strength breaks down in the discovery that one is unable to make a significant choice. Progressive vulgarization of society may deprive man of his ability to appreciate the sublime burden of freedom. Like Esau he may be ready to sell his birthright for a pot of lentils.

A major root of freedom lies in the belief that man, every man, is too good to be the slave of another man. However, the dynamics of our society, the cheapening and trivialization of existence, continues to corrode that belief. The uniqueness and sacred preciousness of man is being refuted with an almost cruel consistency. I do not mean the anthropological problem whether or not we are descendants of the monkeys. What I have in mind is the fact that we are being treated as if there were little difference between man and monkey. Much that is being done, e.g., in the name of entertainment, is an insult to the soul. What is involved is not demoralization; much of it may be morally neutral. What is involved is dehumanization; so much of it is a continual process of intellectual deprivation. Sensitivity to words is one of the many casualties in that process.

Words have become pretexts in the technique of evading the necessity of honest and genuine expression. Sometimes it seems as if we were all engaged in the process of liquidating the English language. But words are the vessels of the spirit. And when the vessels are broken, our relationship to the spirit becomes precarious.

To be free one must attain a degree of independence. Yet the complexities of society have enmeshed contemporary man in a web of relationships which make his independence most precarious.

Inherent in man is the desire to be in agreement with others. Yet today with a mass of miscellaneous associations and unprecedented excitements, it is a grim task, indeed, to agree with all and to retain the balance of integrity.

Loaded with more vulnerable interests than he is able to protect, bursting with fears of being squeezed by a multiplicity of tasks and responsibilities, modern man feels too insecure to remain upright.

Good and evil have always had a tendency to live in promiscuity, but in more integrated societies man, it seems, found it easier to discriminate between the two, while in our turbulent times circumstances often stupefy our power of discernment; it is as if many of us have become value-blind in the epidemics of needs.

The glory of a free society lies not only in the consciousness of *my* right to be free, and *my* capacity to be free, but also in the realization of *my fellow man's* right to be free, and *his* capacity to be free. The issue we face is how to save man's belief in his capacity to be free. Our age may be characterized as the *age of suspicion*. It has become an axiom that the shortest way to the understanding of man is to suspect his motives. This seems to be the contemporary version of the Golden Rule: *Suspect thy neighbor as thyself*. Suspicion breeds suspicion. It creates a chain-reaction. Honesty is not necessarily an anachronism.

The righteous man shall live by his faith. Can he live by his suspicion and be righteous? It is dangerous to take human freedom for granted, to regard it as a prerogative rather than as an obligation, as an ultimate fact rather than as an ultimate goal. It is the beginning of wisdom to be amazed at the fact of our being free.

Freedom is a gift which may be taken away from us. It is not an absolute but a relative possession, an opportunity. We are free only when living in attachment to the spirit. The blessings and opportunities of living in a free society must not make us blind to those aspects of our society which threaten our freedom: the tyranny of needs, the vulgarization of the spirit are a particular challenge.

The insecurity of freedom is a bitter fact of historical experience. In times of unemployment, vociferous demagogues are capable of leading the people into a state of mind in which they are ready to barter their freedom for any bargain. In times of prosperity hidden persuaders are capable of leading the same people into selling their conscience for success. Unless a person learns how to rise daily to a higher plane of living, to care for that which surpasses his immediate needs, will he in a moment of crisis insist upon loyalty to freedom?

The threat to freedom lies in the process of reducing human relations to a matter of fact. Human life is no longer a drama; it is a routine. Uniqueness is suppressed, repetitiveness prevails. We teach our students how to recognize the labels, not how to develop a taste. Standardization corrodes the sense of ultimate significance. Man to his own self becomes increasingly vapid, cheap, insignificant. Yet without the sense of ultimate significance and ultimate preciousness of one's own existence, freedom becomes a hollow phrase.

We are losing our capacity for freedom. New forces have emerged which regulate our actions. Modern man is not motivated anymore, he is being propelled; he does not strive anymore, he is being driven.

The principle of majority decision, the binding force of a majority, depends upon the assumption that the individuals who make up the majority are capable of discerning between right and wrong. But we are gradually led to believe that man is incapable of making a significant moral judgment.

We have made great contributions to the spiritual defamation of man. Far from eliminating the fear of man, our novels and theories depict man as untrustworthy, passion-ridden, self-seeking, and disingenuous.

Reverence for man has been strenuously refuted as sentimental eyewash. We all ride on the highways of debunking. There seems to be no question in our mind that there is no depth to virtue, no reality to integrity; that all we can do is to graft goodness upon selfishness, to use truth as a pragmatic pretext, and to relish self-indulgence in all values.

Contemporary man is told that his religious beliefs are nothing but attempts to satisfy subconscious wishes, that his conception of God is merely a projection of self-seeking emotions, an objectification of subjective needs; God is the Ego in disguise. We have not only forfeited faith; we have also lost faith in the meaning of faith. This tendency to question the genuineness of man's concern for God is a challenge more serious than the tendency to question God's existence.

One of the chief problems of contemporary man is the problem: What to do with time? Most of our life we spend time in order to gain space, namely things of space. Yet when the situation arrives in which no things of space may be gained, the average man is at a loss as to what to do with time.

With the development of automation the number of hours to be spent professionally will be considerably reduced. The four-day week may become a reality within this generation. The problem will arise: What to do with so much leisure time? The problem will be *too much* time rather than too little time. But too much time is a breeding ground for crime.

The modern man has not only forgotten how to be alone; he finds it even difficult to be with his fellow man. He not only runs away from himself; he runs away from his family. To children, "Honor your father and your mother," is an irrational suggestion. The normal relationship is dull; deviation is where pleasure is found.

. . . .

Religion's major effort must be to counteract the deflation of man, the trivialization of human existence. Our religious traditions claim that man is capable of sacrifice, discipline, of moral and spiritual exaltation, that every man is capable of an ultimate commitment.

Ultimate commitment includes the consciousness of being accountable for the acts we perform under freedom; the awareness that what we own we owe; the capacity for repentance; that a life without the service of God is a secret scandal.

Faith in God cannot be forced upon man. The issue is not only lack of faith but the vulgarization of faith, the misunderstanding and abuse of freedom. Our effort must involve a total reorientation about the nature of man and the world. And our hope lies in the certainty that all men are capable of sensing the wonder and mystery of existence, that all men have a capacity for reverence. Awe, reverence precedes faith; it is at the root of faith. We must grow in awe in order to reach faith. We must be guided by awe to be worthy of faith. Awe is "the beginning and gateway of faith, the first precept of all, and upon it the whole world is established."

The grandeur and mystery of the world that surrounds us is not something which is perceptible only to the elect. All men are endowed with a sense of wonder, with a sense of mystery. But our system of education fails to develop it and the anti-intellectual climate of our civilization does much to suppress it. Mankind will not perish for lack of information; it may collapse for want of appreciation.

Education for reverence, the development of a sense of awe and mystery, is a prerequisite for the preservation of freedom.

We must learn how to bridle the outrageous presumption of modern man, to cultivate a sense of wonder and reverence, to develop an awareness that something is asked of man. Freedom is a burden that God has thrust upon man. Freedom is something we are responsible for. If we succeed, we will help in the redemption of the world; if we fail, we may be crushed by its abuse. Freedom as man's unlimited lordship is the climax of absurdity, and the central issue we face is man's false sense of sovereignty.

DISCUSSION QUESTIONS

1. Must "freedom" have a theological base?
2. How do we "know" or "test" the validity of human action in terms of divine will?
3. Is Heschel's presentation of the concept of freedom inherently repugnant to the agnostic, the atheist, and the traditional democratic thinker?

WILLIAM F. O'NEILL

Existentialism and Education for Moral Choice

> *. . . what there is of free will in individual determination begins only on a rather high human level. . . . The broadly developed intelligence is needed to ponder moral problems, to have moral problems, and only he who feels ethics as a continuous problem is a person to*

Reprinted from *Phi Delta Kappan,* Vol. XLVI, No. 2 (October 1964), pp. 48–53, with permission of the publisher.

whom ethics is a real concern—just as the only blasphemers or near-unbelievers, like Job, Kierkegaard, Hopkins, Dostoievsky, Kafka, Simone Weil, are the only ones to deal deeply with religion. The Prussian king Frederick II, an atheist, was the only one among his devout dynasty who took religion quite seriously.

Erich Kahler, "The Tower and Abyss"

We have values, and we judge values. Of course, having them is not an intellectual or cognitive process; but judging is. . . . The rational man is one who values only what evaluation reveals to be worthy of it. A value judgment is not a mere expression of the fact that we then and there find something satisfying, but a hypothesis that it will prove to be satisfactory; not merely that we are interested in it, but that indeed it is our interest.

Abraham Kaplan, "New World of Philosophy"

To sum up, *good in humanistic ethics is the affirmation of life, the unfolding of man's powers. Virtue is responsibility toward his own existence.* Evil constitutes the crippling of man's powers; *vice is irresponsibility toward himself.*

Erich Fromm, "Man for Himself"

In the last ten or fifteen years educators have become increasingly aware of just how little they know, not only about ethics in general, but about the whole process of education for the development of moral character. It is probably true that to some degree this discomfiting sense of disorientation stems from a radical new sense of urgency with respect to the whole question of human values which has in part grown out of the activities of a relatively small group of intellectuals who are frequently referred to as "the existentialists."

Existentialism is a difficult term to define. In perhaps the most basic sense, it is a sort of metaphysical first principle which holds that all meaning is a product of direct personal experience. Existentialism at its broadest does not necessarily imply any particular concepts of value. On the other hand, most existentialist philosophers have clearly developed their theories beyond the bare assertion that "existence precedes essence" and most are in fundamental agreement on what might be termed a sort of minimum existentialist theory of value. In a very general sense, this theory can be reduced to three basic principles:

1. Man exists—experiences the world—through the medium of choice.
2. His moral standards are also choices, by means of which he regulates his responsibility with respect to others.

3. A *good choice* (including a good *moral* choice), is one which has been derived "authentically"—that is, on the basis of active, conscious and self-determined experience.[1]

Virtually all of the existentialist philosophers have developed some ethical point of view which encompasses these basic assumptions. The fundamental differences between these theories are those which exist between the *theistic* (religious) existentialists, who are perhaps best represented by such individuals as Kierkegaard and, more recently, Jaspers, Tillich, Marcel, and Buber, and the *non-theistic* (agnostic and/or atheistic) existentialists such as Heidegger and Sartre.

It goes without saying that there are vast and significant differences between the fully developed ethical viewpoints expressed by these men and particularly, of course, by the viewpoints which characterize the extreme poles of existentialist thought. On the other hand, there are certain general assumptions which the major representatives of the existentialist point of view hold in common and which, supplemented by the more recently developed views of the existentialist psychologists and psychoanalysts such as Frankl and May, seem to represent a reasonably reliable source of warrantable assertions with respect to the more general position which most existentialists share with respect to the problems posed by moral education. This position, while it has never been explicitly developed by any of the major representatives of the existentialist point of view, is, on the whole, implied by the theories developed by the major existentialists and may be summarized in the following six basic points.

1. Man is potentially autonomous.[2] The only value which applies categorically to all men *as men* is the actualization of the self as a free agent. This is the so-called value of "authenticity," or "authentic existence." A man who lives authentically exists in the autonomous mode. Such an individual is capable of choosing his own acts and is, in a sense, the author of his own destiny.

2. The basic function of the school is normative. It should act to encourage the maximum development of individual autonomy, or free choice. The fundamental problem confronted by the school is, as Heidegger states, "*Wie man wird, was man ist*—how one becomes what one is."[3]

Developing the capacity for free choice encompasses two basic steps: (1)

[1] The existentialists hold that man is "free"—that he is capable of "free choice," which is actually a sort of epistemological self-selection.

[2] The question of how and to what extent man is autonomous is a point of argument even among the existentialists themselves. All would seem to hold to the position that man is at least *capable* of free choice. Some would go so far as to assert that man is *absolutely free* and is, therefore, incapable of augmenting his free choice through any sort of volitional activity whatsoever.

[3] Martin Heidegger, *Being and Time*. As quoted in Rollo May, Ernest Angel, and Henri F. Ellenberger, eds., *Existence: A New Dimension in Psychiatry and Psychology*. New York: Basic Books, Inc., 1958, p. 31.

cultivating the *ability* to make free and rational decisions and (2) developing the *inclination* to make such decisions in the first place. Of these, the latter is clearly the more important phase. The basic aim of existentialist education is to develop a sense of commitment to free choice. The existentialist agrees that dullness is generally an achievement and not a gift.[4] The aim of existentialist education is not simply to help the individual *cope* with his existence. Its primary purpose is to help him to *experience his existence* by confronting it with a sense of defined purpose. For the existentialist, the proper outcome of education is a certain sort of attitude toward life. Such an attitude includes more than "openness," however; it also implies an "eagerness." The educated man is characterized not only by what he *knows* but also, and perhaps even more, by what he is *capable of knowing and experiencing*. In a basic sense, then, the hallmark of an existentialist education is not knowledge as such but rather "educability."

The existentialist advocates "education for choice" because he has a clear awareness that the most basic educational problem pertains to the criteria for selecting appropriate knowledge and not with the techniques for disseminating knowledge as such. The existentialist is concerned, above all, with "the habit of growth." He focuses on values precisely because he recognizes that values are directive and, therefore, determinative of more subsequent knowledge.

3. The school should be basically concerned with "moral education"—that is, with developing not only the *capacity for* but also the *inclination toward* moral choice—and not with "moral training"—that is, the conditioning of "acceptable behavior" as such.[5] From the existentialist point of view it is far more important that a child be taught to be "moral"—that he become capable of moral *choice,* and hence, become fully "human"—than that he be "right" in the sense of conforming to the established dictates of society.

This position is based on two underlying assumptions about the nature of moral choice: (a) A "moral act" is necessarily an autonomous act, and (b) an autonomous (authentic) act may be either good *or* bad, but is in any event preferable to an inauthentic "non-act," which can be *neither* good nor bad, since it is never really "chosen" at all but merely "performed" on a more or less unreflective basis.

In a general sense, then, existentialism is more concerned with developing the capacity for *moral choice* than with the *moral nature*—i.e., the goodness

---

[4] Earl Kelley, *In Defense of Youth.* New York: Spectrum, 1963, p. 129.

[5] This is not to suggest that "moral education" and "moral training" are in any sense mutually exclusive. In many instances they are mutually reinforcing. As Ryle points out, the capacity to appreciate a performance is generally, if qualifiedly, one in type with the capacity to execute it. (Gilbert Ryle, *The Concept of Mind.* New York: Barnes and Noble, 1949, p. 56.) On the other hand, the fact that moral education may expedite moral training and vice versa does not mean that they are the same thing.

and badness—of the choice made. For the existentialist there can be morality without goodness, but there cannot be goodness without morality.

As a general rule, then, the existentialist takes the position that we should not try to anticipate all moral problems in an attempt to pre-formulate decisions to every conceivable sort of moral conflict but should seek to produce the sort of individual who is capable of improvising enlightened solutions to various moral questions as they emerge. The existentialist would not say that lying, for example, is *not* a moral problem. He would, however, characteristically take the position that *whether* lying is or is not a moral problem for any particular person depends upon three basic conditions: (a) whether that individual is capable of making a real moral choice—that is, of making a decision in the rational-autonomous mode; (b) whether truthfulness is a value which is logically required by the goal of autonomous behavior as such (i.e., whether it is a condition necessary for autonomous choice to take place); and (c) whether truthfulness is otherwise logically implied by any additional value-commitments which have been made. In all events, for the existentialist the basic moral question involved would not be whether one should or should not lie, but, rather, whether one is willing and able to decide *whether* one should lie or not—that is, whether one is capable of making a moral choice with respect to the advisability of lying in the first place.

4. There is no basic and irreconcilable conflict between self-interest and the interests of others. A concern for others is a logical development of self-interest clearly conceived, since personal autonomy requires a complex set of supportive social conditions, including a fully functioning democratic process and a high degree of civil liberty. Real autonomy precludes license and, to be effective,

> . . . every pupil must be convinced that discipline is the best way of attaining the aims of the community. . . . A logic of . . . discipline confirms that discipline places each individual personality in a position of greater security and freedom. Children easily understand the apparent paradox that discipline means freedom. . . .[6]

5. Any real commitment to free choice as an educational goal both implies and entails a certain type of self-discipline on the part of the students themselves. If the school succeeds in making rational self-determination a dominant value, two important consequences arise: (a) Most of the more traditional ethical objectives of the school, such as honesty and responsibility, tend to emerge automatically as conditions necessary for the full realization of rational-autonomous behavior, and (b) the need for the usual sort of externalized discipline is largely precluded.

The existentialist would tend to agree that "a single moral principle hammered out in discussion and applied to real situations is worth tons of

---

[6] Anton S. Makarenko, *The Road to Life*. As quoted in National Society for the Study of Education: The Fifty-fourth Year Book, Part I. Nelson B. Henry, ed., *Modern Philosophies and Education*. Chicago: University of Chicago Press, 1955, p. 209.

affirmed values which are never put to a natural test."[7] It is best that a few really significant ideas, a few truly generative principles, should be developed and reinforced through direct practice over a period of time than that the really significant issues should be obscured behind a multiplicity of trivial and legalistic rules.

These values (with the possible exception of the value of autonomy itself) are available to common sense and can be affirmed on the basis of relatively undirected and informal experience. Once autonomous behavior has been allowed to develop, other types of moral behavior tend to emerge more or less spontaneously out of the natural process of trial-and-error experience and are either confirmed or denied on the basis of their own natural consequences.[8]

This position deviates from the traditional Rousseauistic concept of "negative education" in two basic respects. First, existentialism precludes any naive concept of goodness as an innate quality (although some existentialists would take the position that man's basic capacity for rational self-determination, in conjunction with his preinclination to conform to such a constructive potential, predisposes him toward "goodness"). Second, the existentialist is ordinarily little inclined to the idea that the individual recapitulates the history of the race in his natural development. Most existentialists are, if anything, somewhat *anti*historical in inclination, frequently taking the position that much, if not most, past knowledge is actually noncontributive and possibly even dysfunctional with respect to the fulfillment of basic human freedom. Their fundamental objection would seem to center on the idea that much of what presently passes for "education" is simply an attempt to obscure the real (existential) problems relating to the *human condition* behind a great deal of irrelevant or erroneous data about the past and present *human situation.*

---

7 T. V. Smith and Eduard C. Lindeman, *The Democratic Way of Life.* New York: New American Library, 1951, p. 134.

8 It goes more or less without saying that this is a controversial position. What so many existentialists are suggesting is essentially (a) that there are actually very few categorical (intercontextual) problems which are shared by all men and (b) that the "answers" to those that do exist are for the most part (and providing the situation remains uncontaminated by gratuitous theory) relatively self-evident on the basis of common-sense trial-and-error experience conducted in the sort of learning situation which makes such experience possible. Perhaps the best example of this point of view in action is A. H. Neill's well-known school, Summerhill, where all moral training is allowed to evolve as a product of direct experience in response to practical problems encountered in what approximates a life-like learning situation. It should be noted that Neill does not take the position that there are no errors under such a procedure but rather that all learning requires practice; that all practice involves error or at least the possibility of error; and that to eliminate error (or at least *significant* error) is to curb learning drastically. He does not, in other words, say, "This is the ideal way in which it is possible to conceive of learning taking place," but rather, "This is the way learning *does* take place whether we like it or not." Much of progressive pedagogy was, of course, based upon much the same point of view—that is, not that you cannot teach *more,* but that children can only learn so much effectively, based upon the necessary conditions for any sort of responsible learning.

The schools have traditionally made the error of trying to change behavior directly, that is, of trying to make children do and say those things which would ostensibly alter their values in an immediate and observable manner. Unfortunately, and as the great educational theorists have observed repeatedly for many centuries, the most effective way to change belief and behavior is not to deal with belief and behavior as such, but rather to use the "seed crystal effect"—that is, to concentrate upon the values which make any given individual susceptible to certain kinds of experience rather than others.

James once said that it is nonsense to suppose that every step in education *can* be interesting.[9] He might well have added, however, that those things which are not interesting in and of themselves can at least be made *necessary* and, hence, turned into a source of secondary interest when they have been implicated in the total life-process through a sense of overriding purpose. In other words, intellectual knowledge conduces to change only by being transmuted into emotional knowledge. As Wiener has indicated, ". . . it is not the quantity of information sent that is important for action, but rather the quantity of information which can penetrate into a communication and storage apparatus sufficiently to serve as a trigger for action."[10]

Moral education, properly developed, is self-corroborating. It channels perception into prescribed routes and generates the kind of moral training compatible with its own underlying presuppositions. As Comenius said as far back as the beginning of the 17th century,

> Most teachers are at pains to place in the earth plants instead of seeds, and trees instead of shoots, since, instead of starting with the fundamental principles, they place before their pupils a choas of diverse conclusions or the complete texts of authors.
>
> . . . .
>
> Hitherto the schools have not taught their pupils to develop their minds like young trees from their own roots, but rather to deck themselves with branches plucked from other trees, and, like Aesop's crow, to adorn themselves with the feathers of other birds; they have taken no trouble to open the fountain of knowledge that is hidden in the scholars, but instead have watered them with water from other sources.[11]

Certain types of moral choice cannot be forced. The young child is incapable of undertaking a meaningful sort of religious commitment for the simple reason that he is incapable of comprehending the various options involved in any but the most superficial sense. Premature education is shallow because it tends toward empty verbalization. A fact which few

---

[9] William James, *Talks to Teachers on Psychology: and to Students on Some of Life's Ideals*. New York: W. W. Norton and Company, 1958, p. 51.

[10] Norbert Wiener, *The Human Use of Human Beings: Cybernetics and Society*. Garden City, N.Y.: Doubleday Anchor Books, 1950, p. 94.

[11] Comenius, *The Great Didactic*. Trans. by M. W. Keatings. Quoted in Ronald Gross, *The Teacher and the Taught*. New York: Dell Publishing Company, 1963, p. 38.

educators have ever really faced up to is that much significant learning simply cannot be acquired during the school years at all because it is totally unrelated to the needs and problems of school children. Every year we manage to distort, obscure, and otherwise mishandle a great deal of religion, philosophy, and literature by force-feeding it to children who haven't the foggiest notion of what it really *means* and whose only adequate defense lies in either total indifference or naive misinterpretation. It is simply not true, as many high school students would be willing to testify, that *Moby Dick* is actually an excellent sea story even if its real meaning is overlooked or that *Hamlet* is basically an exciting mystery in addition to everything else. The sad fact is that *Moby Dick* is a pretty dull sea story unless it is understood as precisely the intellectually provocative and deeply intense moral and psychological drama it was intended to be in the first place and that *Hamlet* doesn't really hold a candle to the average paperback thriller in the eyes of the typical adolescent.

6. Moral *content* cannot be separated from the moral *procedures* that are used to establish and maintain classroom discipline. The development of free choice is incompatible with arbitrary or externalized control. Autonomy is not derived through a system characterized by habituation to unquestioning obedience. Authoritarian control, regardless of how ostensibly "efficient" it may seem to be, undermines the basic human values which should motivate the entire educational process and even serves to subvert the basic goal of student *self*-determination. As Edgar Friedenberg indicates with reference to the contemporary high school,

> . . . the consequence of continuing through adolescence to submit to diffuse authority that is not derived from the task at hand—as a doctor's orders or the training regulations of an athletic coach, for example, usually are—is more serious than political incompetence or weakness of character.[12]

It is difficult to elicit a real enthusiasm for solving problems and making choices where the problems and choices with which one is habitually confronted are essentially *fait accompli* which have been disseminated from above and in which professed and real values are perceived to be clearly incompatible. As Erich Fromm suggests,

> "Liberal" or "progressive" systems of education have not changed this situation as much as one would like to think. Overt authority has been replaced by anonymous authority, overt commands by "scientifically" established formulas; "don't do this" by "you will not like to do this." In fact, in many ways, this anonymous authority may be even more oppressive than the overt one. The child is no longer aware of being bossed (nor are the parents of giving orders), and he cannot fight back and thus develop a sense of independence. He is coaxed and persuaded in the name of science, common sense, and cooperation—and who can fight against such objective principles?[13]

---

[12] Edgar Z. Friedenberg, "The Modern High School: A Profile," *Commentary,* November, 1963, p. 379.
[13] Erich Fromm, *Man for Himself.* New York: Rinehart, 1947, p. 156.

Or as philosopher T. V. Smith comments,

A few years after graduation from high school we expect students to be mysteriously transformed into citizens. When they reach the magic age of twenty-one, they are expected to participate. But the sad truth is that in our last national elections only slightly more than one-half of the legal voters took the trouble to cast their ballots. They had not acquired the habit of participation.[14]

. . . .

Democracy may be defended on battlefields but it can become a way of life worth defending only through intelligent practice.[15]

The existentialist takes the point of view that moral choice cannot be taught didactically. The danger with vicarious morality is, as Wendell Johnson has suggested, that while waiting for Moses to lead them into the promised land, the children may forget how to walk.[16]

One of the most astonishing sights to be seen all too often in our schools is a teacher of civics or political science conducting a class in "democratic government" with the pupils sitting in neat rows dutifully giving answers prescribed by the teacher and the book. A dictator can't teach democracy. It just can't be taught with a hickory stick any more than it can be taught with a bayonet. It can only be taught by a good listener.[17]

Certainly one of the great but virtually incomprehensible truths of all times is that which holds that formative moral principles can only be acquired through direct personal experience. Basic moral truths may be *communicated* verbally, but they can never acquire any full and personal *significance* in this way. As Kierkegaard has said, genuine moral insight is always a profoundly personal thing which can only be shared with others who have also come to experience it as a profoundly intimate sort of *self*-discovery.

Whatever the one generation may learn from the other, that which is genuinely human no generation learns from the foregoing. . . . Thus, no generation has learned from another to love, no generation begins at any other point than at the beginning, no generation has a shorter task assigned to it than had the previous generation. . . . In this respect every generation begins primitively, has no different task from that of every previous generation, nor does it get further, except insofar as the preceding generation shirked its task and deluded itself.[18]

There is, however, something about a man that does not love a paradox—even one that has been amply confirmed by the best psychological evidence.

---

[14] T. V. Smith and Eduard C. Lindeman, *The Democratic Way of Life*. New York: New American Library, 1951, p. 151.

[15] *Op. cit.*, p. 154.

[16] Wendell Johnson, *People in Quandaries*. New York: Harper, 1946, p. 342.

[17] *Op. cit.*, pp. 480–81.

[18] Soren Kierkegaard, *Fear and Trembling*. As quoted in Rollo May, Ernest Angel, and Henri F. Ellenberger (eds.), *Existence: A New Dimension in Psychiatry and Psychology*. New York: Basic Books, Inc., 1958, p. 70.

We insist on holding tight to our Euclidean certainties in a post-Euclidean age. Stubbornly, we continue to confuse the "logic of discovery" with the "logic of presentation," overlooking the fact that "trials terminate in verdicts, they do not consist of them."[19] Unwilling to accept the conclusions of our own best research, we continue to reject the fact that learning is a highly devious, indirect, and complex phenomenon and persist in placing our reliance on the all too easy, if frequently misleading, techniques of traditional "telling" in which morality is conceived to emerge through a sort of spontaneous combustion out of the friction arising from repeated moral admonition.

For the existentialists, autonomy is not a *fact* to be learned but a *process* to be mastered. A system of moral education based upon the unreflective assimilation of the conclusions of others unfortunately provides no basis for deriving one's own conclusions. Rational assent is an insufficient basis for authentic existential commitment.

DISCUSSION QUESTIONS

1. Should education have as a basic aim the development in the individual of "a sense of commitment to free choice"?
2. If so, how would you accomplish this goal in your classroom?
3. What is your "defined purpose" in life? How helpful was your schooling in arriving at this definition?
4. What is "authentic existential commitment"? What is its relationship to freedom?

SIDNEY HOOK

Student Revolts Could Destroy Academic Freedom

Colleges Should Not Yield to Militants' Blackmail, Professor Warns; Only Courage Tames Fanatics

I began my college career in the fall of 1919, almost a half century ago. My academic lifetime spans half a dozen revolutions in American education. But have no fear, I am not going to reminisce. I want to stay young, at least in spirit, and I learned from my teacher, John Dewey, whom I observed closely for the last 25 years of his life, what the secret of staying

Reprinted from *The New York University Alumni News,* May 1968, with permission of the publisher.

[19] Gilbert Ryle, *The Concept of Mind.* New York: Barnes and Noble, 1949, pp. 298–99.

young is, and that is *not* to reminisce about the past. Actually, I never heard John Dewey reminisce until he was in his nineties, and that was as a reluctant response to my deliberate prodding in order to extract biographical data from him.

However, there is a way of talking about the past that is not merely reminiscence or idle reverie. It occurs when we make comparisons of the past and present for the sake of a present purpose or for the sake of finding a new way out of present difficulties.

Fifty years ago when I began my college studies, it would be no exaggeration to say that the belief in academic freedom was regarded as faintly subversive even in many academic circles. The AAUP [American Association of University Professors], organized by two philosophers, Arthur Lovejoy and John Dewey, was in its infancy without influence or authority. Today, except in some of the cultural and political backwaters of the U.S., academic freedom, although not free from threats, is firmly established. In some regions it has the support of law.

Fifty years ago, the power of the chief university administrator was almost as unlimited as that of an absolute monarch. Today the administrator is a much harried man with much less power and authority among faculty, and especially students, than his forebears. Today there may be temperamentally happy administrators but their present life is an unhappy one. There seems to be an open season on them, and to such a degree that for the first time in history there is an acute shortage of candidates for the almost 300 vacant administrative posts in institutions of higher learning. When I did my graduate work at Columbia, Nicholas Murray Butler was both the reigning and ruling monarch. I don't believe that in his wildest dreams he could have conceived of the Columbia scene today. The strongest argument I know against the resurrection of the body is that if it were within the realm of possibility, Nicholas Murray Butler would have risen from his grave and would now be storming Morningside Heights.

Having been an administrator in a small way myself, I have learned what an ungrateful job it is, and at the same time how necessary. Without administrative leadership, every institution (especially universities, whose faculties are notoriously reluctant to introduce curricular changes) runs downhill. The greatness of a university consists predominantly in the greatness of its faculty. But faculties, because of reasons too complex to enter into here, do not themselves build great faculties. To build great faculties, administrative leadership is essential. In the affairs of the mind and in the realm of scholarship, the principles of simple majority rule or of "one man, one vote" do not apply. The most "democratically" run institutions of learning are usually the most mediocre. It takes a big man to live comfortably with a still bigger man under him, no less to invite him to cast his shadow over the less gifted.

TARGETS OF ABUSE

The paradox today is that as administrative power decreases and becomes more limited, the greater the dissatisfaction with it seems to grow. The memory of favors or requests denied remains much stronger than the memories of requests granted. Faculties are fickle in their allegiance. Overnight the most beloved of administrators can become the target of abuse, a figure of obloquy in the eyes of the very faculty, or a large section of it, which he himself has helped to build. In the very year that Clark Kerr received the Meikeljohn medal for academic freedom, the faculty at the University of California campus at Berkeley panicked in consequence of the events resulting from the *fourth* student sit-in.

In effect it repudiated him by adopting a set of resolutions that made him the scapegoat for the student lawlessness that it conspicuously refused to condemn. The faculty even voted down a motion that would have given the students complete freedom of speech except to urge the commission of *immediate acts* of force and violence. Another example: Vice President Truman of Columbia University was vigorously applauded at Columbia's commencement last June for, among other things, opening new avenues of communication with students. Only a few days ago he was roundly booed by a section of the Columbia faculty.

Why any scholar (and administrators are largely recruited from the ranks of scholars) should want to become a *full-time* administrator has always puzzled me. The duties, sacrifices and risks seem altogether disproportionate to the rewards. In speaking of administrators, one is tempted to characterize them with the words Lecky used in his great history of European morals about the fallen women of Europe . . . "The eternal priestesses of humanity blasted for the sins of their people." Well, university administrators are no longer priests, but whenever a crisis arises they are sure to be damned if they do and damned if they don't.

SYNTHETIC STORMS

One thing seems clear. In the crisis situations shaping up throughout the country, administrators are not going to enjoy a peaceful life. Their prospect of weathering the storms that will be synthetically contrived for them depends upon their ability and willingness to win the faculty for whatever plans and proposals they advance in the name of the university. For if they permit students or any other group to drive a wedge between them and the faculty, they will discover the sad fact of academic life that in such rifts the faculty will either play a neutral role or even assume a hostile one.

Not only on good educational grounds, therefore, but on prudential ones as well, the administration must draw the faculty into the formulation of institutional educational policy. I say this with reluctance because it means the proliferation of committee meetings, the dilution of scholarly interest, and even less time for students. But this is a small price to pay for academic freedom and peace.

In talking about academic freedom, nothing signifies the distance we have come in the space of my lifetime so much as the fact that we now are concerned with the academic freedom of *students.* For historical reasons I cannot now explore, academic freedom in the United States meant *Lehrfreiheit,* freedom to teach. *Lernfreiheit,* freedom to learn, has only recently been stressed. It does not mean the same as it meant under the German university system that presupposed the all-prescribed curriculum of studies of the *Gymnasium.* If academic freedom for students means freedom to learn, then two things should be obvious. There is no academic freedom to learn without *Lehrfreiheit* or academic freedom to teach. Where teachers have no freedom to teach, students have obviously no freedom to learn, although the converse is not true.

Second, students' freedom to learn was never so widely recognized, was never so pervasive in the United States as it is today—whether it be construed as the freedom to attend college or not, or the freedom to select the *kind* of college the student wishes to attend or his freedom of curricular choice *within* the kind of college he selects. Above all, if academic freedom for students means the freedom to doubt, challenge, contest and debate within the context of inquiry, American students are the freest in the world, and far freer than they were when I attended college.

I recall an incident when I was a student in a government class at CCNY. The teacher conducted the class by letting the students give reports on the themes of the course. All he contributed was to say "next" as each student concluded. But when in reporting on the Calhoun-Webster debates, I declared that it seemed to me that Calhoun had the better of the argument, that his logic was better than Webster's although his *cause* was worse, the instructor exploded and stopped me. After emotionally recounting his father's services in the Civil War, he turned wrathfully on me and shouted: "Young man! When you're not preaching sedition, you are preaching secession!" Whereupon he drove me from the class. (The "sedition" was a reference to an earlier report on Beard's economic interpretation of the Constitution that he had heard with grim disapproval.) And this was at CCNY in 1920! The incident wasn't typical, but that it could happen at all marks the profundity of the changes in attitudes toward students since then. John Dewey's influence has made itself felt even in the colleges today.

MORAL PREMISE

Of course, there is still a large group of potential college students who are deprived of freedom to learn because of poverty or prejudice or the absence of adequate educational facilities. And as citizens of a democratic society whose moral premise is that each individual has a right to that education that will permit him to achieve his maximum growth as a person, our duty is to work for, or support, whatever measures of reconstruction we deem necessary to remove the social obstacles to freedom of learning. It is perfectly legitimate to expect the university to study these problems and propose solutions to them. All universities worthy of the name already do. This is one thing. But to therefore conclude that these problems must become items not only on the agenda of study but for an agenda of action is quite another.

For it therewith transforms the university into a political action organization and diverts it from its essential task of discovery, teaching, dialogue and criticism. Since there are profound differences about the social means necessary to achieve a society in which there will be a maximum freedom to learn, the university would become as partisan and biased as other political action groups urging their programs on the community. Its primary educational purpose or mission would be lost. It would be compelled to silence or misrepresent the position of those of its faculty who disagreed with its proposals and campaigns of action. Class and group conflicts would rend the fabric of the community of scholars in an unceasing struggle for power completely unrelated to the quest for truth.

OBJECTIVITY IMPERILED

If the university is conceived as an agency of action to transform society in behalf of a cause, no matter how exalted, it loses its *relative* autonomy, imperils both its independence and objectivity, and subjects itself to retaliatory curbs and controls on the part of society on whose support and largesse it ultimately depends.

This is precisely the conception of a university that is basic to the whole strategy and tactics of the so-called Students for a Democratic Society. I say "so-called" because their actions show that they are no more believers in democracy than the leaders of the so-called Student Non-Violent Coordinating Committee are believers in non-violence. And indeed the leaders of the SDS make no bones about that fact. In manifesto after manifesto they have declared that they want to use the university as an instrument of revolution. To do so, they must destroy the university as it exists today.

I wish I had time to list some of the clever stratagems they have devised to focus their opposition. On every campus there are always some grievances. Instead of seeking peacefully to resolve them through existing channels of consultation and deliberation, the SDS seeks to inflame them. Where grievances don't exist, they can be created. In one piece of advice to chapter members, they were urged to sign up for certain courses in large numbers, and then denounce the university for its large classes!

Freedom of dissent, speech, protest is never the real issue. They are, of course, always legitimate. But the tactic of the SDS is to give dissent the immediate form of violent action. The measures necessarily adopted to counteract this lawless action then become the main issue, as if the original provocation hadn't occurred. Mario Savio admitted after the Berkeley affair that the issue of "free speech" was a "pretext"—the word was his—to arouse the students against the existing role of the university in society.

SEEK TO DESTROY

One of the leaders of the SDS at Columbia is reported to have said: "As much as we would like to, we are not strong enough as yet to destroy the United States. But we are strong enough to destroy Columbia!" He is wrong about this, too—the only action that would destroy Columbia would be faculty support of the students!—but his intent is clear.

Actually, the only thing these groups, loosely associated with the New Left, are clear about is what they want to destroy, not what they would put in its stead. In a debate with Gore Vidal, Tom Haydon, one of the New Left leaders, was pointedly asked what his revolutionary program was. He replied: "We haven't any. First we will make the revolution, and *then* we will find out what for." This is truly the politics of absurdity.

The usual response present-day academic rebels make to this criticism is that the university today is nothing but an instrument to preserve the status quo, and therefore faithless to the ideals of a community of scholars. Even if this charge were true, even if the universities today were bulwarks of the status quo, this would warrant criticism and protest, not violent and lawless action in behalf of a contrary role, just as foreign to their true function. But it is decidedly *not* true!

There is no institution in the country in which dissent and criticism of official views, of tradition, of the conventional wisdom in all fields, is freer and more prevalent than in the university. The very freedom of dissent that students today enjoy in our universities is in large measure a consequence of the spirit of experiment, openness to new ideas, absence of conformity and readiness to undertake new initiatives found among them.

ARROGANT CLAIM

The first casualty of the strategy of the campus rebels is academic freedom. It is manifest in their bold and arrogant claim that the university drop its research in whatever fields these students deem unfit for academic inquiry and investigation. This note was already sounded in Berkeley. It is focal at Columbia. It is a shameless attempt to usurp powers of decision that the faculty alone should have. After all, it is preposterous for callow and immature adolescents who presumably have come to the university to get an education to set themselves up as authorities on what research by their teachers is educationally permissible.

Unless checked, it will not be long before these students will be presuming to dictate the conclusions their teachers should reach, especially on controversial subjects. This is standard procedure in totalitarian countries in which official student organizations are the political arm of the ruling party. Already there are disquieting signs of this. At Cornell a few weeks ago—*before* the martyrdom of Dr. King—a group of Black Nationalist students invaded the offices of the chairman of the economics department and held him captive in order to get an apology from a teacher whose views on African affairs they disagreed with. Only yesterday, another group at Northwestern demanded that courses in "black literature" and "black art" be taught by teachers approved by the Negro students.

And there are spineless administrators and cowardly members of the faculty who are prepared to yield to this blackmail. Under the slogans of "student rights" and "participatory democracy" the most militant groups of students are moving to weaken and ultimately destroy the academic freedom of those who disagree with them.

Let us not delude ourselves. Even when these militant students fail to achieve their ultimate purpose, they succeed in demoralizing the university by deliberately forcing a confrontation upon the academic community that it is not prepared to face and the costs of which it is fearful of accepting. In forcing the hand of the academic community to meet force with force, the citadel of reason becomes a battlefield. The students glory in it, but the faint of heart among their teachers turn on their own administrative leaders. These militants succeed in sowing distrust among students who do not see through their strategy. They also succeed in dividing the faculties.

EMBITTER RELATIONS

There is always a small group—a strange mixture of purists and opportunists desirous of ingratiating themselves with students—who will *never* condemn the violence of students but only the violence required to stop it. These students succeed, even when they fail, in embittering relations between the administration and some sections of the faculty. They succeed, even when they fail, in antagonizing the larger community of which the university is a part, and in arousing a vigilante spirit that demands wholesale measures of repression and punishment that educators cannot properly accept.

How is it possible, one asks, for events of this character to happen? There have always been extremist and paranoidal tendencies in academic life, but they have been peripheral—individuals and small groups moving in eccentric intellectual orbits. But not until the last four or five years has the norm of social protest taken the form of direct action, have positions been expressed in such ultimatistic and intransigent terms, have extremist elements been strong enough to shut down great universities even for a limited time.

There are many and complex causes for this. But as I see it, the situation in the university is part of a larger phenomenon, viz., the climate of intellectual life in the country. I do not recall any other period in the last 50 years when intellectuals themselves have been so intolerant of each other, when differences over complex issues have been the occasion for denunciation rather than debate and analysis, when the use of violence—in the right cause, of course!—is taken for granted, when dissent is not distinguished from civil disobedience, and civil disobedience makes common cause with resistance, and readiness for insurrection. A few short years ago, anti-intellectualism was an epithet of derogation. Today it is an expression of revolutionary virility.

FANATICISM RAMPANT

In the fifties I wrote an essay on "The Ethics of Controversy," trying to suggest guidelines for controversy among principled democrats no matter how widely they differed on substantive issues. Today I would be talking into the wind for all the attention it would get. Fanaticism seems to be in the saddle. That it is a fanaticism of conscience, of self-proclaimed virtue, doesn't make it less dangerous. This past year has presented the spectacle of militant minorities in our colleges from one end of the country to another, preventing or trying to prevent representatives of positions they disapprove of from speaking to their fellow-students wishing to listen to them.

The spectacle shows that we have failed to make our students understand the very rudiments of democracy, that to tolerate active intolerance is to compound it. If we judge commitment by action, the simple truth is that the great body of our students is not firmly committed to democracy or to the liberal spirit without which democracy may become the rule of the mob.

I do not know any sure way or even a new way of combatting the dominant mood of irrationalism, especially among students and even among younger members of the faculty whose political naiveté is often cynically exploited by their younger, yet politically more sophisticated, allies. What is of the first importance is to preserve, of course, the absolute intellectual integrity of our classrooms and laboratories, of our teaching and research against any attempt to curb it. We must defend it not only against the traditional enemies, who still exist even when they are dormant, but also against those who think they have the infallible remedies for the world's complex problems, and that all they need is sincerity as patent of authority. Fanatics don't lack sincerity. It is their long suit. They drip with sincerity—and when they have power, with blood—other people's blood.

We need more, however, than a defensive strategy, safeguarding the intellectual integrity of our vocation against those who threaten it. We need—and I know this sounds paradoxical—to counterpose to the revolt of the emotionally committed the revolt of the rationally committed. I do not want to identify this with the revolt of the moderates. There are some things one should not be moderate about. In the long run, the preservation of democracy depends upon a passion for freedom, for the logic and ethics of free discussion and inquiry, upon refusal to countenance the measures of violence that cut short the processes of intelligence upon which the possibility of shared values depends.

These are old truths but they bear repeating whenever they are denied. Even tautologies become important when counterposed to absurdities.

We as teachers must make our students more keenly aware of the centrality of the democratic process to a free society and of the centrality of intelligence to the democratic process. Democracy has our allegiance because of its cumulative fruits, but at any particular time the process is more important than any specific program or product. He who destroys the process because it does not guarantee some particular outcome is as foolish as someone who discards scientific method in medicine or engineering or any other discipline because of its failure to solve altogether or immediately a stubborn problem.

COURAGE NEEDED

There is one thing we cannot deny to the intransigent and fanatical enemies of democracy. That is courage. Intelligence is necessary to overcome foolishness. But it is not sufficient to tame fanaticism. Only courage can do that. A handful of men who are prepared to fight, to bleed, to suffer and, if need be, to die, will always triumph in a community where those whose freedom they threaten are afraid to use their *intelligence* to resist and to fight, and ultimately to take the same risks in action as those determined to destroy them.

Yes, there is always the danger that courage *alone* may lead us to actions that will make us similar to those who threaten us. But that is what we have intelligence for—to prevent that from happening! It is this union of courage and intelligence upon which the hope of democratic survival depends.

DISCUSSION QUESTIONS

1. Do you agree with Hook that "in the affairs of the mind and in the realm of scholarship, the principles of simple majority rule . . . do not apply"?
2. What does "freedom to learn" mean to you? What is your concept of "freedom to teach"? Do they imply a contradiction?
3. Are you in sympathy with Hook's evaluation of Students for a Democratic Society?

4. Who should decide on what research is to be conducted at a university?
5. Should students have the power to "approve" who should teach specific courses?
6. Is Hook's contention true that "we have failed to make our students understand the very rudiments of democracy"? How would you bring about an understanding of true democracy in students?

EDITORIAL | *The Chisholm Case*

John Dewey said, "Democracy must be reborn every 20 years and education is the midwife."

Start boiling water, friend, and better ride shotgun. On the way to the accouchement you might meet the great beast of antidemocracy. Items:

Jacksboro, Tenn., April 14. A 24-year-old science teacher accused of teaching evolution in violation of state law was dismissed today from his $4,700-a-year job at the high school in this Cumberland Mountain community. As he left school at the end of the day, the teacher, Gary Lindle Scott, was handed a note informing him of the charges. They included the statement that he had violated Section 49-1922 of the Tennessee Code. (It was in 1922 that the Monkey Law was passed, setting the stage for the antic Scopes trial of 1924. Yes, that law is still on the books.)

Washington, D.C., April 26. The Catholic University Board of Trustees reversed their decision to fire the Rev. Charles E. Curran, following student and faculty protests and boycotts. The board had given Father Curran no hearing and apparently disregarded the judgment of his faculty peers. It seems certain that he was fired largely because of his liberal position on the question of birth control. Although the bishops gave the job back, they granted no reforms to guarantee that this violation of academic freedom would not happen again.

Bloomfield, Ind., April 26. Mrs. Patricia L. Reilly, 22, an English teacher in Bloomfield High School and nominee for "Young Career Woman of the Year" in Indiana,* was relieved of her duties amid accusations that she condoned the burning of an American flag by an Indiana State University professor in Terre Haute. It took the school board only a few minutes to fire Mrs. Reilly after hearing parental charges that she was a "liberal with preconceived ideas" and "led our children to believe in free thinking." The local American Legion Post demanded immediate dismissal. Mrs. Reilly herself wasn't given a hearing.

Because it reeks with implications, ramifications, and significance, let's take a brief look at the incident which touched off Mrs. Reilly's dismissal, as reported in *The Indiana Statesman,* a student newspaper at Indiana State University:

Reprinted from *Phi Delta Kappan,* Vol. XLVIII, No. 10 (June 1967), pp. 481–484, with permission of the publisher.

* Later withdrawn at the request of the Bloomfield Business and Professional Women's Club.

On April 12 Scott A. Chisholm lectured his English 102 class on the difference between a concrete, material object and that object's abstract, symbolic meanings.

Later in the day the parent of an ISU student warned President Alan G. Rankin that a U.S. flag might be burned in the same class on April 14. Chisholm was not told of the warning.

On April 14 a girl student who had recently asked permission to attend Chisholm's class but was absent on April 12 brought a small flag and matches to the classroom. Chisholm burned the flag after telling the class his action was not to be taken as an unpatriotic action or as one critical of the U.S. government.

The class was dismissed at 8:50 A.M. At 9:30 a parent called President Rankin's office, telling of the classroom incident. By 3:30 that afternoon, after interviewing some students from the class and conferring with an attorney, but without talking with Chisholm, the university administration informed Chisholm of his suspension for unprofessional conduct. The story was in the evening Terre Haute *Tribune*.

A Faculty Council hearing was held on April 18, but as this is written the transcript is not available and no decision has been made with respect to the case.* A statement drafted by Chisholm is available, however, and is published herewith.

It is interesting to note that the Indiana legislature recently updated its 1901 statute on mutilation of the flag, raising the penalty for a first offense from a maximum of $10 to $1,000 or a year in jail. The new law goes into effect next month.

It is also interesting that Indiana's U.S. Congressman Richard L. Roudebush has publicly demanded that Chisholm, a Canadian, be dismissed at once and sent back to Canada.

The following is Chisholm's statement in full, released at the request of the KAPPAN editors:

On Friday, April 7, 1967, I began a transition in my English 102 classes from Vance Packard's *The Hidden Persuaders* to Daniel Boorstin's *The Image: A Guide to Pseudo-Events in America*. My basic point of discussion was that the ethical responsibility of Packard's book is placed totally upon the advertiser, while the responsibility in Boorstin is placed upon the individual and his failure to examine the images by which he lives. In the former, the responsibility lies outside the individual, who regards himself as victim; in the latter, the individual becomes the victim of his own unexamined abstractions and is responsible for his own self-deceit. The emphasis in making the transition was to call into question the examined life as opposed to the unexamined life, the examined images as opposed to the unexamined images, the examined values as opposed to unexamined values.

---

* Indiana State University's Board of Trustees discharged Mr. Chisholm on May 20, on the recommendation of President Rankin. A faculty committee had recommended "censure for unprofessional conduct." It also said the flag burning was not done maliciously but demonstrated "bad judgment." Chisholm had not appealed the decision as of May 22.

On Monday, April 10; Tuesday, April 11; Wednesday, April 12, and Thursday, April 13, I continued this discussion in class. Two additional points were made: 1) that Vance Packard's book was in part a success because the language he uses is less stylistic and more simple than that in Boorstin, thus appealing to a larger segment of society, and 2) that Packard deals with more immediately provocative material of a more concrete and inflamatory nature, thus trapping his reader with psychological appeals—the very subject of his book's attack. Boorstin's *The Image* was then contrasted with Packard, with specific reference to style and the more abstract treatment of ideas. While being the more difficult book to read, it was conceded to be the better of the two.

The discussion of Boorstin's style—his use of various sentence forms, his preference for parallel rhythms, his use of catalogued details for compression, his effective use of the stylistic fragment sentence—precipitated the discussion of the relationship between the *abstract* and the *concrete,* since it was generally agreed that qualities of abstract thought are necessary to effective thinking and writing. Care was taken to mention that concrete objects could also have abstract meaning, in which case they function as symbols, but that *the two essential qualities could be separated.* Thus, it was emphasized that a person who evaluates his abstractions before making a judgment is often better prepared to make more reasonable decisions than a person who makes decisions based upon an irrational reaction to a concrete symbol.

It was in this context that I introduced the example of the recent burning of an American flag by French political leftists. At the time, it was the best available example because of its timely interest. Since students in all my 102 classes subscribe to the *Christian Science Monitor,* I assumed they would have some knowledge of the coverage given to the incident and it was within this framework that I discussed the flag as a symbol of the abstract ideas for which the nation stands—concepts which involve democracy, justice, equality before the law, respect for human rights, civil liberties, freedom of speech, and so forth. But it was emphasized that the flag is also a *concrete* object; that is, its *real value* as opposed to its *symbolic value* is little more than its wood and cloth. I emphasized that the French leftists who had burned the American flag did so because they objected to the abstract ideas which the flag represents, and that they were using a non-verbal rhetoric through the implied associations to defame, abuse, and destroy the abstract principles upon which the nation and its symbol rests. I further discussed the retaliatory action by several American citizens in Connecticut, in which a French flag was similarly defaced and burned. However, I commented that such an action on our part was somewhat childish, since it smacked of an "I'll show you!" attitude. I pointed out that the Americans who burned the French flag were probably burning not the abstract political and social ideals of the French people, but the effigies of those Frenchmen who had burned our flag. In each instance I was careful to separate the two functions of the symbol into the *concrete* (its real value) and the *abstract* (its idea value). I concluded, therefore, that when a man burns a flag or a draft card or a cross we should be more concerned with the abstractions he attacks than with the object itself, since these objects are only the symbol of larger abstract ideas which have serious implied meanings for every citizen. To react solely to the object is irrational, and when we become trapped by our symbols and do not think about the ideas which they represent we abandon reason and replace it with misplaced emotion. Thus I stated that "any man could burn any flag so long as it is understood that he is not attacking the abstract value for which the flag stands—that he is not entering into an unpatriotic act or a quarrel with his government or with its principles—that he is merely burning a concrete object." Continuing, I said, "I would be willing to burn any flag—British, American, Canadian, Dutch, Russian, Australian, South African—so long as the context in which I am burning it is understood—that I am burning it as a concrete object as opposed to a symbol of abstract values—that I am not burning it as an unpatriotic act."

Following this statement, I moved to a concluding illustration in which I examined two statements for their concrete and abstract content. The intent was to show that within the context of stated ideas words themselves have values which can be fixed as more or less abstract and which, if studied, can limit our judgment or free it, can make us less aware, less confused, or more confused. Thus in discussing the differences between "Thou shalt not kill!" and "Blessed are the peacemakers for they shall inherit the earth!" any distinction involves not only the choice of terms but the abstract evaluation of those terms. In the first statement, it was pointed out that the choice of words permits only two choices of action, and the language is used in such a way that the evaluation is more concrete—that is, in the Hebrew sense it becomes a law that is fixed and rigid. Thus the language enforces behavior while restricting the abstractions. In the second statement, however, the terms "blessed," "peacemakers," and "inherit" are more abstract. Thus the reader is under an obligation to emphasize certain qualities of abstract thought in order to arrive at an understanding of the beatitude, with any adjustments in his behavior following an abstract evaluation. The terms are more expansive, the value implications less restrictive, and the judgment more inclusive of experience. In this respect, I indicated that a man often behaves more ethically because he has been aided by words calling for abstract thinking than he would behave if his choice and his thought were limited by the negating and more concrete qualities of "Thou shalt not kill!" The irony in this is, of course, that we do kill—often in defense of the flag. Thus our choices and our behavior can be qualified by thought. These examples were used and related to effective writing—specifically, that one writes better when he learns to think in a more abstract and nonrestrictive manner because thought has a relationship to language and vocabulary. Generally, this was the extent of the background lectures.

On Friday morning, April 14, 1967, I arrived at my 8:00 a.m. English 102 class in the Science Building and found a flag-like object on my desk. I call the object *flag-like* because, while it had the appearances of a flag, I did not carefully examine it. Therefore, I cannot attest to its legality. The object in question was mounted upright in a cup with a book of blue bookstore matches beside it. Within the context of my previous lectures, there was but one choice of any honesty. Rather than compromise myself and the class in order to preserve the ignorance of one or two students, I struck a match and burned it. As I did so, I repeated, "This is not to be misconstrued as an unpatriotic act, because I am not herein involved with abstract questions about the values of my government, about its foreign policy, or about its actions. I am not attacking the principles for which it stands, nor am I making a political comment about democracy. I am burning a concrete object—a stick and a piece of cloth—not my country or its principles." Thereafter, I repeated this injunction three or four times during the course of the hour's class.

In order to strengthen the position I had taken, I used at least two additional examples to point out the difference between the concrete and the abstract. In the first of these, I mentioned that it was necessary for a person to realize that there exists a difference between "the concept of a chair and the chair itself." "The idea and the object are not the same thing," I insisted. I pointed out that while the chair is the result of the abstract concept which first understood the function of sitting down, it is nonetheless an object given concrete existence out of a world of concrete objects—wood, stone, trees, mountains, and so forth. I explained that to burn a chair is not to destroy the concept of sitting down. In subsequent encounters with students and faculty who have asked for my logic in this matter, I have explained it this way: "If I burn the cover of a book entitled *19th Century Political Thought,* I have not burned political thought, nor have I abused the community of political thinkers." I did not, however, use this example in the Friday morning class.

After discussing the differences between the concept of a chair and the chair itself, I asked the class to consider the statement, "Man shall not live by bread alone, but by every word that proceeds from the mouth of God." Again, my intent was to get them to analyze the statement in terms of its essential concrete and abstract word values in order to better reach an evaluation of its meaning. It was pointed out that the context of an evaluation would need to consider at least four nouns—*man, bread, word,* and *God.*

Within this framework, I asked the class to reduce these terms to their actual concrete or abstract values. There was little response. I continued, pointing out that both *man* and *bread* have an actual physical existence which can continuously be demonstrated; thus, I assigned them a *concrete* value. It is understood, of course, that the word *bread* as used here is symbolic. Nonetheless, it refers to material values, all of which have concrete equivalents.

In assigning a value to the remaining nouns *word* and *God,* it became necessary to discuss in elementary terms the function of language as symbol. In the case of the noun *word,* it was pointed out that there is no actual physical existence but that language symbols can either assign concrete values or can be used to frame abstract ideas. In this case, it was agreed that *word* represented language in general and specifically ideas, in which case I assigned it an abstract value. But the noun *God* threatened to present trouble, since in assigning it a value as an abstraction, I encountered one student who insisted it was a thing "just like us." I countered by saying that "many abstract ideas reduce themselves to concrete realities." As examples, I pointed to such things as automobiles, space capsules, and washing machines. "However," I continued, "in such cases the relationship between the abstract idea and the concrete object can continuously be demonstrated—like an experiment. Through the scientific method, man demonstrates that his abstractions can often be reduced to concrete realities." I continued to point out that the concrete objects could be used as a verification of the abstraction and that in the case of the noun *God* no such concrete value had continuously been demonstrated. Thus I indicated that the word *God* remains an abstraction upon which we unscientifically impose elements of concrete form none of which can be continuously verified.

Recognizing that this water was a little too deep for the boy in the back row, I shifted my emphasis from the word *God* to a new example in which I hoped to demonstrate how a particular word in the Old Testament can be understood only in terms of the abstractions which it symbolizes. To take it on a literal level rather than on a symbolic level reduces the implied behavior to an ethical ideal which even the most narrow of men would assume ridiculous. "Why," I asked the boy in the back row, "did God banish Adam and Eve from the garden of Eden?"

"For eating the forbidden fruit?" he replied.

"What was the forbidden fruit?"

"An apple," he said.

"Was it a literal apple?" I asked.

"It could have been," he answered.

"Could it have been a banana?" I asked.

"It might have been," he answered. "Anyway, it was some kind of fruit."

"Then my behavior is more ethical than God's," I said, "because I would not run you out of my back yard for eating an apple." I then attempted to point out that the apple had symbolic value and that the ideas involved in the Garden of Eden story could not be understood if we accepted it literally. I further defended this position by arguing that in a primitive world in which abstract thought was relatively undeveloped and in which language was limited in vocabulary and in which information was generally transmitted by word of mouth and in which writing was virtually nonexistent, difficult concepts had to be framed in symbolic concrete objects. Thus, the word *apple,* while meaning fruit, involved other ideas as well—ideas which developed as language developed through which to express them: the ideas of lushness or ripeness or freshness or of pleasure and joy and delight. Once this image was established, it was easy for the class to get other associations. But only one student ventured the word *sex* as an equivalent.

Having established the symbolic abstraction for which the word *apple* stood, I returned to my original statement, "Man shall not live by bread alone, but by every word which proceeds from the mouth of God," and reduced it to these terms: "Man shall not live by concrete values, but by abstract values." I did not push it further because I did not wish to discuss the implications of the finite (man) and the infinite (God). But I might have expressed it this way: "Although finite himself, man should not live by equally finite and concrete values, but by abstractions which allow him recourse to infinite ideas."

At this point, however, I was about to run out of time. Taking advantage of the time I had left, I attempted to summarize what I had said about the differences between the abstract and the concrete. I related the value of abstract thinking to writing, I repeated the example of the chair and the concept of the chair, and I indicated that all of our images must be understood in terms of their basic value (concrete) as well as their ideological value (abstract). I repeated as well my motives for having burned the object on my desk and reiterated that it was "not to be misconstrued as an unpatriotic act." The bell rang and I dismissed the class.

As to the charge of unprofessional conduct, I would like to refute it as follows:

1. The incident in question was performed in an academic setting, devoted to academic issues which have practical application to the student. Any attempt to consider the action beyond the classroom involves the public and is thus disruptive of the very climate in which the free association of ideas is supposed to take place.

2. The incident was conducted within the context of a series of lectures establishing its validity and its meaning both intellectually and morally. It was neither rash nor unqualified in its context.

3. The spoken intentions of the instructor involved were not unpatriotic in any sense. Rather, he sought throughout his lectures and during the incident itself to establish that the context of the action was merely to illustrate that objects have both concrete and abstract value, and that it is reasonable to assume that any object, even the flag, can be destroyed on a concrete level without impugning either the nation or one's own patriotism.

4. The instructor himself did not choose the symbol. Thus the entire class is involved by implication. With specific reference to flags, he listed several and was brought one in particular. In such a case, it is not unreasonable to assume a less academic intent on the part of the party or parties who placed the object in the room.

5. The act was undertaken, beyond the level of its academic context, in order not to compromise the integrity of the class or its instructor through the ignorance of one or two students. It points more clearly to the fact facing many of us that we

are victimized by the students themselves and, in part, by the willingness of an administration to encourage and even to support hearsay evidence unqualified and supported out of context.

DISCUSSION QUESTIONS

1. If you were in Chisholm's place, how would you have reacted when the flag was brought in to be burned?
2. If you were a student in this class, what would have been your contribution in this confrontation? What would have been your position as a parent of a student in the class?
3. Defend the removal of all restraints upon the actions of the teacher.

NEWSWEEK | *The Dissent Threshold*

Chicago State College is a streetcar school for 4,000 students crowded into two deteriorating red-brick buildings on the city's déclassé South Side. A teacher-training institution through most of its 96 years and six changes of name, it shares a 25-acre campus with a high school and an elementary school and usually manages to avoid any hint of fame—or whisper of notoriety. Last week, by denying a teaching job to historian Staughton Lynd because he illegally visited North Vietnam in 1965, Chicago State put itself on the map.

The 37-year-old pacifist, whose parents Robert and Helen wrote the classic study "Middletown," had taken a one-year unpaid leave of absence as assistant professor at Yale; it was understood that Lynd was leaving the Ivy League to confront directly the problems of the "inner city." Attracted to Chicago, he first applied for jobs at the West Side campus of the University of Illinois and then at Northern Illinois University in nearby DeKalb—and was turned down without explanation by their administrations. It looked as if his luck had changed, however, when he tried Chicago State. The Arts and Sciences Department sent him a letter informing him that he was hired for a $14,000-a-year job pending routine approval from the Board of Governors of State Colleges and Universities. Three weeks ago Lynd moved his wife and three children from Connecticut to a six-room house on the South Side.

Reprinted from *Newsweek,* July 31, 1967, with permission of the publisher.

COURSE OF MEDIOCRITY

Once there, his luck ran out. Informed by reporters that Lynd's name was on the list of proposed new faculty members, the board met privately in a Holiday Inn on Lake Shore Drive. In a paneled meeting room, Milton Byrd, the college's president since September, made a strong personal appeal for Lynd's appointment. "His espousal of an unpopular position has in no way adversely colored his teaching or his scholarship," Byrd said. Lynd, he added, is "A historian of prodigious and imposing scholarly productivity." Board president Richard Nelson, former administrative assistant to Adlai Stevenson when he was governor of Illinois, also backed Lynd. The appointment, said Nelson, now director of public relations for Inland Steel Corp., would help the school avoid a "course of convention, conformity and mediocrity."

The board's final decision, however, was that Lynd would not be hired because he had violated the law (he defied Federal regulations by visiting Hanoi without a valid passport). The governors did not question his ability as a scholar or teacher, but said in a statement that his visit to North Vietnam and his advocacy of nonviolent civil disobedience "goes beyond mere dissent." A teacher, the board added, "has a responsibility to stay within the laws of the country."

UNHEALTHY VIEW

A few board members explained their votes individually. J. Bon Hartline, a fruit grower from downstate Anna, Ill., said he had read magazine stories about Lynd and decided the professor's views "weren't healthy." Dr. W. I. Taylor, a physician from Canton, feared that Lynd's philosophy "might indirectly influence students." Nelson, the only board member from the Chicago area voting, cast the sole vote to hire Lynd. "The other board members apparently felt that it's all right to dissent, but you shouldn't go so far as going to North Vietnam." Nelson said later, "I guess my dissent threshold is a little higher than theirs."

Lynd protested that the board has adopted a "narrow-minded, provincial view." "Martin Luther King, Thomas Jefferson and many other teachers also have been deliberate lawbreakers," he added, "and the board has not quite come to grips with that." Lynd's academic future is uncertain, but he probably will stay in Chicago, teaching at the New Center of Radical Research and also conducting a graduate history seminar at Roosevelt University.

Reaction in Chicago was mixed. "We had hoped that Lynd would be with us to help us build this school into something," said one faculty member. But The Chicago Tribune said it saw "no reason why the taxpayers of Illinois should be required to pay $14,000 for the services of . . . an activist of the left who hasn't missed a 'cause' in years."

DISCUSSION QUESTIONS

1. Is Lynd's dismissal a violation of academic freedom?
2. Should a teacher be able to say what he believes in a classroom? Outside of the classroom?
3. Would you vote to hire Lynd at Chicago State? Defend your vote.
4. Are there legal or constitutional precedents that might be cited by the board member who voted to hire Lynd?
5. To what extent do our schools provide a free marketplace for ideas? To what extent should they do so?

PART TWO *The Issues*

CHAPTER 3 *Education of the Culturally Different*

Immediately after World War II, the schools of the large urban ghettos throughout the United States became a major social problem. In the period of mass European immigration of the early 1900's, urban schools had accepted and processed large numbers of children. The quality of the education they gave these children is debatable, but the society of the day was amorphous and expansive enough to absorb the school's mistakes. The shocking failure of slum schools cannot now be hidden. Black children who before had been educated in the segregated schools of the rural South, and Spanish-speaking children from Puerto Rico and from the Southwest, present a problem that the schools have bitten off, chewed, but cannot swallow.

Basic to the plight of the schools is the broader social problem of the integration of the newcomers into the social body. Housing patterns and the neighborhood school concept have resulted in "de facto" segregation, northern style. The "Harlems" of America have had schools characterized by old and inferior physical plants, overcrowded classes, underpaid, poorly prepared, and transient teachers, and lack of flexibility of organization and administration, among other ills. This is not to say that other social agencies have been any more capable or visionary in outlook or performance. Taken together, the collective ineptitude demonstrates a deep-seated social breakdown stemming from the second-class citizenship of a large segment of the people.

It might be asked why education is most severely under attack. Perhaps the poor are most angered at the schools because, besides being visible and vulnerable, they are supposed to hold the key to social mobility and eventual affluence. Television has shown the "disadvantaged" what they are lacking; education ought to provide the means for attaining it. Instead, very few are even "making it" out of the ghetto. Education has failed the poor and they are not loath to point the finger of blame.

The poor demand for their children the education that "advantaged" children get. They will be tragically "shortchanged" if they get no more than this. Education for ghetto children will be a mockery until society will no longer tolerate penalizing children for their parents' poverty and the circumstance of their birth. Slum children will become "children" when the ghetto walls, like the walls of Jericho, come tumbling down.

Education for all children calls for bold, new, innovative thinking, deeply rooted in humanity. It must be part of the vision that sees all men joined together as parts of humanity. Only then can democracy be made meaningful. And education is the heart of democracy.

URIE BRONFENBRENNER

The Psychological Costs of Quality and Equality in Education

A review of research indicates that the serious inadequacies experienced in school by disadvantaged children, especially Negro boys, have their origins primarily in prenatal damage, father absence, impoverished home environment, and dysfunctional patterns of child rearing. In an integrated classroom, these inadequacies present problems not only to the Negro child but also to his white companion, who is exposed to the contagion of disorganized and antisocial behavior. Findings of social psychological research call for a counterstrategy of active involvement in work with disadvantaged children on the part of middle-class children and adults of both races. The results are seen as benefiting not only the disadvantaged but also the advantaged child by providing him with needed training in actual behavior consistent with the democratic values of human dignity and social responsibility.

The costs of quality and equality in education—calculated, as they usually are, in dollars and cents—invariably turn out to be higher than expected. Not infrequently the public is unwilling to pay the price, and even when it does so, it is often with reluctance, pain, and resentment, toward both those who impose the payment and those who receive the benefits. The reasons for resistance are well known. Personal financial resources are slow to acquire, the demand invariably exceeds the supply, and what little we have is urgently needed to provide for ourselves and our families.

The sobering burden of this paper is to show that all these considerations apply with even greater force when the costs of quality and inequality are reckoned in psychological rather than economic terms. Here, too, the price turns out to be far higher than anticipated, but the available resources are even more limited, the needs of self and family more pressing, and the pain and resentment at having to pay the price far more acute. Yet, these costs will have to be met, for unless they are, no increase in school budget, however generous, no regrouping of pupils, however democratic, no new curriculum, however adapted to the child's environment, can bring either quality or equality in education to those who do not have them, or, as I hope to demonstrate, even for those who do.

Reprinted from *Child Development,* Vol. XXXVIII, No. 4 (December 1967), pp. 909–925, with permission of the publisher. This paper was presented at the Conference on Psychological Factors in Poverty held in Madison, Wisconsin, June 22–24, 1967.

To understand why this is so, we must come to terms with an unwelcome but nonetheless inexorable reality: whatever their origin, the most immediate, overwhelming, and stubborn obstacles to achieving quality and equality in education now lie as much in the character and way of life of the American Negro as in the indifference and hostility of the white community. The first part of this paper summarizes the bases for this assertion.

THE PSYCHOLOGICAL CHARACTERISTICS OF THE NEGRO CHILD

Recognition in actual practice of the critical role played by psychological factors in the education of the Negro child begins with implementation of the 1954 Supreme Court decision that separate facilities are inherently unequal. Unfortunately, it all too often ends there. In many American communities the enlightened leadership, both Negro and white, and their supporters operate on the tacit assumption that once the Negro child finds himself in an integrated classroom with a qualified teacher and adequate materials, learning will take place, and with it the deficiencies of the American Negro, and the judgments of inferiority which they in part encourage, will be erased.

Regrettably, this is not the case. Neither the scars of slavery which the Negro child still bears nor the skills and self-confidence of his white companion rub off merely through contact in the same classroom. This is not to imply that integration is impotent as an instrument of change. On the contrary, it is a desperately necessary condition, but not a sufficient one. Objective equality of opportunity is not enough. The Negro child must also be able to profit from the educational situation in which he finds himself. This he cannot do if he lacks the background and motivation necessary for learning. And the evidence indicates that these essentials are often conspicuously absent.

Let us examine the data. Fortunately, most of the relevant facts are already brought together for us in Pettigrew's (1964) recent volume, *A Profile of the Negro American,* a masterful compendium and interpretation of the available research findings. We shall not concern ourselves here with the full array of facts which Pettigrew presents; they are eloquent testimony to the crippling psychological costs to the Negro of the inequality imposed upon him by slavery and its contemporary economic and social heritage. For our purposes, we select those findings that bear directly and indirectly on the educability of the Negro child of poverty.

The first of these is the sobering statistic that the longer such a child remains in school, even in integrated classrooms, the further behind he falls in relation to the norms for his age and grade. Such progressive retardation is reported not only for measures of academic achievement (Coleman, 1966; Deutsch, 1960; Kennedy, Van de Riet, & White, 1963) but also for scores on

34094

tests of general intelligence (Coleman, 1966; Deutsch & Brown, 1964; Kennedy et al., 1963; Pettigrew, 1964, chap. v). Moreover, the discrepancies between Negro and white children are not limited to poverty-stricken families. They are not only present across the socioeconomic spectrum but "the Negro-White differences increase at each higher SES level" (Deutsch & Brown, 1964, p. 27).

In analyzing the factors producing these results, investigators call attention to the inappropriateness of many test items to lower-class Negro culture. But at the same time, they make clear that improvements in test construction will not change the fact of the Negro child's inferiority; he suffers from handicaps that are real and debilitating. For example, Deutsch (1960) cites evidence that, in comparison with white children from deprived socioeconomic backgrounds, lower-class Negro youngsters are especially retarded in reading and language skills. They also show a shorter attention span in any task which requires concentration and persistence. Deutsch's observations indicate that the failure in persistence reflects not only an inability to concentrate but also a lack of motivation and an attitude of futility in the face of difficulty. Thus he reports:

> Time after time, the experimental child would drop a problem posed by the teacher as soon as he met any difficulty in attempting to solve it. In questioning after, the child would typically respond "so what?" or "who cares" or "what does it matter?" In the control group [white children of "similar socio-economic level"], there was an obvious competitive spirit, with a verbalized anticipation of "reward" for a correct response. In general, this anticipation was only infrequently present in the experimental group and was not consistently or meaningfully reenforced by the teachers [Deutsch, 1960, p. 9].

Deutsch's observations are confirmed by a series of studies, cited by Pettigrew, showing that "lower class Negro children of school age typically 'give up the fight' and reveal unusually low need for achievement" (1964, pp. 30–31).

Not only does the Negro child feel powerless; he feels worthless as well. At the core of this sense of inferiority is the awareness of being black. From the age of 3 onward, Negro children begin to prefer white skin to black and to think of Negroes in general and themselves in particular as ugly, unwanted, and "bad." Results of the numerous studies of this phenomenon, summarized by Pettigrew (1964, chap. i), are epitomized in an example he cites of a small Negro boy who served as a subject in one of these investigations. "Asked if he were white or colored, he hung his head and hesitated. Then he murmured softly, 'I guess I'se kind o' colored' " (Pettigrew, 1964, p. 8).

It is this "mark of oppression" (Kardiner & Ovesey, 1951) which distinguishes the personality development of the Negro child from that of his white counterpart, especially in lower-class families. The psychological process and its consequences are summarized by the following excerpt from a more extended analysis by Ausubel.

> The Negro child . . . gradually becomes aware of the social significance of racial membership. . . . He perceives himself as an object of derision and disparagement, as socially rejected by the prestigeful elements of society, and as unworthy of succorance and affection. Having no compelling reasons for not accepting this officially sanctioned, negative evaluation of himself, he develops ingrained feelings of inferiority [Ausubel, 1958, p. 35].

It is all these intellectual, motivational, and emotional problems that the Negro child brings with him when he goes to school. The obstacles they place to the learning process are reflected in the marked contrast in classroom atmosphere reported by Deutsch (1960) in his study of schools in Negro and white lower-class neighborhoods. In the former setting, 50–80 per cent of all classroom time was devoted to disciplinary and various essentially nonacademic tasks, whereas the corresponding percentage for the white control group was about 30.

What factors account for the special debilities and behavior difficulties of Negro children? The thesis, still militantly upheld by some investigators (Garrett, 1960; 1961; 1962a; 1962b; McGurk, 1956; 1959; Shuey, 1958; Van den Haag, 1964), that such deficiencies have an innate basis in race differences, has been so thoroughly discredited (Anastasi, 1956; Chein, 1961; Pettigrew, 1964) that it needs no extended consideration here. We would call attention, however, to one additional fact which, if acknowledged, presents an interesting problem to those who seek to account for Negro inferiority in genetic terms. The intellectual, emotional, and social deficiencies observed in Negro children are considerably more pronounced in boys than in girls. Systematic data on this point are cited by Deutsch (1960). For instance, in his sample of Negro schoolchildren in grades 4–6, the proportion who scored below fourth-grade norms on the Stanford Achievement Test was 38 per cent for girls and 68 per cent for boys, the discrepancies being greatest on the reading subtest. No differences approaching this magnitude were found for the white controls. Similarly, in repeating digits forward or backward, Negro girls performed at about the same level as white controls, whereas Negro boys were markedly inferior to their white counterparts. Deutsch stresses the psychological significance of this difference in view of "the importance of attention for any academic learning and therefore the potential contribution of lowered attentivity to the achievement differences found" (Deutsch, 1960, p. 12). It is noteworthy that these sex differences in achievement are observed among Southern as well as Northern Negroes, are present at every socioeconomic level, and tend to increase with age (Kennedy et al., 1963, see especially Tables 68 and 69).

THE SOURCES OF INADEQUACY

Clearly any satisfactory explanation for the debilities of the Negro child must also account for the special ineptitude of the Negro male. Several lines of evidence are pertinent in this regard: the first is biological, the remainder social.

Organic bases of inadequacy

Though the Negro infant is not biologically inferior at the moment of conception, he often becomes so shortly thereafter. The inadequate nutrition and prenatal care received by millions of Negro mothers result in complications of pregnancy which take their toll in extraordinarily high rates of prematurity and congenital defect (Knobloch, Rider, Harper, & Pasamanick, 1956; Pasamanick & Knobloch, 1958; Pasamanick, Knobloch, & Lilienfeld, 1956). Many of these abnormalities entail neurological damage resulting in impaired intellectual function and behavioral disturbances, including hyperactivity, distractibility, and low attention span. Of particular relevance is the significant role played by paranatal and prenatal factors in the genesis of childhood reading disorders. In a retrospective comparison of hospital records, Kawi and Pasamanick (1959) found that instances of two or more complications of pregnancy were over nine times as frequent in the records of mothers whose children later exhibited severe reading difficulties as in a control population matched on social class and other relevant variables. Finally, it is a well established, though not thoroughly understood, fact that neurological disorders resulting from complications of pregnancy and birth are considerably more frequent for males than females. This differential rate has been identified as a major factor in contributing to the consistent sex differences observed in incidence of neuropsychiatric disorders and psychological disturbances in children (Kawi & Pasamanick, 1959, p. 19). Of special relevance in this connection is the statistic that "behavior disorders are two to three times more common in boys, reading disorders as much as eight or nine times" (Pasamanick & Knobloch, 1958, p. 7). These authors see in "reproductive casualty" and its sequelae a major factor contributing to school retardation in Negro children generally and Negro males in particular. Organic debilities, of course, result not only in intellectual dysfunction but also in discouragement. In this manner, they play a part in evoking the expectations of failure, the readiness to give up in the face of difficulty, and the low level of aspiration observed in Negro children, especially among boys.

The impact of paternal absence

But even where organic factors do not set in motion the vicious circle of defeat and disinterest in achievement, social circumstances can be counted on to instigate and accelerate a similar downward spiral. A growing body of research evidence points to the debilitating effect on personality development in Negro children, particularly males, resulting from the high frequency of father absence in Negro families. The extent of such absence is eloquently reflected in census figures summarized by Pettigrew (1964).

Census data for 1960 illustrate the depth of this family disorganization among Negroes: over a third (34.3 per cent) of all non-white mothers with children under six years of age hold jobs as compared with less than a fifth (19.5 per cent) of white mothers with children under six; only three-fourths (74.9 per cent) of all non-white families have both the husband and the wife present in the household as compared with nine-tenths (89.2 per cent) of white families; and only two-thirds (66.3 per cent) of non-whites under eighteen years of age live with both of their parents as compared with nine-tenths (90.2 per cent) of such whites. . . .

The vast majority of incomplete Negro households is lacking the husband. Frazier estimated in 1950 that the male parent was missing in roughly 20 per cent of Negro households. In addition to divorce and separation, part of this phenomenon is due to a higher Negro male death rate. The percentage of widows among Negro women fifty-four years old or less is roughly twice that of white women [Pettigrew, 1964, pp. 16–17].

The consequence of this state of affairs for the personality development of the Negro child is indicated by several lines of investigations. First, a series of studies conducted in the United States (Bach, 1946; Barclay & Cosumano, 1967; Kuckenberg, 1963; Sears, 1951; Sears, Pintler, & Sears, 1946; Stolz, 1954) and in Norway (Grønseth, 1957; Lynn & Sawrey, 1959; Tiller, 1957; 1961) showed that father absence has far greater impact on sons than on daughters. The results, and their implications, are summarized by Pettigrew as follows:

. . . father-deprived boys are markedly more immature, submissive, dependent, and effeminate than other boys. . . . As they grow older, this passive behavior may continue, but more typically, it is vigorously overcompensated for by exaggerated masculinity. Juvenile gangs, white and Negro, classically act out this pseudo-masculinity with leather jackets, harsh language, and physical "toughness" [Pettigrew, 1964, p. 18].

Consistent with this same line of evidence are the results of a substantial number of studies pointing to the importance of paternal absence and inadequacy in the genesis of delinquent behavior (Bacon, Child, & Barry, 1963; Bandura & Walters, 1959; Burton & Whiting, 1961; Glueck & Glueck, 1950; 1956; Miller, 1958; Rohrer & Edmonson, 1960; Scarpitti, Murray, Dinitz, & Reckless, 1960). In seeking an explanation for this relationship, several of the major investigators have concluded that the exaggerated toughness, aggressiveness, and cruelty of delinquent gangs reflect the desperate effort of males in lower-class culture to rebel against their early overprotective, feminizing environment and to find a masculine identity. For example, Miller analyzes the dynamics of the process in the following terms:

The genesis of the intense concern over "toughness" in lower class culture is probably related to the fact that a significant proportion of lower class males are reared in a predominantly female household, and lack a consistently present male figure with whom to identify and from whom to learn essential components of a "male" role. Since women serve as a primary object of identification during preadolescent years, the almost obsessive lower class concern with "masculinity" probably resembles a type of compulsive reaction-formation. . . . A positive overt evaluation of behavior defined as "effeminate" would be out of the question for a lower class male [Miller, 1958, p. 9].

The special relevance of this dynamic for public education is indicated in a similar conclusion drawn by Rohrer and Edmonson in their follow-up study of Negro youth in New Orleans. "The gang member rejects this femininity in every form, and he sees it in women and in effeminate men, in laws and morals and religion, in schools, and occupational striving" (Rohrer & Edmonson, 1960, p. 163).

Despite their desperate effort to prove the contrary, a latent femininity is nevertheless present in "fatherless" youngsters and results in a confused sex identity. Substantial support for this argument is found in the impressive number of studies, summarized by Pettigrew, which show that Negro men, especially those from lower-class homes, obtain high scores on indirect measures of femininity. Additional evidence points to father absence as a critical factor. In comparison with a control group from intact homes, Negroes whose fathers were absent during early childhood were far more likely to be either single or divorced; in addition, "they also felt more victimized, less in control of the environment, and more distrustful of others" (Pettigrew, 1964, p. 20).

Nor are the consequences of paternal absence limited to the emotional and social sphere. A series of investigations by Mischel (1958; 1961a; 1961b; 1961c) points to the crucial role of this same factor in the development of a capacity essential to achievement generally and academic achievement in particular—the ability to delay immediate gratification in order to obtain a later reward. The systematic investigation of this phenomenon was suggested to the investigator by anthropological reports alleging "a major personality difference" between Negro and East Indian groups on the island of Trinidad.

This difference, as expressed by numerous informants, is that the Negroes are impulsive, indulge themselves, settle for next to nothing if they can get it right away, do not work or wait for bigger things in the future but, instead, prefer smaller gains immediately (Mischel, 1958, p. 57).

In a series of ingenious experiments (e.g., a child is offered a choice between a tiny candy bar now, and a larger bar in a week's time), Mischel (1958, 1961c) demonstrated that the preference for immediate gratification was a distinguishing characteristic observable in Negro children of 10 years of age and that the cultural difference could be attributed primarily, but not entirely, to the greater absence of the father among Negro families. In addition, the same investigator has shown that the desire for immediate gratification is associated with poorer accuracy in judging time, less achievement drive, lower levels of social responsibility, and a greater propensity toward delinquent behavior (Mischel, 1961a, 1961b).

The impact of paternal absence on actual school performance is reflected in Deutsch's (1960) finding that lower-class Negro children from broken homes were far more likely to score below grade level on tests of academic achievement than their classmates from intact families, and that the higher frequency of broken homes among Negro families accounted for most of the difference in achievement between the Negro and white samples. Moreover, children from intact families did better in school than those from broken homes, despite the fact that intact homes were more crowded, a circumstance which leads Deutsch to conclude that "*who* lives in the room is more important than *how many*" (Deutsch, 1960, p. 10). In a subsequent study, Deutsch and Brown (1964) have shown that a significant difference of about 8 points in IQ is specifically attributable to absence of the father from the home.

Finally, it is not only the absence of the Negro father that prevents the son from seeing the future realistically. Also relevant is the inferior position held by the adult Negro male in the economic world. In the matter of occupational choice, the Negro boy has few models to emulate that are actually within the realm of his possible achievement. This circumstance is reflected in a study of occupational aspirations among lower-class children (Deutsch, 1960, pp. 11–14). When asked what they wanted to be when they grew up, 25 per cent of the Negro boys named high-prestige professions, such as doctor or lawyer, etc.—goals completely beyond practical realization and hence reflecting idle wish fulfilment rather than an active achievement drive. In contrast, Negro girls were more realistic in scaling down their aspirations to occupations within their reach. Deutsch accounts for this difference in terms of the greater availability for the girls of an accepted role model both within the family and in the outside world.

The impoverished environment

We see, then, that both the high incidence of perinatal pathology and of paternal absence among lower-class Negroes have produced psychological deficits and disturbances in Negro children, particularly boys. But there are other early influences, equally baneful, which do not discriminate between the sexes. Among these is another product of poverty, the absence of an educationally stimulating environment during the preschool years. Studies of this phenomenon, summarized by Bloom, Davis, and Hess (1965), indicate that the lower-class Negro home is barren of objects (books, newspapers, pencils, paper, toys, games) and of coherent social interaction. For example, in a study of the "Social World of the Urban Slums," Keller (1963) reports that the children had little sustained contact with adults, few organized conversations, and little shared family activity. In the same vein, a comparison of Negro and white lower-class children (Deutsch, 1960) revealed that the former had fewer books in the home, got less help with their homework, took fewer trips beyond a 25-block radius from their home, ate less frequently with their parents, and spent less time with them on Sundays. Also, such verbal interaction with parents as did occur tended to be limited in complexity and completeness. For example, commands were likely to be one or several words rather than complete sentences and were typically given without explanation or elaboration.

Patterns of child rearing

An additional factor contributing to the inadequacies and problems of the Negro child is the alternately repressive and indulgent pattern of upbringing found in lower-class families in general (Bronfenbrenner, 1958) and Negro lower-class families in particular (Davis, 1941; Davis & Dollard, 1940; Davis & Havighurst, 1946; Frazier, 1957, Rohrer & Edmonson, 1960. Discipline is exercised principally by the mother, is focused on overt acts rather than motives or goals, and is mainly inhibitory in character; that is, the child is told *not* to do this or that, to keep quiet, not ask questions, stay out of trouble. The effect of such negative reinforcement is to discourage early initiative, curiosity, and exploration, as well as cooperative interaction with a guiding adult.

The legacy of slavery

It is noteworthy how many of the characteristics of the Negro family of today which are dysfunctional for modern society were functional for, or at least adaptive to, the conditions of bondage (Frazier, 1957). With the father constantly in risk of being sold to another owner, a matriarchal family structure became almost inevitable. But since the mother, too, had to work, it was necessary to keep the child from interfering by his activity, questions, or misbehavior. Moreover, as McClelland (1961) has pointed out, slavery is incompatible with and destructive of a high drive for achievement, since the rewards of the slave come not from initiative and independence but compliance. "Negro slaves should, therefore, have developed child-rearing practices calculated to produce obedience and responsibility not n-Achievement, and their descendents, while free, should still show the effects of such training in lower n-Achievement" (McClelland, 1961, pp. 376–377). In keeping with this prediction, Negro adolescents have the lowest scores in achievement motive among youth from six different ethnic groups in the United States (Rosen, 1959).

But the most important legacies of slavery were the conditions in which the American Negro found himself upon release from bondage—economic poverty and racial discrimination. The three together—slavery, poverty, and discrimination—lie at the root of the biological and social forces which produce widespread psychological debility and disturbance in the Negro child. From this perspective, it is the white man who is in the first instance primarily responsible for the inadequacies of the Negro and his way of life.

THE INTEGRATED CLASSROOM AND THE DISINTEGRATED CHILD

But allocation, or even acceptance, of responsibility for damage does not do away with the Negro child's deficiencies. Nor does placing him in an integrated classroom. On his arrival there he brings with him his full array of defects and disruptive behaviors. True, being able at least to sit with his white age mates may, under certain circumstances (Katz, 1964), bolster his self-esteem, provide him with more competent models to emulate, and significantly improve his academic performance (Coleman, 1966). But integration cannot repair a damaged brain, supply a father, equip a home with books, or alter a family's values, speech habits, and patterns of child rearing. Thus, in many cases, the Negro child in the integrated classroom is, and continues to be, intellectually retarded, unable to concentrate, unmotivated to learn; at first apathetic, but as he gets older, becoming resentful, rebellious, and delinquency-prone.

What is more, in the integrated classroom, all of these characteristics of the Negro child have their impact on his white companion. To begin with, unless countermeasures are introduced, they provide an objective basis and emotional provocation for devaluating and rejecting the Negro, thus reactivating and reinforcing the vicious circle of discrimination and defeat (Coles, 1963; Katz, 1964). But the white child is affected in other ways as well. Although the findings of the Coleman report (1966) indicate that middle-class white children do not suffer academically from attending the same schools as lower-class Negroes, the analysis was not carried out on a classroom basis, nor did it examine other aspects of behavior besides test performance. As has been demonstrated both in field (Polansky, Lippitt, & Redl, 1954) and experimental (Bandura & Walters, 1963) studies, disintegrative and destructive behavior of peers is highly subject to contagion, against which contrasting values and practices of the family provide little immunity. In other words, the white child is likely to take on some of the aggressive and disruptive activities of his Negro classmates. Such developments are, of course, viewed with alarm by many white parents, who become understandably concerned about the consequences of integration for character development of their children. In short, in the integrated classroom, the problems of the Negro child become, at least in part, those of the white child as well. Thus, the costs of inequality to the Negro become the costs of equality to the white.

COUNTERMEASURES AND CONSEQUENCES

Nor do these costs end with the impact on the classroom of the inappropriate behavior of the Negro child. While the damage already done to the latter by the time he enters school cannot be undone completely, some counteractive measures can be taken within the school environment, or under its auspices, which may entail still further psychological problems for the white community. For example, to a limited but significant extent, a male teacher can serve some of the functions of the absent or inadequate father. The high incidence of fatherless families in the Negro lower class argues strongly for the involvement of many more men as teachers at the elementary level. The psychological costs here, to the extent that any exist, lie in the low prestige and consequent threat to self-esteem which elementary teaching still holds for men in American society. This threat may be alleviated in part by the special need for Negro men as primary teachers, and these are not so likely to resent the role. But they themselves may often be resented by the white community, not only on grounds of racial prejudice, but also on the basis of their teaching effectiveness. Only a small proportion of Negro teachers have been able to enjoy the same educational opportunities, from early childhood on, as were available to their white colleagues; and, for the reasons already outlined, it is the Negro male who is most likely to have been disadvantaged. For this reason, if Negro teachers—especially Negro men—are employed in the large numbers in which they are needed, there will be a drop in the general level of instruction, for these teachers will not have as good command of subject matter as their predecessors, and their speech will deviate from the white middle-class norm. Yet, despite these deficiencies, such persons can do much more for the education of the Negro child than the better-educated, more middle-class-acculturated white or Negro female who would otherwise be their teacher.

But exposing the Negro child to a male teacher of his own race is not enough. Given the absence of positive male figures in his out-of-school environment, the young Negro requires additional acquaintance with men, especially of his own race, who, by their example, demonstrate the possibility and attraction of masculine competence and constructive conduct in a variety of spheres. This need could be met through programs of after-school activities conducted by persons—both Negro and white—who possess such diverse skills and who have found a place in their community. The objective of such programs would be not so much to take the youngster off the streets (although they would have this effect if successful) as to involve him in patterns of interaction which can develop the basic skills, motives, and qualities necessary for a child to be able to profit from the classroom experience. In other words, these after-school activities are to be viewed as an essential part of the educational process, falling within the responsibility of those agencies charged with providing public instruction.

It should be stressed that the after-school program here invisioned is not offering pre-vocational training. Quite the contrary. The activities would be nontechnical in nature and would begin at levels accessible and attractive to the lower-class child—sports, games, selected movies, outings. In the beginning, such activities would have to be conducted by persons trained or experienced in recreational activities; but gradually other adults would participate in them; and the child would discover that one was a machinist, another worked in a bank, a third was a reporter on a newspaper, etc. The objective is to expose the child to and induce him to emulate models embodying the values, skills, and aspirations necessary for achievement in school and society.

There is no question that such programs would be difficult to develop and to administer, but there is some evidence that they are practicable. For example, in Soviet schools (Bronfenbrenner, 1962), members of the community are frequently invited to accompany and participate with children in after-school activities, hikes, expeditions, etc., with the explicit aim of exposing the youngster to intimate contact with adults who combine specialized knowledge or skill with sterling and attractive qualities of character (of course, from the Communist point of view). A related practice long employed in Soviet schools is the involvement of adolescents and preadolescents in activities with young children. Recently, similar utilization of this age group, under appropriate supervision, has been urged in our own country in connection with Project Headstart—the federally sponsored preschool program for children in economically deprived areas. An issue of the *Headstart Newsletter* (1965) points to the fact that high school students can, in certain respects, function more effectively than adults in working with young children: "Grown-ups, no matter how friendly and helpful, are in an important sense, in a world apart. Their abilities, skills, and standards are so clearly superior to those of the child as to appear beyond his grasp."

It is, of course, important that persons working in such programs, be they adults or teen-agers, not be restricted to one race; but the same consideration applies for the children as well. Unless white youngsters are also involved in after-school programs, the activity once again becomes identified as an operation for second-class, second-rate citizens. Nor is it sufficient if participation is limited to children—Negro and white—coming from deprived backgrounds. A growing body of research (summarized in Bronfenbrenner, 1962; Millsom, 1966) points to the conclusion that peers are at least as effective if not more potent than adults in their capacity to influence the behavior of the child. From this point of view, it is desirable that children from more favored environments also be included in after-school activities; and, if they are, they are of course exposed to the deleterious as well as constructive influences present in that situation.

The after-school program has other difficulties as well. Indeed, some of these difficulties are a direct function of the degree to which the program achieves its objectives. For, to the extent that the Negro child acquires the skills and values of his new companions, he becomes further removed from his own family. The conflict which such separation can arouse both within the family and within the child himself can undermine whatever progress has been made and lead ultimately to debilitating problems of self-identity. Regrettably, this phenomenon has not yet been investigated systematically by psychologists. The best available data and analyses of the Negro's identity crisis appear in the works of such gifted Negro writers as Richard Wright (1945) and James Baldwin (1962). Because of this danger, it is necessary that, insofar as possible, the child's parents become actively involved in their child's new activities and new world. To modify the pattern of life of parents is, of course, far more difficult than to influence their children, but some opportunities nevertheless exist. One approach is that being employed in Project Headstart (*Report of the Planning Committee,* 1965), where parents from low-income families participate as "paid volunteers" in a variety of tasks requiring little formal education or experience but, at the same time, involving close contact with professional workers as they interact with children. In this manner, some parents—or more realistically, some mothers—are exposed to new and different attitudes and methods in dealing with young children. The device employed in Project Headstart illustrates a general principle, the validity of which has been demonstrated in a substantial body of research in behavioral science generally and in the study of intergroup relations in particular, namely, that attitudes and behaviors are changed most readily when people work together in pursuit of a common goal to which they are committed (Sherif, 1958; Williams, 1947; 1964). And the goal of bettering life for children is one which most parents are willing to pursue.

If we apply the foregoing principle more generally to the role of parents in programs for disadvantaged children in school and out, we come to a conclusion that should properly give us pause; namely, the principle implies that parental involvement is necessary, not only on the part of underprivileged families, but of the privileged as well. It is only through nonantagonistic exposure to the different view and the different practice that the lower-class parent can come to tolerate, understand, and perhaps adopt the different way of dealing with his child employed by those charged with responsibility for his education. Accordingly, it becomes highly desirable for parents from more privileged circumstances—Negro as well as white—to become actively involved in programs concerned with the education of their children both in school and out.

We are asking a great deal. As we said at the outset of this paper, the psychological costs of quality and equality in education for *all* the children are high. They require a new conception of the scope of public education as extending beyond school walls and school hours. They call for a far greater involvement in education of parents and other members of the adult community. They may even require some sacrifice in academic advancement for children from advantaged families to make possible academic survival for children from disadvantaged families. In short, they demand heavy payment from the Haves in favor of the Have-nots, not just in money, but in the far harder coin of psychological security and status.

And if we who have are willing to pay, what is achieved? Whatever we pay cannot be enough. Those who receive payment will still feel cheated, and rightly so. One cannot repay to the children of slaves the present costs of ancient bondage.

It is the tragedy and irony of injustice that those who seek to right it gain as much if not more than those who have been wronged. Paradoxically, it is not the disadvantaged Negro alone who would benefit from equality in education, were we truly to achieve it. For the only way in which we can give the Negro child equality is to teach the white child how to treat him equally. This will not happen from mere physical association in the classroom. It will require the actual teaching and practice, in school and out, of the principles of human dignity to which our society is dedicated. It is a sobering fact that in Communist schools a deliberate effort is made to teach the child, through concrete experience, the values and behaviors most consistent with Communist ideals (Bronfenbrenner, 1962; 1966). In American schools, training for action consistent with social responsibility and human dignity is at best an extracurricular activity. The belated recognition of our educational obligations to the child of poverty, white or black, offers us a chance to redress this weakness and to make democratic education not only a principle but a process.

REFERENCES

Anastasi, Anne. Intelligence and family size. *Psychological Bulletin,* 1956, **53**, 187–209.

Ausubel, D. P. Ego development among segregated Negro children. *Mental Hygiene,* 1958, **42**, 362–369.

Bach, G. R. Father-fantasies and father-typing in father-separated children. *Child Development,* 1946, **17**, 63–79.

Bacon, M. K. Child, I. L., & Barry, H., III. A cross-cultural study of correlates of crime. *Journal of Abnormal and Social Psychology,* 1963, **66**, 291–300.

Baldwin, J. *Another country*. New York: Dial, 1962.

Bandura, A., & Walters, R. H. *Adolescent aggression*. New York: Ronald, 1959.

Bandura, A., & Walters, R. H. *Social learning and personality development.* New York: Holt, Rinehart & Winston, 1963.

Barclay, A., & Cosumano, D. R. Father absence, cross-sex identity, and field dependent behavior in male adolescents. *Child Development,* 1967, **38**, 243–250.

Bloom, B. S., Davis, A., & Hess, R. *Compensatory education for cultural deprivation.* New York: Holt, Rinehart & Winston, 1965.

Bronfenbrenner, U. Socialization and social class through time and space. In E. Maccoby, T. M. Newcomb, & E. L. Hartley (Eds.), *Readings in social psychology*. New York: Holt, Rinehart & Winston, 1958. Pp. 400–425.

Bronfenbrenner, U. Soviet methods of character education. *American Psychologist,* 1962, **17**, 550–564.

Bronfenbrenner, U. Response to pressure from peers versus adults among Soviet and American school children. In *Social factors in the development of personality.* XVIII International Congress of Psychology, Symposium 35, 1966, Moscow. Pp. 7–18.

Burton, R. V., & Whiting, J. W. M. The Absent father and cross-sex identity. *Merrill-Palmer Quarterly,* 1961, **7**, 85–95.

Chein, I. The roots of conspiracy, *SPSSI Newsletter,* December, 1961.

Coleman, J. S. *Equality of educational opportunity.* Washington: U.S. Office of Education, 1966.

Coles, R. *The desegregation of southern schools: a psychiatric study.* New York: Anti-Defamation League, 1963.

Davis, A. *Deep south.* Chicago: University of Chicago Press, 1941.

Davis, A., & Dollard, J. *Children of bondage.* Washington, D.C.: American Council on Education, 1940.

Davis, A., & Havighurst, R. J. Social class and color differences in child-rearing. *American Sociological Review,* 1946, **11,** 698–710.

Deutsch, M. Minority group and class status as related to social and personality factors in scholastic achievement. *Monograph of the Society for Applied Anthropology,* 1960, No. 2, 1–32.

Deutsch, M., & Brown, B. Social influences in Negro-white intelligence differences. *Journal of Social Issues,* 1964, **20,** (2), 24–35.

Frazier, E. F. *The Negro in the United States.* New York: Macmillan, 1957.

Garrett, H. E. Klineberg's chapter on race and psychology: a review. *Mankind Quarterly,* 1960, **1,** 15–22.

Garrett, H. E. The equalitarian dogma. *Mankind Quarterly,* 1961, **1,** 253–257.

Garrett, H. E. Rejoinder by Garrett. *Newsletter of the Society for the Psychological Study of Social Issues,* May, 1962, 1–2. (a)

Garrett, H. E. The SPSSI and racial differences. *American Psychologist,* 1962, **17,** 260–263. (b)

Glueck, S., & Glueck, E. T. *Unreveling juvenile delinquency.* New York: Commonwealth Fund, 1950.

Glueck, S., & Glueck, E. T. *Physique and delinquency.* New York: Harper, 1956.

Grønseth, E. The impact of father absence in sailor families upon the personality structure and social adjustment of adult sailor sons. Part I. In N. Anderson (Ed.), *Studies of the family.* Vol. 2. Göttingen: Vandengoeck & Ruprecht, 1957. Pp. 97–114.

Headstart Newsletter. No. 2. Published by the Office of Economic Opportunity, July, 1965.

Kardiner, A., & Ovesey, L. *The mark of oppression.* New York: Norton, 1951.

Katz, I. Review of evidence relating to effects of desegregation on the intellectual performance of Negroes. *American Psychologist,* 1964, **19,** 381–399.

Kawi, A. A., & Pasamanick, B. Prenatal and paranatal factors in the development of childhood reading disorders. *Monographs of the Society for Research in Child Development,* 1959, **24,** No. 4 (Serial No. 73).

Keller, S. The social world of the urban slum child: some early findings. *American Journal of Orthopsychiatry,* 1963, **33,** 823–831.

Kennedy, W. A., Van de Riet, V., & White, J. C., Jr. A normative sample of intelligence and achievement of Negro elementary school children in the Southeastern United States. *Monographs of the Society for Research in Child Development,* 1963, **28,** No. 6 (Serial No. 90).

Knobloch, H., Rider, R., Harper, P., & Pasamanick, B. Neural psychiatric sequelae of prematurity. *Journal of the American Medical Association,* 1956, **161,** 581–585.

Kuckenberg, C. Effect of early father absence on scholastic aptitude. Unpublished doctoral dissertation, Harvard University, 1963.

Lynn, D. B., & Sawrey, W. L. The effects of father-absence on Norwegian boys and girls. *Journal of Abnormal and Social Psychology,* 1959, **59,** 258–262.

McClelland, D. C. *The achieving society.* Princeton, N.J.: Van Nostrand, 1961.

McGurk, F. Psychological tests: a scientist's report on race differences. *United States News and World Report,* September 21, 1956, 92–96.

McGurk, F. Negro vs. white intelligence—an answer. *Harvard Educational Review,* 1959, **29,** 54–62.

Miller, W. B. Lower class culture as a generating milieu of gang delinquency. *Journal of Social Issues,* 1958, **14,** (3), 5–19.

Millsom, C. *Conformity to peers versus adults in early adolescence.* Ph.D. Dissertation, submitted to the Graduate School of Cornell University, February, 1966.

Mischel, W. Preference for delayed reinforcement and experimental study of a cultural observation. *Journal of Abnormal and Social Psychology,* 1958, **56,** 57–61.

Mischel, W. Delay of gratification, need for achievement, and acquiescence in another culture. *Journal of Abnormal and Social Psychology,* 1961, **62,** 543–552. (b)

Mischel, W. Father-absence and delay of gratification: cross-cultural comparison. *Journal of Abnormal and Social Psychology,* 1961, **63,** 116–124. (c)

Pasamanick, B., & Knobloch, H. The contribution of some organic factors to school retardation in Negro children. *Journal of Negro Education,* 1958, **27,** 4–9.

Pasamanick, B., Knobloch, H., & Lilienfeld, A. M. Socionomic status and some precursors of neuropsychiatric disorder. *American Journal of Orthopsychiatrics,* 1956, **26,** 594–601.

Pettigrew, T. F. *A profile of the Negro American.* Princeton, N.J.: Van Nostrand, 1964.

Polansky, N., Lippitt, R., & Redl, F. An investigation of behavioral contagion in groups. In W. E. Martin & C. B. Stendler (Eds.), *Readings in child development.* New York: Harcourt, Brace, 1954. Pp. 413–513.

Report of the planning committee. Project Head Start, Office of Economic Opportunity, 1965.

Rohrer, J. H. & Edmonson, M. S. (Eds.) *The eighth generation.* New York: Harper, 1960.

Rosen, B. C. Race, ethnicity, and the achievement syndrome. *American Sociological Review,* 1959, **24,** 47–60.

Scarpitti, F. R., Murray, E., Dinitz, S., & Reckless, W. C. The "good" boy in a high delinquency area: four years later. *American Sociological Review,* 1960, **25,** 555–558.

Sears, P. S. Doll play aggression in normal young children: influence of sex, age, sibling status, father's absence. *Psychological Monographs,* 1951, **65,** No. 6 (Whole No. 323).

Sears, R. R., Pintler, M. H., & Sears, P. S. Effects of father-separation on pre-school children's doll play aggression. *Child Development,* 1946, **17,** 219–243.

Sherif, M. Superordinate goals in the reduction of intergroup tensions. *American Journal of Sociology,* 1958, **53,** 349–356.

Shuey, A. *The testing of Negro intelligence,* Lynchburg, Va.: Bell, 1958.

Stolz, L. M. *Father relations of warborn children.* Palo Alto, Calif.: Stanford University Press, 1954.

Tiller, P. O. Father absence and personality development of children in sailor families: a preliminary research report. Part II. In N. Anderson (Ed.), *Studies of the family.* Vol. 2, Göttingen: Vandenhoeck & Reprecht, 1957. Pp. 115–137.

Tiller, P. O. *Father-separation and adolescence.* Oslo: Institute for Social Research, 1961. (Mimeographed)

Van den Haag, E. Negroes' intelligence and prejudice. *National Review,* December 1, 1964.

Williams, R. M., Jr. *The reduction of intergroup tensions.* Bull. **57.** New York: Social Science Research Council, 1947.

Williams, R. M., Jr. *Strangers next door.* Englewood Cliffs, N.J.: Prentice-Hall, 1964.

Wright, R. *Black boy.* New York: Harper, 1945.

DISCUSSION QUESTIONS

1. What new forms of social engineering could you suggest to overcome the organic deficiencies, the intellectual starvation, and the psychological maiming delineated by Bronfenbrenner?

2. Are we willing to pay the price for dealing adequately with our educational problems? What priority should the schools have in the national scheme?
3. What steps can the schools take immediately to make education for the "disadvantaged" more meaningful, more relevant, and more successful?
4. Bronfenbrenner describes as a major problem the absence of the male parent. Should the school recognize this problem? What should be done about it?

HERBERT KOHL | *36 Children*

My alarm clock rang at seven thirty, but I was up and dressed at seven. It was only a fifteen-minute bus ride from my apartment on 90th Street and Madison Avenue to the school on 119th Street and Madison.

There had been an orientation session the day before. I remembered the principal's words. "In times like these, this is the most exciting place to be, in the midst of ferment and creative activity. Never has teaching offered such opportunities . . . we are together here in a difficult situation. They are not the easiest children, yet the rewards are so great—a smile, loving concern, what an inspiration, a felicitous experience."

I remembered my barren classroom, no books, a battered piano, broken windows and desks, falling plaster, and an oppressive darkness.

I was handed a roll book with thirty-six names and thirty-six cumulative record cards, years of judgments already passed upon the children, their official personalities. I read through the names, twenty girls and sixteen boys, the 6-1 class, though I was supposed to be teaching the fifth grade and had planned for it all summer. Then I locked the record cards away in the closet. The children would tell me who they were. Each child, each new school year, is potentially many things, only one of which the cumulative record card documents. It is amazing how "emotional" problems can disappear, how the dullest child can be transformed into the keenest and the brightest into the most ordinary when the prefabricated judgments of other teachers are forgotten.

The children entered at nine and filled up the seats. They were silent and stared at me. It was a shock to see thirty-six black faces before me. No preparation helped. It is one thing to be liberal and talk, another to face something and learn that you're afraid.

The children sat quietly, expectant. *Everything must go well; we must like each other.*

Hands went up as I called the roll. Anxious faces, hostile, indifferent, weary of the ritual, confident of its outcome.

The smartest class in the sixth grade, yet no books.

"Write about yourselves, tell me who you are." (I hadn't said who I was, too nervous.)

Slowly they set to work, the first directions followed—and if they had refused?

Then arithmetic, the children working silently, a sullen, impenetrable front. *To talk to them, to open them up this first day.*

"What would you like to learn this year? My name is Mr. Kohl."

Silence, the children looked up at me with expressionless faces, thirty-six of them crowded at thirty-five broken desks. *This is the smartest class?*

Explain: they're old enough to choose, enough time to learn what they'd like as well as what they have to.

Silence, a restless movement rippled through the class. *Don't they understand? There must be something that interests them, that they care to know more about.*

A hand shot up in the corner of the room.

"I want to learn more about volcanoes. What are volcanoes?"

The class seemed interested. I sketched a volcano on the blackboard, made a few comments, and promised to return.

"Anything else? Anyone else interested in something?"

Silence, then the same hand.

"Why do volcanoes form?"

And during the answer:

"Why don't we have a volcano here?"

A contest. The class savored it, I accepted. Question, response, question. I walked toward my inquisitor, studying his mischievous eyes, possessed and possessing smile. I moved to congratulate him, my hand went happily toward his shoulder. I dared because I was afraid.

His hands shot up to protect his dark face, eyes contracted in fear, body coiled ready to bolt for the door and out, down the stairs into the streets.

"But why should I hit you?"

They're afraid too!

Hands relaxed, he looked torn and puzzled. I changed the subject quickly and moved on to social studies—How We Became Modern America.

"Who remembers what America was like in 1800?"

A few children laughed; the rest barely looked at me.

"Can anyone tell me what was going on about 1800? Remember, you studied it last year. Why don't we start more specifically? What do you think you'd see if you walked down Madison Avenue in those days?"

A lovely hand, almost too thin to be seen, tentatively rose.

"Cars?"

"Do you think there were cars in 1800? Remember that was over a hundred and fifty years ago. Think of what you learned last year and try again. Do you think there were cars then?"

"Yes . . . no . . . I don't know."

She withdrew, and the class became restless as my anger rose.

At last another hand.

"Grass and trees?"

The class broke up as I tried to contain my frustration.

"I don't know what you're laughing about—it's the right answer. In those days Harlem was farmland with fields and trees and a few houses. There weren't any roads or houses like the ones outside, or street lights or electricity. There probably wasn't even a Madison Avenue."

The class was outraged. It was inconceivable to them that there was a time their Harlem didn't exist.

"Stop this noise and let's think. Do you believe that Harlem was here a thousand years ago?"

A pause, several uncertain Noes.

"It's possible that the land was green then. Why couldn't Harlem also have been green a hundred and fifty or two hundred years ago?"

No response. The weight of Harlem and my whiteness and strangeness hung in the air as I droned on, lost in my righteous monologue. The uproar turned into sullen silence. A slow nervous drumming began at several desks; the atmosphere closed as intelligent faces lost their animation. Yet I didn't understand my mistake, the children's rejection of me and my ideas. Nothing worked, I tried to joke, command, play—the children remained joyless until the bell, then quietly left for lunch.

There was an hour to summon energy and prepare for the afternoon, yet it seemed futile. What good are plans, clever new methods and materials, when the children didn't—wouldn't—care or listen? Perhaps the best solution was to prepare for hostility and silence, become the cynical teacher, untaught by his pupils, ungiving himself, yet protected.

At one o'clock, my tentative cynicism assumed, I found myself once again unprepared for the children who returned and noisily and boisterously avoided me. Running, playing, fighting—they were alive as they tore about the room. I was relieved, yet how to establish order? I fell back on teacherly words.

"You've had enough time to run around. Everybody please go to your seats. We have work to begin."

No response. The boy who had been so scared during the morning was flying across the back of the room pursued by a demonic-looking child wearing black glasses. Girls stood gossiping in little groups, a tall boy fantasized before four admiring listeners, while a few children wandered in and out of the room. I still knew no one's name.

"Sit down, we've got to work. At three o'clock you can talk all you want to."

One timid girl listened. I prepared to use one of the teacher's most fearsome weapons and last resources. Quickly white paper was on my desk, the blackboard erased, and numbers from 1 to 10 and 11 to 20 appeared neatly in two columns.

"We're now going to have an *important* spelling test. Please, young lady"—I selected one of the gossipers—"what's your name? Neomia, pass out the paper. When you get your paper, fold it in half, put your heading on it, and number carefully from one to ten and eleven to twenty, exactly as you see it on the blackboard."

Reluctantly the girls responded, then a few boys, until after the fourth, weariest, repetition of the directions the class was seated and ready to begin—I thought.

Rip, a crumpled paper flew onto the floor. Quickly I replaced it; things had to get moving.

Rip, another paper, rip. I got the rhythm and began quickly, silently replacing crumpled papers.

"The first word is *anchor*. The ship dropped an *anchor*. Anchor."

"A what?"

"Where?"

"Number two is *final*. *Final* means last, *final*. Number three is *decision*. He couldn't make a *decision* quickly enough."

"What *decision?*"

"What was number two?"

"Final."

I was trapped.

"Then what was number one?"

"Anchor."

"I missed a word."

"Number four is *reason*. What is the *reason* for all this noise?"

"Because it's the first day of school."

"Yeah, this is too hard for the first day."

"We'll go on without any comments whatever. The next word is——"

"What number is it?"

"——*direction*. What *direction* are we going? *Direction.*"

"What's four?"

The test seemed endless, but it did end at two o'clock. What next? Once more I needed to regain my strength and composure, and it was still the first day.

"Mr. Kohl, can we please talk to each other about the summer? We won't play around. Please, it's only the first day."

"I'll tell you what, you can talk, but on the condition that everyone, I mean *every single person in the room,* keeps quiet for one whole minute."

Teacher still had to show he was strong. To prove what? The children succeeded in remaining silent on the third attempt; they proved they could listen. Triumphant, I tried more.

"Now let's try for thirty seconds to think of one color."

"You said we could talk!"

"My head hurts, I don't want to think anymore."

"It's not fair!"

It wasn't. A solid mass of resistance coagulated, frustrating my need to command. The children would not be moved.

"You're right, I'm sorry. Take ten minutes to talk and then we'll get back to work."

For ten minutes the children talked quietly; there was time to prepare for the last half hour. I looked over my lesson plans: Reading, 9 to 10; Social Studies, 10 to 10:45, etc., etc. How absurd academic time was in the face of the real day. *Where to look?*

"You like it here, Mr. Kohl?"

I looked up into a lovely sad face.

"What do you mean?"

"I mean do you like it here, Mr. Kohl, what are you teaching us for?"

What?

"Well, I . . . not now. Maybe you can see me at three and we can talk. The class has to get back to work. All right, everybody back to your seats, get ready to work."

She had her answer and sat down and waited with the rest of the class. They were satisfied with the bargain. Only it was I who failed then; exhausted, demoralized, I only wanted three o'clock to arrive.

"It's almost three o'clock and we don't have much time left."

I dragged the words out, listening only for the bell.

"This is only the first day, and of course we haven't got much done. I expect more from you during the year . . ."

The class sensed the maneuver and fell nervous again.

"Take out your notebooks and open to a clean page. Each day except Friday you'll get homework."

My words weighed heavy and false; it wasn't my voice but some common tyrant or moralizer, a tired old man speaking.

"There are many things I'm not strict about but homework is the one thing I insist upon. In my class *everybody always* does homework. I will check your work every morning. Now copy the assignment I'm putting on the blackboard, and then when you're finished, please line up in the back of the room."

What assignment? What lie now? I turned to the blackboard, groping for something to draw the children closer to me, for something to let them know I cared. *I did care!*

"Draw a picture of your home, the room you live in. Put in all the furniture, the TV, the windows and doors. You don't have to do it in any special way but keep in mind that the main purpose of the picture should be to show someone what your house looks like."

The children laughed, pointed, then a hand rose, a hand I couldn't attach to a body or face. They all looked alike. I felt sad, lonely.

"Do you have to show your house?"

Two boys snickered. *Are there children ashamed to describe their homes? —have I misunderstood again?* The voice in me answered again.

"Yes."

"I mean . . . what if you can't draw, can you let someone help you?"

"Yes, if you can explain the drawing yourself."

"What if your brother can't draw?"

"Then write a description of your apartment. Remember, *everybody always* does homework in my classes."

The class copied the assignment and lined up, first collecting everything they'd brought with them. The room was as empty as it was at eight o'clock. Tired, weary of discipline, authority, school itself, I rushed the class down the stairs and into the street in some unacknowledged state of disorder.

The bedlam on 119th Street, the stooped and fatigued teachers smiling at each other and pretending *they* had had no trouble with their kids relieved my isolation. I smiled too, assumed the comfortable pose of casual success, and looked down into a mischievous face, the possessed eyes of the child who had thought I would hit him, Alvin, who kindly and thoughtfully said: "Mr. Kohl, how come you let us out so early today? We just had lunch . . ."

Crushed, I walked dumbly away, managed to reach the bus stop and make my way home. As my weariness dissolved, I only remembered of that first day Alvin and the little girl who asked if I liked being "there."

The books arrived the next morning before class. There were twenty-five arithmetic books from one publisher and twelve from another, but in the entire school there was no complete set of sixth-grade arithmetic books. A few minutes spent checking the first day's arithmetic assignment showed me that it wouldn't have mattered if a full set had existed, since half the class had barely mastered multiplication, and only one child, Grace, who had turned in a perfect paper, was actually ready for sixth-grade arithmetic. It was as though, encouraged to believe that the children couldn't do arithmetic by judging from the school's poor results in teaching it, the administration decided not to waste money on arithmetic books, thereby creating a vicious circle that made it even more impossible for the children to learn.

The situation was almost as dismal in reading—the top class of the sixth grade had more than half its members reading on fourth-grade level and only five or six children actually able to read through a sixth-grade book. There were two full sets of sixth-grade readers available, however, and after the arithmetic situation I was grateful for anything. Yet accepting these readers put me as a teacher in an awkward position. The books were flat and uninteresting. They only presented what was pleasant in life, and even then limited the pleasant to what was publicly accepted as such. The people in the stories were all middle-class and their simplicity, goodness, and self-confidence were unreal. I couldn't believe in this foolish ideal and knew that anyone who had ever bothered to observe human life couldn't believe it. Yet I had to teach it, and through it make reading important and necessary. Remembering the children, their anxiety and hostility, the alternate indifference, suspicion, and curiosity they approached me with, knowing how essential it is to be honest with children, I felt betrayed by the books into hypocrisy. No hypocrite can win the respect of children, and without respect one cannot teach.

One of the readers was a companion to the social studies unit on the growth of the United States and was full of stories about family fun in a Model T Ford, the first wireless radio in town, and the joys of wealth and progress. The closest the book touched upon human emotion or the real life of real children was in a story in which children accepted a new invention before their parents did, even though the adults laughed at the children. Naturally, everything turned out happily.

The other reader was a miscellany of adventure stories (no human violence or antagonists allowed, just treasure hunts, animal battles, close escapes), healthy poems (no love except for mother, father, and nature), and a few harmless myths (no Oedipus, Electra, or Prometheus). I also managed to get twenty dictionaries in such bad condition that the probability of finding any word still intact was close to zero.

The social studies texts (I could choose from four or five) praised industrial America in terms that ranged from the enthusiastic to the exorbitant. Yet the growth of modern industrial society is fascinating, and it was certainly possible to supplement the text with some truth. I decided to work with what was given me and attempt to teach the sixth-grade curriculum as written in the New York City syllabus, ignoring as long as possible the contradictions inherent in such a task.

The class confronted me, surrounded by my motley library, at nine that second morning and groaned.

"Those phoney books?"

"We read them already, Mr. Kohl."

"It's a cheap, dirty, bean school."

My resolve weakened, and I responded out of despair.

"Let me put it straight to you. These are the only books here. I have no more choice than you do and I don't like it any better. Let's get through them and maybe by then I'll figure out how to get better ones."

The class understood and accepted the terms. As soon as the books were distributed the first oral reading lesson began. Some children volunteered eagerly, but most of the class tried not to be seen. The children who read called out the words, but the story was lost. I made the lesson as easy as possible by helping children who stumbled, encouraging irrelevant discussion, and not letting any child humiliate himself. It was bad enough that more than half the class had to be forced to use books they couldn't read.

The lesson ended, and a light-skinned boy raised his hand.

"Mr. Kohl, remember that ten minutes you gave us yesterday? Couldn't we talk again now? We're tired after all this reading."

I wasn't sure how to take Robert's request. My initial feeling was that he was taking advantage of me and trying to waste time. I felt, along with the official dogma, that no moment in school should be wasted—it must all be pre-planned and structured. Yet why shouldn't it be "wasted"? Hadn't most of the class wasted years in school, not merely moments?

I remembered my own oppressive school days in New York City, moving from one subject to another without a break, or at most, with a kind teacher letting us stand and stretch in unison; I remember reading moving into social studies into arithmetic. How hateful it seemed then. Is it a waste to pause, talk, or think between subjects? As a teacher I, too, needed a break.

"You're right, Robert, I'm tired, too. Everybody can take ten minutes to do what you want, and then we'll move on to social studies."

The class looked fearful and amazed—freedom in school, do what you want? For a few minutes they sat quietly and then slowly began to talk. Two children walked to the piano and asked me if they could try. I said of course, and three more children joined them. It seemed so easy; the children relaxed. I watched closely and suspiciously, realizing that the tightness with time that exists in the elementary school has nothing to do with the quantity that must be learned or the children's needs. It represents the teacher's fear of loss of control and is nothing but a weapon used to weaken the solidarity and opposition of the children that too many teachers unconsciously dread.

After the ten minutes I tried to bring the children back to work. They resisted, tested my determination. I am convinced that a failure of will at that moment would have been disastrous. It was necessary to compel the children to return to work, not due to my "authority" or "control" but because they were expected to honor the bargain. They listened, and at the moment I learned something of the toughness, consistency, and ability to demand and give respect that enables children to listen to adults without feeling abused or brutalized and, therefore, becoming defiant.

I tried How We Became Modern America again. It was hopeless. The children acted as if they didn't know the difference between rivers, islands, oceans, and lakes; between countries, cities, and continents; between ten years and two centuries. Either their schooling had been hopeless or there was a deeper reason I did not yet understand underlying the children's real or feigned ignorance. One thing was clear, however, they did not want to hear about the world and, more specifically, modern America from me. The atmosphere was dull as I performed to an absent audience.

"The steam engine was one of the most important . . . Alvin, what was I talking about?"

"Huh?"

He looked dull, his face heavy with resignation, eyes vacant, nowhere. . . .

The morning ended on that dead note, and the afternoon began with an explosion. Alvin, Maurice, and Michael came dashing in, chased by a boy from another class who stuck his head and fist in the room, rolled his eyes, and muttered, "Just you wait, Chipmunk."

As soon as he disappeared the three boys broke up.

"Boy, is he dumb. You sure psyched him."

"Wait till tomorrow in the park."

The other children returned and I went up to the three boys and said as openly as I could, "What's up?"

They moved away. Alvin muttered something incomprehensible and looked at the floor. As soon as they reached the corner of the room the laughter began again. Maurice grabbed Michael's glasses and passed them to Alvin. Michael grabbed Alvin's pencil and ran to the back of the room as one of the girls said to me:

"Mr. Kohl, they're bad. You ought to hit them."

Refusing that way out I watched chaos descend once more. Only this time, being more familiar with the faces and feeling more comfortable in the room, I discerned some method in the disorder. Stepping back momentarily from myself, forgetting my position and therefore my need to establish order, I observed the children and let them show me something of themselves. There were two clusters of boys and three of girls. There were also loners watching shyly or hovering eagerly about the peripheries of the groups. One boy sat quietly drawing, oblivious to the world. As children entered the room they would go straight to one group or another, hover, or walk over to the boy who was drawing and watch silently. Of the two boys' groups, one was whispering conspiratorially while the other, composed of Alvin, Maurice, Michael, and two others, was involved in some wild improbable mockery of tag. Alvin would tag himself and run. If no one was watching him he'd stop, run up to one of the others, tag himself again, and the chase was on—for a second. The pursuer would invariably lose interest, tag himself, and the roles would be switched until they all could collide laughing, slapping palms, and chattering. The other group paid no attention—they were talking of serious matters. They looked bigger, older, and tougher.

There wasn't time to observe the girls. The tag game seemed on the verge of violence and, frightened, I stepped back into the teacherly role, relaxed and strengthened with my new knowledge of the class, and asked in a strong quiet voice for the homework. I felt close to the children—observing them, my fear and self-consciousness were forgotten for a moment. It was the right thing. The girls went to their desks directly while the boys stopped awkwardly and made embarrassed retreats to their seats.

I am convinced that the teacher must be an observer of his class as well as a member of it. He must look at the children, discover how they relate to each other and the room around them. There must be enough free time and activity for the teacher to discover the children's human preferences. Observing children at play and mischief is an invaluable source of knowledge about them—about leaders and groups, fear, courage, warmth, isolation. Teachers consider the children's gym or free play time their free time, too, and usually turn their backs on the children when they have most to learn from them.

I went through a year of teacher training at Teachers College, Columbia, received a degree, and heard no mention of how to observe children, nor even a suggestion that it was of value. Without learning to observe children and thereby knowing something of the people one is living with five hours a day, the teacher resorts to routine and structure for protection. The class is assigned seats, the time is planned down to the minute, subject follows subject—all to the exclusion of human variation and invention.

I witnessed the same ignorance of the children in a private school I once visited, only it was disguised by a progressive egalitarian philosophy. The teachers and students were on a first-name basis; together they chose the curriculum and decided upon the schedule. Yet many of the teachers knew no more of their classes than the most rigid public-school teachers. They knew only of their pupils and their mutual relationships in contexts where the teacher was a factor. It was clear to me, watching the children when the teacher left the room, that the children's preferences "for the teachers" were not the same as their human preferences (which most likely changed every week). That is not an academic point, for observation can open the teacher to his pupils' changing needs, and can often allow him to understand and utilize internal dynamic adjustments that the children make in relation to each other, rather than impose authority from without.

After the first few days of the year, my students are free to move wherever they want in the room, my role being arbiter when someone wants to move into a seat whose occupant does not want to vacate or when health demands special consideration. I have never bothered to count the number of continual, self-selected seat changes in my classes, yet can say that they never disrupted the fundamental fabric of the class. Rather, they provided internal adjustments and compensations that avoided many possible disruptions. Children fear chaos and animosity. Often they find ways of adjusting to difficult and sensitive situations (when free to) before their teachers are aware they exist.

Only fourteen of the thirty-six children brought in homework that second afternoon, and twelve of them were girls. One of the boys, I noticed, was the quiet artist. Here was a critical moment that plunged me back into the role of participant and destroyed my objective calm. What was the best reaction to the children's lack of response, especially after I'd been so pompous and adamant about homework the first day? How many of the twenty-two missing homeworks were the result of defiance (perhaps merited), of inability, of shame at what the result might reveal? Was there a simple formula: *Good = do homework* and another *Bad = not do homework?* Or would these formulas themselves negate the honesty and sincerity that could lead the children to find a meaningful life in school? At that moment in the classroom I had no criteria by which to decide and no time to think out my response. It would have been most just to react in thirty-six different ways to the thirty-six different children, but there was no way for me to be most just at that moment. I had to react intuitively and immediately, as anyone in a classroom must. There is never time to plot every tactic. A child's responses are unpredictable, those of groups of children even more so, unless through being brutalized and bullied they are made predictable. When a teacher claims he knows exactly what will happen in his class, exactly how the children will behave and function, he is either lying or brutal.

That means that the teacher must make mistakes. Intuitive, immediate responses can be right and magical, can express understanding that the teacher doesn't know he has, and lead to reorganizations of the teacher's relationship with his class. But they can also be peevish and petty, or merely stupid and cruel. Consistency of the teacher's response is frequently desirable, and the word "consistency" is a favorite of professors at teacher training institutions. Consistency can sometimes prevent discovery and honesty. More, consistency of response is a function of the consistency of a human personality, and that is, at best, an unachievable ideal.

I've said many stupid, unkind things in my classroom, hit children in anger, and insulted them maliciously when they threatened me too much. On the other hand, I've also said some deeply affecting things, moved children to tears by unexpected kindnesses, and made them happy with praise that flowed unashamedly. I've wanted to be consistent and have become more consistent. That seems the most that is possible, a slow movement toward consistency tempered by honesty. The teacher has to live with his own mistakes, as his pupils have to suffer them. Therefore, the teacher must learn to perceive them as mistakes and find direct or indirect ways to acknowledge his awareness of them and of his fallibility to his pupils.

The ideal of the teacher as a flawless moral exemplar is a devilish trap for the teacher as well as a burden for the child. I once had a pupil, Narciso, who was overburdened by the perfection of adults, and especially, of teachers. His father demanded he believe in this perfection as he demanded Narciso believe in and acquiesce to absolute authority. It was impossible to approach the boy for his fear and deference. I had terrified him. He wouldn't work or disobey. He existed frozen in silence. One day he happened to pass by a bar where some other teachers and I were sitting having beers. He was crushed; *teachers don't do that.* He believed so much in what his father and some teachers wanted him to believe that his world collapsed. He stayed away from school for a while, then returned. He smiled and I returned the smile. After a while he was at ease in class and could be himself, delightful and defiant, sometimes brilliant, often lazy, an individual reacting in his unique way to what happened in the classroom.

It is only in the world of Dick and Jane, Tom and Sally, that the *always* right and righteous people exist. In a way, most textbooks, and certainly the ones I had to use in the sixth grade, protect the pure image of the teacher by showing the child that somewhere in the ideal world that inspires books all people are as "good" as the teacher is supposed to be! It is not insignificant that it is teachers and not students who select school readers, nor that, according to a friend of mine who edits school texts, the books were written for the teachers and not for children for this very reason.

Of course the teacher is a moral exemplar—an example of all the confusion, hypocrisy, and indecision, of all the mistakes, as well as the triumphs, of moral man. The children see all this, whatever they pretend to see. Therefore, to be more than an example, to be an educator—someone capable of helping lead the child through the labyrinth of life—the teacher must be honest to the children about his mistakes and weaknesses; he must be able to say that he is wrong or sorry, that he hadn't anticipated the results of his remarks and regretted them, or hadn't understood what a child meant. It is the teacher's struggle to be moral that excites his pupils; it is honesty, not rightness, that moves children.

I didn't know all of this when I decided that second day to forget the twenty-two undone homeworks and remark that the first homework wasn't that important. I was just feeling my way.

I accepted the twelve homeworks that were completed without ceremony or praise. At that moment it seemed as wrong to overpraise the children who did the work as to degrade those who didn't, since I didn't understand why they did it.

DISCUSSION QUESTIONS

1. How would you begin your first day of teaching in Harlem? Can you begin to prepare for it now?
2. What would successful teaching in Harlem mean, in your eyes?
3. Faced with the realities of the situation that Kohl describes, why should anyone undertake to teach in Harlem? What might motivate you to accept this assignment?
4. What did you learn about Herbert Kohl from this excerpt?

THEODORE JONES | *Youths Explain Dropout Causes*

Discrimination, Schools and Parents Share in Blame

A group of teen-agers said yesterday that the chief factors producing school dropouts were parental apathy, racial discrimination and a failure by the schools to provide incentive.

These youngsters were participants in an all-day forum of teen-agers sponsored by the Children's Aid Society at its Frederick Douglass Children's Center at 885 Columbus Avenue, near 104th Street.

"Parents seem to be less interested in your report card when you're in high school," observed Rudolph Mitchell, who is 18 years old and attending night school. "They just want to know, 'Did you pass?' "

Cheryl Davis, 17, a student at Julia Richman High School said that "a lot of kids from minority groups figure, why should they go through all the years of high school and further education when they know they're not going to get the job because of discrimination."

ADULT PROGRAMS URGED

"Teachers don't tell the parents when they come to visit just how important school is. They just talk about grades," declared Anthony Petro, a 15-year-old student at St. Peter's High School in Staten Island.

This could be solved, Anthony continued, "by having programs for parents to teach them how important school is for their children."

More than 100 youths, Negro and white, took part in the forum's four workshops, which examined the roles of the parent, the school, the community and the civil rights movement in providing incentive to the student to remain in school.

The workshop discussions followed a keynote address by Mrs. Mary Conway Kohler, a member of the city's Board of Education. Mrs. Kohler told the forum that "the big cause of school dropouts was not financial distress, but educational failure."

She explained that the majority of dropouts fell in those categories of persons, "who had got bored with school; who just wanted to get out, and, to our regret, whom the schools wanted to get rid of for one reason or another."

Reprinted from *The New York Times,* April 5, 1964, with permission of the publisher.

PERSONAL LIFE CITED

During the discussions, several participants volunteered personal answers to some of the problems cited as factors for school dropouts.

"Up to six months ago, I would have dropped out," said Mike Anglin, 17, a student at Charles M. Hughes High School," but I became interested in CORE [the Congress of Racial Equality] and now I'm thinking of going on to college."

The Negro youngster explained that because of job discrimination it was important to get as much education as possible.

"That's what the civil rights movement is all about," he said—"to get us those jobs. But we have to be qualified for these jobs if we want to better ourselves."

Jacob Smith, who did drop out of school and is now taking night courses to obtain an equivalent high school degree, felt that family problems at home made it difficult for a student to do his best in school.

Asked if talking the problem over with the teacher would help, the 19-year-old replied that it might if "a fellow had the nerve to tell his problem to an outsider."

A youth needs a push, Smith explained, "to be that one out of a hundred kids to ask the teacher for help on a home problem. And it's that first time that hurts," he said.

DISCUSSION QUESTIONS

1. What is the school's responsibility toward the child who is "bored"?
2. What responsibility does it have for the child who is affected by adverse home conditions?
3. Should the school be concerned about job discrimination and the civil rights movement? What should it do about them?
4. Who has failed when a youngster "drops out"? How can such failure be prevented?

SARA MURPHY | *First Come Love and Understanding*

When Mike Zotti, a transplanted Yankee who still has traces of a New Jersey accent, sent out a memorandum about the first Springdale, Ark., Summer School for Migrant Children, he wrote unabashedly:

"Our main purpose is to furnish the *successful* atmosphere for these

Reprinted from Southern Education Report (March 1968), pp. 24–27, with permission of the publisher, the Southern Education Reporting Service.

students that eludes them during regular school. We furnish food service, medical service, educational service, but even more important we furnish *love* and *understanding*."

Neither love nor understanding was spelled out in the budget on the detailed forms for the $108,000 program financed under Title I of the Elementary and Secondary Education Act. Zotti's teachers were not sure what he had in mind. A few of them balked when he prescribed a minimum of two home visits during the summer term. They thought it was exhausting enough to parcel out large quantities of love and understanding during the normal school day to children starved for such attention. But the home-visiting time after school came to be the most important part of the school day. Teachers went, not twice, but many times into the homes of some of the problem children. These visits turned out to be a better course in what a poverty environment can do to a child than any number of in-service lectures.

One junior-high-school teacher, returning to school with her principal after a visit to a particularly depressing, unkempt rural home, wept quietly all the way back to town. She tried to explain that it is one thing to see a girl in an ill-fitting dress with her hair curled too tightly doing sixth-grade work in the ninth grade. You become impatient with her for not performing better. It is quite another matter when you see the unpapered, dirty walls of her living room, the chicken strolling through the kitchen and the flies everywhere. Then you meet a retarded brother who only makes sounds and you hear the girl's mother complain that the girl reads too much. With so little going for her at home, why should the girl try at all at school?

Junior-high-school coach Scott Van Hoose, a slender, energetic young man with a blond crew cut, was chosen to be principal of the Springdale Summer School for Migrant Children because of his previous interest in disadvantaged youngsters. There was his friend, Martin, for instance, an eighth-grader who attended the summer school at the insistence of Van Hoose.

"Martin was on the road to becoming a dropout when I first saw him standing in the door to my office at the gym," recalled Van Hoose (whose name rhymes with "noose"). "He had been in trouble with the police for stealing money from newspaper coin boxes. I invited him to go on a basketball trip with us to Fort Smith on the bus and that did it. He rode his first elevators and he was amazed to see the table at the restaurant set up for the team after the game. He had never been in a restaurant before. Martin wanted a new bicycle, and I helped him arrange with the store to put it in layaway so that he could pay for it himself with the money he gets from his job at a grocery store. It cost about $50 and he now lacks only $5 of completing his payments."

Springdale operates on a three-track system—honors for the bright students, general for the average achievers and practical for the slow children. As a result of his summer school experience and the extra help from sympathetic teachers, Martin will be moving out of the practical into the general program next year. He has made up his mind that he wants to stay in school until he finishes.

Another eighth-grader named Jim was not so lucky.

"We have an archaic state law which requires children to remain in school only until they are 16 or finish the eighth grade," said Zotti. "Around here, we start losing many of them as soon as they reach one or the other of those marks."

Zotti and Van Hoose found Jim one night working with a chicken-catching crew a year after he disappeared from school. Jim began catching chickens while he was still in the eighth grade. He was covered with dirt and chicken feathers and he was perspiring when Zotti and Van Hoose stopped by the poultry farm. He earns $70 a week; he had quit school to add to the family income.

"Catching chickens is back-breaking work," said Van Hoose, who knows because he worked at it himself when he was in high school. "A crew of 10 will catch 20,000 to 25,000 chickens in a night working eight or nine hours, loading them into coops stacked on a trailer," he said.

"After working all night carrying loads of squawking, flopping chickens these boys are exhausted," said Van Hoose. "I've seen them come to classes the next day too sleepy to listen. I tell them to put their heads down and take a nap."

Zotti and Van Hoose urged Jim to come back to school and talk with them. They pointed to his older fellow workers who had stayed with chicken-catching rather than school, for whom home was still a migrant camp or a rundown shack. Zotti recalled that he had dropped out of school at the 10th grade to go to work, only to realize the dead end ahead. He now lacks only his dissertation toward his doctorate at the University of Arkansas.

Jim was impressed. "I've been thinking about it a lot since," he said. "I'm coming back to school to talk to you."

"We may not be able to hold him for more than a year or so," said Van Hoose. "But if we get him back in school, we have a chance to get him interested in going on to finish. Otherwise, it would be hopeless."

Springdale, in northwest Arkansas, has only white poverty. There are no Negro families in the town. Across the state in the middle of the eastern farmland, however, Wynne School District has tried a similar parent visitation program. Wynne is one-third Negro and two-thirds white, but the poverty statistics are almost exactly the reverse. Thirty per cent of the white children and 70 per cent of the Negro children qualify for Title I help.

Supt. M. D. Forrest began his parent visitation program last year during an August workshop for teachers. The workshop was conducted with Title I funds and this year, when the funds were running short, he considered dropping the program but the teachers insisted on holding it again. They said they were willing to participate without pay. At the last minute, a partial funding was made available and the workshop came off on schedule the last two days in August.

Wynne teachers, after picking up their lists of students for the coming year at school, went by the post office to get rural route locations, then set out to search for remote homes, some of which were many miles from paved roads.

The teachers went in teams of two or three, some of them both white and Negro, and they visited both white and Negro homes. They learned that many children miss breakfast to catch a bus at 7 o'clock in the morning and that they must walk three-quarters of a mile or more to catch the bus. This helps to explain why attendance drops in bad weather.

Two teachers from the all-Negro Childress High School at Wynne, Mrs. LaEunice Pearson and Carlton Adams, called on a family that lived a mile off the highway on Crowley's Ridge. The tiny three-room shack housed nine children, the parents and a grandmother. A social worker's report on the family showed that the family income for the previous year, which the father earned from day work, was $1,233. Six boys share one bedroom.

"With no electricity and with six boys in one small room, there is no chance for study at night," said Mrs. Pearson. "Yet one of these boys and one of the girls in this family are both 'B' students. They have to carry their drinking water a mile and a half, but they are always neat and clean-looking at school. You can really appreciate what they do at school when you see how hard it is for them at home."

One teacher, making the rounds at Wynne, commented that a visit in and out of a poverty home provided insufficient understanding of the child's dilemma. "For him this is reality; this is what he comes home to every day," she said as she looked back at the old car without wheels in the front yard. "If there is any hope for him, it has to be at school and it will be there only if we understand what it is like for him here at home."

Wynne's program includes another phase. Parents were notified to come to school between 8 A.M. and 1 P.M. or 4 P.M. and 9 P.M. on Dec. 7 while their children were given a full holiday. Report cards were held for the parents to pick up, and individual conferences were held with teachers. Because of the prior home visits, a high percentage of the low-income parents showed up for visits with their children's teachers. Parent participation was a little higher at the two all-Negro schools than at the three others attended mostly by whites. Some rooms at Childress elementary and high schools had as high as 90 per cent participation by mothers or fathers. Some parents saw the inside of their children's schools for the first time.

Forrest said the dropout rate had been approximately 50 per cent in the Negro school and 10 to 15 per cent in the formerly all-white Wynne High School but that the increased parent participation was making its impact. More students are staying in school to finish. He also gives credit to the young principal at Childress, Henry Akins. Akins pointed out that the dropout rate was high beginning at the ninth grade because the children were old enough to start working then and some of them had to work. He pointed out, however, that 23 of his 50 graduates last year would be going on to college this fall.

Springdale and Wynne teachers know now why students' hands are often scratched and bleeding during grape season, why so many arms and legs are covered with infected sores. They know why students start disappearing from their classes in October and November when the families move on to follow the crops farther south during the winter. They know why some children have been enrolled in as many as six or eight different schools during one school term.

The Springdale Summer School for Migrant Children was the result of a study made by Bill Pate, a special programs supervisor for the Arkansas State Department of Education, on the needs of migrant children in Arkansas. He chose Springdale as a target area because of the location of a migrant labor camp there, built in 1941 by the War Manpower Commission of the U.S. Labor Department and leased to the city of Springdale in 1947. Working closely with Supt. Thurman D. Smith and Asst. Supt. Leon Gaines, he drew up the request for the special summer program, which was approved. Smith and Gaines turned over to Zotti the job of implementing the original plans.

Crop-picking jobs around Springdale have dropped off in recent years because of the mechanical bean pickers which came into use and because of the decrease in apple and peach orchards in the area. Grapes are now the principal seasonal crop. Many parents work in canneries, a local soup plant and a grape juice plant, in addition to the chicken industry. The labor camp, which is open from April 15 to Oct. 15, had only 40 families in it at the height of the summer season although it has space for 160. Many of the families in nearby poverty areas, however, stay only until cold weather comes.

The girl with the tightly curled hair shrugged when the teacher mentioned during the home visit that she should stay in school until she got her high-school diploma. "But I know I can't go to college," she said. "Why should I finish?"

"If you make good grades, we'll find a way for you to go," the teacher said, conscious of how far away college seemed from the drab, sparsely furnished room. "There are also other things you can do after high school, such as nursing."

The girl's face lit up. "I have thought about becoming a Red Cross nurse," she said. The teacher promised to get her literature on nursing.

Back in town, Van Hoose brought his car to a sudden stop as a motorcycle shot through an intersection in front of him. "That's one of our boys who ought to be in summer school. We are going to lose him if something isn't done. I'll go by and see him tomorrow."

The nonfederal side of Zotti's federally funded program was in action again.

DISCUSSION QUESTIONS

1. Do you agree that "first come love and understanding"? Should this priority be established for all teachers?
2. How shall teachers of the "disadvantaged" be selected? What should be their preparation for teaching? Are they entitled to special compensation?
3. Would you recommend an extension of Title I of the Elementary and Secondary Education Act of 1965, under which the Springdale program was financed? What additional programs could you suggest to meet the needs of the children described here?
4. How well must teachers understand their children?

JEAN D. GRAMBS

The Self-Concept: Basis for Reeducation of Negro Youth

The human personality is a bundle of dynamic forces about which we have many conjectures and few certainties. Like the inner particles of the atom, which are seen only by the shadows they cast, so we have only the shadows of the workings of the human psyche. We are not always sure, and certainly not always in agreement, as to what these shadows represent. But whatever components there may be to personality, in the words of Park and Burgess, "it is an organization of traits and attitudes of which the individual's conception of himself is central."[1]

There are unresolved differences of opinion among psychologists as to the sources of behavior. Whatever it is that impels an individual to act or not to act, a significant role is played in this determination by what the person thinks about himself.[2] He may be able to tell us something about his view of himself, or he may be able to tell us very little. What he tells us may be what he really thinks, or it may be a selective version for a particular public; on what appears to be safer ground, he may reveal a different version of what he thinks he is. Or he may be completely unaware of what his true feelings about himself are. We are assuming, however, that the person acts and can only act in terms of what he thinks about himself in a

---

Reprinted from William C. Kvaraceus, John S. Gibson, Franklin K. Patterson, Bradbury Seasholes, and Jean D. Grambs, *Negro Self-Concept: Implications for School and Citizenship* (New York: McGraw-Hill Book Co., 1965), pp. 11–23, 30, with permission of the publisher.

given situation, and he cannot assess that situation and its action requirements except in terms of his own view of himself.

Contemporary research in child growth and development has highlighted the central significance of the individual's concept of himself.[3] The way a person views himself is the way he will behave. If he sees himself as successful, as someone whom others like, as good-looking, then his behavior will reflect these views. If the person considers himself to be inadequate, as someone whom others probably won't like, as unattractive, then again his behavior will reflect these valuations. The factual truth of any of these statements is irrelevant. A very beautiful girl may consider herself unattractive; children with adequate intellectual endowment may do poorly in school because they perceive themselves as not able.[4]

The source of one's self-image is, of course, not internal; it is learned. The way a mother responds to her newborn baby—with delight or with weary acceptance—will be apparent in the behavior of the baby before very long. A child whose parents trust and love him will be a loving and trustful individual who will tend to go out to greet the world and its many new experiences.

We have some research insights into the differential treatment that parents accord their children from the very beginning.[5] It is true, too, that different cultures produce different personality types. The ways in which children are reared, the things that they are told to do or not to do, the rewards for various kinds of competencies or their lacks, differ from one culture to another.[6] This produces, as Kardiner has pointed out, what might be termed a basic personality type consistent for a given culture.[7]

Venturing outside the family provides the child with additional clues to his self-worth. As he meets teachers, policemen, and storekeepers, he is told what these powerful persons think of people like him. He learns about himself from other children on the block who report to him how they feel on seeing him and playing with him. Out of countless messages, the individual contrives a picture of who he is.[8]

It is obvious that individuals develop different concepts of themselves and that the concept of self is always in terms of degrees of *adequacy*. Everyone must have some sense of adequacy, no matter how minimal, or he cannot cope with his own existence and then must escape into psychosis or suicide. "*We can define man's basic need, then, as a need for adequacy.*"[9] Jersild refines this further: "The needs associated with a person's idea and appraisal of himself include both desires for enhancing his self-esteem and also striving to preserve the integrity or consistency of the self."[10]

There is agreement that the contemporary situation of the American Negro is deplorable. A nationwide, continuing debate is concerned with ways of ameliorating this condition. As educators, we need to develop strategies for change which will aid the individual in achieving more adequate adjustment to and control of his environment. The role of the concept of self in achieving this sense of adequacy thus appears to be central. The questions that must be considered are these:

1. How do Negro children and youth now achieve a sense of who and what they are?
2. What is the role of education in the school in developing this sense of self?
3. What is the potential within the educational setting of achieving a desirable shift in self-image?

These questions can only be answered by further research. Our purpose here is a brief review of the relevant research and speculation.

THE QUESTION OF DIFFERENCES BETWEEN NEGROES AND WHITES

One of the clearest differences between Negro and white is that society in the contemporary United States continually tells the groups that they are different. Not only are the groups different, but the Negro group is considered inferior to the white group. This message has been communicated in different ways via different social media ever since the Negro was first brought to America. It is obvious that this kind of differential social communication is going to have a differential impact on the personality. As Allport asks:

> . . . what would happen to your own personality if you heard it said over and over again that you were lazy, a simple child of nature, expected to steal, and had inferior blood. Suppose this opinion were forced on you by the majority of your fellow-citizens. And suppose nothing you could do would change this opinion—because you happen to have black skin.[11]

Or, stated in the words of the late President Kennedy:

> If an American, because his skin is dark, cannot eat lunch in a restaurant open to the public; if he cannot send his children to the best public school available; if, in short, he cannot enjoy the full and free life which all of us want, then who among us would be content to have the color of his skin changed and stand in his place?[12]

The self-concept of the Negro is contaminated by the central fact that it is based on a color-caste complex. The American color-caste system was evolving at the same time that the brave concepts of the American and French revolutions about human equality were also born. It was thus almost inevitable that the racial situation would cause trouble. The first drafts of the Declaration of Independence contained a clause objecting to the imposition of slavery upon the American colonies by the English power. The clause was stricken from the final version for fear of alienating Southern support. Shades of contemporary political maneuverings over civil rights legislation in Congress!

In order to cope with the obvious discrepancy between Christian beliefs about the oneness of the human family, slaveholders had to resort to the idea of the supposed inferiority of the Negro, preaching in some instances that he really was a subhuman breed of animal. Even today there continue to be strenuous efforts to convince those who require scholarly evidence that the Negro is, in fact, inferior.[13]

The social system that emerged out of the need to rationalize the owning of slaves and, following the Civil War, refusal to accord the Negro full citizen status was a clear development of a caste system. Unlike the caste system of India based on religious beliefs, the caste system in the United States was based on color and on the assumption of inferiority due to color. The Brazilian melting pot, unlike that in the United States, classifies anyone with any amount of white ancestry as white; in the United States, the smallest amount of Negro ancestry classifies an individual as Negro.

In the evolution of institutions, those provided for the Negro in the United States, therefore, had to be *separate,* but also *unequal.* It is possible that there are caste systems in which parallel caste-class groups exist without any presumption of superiority or inferiority for one caste over another; this certainly has not been true in America.[14] Of course, the South had to refuse to provide equal educational opportunity for the Negro; the Negro was *not equal.*

THE IMPACT OF INEQUALITY IN VALUATION

It does not take much imagination to understand what generations of being told one is unworthy do to a group's own valuation of its worth. From the first slave revolts, Negro leaders have continually fought against this self-view; but there have been relatively few leaders, a condition also produced by the effect of inferior caste status. Only in recent decades have there been enough Negroes who have overcome these multiple barriers to challenge the general valuation of the Negro.

To quote Dollard, whose original study of caste first focused general attention on this problem:

> Nothing has happened since 1936 [the date of the original study] which has served to unconvince me about what I saw. It seems as real now as then. We are still in the hot water of conflict between our democratic ideals and our personal acceptance of caste status for the Negro. We are still deliberately or unwittingly profiting by, defending, concealing or ignoring the caste system.[15]

Interestingly enough, a recent comprehensive review and evaluation of the research in the area of self-concept does not include any discussion of research that considers race as an aspect of self-concept, though research relating to other factors, such as sex, religious affiliation, social-class status, is discussed.[16] Blindness to, or avoidance of, the implications of the caste system on the self-concept of the Negro, and of the white, which is thus seen to occur at the most- and least-sophisticated levels of society, is symptomatic of the difficulty of dealing with color discrimination in American life and thought.

The Negro personality *cannot* be unmarked by the experience of caste discrimination based upon color.[17] One of the first family learnings of the Negro child has to do with his color. The more white a Negro child is, the more he will be accepted by his family, the greater his opportunity will be to use his talents, the more likely it is that he will be able to make the most of the limited opportunities of his environment. The love that his family will accord him can be calibrated on the same scale as one calibrates color differences. To be most loved as a Negro child, one has to appear least Negro.

In one of their cases, Kardiner and Ovesey describe the reactions of a middle-class Negro woman, herself light, on giving birth to a dark baby. She was sure she had been given the wrong baby; later she tried to bathe it in bleaches of various kinds; she refused to appear in public with it. She reacted almost the same way with a second baby.[18]

In the early drawings and stories and dreams of Negro children appear many wishes to be white. Negro children have a harder time than white children in identifying themselves correctly in terms of race.[19] This identification is also related to color: the darker Negro is able to see himself as a Negro earlier than a light-colored one. In the latter instance, is the nearness to being white such as to make the acceptance of being Negro that much harder?

The self-esteem of the Negro is damaged by the overwhelming fact that the world he lives in says, "White is right; black is bad." The impact on the Negro community is to overvalue all those traits of appearance that are most Caucasian. Evidence is clear that in almost every Negro family, the lighter children are favored by the parents. It is interesting to note that most of the Negro leadership group today are not Negroid in appearance, many being almost completely Caucasian in terms of major physical appearance.

What effect does this have on the child? Of course, his own color becomes extremely important to him. As Dai points out, ". . . the color of one's skin, which does not occupy the consciousness of children of other cultures, is here made an issue of primary importance, and the personality problems thus created are almost as difficult to get rid of as the dark skin itself."[20] The Negro press is replete with advertisements for skin lighteners and hair straighteners. It strikes some Negroes as ironic that, while they strive to become lighter and to make their hair less curly, whites go to great pains to stay out in the sun in order to become darker and spend endless amounts of money on getting their hair to curl! Unfortunately, the efforts of the whites do not assume an acceptance on their part of the features of the Negro which appear to be desirable: darker color and curly hair. But the efforts of the Negro do spring from a deeply ingrained view regarding appearance: it is better to be more white.

One interesting feature of the current Negro revolution has been a small but persistent insistence that the Negro cease trying to make himself white. The Black Muslim group is an almost pure expression of the need to reject all that is white and replace Negro self-hatred with justified hatred of whites, including the dominant white Christian religion.[21] With some Negroes, it is now considered a matter of racial pride to refuse to straighten the hair or to use cosmetics to lighten the skin. It is possible that this movement will reach other Negroes, and with it will come a lessening of the rejection of color and the personal devaluation that this has carried. But unfortunately it hardly seems possible that a reversal of the value system will occur for many, and certainly not for a long time to come.

Thus we see the central ambivalence that makes the world of the Negro so baffling, frustrating, confusing, and demeaning. On the one hand, he is told that white is better, and he relates this to his own social system in which the Negro who is most white, but still a Negro, has highest status. But to *be* white is not good. Whites are not to be trusted; they are, in fact, hated as much as they are feared.

Hatred breeds aggression. Aggression seeks an outlet. A major focus of the hatred of Negroes is the white group, but this group is almost completely protected because of the potency and immediacy of white retaliation.[22] One must remember that the antilynch laws are quite recent. Pictures of burning buses, fire hoses; mounted police with electric cattle prods, and attacking police dogs show only too well that the Negro is still not protected from the quick and vicious reactions of the white group when this power is challenged in any way. Incapable of attacking the white group, the Negro has several psychological alternatives: to hate himself, to act out his aggressive needs within his own group, and to escape into apathy and fantasy. All these paths are utilized, and often by the same individual, depending on the situation. As Combs and Snygg point out, responses to feelings of inadequacy range from the neurotic through perceptual distortions and may result in actual psychosis. The production of "multiple personalities" is, as they see it, one response to feelings of loss of self-esteem.[23] This splitting of the personality in response to the social disvalue placed on being a Negro is graphically stated by Redding:

> From adolescence to death there is something very personal about being a Negro in America. It is like having a second ego which is as much the conscious subject of all experience as the natural self. It is not what the psychologists call dual personality. It is more complex and, I think, more morbid than that. In the state of which I speak, one receives two distinct reactions—the one normal and intrinsic to the natural self; the other, entirely different but of equal force, a prodigy created by the accumulated consciousness of Negroness.[24]

As the gifted Negro writer James Baldwin puts it, in commenting on his own childhood:

In order for me to live, I decided very early that some mistake had been made somewhere. I was not a "nigger" even though you [whites] called me one. . . . I had to realize when I was very young that I was none of those things I was told I was. I was not, for example, happy. I never touched a watermelon for all kinds of reasons. I had been invented by white people, and I knew enough about life by this time to understand that whatever you invent, whatever you project, that is you! So where we are now is that a whole country of people believe I'm a "nigger" and I *don't*.[25]

It does not escape the Negro observer that Negro crimes against Negroes are considered far less serious by the law in many areas than similar crimes of whites against whites, and certainly not nearly so serious as Negro crimes against whites. And white crimes against Negroes are the least serious of all. Again, these social symptoms report to the Negro that he is not valued as a person; he cannot, against such massive evidence, counter by his own feelings of self-esteem, since in truth he can typically show little factual support for a contrary view.[26]

CRUCIAL SOCIAL FORCES CREATING THE NEGRO SELF-IMAGE: THE FAMILY AND POVERTY

The potency of the family in producing the culturally approved person has tempted social manipulators since the dawn of history. Sparta intervened at a very early age in the child-rearing functions of the family. Recent attempts to supplant the family have been unsuccessful. The most enduring such contemporary situation, the Kibbutz of Israel, appears to have produced a rather special kind of person whose social potential can be questioned.[27] So far, no adequate substitute for the family has been found, despite Huxley's predictions.[28]

That there are unique stresses and strains in the modern family is agreed; but the stresses in a Negro family are qualitatively different from those in a white family, even when we hold socioeconomic status constant. The poor have never lived in comfort, and the struggle for material survival has certainly made psychologically adequate survival extremely problematical anywhere in the world. The situation of the Negro family today in the United States is qualitatively different on a number of important counts.

The Negro family is much more likely than the white family to be on the lowest economic rung. Furthermore, we could say that no more than a very small percentage of Negroes is more than one generation removed from abject poverty, so that "Negroes have [a] deeply ingrained sense of impoverishment."[29] It is a rather special kind of impoverishment, too; it is almost inescapable. Although we have seen in recent generations the rise of a Negro middle class, and even a few very wealthy Negroes, most Negroes remain in the "last hired, first fired" category of employment—and if not this generation, their parental generation. Most Negro children, then, inherit a family which is economically insecure from the very start. Most of them live at the edge of survival; and those who have moved a little bit away have a constant fear of a future which may reduce them, too, to desperation.

It is almost impossible for one not reared in a slum to understand its awfulness. Middle-class America flees from a true picture of slum degradation.[30] But as Riessman points out, children reared in these environments will soon constitute 50 percent of all children enrolled in schools in large cities.[31] Most of these children will be Negroes, unless something drastically changes the housing situation which exists in urban centers.

The Negro slum child is far more liable than a white slum child to experience also an unstable home.[32] The self that the Negro child learns early in life is one exposed to the most difficult of all situations for the human being to cope with: an inadequate family living on the edge of economic insufficiency. The impact of family disruption is accentuated by the incapacity of those involved in the rearing of the children to do an adequate job of it because they have had few experiences with family stability and adequacy to guide them.

The circle is indeed a vicious one. The case studies reported by Riese provide appalling accounts of generation after generation of defeat in Negro families.[33] Often neither mother nor father is able to provide the minimum of affection and attention that an infant needs in order to grow into a person able to like himself and others, because, of course, his parents do not like themselves. Too many of these marriages are the result of impulsive escape wishes and lack a secure base in personal regard for the marital partner.[34] Poignant testimony to the difficulties facing the Negro wife and husband is given by talented Negro singer Lena Horne.[35]

As she describes it, her marriage was an effort to get away from the miseries of being a Negro singer in a white man's world. Yet she was not able to accept her role as a Negro wife. The needs her husband brought home from his work, mainly with white colleagues, she felt quite unable and unwilling to deal with. Not only had she to cope with the ordinary problems of running a home and rearing children, she had to absorb the anger and hurt her husband bore on his job, the countless humiliations and degradations that he, a Negro, experienced daily in his contact with white people.

What Lena Horne tells us provides a needed window into the inner reality of Negro family life. The normal hazards of the working world are multiplied many times over by the pervasive insecurity attendant on almost all of the Negro's economic activities. Not only is the Negro the last to be hired and the first to be fired, but he pays more for insurance premiums, he has a much harder time obtaining home mortgage money and any kind of bank or credit loans. Even the slum store preys upon the poor with higher prices for shoddier stuff. In such an environment, it is hard indeed for the Negro male to achieve a sense of self-worth as a breadwinner and provider for his family.

The woman typically is aggressive and hostile; the man is hostile and dependent. Because his economic situation is so insecure, the husband-father cannot be sure that he will provide the economic base for a family; and in a majority of cases, he is right. He cannot assure his wife of support or his children of food and shelter. Who can feel pride of self in such circumstances, and who can pass on feelings of adequacy to anyone else?

The economic security of the Negro family rests primarily with the mother. This is one outgrowth of slavery, when at least the mother could keep the children with her until they could be physically independent and able to work, while the father was often not even accorded the recognition of paternity. Certainly the family as the white population knew it was prohibited for slaves. The patterns of employment in today's urban centers have continued to make economic stability more available to the women than to the men. The significance of this family situation appears in study after study.

The home life reported in many case studies of Negro youth is one of constant bickering and fighting. One father leaves; a stepfather or father substitute appears. The family conflict continues. Because of death or illness or desertion, children often are left with grandparents or other relatives. If an attachment occurs, it may not last until adulthood. Thus many Negro children have few experiences with stability, warmth, attention—all of the things that are taken for granted as part of the necessary environment for healthy personality development.

The important point, of course, is that while many of the conditions reported are a result of acute and continued poverty, a major ingredient is also the color-caste of the Negro. One of the child's early racial learnings is that he cannot turn to his parents for help and retaliation if he is hurt.

> A white man yanked me off a streetcar because I got on ahead of a white woman. He shook me good and tore my clothes. I walked home crying, knowing that my father would do something about it. (But his father could do no more than remark, "You should have known better.") [36]

The denial to a parent of his role in protecting his own child is deeply destructive, not only to the parental feeling but to the possibility that the child will look to his parents as adult models. Nor will the growing child be able to internalize the parental feeling without which having children of one's own is a dangerous enterprise.

What the Negro child is likely to learn is that no one is to be trusted. He is given such small ingredients of affection and attention that he has too meager a hoard to share with anyone else. He learns, too, that his family is only partly responsible for the horrors of his existence; it is the whites who have created this situation, and it is they who keep him in abasement. The burden of hatred for the whites is increased because he is also told that he cannot do anything about that hatred; in fact, he must be particularly careful and watchful in all his relations with whites. These persons hold the key to all that is desirable and good. If only one were white, too!

The earliest learnings, then, of the Negro child, particularly one in the rural or urban slums, is that the family is not a source of basic nurture and support. He seeks his gratifications, therefore, on the street and among peers.[37] But as Kardiner and Ovesey point out, at no time are these relationships such as to produce a feeling of comfort and safety. No one can find in the street a substitute for parental and adult guidance and parental affection. If the child does not necessarily become antisocial, he is asocial.[38]

The damage to the child's self-esteem appears greater for Negro boys than for girls.[39] Though it is debatable whether, in general, it is more or less difficult to grow up as a boy or as a girl in our culture,[40] it seems clear from the evidence that during early childhood and school years, the Negro girl accommodates better to the circumstances of existence. Certainly in school performance the Negro girl exceeds the Negro boy. In most measures of social disorganization, the Negro boy appears to be far more vulnerable. This can be accounted for in part by the fact that the male models available for the growing boy are themselves demoralized. A father who feels defeated by the world is not in a good position to give his son a sense of optimism and a feeling that he can achieve something himself. The fact that the father is most likely to be the absent member of the family and often is replaced by a succession of fathers or father substitutes also tends to militate against the establishment of a view of the male as a reliable, responsible individual. If the boy sees around him men who are unable to sustain a consistent and positive social and economic role, it is hard for the youngster to build a different pattern out of his limited experiences.

Recent efforts to equalize educational opportunities for Negroes in the South should not obscure the fact that these efforts are indeed very recent, and still fall far short of providing, even on a segregated basis, an adequate education for all Negro young people. The fact that even today many Negro children and youth have far from adequate schooling, whether they live in the rural South or the urban North, Midwest, West, or Southwest, should not make us forget that, with few exceptions, the story of Negro education to this day has been one of gross lacks.[41] As Horace Mann said over a hundred years ago, "No educated body of men can be permanently poor"[42]; and the obverse is that no uneducated group can expect to rise out of poverty.

Although the Ausubels state that "Negro girls in racially incapsulated areas are less traumatized than boys by the impact of racial discrimination,"[43] further evidence is needed to support such a statement. On the surface, Negro girls seem more able to cope with some of the demands of middle-class society: going to school, behaving in school, keeping out of serious trouble with the law, showing responsibility for child rearing, and keeping a job.[44] It is nevertheless possible that the impact of their situation is just passed on to the men in the household. Certainly a mother is a prime source, as we have stated, of the child's self-concept. It is communicated to Negro boys, somehow, that they are less wanted, less able to deal with their world, bound to fail in their efforts to be men. We cannot lay the major blame for the way Negro boys develop on the lack of adequate male models. It is highly probable that the trauma suffered by Negro females is passed on and displaced upon the males in the situation. Certainly the case material of Kardiner and Ovesey shows much personal trouble experienced by female as well as male Negroes.[45] The fact that so many Negroes become contributing and stable members of society is an extraordinary tribute to the resilience of the human psyche.

EDUCATIONAL PROCESSES AND SELF-CONCEPT

It is clear that the life experiences of the Negro child are not such as to aid him in developing a positive sense of himself or of his place in his world. What does this suggest to us? It would seem that a very compelling hypothesis is that *the Negro child, from earliest school entry through graduation from high school, needs continued opportunities to see himself and his racial group in a realistically positive light. He needs to understand what color and race mean, he needs to learn about those of his race (and other disadvantaged groups) who have succeeded, and he needs to clarify his understanding of his own group history and current group situation.*

At the moment, these are missing ingredients in the American public school classroom. Numerous studies of textbooks have shown them to be lily-white.[46] Pictures do not show Negro and white children together; when Negroes appear they are usually either Booker T. Washington, George Washington Carver, or foreign.[47] Neither whites nor Negroes have an accurate picture of the American Negro and his history.[48] One observer noted that a commonly used contemporary civics book had no index entry for *urban renewal, transportation, transit,* or *Negro.*[49] The lily-white nature of text materials is true also of other visual aids used in the schools. If Negroes appear in school films, they are in stereotyped roles. One film, for instance, showing "community helpers" illustrated the work of repairing the street with a Negro crew and a white foreman. The educational consultant, incidentally, who worked with the film company to produce the film was surprised at his own blindness. This kind of presentation merely reinforces the many communications to children that Negro work is inferior work.

That these materials can and do have a strong impact on the child's perception of himself and others was well documented in the study by

Trager and Yarrow. When a story describing a Negro child as a funny savage (*Little Black Sambo*) was read aloud to young children, white and Negro children's feelings were affected, particularly when the white children pointed this out in the schoolyard.[50] The only thing that is surprising about these findings is that educators and others have consistently ignored them. It is interesting that the Trager-Yarrow research report is probably the only study made of the differences in education (textbook) content that is reported in the literature. As a matter of fact, it is claimed by one of the very knowledgeable experts in the field, that *no* experimental study has been done of differences in textbook content, despite the fact that the textbook is the most consistently and constantly used educational aid in the classroom, other than the teacher.[51]

If teaching materials present a slanted view of him and his place in the world to the Negro child, what does the teacher tell him? It is not a very startling piece of news that teachers, too, bear the majority version of the Negro. Studies of their attitudes toward children show that the Negro child is rated lowest in all rankings of groups on a Bogardus-type social-distance scale.[52] The original study was completed thirteen years ago; teachers in training in 1963 give the same responses. Attempts to change teachers' attitudes through human relations workshops and special courses have reached very few. In formulating some guidelines for the education of the culturally disadvantaged, Niemeyer stated:

> Our hypothesis is that the chief cause of the low achievement of the children of alienated groups is the fact that too many teachers and principals honestly believe that these children are educable only to an extremely limited extent. And when teachers have a low expectation level for their children's learning, the children seldom exceed that expectation, which is a self-fulfilling prophecy.[53]

Nor is the situation made easier where Negro teachers are employed. The Negro teacher represents a middle-class position, and there is evidence that virulent anti-Negro feelings are expressed by middle-class Negroes for lower-class Negroes. Unfortunately, most Negro children come from lower-class homes. Dai makes the point that, denied access to other rewards in life, the Negro tends to put an overemphasis upon status.[54] The Negro professional, who may have many contacts with white professionals, must even in these professional relationships maintain an etiquette which prevents showing resentment or rage; but this is not necessarily controlled to the same extent when dealing with fellow Negroes. Children, particularly, are available targets of all the displaced self-hatred of the professional middle-class Negro teacher. If they are lower-class children, they typically will demonstrate everything the middle-class Negro most despises about the race from which he cannot dissociate himself. The warmth, welcome, and support which children should find, particularly in the early elementary school grades, and which the Negro child needs in abundance because of so much deprivation at home, is exactly what teachers, Negro or white, as presently oriented, can least provide.

In this necessarily brief discussion of the factors that enter into the development of the self-concept of the Negro, we have utilized only a small sampling of the wealth of research literature and other documentation which bears on this subject. We have merely tried to suggest some of the crucial situations which help to mold the Negro child. It is these of which educational practitioners must be aware.

EDUCATIONAL INTERVENTION

The child with a negative view of self is a child who will not be able to profit much from school. Once a child is convinced that school is irrelevant to his immediate needs and future goals, the task of education becomes almost impossible. As one junior high student said, after having failed all his subjects for two years:

> I just don't like it. It seems to bore me. It seems silly just going there and sitting. And most of the time it is so hot and they don't do anything about it and the teachers just talk, talk, and you never learn anything.[55]

Deutsch's research points out that the lower-class Negro child probably received about one half to one third less instructional time in the primary grades than did white children from the same slum environment: "our time samples indicated that as much as 80% of the school day was channeled into disciplining, and secondarily, into ordinary organizational details. . . ."[56]

. . . .

CONCLUSION

If today we note a change of tone, a militancy and impatience on the part of Negro youth, it is not because schools are any different. For the first time, the Negro, via TV, is beginning to see that the world of comfort, luxury, and fun is all around him. He wants some of it, too. As Hayakawa pointed out in a speech at a recent American Psychological Association convention in Philadelphia, the ads that beckon one to join the fun on the picnic do *not* add "for whites only."[88]

But the militancy, welcome as it may be, cannot erase the burden of self-hatred that has accumulated through so many generations. And many who most need to hear the call to challenge the racial status quo may already be too deeply sunk in despair and apathy. These feelings are so quickly communicated to the infant and child that intervention by the school even as early as kindergarten or the first grade may be too late. But if many older adolescents can respond to a new concept of their role in the world, then certainly the younger child can be reached, too, by deliberate efforts to change the way in which he views himself. These, then, are the challenges we must meet.

REFERENCES

1. Bingham Dai, "Minority Group Membership and Personality Development," in Jitsuichi Masuoka and Preston Valien (eds.), *Race Relations: Problems and Theory,* Chapel Hill, N.C., The University of North Carolina Press, 1961, p. 183.
2. Ruth C. Wylie, *The Self-Concept,* Lincoln, Nebr., University of Nebraska Press, 1961, pp. 1–22.
3. Arthur T. Jersild, "Emotional Development," in L. Carmichael (ed.), *Manual of Child Psychology,* 2d ed., New York, John Wiley & Sons, Inc., 1954, p. 837. "Selective Bibliography on Self," *Childhood Education,* vol. 35, October, 1958, pp. 80–81.
4. M. B. Frink, "Self-Concept as It Relates to Academic Underachievement," *California Journal of Educational Research,* vol. 13, March, 1962, pp. 57–62.
5. Robert R. Sears, Eleanor E. Maccoby, and Harry Levin, *Patterns of Child Rearing,* New York, Harper & Row, Publishers, 1957.
6. John W. M. Whiting and Irvin L. Child, *Child Training and Personality: A Cross-Cultural Study,* New Haven, Conn., Yale University Press, 1953.
7. Abram Kardiner et al., *The Psychological Frontiers of Society,* New York, Columbia University Press, 1945.
8. Helen G. Trager and Marian Radke Yarrow, *They Learn What They Live: Prejudice in Young Children,* New York, Harper & Row, Publishers, 1952.
9. Arthur W. Combs and Donald Snygg, *Individual Behavior* (rev. ed.), New York, Harper & Row, Publishers, 1959, p. 46.
10. Jersild, *op. cit.*
11. Gordon W. Allport, *The Nature of Prejudice,* Reading, Mass., Addison-Wesley Publishing Company, Inc., 1954, p. 142.
12. John F. Kennedy, "A Time to Act," an address to the American people, June 11, 1963. Reprinted by Anti-Defamation League of B'nai B'rith, New York.
13. Robert D. North, "The Intelligence of American Negroes," *Research Reports,* Anti-Defamation League of B'nai B'rith, vol. 3, no. 2, November, 1956; Melvin M. Tumin (ed.), *Race and Intelligence: A Scientific Evaluation,* New York, Anti-Defamation League of B'nai B'rith, 1963.
14. John Dollard, *Caste and Class in a Southern Town,* 3d ed., Garden City, N.Y., Doubleday & Company, Inc., 1957.
15. *Ibid.,* p. viii.
16. Wylie, *op. cit.*
17. Abram Kardiner and Lionel Ovesey, *The Mark of Oppression: Explorations in the Personality of the American Negro,* Cleveland, The World Publishing Company (a Meridian Book), 1962.
18. Kardiner and Ovesey, *op. cit.,* pp. 252–253.
19. Kenneth Clark and Mamie P. Clark, "Racial Identification and Preference in Negro Children," in Eleanor Maccoby et al. (eds.), *Readings in Social Psychology,* New York, Holt, Rinehart and Winston, Inc., 1958, pp. 602–611.
20. Bingham Dai, "Problems of Personality Development Among Negro Children," in Clyde Pluckhohn and Henry A. Murray (eds.), *Personality in Nature, Society and Culture,* New York, Alfred A. Knopf, Inc., 1953, p. 560.
21. C. Eric Lincoln, *The Black Muslims in America,* Boston, The Beacon Press, 1961; E. U. Essien-Udom, *Black Nationalism,* Chicago, The University of Chicago Press, 1962; James Baldwin, *The Fire Next Time,* New York, The Dial Press, Inc., 1963, pp. 61–120.

22. Baker M. Hindman, "The Emotional Problems of Negro High School Youth Which Are Related to Segregation and Discrimination in a Southern Urban Community," *Journal of Educational Sociology,* vol. 27, November, 1953, pp. 115–127.
23. Combs and Snygg, *op. cit.,* pp. 265–303.
24. J. Saunders Redding, *On Being Negro in America,* Indianapolis, Ind., The Bobbs-Merrill Company, Inc., 1962, p. 12.
25. James Baldwin, "A Talk to Teachers," *Saturday Review,* vol. 46, December 21, 1963, pp. 42–44+.
26. Walter Reckless et al., "Self-concept as Insulator Against Delinquency," *American Sociological Review,* vol. 21, no. 6, 1956.
27. Abram Kardiner, "When the State Brings up the Child," *Saturday Review,* vol. 44, August 26, 1961, pp. 9–11; Albert J. Rabin, "Culture Components as a Significant Factor in Child Development: Kibbutz Adolescents," *American Journal of Orthopsychiatry,* vol. 31, 1961, pp. 493–504.
28. Aldous Huxley, *Brave New World,* New York, Harper & Row, Publishers, 1932.
29. Kardiner and Ovesey, *op. cit.,* p. 366.
30. Michael Harrington, *The Other America: Poverty in the United States,* New York, The Macmillan Company, 1963, Chap. 4, "If You're Black, Stay Black," pp. 61–81.
31. Frank Riessman, *The Culturally Deprived Child,* New York, Harper & Row, Publishers, 1962, p. 1.
32. Martin Deutsch, *Minority Group and Class Status as Related to Social and Personality Factors in Scholastic Achievement,* monograph 2, Ithaca, N.Y., The Society for Applied Anthropology, Cornell University Press, 1960; E. Franklin Frazier, *The Negro Family in the United States* (rev. ed.), New York, The Dryden Press, Inc., 1951; Nathan Glazer and D. P. Moynihan, *Beyond the Melting Pot,* Cambridge, Mass., The M.I.T. Press and Harvard University Press, 1963, pp. 25–85.
33. Bertha Riese, *Heal the Hurt Child,* Chicago, The University of Chicago Press, 1962.
34. Kardiner and Ovesey, *op. cit.,* pp. 345–349.
35. Lena Horne, "I Just Want To Be Myself," *Show,* vol. 3, September, 1963, pp. 62–65+.
36. Robert L. Sutherland, *Color, Class and Personality,* Washington, D.C., American Council on Education, 1942, p. 41.
37. David and Pearl Ausubel, "Ego Development Among Segregated Negro Children," in A. Harry Passow (ed.), *Education in Depressed Areas,* New York, Bureau of Publications, Teachers College, Columbia University, 1963, p. 113.
38. Kardiner and Ovesey, *op. cit.,* p. 380.
39. David and Pearl Ausubel, *op. cit.,* pp. 127–128.
40. Walter Waetjen and Jean D. Grambs, "Sex Differences: A Case of Educational Evasion?" *Teachers College Record,* December, 1963.
41. Virgil Clift, Archibald W. Anders, H. Gordon Hullfish (eds.), *Negro Education in America,* New York, Harper & Row, Publishers, 1962.
42. Majorie B. Smiley and John S. Diekoff, *Prologue to Teaching,* Fair Lawn. N.J., Oxford University Press, 1959, p. 286.
43. David and Pearl Ausubel, *op. cit.,* p. 128.
44. Albert J. Lott and Bernice E. Lott, *Negro and White Youth,* New York, Holt, Rinehart and Winston, Inc., 1963.
45. Kardiner and Ovesey, *op cit.*
46. Abraham Tannenbaum, "Family Living in Textbook Town," *Progressive Education,* vol. 31, no. 5, March, 1954, pp. 133–141; Martin Mayer, "The Trouble with Textbooks," *Harper's Magazine,* vol. 225, July, 1962, pp. 65–71; Otto Klineberg, "Life Is Fun in a Smiling, Fair-Skinned World," *Saturday Review,* February 16, 1963; Albert Alexander, "The Gray Flannel Cover on the American History Textbook," *Social Education,* vol. 24, January, 1960, pp. 11–14.

47. Lloyd Marcus, *The Treatment of Minorities in Secondary School Textbooks,* New York, Anti-Defamation League of B'nai B'rith, 1961; Jack Nelson and Gene Roberts, Jr., *The Censors and the Schools,* Boston, Little, Brown & Company, 1963.
48. Melville J. Herskovits, *The Myth of the Negro Past,* Boston, The Beacon Press, 1958.
49. Atlee E. Shidler, "Education for Civic Leadership: The School's Responsibility," an address presented to the 68th National Conference on Government, The National Municipal League, Washington, D.C., November 16, 1962, mimeo.
50. Trager and Yarrow, *op. cit.*
51. A. A. Lumsdaine, "Instruments and Media of Instruction," in N. L. Gage (ed.), *Handbook of Research on Teaching,* Chicago, Rand McNally & Company, 1963, p. 586.
52. Jean D. Grambs, "Are We Training Prejudiced Teachers?" *School and Society,* vol. 71, April 1, 1950, pp. 196–198.
53. John Niemeyer, "Some Guidelines to Desirable Elementary School Reorganization," in *Programs for the Educationally Disadvantaged,* Washington, D.C., U.S. Office of Education Bulletin, 1963, no. 17, p. 81.
54. Bingham Dai, "Minority Group Membership and Personality Development," *op. cit.*
55. Kardiner and Ovesey, *op. cit.,* p. 264.
56. Deutsch, *op. cit.,* p. 23.
88. *Washington Post,* September 10, 1963.

DISCUSSION QUESTIONS

1. Should we absolve the schools from the responsibility of creating a wholesome self-image for the culturally different child, since the school, as a social organism, generally reflects the public conviction of the ghetto child's worthlessness?
2. Are the inadequacies of our slum schools basically rooted in our willingness to have our poor remain invisible and uneducated?
3. How do we educate the public as to what desirable education is and how it is achieved?
4. How do you recruit teachers for slum schools?

JAMES KILPATRICK | *It's Time to Teach Self-Help*

Washington—The thought occurs, and can no longer be repressed, that it's time for some of us who write for a living to stop writing so nicey-nice about this summer's riots and the Negro leadership. This is a summer of outrage, scored for kettle drums of violence; but such is our sense of genteel restraint that most of us have been playing our typewriters pianissimo. We have settled for murmuring my-my and oh-oh, and they certainly do have grievances, don't they.

Well, nuts. There comes a time when the law-abiding majority of this country, imperfect as it is, ought to put a hard question to large elements of the Negro community: When in the name of God are you people going to shape up? One is tempted to exempt from the thrust of that question many thousands of Negro citizens who have played no active part in the recent violence and indeed have been victims of it. They can't be left out. Who has given sanctuary to the Negro snipers? Fellow Negroes. They share in the guilt.

What's the matter with the Negro leadership? Since the first torch was put to Newark, one has waited—and waited in vain—for some high-level expression of shame, apology, contrition. Non est. Perhaps nothing was to be expected from H. Rap Brown; his theme is "Get you some guns and burn this town down." The sullen Stokely Carmichael yearns "to kill the whites first." But what of Roy Wilkins, Whitney Young, Martin Luther King? They are full of excuses, and in King's case, something more. It's all the fault, he says, of "the policy-makers of white society." He proposes strikes and sit-ins to "dislocate" the cities without actually destroying them. He will do this "lovingly."

At every hand, the cry goes up for crash spending programs in the slums. Most of the money would go toward jobs and housing. The *New Republic* tells us what kind of jobs—not merely jobs for "black waiters, dishwashers and busboys, but jobs that will restore Negro self-respect."

What's wrong with being a waiter, a dishwasher, or a busboy, if one qualifies for the work? Hundreds of thousands of white men and women perform these humble but essential labors. What's the matter with a teen-ager's starting as a bootblack? It's an honest trade.

And what of "jobs that will restore Negro self-respect"? Employers increasingly are searching for Negroes as sales clerks, bank tellers, drafts-men, technicians. They may not be overcome with altruism; it may be only the Equal Employment Opportunity Commission breathing down their necks. But the jobs are there. Where are qualified Negro applicants to fill them?

The excuse is that the "ghetto schools" are so bad, and the Negro teenagers so "insufficiently motivated," that they drop out. It's a feeble excuse. Many a middle-aged American looks at some of these "ghetto schools" and is dimly reminded of the elementary schools of his own unfair nonage. The opportunity for an education lies within them. What's asked of the Negro? Ambition. Hard work.

The cry is that "ghetto housing" is so bad. Okay. Some of it is awful. Some of it is not. But there are twice as many poor whites as poor blacks; the poor colored neighborhoods of Watts and Detroit have their counter-parts—and their rats—in poor white neighborhoods across the land. The blunt truth is that self-help could cure at least a part of the ills. If some of Jesse Gray's complainers would spend more time with a dollar rake or a 50-cent broom, and less time with a $2 pint of gin, maybe a sense of mutual respect would start to grow. Heresy, one supposes, to say such things. But they need to be said.

DISCUSSION QUESTIONS

1. Kilpatrick asks of the Negro that he be ambitious and work hard, if he wishes to get an education. How reasonable is his request?
2. What contribution do you think Kilpatrick's arguments will make in bridging the ever-widening gap between blacks and whites in America?
3. Can society sit back and wait for the "disadvantaged" to become "advantaged"?

FRED M. HECHINGER

The Teacher Gets What He Expects

"You see, really and truly, apart from the things anyone can pick up (the dressing and the proper way of speaking, and so on), the difference between a lady and a flower girl is not how she behaves, but how she's treated. I shall always be a flower girl to Professor Higgins, because he always treats me as a flower girl, and always will; but I know I can be a lady to you, because you always treat me as a lady, and always will."

So spoke Eliza Doolittle to Colonel Pickering in George Bernard Shaw's "Pygmalion." Last week, a 34-year-old Harvard social psychologist showed through a series of experiments how the words apply to the classroom. If teachers are made to believe that certain children have exceptional promise, the children will outperform classmates of equal or even greater talent.

Dr. Robert Rosenthal discovered, some time ago, that rats perform more intelligently if their human mentors, the researchers, are made to believe that the rats have been bred for special intelligence. When he put the theory to the human test in a South San Francisco elementary school and a number of other places, the effect was the same. Teachers were told that certain children were likely, according to fictitious pretesting, to "spurt ahead." The children did spurt ahead.

"The difference between the special children and the ordinary children, then, was only in the mind of the teacher," said Dr. Rosenthal in a study which will be published as a book, "Pygmalion in the Classroom," by Holt, Rinehart & Winston, in the spring.

Reprinted from *The New York Times,* August 13, 1967, with permission of the publisher.

Cynics may say that, like so much sociological research, this study proves only what everybody has long known. Shaw was not alone.

KEY IS EXPECTATION

Children of upper middle class families are virtually without exception, "college material." While it is undoubtedly true, as biologists have shown, that intermarriage among the college-educated raises the intellectual level of the next generation, the hereditary upgrading is by no means as total as the college-going (and succeeding) record shows. The key is the expectation.

What makes the experimentally documented findings valuable is not that they tell something radically new but rather that they offer documented evidence of the shortcomings in present attitudes. Thus they may focus on unnecessary failures which result from low expectation.

How relevant such research is was shown less than two weeks ago, when teenagers in a Brooklyn high school publicly voiced their criticism of some teachers' attitudes.

"This area [a slum neighborhood] may be physically repugnant to you, but a lot of the people are beautiful," said one student.

The only time the principal's voice is ever heard is over the public address system, complained another.

The clincher came from a student who suggested: "I think a lot of the trouble comes from a lack of love between students and teachers."

An angry teacher, ignoring the fact that the student had blamed both parties, shouted back: "It's not my job to love my pupils—it's my job to teach them."

The Rosenthal thesis, however, while not demanding "love," calls for respect and a teacher's subtly transmitted faith in the students' ability to succeed.

The thesis applies to all children, but it is of special importance for the disadvantaged. Dr. Rosenthal wrote: "If [the teacher] is to teach a 'slow group,' or children of darker skin color, or children whose mothers are 'on relief,' she will have different expectations for her pupils' performance than if she is to teach a 'fast group,' of children of an upper middle class community."

In the " 'Pygmalion" experiment, children "falsely" labeled as potential "bloomers," tended to bloom with extraordinary frequency—without any special tutoring or crash programs. The tests on which the findings were based were externally administered to avoid the risk of favoritism. But it turned out that the teachers tended to grade their "special" children more severely than the others and to spend less time babying them. In other words, they respected them more but spoon-fed them less. Incidentally, the performance of the "ordinary" pupils in the same classroom tended to improve, too, although not as dramatically. The infusion of confidence seemed contagious.

The temptation then is to suggest that the remedy for the disastrously low level of achievement in many slum schools is simple—exhort teachers to expect more of their pupils.

The cure is not likely to be so easy. Even assuming that it is feasible to persuade all teachers to overcome the many human, often subconscious antipathies—toward the unkempt, poor, different, unruly, antagonistic, etc.—other obstacles remain.

Steep hurdles have been set up by a general deterioration of the classroom atmosphere and a misinterpretation of the role of the teacher in many American schools. A trend of well-intentioned egalitarianism has brought into disrepute the idea of the teacher as a person of authority—not authoritarian, but endowed with a dominant position akin to that of father or mother in a well-ordered, mutually respectful, non-permissive family.

Teachers must establish their authority by special cunning or force, and only the exceptional ones by special talent. It is utopian to expect a mass-education system to be staffed by a majority of exceptional teachers.

The result then is inevitably that in more and more classrooms teachers emerge either as the pupils' antagonists or pals, relying either on fear or popularity. Neither fear nor palship lead to the kind of respect and high expectations which, is the Rosenthal experiments indicate, are crucial to success.

"What was done in our program of educational change was done directly for the teacher, only indirectly for her pupils," Dr. Rosenthal wrote. "Perhaps, then, it is the teacher to whom we should direct more of our research attention."

This is undoubtedly true—as is Dr. Rosenthal's suggestion that this, in turn, calls for a more sophisticated selection of future teachers who are most likely to raise their pupils' aspirations. But in order to be able to transmit faith and respect, these teachers must also be assured of an environment free of the de-humanized bureaucracy that is symbolized by the principal's voice over the loudspeaker and free, too, of the pseudo-democratic concept that the teacher is just a hired hand rather than a strong father or mother figure.

Unless the atmosphere in many American schools can be improved, too many teachers, under combat conditions, will continue to give children enough rope to hang themselves instead of—as Dr. Rosenthal properly demands—a rope ladder on which to climb.

DISCUSSION QUESTIONS

1. Hechinger states that, "It is utopian to expect a mass-education system to be staffed by a majority of exceptional teachers." Is it impractical to do so, or impossible?

2. Have we ever seriously attempted to staff our schools with outstanding teachers? If you believe that we have, delineate the inducements we have offered them. If not, how would you go about attracting and holding exceptional people?
3. Is it possible for teachers to respect all children, and to have faith in the ability of every child to succeed? Should these two factors be used as criteria for admittance into teaching?

CHAPTER 4 *School Desegregation*

Segregation in the schools of America has been a fact of life throughout the history of public education. It has been a major political assumption, reflecting a generalized point of view deeply rooted in the group ethos. American patterns of segregation have been based on sex, color, religion and economic status; the schools have reflected the general bias.

Until 1954, racial segregation enjoyed legal sanction under the "separate but equal" doctrine enunciated by the Supreme Court. In that year the Court, in *Brown* v. *The Board of Education,* reversed itself and stated an entirely different national intent; to be separate is to be unequal, per se. The Court ruled that the nation's schools must desegregate with all reasonable speed.

Racial segregation has been cast in two major models, *de jure* in the South and *de facto* in the North. *De jure* segregation can be countered on a legalistic plane, and the South has moved haltingly, painfully toward desegregation. Northern-style segregation is the creation not of statute but of circumstance and intent. Desegregation efforts in the large urban centers of the North have been piecemeal, ineffectual, and even self-defeating. No workable, generally acceptable pattern of action has evolved, although there have been a number of seemingly successful desegregation efforts under carefully controlled conditions, in smaller communities.

From an earlier trend toward centralization through the creation of educational centers and "parks," the large cities at the insistence of the black community seem to be moving toward decentralization as a politically more acceptable pattern. All-black schools are deemed acceptable, even desirable, if they are locally controlled by black parents. The argument is that local control will inevitably result in quality education. Quality now, integration later, is the cry. Whether or not either or both of these goals will be achieved remains for the future to reveal.

JAMES BALDWIN | *The Fire Next Time*

Letter to my Nephew on the One Hundredth Anniversary of the Emancipation

Dear James:

Well, you were born, here you came, something like fourteen years ago; and though your father and mother and grandmother, looking about the streets through which they were carrying you, staring at the walls into which they brought you, had every reason to be heavyhearted, yet they were not. For here you were, Big James, named for me—you were a big baby, I was not—here you were: to be loved. To be loved, baby, hard, at once, and forever, to strengthen you against the loveless world. Remember that: I know how black it looks today, for you. It looked bad that day, too, yes, we were trembling. We have not stopped trembling yet, but if we had not loved each other none of us would have survived. And now you must survive because we love you, and for the sake of your children and your children's children.

This innocent country set you down in a ghetto in which, in fact, it intended that you should perish. Let me spell out precisely what I mean by that, for the heart of the matter is here, and the root of my dispute with my country. You were born where you were born and faced the future that you faced because you were black and *for no other reason.* The limits of your ambition were, thus, expected to be set forever. You were born into a society which spelled out with brutal clarity, and in as many ways as possible, that you were a worthless human being. You were not expected to aspire to excellence: you were expected to make peace with mediocrity. Wherever you have turned, James, in your short time on this earth, you have been told where you could go and what you could do (and *how* you could do it) and where you could live and whom you could marry. I know your countrymen do not agree with me about this, and I hear them saying, "You exaggerate." They do not know Harlem, and I do. So do you. Take no one's word for anything, including mine—but trust your experience. Know whence you

---

Reprinted from James Baldwin, *The Fire Next Time* (New York: The Dial Press, Inc., 1962), pp. 20–24, with permission of the publisher.

came. If you know whence you came, there is really no limit to where you can go. The details and symbols of your life have been deliberately constructed to make you believe what white people say about you. Please try to remember that what they believe, as well as what they do and cause you to endure, does not testify to your inferiority but to their inhumanity and fear. Please try to be clear, dear James, through the storm which rages about your youthful head today, about the reality which lies behind the words *acceptance* and *integration*. There is no reason for you to try to become like white people and there is no basis whatever for their impertinent assumption that *they* must accept *you*. The really terrible thing, old buddy, is that *you* must accept *them*. And I mean that very seriously. You must accept them and accept them with love. For these innocent people have no other hope. They are, in effect, still trapped in a history which they do not understand; and until they understand it, they cannot be released from it. They have had to believe for many years, and for innumerable reasons, that black men are inferior to white men. Many of them, indeed, know better, but, as you will discover, people find it very difficult to act on what they know. To act is to be committed, and to be committed is to be in danger. In this case, the danger, in the minds of most white Americans, is the loss of their identity. Try to imagine how you would feel if you woke up one morning to find the sun shining and all the stars aflame. You would be frightened because it is out of the order of nature. Any upheaval in the universe is terrifying because it so profoundly attacks one's sense of one's own reality. Well, the black man has functioned in the white man's world as a fixed star, as an immovable pillar: and as he moves out of his place, heaven and earth are shaken to their foundations. You, don't be afraid. I said that it was intended that you should perish in the ghetto, perish by never being allowed to go behind the white man's definitions, by never being allowed to spell your proper name. You have, and many of us have, defeated this intention; and, by a terrible law, a terrible paradox, those innocents who believed that your imprisonment made them safe are losing their grasp of reality. But these men are your brothers—your lost, younger brothers. And if the word *integration* means anything, this is what it means: that we, with love, shall force our brothers to see themselves as they are, to cease fleeing from reality and begin to change it. For this is your home, my friend, do not be driven from it; great men have done great things here, and will again, and we can make America what America must become. It will be hard, James, but you come from sturdy, peasant stock, men who picked cotton and dammed rivers and built railroads, and, in the teeth of the most terrifying odds, achieved an unassailable and monumental dignity. You come from a long line of great poets, some of the greatest poets since Homer. One of them said, *The very time I thought I was lost, My dungeon shook and my chains fell off.*

You know, and I know, that the country is celebrating one hundred years of freedom one hundred years too soon. We cannot be free until they are free. God bless you, James, and Godspeed.

Your uncle,
James

DISCUSSION QUESTIONS

1. Is it true, in your eyes, that ". . . what they [white people] do and cause you [the Negro] to endure, does not testify to your inferiority, but to their inhumanity and fear"?
2. Is it possible to have "integration" without "acceptance"? Who must accept whom?
3. Have we celebrated "one hundred years of freedom one hundred years too soon," as Baldwin states?

JAMES S. COLEMAN — *Segregation in the Public Schools*

The great majority of American children attend schools that are largely segregated—that is, where almost all of their fellow students are of the same racial background as they are. Among minority groups, Negroes are by far the most segregated. Taking all groups, however, white children are most segregated. Almost 80 percent of all white pupils in 1st grade and 12th grade attend schools that are from 90 percent to 100 percent white. And 97 percent at grade 1, and 99 percent at grade 12, attend schools that are 50 percent or more white.

For Negro pupils, segregation is more nearly complete in the South (as it is for whites also), but it is extensive also in all the other regions where the Negro population is concentrated: the urban North, Midwest, and West.

More than 65 percent of all Negro pupils in the 1st grade attend schools that are between 90 and 100 percent Negro. And 87 percent at grade 1, and 66 percent at grade 12, attend schools that are 50 percent or more Negro. In the South, most students attend schools that are 100 percent white or Negro.

The same pattern of segregation holds, though not quite so strongly, for the teachers of Negro and white students. For the Nation as a whole the

Reprinted from "Summary Report" of the publication *Equality of Educational Opportunity* (Washington, D.C.: United States Office of Education, Department of Health, Education, and Welfare 1967), pp. 3, 8, 9, 14, 20, 21, 22, 24, 27, 28, 32, 33. (In the interests of brevity, published tables and references to them have been omitted, in the main.)

average Negro elementary pupil attends a school in which 65 percent of the teachers are Negro; the average white elementary pupil attends a school in which 97 percent of the teachers are white. White teachers are more predominant at the secondary level, where the corresponding figures are 59 and 97 percent. The racial matching of teachers is most pronounced in the South, where by tradition it has been complete. On a nationwide basis, in cases where the races of pupils and teachers are not matched, the trend is all in one direction: white teachers teach Negro children but Negro teachers seldom teach white children; just as, in the schools, integration consists primarily of a minority of Negro pupils in predominantly white schools but almost never of a few whites in largely Negro schools.

In its desegregation decision of 1954, the Supreme Court held that separate schools for Negro and white children are inherently unequal. This survey finds that, when measured by that yardstick, American public education remains largely unequal in most regions of the country, including all those where Negroes form any significant proportion of the population. Obviously, however, that is not the only yardstick. The next section of the summary describes other characteristics by means of which equality of educational opportunity may be appraised.

THE SCHOOLS AND THEIR CHARACTERISTICS

The school environment of a child consists of many elements, ranging from the desk he sits at to the child who sits next to him, and including the teacher who stands at the front of his class. A statistical survey can give only fragmentary evidence of this environment.

Great collections of numbers such as are found in these pages—totals and averages and percentages—blur and obscure rather than sharpen and illuminate the range of variation they represent. If one reads, for example, that the average annual income per person in the State of Maryland is $3,000, there is a tendency to picture an average person living in moderate circumstances in a middle-class neighborhood holding an ordinary job. But that number represents at the upper end millionaires, and at the lower end the unemployed, the pensioners, the charwomen. Thus the $3,000 average income should somehow bring to mind the tycoon and the tramp, the showcase and the shack, as well as the average man in the average house.

So, too, in reading these statistics on education, one must picture the child whose school has every conceivable facility that is believed to enhance the educational process, whose teachers may be particularly gifted and well educated, and whose home and total neighborhood are themselves powerful contributors to his education and growth. And one must picture the child in a dismal tenement area who may come hungry to an ancient, dirty building that is badly ventilated, poorly lighted, overcrowded, understaffed, and without sufficient textbooks.

Statistics, too, must deal with one thing at a time, and cumulative effects tend to be lost in them. Having a teacher without a college degree indicates an element of disadvantage, but in the concrete situation, a child may be taught by a teacher who is not only without a degree but who has grown up and received his schooling in the local community, who has never been out of the State, who has a 10th grade vocabulary, and who shares the local community's attitudes.

One must also be aware of the relative importance of a certain kind of thing to a certain kind of person. Just as a loaf of bread means more to a starving man than to a sated one, so one very fine textbook or, better, one very able teacher, may mean far more to a deprived child than to one who already has several of both.

Finally, it should be borne in mind that in cases where Negroes in the South receive unequal treatment, the significance in terms of actual numbers of individuals involved is very great, since 54 percent of the Negro population of school-going age, or approximately 3,200,000 children, live in that region.

All of the findings reported in this section of the summary are based on responses to questionnaires filled out by public school teachers, principals, district school superintendents, and pupils. The data were gathered in September and October of 1965 from 4,000 public schools. All teachers, principals, and district superintendents in these schools participated, as did all pupils in the 3d, 6th, 9th, and 12th grades. First grade pupils in half the schools participated. More than 645,000 pupils in all were involved in the survey. About 30 percent of the schools selected for the survey did not participate; an analysis of the nonparticipating schools indicated that their inclusion would not have significantly altered the results of the survey. The participation rates were: in the metropolitan North and West 72 percent, metropolitan South and Southwest 65 percent, nonmetropolitan North and West 82 percent, nonmetropolitan South and Southwest 61 percent.

All the statistics on the physical facilities of the schools and the academic and extracurricular programs are based on information provided by the teachers and administrators. They also provided information about their own education, experience, and philosophy of education, and described as they see them the socioeconomic characteristics of the neighborhoods served by their schools.

The statistics having to do with the pupils' personal socioeconomic background, level of education of their parents, and certain items in their homes (such as encyclopedias, daily newspapers, etc.) are based on pupil responses to questionnaires. The pupils also answered questions about their academic aspirations and their attitudes toward staying in school.

All personal and school data were confidential and for statistical purposes only; the questionnaires were collected without the names or other personal identification of the respondents.

Data for Negro and white children are classified by whether the schools are in metropolitan areas or not. The definition of a metropolitan area is the one commonly used by Government agencies: a city of over 50,000 inhabitants including its suburbs. All other schools in small cities, towns, or rural areas are referred to as nonmetropolitan schools.

Finally, for most tables, data for Negro and white children are classified by geographical regions. For metropolitan schools there are usually five regions defined as follows:

Northeast—Connecticut, Maine, Massachusetts, New Hampshire, Rhode Island, Vermont, Delaware, Maryland, New Jersey, New York, Pennsylvania, District of Columbia. (Using 1960 census data, this region contains about 16 percent of all Negro children in the Nation and 20 percent of all white children age 5 to 19.)

Midwest—Illinois, Indiana, Michigan, Ohio, Wisconsin, Iowa, Kansas, Minnesota, Missouri, Nebraska, North Dakota, South Dakota (containing 16 percent of Negro and 19 percent of white children age 5 to 19).

South—Alabama, Arkansas, Florida, Georgia, Kentucky, Louisiana, Mississippi, North Carolina, South Carolina, Tennessee, Virginia, West Virginia (containing 27 percent of Negro and 14 percent of white children age 5 to 19).

Southwest—Arizona, New Mexico, Oklahoma, Texas (containing 4 percent of Negro and 3 percent of white children age 5 to 19).

West—Alaska, California, Colorado, Hawaii, Idaho, Montana, Nevada, Oregon, Utah, Washington, Wyoming (containing 4 percent of Negro and 11 percent of white children age 5 to 19).

The nonmetropolitan schools are usually classified into only three regions:

South—as above (containing 27 percent of Negro and 14 percent of white children age 5 to 19).

Southwest—as above (containing 4 percent of Negro and 2 percent of white children age 5 to 19).

North and West—all States not in the South and Southwest (containing 2 percent of Negro and 17 percent of white children age 5 to 19).

Data for minority groups other than Negroes are presented only on a nationwide basis because there were not sufficient cases to warrant a breakdown by regions.

Facilities

. . . For the Nation as a whole white children attend elementary schools with a smaller average number of pupils per room (29) than do any of the minorities (which range from 30 to 33). . . . In some regions the nationwide pattern is reversed: in the nonmetropolitan North and West and Southwest for example, there is a smaller average number of pupils per room for Negroes than for whites. . . . One finds much more striking differences than the national average would suggest: in the metropolitan Midwest, for example, the average Negro has 54 pupils per room—probably reflecting considerable frequency of double sessions—compared with 33 per room for whites. (Nationally, at the high school level the average white has one teacher for every 22 students and the average Negro has one for every 26 students.) . . .

There is not a wholly consistent pattern—that is, minorities are not at a disadvantage in every item listed—but there are nevertheless some definite and systematic directions of differences. Nationally, Negro pupils have fewer of some of the facilities that seem most related to academic achievement: they have less access to physics, chemistry, and language laboratories; there are fewer books per pupil in their libraries; their textbooks are less often in sufficient supply. To the extent that physical facilities are important to learning, such items appear to be more relevant than some others, such as cafeterias, in which minority groups are at an advantage.

Usually greater than the majority-minority differences, however, are the regional differences. . . . 95 percent of Negro and 80 percent of white high school students in the metropolitan Far West attend schools with language laboratories, compared with 48 percent and 72 percent respectively, in the metropolitan South, in spite of the fact that a higher percentage of Southern schools are less than 20 years old.

Finally, it must always be remembered that these statistics reveal only majority-minority average differences and regional average differences; they do not show the extreme differences that would be found by comparing one school with another.

Programs

. . . Just as minority groups tend to have less access to physical facilities that seem to be related to academic achievement, so too they have less access to curricular and extracurricular programs that would seem to have such a relationship.

Secondary school Negro students are less likely to attend schools that are regionally accredited; this is particularly pronounced in the South. Negro and Puerto Rican pupils have less access to college preparatory curriculums and to accelerated curriculums; Puerto Ricans have less access to vocational curriculums as well. Less intelligence testing is done in the schools attended by Negroes and Puerto Ricans. Finally, white students in general have more access to a more fully developed program of extracurricular activities, in particular those which might be related to academic matters (debate teams, for example, and student newspapers).

Again, regional differences are striking. For example, 100 percent of Negro high school students and 97 percent of whites in the metropolitan Far West attend schools having a remedial reading teacher (this does not mean, of course, that every student uses the services of that teacher, but simply that he has access to them) compared with 46 and 65 percent, respectively, in the metropolitan South—and 4 and 9 percent in the nonmetropolitan Southwest.

Principals and teachers

. . . 1 percent of white elementary pupils attend a school with a Negro principal, and . . . 56 percent of Negro children attend a school with a Negro principal. . . . The average white student goes to an elementary school where 40 percent of the teachers spent most of their lives in the same city, town, or country; the average Negro pupil goes to a school where 53 percent of the teachers have lived in the same locality most of their lives. . . . Other characteristics which offer rough indications of teacher quality, [include] the types of colleges attended, years of teaching experience, salary, educational level of mother, and a score on a 30-word vocabulary test. The average Negro pupil attends a school where a greater percentage of the teachers appears to be somewhat less able, as measured by these indicators, than those in the schools attended by the average white student.

Other items . . . reveal certain teacher attitudes. Thus, the average white pupil attends a school where 51 percent of the white teachers would not choose to move to another school, whereas the average Negro attends a school where 46 percent would not choose to move.

Student body characteristics

. . . The average white high school student attends a school in which 82 percent of his classmates report that there are encyclopedias in their homes. This does not means that 82 percent of all white pupils have encyclopedias at home, although obviously that would be approximately true. . . . Clear differences are found on these items: the average Negro has fewer classmates whose mothers graduated from high school; his classmates more frequently are members of large rather than small families; they are less often enrolled in a college preparatory curriculum; they have taken a smaller number of courses in English, mathematics, foreign language, and science.

On most items, the other minority groups fall between Negroes and whites, but closer to whites, in the extent to which each characteristic is typical of their classmates.

Again, there are substantial variations in the magnitude of the differences, with the difference usually being greater in the Southern States.

ACHIEVEMENT IN THE PUBLIC SCHOOLS

The schools bear many responsibilities. Among the most important is the teaching of certain intellectual skills such as reading, writing, calculating, and problem-solving. One way of assessing the educational opportunity offered by the schools is to measure how well they perform this task.

Table 1. Nationwide Median Test Scores for First- and Twelfth-Grade Pupils

Text	Racial or ethnic group					
	Puerto Ricans	Indian-Americans	Mexican-Americans	Oriental-Americans	Negro	Majority
First grade:						
Nonverbal	45.8	53.0	50.1	56.6	43.4	54.1
Verbal	44.9	47.8	46.5	51.6	45.4	53.2
Twelfth grade:						
Nonverbal	43.3	47.1	45.0	51.6	40.9	52.0
Verbal	43.1	43.7	43.8	49.6	40.9	52.1
Reading	42.6	44.3	44.2	48.8	42.2	51.9
Mathematics	43.7	45.9	45.5	51.3	41.8	51.8
General information	41.7	44.7	43.3	49.0	40.6	52.2
Average of the 5 tests	43.1	45.1	44.4	50.1	41.1	52.0

Standard achievement tests are available to measure these skills, and several such tests were administered in this survey to pupils at grades 1, 3, 6, 9, and 12.

These tests do not measure intelligence, nor attitudes, nor qualities of character. Furthermore, they are not, nor are they intended to be, "culture-free." Quite the reverse: they are culture-bound. What they measure are the skills which are among the most important in our society for getting a good job and moving up to a better one, and for full participation in an increasingly technical world. Consequently, a pupil's test results at the end of public school provide a good measure of the range of opportunities open to him as he finished school—a wide range of choice of jobs or colleges if these skills are very high; a very narrow range that includes only the most menial jobs if these skills are very low.

The above table gives an overall illustration of the test results for the various groups by tabulating nationwide median scores (the score which divides the group in half) for 1st-grade and 12-grade pupils on the tests used in those grades. For example, half of the white 12th-grade pupils had scores above 52 on the nonverbal test and half had scores below 52. (Scores on each test at each grade level were standardized so that the average over the national sample equaled 50 and the standard deviation equaled 10. This means that for all pupils in the Nation, about 16 percent would score below 40 and about 16 percent above 60.)

With some exceptions—notably Oriental Americans—the average minority pupil scores distinctly lower on these tests at every level than the average white pupil. The minority pupils' scores are as much as one standard deviation below the majority pupils' scores in the first grade. At the 12th grade, results of tests in the same verbal and nonverbal skills show that, in every case, the minority scores are *farther below* the majority than are the 1st graders. For some groups, the relative decline is negligible; for others, it is large.

Furthermore, a constant difference in standard deviations over the various grades represents an increasing difference in grade level gap. For example, Negroes in the metropolitan Northeast are about 1.1 standard deviations below whites in the same region at grades 6, 9, and 12. But at grade 6 this represents 1.6 years behind, at grade 9, 2.4 years, and at grade 12, 3.3 years. Thus, by this measure, the deficiency in achievement is progressively greater for the minority pupils at progressively higher grade levels.

For most minority groups, then, and most particularly the Negro, schools provide no opportunity at all for them to overcome this initial deficiency; in fact, they fall farther behind the white majority in the development of several skills which are critical to making a living and participating fully in modern society. Whatever may be the combination of nonschool factors—poverty, community attitudes, low educational level of parents—which put minority children at a disadvantage in verbal and nonverbal skills when they enter the first grade, the fact is the schools have not overcome it.

Some points should be borne in mind in reading the table. First, the differences shown should not obscure the fact that some minority children perform better than many white children. A difference of one standard deviation in median scores means that about 84 percent of the children in the lower group are below the median of the majority students—but 50 percent of the white children are themselves below that median as well.

A second point of qualification concerns regional differences. By grade 12, both white and Negro students in the South score below their counterparts—white and Negro—in the North. In addition, Southern Negroes score farther below Southern whites than Northern Negroes score below Northern whites. The consequences of this pattern can be illustrated by the fact that the 12th grade Negro in the nonmetropolitan South is 0.8 standard deviation below—or in terms of years, 1.9 years behind—the Negro in the metropolitan Northeast, though at grade 1 there is no such regional difference.

Finally, the test scores at grade 12 obviously do not take account of those pupils who have left school before reaching the senior year. In the metropolitan North and West, 20 percent of the Negroes of ages 16 and 17 are not enrolled in school, a higher dropout percentage than in either the metropolitan or nonmetropolitan South. If it is the case that some or many of the Northern dropouts performed poorly when they were in school, the Negro achievement in the North may be artificially elevated because some of those who achieved more poorly have left school.

RELATION OF ACHIEVEMENT TO SCHOOL CHARACTERISTICS

If 100 students within a school take a certain test, there is likely to be great variation in their scores. One student may score 97 percent, another 13; several may score 78 percent. This represents variability in achievement *within* the particular school.

It is possible, however, to compute the average of the scores made by the students within that school and to compare it with the average score, or achievement, of pupils within another school, or many other schools. These comparisons then represent variations *between schools.*

When one sees that the average score on a verbal achievement test in School X is 55 and in School Y is 72, the natural question to ask is: What accounts for the difference?

There are many factors that in combination account for the difference. This analysis concentrates on one cluster of those factors. It attempts to decribe what relationship the school's characteristics themselves (libraries, for example, and teachers and laboratories and so on) seem to have to the achievement of majority and minority groups (separately for each group on a nationwide basis, and also for Negro and white pupils in the North and South).

The first finding is that the schools are remarkably similar in the effect they have on the achievement of their pupils when the socioeconomic background of the students is taken into account. It is known that socioeconomic factors bear a strong relation to academic achievement. When these factors are statistically controlled, however, it appears that differences between schools account for only a small fraction of differences in pupil achievement.

The schools *do* differ, however, in the degree of impact they have on the various racial and ethnic groups. The average white student's achievement is less affected by the strength or weakness of his school's facilities, curricula, and teachers than is the average minority pupil's. To put it another way, the achievement of minority pupils depends more on the schools they attend than does the achievement of majority pupils. Thus, 20 percent of the achievement of Negroes in the South is associated with the particular schools they go to, whereas only 10 percent of the achievement of whites in the South is. Except for Oriental Americans, this general result is found for all minorities.

The conclusion can then be drawn that improving the school of a minority pupil will increase his achievement more than will improving the school of a white child increase his. Similarly, the average minority pupil's achievement will suffer more in a school of low quality than will the average white pupil's. In short, whites, and to a lesser extent Oriental Americans, are less affected one way or the other by the quality of their schools than are minority pupils. This indicates that it is for the most disadvantaged children that improvements in school quality will make the most difference in achievement.

All of these results suggest the next question: What are the school characteristics that account for most variation in achievement? In other words, what factors in the school are most important in affecting achievement?

It appears that variations in the facilities and curriculums of the schools account for relatively little variation in pupil achievement insofar as this is measured by standard tests. Again, it is for majority whites that the variations make the least difference; for minorities, they make somewhat more difference. Among the facilities that show some relationship to achievement are several for which minority pupils' schools are less well equipped relative to whites. For example, the existence of science laboratories showed a small but consistent relationship to achievement . . . minorities, especially Negroes, are in schools with fewer of these laboratories.

The quality of teachers shows a stronger relationship to pupil achievement. Furthermore, it is progressively greater at higher grades, indicating a cumulative impact of the qualities of teachers in a school on the pupils' achievement. Again, teacher quality is more important for minority pupil achievement than for that of the majority.

It should be noted that many characteristics of teachers were not measured in this survey; therefore, the results are not at all conclusive regarding the specific characteristics of teachers that are most important. Among those measured in the survey, however, those that bear the highest relationship to pupil achievement are first, the teacher's score on the verbal skills test, and then his educational background—both his own level of education and that of his parents. On both of these measures, the level of teachers of minority students, especially Negroes, is lower.

Finally, it appears that a pupil's achievement is strongly related to the educational backgrounds and aspirations of the other students in the school. Only crude measures of these variables were used (principally the proportion of pupils with encyclopedias in the home and the proportion planning to go to college). Analysis indicates, however, that children from a given family background, when put in schools of different social composition, will achieve at quite different levels. This effect is again less for white pupils than for any minority group other than Orientals. Thus, if a white pupil from a home that is strongly and effectively supportive of education is put in a school where most pupils do not come from such homes, his achievement will be little different than if he were in a school composed of others like himself. But if a minority pupil from a home without much educational strength is put with schoolmates with strong educational backgrounds, his achievement is likely to increase.

This general result, taken together with the earlier examinations of school differences, has important implications for equality of educational opportunity. For the earlier tables show that the principal way in which the school environments of Negroes and whites differ is in the composition of their student bodies, and it turns out that the composition of the student bodies has a strong relationship to the achievement of Negro and other minority pupils.

This analysis has concentrated on the educational opportunities offered by the schools in terms of their student body composition, facilities, curriculums, and teachers. This emphasis, while entirely appropriate as a response to the legislation calling for the survey, nevertheless neglects important factors in the variability between individual pupils within the same school; this variability is roughly four times as large as the variability between schools. For example, a pupil attitude factor, which appears to have a stronger relationship to achievement than do all the "school" factors together, is the extent to which an individual feels that he has some control over his own destiny. . . . The responses of pupils to questions in the survey show that minority pupils, except for Orientals, have far less conviction than whites that they can affect their own environments and futures. When they do, however, their achievement is higher than that of whites who lack that conviction.

Furthermore, while the characteristic shows little relationship to most school factors, it is related, for Negroes, to the proportion of whites in the schools. Those Negroes in schools with a higher proportion of whites have a greater sense of control. Thus such attitudes, which are largely a consequence of a person's experience in the larger society, are not independent of his experience in school.

OTHER SURVEYS AND STUDIES

A number of studies were carried out by the Office of Education in addition to the major survey of public elementary and secondary schools. Some of these were quite extensive investigations with book-length final reports; certain of them will be published in full as appendixes to the main report. There will be other appendixes containing more detailed analyses of the public school data than could be included in the main report. Still other appendixes will contain detailed tabulation of the data gathered in the survey so that research workers will have easy access to them.

OPPORTUNITY IN INSTITUTIONS OF HIGHER EDUCATION

The largely segregated system of higher education in the South has made comparison between colleges attended mainly by Negro students and mainly by majority students easy in that region. Elsewhere it has not been possible in the past to make comparison between educational opportunities because of the general policy in Federal and State agencies of not collecting data on race. In the fall of 1965, however, the Office of Education reversed this policy as a result of the interest of many agencies and organizations in the progress of minority pupils in gaining access to higher education. The racial composition of freshmen of all degree-seeking students was obtained from nearly all of the colleges and universities in the Nation.

These racial compositions have been cross-tabulated against a variety of characteristics of the institutions in the report itself. . . . Over half of all Negro college students attend the largely segregated institutions in the South and Southwest. About 4.6 percent of all college students are Negro. . . . Negro students are in colleges with substantially lower faculty salaries. The institutions in the South and Southwest generally pay lower salaries than those in other regions, and the colleges serving primarily the Negro students are at the bottom of this low scale.

Other findings of the study are that— (1) in every region Negro students are more likely to enter the State College system than the State University system, and further they are a smaller proportion of the student body of universities than any other category of public institutions of higher education, (2) Negro students are more frequently found in institutions which have a high dropout rate, (3) they attend mainly institutions with low tuition cost, (4) they tend to major in engineering, agriculture, education, social work, social science, and nursing.

Future teachers

Since a number of investigations of teacher qualification in the past few years have indicated that teachers of Negro children are less qualified than those who teach primarily majority children, this survey investigated whether there might be some promise that the situation may be changed by college students now preparing to become teachers. To this end, questionnaire and achievement test data were secured from about 17,000 college freshmen and 5,500 college seniors in 32 teacher training colleges in 18 States that in 1960 included over 90 percent of the Nation's Negro population. Some of the findings of this survey are:

1. At both the freshman and senior levels, future teachers are very similar to students in their colleges who are following other career lines. (It should be remembered that these comparisons are limited to students in colleges that have a primary mission in the training of teachers, and is not, of course, a random sample of all colleges.)

2. Majority students being trained at the college level to enter teaching have a stronger preparation for college than have Negro students; that is, they had more courses in foreign languages, English, and mathematics, made better grades in high school, and more often were in the highest track in English.

3. Data from the senior students suggest that colleges do not narrow the

gap in academic training between Negro and majority pupils; indeed, there is some evidence that the college curriculum increases this difference, at least in the South.

4. Substantial test score differences exist between Negro and white future teachers at both freshman and senior levels, with approximately 15 percent of Negroes exceeding the average score of majority students in the same region. (This figure varies considerably depending on the test, but in no case do as many as 25 percent of Negroes exceed the majority average.)

5. The test data indicate that the gap in test results widens in the South between the freshman and senior years. The significance of this finding lies in the fact that most Negro teachers are trained in the Southern States.

6. The preferences of future teachers for certain kinds of schools and certain kinds of pupils raise the question of the match between the expectations of teacher recruits and the characteristics of the employment opportunities.

The preferences of future teachers were also studied. Summarized in terms of market conditions, it seems apparent that far too many future teachers prefer to teach in an academic high school; that there is a far greater proportion of children of blue-collar workers than of teachers being produced who prefer to teach them; that there is a very substantial number of white teachers-in-training, even in the South, who prefer to teach in racially mixed schools; that very few future teachers of either race wish to teach in predominantly minority schools; and finally, that high-ability pupils are much more popular with future teachers than low-ability ones. The preferences of Negro future teachers are more compatible with the distribution of needs in the market than are those of the majority; too few of the latter, relative to the clientele requiring service, prefer blue-collar or low-ability children or prefer to teach in racially heterogeneous schools, or in special curriculum, vocational, or commercial schools. These data indicate that under the present organization of schools, relatively few of the best prepared future teachers will find their way into classrooms where they can offset some of the environmental disadvantage suffered by minority children.

School enrollment and dropouts

Another extensive study explored enrollment rates of children of various ages, races, and socio-economic categories using 1960 census data. The study included also an investigation of school dropouts using the October 1965 Current Population Survey of the Bureau of the Census. This survey uses a carefully selected sample of 35,000 households. It was a large enough sample to justify reliable nationwide estimates for the Negro minority but not for other minorities. In this section the word "white" includes the Mexican American and Puerto Rican minorities.

According to the estimates of the Current Population Survey, approximately 6,960,000 persons of ages 16 and 17 were living in the United States in October 1965. Of this number 300,000 (5 percent) were enrolled in college, and therefore, were not considered by this Census Bureau study. Of the remaining, approximately 10 percent, or 681,000 youth of 16 and 17 had left school prior to completion of high school. . . . About 17 percent of Negro adolescents (ages 16 and 17) have dropped out of school whereas the corresponding number for white adolescents is 9 percent. . . . Most of this difference comes from differences outside the South; in the South the white and Negro nonenrollment rates are much the same. . . . Whereas the nonenrollment rate was 3 percent for those 16- and 17-year-olds from white-collar families, it was more than four times as large (13 percent) in the case of those from other than white-collar families (where the head of household was in a blue-collar or farm occupation, unemployed, or not in the labor force at all). Furthermore, this difference in nonenrollment by parental occupation existed for both male and female, Negro and white adolescents.

The racial differences in the dropout rate are thus sharply reduced when socioeconomic factors are taken into account. Then the difference of 8 percentage points between all Negro and white adolescent dropouts becomes 1 percent for those in white-collar families, and 4 percent for those in other than white-collar families. . . . The largest differences between Negro and white dropout rates are seen in the urban North and West; in the nonurban North and West there were too few Negro households in the sample to provide a reliable estimate. In the South there is the unexpected result that in the urban areas, white girls drop out at a greater rate than Negro girls, and in the nonurban area white boys drop out at a substantially greater rate than Negro boys.

Effects of integration on achievement

An education in integrated schools can be expected to have major effects on attitudes toward members of other racial groups. At its best, it can develop attitudes appropriate to the integrated society these students will live in; at its worst, it can create hostile camps of Negroes and whites in the same school. Thus there is more to "school integration" than merely putting Negroes and whites in the same building, and there may be more important consequences of integration than its effect on achievement.

Yet the analysis of school effects described earlier suggests that in the long run, integration should be expected to have a positive effect on Negro achievement as well. An analysis was carried out to examine the effects on achievement which might appear in the short run. This analysis of the test performance of Negro children in integrated schools indicates positive effects of integration, though rather small ones. . . . [I]n every case but one the highest average score is recorded for the Negro pupils where more than half of their classmates were white. But . . . often those Negro pupils in classes with only a few whites score lower than those in totally segregated classes. . . . Those [Negro] pupils who first entered integrated schools in the early grades record consistently higher scores than the other groups, although the differences are again small.

No account is taken in these tabulations of the fact that the various groups of pupils may have come from different backgrounds. When such account is taken by simple cross-tabulations on indicators of socioeconomic status, the performance in integrated schools and in schools integrated longer remains higher. Thus although the differences are small, and although the degree of integration within the school is not known, there is evident even in the short run an effect of school integration on the reading and mathematics achievement of Negro pupils.

Tabulations of this kind are, of course, the simplest possible devices for seeking such effects. It is possible that more elaborate analyses looking more carefully at the special characteristics of the Negro pupils, and at different degrees of integration within schools that have similar racial composition, may reveal a more definite effect. Such analyses are among those that will be presented in subsequent reports.

Case studies of school integration

As part of the survey, two sets of case studies of school integration were commissioned. These case studies examine the progress of integration in individual cities and towns, and illustrate problems that have arisen not only in these communities but in many others as well. The complete case studies are maintained on file at the Office of Education. In addition, publication of all or some of the reports by their authors will be carried out through commercial publishers.

In the main report, excerpts from these case studies are presented to illustrate certain recurrent problems. A paragraph which introduces each of these excerpts is given below, showing the kinds of problems covered.

LACK OF RACIAL INFORMATION. In certain communities the lack of information as to the number of children of minority groups and of minority group teachers, their location and mobility, has made assessment of the equality of educational opportunity difficult. In one city, for example, after a free transfer plan was initiated, no records as to race of students were kept, thereby making any evaluation of the procedure subjective only. Superintendents, principals, and school boards sometimes respond by declaring racial records themselves to be a mark of discrimination.

A narrative of "the racial headcount problem" and the response to the search for a solution is given in the excerpt from the report on San Francisco.

PERFORMANCE OF MINORITY GROUP CHILDREN. One of the real handicaps to an effective assessment of equality of education for children of minority groups is the fact that few communities have given systematic testing and fewer still have evaluated the academic performance and attitudes of these children toward education. Yet quality of education is to be estimated as much by its consequences as by the records of the age of buildings and data on faculty-student ratio. A guide to cities now planning such assessment is a pupil profile conducted in Evanston, Ill.

In 1964, the Director of Research and Testing for District 65 gathered and analyzed data on "ability" and "achievement" for 136 Negro children who had been in continuous attendance at either Central, Dewey, Foster, or Noyes school through the primary years. A group of 132 white children in continuous attendance for the same period at two white primary schools was compared. Seven different measures from kindergarten through seventh grade were correlated and combined by reducing all measures to stanines. The excerpt from the Evanston report examines in detail the performance of these two groups of children.

COMPLIANCE IN A SMALL COMMUNITY. Many large metropolitan areas North and South are moving toward resegregation despite attempts by school boards and city administrations to reverse the trend. Racial housing concentration in large cities has reinforced neighborhood school patterns of racial isolation while, at the same time, many white families have moved to the suburbs and other families have taken their children out of the public school system, enrolling them instead in private and parochial schools. Small towns and medium-sized areas, North and South, on the other hand, are to some extent desegregating their schools.

In the Deep South, where there has been total school segregation for generations, there are signs of compliance within a number of school systems. The emphasis on open enrollment and freedom of choice plans, however, has tended to lead to token enrollment of Negroes in previously white schools. In school systems integrated at some grade levels but not at others, the choice of high school grades rather than elementary grades has tended further to cut down on the number of Negroes choosing to transfer because of the reluctance to take extra risks close to graduation.

The move toward compliance is described in the excerpt from the report on one small Mississippi town.

A VOLUNTARY TRANSFER PLAN FOR RACIAL BALANCE IN ELEMENTARY SCHOOLS. The public schools are more rigidly segregated at the elementary level than in the higher grades. In the large cities, elementary schools have customarily made assignments in terms of neighborhood boundaries. Housing segregation has, therefore, tended to build a segregated elementary school system in most cities in the North and, increasingly, in the South as well, where *de facto* segregation is replacing *de jure* segregation.

Various communities have been struggling to find ways to achieve greater racial balance while retaining the neighborhood school. Bussing, pairing, redistricting, consolidation, and many other strategies have been tried. Many have failed; others have achieved at least partial success. In New Haven, Conn., considerable vigor has been applied to the problem: Whereas pairing was tried at the junior high level introducing compulsory integration, a voluntary transfer plan was implemented at the elementary level. Relief of overcrowding was given as the central intent of the transfer plan, but greater racial balance was achieved since it was the Negro schools that were overcrowded. With the provision of new school buildings, however, this indirect stimulus to desegregation will not be present. In New Haven the transfer plan was more effective than in many other communities because of commitment of school leadership, active solicitation of transfers by door-to-door visits, provision of transportation for those transferring, teacher cooperation, heterogeneous grouping in the classrooms, and other factors.

The original plan provided that a student could apply to any one of a cluster of several elementary schools within a designated "cluster district," and the application would be approved on the basis of availability of space, effect on racial balance and certain unspecified educational factors; that students "presently enrolled" at a particular school would be given priority; and that transportation would be provided where necessary.

DESEGREGATION BY REDISTRICTING AT THE JUNIOR HIGH SCHOOL LEVEL. The junior high schools, customarily grades 7 to 9, have been the focus of considerable effort and tension in desegregation plans in many communities. With most areas clinging to the neighborhood school at the elementary level with resultant patterns of racial concentration, and with high schools already more integrated because of their lesser reliance upon neighborhood boundaries and their prior consolidation to achieve maximum resources, junior high schools have been a natural place to start desegregation plans. Like the elementary schools, they have in the past been assigned students on the basis of geography; but on the other hand, they tend to represent some degree of consolidation in that children from several elementary schools feed one junior high school. Further, parental pressures have been less severe for the maintenance of rigid neighborhood boundaries than at the elementary level.

Pairing of two junior high schools to achieve greater racial balance has been tried in a number of communities. Redistricting or redrawing the boundaries of areas that feed the schools has been tried in other areas. In Berkeley, Calif., after considerable community tension and struggle, a plan was put into effect that desegregated all three junior high schools (one had been desegregated previously). All the ninth graders were sent to a single school, previously Negro, and the seventh- and eighth-graders were assigned to the other two schools. The new ninth grade school was given a new name to signal its new identity in the eyes of the community. The excerpt describes the period following initiation of this plan and the differential success of integration in the different schools.

A PLAN FOR RACIAL BALANCE AT THE HIGH SCHOOL LEVEL. In a number of communities, students are assigned to high schools on the basis of area of residence and hence racial imbalance is continued. In Pasadena, Calif., a plan was initiated to redress this imbalance by opening places in the schools to allow the transfer of Negroes to the predominantly white high school. A measure of success was achieved but only after much resistance. Of interest particularly in this situation was the legal opinion that attempts to achieve racial balance were violations of the Constitution and that race could not be considered as a factor in school districting. Apparently previous racial concentration, aided by districting, had not been so regarded, yet attempts at desegregation were. The school board found its task made more difficult by such legal maneuvering. The excerpt describes the deliberations and controversy in the school board, and the impact of the court decision, which finally upheld the policy of transfers to achieve racial balance.

SEGREGATION AT A VOCATIONAL SCHOOL. The Washburne Trade School in Chicago seems to be effectively segregated by virtue of the practices and customs of the trade unions, whose apprenticeship programs have been characterized by racial isolation. Washburne has presented the same picture since its founding in 1919 after the passage of the Smith-Hughes Act by Congress. That Act provides for the creation of apprenticeship programs in which skilled workers are trained both in school and on the job. For example, a young man who wishes to be certificated as a plumber may work at his job 4 days a week and attend a formal training program 1 day or more or evenings.

The apprenticeship programs are heavily financed and regulated by the Federal Government through the Department of Labor and the Department of Health, Education, and Welfare. In recent years the regulations have focused increasingly upon racial segregation within the union structures. One of the causes for this concern has been the rather discouraging racial pattern in the apprenticeship schools. Washburne seems to preserve that pattern. In 1960 an informal estimate showed that fewer than 1 percent of the 2,700 Washburne students were Negroes. Half of the apprenticeship programs conducted at the school had no Negroes whatsoever. This excerpt describes the state of racial segregation at Washburne and at Chicago's vocational schools.

RELATION OF A UNIVERSITY TO SCHOOL DESEGREGATION. Education is a continuum—from kindergarten through college—and increasingly public school desegregation plans are having an impact on colleges in the same area, particularly those colleges which are city or State supported. Free tuition, as in the New York City colleges, has no meaning for members of minority groups who have dropped out of school in high school and little meaning for those whose level of achievement is too low to permit work at the college level. A number of colleges, through summer tutorials and selective admittance of students whose grades would otherwise exclude them, are trying to redress this indirect form of racial imbalance.

In Newark, Del., the pressures for desegregation in the public schools have had an effect on the nearby University of Delaware indicated by the following excerpt:

There are striking parallels in reactions to integration among Newark's civic agencies, school district, and the University of Delaware. Because the university plays such a large part in Newark's affairs, this excerpt examines its problems with school integration.

This section concludes the summary report on the survey; the summary report is the first section of the full report, and it is also printed separately for those who desire only an overview of the main findings of the survey. The full report contains a great deal of detailed data from which a small amount has been selected for this summary. It also contains a full description of the statistical analysis which explored the relationships between educational achievement and school characteristics.

DISCUSSION QUESTIONS

1. What do you consider to be the major findings of The Coleman Report?
2. Which of these can be translated into improved education for the children of the poor and the deprived in America?
3. What resistances do you forsee to the possibilities for change that are implicit in The Coleman Report?

PETER SCHRAG — *Why Our Schools Have Failed*

In the context of traditional American belief, Section 402 of the Civil Rights Act of 1964 is one of the simplest, most unambiguous directives ever issued to a government agency. It instructs the United States Commissioner of Education to carry out a survey "concerning the lack of availability of equal educational opportunities for individuals by reason of race, color, religion, or national origin in educational institutions" in the United States and its possessions. Presumably, the wording of Section 402 merely pointed

---

Reprinted from *Commentary*, March 1968, pp. 31–38, with permission of the publisher.

toward an examination of the effects of overt racial discrimination in American schools. What it produced instead was a 737-page document that demonstrated not only the ineffectiveness of schools in overcoming the handicaps of poverty and deprivation, but also the fact that no one knows what the phrase "equal educational opportunities" means, and that, given the conditions of contemporary American society, it can have no meaning. Education in America is patently unequal, it is structured to be unequal, and it can only define its successes by its failures. On the dark side of every conception of "opportunity" lies an equal measure of exclusion and rejection.

No one needs another set of statistics to prove that American Negro children—and many others—are being miseducated, that they are behind in the elementary grades, and that they fall further behind as they move through school. In the twelfth grade more than 85 per cent of Negro children score below the average white on standardized tests of achievement, their dropout rates are higher, and their self-esteem is lower. We can dispute the validity of the tests as indicators of intelligence, but there is not the slightest doubt that if they measure educational achievement, and if they predict future success in school and college (as they do), then the children of the poor minorities in America perform well below average. What the new statistics do provide is solid evidence for the repeated assertion by civil-rights leaders and others that what children learn in school are the rules and attitudes of second-class citizenship, and that the school is a highly effective mechanism not only for advancement but for selecting people out.

Historically, "equality of educational opportunity" simply demanded that all individuals were to have access to similar resources in similar public schools: where children failed, it was because of their own limitations, their lack of ambition and intelligence, not because of the inadequacies of the schools or the society. If the schools were found to favor a particular race or economic group (as they were in many of the desegregation cases), one could rectify the inequities through application of relatively simple standards: the appropriation of equal resources to the education of children of all races, the integration of schools, or the reassignment of teachers. The definition never contemplated the difficulties children might bring from home or the fact that even the best teachers and resources, according to the conventional standards, were keyed to middle-class experience, motivation, and attitude. More important, it never contemplated genuine integration: what it presumed was that only the white middle-class society offered ideals and standards of value, and that whatever the ghetto offered, or what minority children brought with them, was to be disregarded, deflated, or denied. The traditional melting pot was stirred by Protestant hands with a white ladle.

It will be years before the sociologists and statisticians get through with the data in the government's report, "Equality of Educational Opportunity" that was prompted by Section 402. The study, headed by Professor James S. Coleman of the Johns Hopkins University, was eighteen months in the making, cost $2 million to produce, and included data on 600,000 children and 60,000 teachers in 4,000 schools. It is written, as Christopher Jencks said, "in the workmanlike prose of an Agriculture Department bulletin on fertilizer," and it is so thoroughly crammed with tables, regression coefficients, and standard deviations as to make all but the most passionate statisticians shudder. (Ultimately, it turned out, even some of the statisticians began to shudder.) Nonetheless, the Coleman Report has probably become the most influential educational study of the decade. It formed the basis of the recent report of the United States Civil Rights Commission, "Racial Isolation in the Public Schools," it provided ammunition for a federal court opinion on segregation in the Washington schools, it is the topic of conferences and seminars, it is endlessly quoted at meetings, and it became the subject of a year-long study at Harvard under the direction of Daniel P. Moynihan and Thomas Pettigrew (who also wrote the Civil Rights Commission Report). It may be a measure of the times that, where forty years ago we produced educational philosophy and ideology, we are now producing statistics.

The Coleman Report comes to two central conclusions:

1. That the most significant determinant of educational success (as measured by standardized tests of mathematical and verbal performance) is the social and economic background of the individual student, that formal instructional inputs—which are not as unequally distributed between races as supposed—make relatively little difference, and that the social and economic composition of fellow students, not materials or libraries, is the most important in-school resource.
2. That children from disadvantaged backgrounds (regardless of race) benefit from integration with advantaged kids (regardless of race), but that the latter are not harmed by such integration. Proper integration mixes rich and poor and produces a general social gain: the poor learn more; the performance of the rich does not go down.

The Coleman conclusions substantiate propositions that have been gaining currency in the last few years. If racial integration is pedagogically desirable, then clearly social and economic integration, and the interplay of cultural styles, are even more important. Poor blacks and whites can learn from each other, but rich and poor—under the proper conditions—can benefit even more. The Report's conclusions on the impact of teachers are not entirely clear, but they do indicate that good teachers and effective educational environments are more important to the disadvantaged than to those who have access (in the home, for example) to other resources. Even so, teachers, libraries, laboratories, and other formal inputs are not as important as fellow students.

Carried to its ultimate, the Coleman Report seems to indicate that schools make relatively little difference, except as a place where kids learn from each other, and that money spent in improving them is likely, at best, to yield marginal results. The first temptation, of course, is to dismiss that assertion as an absurdity: we take it as an article of faith that the public school has always been the great American social instrument, the device that converted the raw material of immigration into an endless stream of social success. Now, oddly enough, the school seems to be failing in the very functions on which its reputation has always been based. It does not seem to be able to bring the most indigenous and American of all "immigrants" into the mainstream or even to give them the educational qualifications that life in the mainstream requires. Given the insights of recent experience, we might now properly ask whether the school was ever as successful or important in the process of Americanization and education as the history textbooks sentimentally picture it. With the possible exception of the Jews, did the school ever become a major avenue of entry for the ethnic minorities of the urban centers? How effective was it for the Irish, the Italians, the Poles? Was it the school or the street that acculturated our immigrants? What about such Americanizing institutions as the political ward, the shop, and the small town? A half-century ago American society provided alternatives to formal education, and no one became officially distressed about dropouts and slow readers. Now the school has become *the* gatekeeper to advancement, and while it is being blamed for obvious failures, it may actually be doing better than it ever did before.

And yet, despite the accumulation of studies and statistics, we still don't know how much difference formal instruction makes, except to amplify characteristics that have already been determined somewhere else. The Coleman *conclusions* indicate that it doesn't make much difference, but here semantic problems and statistical difficulties begin to get in the way. What the Coleman group did was, in essence, to take schools with students of similar background and try to determine how much difference varying inputs seemed to make. (E.g., given two all-Negro schools, did children in the school where teachers had better training, higher degrees, for example, perform better than those in the other school?) In controlling for student background, however, Coleman and his colleagues may have underestimated the crucial fact that almost all schools are internally harmonious systems, and that where children come from disadvantaged backgrounds their teachers are also likely, in some respects, to be disadvantaged. Two economists, Samuel Bowles of Harvard and Henry M. Levin of The Brookings Institution, point out in the *Journal of Human Resources** that if the methodology of the study had been reversed, so would the conclusions: that is, if Coleman had controlled for such educational inputs as teacher

* "The Determinants of Scholastic Achievement—An Appraisal of Some Recent Evidence," Winter 1968.

training, the social background of the students would have appeared to make little difference. They point out, moreover, that Coleman's Report, despite the vast sample, was unavoidably biased through the refusal of many school systems to furnish data: suburban systems were statistically over-represented while big cities, which have the most severe problems, were under-represented. The most vicious attribute of urban school systems, until recently, has not been their consistent failure with the disadvantaged, but their refusal to produce honest data on that failure. In case after case, they pretended (perhaps because of the historical definition of "equality") that, despite statistical evidence to the contrary, it was individual children, not schools, that failed. Bowles and Levin contend, moreover, that the Coleman Report's conclusions that teachers' traits (verbal facility, educational level, etc.) are relatively unimportant is not supported by the data, which suggests exactly the opposite; that the Report's data on the importance of class size are useless, and that its conclusions about the effect of integration are questionable since "the processes of residential and academic selection imply that those Negroes who attend predominantly white schools are drawn largely from higher social strata." In brief, integration is educationally effective among those who are already educationally and socially "advantaged."

The most significant difficulty, however, is one that the Coleman Report did not create and cannot solve. What does equality mean in education? Does it mean that the average Negro should be doing as well as the average white, and that the resources devoted to his education should be improved until he does? Or does it point to some sort of parity in resources? Or to something else? Coleman himself said that the focus of his report was not on "what resources go into education, but on what product comes out." He then goes on to say (in an article in *The Public Interest***) that "equality of educational opportunity implies not merely 'equal' schools but equally effective schools, whose influences will overcome the differences in starting point of children from different social groups."

Pedagogically and politically, Coleman's suggestion is pleasant, impossible, and probably undesirable. Pleasant because it has a nice democratic ring, impossible because the haves in the society won't allow it to happen, undesirable because it assumes that all social and cultural differences should be equalized away, that Negro children (or Chinese or Jews) have nothing to offer *as Negroes* except problems and disadvantage, and that their culture (or perhaps even their genes) gives them nothing special that might be socially, educationally, or personally valuable. A Negro in this context is nothing but a disadvantaged white.

Since we are now beginning to discover the crucial importance of the very early years of childhood, it is likely that we can achieve a greater measure of

** "Toward Open Schools," Fall 1967.

equality—to narrow the gap between the advantaged and disadvantaged. More effective preschool programs, and a general extension of the social responsibility of the school for children from deprived homes, may make the classroom more effective. But the matter of achieving genuine equality is another question.

As to the politics: the most effective way that a middle-class parent can endow his children is by buying them a superior education, by giving them the head start his advantages can provide, and he is not likely to run slower to let the poor catch up. Given Coleman's standards, the only way to determine whether schools "overcome the differences in starting point of children from different social groups" is when Negro children from Harlem do as well in College Board scores or reading achievement as whites from Scarsdale. Yet when that happens, Scarsdale will have lost its reason to exist. Is the average white afraid of integration or "equality" only because the Negroes would, as he often says, "drag down the standards" or also because, ultimately, they might succeed? What would happen if the prep schools and suburban high schools, let alone the Ivy League universities, were no longer a guarantee of advantage and ultimate success? What if the game were genuinely open? It has often been said that American economic viability depended in part on the existence of a class of individuals who were available for the dirty jobs that the society requires (try the suggestion that we guarantee everyone a living wage, and listen to the prophecies of economic doom), but is it not equally conceivable that, for many, self-esteem and success are themselves defined by the failures of others? We can assert that technology is taking us to some sort of economic nirvana in which menial work is superfluous and we will no longer require Negroes to do it. And yet, doesn't the psychology of success always require a class of failures, and aren't the black, by virtue of their cultural inheritance, always the best candidates? Can we ever maintain a middle class without a lower class, or does it thrive, like Alcoholics Anonymous, on the continued presence of a group of people who, it is assumed, need reform, and from whose failures the successful can draw esteem? Even if we dismiss that as the bleakest kind of cynicism, we are still confronted by the difficulty of a system where cash and power are convertible into educational assets, where educational assets are, in turn, the major qualifications for entry into the life and prerogatives of the middle class, and where the poor have neither. No governmental program is likely to alleviate the inequities.

As to the pedagogy: Coleman's assumption in talking about the different starting points of children "from different social groups" is that all talent is equally distributed through the population, and that inequities are generated only by social, rather than ethnic or cultural characteristics. The current evidence seems to make the assumption doubtful: it points, indeed, to a very different course of action from the one Coleman advocates. For years there was a lot of condescending talk about the attributes and activities of different ethnic groups (all Jews were tailors, the Chinese ran laundries, the Negro had "rhythm"), and we properly reacted with egalitarian indignity when we decided how silly and pernicious that talk had become. Are we now going overboard the other way by suggesting that all talents and interests, of whatever kind, are distributed absolutely equally through the different ethnic sectors of the population? In establishing criteria for academic success—indeed for social success generally—are we emphasizing certain skills and measures at the expense of others that may be equally valuable not only to the individual's personality and self-esteem but to the society generally? In a recent article in the *Harvard Educational Review*,† Susan S. Stodolsky and Gerald Lesser report on research that indicates that the relative strengths and weaknesses in different attributes remain constant for various ethnic groups, regardless of whether they are middle- or lower-class. Jews, for example, score higher, relative to the general population, in verbal ability than they do in space conceptualization. For Chinese children, the relative strengths and weaknesses in verbal ability and space conceptualization are reversed. (Similarly, Negroes seem to perform somewhat better in arithmetic skills and space conceptualization than they do in verbal tests; for Puerto Ricans, the pattern is almost the reverse.) Although middle-class children score higher in *all categories*, the relative ethnic differences are not eliminated. To Lesser and Stodolsky, these findings suggest new distinctions, definitions, and a new course of action. To Coleman's call for equalization, they want to add what they consider the equally important objective of diversification, of trading on the strengths of different ethnic groups, and helping them to develop those strengths to the maximum. "Beyond deploying all necessary resources to achieve minimal equality in essential goals, further development of students may well be diverse," they write. "Following our principle of matching instruction and ability we incidentally may enhance the initial strengths which each group possesses. For example, through the incidental enhancement of the space-conceptualization skills of the Chinese children, we may produce proportionally more Chinese than Jewish architects and engineers. Conversely, through incidental enhancement of verbal skills of the Jewish children, we may produce proportionally more Jewish than Chinese authors or lawyers." There is no suggestion here about producing a Jewish or a Chinese curriculum; what they do propose is tailoring the mode and techniques of instruction to the strengths of particular children.

Studies like this are a long way from producing comprehensive solutions, but they demonstrate how complex the problem has become, how little we know about learning, and how ineffective most current remedial programs seem to be. One of the difficulties, indeed, is determining just what the problem really is. The Coleman Report, whatever its weaknesses, has made

† "Learning Patterns in the Disadvantaged," Fall 1967.

the definitional problem painfully clear. When we talk about the education of Negroes, or urban schools, or the ghetto, are we talking about ethnic minorities, a social class, or simply the universal difficulties of operating effective schools, no matter who their pupils happen to be? Clearly there is validity in the charge that some teachers are racially and socially biased, and that the phrase "cultural disadvantage" can be used, like assertions about Negro inferiority, as an excuse for failure, a cop-out for bad teachers. The psychologist Kenneth B. Clark has often pointed out that statements about uneducable children tend to become self-fulfilling prophecies, and that teachers who talk this way don't belong in the classroom. At the same time, it's hard to believe that the same attitudes don't operate in classrooms full of lower-class Italians or Appalachian mountaineers, or that the Protestant schoolmarms of the year 1900 were altogether openminded about the Jews and the Catholics.

Before anyone comes back with the declaration that "we made it on our own, why can't they?" let's quickly add that the economy that permitted making "it" on one's own is dead and gone, and that when it comes to many contemporary school systems, *all children* tend to be disadvantaged. What I'm suggesting is that many schools are not educational but sociological devices which destroy learning and curiosity and deny differences as often as they encourage them, and which value managerial order above initiative, good behavior above originality, and mediocrity above engagement. (Yes, of course, there are exceptions.) All too often, they demand styles of behavior antithetical not only to social and ethnic minorities, but also to most other original or "difficult" children, no matter what their background. They are instruments of social selection and as such they screen out misfits for the middle class, regardless of race, color, or national origin. In performing this function, every guidance counselor becomes an immigration officer and every examination a petition for a passport. Lower-class youngsters, wrote Edgar Z. Friedenberg in *The Vanishing Adolescent,* "are handy with their fists and worse; but they are helpless in the meshes of middle-class administrative procedure and are rapidly neutralized and eliminated by it. . . . They quickly learn that the most terrifying creatures are those whose bite passes unnoticed at the time and later swells, festers, and paralyzes; they cannot defend themselves against the covert, lingering hostility of teachers and school administrators." This hostility, says Friedenberg, is generated by a reaction to the personal intensity of young men and women who resist personal repression offered in the name of adjustment. "Any individual through whom subjective intensity may intrude into the processes of bureaucratic equilibrium is extremely threatening to our society." The school, in short, is not an instrument of pluralism, but of conformity. It turns out shoddy goods for the dime store trade; its teachers are not professionals but petty civil servants who teach children to deny their own instincts and honesty, teach them little tricks of evasion, and reject those who are not acceptable for the mold. While the deviants of the upper class may have access to special schools in the suburbs or the hills of New England, the poor have no choice: the law *requires* them to go to one particular school in one community which, as often as not, treats them as inmates. The school in this instance becomes a sort of colonial outpost manned by a collection of sahibs from downtown. Their idea of community relations is telling parents to encourage their kids to stay in school, help them with their homework, and live the life of Dick and Jane. As a result, the neighborhood school is in, but not of or by the neighborhood.

Given these conditions and the failures of the ghetto schools, the current demands for decentralization and community control are hardly surprising. There is nothing radical about them, except in the view of school personnel who have been trained to suspect community pressure and who regard any overt mixture of politics and education as the ultimate evil. The advocates of decentralization, who feel that ghetto parents should have as much control over the education of their children as the parents of the small suburb, see political action as the only way to make the school effective and responsible: the issue is not a black principal or a black curriculum for their own sake, but making the schools accountable, and developing the sense of participation that is expected to come with it. If parents are involved, they may provide the interest and support that the education of their children requires. The schools will then become *their* schools, the teachers *their* teachers. A principal working for parents is going to try harder than one who is responsible only to bureaucrats downtown.

For many militants, the appeal of decentralization—as an essential component of community power (read Black Power, if preferred)—is extremely powerful. At the same time, the concept of decentralization suffers from some serious ambiguities. There are people like Roy Innis, a leader in CORE, who favor a single Negro school district in Harlem, a system as distinct from that of New York City as the schools of Buffalo. For most others, including white liberals, the model is a collection of small districts, each hopefully resembling those of the suburbs or the small town, each immediately accessible to the parents and community. The difference between the two is as large as the difference between Thomas Jefferson and John C. Calhoun: one visualizes a thoroughgoing decentralization—educational federalism; the other calls forth the ghost of the doctrine of the concurrent majority. It is based on the presumption that the Negro community is as distinct from the mainstream as the peculiar institution which helped give it birth and on which Calhoun founded his brand of separatism more than a century ago. Both suffer from what may be an excessive belief in the power of formal education and a conviction that racism and bad intentions, rather than educational incompetence, are the major sources of educational inadequacy.

Yet if this were the whole problem—if teachers and schools were guilty of nothing more than middle-class bias or political irresponsibility toward the poor—the situation would not be as difficult as it is. Even if one grants the possibility of effective decentralization as a *political* solution (assuming that parents can run schools without turning them into political battlegrounds or hothouses of nepotism), what of the educational solutions? The pressure for decentralization does not stem from some specific educational program that large systems refuse to adopt and which the militants consider appropriate to the problems of their neighborhoods and children. Indeed, if the Coleman Report has any validity—and there is little reason to doubt that children from different social backgrounds do learn from each other—then decentralization, which will help institutionalize segregation, is a step backward. Thus, the Bundy Report, which outlines a plan of decentralization for New York City, and the Coleman Report, one might think, were composed on different planets.

The great possibility of decentralization (in New York, the proposal is to establish between thirty and sixty semi-autonomous districts) is not some large educational breakthrough, but no more, and no less, than the immediate objective itself: giving the community a greater sense of participation and voice in the management of one of its institutions. (In this respect, it is no different from increasing community control over planning, street-cleaning, or the administration of the local precinct of the police.) It is thus a revolt against the "professionals"—the people who took charge, in the name of reform and good government, and apparently failed to deliver the goods. In its unwillingness to trust the experts, the demand for decentralization is frontier populism come to the city, a rejection of outside planning and expertise. Parents whose children attend decentralized schools may (with luck) learn more about political action and school management than their children learn about reading or mathematics: so far, at any rate, the chances for the first outweigh those of the second. The mystery of power is, for the moment, more fascinating than the problems of instruction.

The fact is that no one, in the ghetto or out, has yet developed a vision of what the ghetto schools ought to do, how they should operate, or what an educated Negro child ought to be if he is to be something different from a dark-skinned middle-class white. The existing ghetto schools fail Negroes not so much because they are different from all other schools—as the integrationists once assumed—but because they are too much like them. Local control may introduce diversity and new ideas, but those changes are far from clear. At this point there are few alternative models to the existing public-school program. The current talk about relevance in Negro education—about more Afro-Americanism in the curriculum, about Negro history, about urban problems—and the peripheral efforts to use the arts (painting, the dance, music) as ways of engaging children's interests have not taken us very far toward genuine educational integration, toward the point, that is, where ghetto children have the skills to compete effectively in the larger world. It has been said again and again that conventional instruction in formalized academic skills is difficult for children whose lives provide few examples of the value of formal education and little reinforcement for work that might pay off in some vague abstract future. Middle-class kids are, in some measure, to the manner born, and they find plenty of reinforcement around them: they often succeed regardless of school. For many ghetto children, instruction, to be successful, has to be immediately attractive or interesting. (There are, to be sure, many ghetto children from families whose ambitions are identical to those of the middle class.) Whether or not "enjoyment," as someone said, "is a prerequisite to competence," it is plain that skills for the larger world may appear only remotely valuable in the immediate life of a child. The humanity of children may be very distant from the problems of negotiating the economy. The problem is how to get from one to the other.

The proposals for solving the problem are endless and, as might be expected, they are often contradictory. There is no consistent Negro demand in education, any more than there is a white one. Some Negro parents are as committed to authoritarian teachers and rote learning as the village schoolmarm; others regard them as racially repressive and pedagogically useless. (Most Negro parents are probably as conservative about education as any others.) I suspect that part of the anger and frustration in all racial school disputes stems from the inability of the parties to be entirely clear about what they want. Should the schools be more middle class, more white than white, turning out suburban doctors and lawyers, or should they be training men and women who can cope with the outside world but whose energies are directed to the black community and whose loyalties remain in the ghetto? (The controversy is similar to a conventional school debate between advocates of vocational training and college preparation, but the race aspect charges it with explosive overtones.) Whatever the position, the issue is clear: almost inevitably it revolves around the problem of moving the child from where he is to the larger world—resolving the inconsistencies between the attitudes and experience of poverty and the formalized skills and motivation that the world demands. There is no disagreement anywhere that there is a common culture that demands certain levels of verbal and social ability. The question slowly emerging from the current debates, however, is whether that ability must become a universal virtue. Should we be concerned only with the preparation of economic functionaries and the development of conventional academic skills, or also with the growth of human beings whose dignity is not necessarily dependent on middle-class standards of success? Is an understanding of algebraic functions any more desirable than the ability to paint or dance? (The mandated requirements for many jobs—nursing, for example—include verbal abilities that are higher than those the job actually require; the stipulated credentials are not necessarily related to the characteristics the jobs demand.) Are we establishing norms that tend to undervalue characteristics that all of society could well use, and for which certain children might be especially well prepared, or do we have to make *all* children into replicas of the middle class?

For the next several years we are likely to hear more and more along this line. In its most extreme form, the argument says that not only is the American school an instrument of the white middle class, but that the overriding emphasis—in school and out—on high verbal and cognitive skills is itself a form of racial and social bias. The rational mind, with its emphasis on a high degree of verbal and analytical facility is, in a manner of speaking, our thing. We invented and perfected it, and for the last fifteen years most curricular reform has been directed to the task of putting a larger and more powerful dose of it into the classroom. Thus we have, even more thoroughly than before, arranged education to separate the sheep of privilege from the goats of deprivation. Increasingly, we will now have to confront questions about what has been excluded: Are we missing something more intuitive, personal, and intangible? Is it possible to extend the Lesser-Stodolsky kind of analysis to include—along with assessments of verbal and mathematical characteristics, and the ability to conceptualize space—things like affective and intuitive qualities, creativity, and some general feeling for the poetic, the visual, and the musical?

Because these things are difficult to test, and because their cash value has usually been remote, the schools tend to disregard them, or to assign them to a secondary level of importance. Of all the things that make life rich—the arts, the various elements of literary and personal sensitivity, social and political involvement, philosophy, religion—very few have even a minimal place (except as lip service) in the public school program. One may not be able to mandate such activities in a large compulsory school system, but it is possible to offer them as alternatives to the public school, and one can conceive of all sorts of programs for doing so. The issue here is not to turn every ghetto school into an academy of the arts, but to offer diversity—teaching the skills of a trade or of an art with as much of a sense of importance as we teach mathematics or history. The objective, in each instance, is to draw upon the experiences and interests of the kids, to give them a sense of motion and relevance, and to provide choices, not only as to school and school control, but also as to style of learning. We have, with the single public system, and the instruction it offers, created a single standard of success and failure (and the large hippie element seems to indicate that the standard is not acceptable even to some of those who might meet it). Perhaps we have to recognize the principle of pluralism not only in a cultural context but in an educational one as well. A few years ago such suggestions would have been regarded as racist slurs, but it is now the black militant who regards Swahili as desirable for Negroes as Latin.

Carried to its extreme, the argument leads to a romantic trap, a wishful attempt to arm the weakest members of a technological society with the least effective weapons for dealing with it. It may be nice to think that there are dishwashers with the souls of poets (or even with the skills of poets), but that thought provides no foundation on which to base an educational system. There are, in our culture, a variety of important and rewarding functions that require no extensive verbal or mathematical skills (despite the exclusionist tendency of certain trades and professions to impose arbitrary educational standards for membership). Nonetheless, there remain certain levels of verbal ability without which few people can survive, except in the most menial situations. In our ambiguity and guilt about middle-class life, many of us hold a corresponding ambiguity about those who are left outside the mainstream: the happy hillbilly, the engagement and passion of the ghetto, the uninhibited poor. What we disregard is that, given the choice, most of them would elect to live like us; because of educational deficiencies, they do not have the choice. There is, said a Negro sociologist, only one way out of the ghetto, "and that's out." The reason, finally, that so few of them make it has little to do with differences in culture, or the fact that teachers and administrators are ignorant about the lives of the children assigned to them; it is because they still don't know how to teach. Negro schools are bad because all schools are bad. We simply don't know very much about how children learn. This is, in the end, what the Coleman Report proved. It may also be the greatest single contribution of the civil-rights movement.

But to say that great diversity, the provision of educational options, and a new emphasis on intuitive learning can be carried to extremes is not to deny the validity of the idea, either in the ghetto or anywhere else. For the past decade we masculinized the schools with mathematics, physics, and with a variety of new toughminded curricula. Educational criticism in the next decade may well concern itself more with the soft side of things—with non-cognitive approaches, and with a reaffirmation of Deweyan ideas. There are a number of people who are talking seriously about a "curriculum of concerns," educational programs that begin with the interests and experience of kids, not with predetermined sets of skills to be learned. Most of the ghetto experiments that seem to have potential are pure Dewey: letting children talk their own stories and developing vocabulary and writing skills from them; trips to factories, galleries, and museums; stories and poems about the streets of the city, and even about addicts and junkies: These things, too, can be carried to undisciplined extremes. None is a cure-all, but nothing in education ever is. The very nature of the enterprise is unsettling and troublesome. Education and maturation mean change, and that, in turn, means dealing with new problems, new elements every day. Equality is relatively easy to define in employment, in housing, or in medicine. It is impossible to define in education because the very nature of the enterprise demands distinctions and produces diversity.

Are we then to abandon integration and concentrate exclusively on the problems of the classroom? Plainly the answer is no. No, because it still seems—at least to some of us—morally important; no, because, lacking better tools, it still appears to be an effective technique for education; no, because any alternative to integration is, despite immediate attractions to the contrary, unthinkable. Yet if integration is to have any meaning, it must be a two-way street—integration not only *between* races, going both ways, but also between the school and the community, school and job, culture and culture. If equality of educational opportunity means merely an effort to improve the chances of the disadvantaged to run the race on our terms, things will never be equal and whatever they have to offer will be lost. Are we really courageous enough to provide a broad range of educational options and not to worry about who's at what level in which track? Are we really interested in education or merely in grades, credits, and diplomas? In the structure of the existing school system, segregation, repression, competition, and failure are all essential parts. Every class has a bottom half, and it tends to include, numerically, as many whites as blacks. Until we are ready to stop selecting people out, almost any conception of education is going to involve some sort of segregation. Our democratic professions might be vindicated if the ranks of the successful were as well integrated as the ranks of the failures, but would that solve the problem of education? What would we do with the failures if they were a statistically average shade of tan? The fundamental issue is not the equality of Negro schools, but the lives of all young men and women, no matter what their category of stigma. "If urban educators are failing," says Robert Dentler, the director of the Center for Urban Education, "they are failing where the newly emergent culture of the urban society itself has failed to specify either ends or means for the educator or his clientele. . . . We are in a period when the place of all children in this culture is in transition." What the problem of Negro education has done, or should be doing, is to alert us to a far larger range of social and educational questions, and to the fact that the goal of maximizing human potential is still a long way off.

DISCUSSION QUESTIONS

1. What kind of education is it that will accept all children as they are and, without stigma or malice, help them to develop to their fullest potential, in their own style?
2. Would you assume, as Schrag does, that "equally effective schools, whose influences will overcome the differences in starting point of children from different social groups" will equalize away "all social and cultural differences" among children?
3. Do you accept the Stodolsky and Lesser thesis of ethnic differences remaining constant for groups, regardless of class? Would you be in favor of "tailoring the mode and techniques of instruction to the strengths of particular children"?
4. How valid is Friedenberg's indictment of the schools? Does your own experience bear him out?

5. Is decentralization a power ploy, rather than a meaningful way of improving ghetto schools?
6. Are ghetto schools failing not because they are different from all other schools, but because they are too much like them?

ALICE MIEL and EDWIN KIESTER, JR.

The Shortchanged Children of Suburbia

At first glance, the community of New Village, not far from New York City, seems an idyllic place for American children to grow up in. The homes are mostly ranged along quiet, winding streets. There are open spaces, greenery, woods to explore. The churches and community centers run dances, teen programs and other youth activities. The schools are new and modern, with well-kept lawns and the latest in playground facilities; they boast a curriculum tailored mostly to students headed for college. PTA meetings are among the best-attended events in town.

Yet children miss something in New Village. You do not recognize it at first, but as you drive along the streets, you suddenly realize that all the homes are pretty much of a stripe. None are very lavish, none are very poor. The people are of a stripe, too—almost all of them are white and young or fairly young. You will look long for a dark face or an old one. New Village has many things to offer young people, but diversity is not one of them.

The residents of New Village (which is not its real name) would resent hearing their town characterized as a look-alike suburb. And indeed the community, which began as a cluster of city people's summer cottages, does have a character, individuality and charm of its own that set it apart from other suburbs—even adjoining ones. Just the same, New Village is representative of America's postwar rush to "the country"—with all that is promising and all that is disquieting about that movement. Like hundreds of other new communities, it is made up largely of white middle-income families, clustering together and raising their children in an atmosphere where many of the basic differences among people are fenced out.

In another period of history, this sort of self-segregation might not have mattered. But today Americans cannot afford to shut themselves off from human differences, for these differences are precisely what the chief problems of our time are about. On the domestic scene, the crucial issues of the sixties include the Negroes' drive for equality, the Government's effort to

Reprinted from Alice Miel and Edwin Kiester, Jr., *The Shortchanged Children of Suburbia* (New York: The Institute of Human Relations Press, 1967), pp. 10–15, with permission of the publisher.

bring a share of prosperity to the impoverished, the nation's concern with the welfare of the elderly, the ecumenical movement in organized religion. On the world stage we see the growing aspirations of the underdeveloped nations, the rise of nationalism and the ascendancy of the colored races. Moreover, hardly anyone believes these prickly questions can be solved during the present generation; our children and perhaps our children's children will have to face up to them as well.

How well is suburbia—the home of vast numbers of Americans, and increasingly the trend-setter for the entire population—preparing the young people of today for such a future? Lacking first-hand contact, how do suburban children learn about human difference, and what do they think about it? How can they acquire respect for persons whom their middle-class society brands less acceptable than themselves? And what can adults—parents, school administrators, classroom teachers, community organizations—do to groom the coming generation for a proper role in a multicultural society?

The study: why and how

Some time ago, a group of us—teachers, sociologists and researchers from Teachers College, Columbia University—set out to shed some light on these questions. We focused on New Village as a reasonably typical American suburb.

Of course, we knew that New Village was not a precise counterpart of every suburb. No single community could be, for each has developed according to its own pattern. Some were built on open land, others grew up around an existing community. Some belong almost wholly to one social class, others have at least a small range of socio-economic difference. In some, one faith predominates; in others, religious groups are more evenly represented. Some have stopped growing while others are still increasing in size. Yet, all seem to have a number of characteristics in common. They consist almost wholly of young adults and children. Fathers commute, and mothers dominate the children's upbring. Adults have at least a high-school education and own their homes. Parents are greatly concerned with how their youngsters are raised. In all these respects, we found, New Village strongly resembles suburbs around the country.

Our study concentrated chiefly on the elementary schools as the chief training ground for American children today. We sought to discover how suburban youngsters are taught (or not taught) about human difference, and how their attitudes toward it are shaped and molded. We hoped to find out what opportunities for such "social learning" are available in the schools, and how teachers capitalize on them. We tried to delve into the values and predispositions of parents and teachers, and to gauge their awareness of problems connected with group differences. In short, we set out to learn what kind of background a suburb provides for educating children to live in a multicultural society. We also wanted to point up the need for social lessons in schools today, and to suggest how they might be included in the curriculum.

The actual study covered four years. In that time all the teachers in three elementary schools took part in group interviews, and over 200 teachers in seven schools filled out a lengthy questionnaire. Teachers were asked what their pupils seemed to know about human difference, and also how they taught about it. Numerous meetings were held with administrators. One researcher concentrated on the students themselves, using what are known as projective techniques—for example, asking the children to comment on or interpret photographs or imaginary situations. A sociologist on our research team talked to parents of children in three schools; and two other team members (one of them the study director) conducted a workshop for members of the faculty. In addition, some comparative research was done in urban, suburban and rural localities outside New Village.

The information obtained was then sorted out according to whether it had to do with racial, socio-economic, religious, ethnic or other differences between people. The next few chapters in this pamphlet set out our findings according to the same grouping. In later chapters we outline certain broader attitudes of suburban children (and, incidentally, their elders) that bear on our subject, and discuss the potential role of schools in helping the young get better prepared for life in the modern world. The concluding chapter suggests action programs which should prove useful to educators, parents and community groups in many places besides New Village.

Some general impressions

The study points up certain troubling aspects of growing up in New Village—and, by extension, in any suburban community. To begin with, it was found that extraordinary effort was required to bring about any encounter between a child of the suburbs and persons different from himself. In big cities today—as in the small towns of the past—youngsters are virtually certain to encounter ethnic, economic or racial diversity, in the course of their school or social life. But the suburban child's life and social contacts are far more circumscribed; in fact they are almost totally controlled by his parents, whether or not the parents recognize this. He depends on his mother to chauffeur him wherever he goes. As a result, he knows little beyond his own home, the very similar homes of friends, the school, and the inside of the family car; he is largely insulated from any chance introduction to a life different from his own.

Second, we observed that children learn to be hypocritical about differences at a very early age. At first, many said things like "I wouldn't care if a person were white or black, I'd play with him if I liked him." But on further probing, it became evident that this supposed tolerance was only skin-deep: when the same children were given any test which involved just such a choice, they almost invariably shied from choosing the Negro. The prejudices of their society were still very much with them, but they had had it drilled into them that it was "not nice" to express such feelings.

Third, group prejudices, of whatever nature, evidently take root early and go deep. Many stereotypes about race and religion cropped up even among the youngest children. Six- and seven-year-olds, for instance, pictured Negroes as poor, threatening or inferior. With such early beginnings, any fight against prejudice is bound to be a difficult uphill struggle.

Fourth, and more hopefully, the study found a good many parents united in desiring more emphasis on certain kinds of human difference. For example, they were greatly in favor of children's learning about nationality differences; many also hoped the schools would help youngsters achieve respect for other faiths and even teach what the beliefs of these faiths were.

Finally, it appears that one area of human difference is almost completely ignored in the American suburb. Many parents and teachers were found eager to bridge religious differences; many recognized, however uneasily, the need for discussion of racial differences. But with a few notable exceptions, neither parents nor schools were facing up to economic inequality. Occasionally, a social-studies class would take up the poor of other nations, or a fund drive would focus attention on the less fortunate in the United States; but the fact that there were impoverished families within a stone's throw of New Village was seldom noted, and how they got there or what kept them impoverished was seldom investigated.

The overall impression one carries away is that something is missing in New Village. People who have moved to the suburbs since the Second World War often say proudly that they did so "for the children." And, of course, the children of communities like New Village do have a host of advantages, by no means all of them material. But in one aspect of their education suburban children are underprivileged. Though other races, other nationalities, other generations have a great deal to teach them, there is little in their education, formal or otherwise, to familiarize them with the rich diversity of American life.

In this sense, despite the many enviable features of their environment, the children of suburbia are being shortchanged.

BLACK AND WHITE

The average elementary-school child in New Village does not know and has never known a Negro his own age. The school population includes several hundred "non-whites," most of them Negroes, but they are concentrated in one school in the least desirable section of the community and have little or no contact with children outside that section. When our study began, the school in the Negro neighborhood was closed for remodeling, and the pupils were being transported by bus to another, but by the later phases of our work they had been resegregated in their old school.

In one area sampled, all families were white except for one Chinese-American household. When parents were asked if their children had contact with other races, they declared they had indeed—the Chinese family, one Negro teacher and one Negro bus driver. But actually, as the study showed only too clearly, racial ignorance and racial prejudice flourished among the young children there. In fact, throughout New Village, children at the very earliest age had learned to look upon Negroes as different, inferior, undesirable and even violent. Some, as noted above, had learned to be hypocritical and to conceal any such feeling; but it was scarcely difficult to establish its prevalence.

None of this, actually, is surprising, for it clearly mirrors the attitudes of the adult community. When we interviewed the parents of children in the New Village schools, we found that most paid lip service to ideas of racial justice, but admitted to prejudice on closer questioning. Several said candidly that they did not want their children to associate with Negroes. On the other hand, parents agreed that Negroes were "entitled to their rights" and that it was "not nice" to make slurring remarks about them.

DISCUSSION QUESTIONS

1. Are white children educationally shortchanged in our finer suburbs?
2. Is it vital to our nation—and to the world—that our children learn about human difference, as Miel and Kiester state?
3. Do you agree that group prejudices "take root early and go deep"? As a teacher, what is your responsibility for combating such prejudice? How would you go about it in a wealthy suburban school?
4. Are the children of our suburbs likely, when they become adults, to opt for open-housing laws and integrated schools?

SHELDON STOFF

The Two-Way Street: A History of the Main Trends in School Desegregation in the United States

A theory of social change

A study of past school desegregations has convinced me that where racial desegregation of public schools has been brought about in a nonviolent manner, either positive action has been taken by persons in leadership positions or specific conditions in the transition communities have precluded the outcropping of violence. In other words, specific factors, events, or deeds are associated with nonviolent school desegregation. This research seeks the isolation and description of these factors.

I have supported a theory of social change that agrees with Professor Kenneth Clark's: "Desired changes in the behavior of individuals and groups can be brought about by a change in the social situation in which they are required to function."[1] He believed that skilled persons, with accurate information, could act so as to vary some community situations, utilize and recognize others, and institute a community situational set which would support nonviolent school desegregation.

A prior claim, now supported by this research, stated that social change in school desegregation could be brought about in a less disruptive, nonviolent manner when there is—

1. Open communication between groups, in good faith working toward common goals
2. Firm leadership for non-violent desegregation to serve as a unifying force in this direction
3. Allegiance to the American Creed, upheld and explained
4. An understanding attitude when implementing change and respect for the dignity of the opposition.

Early efforts for Negro education

The early history of the education of the Negro American is characterized by a large zero. Education was denied Negroes by white men. In part, this denial was based on the fear that educated Negroes would not, in all probability, accept their position as slaves. The very structure of slavery would be threatened, which would in turn affect the white man's economic life. As pointed out by Knight and Hall, the denial of education for the Negro was often supported by legal statute. South Carolina imposed a fine of "one hundred pounds current money" on anyone who would "teach, or cause any slave or slaves to be taught, to write, or shall use or employ any slave as a scribe in any manner of writing whatsoever."

This attitude was maintained, with notable exceptions, for years to come. The General Assembly of Virginia, in 1831, prohibited the teaching of slaves, free Negroes, or Mulattoes to read or write. Before and during this time there were also state laws prohibiting the education of Negroes or prohibiting their attendance in public schools in Georgia and Louisiana. Similar prohibitions were enacted in Alabama (1832), South Carolina (1834), Washington, D.C. (1834), Missouri (1847), and Texas (1866). The usual punishment for teaching Negroes was a fine, imprisonment, or

Reprinted from Sheldon P. Stoff, *The Two Way Street* (Indianapolis, Ind.; David-Stewart Publishing Co., 1967), pp. 1–6, 66–68, with permission of the publisher.

[1] Kenneth B. Clark, "Desegregation: An Appraisal of the Evidence," *Journal of Social Issues,* 1953, No. 4, p. 72.

lashes; however, a Methodist minister who had taught Negroes was pulled from his pulpit on a Sunday morning by an angry mob and subjected to abuses at the town water pump.

Some of the notable exceptions to this attitude were the early attempts at Negro education which were inspired by religious groups.

> An early catechizing school was founded in New York City at Trinity Church in 1704. Instruction was given by Elia Neau regularly until 1712, when blame for a local slave uprising was attributed by some masters to Neau's work.[2]

At this point, he was forced to cease his work. Efforts at educating the Negro were continued by Catholics, and a strong effort was launched by the Quakers. In no Northern states were laws passed against teaching Negroes even though such education was often feared. Still the educational level of Negroes in the North was well below that of their white brethren.

Education permitted

Following the close of the Civil War, efforts were increased to provide greater educational opportunities for the Negro. The new attempts were usually made within the context of white supremacy and were not aimed at equality of opportunity.

> It must be remembered, nevertheless, that violent opposition abated as years passed. Though barriers of caste were to be raised in the New South (1877–1913) as Southern white rule was destroyed, the idea of support for the academic education of the Negro began to receive sympathetic acceptance. By the turn of the century, some communities of the South were giving limited financial support to a segregated Negro education that was controlled by whites, unequally supported, and devoted almost exclusively to elementary or industrial education.[3]

During this period of time increased efforts for the education of the Negro were made in New York, Michigan, Massachusetts, Connecticut, Alabama, Iowa, Louisiana, South Carolina, New Jersey, Pennsylvania, and California. Efforts to provide for segregated education were instituted in Nevada, Georgia, Mississippi, North Carolina, Texas, Virginia, Indiana, and Ohio.[4]

Education and desegregation

Many Northerners are surprised to discover that the "separate but equal" doctrine was apparently born in the North rather than in the South. It is interesting that a key court case arose in a stronghold of the abolitionists, Boston, Massachusetts.

Many communities in Massachusetts had abolished racially segregated

---

[2] Virgil A. Clift, *et al.* (eds.), *Negro Education in America* (New York: Harper and Brothers, 1962), p. 34.

[3] *Ibid.*, p. 39.

[4] William Brickman and Stanley Leher (eds.), *The Countdown on Segregated Education* (New York: Society for the Advancement of Education, 1960), p. 154.

schools prior to 1849. Then Benjamin Roberts, a Boston Negro, tried to enroll his five-year-old daughter in a white elementary school. Five white schools were closer to his home than the nearest Negro school. His bid was rejected. His attorney contended that the school board had no authority to maintain segregation and "brand a whole race with the stigma of inferiority."[5] He further contended that schools should foster understanding, and that separation of the races would lead to bias and ignorance.

Massachusetts State Chief Justice Shaw delivered the unanimous opinion of the court and held that the school board did have the power to enforce segregation. He further held that the legal authority and power in education was "exclusively with them [the board]."[6]

The ruling stated—

> The "great principle" that "all persons without distinction of age or sex, birth or color, origin or condition are equal before the law," when applied "to the actual and various conditions of persons in society," does not lead to the conclusion that all persons "are legally clothed with the same civil and political powers." Laws may be enacted that are "adapted" to the "respective relations and conditions" of people or classes of people.[7]

This reasoning was later applied to other court cases which strongly supported the "separate but equal" doctrine (in New York, Arkansas, Missouri, Louisiana, and West Virginia). It constituted a precedent for upholding segregated education. And his view was in the fabric of the thinking of white Americans' attitudes in regard to Negroes in all phases of their life, including education.

As the efforts to educate the Negro increased, support for education arose from several quarters. The churches continued their previous efforts. Among them were the American Missionary Association, the Friends Association for Aid to Freedmen, the Presbyterian Church, the Methodist Church, and the Baptist and Episcopal Churches. Wealthy Northerners provided financial aid. Among the leaders were the Peabody fund with a contribution of $3,500,000, the Slater fund with a contribution of $2,000,000, the Carnegie fund with a contribution of $10,000,000, the Rockefeller fund with a contribution in excess of $1,000,000, and the Rosenwald and Jeanes funds. These grants aided school construction, scholarships, endowments, teacher training, and industrial development.[8]

The Southern states also made efforts in this direction, but, before 1900, many of the efforts were completely inadequate. "The Southern states were spending an average of $4.92 per year on a white child in 1900 and $2.71 on a Negro child."[9]

---

[5] Milton R. Konvitz, *A Century of Civil Rights* (New York: Columbia University Press, 1961), p. 126.
[6] *Ibid.*, p. 127.
[7] *Ibid.*, p. 127.
[8] Clift, *op. cit.*, pp. 40–42.
[9] *Ibid.*, p. 44.

Under the influence of Samuel C. Armstrong and Booker T. Washington the Negroes were apparently willing to accept segregation in their schools, churches, and industry as long as improvements and a sense of equality could be provided in these areas. To do otherwise in the South, at that time, was unsafe and unrealistic.

The Supreme Court case of *Plessy* v. *Ferguson* in 1896 upholding racial segregation in transportation seemed to settle the issue for a period of time. The question of concern to the court was the reasonableness of the regulation, not the issue of properness of segregation *per se.* The dissenting opinion by Justice Harlan criticized this ruling which seemingly branded Negroes an inferior class of citizens. Here is an excerpt from his decision:

> Americans boast of the freedom enjoyed by our people above all other people. But it is difficult to reconcile that boast with a state of the law which, practically, puts the brand of servitude and degradation upon a large class of our fellow citizens, our equals before the law. . . .
>
> Our Constitution is color blind, and neither knows nor tolerates classes among citizens.[10]

The *Plessy* v. *Ferguson* decision enabled states, such as Kentucky, to prohibit mixed schools with the sanction of the U.S. Supreme Court. There was no doubt of Kentucky's position.

> It shall be unlawful for any white person to attend any schools or institutions where negroes are received as pupils or receive instruction, and it shall be unlawful for any negro or colored person to attend any school or institution where white persons are received as pupils or receive instruction. Any person so offending shall be fined fifty dollars for each day he attends such institution or school.[11]

Though the promise was "separate but equal," inequality in financial support prevented the Negroes from achieving this equality. The U.S. Supreme Court even held constitutional a Georgia school segregation law providing state funds for white schools although there were no provisions made for Negro schools.

Even with these shortcomings, there was some improvement of Negro schools. But equality was never achieved. In recent years some Southern states have spent from 21 percent to 94 percent as much on their Negro students as on their white students.[12]

During later years there was still a strong carry-over from previous days. There are many recorded reports of threats to white teachers of Negro students, such as the note quoted here:

> Mr. Banks we thought we would give you a chance to save yourself one of the worst scourings that a man ever got and you can do so by reading this note and acting

---

[10] U.S. Supreme Court Justice Harlan, *Plessy* v. *Ferguson* (163 U.S. 537, 1896).

[11] Acts of the General Assembly of the Commonwealth of Kentucky (1904), pp. 181, 182.

[12] U.S. Dept. of Health, Education and Welfare, Office of Education, *Statistics of State School Systems, Organization Staff, Pupils and Finances 1953–1957* (Washington, D.C.: U.S. Government Printing Office, 1954), Ch. 2, p. 114, Table 48.

upon its contents. You have set up a nigger school in the settlement which we will not allow you to teach if you were a full blooded negro we would have nothing to say but a white skin negro is a little more than we can stand you can dismiss the school immediately or prepar yourself to travail we will give you a chance to save yourself and you had better move instanter.[13]

. . . .

FINAL THOUGHTS

In this study some of the variables significantly related to nonviolent desegregation have been identified. Twenty-three variables have been organized into six factors. Examples for most of the variables have been presented.

It is obvious that important differences in community settings did exist between violent and nonviolent public school desegregation situations. The variables significantly associated with nonviolence in public school desegregations in this study were these:

Factor I: Favorable School Leadership

1. The chief school administrator led in the development of a school desegregation plan.
2. The chief school administrator supported the desegregation plan.
3. The school board supported the desegregation.

Factor II: The Opposition

1. There was a lack of active opposition to school desegregation by the governor.
2. There was a lack of active opposition to school desegregation by outside organizations.
3. There was a lack of active opposition to school desegregation by local organizations.
4. There was a lack of opposition to school desegregation by the state education department.
5. There was a lack of opposition to school desegregation by local individuals.

Factor III: The Urban Center

1. Smaller communities (under 50,000 persons) had better success.
2. There were no Negroes on the police force.[14]
3. There were no police on duty in plain clothes.
4. Negro and white schools were comparable.
5. Nearby schools desegregated at the same time.

---

[13] *State Journal* (Alabama, 1875); given in E. Knight and Clifton Hall, *Readings in American Educational History* (New York: Appleton-Century-Crofts, Inc., 1951), p. 679.
[14] Apparently not substantiated by further in-depth probing and thus discounted.

Factor IV: The Practical Community

1. Desegregation was voluntary (not specifically ordered by a court).

2. There was preparation by the white faculty of white students for nonviolent school desegregation.

3. There were nearby desegregated schools.

4. There was a high employment level among the male, nonwhite population.

Factor V: Active Community Support

1. The white clergy supported school desegregation.

2. Respected white community members supported nonviolent school desegregation.

3. School transportation facilities were desegregated.

4. Local newspapers advocated nonviolent school desegregation.

Factor VI: Residual Support

1. There were desegregated labor unions.

2. The state educational agencies supported school desegregation.

It is evident, on the basis of this broad study of school desegregation, that nonviolence does not simply happen. Careful preparation very often precedes its achievement. There are many factors which provide a favorable social set for nonviolent school desegregation. If a favorable social set is to be provided, many forces and individuals in the community must actively fulfill their responsibilities.

It is equally apparent that nonviolent school desegregation can be attained even if many persons in the community do not favor school desegregation. When it is recognized that the present operational issue is violent vs. nonviolent desegregation, those forces favoring nonviolence can act so as to increase the possibility of achieving this goal. One important step is to identify the forces of active opposition and then act so as to mitigate or control their influences.

The related variables identified in this study would indicate that the burden of social action has a certain specificity. But the implications are that every man has an obligation to fulfill. Even in a modern technological society, man is still his brother's keeper.

Some citizens of modern society seem self-condemned to apathy; they think that individual actions don't count or don't matter. Certainly it would be ambitious to seek an answer to that primary question in empirical research. The knowledge that what man becomes is determined by his "turning to the other," by the "I-Thou" relationship of mutuality, and the attempt to provide for the worthwhile needs of one's fellow-man, is gained only through inner experience. For those who do not or cannot look within for these answers, this study may provide a statistical basis for action, may demonstrate the broad responsibilities occasioned by interactions between individuals and groups. The examples of individual action which "did count" may indicate guidelines for the responsible citizen in a community in flux.

In an age when we often take social action on the basis of scientific research, studies like this one are necessary, even essential. But if one asked that all his actions be founded only in science, the consequences would be paralyzing. The combination of scientific method, used in this study, and the inner vision of each individual, vital to the development of the balanced person, is for now the best hope for the individual and the community seeking change with dignity, respect, and cohesion.

DISCUSSION QUESTIONS

1. Do you believe that Stoff's guidelines would apply in planning the desegregation of your community?
2. As an educator, do you believe that the responsibilities that Stoff details for educators are a valid charge on the educational profession?
3. Can we insist that small communities desegregate their schools now, while we postpone desegregation and subscribe to "quality segregated education" for ghetto schools, such as those of Harlem?
4. Stoff calls for firm, skilled leadership to bring about reasonable, nonviolent desegregation. Can this be furnished by local civic leadership?

KEITH WHEELER

Integration Vendetta in a Northern Town

Until five years ago New Rochelle—the town saluted in George M. Cohan's *Forty-five Minutes from Broadway*—was about as typical as a suburb of New York City could get. A patriarch of a place, with archives stretching back to French Huguenot refugees and their Negro slaves around 1688, it had grown up to be mostly a pleasant and prosperous small city though its older sections were sliding into slums. Then, all at once, New Rochelle saw itself both unique and notorious; it became the first northern city forced by the courts of the United States to desegregate a public school which had become virtually all Negro.

Half a decade has gone. Now it is possible to look back and see how New Rochelle made out in, first, obeying the court, and second, enduring the consequences. New Rochelle is not likely to welcome the scrutiny, for the town—as full of prejudice, fair-mindedness, compassion and cussedness as

---

Reprinted from *Life,* May 6, 1966, with permission of the publisher.

any other—has already had more painful publicity than it wants. A place which likes to call itself the "Queen City" cannot be expected to enjoy the memory of having been also called the "Little Rock of the North."

But a backward look, although possibly wounding, can be useful to all of us. New Rochelle furnishes the pioneer northern case history of an attempt to make cold law mesh with hot blood and passion. Every large urban place outside the South—from Boston to Gary to Los Angeles—is either already face-to-face with something like New Rochelle lived through, or soon has to be.

In New Rochelle the aftermath of the court's order to desegregate sent the public schools through a special kind of hell and, until just recently, they were still suffering it. In the process (1) the board of education was harassed and coerced, (2) teachers were tormented, (3) school discipline went to pot, and (4) most important of all, the business of education—which is the only legitimate endeavor schools are in—was crippled. Only now that New Rochelle's ordeal has finally eased are the schools convalescing satisfactorily.

Full desegregation of all the nation's public schools has been law since 1954. And that concept has been propped and buttressed since by a whole series of remarkable and enlightened court decisions. But law is one thing, the quirky human animal another. Old grievances and old suspicions die in a slow and wretched way. In New Rochelle it was man, not the law, that went sour. And—it has to be said—the spirit of the Negroes, hot at being winners after 100 years of monotonous losing, was such that many could not see—or were damned if they would admit—that having equality carries as heavy a responsibility as the obligation to fight for it.

It was incongruous that the trouble should have come to the New Rochelle schools. For years the town's senior high has maintained one of the highest academic ratings in the country. And the graduates of its college preparatory program have enjoyed a warm welcome at the choosiest colleges and universities in the land.

The order to desegregate struck New Rochelle as both ironic and insulting. In the way a town looks at itself, New Rochelle had considered its public school system entirely integrated ever since 1889, when the last deliberately segregated Negro school was closed down.

In 1960 there were 12 elementary schools, two junior high schools and one senior high for a city population of 77,000. From first through sixth grades, a child went to the elementary school in the district where he lived—to his "neighborhood school," words which these days mean either sacred institution or tool to destroy human dignity, depending on who is speaking. Above sixth grade, everybody merged. The hitch in New Rochelle was one old school—Lincoln Elementary. By all the pressures which bear upon American society, Lincoln had become 94% Negro—that is, *"de facto* segregated," another epithet in the modern social lexicon. This was not entirely by chance. Former school boards had created the district so that Lincoln would serve New Rochelle as a segregated elementary school.

The situation takes various forms in urban areas, but the basic problem remains the same. It is most baffling in bigger cities where the difficulties and confusions of integration are bound to increase. Most large northern urban centers will have nonwhite majorities within a decade. Washington is already more than half Negro; Detroit, Chicago, Cleveland will get there by 1980.

In May 1960, New Rochelle's citizens approved a referendum to tear down Lincoln Elementary, which was 62 years old and decrepit—and to build a new $1.3 million school in the same area. A proposal to build a new Lincoln had been put to vote three years earlier but was turned down. This defeat focused attention on the issue and whites and Negroes alike joined in debate over the need for a new school. By 1960 the proposal had such widespread support that it easily passed. Only in the Lincoln district did the voters, most of them Negroes, oppose the referendum—by a ratio of 1.36 to 1. While some Lincoln parents apparently wanted a new school and others didn't appear to care, many believed that it would serve only to continue segregation. They felt that the education their children were getting at Lincoln didn't amount to much and the only way to improve matters was to get them out of there.

"I went to Lincoln as a kid and I guess I was happy there," a Negro insurance man has recalled. "But I suspect I was shortchanged on education. I doubt if the teachers *wanted* to stunt us, but they asked only a low level of performance. They used to have us sing *Old Black Joe* and *Swanee River* at assemblies. You had to get to high school to find out how much you didn't know."

When the fall term began in 1960, a small group of Negro parents and their children formed themselves into an all-or-nothing wedge to force their way out of Lincoln. They showed up at eight elementary schools with preponderantly all-white enrollment, demanding to register their children. They were refused. After a sitdown at one school they were given summonses for loitering. Within a few days the school board's attorney filed neglect charges against the strikers for "failing to send their children to school in accordance with the compulsory attendance law."

Now it was everybody's issue and it soon developed into a war of every person's fears, convictions and prejudices. An NAACP leader told a meeting of white parents that, unless Negro children were taken into white schools, he would "come through you like a bulldozer." A Negro woman principal was repeatedly called "Aunt Jemima" for supporting the referendum because she felt that the Negroes in the Lincoln School did not have the socioeconomic background to compete with the students in the north end of town. PTA meetings in the all-white sections turned into yelling matches where the clearest sounds to be heard were soaring exchanges of "bigot" and "Communist," "fascist" and "fathead."

Matters might have tapered off in mere vituperation if it had not been for the dedicated involvement of an outsider. He was Paul Zuber, a tall, tough, articulate young Negro lawyer who had already won a civil rights dispute with the New York City school board. Zuber, representing the Negro parents who challenged the Lincoln proposal, has learned to welcome any tool and so the split among the whites interested him. But he did not count upon the split for really substantial strategic help.

"Of course we get support from white liberals," Zuber said. "But it tends to fade off when they realize integration could also get to *their* street. One white woman thought it over and told me, 'I really don't see what our children can have in common. We take ours to Florida for Christmas.' "

Zuber, a gentle and friendly man in private but a battering ram in matters concerning Negro civil rights, knew exactly how he intended to fight his fight in New Rochelle.

"We'll get them into court," he said. "Demonstrations are for babies. You can go out there and march up and down with placards and sing *We Shall Overcome* till you fall down. The other side comes out and yells 'Two, Four, Six, Eight, We don't wanna integrate!' . . . a Mexican standoff. But in court only one man can talk at a time and one man in front of a judge is just as big as a whole damn school board."

He couldn't have been more right. On Jan. 24, 1961, U.S. District Judge Irving Kaufman—rendering a landmark decision—found down the line for the plaintiffs. The New Rochelle board of education, he ruled, had gerrymandered the Lincoln district to keep the Negroes in and, by pursuing the "neighborhood school policy," it had violated the constitutional rights of Lincoln pupils under the 14th Amendment.

The judge ordered the board to offer a plan for desegregation of the school. But the board, which had ignored the racial overbalance at the school in the past and the fact that over an extended period white pupils—but no Negroes—had been allowed to transfer from Lincoln to other schools, kept up its fight for the "neighborhood school" concept. In a stubborn refusal to accept the Kaufman decision, the board decided to carry their argument to higher courts. Three of the nine board members voted against appeal, but the board petitioned all the way to the U.S. Supreme Court—and lost all the way.

That was the end of Lincoln Elementary. Within two years the school was torn down. All that remained was a place where Negro children still assemble in the morning to board their buses for schools all over town.

Lincoln Elementary was dead but the effect of its passing was only beginning to spread through town. Like every other northern city, New Rochelle and its schools would have felt the impact of the drive for Negro equality even without the fight over the school. But the legacy of Lincoln made a difference. An angry minority, battling for its civil rights, had taken on the local establishment and beaten it hands down. And an establishment, once beaten, can be beaten again.

The question was how would the momentum of this new force be directed in New Rochelle? In the next five years, it seemed to be guided more by a severe case of bitterness over old wounds than by any newly acquired sense of responsibility for the welfare of the community as a whole.

In the five-year period New Rochelle's board of education, appointed by the mayor ("When you talked, they made jokes and didn't hear," a Negro leader said of the board) had 10 changes of membership. The turnover in the school administration itself was even more telling. There were three different principals of the senior high school. There were three school superintendents. One superintendent heard from a civil rights militant, "We brought you and we can send you away."

Individuals were able to borrow from the massed vigor. One outraged Negro mother, whose daughter had been sent home for getting into a fight, took the little girl to school the next morning and marched into the principal's office to announce, "I've brought T——— back; she's going to stay back or I'll break your neck." The child stayed.

But the most painful inheritance from Lincoln Elementary was the climate created for the children. In the beginning the struggle had been an adults' contest. But now the children took over from their elders and carried the challenge to constituted authority into the classroom—to nobody's benefit. So began a siege on campus, fought mainly in the junior and senior high schools.

"These kids come in here with a chip on the shoulder," said a faculty member. "They're primed to take offense. You can't keep telling a kid at home that he's the victim of discrimination and expect him not to look for discrimination—and find it whether it's there or not."

The defiant students, aware of the distemper of their elders, knew they could count on adult support when they needed it. And they soon learned that, under pressure, authority—the faculty and the board of education—would back down.

The board itself, ready to acknowledge concern over affairs in the nation's schools generally, shied away from admitting that these problems were particularly pressing at home. Said the board on one occasion: "Throughout the country, parents, teachers and school administrators are becoming increasingly concerned with the maintenance of law and order and respect for adult authority . . . in our public schools. The present unrest and the problems of maintaining good attendance and conduct at our own high school should be viewed in this perspective. Disturbing as it is to us, the behavior of a very small percentage of the New Rochelle students, both white and Negro, is not peculiar to this city."

Some teachers began to agree with the students that the administration was caving in under pressure. A young woman teacher who was cussed at by a pupil in the hall marched him off to his guidance counselor. The boy admitted his profane outburst while the counselor frowned his disapproval and said nothing. The boy shrewdly regarded both teacher and counselor, then with a grin simply turned and walked out, leaving the teacher to sputter her indignation.

"What can you do?" the counselor shrugged. "That's the way *they* are. Let's not make waves."

Student discipline began to deteriorate and, along with it, faculty morale. "School master" is an old and honorable title; but New Rochelle's teachers began to feel they were no longer masters in their own schools.

Faculty members found themselves involved in incidents that might have passed as ordinary breakdowns in discipline—except that too often they took on racial complications. Although the more outrageous acts of defiance and law-breaking were committed by a relatively small group of easily identified hooligans, the example they set encouraged hundreds of other students to disobedience and infected the whole school.

▶ An 18-year-old boy, an 11th grader, swore at a teacher who was trying to herd him and others into their homeroom. Then he disappeared. Around noon the same day he was found and taken to the principal's office. There was liquor on his breath; the boy slouched down in his chair and stared back at the principal.

"Where were you?" the official asked. "Home, sick," the boy said.

"No, you weren't. I called your mother. Where were you?"

The boy lounged deeper, thought a while, then spoke. "If you're so damned smart, you tell me where I was." And so the boy was suspended for five days—the legal limit without board of education sanction.

The boy's mother asked CORE for help. CORE representatives met with school officers three times to discuss the case. Finally, the principal showed them the boy's past record, with 28 teacher complaints about his behavior. At least one CORE representative thought the use of the boy's past record was unethical.

"You're prejudiced, aren't you?" the delegate said.

▶ At a high school football game, a coach spotted a boy in a sweat-shirt stolen from the school's athletic supplies. The coach grabbed the youngster, but was immediately surrounded by other boys, yelling at him to get his hands off the offender. The situation teetered on the edge of explosion until the coach marched the boy away and told him to turn in the pilfered shirt the next day. But when the boy failed to appear, the coach went for advice to a faculty friend, who asked, "Does this involve race?" The coach said no, it involved school property." "Negro?" he was asked. "Yes," said the coach.

"Drop it," the faculty member said. "If you try to get that shirt back, you'll be alone."

The coach appealed to the boy's assistant principal, anyway, and asked him to help recover the shirt. A few days later the assistant principal called to say that he had had the boy in his office. "He admits he took the shirt," the assistant principal told the coach. "But he won't give it back." And with that the administrator simply hung up.

▶ Two white girls rushed into the senior high principal's office and reported that some Negro girls were brandishing knives in one of the lavatories. The principal, a custodian and a teacher took stations outside the door and, with the custodian holding it open, ordered the occupants out. After some scurrying and laughter, a dozen girls, Negro and white, appeared. The white girls were allowed to leave, but the Negroes were taken to an adjacent room, where a teacher searched their purses. She got three knives and a partly filled bottle of liquor. The police were called but made no arrests. Later the girls were suspended.

Prompt protest came from civil rights leaders. The principal's phone began ringing; his callers accused him of invading the girls' lavatory, of searching them personally, of invading their civil rights. The principal later admitted he had been "tactless" in having only the Negro girls searched. A demand for a public apology was sent to the superintendent. The Negro girls' defenders explained that the girls needed the knives to protect themselves when they walked home, past a nearby car-wash emporium whose attendants were forward.

As they have in so many places in recent years, home football games became occasions of such hazard that New Rochelle police and faculty "goon squads"—as they described themselves and getting $10 each for extra duty—were needed to stop gate-crashing and prevent all sorts of violence and abuse during and after the games. The principal, with binoculars, always surveyed the scene from the roof of a nearby school building and at game's end an assistant principal patrolled the field on the jump seat of a cop's motorcycle.

Student outlawry ran through most of the forms young and active imaginations devise. There were cases of extortion by big kids from little ones; most of the demands were petty but a few involved large sums of money. ("Give, or I'll use this can opener on you! Jump up and down and jingle and I'll know how much you have!") The lavatories especially took a beating—from vandals, from fights, from fires, from cherry bombs. "They finally took all the mirrors out; mirrors are dangerous," a student said. A mother, who moved away from New Rochelle because of the school situation, said: "The toilets are where they can get hurt. I trained my kids not to go to the toilet at school; they can wait until they get home."

The students' favorite form of eluding authority—and education at the same time—was to reach school late or not at all. One senior homeroom of 30 members recorded 320 cases of lateness or absence between school opening and Christmas, and one student showed up only twice all semester.

Senior high absenteeism ran up to 600 cases a day—the past average had been around 250—and the school racked up a record of 23,000 students late or absent in the 1964–65 school year.

Teachers were treated with insolence often, ignored frequently, defied on occasion. Seldom were they actually assaulted, but there were exceptions. An elderly male teacher entered a classroom just in time to see a strange Negro boy getting ready to heave a heavy wastebasket at one of the students. He yelled and then grappled with the boy, who dropped the basket and began hammering his fists into the teacher. The racket brought a guidance counselor and several women teachers. The boy was finally wrestled into the hall and to an assistant dean's office. The dean, charged with student discipline but conscious of previous experience, listened to a description of the incident and announced that the boy would be sent home. The outraged teachers demanded that the boy be prosecuted for assault. He was brought to trial on a charge of assault and disorderly conduct. The assault charge was later dropped and the boy, already on probation under a four-year suspended sentence for robbery, pleaded guilty to disorderly conduct. He was given the maximum sentence of 30 days.

Some of the hell-raisers enjoyed distinct advantages. One white pupil, brought to book for school arson, stood mute before an assistant principal. His father, he said, had instructed him that if he ever got into trouble he should refuse to talk until he had his own lawyer. Next day the boy's father telephoned to let the school know that, if the authorities intended to press the matter, he himself would testify that his son hadn't even been in school the day of the fire.

On a basis of proportion it rings oddly that the hoodlums in New Rochelle's school population could have disconcerted the process of education as much as they did. New Rochelle is a concentrated system with 2,900 in the senior high, 1,800 in one junior high, 1,050 in the other. The genuine malefactors were relatively few. And they were not all Negroes by any means; they scarcely could be in a school population where Negroes numbered less than one-fifth. Faculty, who had to deal with the rebels, estimated that the senior high contained only about 100 really hard-core incorrigibles. But those 100 were active and—worse—they attracted the hero worship of many others who were too eager to experiment with slightly milder forms of outlawry.

The vast majority of the school population—white and Negro alike—remained law-abiding citizens, as intent upon getting an education as any other group of individuals. But the hooligans levied a price upon the lawabiding. The first and most obvious damage to all was that the faculty became so preoccupied with maintaining order that the teachers' real function—teaching—had to suffer. One faculty member who finally gave up in frustration commented in her resignation, "I studied to teach English; if I had wanted to be a social worker, I'd have studied that."

"I try to handle every case as an individual and never as a matter of race," another teacher said. "But it won't work when the kid involved is a Negro. Land on a Negro pupil and the civil rights people land on you. I'm a teacher; part of what I'm supposed to teach is that order is essential to civilization. But am I teaching that—if I see kids raising hell in the halls and I have to stop before cooling it off and wonder whether I'm setting off a race crisis?"

In the autumn of 1963 the board of education had installed a new principal in the senior high. He was Dr. John Kelley, a peppery, no-nonsense educator who spent 23 years in public schooling and had an enviable reputation as an administrator. For a while Dr. Kelley felt that things were going well and that, within a couple of years, he could overcome the discipline problem and restore the school to its former place as "one of the finest secondary schools in the country." But early in the next school year, a Negro faculty member warned Dr. Kelley that, by his outspoken firmness, he had offended the civil rights activists and they intended to "get" him. It took time, but in the end Dr. Kelley was "got."

Over a span of five months, 26 students—12 white, 14 Negro—were suspended for various misdeeds. A delegation called the Westchester Joint Committee on Equal Opportunity—representing CORE, the NAACP and four other Negro organizations—decided to act and went to the board of education with a call for Dr. Kelley's "immediate removal."

The group caused to be read a statement resounding with such phrases as: ". . . treatment which minority-group children receive in public schools tends strongly and tragically to be, in effect, not only 'separate' but not 'equal' either . . . board has the immediate responsibility of removing the unwilling and ineffective administrative personnel . . . actions of Dr. Kelly (sic) are arbitrary and capricious . . . serious breaks in his [Dr. Kelley's] judgment. . . . Dr. Kelly's handling is punitive and retaliatory . . . when 75% of disciplinary problems are designated by Dr. Kelly as coming from Negroes, who are less than 17% of the school population, then there is critical need for review of the teachers' obvious failure to motivate and understand their students . . . our strong and unyielding opinion that his unsatisfactory and unprecedented performance as principal mandates his replacement. . . ."

The statement also included this passage: "We find also . . . the presence of unfounded and irrational fear, shown by white teachers, of well-developed, physically fit, attractive, well-dressed young Negro male adolescents, particularly when they are expressive and assertive."

Against this assault, Dr. Kelley got impressive support. The faculty, which included 11 Negro teachers, and all the custodial staff, largely Negro, signed a statement of support that ran in the daily New Rochelle *Standard Star*.

The high school paper, the *Huguenot Herald,* commented: "His [Dr. Kelley's] loss to the high school would be incalculable. . . . To tamper with this [the power to suspend] would be to create so chaotic a situation that learning and living at New Rochelle high school would be impossible. . . . Students who are not capable of living in the school environment should not be permitted to disrupt it for the majority. . . ."

But this support did Dr. Kelley little tangible good. Within 14 weeks he was out, ostensibly after a voluntary resignation—which few really believed.

"We got him. We could get another if we needed to," a CORE activist said later.

Even before Dr. Kelley left, the lack of effective discipline and rehabilitation attempts was deliberately dramatized at a special board meeting in a confrontation between a group of teachers, on the one hand, and the board and the then superintendent, on the other.

A teacher staged this interrogation of Dr. Kelley:

TEACHER: Dr. Kelley, isn't it true that we have had students found with knives in this school?
DR. KELLEY: Yes.
TEACHER: Isn't it true that we have had students found intoxicated in this school?
DR. KELLEY: Yes.
TEACHER: Isn't it true that certain students assaulted other students in school in the presence of witnesses?
DR. KELLEY: Yes.
TEACHER: Isn't it true that these students are back in school?
DR. KELLEY: It would be accurate to say they never left.

In such an atmosphere of "getting" and being "got" there were no winners, but losers abounded. And it was a distasteful paradox of his and the school's condition that the New Rochelle youngster who needed education most—the so-called "disadvantaged child"—lost most.

The term "disadvantaged child" seems to have been manufactured to avoid giving offense in a climate where many stand more than ready to take offense. The way things are, the "disadvantaged child" today is most frequently Negro. The nature of his disadvantagement varies with the individual; but, in practice, it most often means a Negro child from an impoverished, broken-home background, where hopelessness and bitter resentment are the large character-shaping influences. This is a youngster whose only real chance hitherto came through some miracle of luck or pluck.

How ironic, then, that the very pressure of the civil rights drive sometimes worked to the further disadvantage of the already disadvantaged. Swept up in the movement—with its legitimate hunger for full equality, right now, in American society—the people could not tolerate an admission that many of its children were not as ready for existing educational systems as their counterparts from fuller backgrounds.

In New Rochelle the civil rights militants preferred to blame the school system alone for failing to overcome the fundamental social and economic disadvantages of many Negro children. They appeared to feel that a conspiracy in the system was deliberately designed to betray the Negro child.

"There is a definite, conscious intent to keep the Negro male ignorant," declared a Negro minister in New Rochelle. "It is fine for him to play football, but he is encouraged to take the line of least resistance. They [the white establishment] want him so he can't go to anybody's college.

"Education is often slanted for the advantaged child," said a Negro woman psychologist there. "More attention must be given to the children the school doesn't seem able to reach. . . . The teachers must be creative enough to motivate these kids.

"Along with the problems [the Negro child] brings from home are the new problems he encounters in his teachers. Many [teachers] are definitely prejudiced. They seem to ask, 'What can be expected of him?' There is a basic contempt for the Negro child among some teachers."

And it was on this point that constructive dialogue in New Rochelle seriously broke down. "They will never understand that the school is looking for talent, not trying to stifle it," a teacher said. "How the hell am I supposed to motivate a kid I never see more than three times between school opening and Christmas?"

The suspicions, coupled with the common parental inclination to push a child too soon and too hard, often plunged the Negro student in over his head. And then, too often, he sank.

"A man in my job used to carry a lot of weight," said one guidance counselor in New Rochelle. "His function was to analyze a student's needs and capacities. He had the student's school record, his test scores and personal interviews to work with. Then, along with department heads, he would advise the student what courses he ought to take—and, in most cases, that's what he would do.

"It doesn't work that way any more. For instance, Negro girls shy away from home economics; they suspect you're trying to trap them into being domestics. Negro boys don't much want vocational school. The pressure is on them to shoot for white-collar jobs—that is, the ones who are serious about school at all. So the parents and civil rights people insist that a child go into the college preparatory program, the toughest regimen the school has to offer. And that, by golly, is where he goes.

"This is fine—if . . . if he has soaked up enough education to handle it. But if he isn't ready for CP, he soon discovers they might as well be speaking Sanskrit for all he understands. He's flabbergasted and left with nothing much to do but stare at the blackboard or start cutting classes. By the end of the semester, he's ready to be a dropout."

One Negro mother of 10 wanted to send her oldest son through the high school business course; but, suspicious that the school would prejudge him as unqualified, went to the school and "really sat on" the boy's guidance counselor: "They didn't want to give him a chance. Wanted to say ahead of time that he couldn't pass the course."

The counselor surrendered and the boy went where his mother wanted him to go. But he didn't stay long. The mother's explanation: "He was bored. The teachers didn't try to get him interested. He would rather stay in his room and play records. Then he dropped out of school. But he's back now. The Army was going to draft him if he wouldn't go to school."

When asked what had gone wrong to bring her fight for her sons's rights to this sorry end, she said, "I don't know. The children are confused, the parents are confused, the teachers are confused. It just makes a big mess."

Confusion over how to reach a workable, livable, acceptable and fruitful human condition in the nation's schools is hardly limited to New Rochelle. It is only that New Rochelle has had longer and, because of the exacerbation of Lincoln Elementary, possibly more intense experience with the struggle. (Mount Vernon, a cheek-by-jowl Westchester County neighbor of New Rochelle's is right now at the point of anger and bitter no-compromise that New Rochelle was in five years ago. The measure of the bitterness in Mount Vernon was reached a few weeks ago when an enraged CORE spokesman railed at his neighbors that Hitler didn't kill enough of them.)

But in New Rochelle, forced to be a pathfinder in the North, there are beginning to be reasons to rejoice, to nourish hope that, given time, the matter can be resolved. It has not been easy, but progress has been made.

The board of education has created a human relations committee and given it a franchise to hunt out avenues of inter-racial communication. A government "Headstart" program has been instituted within the school system; the idea is to catch children young—under kindergarten age—and demonstrate to them early that education is the thing that must be got.

The PTAs have concluded that they were going at their mission backwards. "Regular meetings get the regular customers. Same people, same speeches, same agenda," a PTA leader said. "We weren't getting anywhere near the people we really needed to reach. Some people are uncomfortable, feel out of place in a big PTA meeting, and some people had never even heard of PTA. We had to go out and get them."

Using the techniques of a door-to-door brush salesman they began to attract more parents. The newcomers were invited to small, intimate kaffeeklatsches in private homes.

"I enjoy those little meetings," a Negro mother said. "No speeches to listen to. I've heard so many speeches I can tune them out, the same way my kids tune me out when they don't want to listen. But in these little groups you can find out things about the schools—and about kids—that are of some use to you."

A group of New Rochelle women started a Volunteer Tutoring Program. These women went into the schools and with advice from the teacher of those students who were having trouble, both academically and emotionally, went to work on them on a one-to-one basis. To prepare themselves, the women had to take courses in the new math and, because the schools were crowded, they sometimes found themselves holding class in the boiler room. The tutors' program eventually had 65 members handling a case load of 136 kids, 103 of them Negroes, from grades 1 to 12.

The high school faculty has agitated to modernize the curriculum for the approximately 12% of the student body who are unable or unwilling to cope with the vocational, business or college preparatory courses. They have also lobbied for a remedial reading program, special classes for the emotionally out-of-kilter and psychological help for those in need of it. These have been tentative steps—and well short of the need—but they have been steps and there has been detectable positive response from the civil rights side of the fence.

"Things are better," Paul Dennis, head of the New Rochelle NAACP chapter, said recently. "Now we have a school board that will listen—not just a stone wall. And there are other improvements in the town and outside the schools. We're getting jobs for Negroes, jobs that were never open to us before."

Even a year ago nobody among the civil rights activists could have afforded to admit that the burden of order and education could rest anywhere but on the schools. Even that has changed—a little.

"The children do have to fight for their rights. They're entitled to that and they're bound to do it," one formerly uncompromising leader said. "They have to strike back when they're discriminated against. But also I know they have to learn respect for the institution, the school system itself. That begins at home."

It may have begun. In the last few months the school system, which for too many years was intimidated by the civil rights pressures, has gradually been putting its house in order. Discipline is now being enforced more stringently and consistently. Two new disciplinary officers have been appointed. Students away from their classes are required to carry cards certifying their right to be abroad. Some of the most lawless have been suspended or expelled. Among those kicked out were several of a kind once considered "untouchable"—including the son of a civil rights leader. No organized protests have been brought in their behalf.

At its essence, the ordeal that the New Rochelle schools underwent, and from which they are now painfully emerging, was a crisis of human relations—the unwillingness and inability to understand, the unwillingness and inability to take responsibility. If the Negro community was defiant in its striving for its civil rights, the white community was complacent in the face of social change.

It may be that the community's best hope lies in the students themselves. Though they fought the system, they never did fight one another except in odd and isolated instances. Students, after all, are what the schools are all about—they and the kind of education they get or don't get. An essential element of that education is, again, human relations. The youngsters of New Rochelle, with the example of the struggle their elders had waged, were offered on a silver platter an invitation to wage race war inside the schools. But they have ignored that invitation.

"Once in a while somebody will yell 'Paleface' or 'Whitey' and mean it nasty, but not often. Or somebody will write hate-Negro stuff on a toilet wall," said a Negro student who is a class officer. "Or a Negro girl will say you are a snob because you have white friends, too. But those are exceptions. I have as many white friends as Negro, and some of the whites I'm more comfortable with than *some* of the Negroes."

There it is—the dividend: the kind of practicing humanity that too many adults are too old and ornery to take upon themselves.

DISCUSSION QUESTIONS

1. Was the confrontation of Negroes and whites in New Rochelle and the conflicts growing out of this confrontation an inevitable step in the development of relationships between Negroes and whites in our society?
2. What preparatory courses of action would you suggest the Board of Education and the Administration of the schools might have taken so that the confrontation might have been made on a different level?
3. Evaluate the steps the school eventually took to accommodate and meet the needs of its Negro children in terms of their cost, adequacy, and timing.
4. Do you agree with the author's estimate of Dr. Kelley's leadership in his crisis role?

CHAPTER 5 *Religion*

Religion is an integral part of our culture and our history. The drama of the founding of the colonies has religionists as its protagonists: Protestants in New England, Catholics in Maryland, Quakers in Pennsylvania, and a host of others elsewhere.

From the beginning, education in the colonies served the cause of religion; the first schools were church schools, established to give religious education. Thayer says of the Massachusetts Educational Act of 1647 that "it reflected more the determination of colonial officials to insure orthodoxy in religion than the stirrings of a democratic conscience."[1]

Education in colonial times "attempted no more than to develop 'an ability to read and to understand the principles of religion and the capital laws of the country.' "[2] Today, while religious education still claims large numbers of adherents, the nature of education is predominantly secular. Pragmatic themes, status, wealth, and vocational preparation looming largely among them, are of major concern.

Perhaps as a reaction to the narrowness and sterility of modern life, young people have become increasingly disenchanted with the affluent society. Many have turned to political activity, out of high ethical and moral principle. Others have joined Vista and the Peace Corps. There are evangelical overtones in the fervor and the dedication of their commitment to render service to mankind. The values displayed are the deep concern of education, but they are part too of the religious sentiment and tradition

---

[1] V. T. Thayer, *Formative Ideas in American Education,* Dodd, Mead, & Co., Inc. New York, 1965, p. 4.
[2] *Ibid.*

that has always been present in American life. Education is never far from religion; the question may be raised whether religion is, or should be, part of education.

Should the state provide financial support for religious schools, to insure and to strengthen religion's contribution to American life? Would such aid be divisive and destructive of the American social fiber? Exactly what does separation of church and state mean? The issue of religion and education is by no means settled, as a reading of the latest Supreme Court decision and any local paper at Christmas time will make obvious. The doubt arises that it ever will be.

SAM DUKER

The Public Schools and Religion

The Supreme Court of the United States occupies a unique role in our society. No parallel to this role can be found in any other time or place. Nine men, appointed for life by the President with the consent of the Senate, have the responsibility for setting social policy in many areas without authority to do so except insofar as this social policy is determined by their legal interpretation of the laws and the Constitution of the United States in the light of present-day needs. Unless the Court itself reverses its ruling in a later case, an event which happens very rarely, there is, in the last analysis, only one appeal from a Supreme Court decision and that is to the process of amending the Constitution. This process is long, difficult, and infrequently successful. The word of the Supreme Court is, therefore, in most cases the final one. It must be accepted, graciously or ungraciously as the case may be, by all other components of American society.

It is not at all surprising that many of the major constitutional decisions of the Supreme Court are unpopular when one considers that it is almost invariably a minority that seeks the protection of its constitutional rights. It is worth noting that in each of the 12 cases excerpted it was a minority group that brought about the Court's decision. Because the protection of the minority so frequently involves the majority, there is often a pained outcry. While the Supreme Court proceeds with great caution and seeks to avoid meeting any issue except when it becomes necessary, it has always been the view of this body that no entering wedge shall be allowed in the matter of a clear violation of a constitutional right.

REVIEW OF THE CASES EXCERPTED

In *Meyer* v. *Nebraska* the issue presented was the validity of a state law prohibiting the teaching of foreign languages in the nonpublic elementary schools. Clearly, it was the majority sentiment in those states passing such laws that Americanization would be promoted by such laws. As has been previously noted, no direct religious question was raised, but actually the schools involved were almost all religiously supported and operated. The Supreme Court held these laws to be beyond the constitutional powers of a state and thus preserved the rights of private schools, whether religiously oriented or not, to determine the content of their curricula. This decision

Reprinted from Sam Duker, *The Public Schools and Religion: The Legal Context* (New York: Harper & Row, Publishers, Inc., 1966), pp. 214–220, with permission of the publisher.

did not imply any impotence on the part of the state in the matter of requiring inclusion of material in that curriculum but dealt solely with exclusion.

In *Pierce* v. *Society of Sisters,* the law requiring all children to attend public school had been adopted by a clear majority of the voters of the State of Oregon. While it is true that this law did not single out religious schools, it was clear to all concerned that religiously oriented schools were the target. Here, as in the *Meyer* case, no mention was made either in the arguments or in the Court's decision of the First Amendment, but in later cases the point is made over and over again that because of this case there is no justification for religious instruction or exercises in the public school classroom.

The only cases decided by the Supreme Court that concern the question of "free exercise" and the schools are those involving compulsory saluting of the flag. Once more it was an expression of the majority will that brought about the adoption of laws and regulations requiring all public school pupils to participate in giving the Pledge of Allegiance to the Flag. The members of the Jehovah's Witnesses sect who found participation in this ceremony to be in conflict with their religious beliefs represented a very small sector of our population. A sharp difference is found between these cases and the *Engel* and *Schempp* cases. Here the Supreme Court held that excusing the objecting children from participation was all that was required, but in the subsequent cases involving devotional exercises the Court held that excusal did not serve to adequately protect the rights of the minority group. The reason for the different holdings clearly lies in the fact that the flag salute cases involved the Free Exercise Clause of the First Amendment while the prayer cases turned on an interpretation of the Establishment Clause.

Just as excusal was held insufficient protection of constitutional rights in the later prayer cases, so in *McCollum* excusal was held not to properly protect the rights of the small minority who did not wish to participate in sectarian religious instruction given in the public school classroom during school hours. The *Zorach* case also involved the appeal of a minority but in this case the ruling was in favor of the majority when the Court held dismissal from school for the purpose of attending sectarian religious instruction elsewhere during school hours to be constitutionally unobjectionable.

The *Cochran* case which did not turn on the First Amendment and the *Everson* case which the Court used as an occasion for its most thorough analysis of the Establishment Clause established the important principle of "child-benefit." It is, of course, obvious that any help, financial or otherwise, given to a parochial school child tends directly or indirectly to aid the parochial school itself as this then becomes a service that that school need not render. By the same token, when the government assumes an expense that would otherwise be a parental one, the parochial school is benefited at least indirectly by the resulting greater share of parental resources available to it. It is, however, exceedingly difficult to draw the line between a governmental expenditure on behalf of the child and one on behalf of the parochial school. Extremes are easily interpreted but in the middle group this becomes an exceedingly sticky question. A few more words will be said about the child-benefit theory later in this chapter.

The last four cases excerpted here deal with devotional exercises in the public school classroom. *Engel* v. *Vitale* stirred the most controversy but actually the decision in that case was the mildest and most restricted of the four. Considerable doubt existed for a year after the decision as to whether the Court would or would not extend the doctrine of that case. *Engel* turned largely on the fact that the prayer in question had been composed by a state agency and there was no intimation one way or another as to the Court's views on Bible reading or on prayers not composed by state agencies.

Schempp and *Murray* squarely presented the Court with the validity of Bible reading and praying in the public school classroom. The Court unequivocably held such activities violative of the Establishment Clause of the First Amendment. Surprisingly, the reaction to the decision in these cases was not nearly so furious and volatile as the reaction had been to *Engel*. This does not imply that it was a popular decision or that the groups reacting unfavorably to *Engel* had been won over.

The *Chamberlin* case presented many issues about which there had been and still are great uncertainties, but in the last analysis the final decision dealt only with prayers and Bible reading and thus did not extend or restrict the *Schempp* ruling in any way whatsoever. The principal point of interest in this case lies in the byplay between the Florida Supreme Court's anxiety to display its deep-seated disagreement with the Supreme Court of the United States' interpretation of the Establishment Clause and the Supreme Court's summary disposition of the case on two separate occasions.

The 12 cases included in this book show the result of a chain of reasoning in which, to a remarkable degree, each case gives support to the decision in the following one. It must be borne in mind, however, that the view contrary to the one adopted by the Court was upheld by learned counsel and almost invariably by one or more members of the Court itself. To say that these decisions were foreordained as an indisputable matter of logic or reasoning would be rash indeed.

It can be argued that the series of decisions tends to have a unifying effect on society in that diversity of opinion is respected and protected. It can also be argued that these decisions have had the effect of polarizing the viewpoints of the factions of society holding varying points of view as to the proper relationship between religion and the public school. Time will have to pass before a fair judgment can be made as to which of these arguments has the most validity. We are now too close to the events to gain the necessary perspective.

CRITERIA EMPLOYED BY THE COURT

Everson, the released time cases, and the prayer cases all rest on the Court's interpretation of the Establishment Clause of the First Amendment which states: "Congress shall make no law respecting an establishment of religion." A great portion of the decisions in these cases deal with attempted analysis of the intentions of the "Founding Fathers" when they inserted this provision into our Bill of Rights. There certainly is no incontrovertible evidence available as to exactly what these intentions were. It is clear that at the time of the drafting and the adoption of the Bill of Rights there was considerable concern lest the newly created federal government usurp greater powers than its constituents intended to bestow upon it. It is also evident that there was strong feeling against the formation by that federal government of a state church supported by taxes and imposed on an unwilling populace.

There had been a great deal written about the intended strength of the concept referred to as the "wall of separation" between church and state, if indeed at the time that concept was generally accepted—which seems very doubtful. From extensive reading in this area one can only conclude that most of our Founding Fathers, if not all of them, would have been amazed at the interpretation now placed on this phrase. This does not mean, however, that they would necessarily be out of sympathy with this construction in the light of present-day conditions. It seems highly likely that men of the strong practical views of Madison and Jefferson would enthusiastically agree that the language of the Constitution should be interpreted in the light of existing conditions and current societal needs. The point would seem to be that the strongest support for the decisions in question does not necessarily come from the intentions of the framers of the Bill of Rights even if those intentions could be ascertained with any degree of certainty.

Similarly, without questioning the desirability of the interpretation given the Due Process Clause of the Fourteenth Amendment, it seems futile to seek historical evidence that its framers meant to incorporate the First Amendment's guarantees of religious freedom in the clause.

It is perfectly clear from the ruling of the Court on the five cases dealing with the Establishment Clause that there is no question about the interpretation of its meaning. There is an unequivocable and consistent view in these opinions to the effect that this clause demands an absolute separation between church and state. It seems most unlikely that the Court will, in the foreseeable future at least, depart to any extent from this view. The question that remains open is only whether a given activity impinges on this separation. In this respect it is not at all impossible that, in time, varying shades of interpretation may arise.

DISCUSSION QUESTIONS

1. Do you agree with the trend of the Supreme Court decisions concerning religion and education?
2. Should the basis for educational decision-making in matters affecting religion in the schools be pragmatic, ethical, or legal? Are these mutually exclusive?

Supreme Court of the United States

NO. 660.—OCTOBER TERM, 1967.

Board of Education of Central School District No. 1, etc., et al., Appellants, v. *James E. Allen, Jr., as Commissioner of Education of New York, et al.*	On Appeal From the Court of Appeals of New York.

[June 10, 1968.]

MR. JUSTICE WHITE delivered the opinion of the Court.

A law of the State of New York requires local public school authorities to lend textbooks free of charge to all students in grades seven through 12; students attending private schools are included. This case presents the question whether this statute is a "law respecting the establishment of religion or prohibiting the free exercise thereof," and so in conflict with the First and Fourteenth Amendments to the Constitution, because it authorizes the loan of textbooks to students attending parochial schools. We hold that the law is not in violation of the Constitution.

Until 1965, § 701 of the Educational Law of the State of New York authorized public school boards to designate textbooks for use in the public schools, to purchase such books with public funds, and to rent or sell the

The majority opinion of the Supreme Court and the separate dissenting opinion of Justice Douglas are offered here as indicative of the diversity and range of opinion in this case.

books to public school students.[1] In 1965 the Legislature amended § 701, basing the amendments on findings that the "public welfare and safety require that the state and local communities give assistance to educational programs which are important to our national defense and the general welfare of the state."[2] Beginning with the 1966–1967 school year, local school boards were required to purchase textbooks and lend them without charge "to all children residing in such district who are enrolled in grades seven to twelve of a public or private school which complies with the compulsory education law." The books now loaned are "text-books which are designated for use in any public, elementary or secondary schools of the state or are approved by any boards of education," and which—according to a 1966 amendment—"a pupil is required to use as a text for a semester or more in a particular class in the school he legally attends."[3]

Appellants, the members of the Board of Education of Central School District No. 1 in Rensselaer and Columbia Counties, brought suit in the New York courts against appellee James Allen.[4] The complaint alleged that § 701 violated both the State and Federal Constitutions; that if appellants, in reliance on their interpretation of the Constitution, failed to lend books to parochial school students within their counties appellee Allen would remove appellants from office; and that to prevent this, appellants were complying with the law and submitting to their constituents a school

---

[1] New York Sess. Laws 1950, c. 239, § 1. New York Education Law § 703, New York Sess. Laws 1950, c. 239, § 3, permitted the qualified voters of any school district to authorize a special tax for the purpose of making available free textbooks. The 1965 amendments that required free textbooks to be provided for grades seven through 12 amended § 703 so that it now permits local voters to approve free books for grades one through six.

[2] New York Sess. Laws 1965, c. 320, § 1.

[3] New York Education Law § 701 (1967 Supp.):

"1. In the several cities and school districts of the state, boards of education, trustees or such body or officer as perform the functions of such boards, shall designate text-books to be used in the schools under their charge.

"2. A text-book, for the purposes of this section shall mean a book which a pupil is required to use as a text for a semester or more in a particular class in the school he legally attends.

"3. In the several cities and school districts of the state, board of education, trustees or such body or officers as perform the function of such boards shall have the power and duty to purchase and to loan upon individual request, to all children residing in such district who are enrolled in grades seven to twelve of a public or private school which complies with the compulsory education law, text-books. Text-books loaned to children enrolled in grades seven to twelve of said private schools shall be text-books which are designated for use in any public, elementary or secondary schools of the state or are approved by any boards of education, trustees or other school authorities. Such text-books are to be loaned free to such children subject to such rules and regulations as are or may be prescribed by the board of regents and such boards of education, trustees or other school authorities."

The present subdivision (2) was added by amendment in 1966, New York Sess. Laws 1966, c. 795. This suit was filed, and the trial court opinion was rendered, prior to the 1966 amendment.

[4] Intervention was permitted on plaintiffs' side by the Board of Education of Union Free School District No. 3 in Nassau County, which appears here as co-appellant, and on defendants' side by parents of certain students attending private schools, who appear here as co-appellees.

budget including funds for books to be lent to parochial school pupils. Appellants therefore sought a declaration that § 701 was invalid, an order barring appellee Allen from removing appellants from office for failing to comply with it, and another order restraining him from apportioning state funds to school districts for the purchase of textbooks to be lent to parochial students. After answer, and upon cross-motions for summary judgment, the trial court held the law unconstitutional under the First and Fourteenth Amendments and entered judgment for appellants. 51 Misc. 2d 297, 273 N. Y. S. 2d 239 (1966). The Appellate Division reversed, ordering the complaint dismissed on the ground that appellant school boards had no standing to attack the validity of a state statute. 27 A. D. 2d 69, 276 N. Y. S. 2d 234 (1966). On appeal, the New York Court of Appeals concluded by a 4–3 vote that appellants did have standing[5] but by a different 4–3 vote held that § 701 was not in violation of either the State or the Federal Constitution. 20 N. Y. 2d 109, 228 N. E. 2d 791, 281 N. Y. S. 2d 799 (1967). The Court of Appeals said that the law's purpose was to benefit all school children, regardless of the type of school they attended, and that only textbooks approved by public school authorities could be loaned. It therefore considered § 701 "completely neutral with respect to religion, merely making available secular textbooks at the request of the individual student and asking no question about what school he attends." Section 701, the Court of Appeals concluded, is not a law which "establishes a religion or constitutes the use of public funds to aid religious schools." 20 N. Y. 2d, at 117; 228 N. E. 2d, at 794, 795; 281 N. Y. S. 2d, at 805. We noted probable jurisdiction. 389 U. S. 1031 (1968).

Everson v. *Board of Education,* 330 U. S. 1 (1947), is the case decided by this Court that is most nearly in point for today's problem. New Jersey reimbursed parents for expenses incurred in busing their children to parochial schools. The Court stated that the Establishment Clause bars a State from passing "laws which aid one religion, aid all religions, or prefer one religion over another," and bars too any "tax in any amount, large or small . . . levied to support any religious activities or institutions, whatever they may be called, or whatever form they may adopt to teach or practice religion." 330 U. S., at 15–16. Nevertheless, said the Court, the Establishment Clause does not prevent a State from extending the benefits of state laws to all citizens without regard for their religious affiliation and does not prohibit "New Jersey from spending tax-raised funds to pay the bus fares of parochial school pupils as part of a general program under

[5] Appellees do not challenge the standing of appellants to press their claim in this Court. Appellants have taken an oath to support the United States Constitution. Believing § 701 to be unconstitutional, they are in the position of having to choose between violating their oath and taking a step—refusal to comply with § 701—that would be likely to bring their expulsion from office and also a reduction in state funds for their school districts. There can be no doubt that appellants thus have a "personal stake in the outcome" of this litigation. *Baker* v. *Carr,* 369 U. S. 186, 204 (1962).

which it pays the fares of pupils attending public and other schools." The statute was held to be valid even though one of its results was that "children are helped to get to church schools" and "some of the children might not be sent to the church schools if the parents were compelled to pay their children's bus fares out of their own pockets." 330 U. S., at 17. As with public provision of police and fire protection, sewage facilities, and streets and sidewalks, payment of bus fares was of some value to the religious school, but was nevertheless not such support of a religious institution as to be a prohibited establishment of religion within the meaning of the First Amendment.

Everson and later cases have shown that the line between state neutrality to religion and state support of religion is not easy to locate. "The constitutional standard is the separation of Church and State. The problem, like many problems in constitutional law, is one of degree." *Zorach* v. *Clauson,* 343 U. S. 306, 314 (1952). See *McGowan* v. *Maryland,* 366 U. S. 420 (1961). Based on *Everson, Zorach, McGowan,* and other cases, *Abington School District* v. *Schempp,* 374 U. S. 203 (1963), fashioned a test ascribed to by eight Justices for distinguishing between forbidden involvements of the State with religion and those contacts which the Establishment Clause permits:

> The test may be stated as follows: what are the purpose and the primary effect of the enactment? If either is the advancement or inhibition of religion then the enactment exceeds the scope of legislative power as circumscribed by the Constitution. That is to say that to withstand the strictures of the Establishment Clause there must be a secular legislative purpose and a primary effect that neither advances nor inhibits religion. *Everson* v. *Board of Education.* 374 U. S., at 222.

This test is not easy to apply, but the citation of *Everson* by the *Schempp* Court to support its general standard made clear how the *Schempp* rule would be applied to the facts of *Everson.* The statute upheld in *Everson* would be considered a law having "a secular legislative purpose and a primary effect that neither advances nor inhibits religion." We reach the same result with respect to the New York law requiring school books to be loaned free of charge to all students in specified grades. The express purpose of § 701 was stated by the New York Legislature to be furtherance of the educational opportunities available to the young. Appellants have shown us nothing about the necessary effects of the statute that is contrary to its stated purpose. The law merely makes available to all children the benefits of a general program to lend school books free of charge. Books are furnished at the request of the pupil and ownership remains, at least technically, in the State. Thus no funds or books are furnished to parochial schools, and the financial benefit is to parents and children, not to schools.[6] Perhaps free

[6] While the record and the state court opinions in this case contained no information about how the books are in fact transferred from the Boards of Education to individual students, both parties suggested in their briefs and on oral argument before this Court

books make it more likely that some children choose to attend a sectarian school, but that was true of the state-paid bus fares in *Everson* and does not alone demonstrate an unconstitutional degree of support for a religious institution.

Of course books are different from buses. Most bus rides have no inherent religious significance, while religious books are common. However, the language of § 701 does not authorize the loan of religious books, and the State claims no right to distribute religious literature. Although the books loaned are those required by the parochial school for use in specific courses, each book loaned must be approved by the public school authorities; only secular books may receive approval. The law was construed by the Court of Appeals of New York as "merely making available secular textbooks at the request of the individual student," *supra,* and the record contains no suggestion that religious books have been loaned. Absent evidence we cannot assume that school authorities, who constantly face the same problem in selecting textbooks for use in the public schools, are unable to distinguish between secular and religious books or that they will not honestly discharge their duties under the law. In judging the validity of the statute on this record we must proceed on the assumption that books loaned to students are books that are not unsuitable for use in the public schools because of religious content.

The major reason offered by appellants for distinguishing free textbooks from free bus fares is that books, but not buses, are critical to the teaching process, and in a sectarian school that process is employed to teach religion. However this Court has long recognized that religious schools pursue two goals, religious instruction and secular education. In the leading case of *Pierce* v. *Society of Sisters,* 268 U. S. 510 (1925), the Court held that although it would not question Oregon's power to compel school attendance or require that the attendance be at an institution meeting State-imposed requirements as to quality and nature of curriculum, Oregon had not shown that its interest in secular education required that all children attend

---

that New York permits private schools to submit to boards of education summaries of the requests for textbooks filed by individual students, and also permits private schools to store on their premises the textbooks being loaned by the Board of Education to the students. This interpretation of the State's administrative procedure is supported by an "Opinion of Counsel" made available by the Board of Regents and the State Department of Education to local school superintendents. For purposes of this case we consider the New York statute to permit these procedures. So construing the statute, we find it in conformity with the Constitution, for the books are furnished for the use of individual students and at their request.

It should be noted that the record contains no evidence that any of the private schools in appellants' districts previously provided textbooks for their students. There is some evidence that at least some of the schools did not: intervenor defendants asserted that they had previously purchased all their children's textbooks. And see statement of then Commissioner of Education Keppel: "Nonpublic schools rarely provide free textbooks." I Hearings on Elementary and Secondary Education Act of 1965 before General Subcommittee on Education of House Committee on Education and Labor 93 (1965).

publicly operated schools. A premise of this holding was the view that the State's interest in education would be served sufficiently by reliance on the secular teaching that accompanied religious training in the schools maintained by the Society of Sisters. Since *Pierce,* a substantial body of case law has confirmed the power of the States to insist that attendance at private schools, if it is to satisfy state compulsory-attendance laws, be at institutions which provide minimum hours of instruction, employ teachers of specified training, and cover prescribed subjects of instruction.[7] Indeed, the State's interest in assuring that these standards are being met has been considered a sufficient reason for refusing to accept instruction at home as compliance with compulsory education statutes.[8] These cases were a sensible corollary of *Pierce* v. *Society of Sisters:* if the State must satisfy its interest in secular education through the instrument of private schools, it has a proper interest in the manner in which those schools perform their secular educational function. Another corollary was *Cochran* v. *Louisiana State Board of Education,* 281 U. S. 370 (1930), where appellants said that a statute requiring school books to be furnished without charge to all students, whether they attended public or private schools, did not serve a "public purpose," and so offended the Fourteenth Amendment. Speaking through Chief Justice Hughes, the Court summarized as follows its conclusion that Louisiana's interest in the secular education being provided by private schools made provision of textbooks to students in those schools a properly public concern: "[The State's] interest is education, broadly; its method,

---

[7] This Court has twice suggested the constitutionality of these state regulations. "[T]he State may 'require teaching by instruction and study of all in our history and in the structure and organization of our government, including the guaranties of civil liberty, which tend to inspire patriotism and love of country.'" *West Virginia State Board of Education* v. *Barnette,* 319 U. S. 624, 631 (1943), quoting *Minersville School District* v. *Gobitis,* 310 U.S. 586, 604 (1940) (Stone, J., dissenting). "This Court has said that parents may, in the discharge of their duty under state compulsory education laws, send their children to a religious rather than a public school if the school meets the secular educational requirements which the state has the power to impose." *Everson* v. *Board of Education,* 330 U. S. 1, 18 (1947) (citing *Pierce* v. *Society of Sisters*). A great many state cases have upheld a wide range of private school regulation. *E.g., Meyerkorth* v. *State,* 173 Neb. 889, 115 N. W. 2d 585 (1962), appeal dismissed for want of a substantial federal question, 372 U. S. 705 (1963); *State* v. *Hoyt,* 84 N. H. 38, 146 A. 170 (1929); *People* v. *Donner,* 199, Misc., 643, 99 N. Y. S. 2d 830 (Dom. Rel. Ct. 1950), aff'd mem., 278 App. Div. 705, 103 N. Y. S. 2d 757, aff'd men., 302 N. Y. 875, 100 N. E. 2d 48, appeal dismissed for want of a substantial federal question, 342 U. S. 884 (1951).

New York State regulates private schools extensively, especially as to attendance and curriculum. New York Education Law §§ 3201–3229 (1953). Regents examinations are given to private school students. *Id.,* § 209. The basic requirement is that the instruction given in private schools satisfying the compulsory attendance law be "at least substantially equivalent to the instruction given to minors of like age and attainments at the public schools of the city or district where the minor resides." *Id.,* § 3204 (2).

New York requires school attendance of "each minor seven to sixteen years of age" unless he has completed high school. *Id.,* § 3205.

[8] *E.g., People* v. *Turner,* 121 Cal. App. 2d 861, 263 P. 2d 685 (1953), appeal dismissed for want of a substantial federal question, 347 U. S. 972 (1954).

comprehensive. Individual interests are aided only as the common interest is safeguarded." 281 U. S., at 375.

Underlying these cases, and underlying also the legislative judgments that have preceded the court decisions, has been a recognition that private education has played and is playing a significant and valuable role in raising national levels of knowledge, competence, and experience. Americans care about the quality of the secular education available to their children. They have considered high quality education to be an indispensable ingredient for achieving the kind of nation, and the kind of citizenry, that they have desired to create. Considering this attitude, the continued willingness to rely on private school systems, including parochial systems, strongly suggests that a wide segment of informed opinion, legislative and otherwise, has found that those schools do an acceptable job of providing secular education to their students.[9] This judgment is further evidence that parochial schools are performing, in addition to their sectarian function, the task of secular education.

Against this background of judgment and experience, unchallenged in the meager record before us in this case, we cannot agree with appellants either that all teaching in a sectarian school is religious or that the processes of secular and religious training are so intertwined that secular textbooks furnished to students by the public are in fact instrumental in the teaching of religion. This case comes to us after summary judgment entered on the pleadings. Nothing in this record supports the proposition that all textbooks, whether they deal with mathematics, physics, foreign languages, history, or literature, are used by the parochial schools to teach religion. No evidence has been offered about particular schools, particular courses, particular teachers, or particular books. We are unable to hold, based solely on judicial notice, that this statute results in unconstitutional involvement of the State with religious instruction or that § 701, for this or the other reasons urged, is a law respecting the establishment of religion within the meaning of the First Amendment.

Appellants also contend that § 701 offends the Free Exercise Clause of the First Amendment. However, "it is necessary in a free exercise case for one to show the coercive effect of the enactment as it operates against him in the practice of his religion," *Abington School District* v. *Schempp,* 374 U. S. 203, 223 (1963), and appellants have not contended that the New York law in any way coerces them as individuals in the practice of their religion.

The judgment is affirmed.

[9] In 1966 in New York State, almost 900,000 students, or 21.5% of total state enrollment, attended nonpublic schools. University of State of New York, Education Statistics New York State, Table I (1968). The comparable statistic for the Nation was at least 10%. United States Bureau of the Census, Statistical Abstract of the United States: 1967, at 111 (1967).

Supreme Court of the United States

NO. 660.—OCTOBER TERM, 1967.

Board of Education of Central School District No. 1, etc., et al., Appellants, v. *James E. Allen, Jr., as Commissioner of Education of New York, et al.*	On Appeal From the Court of Appeals of New York.

[June 10, 1968.]

MR. JUSTICE DOUGLAS, dissenting.

We have for review a statute which authorizes New York State to supply textbooks to students in parochial as well as in public schools. The New York Court of Appeals sustained the law on the grounds that it involves only "secular textbooks" and that that type of aid falls within *Everson* v. *Board of Education,* 330 U.S. 1,[1] where a divided Court upheld a state law which made bus service available to students in parochial schools as well as to students in public schools. 20 N.Y. 2d 109, 281 N.Y.S. 2d 799, 228 N.E. 2d 791.

The statute on its face empowers each parochial school to determine for itself which textbooks will be eligible for loans to its students, for the Act provides that the only text which the State may provide is "a book which a pupil is required to use as a text for a semester or more in a particular class in the school he legally attends." N.Y. Educ. Law § 701 (2). This initial and crucial selection is undoubtedly made by the parochial school's principal or its individual instructors, who are, in the case of Roman Catholic schools, normally priests or nuns.

The next step under the Act is an "individual request" for an eligible textbook (§ 701 (3)), but the State Education Department has ruled that

[1] *Everson,* relied on by the Court of Appeals of New York, did not involve textbooks and did not present the serious problems raised by a form of aid to parochial students which injects religious issues into the choice of curriculum. In the only decision of this Court upholding a state grant of textbooks to sectarian school students, *Cochran* v. *Board of Education,* 281 U.S. 370, the First Amendment issue was not raised. See pp. 370–373; *Everson* v. *Board of Education,* 330 U.S. 1, 29, n. 3 (dissenting opinion).

a pupil may make his request to the local public board of education through a "private school official."[2] Local boards have accordingly provided for those requests to be made by the individual or "by groups or classes."[3] And forms for textbook requisitions to be filled out by the head of the private school are provided.[4]

The role of the local public school board is to decide whether to veto the selection made by the parochial school. This is done by determining first whether the text has been or should be "approved" for use in public schools and second whether the text is "secular," "nonreligious," or "non-sectarian."[5] The local boards apparently have broad discretion in exercising this veto power.[6]

Thus the statutory system provides that the parochial school will ask for the books that it wants. Can there be the slightest doubt that the head of the parochial school will select the book or books that best promote its sectarian creed?

If the board of education supinely submits by approving and supplying

---

[2] State Education Department, letter to school superintendents and principals dated January 10, 1966, by Herbert F. Johnson, ¶ 5.

[3] Manual of Instruction on Recordkeeping Procedures for Textbooks Loaned in Conformance With Provisions of the New York State Textbook Law, ¶ 2.3 (1967).

[4] See Appendix A to this opinion.

[5] The State Court of Appeals used the phrases "secular textbooks" and "nonreligious textbooks" without any elaboration as to what was meant. 20 N.Y. 2d, at 109; 281 N.Y.S. 2d, at 805; 228 N.E. 2d, at 794–795. The legislature, in its "statement of policy" to the Act (Laws of 1965, c. 320, § 1) speaks of aiding instruction in "nonsectarian subjects," and gives as examples "science, mathematics, [and] foreign languages." The State Department of Education has stated that "it is necessary that . . . [t]he textbooks be nonsectarian (this eliminates denominational editions and those carrying the 'imprimatur' or 'nihil obstat' of a religious authority) . . . ." Opinion of Counsel No. 181. There are no other definitions to be found.

The Court was advised at oral argument by the Assistant Attorney General that Opinion of Counsel No. 181 is advisory only and not binding. It would state the policy of the New York Department of Education in event of an appeal to it by a taxpayer of a local board's decision that a certain text was "nonsectarian" or should be "approved." The Regents of the State University, who have the last word on such matters and are specifically authorized by § 701 (3) to promulgate regulations respecting the textbook loan program, have not done so, and their position on what is "nonsectarian" is unknown.

[6] For example the regulations of the Board of Education of the City of New York respecting approval of textbooks for public schools contain no limitations directly relevant to the question of sectarianism. The material is to "promote the objectives of the educational program," "treat the subject competently and accurately," "be in good taste," "have a wholesome tone that is consonant with right conduct and civic values," "be in harmony with American democratic ideals and moral values," "be free of any reflection on the dignity and status of any group, race, or religion, whether expressed or implied, by statement or omission," and "be free of objectionable features of over-dramatization, violence, or crime." Guiding Principles for Schools in the Selection and Use of "Non-Listed" Instructional Materials (1952). Opinion of Counsel No. 181 (see n. 5, *supra*) simply states that the local board, if it finds that no other board has approved the text in question, should "decide if it wishes to approve the same itself." This opinion of counsel also states that if the board is in doubt as to whether a text is "nonsectarian," that is whether it carries an imprimatur or nihil obstat or is a denominational edition, it "must make the appropriate determination."

the sectarian or sectarian-oriented textbooks, the struggle to keep church and state separate has been lost. If the board resists, then the battleline between church and state will have been drawn and the contest will be on to keep the school board independent or to put it under church domination and control.

Whatever may be said of *Everson,* there is nothing ideological about a bus. There is nothing ideological about a school lunch, nor a public nurse, nor a scholarship. The constitutionality of such public aid to students in parochial schools turns on considerations not present in this textbook case. The textbook goes to the very heart of education in a parochial school. It is the chief, although not solitary, instrumentality for propagating a particular religious creed or faith. How can we possibly approve such state aid to a religion? A parochial school textbook may contain many, many more seeds of creed and dogma than a prayer. Yet we struck down in *Engel* v. *Vitale,* 370 U.S. 421, an official New York prayer for its public schools, even though it was not plainly denominational. For we emphasized the violence done the Establishment Clause when the power was given religious-political groups "to write their own prayers into law." *Id.,* at 427. That risk is compounded here by giving parochial schools the initiative in selecting the textbooks they desire to be furnished at public expense.

Judge Van Voorhis, joined by Chief Judge Fuld and Judge Breitel, dissenting below, said that the difficulty with the textbook loan program "is that there is no reliable standard by which secular and religious textbooks can be distinguished from each other." 20 N.Y. 2d, at 122; 281 N.Y.S. 2d, at 809; 228 N.E. 2d, at 798. The New York Legislature felt that science was a nonsectarian subject (see n. 5, *supra*). Does this mean that any general science textbook intended for use in grades 7–12 may be provided by the State to parochial school students? May John M. Scott's Adventures in Science (1963) be supplied under the textbook loan program? This book teaches embryology in the following manner:

> To you an animal usually means a mammal, such as a cat, dog, squirrel, or guinea pig. The new animal or embryo develops inside the body of the mother until birth. The fertilized egg becomes an embryo or developing animal. Many cell divisions take place. In time some cells become muscle cells, others nerve cells or blood cells, and organs such as eyes, stomach, and intestines are formed.
>
> The body of a human being grows in the same way, but it is much more remarkable than that of any animal, for the embryo has a human soul infused into the body by God. Human parents are partners with God in creation. They have very great powers and great responsibilities, for through their cooperation with God souls are born for heaven. (Pp. 618–619.) [7]

[7] Although the author of this textbook is a priest, the text contains no imprimatur and no nihil obstat. Although published by a Catholic press, the Loyola University Press, Chicago, it is not marked in any manner as a "denominational edition," but is simply the general edition of the book. Accordingly, under Opinion of Counsel No. 181, the only document approaching a "regulation" on the issue involved here, Adventures in Science would qualify as "non-sectarian." See nn. 5, 6, *supra.*

Comparative economics would seem to be a nonsectarian subject. Will New York, then, provide Arthur J. Hughes' general history text, Man in Time (1964), to parochial school students? It treats that topic in this manner:

Capitalism is an economic system based on man's right to private property and on his freedom to use that property in producing goods which will earn him a just profit on his investment. Man's right to private property stems from the Natural Law implanted in him by God. It is as much a part of man's nature as the will to self-preservation. (P. 560.)

. . . .

The broadest definition of socialism is government ownership of all the means of production and distribution in a country. . . . Many, but by no means all, Socialists in the nineteenth century believed that crime and vice existed because poverty existed, and if poverty were eliminated, then crime and vice would disappear. While it is true that poor surroundings are usually unhealthy climates for high moral training, still, man has the free will to check himself. Many Socialists, however, denied free will and said that man was a creation of his environment. . . . If Socialists do not deny Christ's message, they often ignore it. Christ showed us by His life that this earth is a testing ground to prepare man for eternal happiness. Man's interests should be in this direction at least part of the time and not always directed toward a futile quest for material goods. (Pp. 561–564.) [8]

Mr. Justice Jackson said, ". . . I should suppose it is a proper, if not an indispensable, part of preparation for a worldly life to know the roles that religion and religions have played in the tragic story of mankind." *McCollum* v. *Board of Education,* 33 U.S. 203, 236 (concurring opinion). Yet, as he inquired, what emphasis should one give who teaches the Reformation, the Inquisition, or the early effort in New England to establish " 'a Church without a Bishop and a State without a King?' " *Ibid.* What books should be chosen for those subjects?

Even where the treatment given to a particular topic in a school textbook is not blatantly sectarian, it will necessarily have certain shadings that will lead a parochial school to prefer one text over another.[9]

---

[8] Man in Time contains a nihil obstat and an imprimatur. Thus, if Opinion of Counsel No. 181 (nn. 5, 6, *supra*) is applicable, this book may not be provided by the State. The Opinion of Counsel, however, is only "advisory," we are told; moreover, the religious endorsements could easily be removed by the author and publisher at the next printing.

[9] Some parochial schools may prefer those texts which are liberally sprinkled with religious vignettes. This creeping sectarianism avoids the direct teaching of religious doctrine but keeps the student continually reminded of the sectarian orientation of his education. In Furlong, Margaret, and Sharkey's American history text, America Yesterday (1963), for example, the student is informed that the first mass to be said in what is now the United States was in 1526 near Chesapeake Bay, that eight French missionaries to Canada in the early 1600's were canonized in 1930, that one of the men who signed the Declaration of Independence and two who attended the Constitutional Convention were Catholic, and that the superintendent of the Hudson Bay Company's outpost in the Oregon country converted to Catholicism in 1842. Pp. 26, 73–74, 102, 140, 235. And Scott's Adventures in Science (1963), in teaching the atmospheric conditions prevailing at the top of Mount

The Crusades, for example, may be taught as a Christian undertaking to "save the Holy Land" from the Moslem Turks who "became a threat to Christianity and its holy places," which "they did not treat . . . with respect" (Wilson, Wilson, Erb and Clucas, Out of the Past 284 (1954)), or as essentially a series of wars born out of political and materialistic motives (see Leinwand, The Pageant of World History 136–137 (1965)).

Is the dawn of man to be explained in the words, "God created man and made man master of the earth" (Furlong, The Old World and America 5 (1937)), or in the language of evolution (see Wallbank, Man's Story 32–35 (1961))?

Is the slaughter of the Aztecs by Cortes and his entourage to be lamented for its destruction of a New World culture (see Caughey, Franklin, & May, Land of the Free 27028 (1965)), or forgiven because the Spaniards "carried the true Faith" to a barbaric people who practiced human sacrifice (see Furlong, Margaret, & Sharkey, America Yesterday 17, 34 (1963))?

Is Franco's revolution in Spain to be taught as a crusade against anti-Catholic forces (see Hoffman, Vincitorio, & Swift, Man and His History 666–667 (1958))[10] or as an effort by reactionary elements to regain control of that country (see Leinwand, The Pageant of World History, *supra,* at 512).[11] Is the expansion of communism in select areas of the world a manifestation of the forces of Evil campaigning against the forces of Good? See Hughes, Man in Time, *supra,* at 565–568, 666–669, 735–748.

It will be often difficult, as Mr. Justice Jackson said, to say "where the secular ends and the sectarian begins in education." *McCollum* v. *Board of*

Everest, informs the student that when Sir Edmund Hillary first scaled this peak he placed there a "tiny crucifix" which a Benedictine monk had supplied. P. 72.

America Yesterday, *supra,* is another example of a text written by the clergy (here a priest and nun together with one layman) that contains no imprimatur and no nihil obstat and is not a denominational edition. See nn. 5–7.

10 "In Spain early in 1936 a popular-front organization won a victory in the national elections. The result was a government made up of discordant political elements that failed to preserve civil order in the country. Violent anti-Catholics attacked and burned churches and monasteries, and the government did not even try to prevent these crimes. As a result, Spaniards who loved their country and were loyal to their religion revolted against the popular-front government of the republic. An able general, Francisco Franco, put himself at the head of the revolt, which began in July 1936."

11 "Spain, at the end of World War I, was a backward, poverty-stricken monarchy. In 1931, the king resigned and the people established a republic. The Spanish tried many reforms, but there were many who wanted to go back to the old ways and old privileges of the monarchy. Those who were rich wanted to hold on to their property. These people thought that Francisco Franco, a Fascist, could help them.

"In 1936, a civil war started which soon came to be called a 'dress rehearsal' for World War II because the Fascist countries of Italy and Germany supported Franco and his rebels. On the other hand, Russia supported the loyalists (as the armies of the republic were called). The democratic countries might have supported the loyalists, too, but fear of communism prevented them from doing so. Franco defeated the loyalists and, in 1938, became dictator of Spain and today as *El Caudillo* ('The Leader') still rules Spain with an iron hand."

Education, 333 U.S., at 237–238. But certain it is that once the so-called "secular" textbook is the prize to be won by that religious faith which selects the book, the battle will be on for those positions of control. Judge Van Voorhis expressed the fear that in the end the state might dominate the church. Others fear that one sectarian group, gaining control of the state agencies which approve the "secular" textbooks, will use their control to disseminate ideas most congenial to their faith. It must be remembered that the very existence of the religious school—whether Catholic or Mormon, Presbyterian or Episcopalian—is to provide an education oriented to the dogma of the particular faith.[12]

Father Peter O'Reilly put the matter succinctly when he disclosed what was happening in one Catholic school:[13] "On February 24, 1954 Rev. Cyril F. Meyer, C. M., then Vice President of the University, sent the following letter to all the faculty, both Catholics and non-Catholics, even those teaching law, science, and mathematics:

Dear Faculty Member:

As a result of several spirited discussions in the Academic Senate, a resolution was passed by that body that a self-evaluation be made of the effectiveness with which we are achieving in our classrooms the stated objectives of the University. . . . The primacy of the spiritual is the reason for a Christian university. Our goal is not merely to equip students with marketable skills. It is far above this—to educate man, the whole man, the theocentric man. As you are well aware, we strive to educate not only for personal and social success in secular society, but far more for leadership toward a theocentric society. . . .

May I, therefore, respectfully request that you submit answers as specific as possible to the following questions:

1. What do you do to make your particular courses theocentric?

2. Do you believe there is anything the Administration or your colleagues can do to assist you in presenting your particular courses more "according to the philoso-

---

12 The purpose of the parochial school in the beginning is clear beyond peradventure. The generally held Roman Catholic position in the matter of education in public and parochial schools has been well summarized by the late Monsignor John A. Ryan (1869–1945):

"'. . . As a matter of fact, the State maintains a system of schools which is not completely satisfactory to Catholics, inasmuch as no place is given to morality and religion. Since the Church realizes that the teaching of religion and instruction in the secular branches cannot rightfully or successfully be separated one from the other, she is compelled to maintain her own system of schools for general education as well as for religious instruction. . . .'" 2 Stokes, Church and State in the United States, 654 (1950).

"The education in the parochial schools follows in general the curriculum in the public schools, the main differences being that about 15 per cent of the time is given to religious instruction, and that the Catholic point of view is brought out in the treatment of historical and other subjects, just as the Protestant point of view might be emphasized in a Protestant school." *Ibid.*

Some, however, think that some parochial schools are changing their character under practical pressures of educational competition. See, *e.g.*, Fleming, Fordham Is Trying To Be catholic with a Small "c," N.Y. Times Magazine, Dec. 10, 1967, p. 32.

13 St. John's I: A Chronicle of Folly, 4 Continuum, 223, 233–234 (1966).

phical and theological traditions of the Roman Catholic Church"? Do not hesitate to let us know. There is no objective of our University more fundamental than this. We must all be aware that "the classroom that is not a temple is a den."

Please try to have your answers, using this size paper, returned to me by March 10.

This tendency is no Catholic monopoly:

The Presbyterian-affiliated Lewis and Clark College seems to have a similar interest in appearances of autonomy, with a view to avoiding possible legal bars to both federal funds and gifts from some foundations. The change, which legitimizes the college as an autonomous educational institution, removes the requirement that each presbytery in Oregon have at least one representative on the board, but it was made clear 'The college wishes to change *only its legal relationship* to the synod and *not its purposes,'* and promised that it still will elect a minister from each presbytery to the board on nomination of the synod, and will consult the synod before making any change in its statement of purpose, which defines it as a Presbyterian-related college.[14]

The challenged New York law leaves to the Board of Regents, local boards of education, trustees, and other school authorities the supervision of the textbook program.

The Board of Regents (together with the Commissioner of Education) has powers of censorship over all textbooks that contain statements seditious in character, or evince disloyalty to the United States or are favorable to any nation with which we are at war. N.Y. Educ. L. § 704. Those powers can cut a wide swathe in many areas of education that involve the ideological element.[15]

In general textbooks are approved for distribution by "boards of education, trustees or such body or officer as performs the function of such boards. . . ." N.Y. Educ. Law § 701 (1). These school boards are generally elected, §§ 2013, 2502 (2), though in a few cities they are appointed. § 2553. Where there are trustees, they are elected. §§ 1523, 1602, 1702. And superintendents who advise on textbook selection are appointed by the board of education or the trustees. §§ 1711, 2503 (5), 2507.

The initiative to select and requisition "the books desired" is with the parochial school. Powerful religious-political pressures will therefore be on the state agencies to provide the books that are desired.

These then are the battlegrounds where control of textbook distribution will be won or lost. Now that "secular" textbooks will pour into religious schools, we can rest assured that a contest will be on[16] to provide those books for religious schools which the dominant religious group concludes best reflect the theocentric or other philosophy of the particular church.

---

14 *Id.*, 234 (emphasis in original).

15 Cf. *Adler* v. *Board of Education,* 342 U.S. 485; *Barsky* v. *Board of Regents,* 347 U.S. 442.

16 The proportions of the contest are suggested in the letter dated November 1, 1967, that the late Cardinal Spellman directed to be read at all the masses on Sunday, November 5, 1967, just before the vote on a proposed Constitution that would have opened wide the door to state aid to parochial schools. I have attached the letter as Appendix B to this opinion.

The stakes are now extremely high—just as they were in the school prayer cases (see *Engel* v. *Vitale, supra*)—to obtain approval of what is "proper." For the "proper" books will radiate the "correct" religious view not only in the parochial school but in the public school as well.

Even if I am wrong in that basic premise, we still should not affirm the judgment below. Judge Van Voorhis, dissenting in the New York Court of Appeals, thought that the result of tying parochial school textbooks to public funds would be to put nonsectarian books into religious schools, which in the long view would tend towards state domination of the church. 20 N.Y. 2d, at 123, 281 N.Y.S. 2d, at 810; 228 N.E. 2d, at 798. That would, indeed, be the result if the school boards did not succumb to "sectarian" pressure or control. So, however the case be viewed—whether sectarian groups win control of school boards or do not gain such control—the principle of separation of church and state, inherent in the Establishment Clause of the First Amendment, is violated by what we today approve.

What Madison wrote in his famous Memorial and Remonstrance against Religious Assessments is highly pertinent here:[17]

> Who does not see that the same authority which can establish Christianity, in exclusion of all other Religions, may establish with the same case any particular sect of Christians, in exclusion of all other Sects? That the same authority which can force a citizen to contribute three pence only of his property for the support of any one establishment,[18] may force him to conform to any other establishment in all cases whatsoever?

DISCUSSION QUESTIONS

1. Would not the rationale that permits lending textbooks to parochial students justify permitting the use of buildings and paying teacher's salaries?
2. Are taxes collected to purchase textbooks for parochial-school use a form of governmental aid to religious organizations?
3. What is your reaction to the religious orientation of John M. Scott's *Adventures in Science?* Would you wish such a viewpoint presented in a public-school text?
4. Do you agree that "the classroom that is not a temple is a den"? Defend your viewpoint.

---

17 2 Writings of James Madison (Hunt, ed., 1901), p. 186.

18 For a recent account of the extent to which public funds are being poured into sectarian schools see S. Rep. No. 473, 90th Cong., 1st Sess., pp. 9–10 (1967).

PHILIP BURTON

Public Funds for Public Schools Only

Many Roman Catholic proponents of tax-subsidized religion are engaging in intricate verbal exercises to invert the meaning of the Constitution's First and Fourteenth amendments and use them against their opponents. Faced with dilemmas posed by expanding population, galloping inflation and canon law imperatives, they are claiming—with amnesiac blandness toward clear dicta of Supreme Court decisions blocking tax-supported religion—that refusal of such support is an unconstitutional limitation of parental rights and religious liberties.

No advocate of tax support for parochial schools denies that such schools are a religious enterprise. *Extra ecclesium nulla salus* is the rationale that accounts for their establishment and compels Catholic parents to use them. Beyond ensuring their right to exist (upheld by the Supreme Court in 1925), the government's obligation toward them is identical with its obligation to the churches themselves. As the Supreme Court has made clear, parochial schools are legally precluded from any tax support whatsoever. If they were to receive such support, the government would thereby acquire the right to regulate them in the same way it regulates public schools, and under such circumstances no religion could be taught in them.

I

Traditional Roman Catholic opposition to public aid to education in general has been modified in recent years by growing anticipation of sharing in larger benefits for public education at public expense. In 1930 the U.S. Supreme Court drew a distinction between child benefits and aid to religion, and rendered a decision permitting parochial school pupils to share in free textbook distribution. Religious school pupils were in some places being transported at public expense even before any legal clarification by the Supreme Court. The Everson case, which came before the court in 1947, culminated in one of the court's most notable verdicts. By a slim majority of one the court adhered to a precedent, drawn first in the 1930 textbook case, distinguishing between child benefits and aid to religion. On this basis it made public transportation of children attending parochial schools permissible. Four members of the court rejected the distinction and declared such use of tax funds violative of the Constitution. And the whole court concurred in the judgment that the First Amendment erects an

Reprinted from *The Christian Century*, April 5, 1961, pp. 313–318, with permission of the publisher.

impregnable wall of separation between church and state and absolutely precludes publicly supported religion. The reasoning of the dissenters was adopted in the McCollum case the following year in an 8–1 decision outlawing the teaching of religion in public classrooms. Taken together, these two Supreme Court decisions settle by a clear negative any real questions as to whether government can subsidize religion.

Comprehensive as this answer seems, those who seek public support for religious enterprises remain undaunted. The extent of their anticipations can be surmised from the nature of the denunciations that have been hurled at the Supreme Court following the Everson and McCollum decisions. The court is charged with departing from tradition and misinterpreting the Constitution. The Constitution, say the accusers, does not prohibit nonpreferential tax support of religion; the court ignores history, logic and law by imposing a novel interpretation upon the First amendment. They further argue that there is no wall of separation between church and state except an imaginary one in the minds of smokers of secular opiums. The misinterpretations the court imposes reject the honored tradition of liberty, deny parental rights and violate freedom of religion. So goes the argument of the proponents of tax-supported religion.

The substance of this argument was articulated last summer by Bishop Lawrence J. Shehan, chairman of the department of education of the National Catholic Welfare Conference. Preaching on August 28 at a Red Mass held at the National Shrine of the Immaculate Conception, Washington, D.C., and attended by three Supreme Court justices (including Chief Justice Earl Warren) and many members of the American Bar Association, Bishop Shehan bluntly posed the question whether the financial burdens of those who send their children to religious schools is an unconstitutional limitation of parental rights and violation of freedom of the practice of religion. While Bishop Shehan put the matter in question form, his own answer was obvious—and clearly contrary to that already established in law by the Supreme Court decisions. Beneath his arcane language is to be found a different concept of the proper relationship between church and state than that which informs the Constitution and guides Supreme Court decisions.

The bishop's logic obviously identifies the Constitution's concern to protect parental and religious rights with a nonexistent governmental duty to incur parents' expenses deriving from exercise of such rights. This kind of logic betrays confusion in the minds of those who invoke its aid. The Constitution upholds the right of parents to send their children to the church of their choice, but maintenance of these legal rights carries no concomitant obligation for the government to, say, pay pew rent in the church chosen. If such a principle were constitutionally valid, legal consistency could claim that the government incurs the obligation to pay any and all expenses involved in a citizen's exercising any one of his constitutional privileges. No claim could be more patently absurd. The financial burden of parochial schools is a private religious problem; nothing relevant to constitutional questions of rights is involved. A clear violation of the Constitution would be perpetrated if the government were to honor the plea for tax support implicit in the presuppositions behind the bishop's question.

II

Bishop Shehan's approach was not born full grown of his homiletic travail last August 28. Inherent in it is Cardinal McIntyre's notion of circumventing the wall that separates parochial schools from the federal treasury by a ruse to gain funds for such schools through scholarship awards to parents of children attending them. Included also is a conception of child welfare benefits that would include everything from erecting religious school plants to stopping leaky toilets in them. Obviously such grab-bag expenditures could be made to cover the major costs of parochial religious education. This method of breaching the wall of separation between church and state is assumed by its proponents to have no constitutional complications and to nullify the Supreme Court's clearest interpretations of the First amendment. They imply that the government's refusal to adopt some such way of nullifying Supreme Court decisions blocking direct or indirect tax support of these schools is equivalent to violation of Catholics' constitutional rights. The assumption ignores the fact that *no person has constitutional rights to religious education at public expense.* Any citizen possesses the legal right to acquire religious education for himself and his children; these rights have been as fully upheld for Roman Catholic citizens as for others. Obviously it is fallacious to confuse legal rights with private economic problems.

Roman Catholic citizens have the legal right to make use of public schools but are prevented by dicta of their church from doing so. The government does not infringe upon their right to act on the insistence of their church's authorities that they send their children to religious schools not entitled to tax support. The germane core of the point at issue here lies in the fact that Roman Catholics accept for themselves an extralegal position that constrains them to go beyond what the government requires and assume for themselves extra educational costs. This is the crux of the dilemma of dual loyalties upon which the government approach to educational responsibility has in many countries foundered.

Contrary to the view of the Roman Catholic hierarchy, the economic disabilities of those required by their churches to assume the burdens incident to religious education are not in any way the result of government discrimination. They are instead incidental costs of the actualization of rights ensured under the First and Fourteenth amendments. The same amendments which set forth these legal rights prohibit the government from collecting taxes to subsidize the individual's exercise of such rights. The government is not a church and cannot act as one in order to collect church school fees. By due process of law the government collects taxes from all its citizens; it treats Roman Catholic citizens on equal terms with all others. If they complain that they are victims of double taxation without representation, they cannot in good conscience lay blame upon the government. If they refuse to accept their share of what the government provides for all on equal terms, the refusal is not one for which the government is responsible.

Advocates of tax-supported religion increasingly recognize the futility of securing direct tax support and tend to cloak their claim for public support under the guise of proposals that speak of child welfare benefits. Their hopes lie in the dubious distinctions discussed herein and appealed to by the slim majority of one which in the Everson case ruled in favor of free transportation of parochial pupils. The dissenting minority of four in that case saw no such distinctions, and in the 1948 McCollum case their reasoning was adopted as the basis for an 8–1 decision outlawing the teaching of religion in public classrooms.

III

When proponents of tax support for religious schools accuse the court of rejecting the tradition of religious liberty, they have in mind the precedents based on dubious distinctions. Carried to logical conclusions, this recent tradition might open the way for vast public expenditures for religion. Such was not the tradition from which James Madison reasoned when he protested federal compensations for chaplains in the House and Senate on the ground that they are unconstitutional. Madison knew more intimately the intent of the tradition that informs the First amendment than do some of those who now appeal to tradition against that amendment! Madison knew of no tradition of nonpreferential aid to religions; he did know that the authors of the Constitution countenanced neither preferential nor nonpreferential aid to religions at public expense. And he knew of no tradition using "benefits to children" as a subterfuge for extending tax support to religious institutions. In the McCollum case the court was wisely sensitive to the tradition known to Madison and others of his day.

Bishop Shehan cites the government's providing chapels and chaplains for the armed forces and special veterans' programs as the kinds of measures needed to facilitate religious freedom. As a matter of fact, the constitutionality of tax-supported chaplaincies and chapels is highly debatable. Madison opposed them as unconstitutional. One can only wait until the Supreme Court takes on and decides a case involving the issue to be certain of its opinion. It is not inconceivable that the practice might be found illegal. As for special programs for veterans, their purpose was not motivated by any concern either to facilitate or hinder practice of religious freedoms. Much less was their purpose to solve the financial dilemmas of administrators of religious schools! That such was the incidental effect in some instances is hardly to be questioned; it is not certain, however, that all aspects of the administration of the programs could pass a constitutional test.

Such problematic cases may yet provide the occasion for future litigations and decisions; nevertheless the fact remains that the kinds of expenditures uppermost in the minds of advocates of tax support for religion are clearly precluded by law. The law which prohibits teaching of religion in a public classroom cannot be bent to accommodate ruses encompassing scholarship awards, child welfare benefits and loans which would in fact constitute financial aid to religion. The answer to questions presupposing that denial of such requests is an unconstitutional violation of parental rights and freedom of religion is contained in these words by Justice Hugo Black (in the Everson decision): "No tax in any amount . . . can be levied to support any religious activities or institutions." Words could not be clearer!

DISCUSSION QUESTIONS

1. How tenable is the distinction drawn in the Everson case between child benefits and aid to religion?
2. Is Burton's distinction between the legal rights and the private economic problems of Roman Catholic citizens borne out in constitutional law?
3. How much justice is there in the complaint of double taxation without representation on the part of parents of children in both public and independent schools?

ROBERT M. HUTCHINS | *Aid to Church Schools*

Federal aid to education is an absolute necessity. But a political argument over funds for parochial schools, masquerading as a constitutional issue, bars the way. Unfortunately President Kennedy, while calling for $5.3 billion in aid to education over a period of years, is himself guilty of jeopardizing aid to all schools by perpetuating the masquerade.

The President and many others, especially liberals, tell us aid to church-school pupils is a constitutional question. They say there is a wall of separation between church and state forbidding any kind of assistance, direct or

Reprinted from the *Saturday Evening Post,* June 8, 1963, with permission of the author.

indirect, to an educational institution operated under the auspices of a church.

In fact, the Constitution says nothing of separation and makes no mention of a wall. The words of the First Amendment are: "Congress shall make no law respecting an establishment of religion, or prohibiting the free exercise thereof. . . ." The Supreme Court has held that the Fourteenth Amendment makes these words applicable to state legislatures as well as to Congress. Nothing in the words necessarily leads to the conclusion that every form of aid, direct or indirect, to educational institutions under religious auspices is unconstitutional.

We owe the wall not to the Constitution but to a letter from Thomas Jefferson to the Baptist Association of Danbury, Connecticut, in 1802, replying to a complimentary address. Jefferson wrote, "Believing with you that religion is a matter which lies solely between man and his God, that he owes account to none other for his faith or his worship, that the legislative powers of Government reach actions only, and not opinions, I contemplate with sovereign reverence that act of the whole American people which declared that their legislature should 'make no law respecting an establishment of religion, or prohibiting the free exercise thereof,' thus building a wall of separation between church and state."

The letter shows that what Jefferson was interested in was freedom of religion. He did not want the Government telling people how or whom or whether they should worship—first, because of the nature of religion, and second, because of the nature of government. Religion was a matter between a man and his God; government should not, if only because it could not, attempt to control the thoughts of men.

The wall Jefferson erected in the name of the First Amendment rose no higher than was necessary to wall off the religious opinions and practices of citizens from interference by government. His letter does *not* suggest that he would have opposed public expenditures that might benefit schools under religious management. And the record shows that he recommended procedures by which students at the University of Virginia, supported by the state and founded by Jefferson, might receive religious instruction.

Jefferson's wall disappeared into the mists of history for 77 years. Then it came back into view when the Supreme Court held that the First Amendment did not protect polygamy among the Mormons. It came back, that is, with a hole in it, through which the Government marched against a practice defended in religion's name. In justifying legislative condemnation of a church's action, Chief Justice Morrison Waite, who wrote the opinion of the court, used the Jefferson doctrine that legislative powers should be limited specifically to regulation of actions.

All was quiet along the wall for 62 years. Then, in 1941 it reappeared, but with another large hole in it, through which a school board in New Jersey drove buses carrying some children to parochial schools. The action was authorized by state law. In 1947 its constitutionality was *upheld.* The majority opinion said, "The First Amendment has erected a wall between church and state. That wall must be kept high and impregnable. We could not approve the slightest breach. New Jersey has not breached it here."

For the last 15 years, whenever there has been a case involving church and state, almost every Supreme Court justice has felt constrained to bow before the wall. The psalms sung in its behalf have grown more eloquent and more moving. It has become one of our more popular figures of speech. But the only effect of the wall on the decisions of the court has been to confuse the opinions of the justices.

The wall is used indiscriminately as a jumping-off point in all cases in which the religion clauses of the First Amendment are invoked. These cases are in general of three quite different kinds: those in which a public agency has used public money in a way benefiting private schools indirectly; those in which a public agency has authorized a program of "released time" for religious instruction in public schools or in connection with public schools; and those in which a public agency has instituted religious exercises in public schools.

Released time and religious exercises put the power of the state behind religion and raise the question of public pressure, direct or indirect, on the consciences of individuals and the consequent limitation of the exercise of their religious freedom. Indirect financial aid to schools under religious auspices does not raise this question. Such aid may actually help the aided pupils to exercise their religious freedom; it cannot be seriously argued that it restricts the religious freedom of those who are not assisted.

For all its talk of the wall, the fact is that the Supreme Court has never held aid to pupils in religious schools unconstitutional. As the court sustained New Jersey in providing transportation for pupils in Catholic schools, so it sustained Louisiana in providing textbooks for children in all schools. The theory in both cases was the same: an overriding public purpose was to be served—the education of the children in the state. The fact that some benefit might incidentally accrue to a private school or to the religious organization that managed it was not significant.

The tax exemption of church schools has never been challenged. Neither have the numerous Government programs of grants, loans, scholarships and tax benefits under such laws as the GI Bill of Rights, the College Housing Act, the School Lunch Act, and the Surplus Property Act, all of which have been available to church-supported institutions. The Kennedy Administration has sonorously opposed Federal aid to church schools. Yet it finds no logical difficulty in recommending in its present bill appropriations to facilitate the recruitment of teachers by parochial as well as by public schools.

My conclusion is that Federal aid to pupils in parochial schools is not a constitutional issue. It is a political issue, a real and important one. It may be stated this way: Will the general welfare be promoted by including parochial-school pupils in a national program of education, or will it be promoted by leaving them out?

In 1961 five and a half million children received education in Catholic elementary and secondary schools. That is a little more than an eighth of all schoolchildren in these categories. If the Constitution does not require us to leave one eighth of our children out of a national program of education, why should we do so?

In the New Jersey bus case, the court said, "It [the state of New Jersey] cannot exclude individual Catholics, Lutherans, Mohammedans, Baptists, Jews, Methodists, Nonbelievers, Presbyterians or the members of any other faith, *because of their faith, or lack of it,* from receiving the benefits of public welfare legislation."

The children in schools supported by religious denominations should not be excluded because of their faith from the benefits of a national program of education. And we can hardly have a national program unless these children are involved in it.

Rep. James J. Delaney of New York has reintroduced a bill to authorize a two-year program of Federal aid to all elementary and secondary schoolchildren in all the states. The bill provides that $20 shall be allotted annually to each pupil to defray part of the cost of his education. Pupils who did not record their intention or desire to attend a private school would be presumed to be destined for a public school, in which case the allotment would be paid to the public educational authority in their community.

This is a GI Bill of Rights for Children in elementary and secondary schools. Over a two-year period it would add $1.7 billion to the resources of these schools. Something more than $100 million a year would go to church-related schools.

Legislation of this sort would quiet the fears of those who are alarmed at the prospect of Federal control. It should calm those who believe that aid to church-related schools means the destruction of the public schools. It should satisfy everybody, except those who hold that a church-related school is the same thing as a church. They might say that legislation authorizing payment of $20 of taxes to a church school was the same as giving a citizen $20 of taxes to put in the plate on Sunday. They might argue that such payments were neither constitutionally possible nor politically wise.

But a school is not an assembly for worship. It does not perform ecclesiastical functions. Payments to a pupil for his education are not payments for the support of worship, of ecclesiastical functions or of the propagation of the faith. The object of education is the development of the mind. This may be conducted under religious auspices, but it is not the same as the development of religion or of the spiritual life. The Supreme Court would not have allowed New Jersey to pay for buses to carry worshipers to church.

A sensational shift in public opinion has been going on over the past two years on the subject of Federal aid to all schools. In March, 1961, the Gallup Poll showed that 57 percent of those interviewed thought Federal aid should go only to public schools; in February, 1963, only 44 per cent of those polled were of this opinion. Apparently the common sense of the American people is winning over the pedantry of their leaders.

DISCUSSION QUESTIONS

1. Do you agree with Hutchins that federal aid to parochial schools is a political rather than a constitutional issue revolving around the question of whether or not it is in the national interest to render the independent school such aid? What is the basic constitutional issue, if any?
2. Discuss Hutchins' statement, "the development of the mind may be conducted under religious auspices, but it is not the same as the development of religion or of the spiritual life."
3. What would be the effect of the $100 million a year available to church-related schools under the Delaney bill?

SHELDON STOFF

How Can the Public Schools Manage Religious Issues?

The Supreme Court ruling against Bible-reading and recitation of the Lord's Prayer in public schools as part of required classroom exercises should cause educators and laymen to evaluate the relationship between religion and the public schools. This Supreme Court ruling is not anti-religious. It is consistent with the basic ideal of a separation of church and state so that both may flourish. It is consistent with past Supreme Court statements in the Zorach case: "We are a religious people whose institutions presuppose a Supreme Being. We guarantee the freedom to worship as one chooses. We make room for as wide a variety of beliefs and creeds as the spiritual needs of man deem necessary. . . . Government may not finance religious groups nor undertake religious instruction nor blend secular and sectarian educators, nor use secular institutions to force one or some religion on any person."[1]

What then should be the role of the public school in the area of religion? It would be wishful thinking to believe that the issue is now clearly resolved. The religious influence in the schools is far deeper than simply Bible-

Reprinted from *The Clearing House,* Vol. XXXVIII, No. 5 (January 1964), pp. 271–274, with permission of the publisher.

[1] *Zorach* v. *Clauson,* 343 U.S. 306, 1952. Mr. Justice Douglas delivered the opinion of the Court.

reading and the recitation of the Lord's Prayer. Basic moral and educational implications must be dealt with.

In many parts of our nation the Christmas season is heralded by emotional controversies regarding certain practices in the public schools. Religious issues become the subjects of heated debate during a period of time in which thoughts of good will are supposed to dominate. For many decades this season of the year has brought forth decorations, trees, crosses, plays, hymns, and nativity scenes for the Christmas celebration in our public schools. This outward display of religious observance quickly brings forth cries for the separation of church and state, and for the public disestablishment of religious favoritism. The results are tears, suspicion, discord, and no concrete solution.

With or without conflict or controversy, the situation is not being properly managed. The Constitutional view is further classified by the Supreme Court in Zorach vs Clauson: "The government must be neutral when it comes to competition between sects. It may not thrust any sect on any person. It may not make a religious observance compulsory. It may not coerce anyone to attend church, to observe a religious holiday, or to take religious instruction."[2]

The public schools, functioning with compulsory attendance laws in a pluralistic society, cannot justify any religious participation and ritual on public property. Religious services and celebrations should be conducted in the home, church, synagogue, or church-supported school. Religious observance should not enter into a pluralistic public forum supported by public funds.

On the other hand, such observances of Christmas celebration cannot often be completely removed from the schools without initiating strong public clamor. The public observance of Christmas has become firmly entrenched in much of our national culture, and many of the population expect its preservation.

A dilemma? Partially, but a third alternative does exist that should satisfy the majority, conform to the Constitution, safeguard minorities, and strengthen the ability of the schools to perform a basic role of enriching and disseminating the culture and enabling the student to grow, mature, and broaden his horizons. Justice Douglas' statement that "We are a religious people" is completely supported by the U.S. Census (95 per cent of those polled classified themselves into one of our three major religious groupings),[3] by *The Catholic Digest* (95 per cent of those interviewed stated that religion was either very important or of medium importance to them),[4] and by statements by every President of the United States (as detailed by James

---

2 *Ibid.*

3 U.S. Bureau of the Census, *Current Population Reports,* Series No. 79 (Washington: Government Printing Office, 1958), p. 20.

4 B. Gaffin and Associates, "Who Belongs to What Church," in *The Catholic Digest* (January, 1953), p. 5.

Keller in *All God's Children*).[5] This religious facet of our lives cannot be ignored without distorting the world culture as it is presented in our schools. It is equally important to remember that it is not the function of the schools to indoctrinate religious dogma. We are historically a nation of many backgrounds and beliefs and we have thrived on this principle. The rights of the religious and the nonreligious should be respected.

> The school cannot and should not try to decide whether the religious need has an answer and, if it does, which one it must be. The school is only obliged, if it would inform its students, to remind them that men have made and lived out a variety of answers. . . .
>
> No man can be regarded as informed, awakened, and free unless he has learned as much as he can about himself and about the examples of others like him in history. No man can call himself educated unless he knows what his religious potentialities are, no matter how unreal, foolish or otherwise objectionable he judges them.[6]

This statement by Professor Harper can be practically applied to our public school situation by assigning the education for a particular religious orientation to the home or church and encouraging the schools to perform the function which neither is performing. I am referring to teaching comparative religion in a specialized course of study. Through this democratic approach, in keeping with our nation's pluralistic and cultural heritages, the school would open students to a broader understanding of life rather than indoctrinate them with specific religious dogma or even force them into a general religious orientation.

The program presented here, to manage the controversy over religious practices in public education, is both practical and educational. It was developed after communication with religious leaders from each of the six religions concerned. A sincere effort was made to meet their recommendations and also meet the general goals many desire for public education.[7] In the development of the program it was desirable to set goals which were compatible with the basic aims of the schools and the nation's Constitution. The goals are these:

1. A greater understanding of other people by the student.
2. A more mature development of the student.
    a. An enriching process for the student because of the broad spectrum of ideas explored.
    b. A more significant insight by the student into his own life, which could lead to a deeper character development.

---

[5] James Keller, *All God's Children* (Garden City, New York: Hanover House, 1953), p. 237.
[6] Ralph Harper, "Significance of Existence and Recognition for Education," in *Modern Philosophies and Education,* N. Henry, Ed. (Chicago, Illinois: The National Society for the Study of Education, 1955), p. 248.
[7] Approval on the part of these religious leaders for this program is not here suggested or rejected.

The basic program is divided into two areas. The first (Part A) could be adopted by the schools immediately. It involves no great expense and would help resolve the pressing issues which have gained the most notoriety. The implementation of the second (Part B) involves the teacher training institutions cooperating with the schools in an attempt to meet their responsibilities in this vital area.

PART A. IMMEDIATE ACTION

The proposals in this phase center on the celebrations of religious holidays in the schools. Christmas is the most notable example. In our society, the schools cannot defend holding religious celebrations on public property. For the most part, Christmas observance cannot be eliminated from the schools without causing considerable public clamor. This total separation should not be attempted. Instead of promoting a religious view by one religious celebration, the schools should seriously consider the several major religious holy days of the world's great religions as resources for the dissemination of knowledge and understanding. The dogma, the ritual, the affirmation is to be avoided; the educational message is to be promoted.

The question which most quickly comes to mind is: "How do you accomplish this education without indoctrination?"

At this preliminary stage in the program I would suggest that a qualified social studies teacher make the presentation to a general assembly or lead a panel discussion in which the "why" of the holy day should be considered. As material becomes more available in the future, dramas could be added to this type of presentation.[8]

We need not have ritual at Christmas in the public schools, but the message inherent in Christmas can be explored. The holy days of Hinduism, Judaism, Buddhism, and Islam could be explained and "respected" in their turns. If the emphasis is placed on promoting broad knowledge and understanding instead of narrow ritual, even the atheist cannot be offended.

A brief understanding of the world's religions is made possible without favoritism, by overcoming existing provincialism. The views of other local religions which are not already represented by the aforementioned should also be considered.

---

[8] Some sources of material are:
The National Conference of Christians and Jews, Inc. 43 West 57th Street, New York 19, New York.
Buddhism: Dr. Kurt F. Leiderker, 306 Caroline Street, Fredericksburg, Virginia; Washington Friends of Buddhism, Washington, D.C.
Islam: The Islamic Foundation of New York, One Riverside Drive, New York 23, New York: Diyanet Isleri Reisligi, Ankara, Turkey.
Hinduism: Ramakrishna-Vivekananda Society, 17 East 94th Street, New York, New York; Vedanta Society, 34 West 71st Street, New York, New York.
For Buddhism, Catholicism, Protestantism, Hinduism, Islam, Judaism: *Great Religions of Modern Man* (6 volumes), published by George Braziller, New York.

The schools would then have the power to outgrow localism. They could continue to fulfill their basic responsibility—education—in the full knowledge that people must learn to live with, and respect, their neighbors.

PART B. THE LONG-TERM SOLUTION

The proposal in this part centers on the role of the school. It is the job of the school and all structures of society to disseminate and enforce that which is beneficial in the culture. The school has responsibilities in the area of knowledge about religion that no other agency can render as well. In outgrowing a concentration on local practices, beliefs, and attitudes, the schools have deep obligations to meet.

Course content

This proposal advocates that a specific course dealing with the religions of mankind be taught in the social studies area of our senior high schools. It would be taught by a specifically trained teacher. The prime content of the course would be concerned with the study of six major religions: Islam, Buddhism, Catholicism, Judaism, Protestantism, and Hinduism. In areas where other religions are present, they would also be explored.

The study of these religions should concern itself with:

A. History and leaders
B. Ethics
C. Rituals and customs
D. Present application

The material for each of the religions under discussion should be provided by or acceptable to the individual religions.

Religious practices

No religious practices would enter into the curriculum. No religious dogmas would be inculcated. This course could develop a broad area of enlightenment and understanding. No one religion would be favored. No expression of faith would be asked of the student. There would be no worship or ritual. The separation of church and state would be maintained as constitutionally intended.

Role of the teacher

The teacher would be sympathetic to each religion as it was studied. He would help his students gain a knowledge and appreciation of each. In the classroom he would not be a partisan supporter of any individual faith.

Teacher training

The teacher should be specifically trained for this task. His training would be in the area of social studies, with a major concentration in the area of comparative religion. Specific knowledge of each of the religions would be included in this training program. The program offered by the Department of Religious Education of New York University could well provide a guide in this area.

CONCLUSION

The above proposal is both practical and far reaching. Interested persons could well take immediate steps toward action. Part A needs no elaborate preparation. Part B would require strong support in order to be executed. This program would help fill a void in present public school curricula. It is designed to present six of the world's great religions as a part of the total world's culture. Some will view this proposal as a program charged with risks. Most certainly some risk is involved. Most steps forward require daring, but the greatest risks are those of inaction. Ignorance should not be preferred to an honest, careful attempt at understanding.

The Supreme Court decision of June 17, 1963, may yet awaken educators and the general public to this serious void existing in much of the American educational system.

DISCUSSION QUESTIONS

1. What is the difference between teaching religion and teaching about religion?
2. What difficulties do you perceive in Stoff's recommendations?
3. What benefits?
4. Do you agree with Stoff that "the greater risks are those of inaction"?
5. Do the schools have any obligations to religion? To the religious?
6. What course of action do you recommend for the schools to take in providing for religion and education?

JOHN F. GARDNER

Education Is Always Religious

From the first, education was the American religion. It was and is—in education that we put our faith: it is our schools and colleges that are the peculiar objects of public largesse and private benefaction; even in architecture we proclaim our devotion, building schools like cathedrals.

. . . .

In a personal statement, written in 1930, John Dewey said philosophy should "focus about educa-

Reprinted from the *Waldorf School News,* 1959, with permission of the author and publisher.

tion as the supreme human interest in which, moreover, other problems, cosmological, moral, logical, come to a head."

Henry Steele Commager

If we have any ground to be religious about anything, we may take education religiously.

John Dewey

The essence of education is that it be religious.

Alfred North Whitehead

Everyone knows that plants turn their leaves and flowers toward the sun, from its rising to its setting. Men only seem to be less heliotropic. The sun is the great fact of cosmic weather for mankind. When we awaken we want to know: where is the sun? One might even say, *how* is the sun? Is it full and warm, or pale and distant? Will it rule the day, or be overlaid and withdrawn from us? Weather from the cosmos is the background of all our living. Though we may forget it later in the day when lesser questions temporarily preoccupy us, we come back to it in many moments. The sun sets the tone of our earth-experience.

What the sun and the sun-filled atmosphere are to our feeling for each day, some conception of divine or ideal being is to our feeling for life as a whole. We can forego the latter as little as the former. We are quite as heliocentric with regard to it. No man gladly takes hold of life until he senses that his existence is lighted and warmed by spiritual sunlight. The heart always asks after the inward weather and the inward weather is always ruled by an ideal sun: that highest value which gives meaning to existence and which blesses it to fruitfulness. It is the value which makes life livable by making lovable what it touches.

This comparison of inner to outer sunlight may help to illustrate what is meant when one maintains, as we do, that mankind is religious *sui generis:* is inveterately and inalienably religious: is religious as the growth of a plant is always heliotropic, or the orbit of a planet is always heliocentric.

Men delude themselves with sophistries when they imagine that they have dispensed with religion. As long as they remain men they will never cease to draw from above and beyond themselves their enthusiasm for living, their power to improve life, their strength and guidance for moral decisions. Men may have different theories about the nature of the sun they see, and these differences may lead to fairly important consequences in action; but sun they will and must see. Dethrone one sun and another rises to take its place by the force of the whole depth of human nature. Behind all the imperfectly visualized suns shines the primordial sun-power itself. Destroy this objective power in the man and you destroy the man fundamentally.

It is possible for an observer on earth to mistake a firefly for a comet, an airplane light for a planet, or a planet for a star. But what is sought and felt, even in mistaken judgments, is still part of the true seeking and feeling, which are matched by truth somewhere. Sunlight shines through diffusely to the seaweeds below the surface of the ocean. Mushrooms are not organized to make the most of light. But even seaweed and mushrooms live toward the sun.

"The sun shines into the eye of an adult, but into the eye and heart of a child," said Emerson. If the grown man needs the sun of the ideal to bring forth his best and deepest, a child is still more dependent. He is more open, more all-one in his devotion.

The child's very existence is trust, hope and belief. He confides himself trustingly to the world because he naturally believes the best of it. He still sees the world in God. People and things are for him still radiant with the invisible light. They yet bear the signature of the divine. They seem as newly coined as he himself from the *fons et origo* of being.

Of course, the religious feeling which is the ground-tone of every normal child's attitude does not direct itself toward abstractions. It is his actual environment that excites the child's wonder. It is his actual father, mother and teacher whose hand he takes in loving trust. He sees the ideal *in* people and things, and *as* people and things, and will not begin to conceive it apart from these until childhood ends. Then the actual will sink to a more prosaic level of reality and the ideal will be sublimated from it. His instinctive love of persons will transform itself into the conscious love of ideal reality: of truth, beauty and goodness as such; the second form of love being strong in proportion to the first.

Grownups need to live with religious awareness, aspiration and discipline, but children need religion still more. If we see this clearly, we are ready to perceive a fundamental truth about education and the institutions of education which are the focus of every modern child's existence from the age of four or five to sixteen or eighteen and beyond. We can perceive that we have been on the wrong track in imagining that a school can ever exclude religion from its teaching. Every school that satisfies children is religious. Through curriculum, methods and attitudes it cultivates a religious life.[1]

We should not let ourselves be deceived by the fact that public schools are supposed to be neutral about religion. Neutral they are not. By the necessity

---

[1] Looking at the matter from quite another point of view I stated the conviction in an earlier article on *Religion and Science in the Waldorf School* that "the religious life cannot be successfully developed by the family and church alone, apart from the school. The time to learn *how* to view the creation as God's handiwork is when created things are being studied for the first time. This occurs in school. Every fact will then speak from its beauty and immediacy the language of God—or none will. And if the school has presented the detail of Nature materialistically, it may be beyond the power of pastor or parents thereafter to bring Deity into a fully credible relationship with the natural order."

of the nature which pulsates and breathes in pupils, teachers, and parents as human beings, every school fosters some form of devotion. The religion that inspires a public school, despite the neutrality taboo, will be one of the traditional faiths, or a crusading zeal for social reform, or some other holy cause.

American public schools are divided chiefly between those which are still rooted in the Protestant Christian impulse that quite consciously and acceptably motivated most of them a century ago, and those which, pressed by changes in the population they serve, have substituted for this religion a new one. The new ideal is generally society-centered; the new faith is called Democracy. It might also be called The American Way of Life. This faith has its hierarchy of power, its credo, its hymn-singing, ceremonies and ritual. It has been brought forward (always with the close support of science, a second sacred cause) to satisfy seeking hearts. Citizenship in the democratic society is increasingly represented as the goal of life. Studies need focus and the preparation for life needs an incentive. These are being found in the earthly paradise which men hope to create.

We have said, then, that education is always religious, in the public school as in a church school. And we have said that the religion which is now coming to the fore with ever-increasing strength in public schools, the sun around which school life is ordered and toward which all eyes are again and again directed with religious feeling, is that of the Ideal.

Society is commonly thought of as a socialized form of democracy in the industrial American image. That these two characterizations are not without support may be seen in the following quotations.

Why should we longer suffer from deficiency of religion? We have discovered our lack: let us set the machinery in motion which will supply it. We have mastered the elements of physical well-being; we can make light and heat to order, and can command the means of transportation. Let us now put a similar energy, good will, and thoughtfulness into the control of the things of the spiritual life. Having got so far as to search for proper machinery, the next step is easy. Education is the modern universal purveyor, and upon the schools shall rest the responsibility for seeing to it that we recover our threatened religious heritage.

. . . .

So far as education is concerned, those who believe in religion as a natural expression of human experience must devote themselves to the development of the ideas of life which lie implicit in our still new science and our still newer democracy . . . In performing this service, it is their business to do what they can to prevent all public educational agencies from being employed in ways which inevitably impede the recognition of the spiritual import of science and of democracy, and hence of that type of religion which will be the fine flower of the modern spirit's achievement.

If one inquires why the American tradition is so strong against any connection of State and Church, why it dreads even the rudiments of religious teaching in state-maintained schools, the immediate and superficial answer is not far to seek . . . The cause lay largely in the diversity and vitality of the various denominations . . .

But there was a deeper and by no means wholly unconscious influence at work. The United States became a nation late enough in the history of the world to profit by the growth of that modern (although Greek) thing—the state consciousness.

John Dewey

Doubtless many of our ancestors would have been somewhat shocked to realize the full logic of their own attitude with respect to the subordination of churches to the state (falsely termed the *separation* of Church and State) : but the state idea was inherently of such vitality and constructive force as to carry the practical result, with or without conscious perception of its philosophy.

. . . .

In such a dim, blind, but effective way the American people is conscious that its schools serve best the cause of religion in serving the cause of social unification; and that under certain conditions schools are more religious in substance and in promise without any of the conventional badges and machinery of religious instruction than they could be in cultivating these forms at the expense of a state-consciousness.

John Dewey

Democracy, therefore is not limited to political, governmental, or economic arrangements. It is a personal, school and civilization ideal . . . Democracy, reconceived, is that quality of experience which pervades social life, and in so doing contributes to the attainment of the fullest possible growth of all toward qualitative ideals. So defined, democracy is a conception about an esthetic-religious affair.

Democratic public education is that form of education which provides this sort of religious experience . . . This esthetic-social objective is one of developing competence in shared qualitative and theoretical intelligence that will enable men to move toward the religious ideal that is democracy.

Francis T. Villemain and Nathaniel L. Champlin writing on behalf of Dewey's educational philosophy in *The Antioch Review,* Fall, 1959

As long as the assumed neutrality of the public schools toward religion masked the situation, one could not see that education is always religious. And one could not go on to draw the inevitable conclusion as regards the proper relation of schools to the state. But the religious nature of public schools is slowly coming at last to be recognized by more and more people who are thoughtful and close to the realities of education. And the time is coming when we shall have to draw conclusions from our observations.

My own conclusion may be expressed as a syllogism:

A. *The state must be neutral with respect to religious institutions.*

The First Amendment to the Constitution of the United States has laid down this true and necessary principle: "Congress shall make no law respecting an establishment of religion . . ."

B. *Schools are religious institutions.*

An education that is not decisively religious is neither serious nor effective. On the other hand, a religious attitude toward life which tries to establish itself only through the influence of church and home, leaving the school out of account, will either fail or will create within the mind, the heart and the will of children a most painful schism. For the sake of education we need religion and for the sake of religion we need education: the two are fundamentally inseparable.

C. *Therefore, the state must become neutral with respect to the support and control of schools.*

Since all serious educational institutions are at the same time religious institutions, the spirit of the First Amendment requires us to realize that the state power must keep hands off the schools as it does the churches. The state schools must eventually—of course by due process, by many small steps, and, as a matter of harmonious evolution—be "disestablished" as state churches have been.

The situation that should arise with regard to schools need not by any means be exactly analogous to the present situation of churches in our culture. But, improbable as it may sound to our ears at the moment, the state school as an ideal must be progressively supplanted by the ideal of full independence for all schools.

DISCUSSION QUESTIONS

1. Does Gardner's description of democracy as a religion stand up in America today?
2. Gandhi believed that religion is an individual experience bringing one face to face with reality. Does Gardner share this concept?
3. What implications do you see for the schools in Gardner's belief in the interrelationship between religion and education?

CHAPTER 6 *The Financing of Education*

The history of federal aid to education predates the Constitution. Yet, ever since the inception of such aid, it has been received in an atmosphere of distrust and suspicion. Today, when federal assistance to education is viewed by many as a matter of the greatest national urgency, its propriety and legality are questioned in an atmosphere suggestive of a rural, isolated America of a time long passed.

From our own point of view, there is little need to document the tremendous inequalities of economic ability and well-being among the fifty states and in the educational subdivisions within the states. To the range in capacity to pay for education must be added an equally broad divergence in willingness to do so, so that the extent and quality of a child's education becomes a concomitant of the economic wealth and the dedication to education of his place of birth.

The proportionately enormous growth in the last few years in the federal effort to bring about some degree of equalization of educational opportunity for America's children merely highlights the magnitude of the task facing us. Our efforts and expenditures are still the proverbial drop in the bucket; if we mean for education to be successful we must commit to it the necessary national resources. We need to rethink through our priorities. Then the question whether states and localities should be permitted to spend on education what they wish to spend or can provide out of their own resources is seen in its proper perspective. In the national interest, we must balance the risks attendant upon massive federal intervention in education against the loss of immediacy of action and involvement that local control and financing are supposed to insure.

SIDNEY W. TIEDT

The History of Federal Aid to Education

Not to know what happened before one is born is always to be a child.

Cicero

Education in this country, it is generally conceded, first developed in the Massachusetts Bay Colony as exemplified by the Massachusetts Bay Law of 1642 and the "Old Deluder Act" of 1647. These acts attempted through education, and more specifically through the reading of the Bible, to prevent the Old Deluder, Satan, from corrupting the minds and hearts of the good men of New England. These early laws required that communities establish common schools whenever it was warranted by the population:

> It is therefore ordered that every township in this jurisdiction, after the Lord hath increased them to the number of fifty householders, shall then forthwith appoint one within their town to teach all such children as shall resort to them to write and read, whose wages shall be paid either by the parents or masters of such children, or by the inhabitants in general. . . .

In this way the Massachusetts laws generated school development in the United States setting the precedent for education as a local responsibility. As one writer stated succinctly: "Education is a local responsibility, a state function, and a national concern." The extent of this concern and the direction it has taken are to be examined in this chapter, for with the growth of the nation and the development of the federal government, activities of the national government inevitably have affected the nation's schools. The questions before us now are: "What has been the role of the federal government in education?" and "How has the federal government's role in education changed throughout the historical development of our schools?"

Organized chronologically, this brief review of the history of the federal government's involvement in education has been divided into three sections: (1) the Early Period (from the beginning of the country's history to the Civil War), (2) the Middle Period (from the Civil War to the Second

---

Reprinted from Sidney W. Tiedt, *The Role of the Federal Government in Education* (New York: Oxford University Press, 1966), pp. 14–19 and 194–200, with permission of the publisher.

World War), and (3) the Contemporary Period (from World War II to the Kennedy-Johnson administration in 1961).

THE EARLY PERIOD

The first suggestion regarding federal aid to education has been attributed to Colonel Timothy Pickering in 1783. Briefly stated, his proposal was that all surplus lands from the Ohio Territory should be the common property of the states and should be disposed of for the common good, that is, the laying out of roads, the construction of public buildings, and the establishment of public schools and academies. Although this suggestion was not enacted, it does indicate the thinking of this period, which resulted in the passage of the Northwest Ordinances.

The Ordinances of 1785 and 1787

The first example of legislation specifically involving the national government in education is the Land Ordinance of 1785. The Continental Congress decided to sell the public lands in the Northwest and decreed that, preparatory to being sold, these lands were to be surveyed and divided into townships comprising 36 sections of 640 acres each. A section was the smallest unit that could be bought, and the price of one section of every township was to be used for maintaining public schools. This policy of governmental support for education was affirmed in 1787 with the passage of the Northwest Ordinance, which stated: "Religion, morality, and knowledge being necessary to good government and the happiness of mankind, schools and the means of education shall forever be encouraged."

The area provided in this ordinance was approximately the size of Texas and was of great assistance in helping to establish our public school system. There remains some question whether these grants were set up to dispose of public lands or whether their purpose was chiefly to aid schools. Daniel Webster, however, recognized the importance of the Northwest Ordinance when he stated:

> I doubt whether any one single law, or any lawgiver, ancient or modern, has produced effects of more distinct, marked and lasting character than the Ordinance of 1787. It set forth and declared it to be a high and binding duty of government to support schools and the means of education.

The United States Constitution

The United States Constitution does not mention education either in its body or in any of the Amendments. There has been much scholarly discussion about this omission. Of the many reasons for the omission the most plausible appears to be that the writers of the Constitution could not foresee the complexity and immensity of the present system of education.

The Tenth Amendment, which reads, ". . . The powers not delegated to the United States by the Constitution, nor prohibited by it to the States, are reserved to the States respectively, or to the people," is usually cited as providing for a state or local system of education.

The General Welfare Clause of the Constitution, Article II, Section 8, reading as follows: "The Congress shall have Power to lay and collect Taxes, Duties, Imposts, and Excises, to pay the Debts and provide for the common Defense and general Welfare of the United States . . .," is used by most authorities to justify the constitutionality of the federal aid programs.

The National Advisory Commission on Education, appointed by Herbert Hoover in 1931, reported finding fourteen warrants for federal activities in the field of education. Historically and legally there appears to be little validity in the argument that any involvement in education by the federal government is unconstitutional.

While education was not mentioned in the Constitution, interest in education was evinced by the founding fathers. Both Washington and Benjamin Rush advocated a national university to prepare young Americans for the duties of self-government. In his will Washington designated stock in the Potomac Navigation Company to be used in developing a university. (Unfortunately, the Potomac Navigation Company failed in 1828.)

Washington's Farewell Address, delivered on September 17, 1796, states clearly his concept of the connection between democracy and education:

> Promote then as an object of primary importance institutions for the general diffusion of knowledge. In Proportion as the structure of a government gives force to public opinion it is essential that public opinion shall be enlightened.

Enabling Acts

Land grants were continued under the Statehood Acts, beginning with the Ohio Enabling Act of 1802 and continuing through the more recent statehood acts of Alaska and Hawaii. Thus Congress confirmed the validity of the Ordinances drawn up under the Continental Congress.

In later Statehood Acts the land grants became even more extensive, with some states receiving two sections and even four sections, as in the case of Utah and Arizona. A total acreage of 98½ million acres has been granted by the federal government to states for public schools. The largest grant of land was made in Alaska, with an estimated acreage of 21 million acres, approximately a fifth of the total acreage granted. The size of the land grant to Alaska may be accounted for by the size of the state and, too, its long status as a territory with the majority of the land being government owned.

THE MIDDLE PERIOD

The Morrill Act

The Middle Period is marked by the historic Morrill Act of 1862, which donated lands to the states and territories for the establishment of colleges. This act represents, according to Gordon Lee, the first attempt to establish through congressional action a national policy with regard to federal aid to education. . . . Introduced first in 1857, and again in 1861, this act was finally passed by the 39th Congress in 1862. The differences between the first bill and the act as passed five years later consist of two points: (1) the original bill specified 20,000 acres per senator and representative in each state, while the final act allotted 30,000 acres per congressman, and (2) the original bill contained no provision for military training which was added later.

Passed by Congress when first introduced, the bill was vetoed by James Buchanan who explained his decision thus:

1. The bill was unconstitutional.
2. It interfered with states' rights.
3. It aided just one aspect of education.
4. The bill was extravagant.

The arguments for the bill as stated more than a hundred years ago were: (1) the need for scientific, agricultural, and industrial training; (2) the fact that most existing colleges were primarily classical; (3) the regional inequalities in the ability to support education; and (4) the belief that too much of the public land was falling into private hands.

The colleges and universities established under the Morrill Act now include sixty-eight institutions whose combined enrollment represents 20 per cent of all undergraduates, while they constitute only 4 per cent of the total number of colleges and universities in the country. Including such outstanding names as Massachusetts Institute of Technology, Ohio State University, and the University of California, these institutions grant close to 40 per cent of the doctoral degrees awarded in all fields of study. . . . It is difficult to overemphasize the significance of the Morrill Act of 1862, which not only determined policy with respect to the federal government's role in education but also granted aid for specific educational purposes.

The United States Office of Education

The post-Civil War period saw President Andrew Johnson establishing a Department of Education in March of 1867, with Henry Barnard as its first commissioner. In 1869, Congress reduced the Department to a Bureau of the Department of the Interior. Later in 1930, it was shifted to the Federal Security Agency, and finally, in 1953, to the Department of Health, Education and Welfare. . . .

The purposes in establishing a federal Office of Education included the collection and diffusion of information about education and the encouragement of education. These purposes were to be effected through the collection and publishing of educational data, through educational research, and through the administration of funds and various programs. The budget for the Office of Education for the fiscal year 1961–62, including salaries and expenses, was $11.5 million.

. . . .

FEDERAL AID TO EDUCATION: A FORECAST

Before we consider the future possibilities of federal involvement in education, it is interesting to note what has been accomplished since the eighteenth century, for it has been said that "the future is but an extension of the past." Following is a chronological summary of federal legislation since 1777 [and until 1965].

Summary of Federal Aid Legislation: 1777–1965

1777 Initiation of direct administration of education programs—the instruction of military personnel, including schooling in mathematics.
1785 Commencement of aid to territories for education by endowment of schools with public lands.
1787 Commencement of endowment of public institutions of higher education with public lands—Northwest Ordinance: "Schools and the means of education shall forever be encouraged."
1802 Establishment of the first federal institution of higher education—Military Academy at West Point.
1804 District of Columbia—federal provision for education begins.
1862 The First Morrill Act—initiated federal policy of aid to states for agricultural and industrial education through land grants for colleges.
1867 Federal Department of Education established by Congress; later the Office of Education.
1874 Introduction of the principle of federal-state matching of funds for education.
1887 Hatch Act—encouraged scientific investigation in agriculture.
1890 The Second Morrill Act—introduction of federal grants of money for college instruction in specified areas of learning.
1914 Smith-Lever Act—matching of funds for agricultural and home economics instruction.
1917 The Smith-Hughes Act—began policy of promoting vocational education below college level through assistance with teachers' salaries.
1918 Rehabilitation training for disabled veterans.
1919 Federal surplus property available to educational institutions.

1920 The National Defense Act of 1920—direct relationship between the federal government and educational institutions.

1920 Smith-Bankhead Act—federal-state cooperation in vocational rehabilitation; education for people disabled in industry.

1933 Federal Emergency Relief Administration—supported educational programs.

1935 National Youth Administration—employment for college students.

1935 Bankhead-Jones Act—increased support for land-grant colleges.

1936 Promotion of Inter-American Cultural Relations Convention—international education exchanges.

1936 George-Deen Act—extended the Smith-Hughes Act.

1937 National Cancer Institute Act—provided fellowship grants.

1937 Civilian Conservation Corps—provided vocational education.

1941 Lanham Act—provided educational assistance for schools in communities affected by the federal government's activities.

1943 Vocational Rehabilitation Act—aid for disabled veterans.

1944 The Servicemen's Readjustment Act—G.I. Bill, educational aid for veterans.

1944 Surplus Property Act—government surplus given to educational institutions.

1946 George-Barden Act—extended Smith-Hughes Act by increasing appropriation.

1946 National School Lunch—gave funds and food to public and nonpublic schools; school milk program added in 1954.

1948 Smith-Mundt Act—program of international educational exchanges.

1949 Federal Property and Administrative Services Act—surplus property disposal for educational, health, and civil defense purposes.

1950 The National Science Foundation Act—promoted progress in science through scholarships and fellowships in fields of science.

1950 The Housing Act—low interest rates for loans to institutions of higher learning for building of housing facilities.

1950 Federal Impact Laws (P.L. 815 and P.L. 874)—extended the Lanham Act of 1941; provided assistance to communities affected by activities of the federal government for construction and operation of schools.

1952 National Science Foundation—fellowship program.

1956 Library Services Act—grants for improvement of library facilities.

1958 United States and Union of Soviet Socialist Republics agree to exchange study groups in educational and cultural fields.

1958 The National Defense Education Act—provided for graduate fellowships in education—science, mathematics, foreign languages, counseling and guidance, educational technology.

1958 Fogarty-McGovern Act—federal grants to train teachers of mentally retarded children.

1961 Area Redevelopment Act—training of persons in redevelopment areas.

1961 Peace Corps Act—supplied teachers and technicians to underdeveloped nations.

1961 Juvenile Delinquency and Youth Offenses Control—study of problem.

1962 Manpower Development and Training Act—up-to-date training for the unemployable.

1963 Health Professions Educational Assistance Act—construction of facilities and student loans.

1963 Mental Retardation Facilities and Community Mental Health Centers Construction Act—training of teachers and demonstration projects.

1963 Higher Education Facilities Act of 1963—grants to all colleges, public and private, for improvement of facilities.

1963 Amendments to the Manpower Development and Training Act—expansion of provisions of law, 1962.

1963 Vocational Education Act of 1963—construction of vocational schools with expanded offerings; extended Impact Laws (1950) and NDEA (1958).

1964 Economic Opportunity Act of 1964—war on poverty through retraining and remedial education and other opportunities.

1964 The Civil Rights Act of 1964—desegregation of the schools enforced and assisted.

1964 Juvenile Delinquency and Youth Offenses Control Act Amendment—new programs and special studies.

1964 The National Commission on Technology and Automation and Economic Progress—commission to study impact of technological change.

1964 Amendments to National Defense Education Act—extended and expanded to include areas of English, reading, history and geography.

1965 Elementary and Secondary Education Act—federal grants to states for allocation to school districts with low income families.

1965 National Foundation for the Arts and Humanities—foundation to support humanities and the arts through grants.

1965 Higher Education Act of 1965—aid to colleges, students, and teachers.

Whatever other predictions are made regarding the future of federal aid to education, this much is certain: The importance of education to the nation has clearly been recognized, and attention will continue to focus on education for all the people and on the general improvement of the quality of that education. The years ahead promise to be the most exciting and challenging in all educational history as we Americans follow the precedents which have been established, for we have the record before us of an American educational system which has moved from provincial beginnings toward a high degree of centralization and federal involvement.

Federal involvement

Despite opposition, the involvement of the federal government will continue at a rapidly increasing rate at all levels of education. One reason for this increased involvement is that the number of individuals directly concerned with education will continue to grow. At the present time, approximately one-fourth of the nation is directly involved in education; this number will soon encompass fully one-third of the national population as enrollments at all levels of education increase. College enrollments alone, for example, are expected to increase 50 per cent before the end of this decade.

With increased enrollments, will come increased spending in education. The cost of education will rise until the educational budget rivals that of the Defense Department. In 1965, educational expenditures were estimated at $30 billion. President Johnson's budget for the fiscal year 1965–66 called for a 75 per cent increase in spending through the U.S. Office of Education.

The basis for the *Great Society* is clearly education. Peter F. Drucker, writing in *Harper's* in 1965, stated: "Education is about to take over from the Welfare State as a basic commitment of the American people. One might call this new phenomenon the Knowledge State. Education is bound to become a focus of political life and political conflict." The administration has obviously placed increased emphasis on domestic affairs, with a definite focus on education.

Not only are we concerned with the sheer quantity of the educational enterprise, but we are also becoming increasingly involved in improving the quality of education—the teaching, the curriculum, and the methodology. Patterned after the very successful National Science Foundation is the National Foundation of the Arts and Humanities, which also attempts to improve the quality of education. The expansion of NDEA in 1964 encompassed broad areas of the curriculum, emphasizing teacher education as well as content and new media. The Elementary and Secondary Education Act of 1965 also stressed research and development in education. It is clear, therefore, that the federal government intends to increase its direct involvement in the general improvement of the nation's education.

Assistance to education by the federal government will continue to be of a pragmatic nature following the course established by previous Congresses, for there has been a close correlation between the federal government's involvement in education and both foreign and domestic crises. Education has been used to solve society's problems, and it will be called upon again to solve the problems posed by automation and leisure.

DISCUSSION QUESTIONS

1. Federal aid to education has increased from $11.5 millions in the 1961–1962 budget to $3 billion, 900 million, exclusive of Head Start and Upward Bound, in 1966–1967. What are the implications of this increase?
2. In reviewing the history of education in the United States, what are the major trends and purposes that become apparant?

EDGAR FULLER

Government Financing of Public and Private Education

There are some federally financed educational activities, all with wholly laudable general objectives, which raise serious problems and require continuing dialogue among the educational partners to resolve. The Higher Education Facilities Act of 1963, for instance, authorizes large federal funds to pay part of the cost of constructing educational facilities for public, private, and sectarian institutions of higher education, all of which are equally eligible to receive these tax funds. Thus our national government finances construction of educational facilities that cannot legally be financed by the states themselves under their own state constitutions. Does this reflect sound national policy?

The Economic Opportunity Act of 1964 authorizes large federal funds for educational programs for young children, youth, and adults. It is directed toward the laudable objective of eliminating poverty, but it impinges strongly and sometimes adversely upon education. What are the issues here? How is it possible for hastily contrived private corporations, composed of and controlled by private interest groups both secular and religious but not representing the entire community, to exercise public authority in conducting educational programs with the tax funds of all the people? If it is possible, is it desirable?

In the Elementary and Secondary Education Act of 1965, Congress has mandated that the local public education agency, as a condition for receiving funds, must first develop its programs and projects in cooperation with the public or private nonprofit agencies operating anti-poverty programs. This approaches definition of cooperation as a one-way street. It does not discourage a few anti-poverty program administrators from pointedly avoiding cooperation with the public schools except to gain assistance for their

Reprinted from *Phi Delta Kappan,* Vol. XLVII, No. 7 (March 1966), pp. 365–372, with permission of the publisher.

own federally financed programs. Would not statutory prescription of mutual cooperation be better?

There are other unsolved problems in connection with administration of portions of such federal laws as the National Defense Education Act of 1958, the Manpower Development and Training Act of 1962 as amended, and Title II of the Elementary and Secondary Education Act of 1965, providing federal funds for library materials, textbooks, and supplementary materials for public and private school pupils and teachers. These and other problems must eventually become involved in determinations of national policy in education, for some aspects of federal activities in education appear to many citizens to be more damaging than helpful to public education.

It is not unusual for federal officials to present strained and legally elusive interpretations of federal requirements that clearly favor private schools. To qualify for federal funds, more than one state attorney general has thus been led to do likewise in interpreting his own state constitution. This is illustrated by a legal opinion on administration of the Elementary and Secondary Education Act of 1965 in Kentucky, interpreting Section 189 of its state constitution, which provides that "no portion of any fund or tax now existing, or that may hereafter be raised or levied for educational purposes, shall be appropriated to, or used by, or in aid of, any church, sectarian or denominational school."

Apparently assuming that the federally financed programs administered by the state educational agency would not be constitutional in Kentucky for the use of state or local funds, the opinion isolated the federal funds from state and local funds so the federal funds could be used in Kentucky. The Attorney General said:

> We are of the opinion that the state and local boards of education and the state department of education are, under Public Law 89–10, likewise only agencies and instrumentalities designated by the Congress to effectuate the present Act. It might be said that these agencies function as trustees or custodians of the federal funds (and property purchased therewith) made available for these programs by the federal government and that in such capacity they are simply administering or disbursing federal funds to carry out the objectives of the federal legislation. In reaching this conclusion we have necessarily determined that the funds provided here essentially retain their character as federal funds though placed in the hands of state and local agencies. We think this is implicit in the Act which retains authority in the Commissioner to revoke, withdraw or set-off funds for non-compliance with the Act and with programs approved thereunder."[1]

The law officers of several states have said that no public agency in their respective states can administer funds under Title II of the Elementary and Secondary Education Act of 1965, thus forcing the U.S. Office of Education to place this responsibility in the hands of private agencies in those states,

[1] Opinion of Attorney General of Kentucky, OAG-865 (December 17, 1965).

unless circuitous methods are adopted. This makes it clear how important it is that our topic here shall become the subject of a continuing federal-state-local governmental and educational dialogue. Even this will not be enough. Eventually decisions must be made by the courts, with the public-private aspects adjudicated by the U.S. Supreme Court under the First Amendment. Because this is the fundamental law for all levels of government, the federal government has a special obligation to expedite this process. Many similar illustrations could be given of the current situation that concerns us.

HISTORY OF RESPONSIBILITY FOR EDUCATION

Let us look at the historical background. Until it became too large and important to leave to chance, education was substantially a private affair. Only in this century has the full development of human resources become an individual need and a public necessity. Some older societies continue to confine most higher education to the few needed to govern and to set social standards, leaving common labor and work requiring only simple skills as the occupational role of most people. Even in our country, serious programs to develop maximum potentialities of all the people are far from complete realization. Such institutions as this college and the school systems it serves are nevertheless based on the imperfectly realized ideal of universal education.

Private education has necessarily been more selective in its purposes, offerings, and clientele. It has been based on desires to have certain kinds of education for certain groups, and to have schools to develop new ideas, to establish richer programs at higher costs than can be afforded for all children and youth, or to make profits as commercial enterprises. We need private educational institutions and approve of them. They deserve the broad constitutional protection they enjoy, but this should not mean protection for them to become both governmentally financed and privately controlled at the same time.

Large private school systems are typically church related. Historically, they have often dominated education. For centuries churches have developed human talent for their own purposes through their own schools. Education established primarily for religious purposes has often received, and in many countries continues to receive, exclusive or special privileges from governments, notably including financial support from tax sources. This was the condition that caused many of our ancestors to flee Europe to settle the American colonies.

Ironically, the same groups that had sought freedom from an established church in Europe had not learned religious tolerance for others, and proceeded to develop their own officially established churches in the American colonies. Thus the Congregational church was established by law in

Massachusetts, New Hampshire, and Connecticut; the Dutch Reformed church in New York; and the Anglican church in Maryland, Virginia, Georgia, and the Carolinas. All groups were welcome in Rhode Island, which provided a notable exception. Pennsylvania and Delaware did not discriminate among Protestant denominations, although there were some restrictions against Catholics.

As the colonies developed pluralistic populations, religious conflict was centered in religiously sponsored schools. Other denominations demanded legal and financial benefits from the government equal to those enjoyed by the established churches. Some states then experimented with multiple establishments of religion by authorizing payments of taxes to additional denominations of the taxpayer's choice. When this arrangement failed to reduce religious conflict in Virginia and tended to favor only the largest denominations, Jefferson and Madison led the historic movement that eliminated special legal ties between the state and all religious denominations in Virginia.

Soon afterward they wrote their principle, which Jefferson called separation of church and state and Madison called separation of religion and government, into the First Amendment to the Constitution of the United States as follows: "Congress shall make no law respecting an establishment of religion or prohibiting the free exercise thereof. . . ."

It is noteworthy that schools of established churches continued relatively unchanged for many years after the adoption of the U.S. Constitution, perhaps because the First Amendment then applied only to the national Congress. Virginia had assured itself of free exercise of religion and had prohibited establishment of religion so that tax funds could not be used by church-related schools, but even here a statewide public school system did not immediately follow. In fact, Jefferson's legislation to establish a Virginia public school system on a statewide basis failed of enactment in 1796.

The last of the American states to abandon legal establishment of religion was Massachusetts, in 1833. Four years later, state-wide public education began when the Massachusetts legislature authorized a state board of education, and Horace Mann gave up his legislative seat and his private law practice to become the executive officer of that board. Thereafter, statewide nonsectarian public school systems developed gradually and became general little more than a century ago.

Following the adoption of the First Amendment, most of the states made similar provisions in their own constitutions as they entered the Union, but they spelled out more specifically the provisions governing tax funds for religious education. This issue had been the most important reason for the First Amendment, but because Madison intended the amendment to cover broader areas of church-state relationships he had drafted it in general terms. The latest state constitution to be adopted—Hawaii in 1962—contains the following:

No law shall be enacted respecting an establishment of religion or prohibiting the free exercise thereof, or abridging the freedom of speech or of the press, or of the right of people peaceably to assemble and to petition the government for redress of grievances.

The State shall provide for the establishment, support and control of a statewide system of public schools free from sectarian control, a state university, public libraries and such other educational institutions as may be deemed desirable, including physical facilities therefor. There shall be no segregation in public educational institutions because of race, religion or ancestry; nor shall public funds be appropriated for the support or benefit of any sectarian or private educational institution.[2]

Most state constitutions and laws, like those of Hawaii, bar tax-raised funds from private nondenominational elementary, secondary, and higher institutions of education, as well as from similar institutions that are sectarian in character. There are a few exceptions to this, notably in Pennsylvania and to some extent in New York in the field of higher education, but most states specify that private nondenominational education is legally the same as private church-related education, so far as use of tax-raised funds is concerned.

COURT APPLICATION OF FIRST AMENDMENT

We must now examine the law of the land that relates to our educational situation. We have seen that the First Amendment as authored by Madison applied only to the Congress, preventing it from enacting any law respecting an establishment of religion or prohibiting the free exercise thereof. The Free Exercise Clause and the Establishment Clause are closely related to each other, but are different enough in regard to education to warrant separate consideration here. We shall consider free exercise first.

The Free Exercise Clause protects freedom of religion in distinctive ways. In regard to education, it was the basis for a 1923 decision which invalidated a Nebraska law that prevented teachers in Lutheran schools and their pupils from engaging in religious activities conducted in the German language.[3] In 1925, an Oregon law requiring most children between 8 and 16 years of age to attend public schools also was declared unconstitutional. Both of these cases were decided under the Fourteenth Amendment as a denial of liberty without due process of law. They clearly established the right of Lutheran and Catholic religious schools to exist.[4] These cases upheld the free exercise of religion within church-related schools and paved the way for the First Amendment cases to come.

The Supreme Court has refused to protect free exercise of religious

---

[2] Constitution of Hawaii, Article 1, Section 3, and Article 9, Section 1. For a summary of provisions in state constitutions, see Beach and Will, *The State and Nonpublic Schools,* Misc. No. 28, U.S. Office of Education, 1958.

[3] *Meyer* v. *Nebraska,* 262 U.S. 390 (1923).

[4] *Pierce* v. *Society of Sisters,* 268 U.S. 510 (1925).

practices performed in the name of religion which are violations of civil law,[5] but it has gone to considerable lengths to protect free exercise of religion. In a leading case, a Jehovah's Witness was upheld in his right to make strong public arguments against other religions in spite of his violation of a law requiring a permit to do so. The censorship law was declared unconstitutional under both the Fourteenth and First Amendments as a governmental interference with free exercise of religion.[6] This was the first time the Supreme Court held that the First Amendment applied to the states and their local subdivisions as well as to the federal government. Since 1940 this has become settled law, and the First Amendment is supreme in its field at every level of government.

The Supreme Court holds that religion is a private matter and that all governments must maintain a position of neutrality in regard to it. This mandates neither governmental hostility to religion nor governmental aid to religion. The reasons for this delicate balance were explained by the court as it invalidated a compulsory flag salute requirement that offended the religious beliefs of a child in a public school as follows:

> Struggles to coerce uniformity of sentiment in support of some end thought essential to their time and country have been waged by many good as well as by evil men. . . . It ends up in racial or territorial security, supported by dynasty or regime, and particular plans for saving souls. . . . As governmental pressure toward unity becomes greater, so strife becomes more bitter as to whose unity it shall be. Probably no deeper division of our people could proceed from any provocation than from finding it necessary to choose what doctrine and whose program public educational officials shall compel youth to unite in embracing. . . . No official, high or petty, can prescribe what shall be orthodox in politics, nationalism, religion or other matters of opinion or force citizens to confess by word or act their faith therein. . . . We think the action of local authorities in compelling the flag salute and pledge transcends constitutional limitations on their power and invades the sphere of intellect and spirit which it is the purpose of the First Amendment . . . to reserve from all official control.[7]

In dealing with freedom of religion we should consider the situation in the United States. The largest church enrolls less than one-fourth of our population, and there are altogether some 250 religious denominations. There are several million Jews, more than 100,000 Buddhists and many other non-Christian denominations that make Christianity only one of many when the law treats all religions alike. Thus we have both religious and educational pluralism, both constitutionally protected. Churches may teach their own religion to the pupils in their own schools, as long as the secular part of their programs meet the minimum requirements set by the state for all its young citizens. In our pluralistic society, blending of religion and education disqualifies the school as an institution eligible for financial

---

5 *Reynolds* v. *United States,* 98 U.S. 145 (1878).
6 *Cantwell* v. *Connecticut,* 310 U.S. 296 (1940).
7 *West Virginia State Board of Education* v. *Barnette,* 319 U.S. 624 (1943).

support by government. Otherwise, taxes would be collected from members of all denominations, as well as many millions of citizens who are not members of any denomination, for the teaching of religions in which they do not believe and over which they are prevented by the Free Exercise Clause from exerting any public control. The issues run far deeper than taxes, too, because most Americans depend on public education that must have general public support for effective survival.

Free exercise of religion constitutionally protects persons having religious faiths espoused by churches, along with a very large minority of Americans who are neither active nor inactive members of any church. Many of these millions who are not church members are conscientious citizens, have personal faiths, believe in God, and are in their own ways religious. Some may choose to follow the exhortation of St. James, who said that religion pure and undefiled consists of comforting the widows and orphans in their affliction and in keeping oneself unspotted from the world. Others may follow the definition of a secular psychologist such as William James, who said that religion is comprised of the feelings, acts, and experiences of an individual in his solitude in relation to whatever he may consider to be the Divine.

The First Amendment goes further. It protects freedom to disbelieve as well as to believe, immune from interference by government. Thus a provision of the Maryland state constitution requiring all holders of public offices to swear to belief in God was invalidated by the U.S. Supreme Court in 1961. The result was to grant a commission as a notary public to an atheist who refused to take an oath that he believed in God.[8] In this way, too, the Free Exercise Clause protects the individual against loss of civil rights or coercion by government, leaving him free to believe as he likes without penalty. It is a major guardian of religious freedom.

The Establishment Clause, on the other hand, is applied even in the absence of personal coercion. Neither does its violation require the complete official establishment of a church. Smaller establishments of government in churches, or of sectarian doctrine in governments also violate the Establishment Clause. It preserves governmental neutrality in religion generally.

The Establishment Clause has been applied specifically to prevent the use of tax-based funds by church-related educational institutions. Justice Black defined it in the case of *Everson* v. *Board of Education*[9] as follows:

> The "establishment of religion" clause of the First Amendment means at least this: Neither a state nor the Federal Government can set up a church. Neither can pass laws which aid one religion, aid all religions, or prefer one religion over another. Neither can force nor influence a person to go to or to remain away from church

[8] *Torcaso* v. *Watkins,* 367 U.S. 488 (1961). For a complete discussion of church-state relationships and freedom of religion, see Stokes and Pfeffer, *Church and State in the United States,* Harper and Row, 1964.
[9] *Everson* v. *Board of Education,* 330 U.S. 1 (1947).

against his will or force him to profess a belief or disbelief in any religion. No person can be punished for entertaining or professing religious beliefs or disbeliefs, for church attendance or non-attendance. No tax in any amount, large or small, can be levied to support any religious activities or institutions, whatever they may be called, or whatever form they may adopt to teach or practice religion. Neither a state nor the Federal Government can, openly or secretly, participate in the affairs of any religious organizations or groups and *vice versa.*

The Everson case decided that a school board in New Jersey could use tax funds to pay bus fares for transporting pupils to and from their parochial school. It is the leading case that approves tax-financed benefits to individual pupils primarily for health or safety purposes. All the justices, both the five who agreed with the Everson decision and the four who dissented, nevertheless agreed with the principles of the Establishment Clause as stated by Justice Black, and all later Supreme Court cases have applied his definition.[10]

In 1963 the Supreme Court reaffirmed the principles supporting this line of cases when it held that Bible reading in public schools is inconsistent with the Establishment Clause because it is an exercise of religion.[11] In a concurring opinion, Justice Brennan made some comments of particular interest to persons in public education. He said:

The public schools are supported entirely, in most communities, by public funds—funds exacted not only from parents, nor alone from those who hold particular religious views, nor indeed from those who subscribe to any creed at all. It is implicit in the history and character of American public education that the public schools serve a uniquely *public* function: the training of American citizens in an atmosphere free of parochial, divisive, or separatist influences of any sort—an atmosphere in which children may assimilate a heritage common to all American groups and religions. . . . This is a heritage neither theistic nor atheistic, but simply civic and patriotic. . . .

Attendance at the public schools has never been compulsory; parents remain morally and constitutionally free to choose the academic environment in which they wish their children to be educated. The relationships of the Establishment Clause of the First Amendment to the public school system is preeminently that of reserving such a choice to the individual parent, rather than vesting it in the majority of voters of each State or school district. The choice which is thus preserved is between a public secular education with its uniquely democratic values, and some form of private, or sectarian education, which offers values of its own. . . .

There are many legally untested practices in education more or less related to those that have been clearly declared constitutional or unconstitutional by the courts. Among these are research and development contracts between federal agencies and sectarian institutions that aid the institutions

10 *McCollum* v. *Board of Education,* 333 U.S. 203 (1948), which invalidated religious teaching in a public school during school hours; *Zorach* v. *Clauson,* 343 U.S. 306 (1952), which upheld released time religious instruction held away from school property during school hours; *Engle* v. *Vitale,* 370 U.S. 421 (1962), which banned public prayers in public schools.
11 *Abington School District* v. *Schempp,* 374 U.S. 203 (1963).

as well as the government, institutional base grants to these institutions for development and improvement of their programs in science,[12] various federal programs to subsidize science teaching in all types of higher institutions, and distribution of surplus real estate and personal property to public, nonprofit private, and sectarian schools and colleges. Others are school lunch programs and grants for hospitals and medical schools that relate to the health of students or patients.

Another area includes individual benefits such as G.I. training grants, and several types of scholarships and fellowships that may be used at any approved public, nonprofit private or sectarian institution of education. These sometimes include federal funds to pay institutional costs beyond the cost of tuition and fees for educating the holders of the scholarships or fellowships. Federal funds are also used to purchase laboratory and other equipment that may be retained by the institution after the federally subsidized program which brought it there has been completed, upon approval of such retention by federal officials.

Other largely untested areas include employment of chaplains for the armed services and government military schools. These provide choices of religious leadership for communicants of a few of the largest religions, and are designed to promote the free exercise of religion with minimum infringements on the rights of others. There are also ceremonial public exercises and observances such as chaplains' prayers in legislative bodies, the pledge of allegiance in its amended form with reference to God, theistic inscriptions on coins and public buildings, and observances of selected religious and secular holidays.[13]

Why is the law of the First Amendment so incomplete? The basic legal rationale for current federal programs that allocate tax funds to religious educational institutions is explained in a "Memorandum on the Impact of the First Amendment to the Constitution upon Federal Aid to Education" dated March 28, 1961. It was released by the Department of Health, Education, and Welfare with the approval of the Department of Justice. The memorandum was in effect a brief to justify constitutionally indirect and some direct federal aids to nonprofit private and sectarian institutions of education, especially those programs authorized by Congress prior to 1961 or under consideration by the Congress in 1961.

The memorandum made a suggestion about legislation Congress might enact to permit judicial review ". . . in the context of an actual case or controversy between the federal government and an institution seeking some form of assistance." It did not suggest any way for taxpayers to bring

---

12 Such as National Science Foundation grants in 1964 to Florida Presbyterian College ($6,801) ; Nebraska Wesleyan University ($10,092) ; St. Mary's College ($4,200) , Indiana; Texas Lutheran College ($5,460) ; Christian Brothers College ($8,400) , Tennessee; Gonzaga University ($4,900) , State of Washington.

13 See *McGowan* v. *Maryland,* 366 U.S. 420 (1961) .

legal actions to enforce the First Amendment, but intimated that Congress could legislate as it pleased unless it provided for the "actual case or controversy" as suggested. The memorandum concluded with the following paragraph: "In the absence of some such statutory provisions, there appears to be no realistic likelihood that federal legislation raising the constitutional issues discussed in this memorandum will be resolved by judicial decision."

The strategy of those who favor increased federal tax support of private and sectarian educational institutions without judicial review under the First Amendment has been to prevent such cases from getting into court. The reason why this strategy has thus far succeeded can be found in a 1923 Supreme Court case decided under the Fourteenth Amendment. The theory there was the taking of property without due process of law, and the monetary loss of the federal taxpayer was held insufficient to give him standing to sue to question the constitutionality of a federal expenditure.[14] This was before the Cantwell case made the First Amendment applicable to the states.

It seems unreasonable to require a substantial monetary loss to support a taxpayer's suit under the First Amendment, which is really a civil rights situation in which monetary loss is relatively inconsequential. Nevertheless, the only avenue for First Amendment cases thus far has been a tortuous route through the state courts. Such a case, begun in Maryland in 1963, may soon reach the Supreme Court, and hearings have been scheduled in the Senate Committee on Constitutional Rights to explore ways to authorize judicial review in federal courts for First Amendment cases involving education.

Those who favor federal financing of private and sectarian education will probably support the position that Congress should determine First Amendment law in education without easier recourse to the courts than the limited scope of judicial review now existing. This would take advantage of only Fourteenth Amendment law prior to 1940 on the issue of the right of taxpayers and citizens to sue under the First Amendment, and unbalance the legislative-executive-judicial branches of the government in favor of the legislative and executive.

IMPORTANCE FOR PUBLIC EDUCATION

It is fair to ask how public education would be damaged if private and sectarian institutions should continue to use and gain additional federal tax funds. Through matching and federal administrative techniques such practices eventually could force the states to grant the same access to state and local tax funds. Such would mean the splintering of education into public,

[14] *Frothingham* v. *Mellon*, 262 U.S. 447 (1923).

nonprofit private, and sectarian sections. For our country, this would be undesirable.

Four decades after the much smaller country of Holland adopted a similar program, enrollment in its public schools had declined from 75 per cent to 30 per cent of the total student population. Only the Protestant and Roman Catholic systems increased greatly in enrollment. A much larger number of denominational and private school systems and special interest private schools operated by nonprofit tax-exempt organizations could be expected in this country. The rate of decline of public education would depend on the amount of tax funds granted to private schools either directly or indirectly and the rate of necessary reduction of services in the public schools due to losses of pupils, teachers, public support, and financial resources.

Should private schools be tax-financed, the elementary and secondary public schools would be left to educate children from denominations too small to operate their own schools, the unchurched, the culturally deprived, and the rejects and problem students from the private schools which can choose their own pupils. Tax funds would be combined with private funds to finance schools segregated on the basis of religion, social status, wealth, and special interests, and would as seriously affect the public schools as an effective educational agency as would segregation by race. The neglect of minorities would be comparable, for both the smaller denominational and other private programs and the public educational programs would necessarily be lean in numerous localities. Community support for financing public school facilities and operation would be on a charity basis from the community power structures whose members would control both public and private funds as patrons of their own private schools.

Most serious would be the religious, social, political, and economic divisiveness that would follow. In Holland almost the whole society is organized along the lines established in the three school systems. It is divided into Catholic, Protestant, and neutral clubs, civic associations, political parties, merchants' groups, labor unions, and trade associations.[15] In our country the splintering of society would probably be even more serious because of the great size and diversity of our country and its people. The minority public school with its underprivileged clientele could no longer be an effective force for unity. It would be disabled in its efforts to supply the "heritage common to all American groups and religions" of which Justice Brennan spoke. The public school could become one divisive school among many divisive denominational and other private schools at a time when its great unifying function is needed more than ever before.

The federal government is today moving into a position from which it may undermine the fiscal base of the public schools within a few years.

[15] See A. Stafford Clayton, "Effects of Public Support of Church-Related Schools," *Phi Delta Kappan*, September, 1965, pp. 19–26.

Should large federal funds be made available to the states to match and distribute, with both private schools and public schools eligible under federal law, federal financial incentives and internal political pressures on the states may become irresistible in making private and sectarian education eligible for full tax support. Already we have seen the beginnings of federal bypassing of the states, passing federal funds through fiscal conduits legally insulated against state and local constitutions and laws.

As Lord Acton said, power corrupts, and absolute power corrupts absolutely. The power of the federal government over education, unless protection is possible under the limitations of the First Amendment, may force the states into a single federally prescribed mold. Should states be led or forced by the power of federal money to amend their state constitutions to permit state matching of federal funds for private nonprofit and religious schools, the next short step could be federal laws requiring that private schools must be eligible under state law for state tax funds before any state can qualify for federal funds either for public or private schools.

Political pressures to bring about a financial merger of church and state are damaging to the spirit of our cooperative religious pluralism, which thrives under the protection of the Free Exercise Clause. Tax support for a multiplicity of private schools will undermine both the tax base and the community support that public education must have to meet its obligations to the people it must serve. For these reasons, it is in the national interest to have judicial definition of the boundaries of the First Amendment in education as soon and as thoroughly as possible.

DISCUSSION QUESTIONS

1. Does federal assistance to private and sectarian schools constitute the threat to the public schools and to the fabric of American social life that Fuller visualizes?
2. Is the Office of Education evading or infringing upon the First Amendment in implementing federal aid to education, as Fuller states?
3. In justifying private educational institutions, Fuller states that they are ". . . based on desires to have certain kinds of education for certain groups, and to have schools to develop new ideas, to establish richer programs at higher costs than can be afforded for all children and youth, or to make profits as commercial enterprises." Evaluate his rationale for private schools, within the framework of an American democratic society.

HENRY M. LEVIN

The Failure of the Public Schools and the Free Market Remedy

The American public schools have been severely criticized in recent years, and no schools more so than those responsible for educating "disadvantaged children" in urban areas. The utter failure of traditional schooling to impart even basic reading skills to substantial numbers of youngsters has stimulated a barrage of proposals, from educators and noneducators alike, to change the educational system.

While some critics suggest that changes within the present structure would cure the impotence of the inner-city schools, others see a necessity for much more radical changes in the structure itself. Among the former group are proponents of new instructional techniques and remedial programs, while some of the latter group would turn over the schools to the community and others would dismantle the present system of public schools altogether, replacing them with private schools that would be—in part—publicly financed.

The aim of this article is to explore those proposals which would replace the public schools with a free market strategy for elementary and secondary schooling. The discussion will be based upon the assumption that basic education yields two types of benefits—those to the student (private benefits) and those to society-at-large (social benefits)—and that any proposal for educational change should be judged on the basis of both criteria. My analysis suggests that the free market approach is likely to increase the private returns of schooling, but that these gains would be largely offset by social costs higher than those received from the present schools or other feasible alternatives. Accordingly, I shall construct a balance sheet that will present both the losses and the gains inherent in replacing our present system with a market scheme. Finally, I shall outline several plans that would implement competition among schools without a framework that might foster both the private and the social goals of education.

Whatever the causes, wherever the blame may be, it seems clear that the traditional public schools are failing to meet the needs and the expectations of vast numbers of their clientele.[1]

In the light of their records of failure in educating the disadvantaged, how is it that these institutions have survived? How is it that even when

Reprinted from *The Urban Review,* Vol. II, No. 7 (June 1968), pp. 32–37, with permission of the publisher, the Center for Urban Education.

[1] A terse, but skillful, description of the "organizational sclerosis" that characterizes the slum schools is found in Christopher Jencks, "Is the Public School Obsolete?" *The Public Interest,* winter 1966, pp. 18–28.

schools do try to adapt to the educational needs of the poor, the major efforts are so limited and unimaginative?

For example, most efforts at compensatory education place principal emphasis on the largely conventional approaches of reduced class size and the addition of specialized remedial services. In the first instance, a typical reduction in class size from 30 students to 20 is very expensive (increasing per pupil expenditure about one-third); yet its effectiveness has yet to be shown in improving educational outcomes for disadvantaged children. On the other hand, remedial services are likely to be helpful to a few individual students, but they are not capable of improving a situation which calls for massive efforts, not minor repairs.

In the main, the continued existence of these schools derives from the fact that they do not have to be effective to survive. In most cases they perform for a captive audience. Pupils are assigned to them for better or for worse, and each school can retain most of its students because the majority of pupils have no other alternatives.

A MARKET FOR SCHOOLING

The proponents of the market approach believe that by giving students and their families a choice of schools, and by requiring schools to compete for students, massive increases in educational effectiveness and output would result. For, if schools had to compete for students, they would likely be much more responsive to the particular needs of their clientele. That is, the private schools—in order to achieve goals of profit, or in the case of nonprofit ones, capacity enrollments—must provide what appears to be good schooling in order to attract students.

The father of this approach is the Chicago economist, Milton Friedman, and it is Friedman's basic scheme that dominates the proposals of others who would also replace the public schools with a market of choices.[2] Before outlining the Friedman plan, however, it is important to point out that all of the advocates of the market approach view basic schooling as a public function. They do so because at the very least, ". . . a stable and democratic society is impossible without widespread acceptance of some common set of values and without a minimum degree of literacy and knowledge on the part of most citizens. Education contributes both."[3] Thus, because of the social benefits derived from a citizenry which has received some basic level of schooling, the responsibility of paying for this education is considered to be a social burden rather than an individual one. But Friedman

2 Christopher Jencks has also endorsed the Friedman plan in the work previously cited. The fact that the "new left" (Jencks) and the "old right" (Friedman) can concur on the same educational palliative is reason enough to consider the market approach to education as a serious alternative to the present system.

3 Milton Friedman, "The Role of Government in Education," in Robert A. Solo ed., *Economics and the Public Interest,* New Jersey: Rutgers University Press, 1955, pp. 124–125.

would separate the financing, which would be public, from the management and operation of schools, which would be private.

Government could require a minimum level of education which they could finance by giving parents vouchers redeemable for a specified maximum sum per child per year if spent on 'approved' educational services. Parents would be free to spend their sum and any additional sum on purchasing educational service from an 'approved' institution of their own choice. The educational services could be rendered by private enterprises operated for profit, or by nonprofit institutions of various kinds.[4]

The result would be that:

. . . Parents could express their views about schools directly, by withdrawing their children from one school and sending them to another to a much greater extent than is now possible.[5]

Indeed, the scheme is based upon the plausible premise that:

Here as in other fields, competitive private enterprise is likely to be far more efficient in meeting consumer demands than either nationalized (publicly run) enterprises or enterprises run to serve other purposes.[6]

It is interesting to note that almost two centuries before Friedman, Adam Smith asserted that while the public should pay some of the costs of teaching children of the working class the 3 R's, the teachers would soon neglect their responsibilities if they were fully paid out of public funds.[7]

In summary then, the government would provide families with a voucher for each school-age child, which would guarantee a maximum specified sum of money which could be paid as tuition to any "approved" school. Nonpublic schools would compete among themselves—and perhaps with the public schools—for students by offering a variety of educational choices.[8] Freedom of entry by schools into the market—provided that they met minimum qualifications—would insure efficiency in the production of schooling, and students and their families would be given a market of

---

[4] *Ibid.*, p. 127.

[5] *Ibid.*, p. 129.

[6] *Ibid.*

[7] More specifically he stated that:

> The public can facilitate this acquisition (of reading, writing, and arithmetic among children of the poor) by establishing in every parish or district a little school, where children may be taught for a reward so moderate, that even a common labourer may afford it; the master being partly, but not wholly paid by the public; because, if he was wholly, or even principally paid by it, *he would soon learn to neglect his business.* (Emphasis provided.)

Adam Smith, *The Wealth of Nations,* Modern Library Edition, New York: Random House, Inc., 1937, p. 737.

[8] Friedman has suggested that under certain conditions it might be desirable to have a mixed system of both public schools and private alternatives. Parents who did not wish to use the public institution would receive a tuition voucher the maximum sum of which would be equal to the cost of educating a child in a government school. See, "The Role of Government in Education," *op. cit.*, p. 130.

educational alternatives in place of the present rigid assignment practices. Moreover, such competition would induce innovation and experimentation in that each school would try to obtain competitive advantages over the others. Thus, the operation of the market would provide far more choices and a greater degree of efficiency in the schooling of all students, especially those pupils who are presently confined to slum schools.[9]

PRIVATE AND SOCIAL BENEFITS

I have already noted that there are two types of benefits associated with basic (elementary and secondary) schooling: private benefits and social ones. The private benefits represent those which accrue to the individual (and his family) tangibly in the form of higher earnings, and intangibly in the form of heightened appreciation, awareness and insights, and so on. If all of the returns to basic education were private ones, a strong case could be made for letting the market determine the production and allocation of schooling among the population.

Yet, as Friedman recognizes, the very reason that basic schooling is considered to be a public responsibility is that it also yields benefits to the society as a whole. In this social context, there are at least two roles which elementary and secondary schooling are supposed to fulfill:

1. Provision of minimum levels of literacy, knowledge, and understanding of our common heritage which are necessary for the functioning of a stable and democratic society, and
2. reduction of disparities in incomes and opportunities presently associated with race and social class.

What, then, are the probable effects of the market approach on the production of both private and social benefits?

In terms of private benefits, it is likely to be true that any measure of competition among schools would lead to increases in their effectiveness. The motive for success—profit maximization—would require that a school meet the need of its students better than its competitors for any given cost. The fact that existing policies would have to be re-examined in the light of their educational contributions would probably engender thorough changes in the administration of the schools. By increasing the number of decision-making units, the probability of schools innovating to gain competitive advantages would be far greater than under the present system. While many examples of such change can be envisioned, a notable one would be the introduction of those new curricula and instructional aids which showed great promise relative to their costs. Most of the existing public institutions have been loath to adopt any but the most modest changes in their educational strategies.

[9] Jencks, "Is the Public School Obsolete?" *op. cit.*

Another fruit of competition among schools might be more imaginative recruitment policies for teachers. At present, teachers are hired on the basis of a single-salary schedule, one which fixes the teachers' salary on the basis of how much schooling he has had and the amount of his teaching experience. Such factors as the quality of his schooling, his actual teaching ability, his expected performance as reflected in his preservice teaching and personality traits or his field of specialization have no effect on his salary. Under this system, the more imaginative persons—who are often able to reap greater returns outside of teaching—either do not enter the schools or leave after short periods of time. On the other hand, those who have few alternatives in the labor market remain in the schools, protected from dismissal by life-long tenure contracts after only three years of experience. Thus, while there are some exceptions, the single-salary schedule fosters mediocrity in teacher selection and retention.

Furthermore, it leads to shortages of teachers with training in some specialties and surpluses of teachers with other training. That is, while mathematics and science majors receive higher starting pay in the market-at-large, they receive the same salaries as do other specialists in the schools. It comes as no surprise, then, to find that schools show a shortage of teachers properly trained in science and mathematics and a surplus of social studies and male physical education teachers.[10] As a result, of course, the social studies and physical education teachers are then often assigned to teach secondary courses in mathematics, physics, chemistry, and other shortage areas. Competitive schools would have to hire on the basis of the realities of the market place rather than on the basis of rigid salary schedules.

Moreover, competitive schools would be more likely to adopt a policy of flexible class size depending upon subject matter, grade level, and type of student, which is a more sensible goal than maintaining uniform class sizes. There would also be more willingness to differentiate staffing by substituting teacher aides, curriculum specialists, and other specialized personnel for classroom teachers wherever accompanied by increases in efficiency *ceteris paribus*. Most important of all, individual differences among teachers might be utilized as an asset in the educational process by enabling teachers to pursue their own teaching styles and approaches in place of the present attempts of the schools to standardize curricula, syllabi, and pedagogy along narrow guidelines.

These are some of the changes that we might realistically envision among competitive schools, changes that are not now feasible given the institutional rigidities of the typical public school system. Since Friedman might leave the public schools as an alternative, only the best of them—those

[10] See Joseph Kershaw and Roland McKean, *Teacher Shortages and Salary Schedules*, New York: McGraw-Hill, 1962. I have also developed an extensive set of data on this phenomenon which will be published in the future.

which could compete effectively—would survive over the long run. That is, competition would keep the remaining public schools on their toes.

In short, it is likely that Friedman is correct in asserting that the market approach is a more efficient device for satisfying the educational preferences of consumers than is the traditional, highly-centralized public school system. Under a competitive market, we could probably expect that greater educational benefits would accrue to students and their families. Yet, increases in private benefits do not necessarily yield similar increases in social benefits.

THE EDUCATIONAL MARKET PLACE AND SOCIAL BENEFITS

Our schools shoulder the primary burden for satisfying at least two social goals: Those of imparting minimum levels of literacy, knowledge and the common values necessary for a stable democracy; and of decreasing disparities in incomes and opportunities associated with race and social class.

Friedman considers only the first of these social objectives. Under his plan, schools would be required to meet minimum standards—such as a common content in their programs—much as restaurants are required to ". . . maintain minimum sanitary standards."[11] But Friedman's analogy is a bad one, for requiring a common content in school programs is more like requiring uniform nutritional offerings in restaurants, not just cleanliness. Who would decide what minimum content was, and how would it be assessed? Would the traditional sequence of courses be considered minimal? Would teachers be required to satisfy certain criteria, or could anyone be hired to teach? All of these issues would have to be reconciled, and it is likely that the common content requirements to which Friedman alludes would lead to far more extensive regulation than he suggests. And obviously the greater the requirements which are imposed, the more alike schools would be; and in the extreme, the very animal which we wish to replace might merely be disguised in the new trappings of a highly regulated private industry.

Beyond the social responsibilities of assuring minimal literacy and basic skills, there is also the responsibility of exposing children to fellow students who are drawn from a variety of social, economic, and racial groups. It has also been asserted that slum children become more highly motivated and are likely to develop greater aspirations when they are exposed to children from the middle-class. Our present system of segregating school populations according to the neighborhoods in which they are located does little to achieve the goal of mixed-class schools. Friedman's approach, however, makes no provision for ensuring that students attend schools in racially and socially diverse environments. Indeed, it is likely that social segregation—one of the by-products of the neighborhood school—would increase under

[11] Friedman, "The Role of Government in Education," *op. cit.*, p. 127.

the market proposal. For, experience with private schools suggests even greater segregation of student bodies on the basis of religious, ethnic, racial, economic, and other social criteria.

The significance of the probability of increased socioeconomic segregation under a free market system is that such a result would work directly against the second social responsibility of the schools—the equalization of opportunity for all racial and social groups. Friedman asserts that: "the widening of the range of choice under a private system would operate to reduce . . . stratification;"[12] and Jencks agrees with him, but neither gives any evidence to support this contention.

It is interesting to note that at least two Southern states, Virginia and Louisiana, adopted tuition plans to circumvent the court edict requiring them to integrate their public schools. In particular, then, how have the poor fared in the market place?

THE POOR AND THE MARKET PLACE

If the public sector has failed the poor in the efficient production and allocation of social services, the private market can hardly claim a greater degree of success in satisfying their needs. For example, a recent study of the Federal Trade Commission showed that goods purchased for $1.00 at wholesale sold for an average of $2.65 in stores located in poor neighborhoods, but only $1.65 in stores located in the "general market."[13] Geographic mobility, education, income, access to capital (credit)—the very things which the poor lack and the middle class possess—are the characteristics that enable one to operate most successfully in the private market. The failure of the market to give rich and poor equal access to privately produced goods and services should, in itself, make us skeptical about applying it to education.

First, while the private market would likely provide many educational alternatives to middle-class children, there would probably be far fewer sellers of educational services to the children of the poor. It is important to note that schooling must be consumed at the point of purchase; therefore geographical location of schools becomes a salient feature of the market place. But if the previous experience of the slums can be used for prediction, few if any sellers of high quality educational services at competitive rates will locate in the ghetto. Not only is there no Saks Fifth Avenue in Harlem; there is no Macy's, Gimbels, Korvettes, or Kleins.

In part the disparities between the slum markets and markets in other areas are the result of differential costs. Those firms or agencies which did elect to build schools in the "inner cities" would face higher land prices, construction costs, and even teacher costs than those in less congested

12 *Ibid.*, p. 130.

13 Leonard Downie, Jr., "FTC Chief Testifies the Poor Pay More," *The Washington Post*, January 31, 1968, p. A1. Other evidence is provided in David Caplovitz, *The Poor Pay More*, Glencoe, Ill.: Free Press of Glencoe, 1963.

areas.[14] Thus students attending schools in the slums would receive less education per dollar than those attending schools in other areas.

In addition, the fact that many families could increase their expenditures on schooling beyond the maximum provided by the state would also tend to bid schooling resources away from the ghettos, particularly in the short run. Not only do the poor lack the incomes to add private expenditures to the proposed public vouchers, but on the average they also have more children to educate. Consequently, public funds will be all they will have to spend on the schooling of their children. Given this situation, the schools which now serve the poor could not hope to obtain the better teachers since such personnel would probably prefer to teach for more money in a middle-class school rather than for less money in a ghetto school.

Even if the slum children were accepted at private schools located outside the ghetto—a highly dubious eventuality given the history of private schools—the poor would have to bear the costs of transportation to such institutions. While the monetary costs of transportation represent only part of such a burden, even $5 a week represents $180 over a school year.[15] Thus, the ghetto resident is likely to face a higher cost of educational services whether he sends his child to a school in or out of the inner city.

Jencks asserts that private schools would spring up to serve Negro children if only money equal to what was spent in the public schools were provided for tuition.[16] Unfortunately, experience with this very approach has suggested that such optimism is probably unwarranted. In order to defy the desegregation order provided by the 1954 Brown decision, Prince Edward County, Virginia, abolished its public schools in 1959 and provided tuition grants to students so that they could attend privately operated schools. While a system of private schools did emerge to serve the needs of white students, no private alternatives became available to black pupils. As a result, those Negro children who could not be sent to relatives or friends in other districts received no regular education at all.[17]

The fact that education as a good is difficult to define or measure also violates an important premise of the competitive market. There is no clear concept of what should be considered "educational output," and data purporting to measure even partial outputs are not wholly satisfactory. Indeed, when schools are referred to as "good" or "bad," such judgments ordinarily reflect the characteristics of the student body, school expendi-

---

[14] At the same salary level, the inner-city schools appear to obtain teachers of lower quality than do schools in middle-class areas. This phenomenon is probably the result of the fact that most teachers prefer middle-class schools to those in the ghetto. See my *Recruiting Teachers for Large-City Schools* (Brookings Institute, in process).

[15] Compare this amount with the average estimated current expenditure per pupil for all educational services in 1967–68 (except capital) of $619. See *Estimates of School Statistics, 1967–68,* Research Report 1967-R18 National Education Association, 1967.

[16] Jencks, "Is the Public School Obsolete?" *op. cit.,* p. 26.

[17] Robert Collins Smith, *They Closed Their Schools: Prince Edward County, Virginia, 1951–1964,* North Carolina: University of North Carolina Press, 1965.

tures, or some other set of input measures rather than measures of output. Or, when "output" measures are utilized, they are generally based upon absolute performance levels of students on standardized tests or the proportion of students who go on to college or win scholarships. But all of these measures are largely a function of the social class of the student body. A more appropriate measure of a school's success would be the "value-added" to the student body along certain cognitive, attitudinal, and other behavioral dimensions. No measures of these are available.

Given the fact that even professional educators have no objective way of rating schools, how are the parents of the poor going to compare them? Friedman has suggested that they will emulate the rich, for "The rich are always the taste makers, and that is the method by which the standards of society are raised."[18] Those of us who have observed the criteria by which families select colleges for their offspring might find this assumption difficult to accept. But even if we were to accept it, and its normative undertones, one might question whether the youngster in Harlem and his counterpart in Great Neck and Scarsdale have the same schooling needs. Further, the only way that the poor could emulate the rich in purchasing education would be if the poor possessed the resources of the rich, as well as their exalted tastes. Indeed, it is the discrepancy in the initial income distribution which is likely to raise the greatest difficulties in a market approach to education.

Friedman tacitly assumes that the initial distribution of income among households is appropriate, and he proposes that individual households should consume educational services according to their own demand functions, rather than by requiring all households to accept the formal schooling allocated by the political process. Friedman considers that a "major merit" of the voucher system is that parents with higher incomes and greater desires for education could add their own monies to the standard tuition grant provided by the government.[19] That is, the middle and upper classes—having higher incomes and fewer children—could purchase much better educations for their offspring than could the poor.

This argument ignores completely the crucial role which has been given education in increasing the future opportunities and incomes of youth. True equality of opportunity implies that—on the average—an individual of any race or social class has the same opportunity to achieve a given income or occupation as a member of any other race or class. Of course, it is sham to assert that any such situation exists today; but under the market approach to education, the disparity in income distribution among rich and poor and among Negroes and whites would probably increase.

---

[18] Quoted from Robert C. Maynard, "The Ultimate Solution Recommended for Schools," *The Washington Post,* November 12, 1967.

[19] Milton Friedman, "A Free Market in Education," *The Public Interest,* spring 1966, p. 107.

Educational expenditures represent investment in "human capital," investment that raises the potentialities and increases the future incomes of those receiving the schooling. By increasing the difference in educational investment between rich and poor, middle- and upper-class children would experience even greater advantages over lower-class children than their parents enjoy at the present time. That is, rather than schooling being utilized as a device for equalizing opportunity, the market would enable it to widen the present disparity between the opportunities afforded the privileged and the disadvantaged.[20]

Even on certain grounds of social efficiency, an unmitigated free market approach to basic schooling might not be desirable. Middle-class children receive a great deal of "educational investment" from their parents and communities prior to and during their formal schooling. The privileged child begins his formal schooling with a far higher level of "educational capital" than does the poor child and he receives greater stimulation and support from his home during the schooling process. Further, it is *a priori* reasonable to believe that the law of diminishing returns is applicable to investment in basic schooling. Since disadvantaged pupils begin their schooling with a smaller amount of "capital" invested in them, it is likely that the marginal returns in future productivity from investing in the schooling of the poor will be greater than those which might be derived from spending the same amount on basic schooling for the advantaged.[21]

Thus, the social goal of maximizing future economic growth—for any given level of educational investment—would imply spending greater amounts on the formal education of the poor than on the rich. Moreover, the goal of future equality of opportunity among groups would also imply greater expenditures on the schooling of the disadvantaged than on the advantaged. Unfortunately, the distribution of expenditures on elementary and secondary education, if left to the free market, would probably yield exactly the opposite results.

Thus the free market remedy as Friedman has proposed it would probably have greater private benefits than does the present system. Even the poor might experience some improvement in their schooling from a market which gave them alternatives to their present schools. Yet offsetting these private gains are the social costs imposed by a system which would tend to change the relative distribution of schooling alternatives in such a way that

---

[20] For a discussion of the distribution of educational resources and equality of opportunity, see Samuel S. Bowles, "Towards Equality of Educational Opportunity?" *Harvard Educational Review* (forthcoming spring 1968).

[21] Evidence which would appear to confirm this phenomenon is the fact that achievement levels of Negro students seem to be far more sensitive to differences in school resources than are achievement levels of white students. See James S. Coleman, *et. al. Equality of Educational Opportunity,* Washington, D.C.: U.S. Dept. of Health, Education, and Welfare. Office of Education, 1966, Chapter III. This finding has been confirmed in reanalysis of the Coleman data by Samuel S. Bowles of Harvard.

the present disparities in income and opportunities among social and racial groups would increase. Moreover, the free market approach would probably lead to greater racial and social segregation of pupils among schools than presently exists. These are tremendous costs to inflict upon a society which is preaching equality on the one hand and on the other hand is reeling from urban riots that are largely attributable to the frustrations of unequal opportunity.

A SIMPLE MODIFICATION

The Friedman approach might nevertheless be modified to avoid some of its deleterious consequences while taking advantage of the benefits of a competitive system. Since we are particularly concerned with the educational deficiencies of the inner-city schools and their disadvantaged clients, we might inquire into how the market approach might be adapted to the specific needs of ghetto children. The simplest way to implement the market approach without putting the poor at a disadvantage would be to grant tuition payments which are inversely related to family income and wealth. Disadvantaged children might be given vouchers which are worth two or three times the value of the maximum grants given children of the well-to-do. Such a redistributive system of grants would overcome many of the initial market handicaps faced by slum families. Thus, differences in tuition would be based upon relative educational needs, costs, and the family resources for fulfilling those needs.

However, since it is unlikely that this differential voucher plan would ever be adopted by the electorate, we ought to consider other market proposals. One of the most meritorious of these is the plan recommended by Theodore Sizer, dean of Harvard's Graduate School of Education. Sizer would have the state provide tuition payments—and thus schooling alternatives—only for children of the poor. These family allowances ". . . would allow that one section of our population that suffers most seriously from segregated schooling—the poor—to move, at their own initiative, and if they want to, into schools of their choice outside their neighborhoods."[22] This specific application of the Friedman proposal appears to be politically feasible and it is likely to spawn both the private and social benefits that we discussed above.

The voucher plan is not the only way of instituting some measure of competition among schools. James S. Coleman has suggested that school districts might contract with private firms for specific educational services such as arithmetic and reading instruction, and the firms would be reimbursed on the basis of their performances in imparting skills to students as measured by standardized tests.[23] These reading and arithmetic programs would be located throughout the city, and they would represent

[22] Theodore Sizer, "Reform and the Control of Education," 1967, p. 14. (Mimeo.)
[23] James S. Coleman, "Towards Open Schools," *The Public Interest,* fall 1967, pp. 20–27.

alternatives to those which are presently offered within each school. "Each parent would have the choice of sending his child to any of the reading or arithmetic programs outside the school, on released time, or leaving him wholly within the school to learn his reading and arithmetic there. The school would find it necessary to compete with the system's external contractors to provide better education, and the parent could . . . have the . . . privileges of consumer's choice."[24]

While this proposal deserves serious consideration, it would have to overcome two obstacles. First, full consumer choice among schooling programs might lead to similar or even greater social, racial and economic segregation among schools than presently exists. Coleman suggests that "One simple control . . ." would solve this problem. "No contractor could accept from any one school a higher proportion of whites than existed in that school, nor a higher proportion of students whose parents were above a certain educational level than existed in the school."[25]

Such a quota system is neither simple (administratively), nor would it tend to reduce segregation. If a student from a school which was 100 per cent white wished to enroll in a particular reading program, the contractor could always accept that student, since undoubtedly no more than 100 per cent of the students in his reading program would be white. That is, whites coming from virtually segregated white schools could enroll in virtually segregated white special programs under Coleman's "open school" criterion. Indeed, even if the quota system were workable, it would tend to perpetuate the existing stratification of students along racial and social class guidelines.

Further, the crudeness of present test instruments and their admitted cultural biases do not suggest that standardized tests should be the only basis on which contractors would be rewarded. Indeed, the Coleman Report found that its "ability" tests appeared to measure achievement far better than its achievement tests did.[26]

Moreover, to the degree that there are educational goals which should be implemented into instructional programs but do not necessarily coincide with changes in test performances *per se,* we might find contractors pursuing goals which are so narrow that they are deleterious to the imparting of broader learning skills. After all, a contractor who is rewarded on the basis of test results has a strong incentive to prepare the student *only* for the limited dimension of the performance to be tested.

COMMUNITY SCHOOLS AND THE MARKET

Recent emphasis on improving the public education system has focused on community involvement in the public schools. The premise on which the

---

[24] *Ibid.*, p. 25.

[25] *Ibid.*

[26] The Coleman Report's extensive analysis of the determinants of *verbal achievment* is based upon the standardized tests of *verbal ability* provided by Educational Testing Service. See Coleman, *et al., Equality of Educational Opportunity, op. cit.*, pp. 292–295.

community approach rests is that a school should serve the particular needs of its clientele rather than some general set of requirements which are defined at a highly centralized level. Several efforts have been made to initiate individual community-run public schools in the large cities; but the boldest overall move in this direction is that recommended for the New York City schools by the Mayor's Advisory Panel on School Decentralization. The Bundy Report—as the New York study is commonly called—proposes that some 60 or so largely autonomous school districts be set up in New York City, each representing a distinct community or set of communities.

Such community school districts would carry out most of the educational functions for their residents and would—in addition—"promote coordination in the planning and operation of health, recreation, and other human resource programs in the city."[27] Responsiveness to the particular educational needs of local residents would be insured by Community School Boards composed of 11 members: "six selected by a panel elected by the parents of children who attend schools in the district; five selected by the Mayor from lists of qualified persons presented by the central education agency after consultation with parents and community organizations."[28]

Given community schools and the promise that they appear to hold in adapting to the special needs of their students, it is possible to suggest a method by which they, too, can benefit from the competitive market. Communities could plan their educational requirements and solicit bids from private industry, universities, and nonprofit groups for fulfilling these needs. Educational contractors would compete for the particular educational services that the community wished to buy, and the most promising proposals would be selected. Contrasts could be awarded to the same groups if the community were satisfied with their performances; or they could be turned over to other firms whose probable performances would be superior to those of the present contractors. Thus, the groups selling educational services to the community schools would have an incentive to perform well or else chance losing a customer.[29]

The purchasing of educational services on the private market by community schools holds particular promise at the present time, for many firms which have been developing educational programs and technology over the last decade have not really had a chance to test their products in a "natural" environment. Such firms appear to be very anxious to show that their approaches are worthy of implementation. Indeed, the potential rewards to be reaped by educational contractors who can show successful implementation are likely to be enormous. Accordingly, the contractor's motive to

[27] *Reconnection for Learning—A Community School System for New York City,* Report of the Mayor's Advisory Panel on Decentralization of the New York City Schools, 1967, p. 16.
[28] *Ibid.* p. 18.
[29] Both Jencks and Sizer have endorsed this approach.

demonstrate the effectiveness of his approach to educational buyers would operate to make competition among sellers keen. In such a market, there is much to be gained by those firms who succeed; there is much to lose for those firms who do not.

A SUMMARY

The replacement of the existing system of publicly operated schools by a market of private ones—supported by government vouchers—would probably yield mixed results. On the one hand, some parents would have greater choices among schools and some schools would have to be productive in order to survive in the competitive framework. The increase in consumer choice and the resultant competition among schools would be likely to lead to greater educational benefits for many students and their families (private benefits) than those which they receive under the present monopolistic system.

On the other hand, the schools are also expected to fulfill certain social functions. It is in these that a market approach to schooling is likely to yield poor results. For example, basic schooling represents the primary device for equalizing opportunities among racial and social groups. Yet, advantaged children would probably receive far better schooling under the market proposal than would disadvantaged ones, and it is likely that this disparity would lead to larger future inequalities in opportunity between the children of the middle class and those of the poor. Further, it is not clear that a set of largely autonomous schools could provide the common set of values and knowledge necessary for the functioning of a democratic society. Finally, it is likely that the market proposal would increase racial and social stratification of students among schools. Whatever the success of the market in meeting consumer preferences, it would be offset by the market's failure to satisfy the social goals of basic schooling.

Fortunately, we are not limited to choosing between the traditional educational bureaucracy on the one hand or an unmitigated free market for educational services on the other. There are several ways to create competition within a public school system. Jencks, Sizer, and Coleman have suggested particular plans based upon the competitive framework, and the proposal for community schools represents a more general framework in which the competition of the market place might be used to advantage. The time is ripe to experiment with at least one of these plans for the children of the ghetto. Do we have any buyers?

DISCUSSION QUESTIONS

1. In an open-market setting, Levin states, schools would compete for students "by offering a variety of educational choices." What are these choices? Who would offer them? How would they be paid for? Would the same amount be allocated for each child's education?

2. How would the competition among a variety of schools resulting from an open-market strategy contribute to the resolution of our educational problems? In what ways might the Detroit design of industrial competition be unsuitable to the educational process?
3. What do you think would be the reaction of Albert Shanker (head of the United Federation of Teachers in New York City) to the free-market approach to the provision of education?

HAROLD HOWE II | *Growth and Growing Pains*

In December of 1964 the United States Office of Education was responsible for an annual budget of $1.5 billion. Now, two years later, its budget for the current fiscal year is $4 billion. Any business which had expanded that fast would have experienced growing pains of the worst kind. So has the Office of Education.

Today the Office is confronted by new and complex questions about its relationships with the world of education. Its money and its programs, and perhaps even its ideas, make it interesting to the schools and colleges, but this interest is tempered by wariness about its intentions and capabilities. Those who operate the public schools of the country—that is, state and local education officials and their governing boards—have a genuine concern about the possibility of shifts in power. They know that in times past the flag has followed the dollar in foreign affairs, and they don't want the "Feds" to follow the dollar in educational affairs.

The relationship of the federal government to state and local education authority is a tender one for three reasons. First and most important is the nature of the school programs supported by money from Washington. They are not "general aid" programs which provide dollars without prescription for their use. Instead they represent efforts to achieve specific ends: Better education for the children of poverty (Elementary and Secondary Education Act); improved teaching of science and mathematics (National Defense Education Act); or support for education leading to employment (Vocational Education Act). In effect, the Congress has voted programs to meet deficiencies in the schools or to enable the schools to make a greater contribution to our national strength or prosperity.

In addition, the Congress has supported programs to help groups of Americans who have missed the opportunities most of our citizens enjoy.

Reprinted from *Saturday Review*, December 17, 1966, pp. 68–70, 87, 88 with permission of the publisher.

Most thoughtful school people recognize the reasons for spelling out the broad purposes for which money is appropriated; but they are concerned lest future federal policy grow more specific in pinpointing activities for the use of federal funds.

Their fears are only partially allayed by declarations from the Congress that no federal control over curriculum, personnel, or administration in local schools is intended or allowed. They think that some aspects of the administration of present programs already reach into these forbidden directions; and they are not overly impressed by declarations of good intentions from the commissioner. They do, however, see virtue in the growing federal expenditure to strengthen state departments of education.

A second reason for abrasions lies in Title VI of the Civil Rights Act. This legislation says that federal money can't go where discrimination is practiced. Particularly in the South, where Office of Education policy seeks an end to the dual school system, charges frequently have been made that the schools are being controlled from Washington.

To meet its legal obligations the Office of Education has had to set standards for school desegregation, and these standards have not been acceptable to many local school authorities. (For entirely opposite reasons they have not been acceptable to the civil rights organizations, either.) There are considerable differences between Office of Education responsibilities in the realm of civil rights and our administration of financial aid programs, but the distinctions have been blurred by the strong feelings which pervade the issue of civil rights. The result of this blurring is additional difficulty in the federal-state-local relationship in education; feelings engendered by the controversy over activity under the Civil Rights Act frequently are transferred to programs sponsored by the Office for totally unrelated purposes.

A third source of strain lies in the decision by Congress to authorize and finance a new educational system which local and state educational authorities do not control. Head Start, the Job Corps, large sections of the Neighborhood Youth Corps, and other endeavors recently appearing on the scene have been somewhat outside the umbrella of duly constituted local and state educational authorities. I am not arguing the merits of these enterprises—merits which I happen to think are considerable—but only observing that the new federally supported education endeavor they represent is disturbing to many of those who operate the schools. Their reservations add to the complexity of federal-state-local relationships concerning education. Paradoxically, some state and local officials see the Office of Education as a source of support in resisting these incursions on education from "outside." Many of these officials would like to see the Office take over and operate the new special educational efforts now under the Labor Department and the U.S. Office of Economic Opportunity.

Higher education, which absorbs a little more than one-third of the funds spent annually by the Office of Education, presents a special problem in relationships. Through the National Science Foundation, the National Institutes of Health, the Defense Department, and other federal sources, higher education long ago learned to live with federal funds without getting nervous indigestion over problems of federal control. It will receive $1.5 billion from the Office this year without many complaints except for the general one of wanting more money. The only issue is the apparent feeling on the part of some university people that the Office isn't really up to the job of handling higher education's major issues. This feeling was evidenced last spring when some university officials and their national organizations opposed placing the new International Center for Educational Cooperation in the Office of Education. Evidently there are university presidents who see the Office of Education as it was ten years ago, and beyond that, as primarily a school-oriented enterprise. Clearly, then, among the many issues needing attention, the confidence of higher education must be developed in the agency of the government principally responsible for serving education in the United States.

The Office of Education also confronts internal problems. Two years ago, it had 1,300 regular full-time employees. Today it has 2,500. In short, taking into account a federal government personnel turnover rate that annually ranges between 20 and 25 per cent, we have been initiating more than seventy-five new people a month into new responsibilities at the very time that the nature and scope of the organization's task have been undergoing rapid and widespread change.

But the personnel situation is only part of the internal problem. The introduction of so many new programs has required a radical change in the basic organization of the Office. It has meant creating some new units and either disbanding or reshuffling others of long standing. The result is that only a handful of people are performing the same duties they were two years ago. The average member of our staff has changed his office, his telephone number, and his boss within the last eighteen months. One division has moved five times! Old hands in our shop have all had to adjust to a major move in the Washington circus—the move from a sideshow to the main tent, a move which can be exhausting as well as exhilarating.

That the Office of Education is today successfully operating some seventy-five separate programs under nineteen different Congressional authorizations, and doing so with reasonable success, is a tribute to the kind of employees the government is able to attract. Clearly they have in large measure qualities which bureaucrats are not supposed to have—adjustability and inventiveness on the one hand and a dedication to the public interest on the other.

Looking beyond internal and external issues of immediate concern to the Office in carrying out its new and complex programs, there are two other matters which require comment. One is the subject of *timing;* the other is the problem of *evaluation*. The first can be dismissed rather quickly without being resolved; the second can be resolved if our political leaders will give the educators time to do so.

By *timing* I refer to the incongruity which exists between the appropria-

The Magnitude of Federal Involvement in Education[a]

Program	Appropriation for the Year Ending June 30, 1966	Appropriation for the Year Ending June 30, 1967
Expansion and improvement of vocational education	$ 253,441,000	$ 278,016,000
Elementary and Secondary Education Act (for deprived children, innovative programs, school libraries, and state education departments)	1,151,000,000	1,342,410,000
Higher education (work-study programs, aid for developing institutions, equipment, and teacher education)	229,923,000	413,900,000
Teacher corps	9,500,000	7,500,000
Student loans	550,000	3,200,000
Higher education facilities (for construction)	632,700,000	722,744,000
Grants for libraries (services and construction)	55,000,000	76,000,000
Impacted areas (payments to school districts serving dependents of government or military employees)	438,078,000	439,137,000
National Defense Education Act (student loans, purchase of equipment, graduate fellowships, summer institutes)	412,608,000	446,357,000
Educational improvement for the handicapped	25,500,000	32,600,000
Research and training	70,000,000	70,000,000
USOE salaries and expenses	30,136,000	35,150,000
Other programs	33,661,000	34,661,000
Total	$3,342,097,000	$3,901,675,000

[a] This does not include programs such as Upward Bound and Head Start, which are not administered by the Office of Education.

tions procedure of the Congress of the United States and the planning cycle of the public schools. Time was when this disparity made no difference because the money appropriated by Congress had almost no effect on decisions by local school authorities. But that time is gone. On the average, about 6 or 7 per cent of elementary-secondary school funding depends on Congressional appropriation, and in many districts the percentage runs much higher. Every indication is that in the years ahead the percentage of federal support will be still larger.

School districts typically operate on a budget year which begins on July 1, and they plan ahead in order to know by early spring what funds will be available for commitment on that date. The typical school district spends 65 to 70 per cent of its funds on salaries, hires its new people in March, April, and May, and fits together a pattern of planned class size and program needs in the light of funds which will be available with the opening of school in the fall. The availability of teachers for new assignments and the continuance of teachers on former jobs are both hitched to this planning cycle.

The timing with which Congress appropriates funds could scarcely be better designed to make the job of the local school superintendent difficult. I hasten to add that Congress intends no inconvenience. It is just doing business as it always has. But somehow the school superintendent must find out in March rather than in November, as he did this year, what federal funds will be available when schools open in September.

Unlike the timing problem, which is an accident of circumstance, evaluation has become a sort of sacred cow in education, in the sense that everyone, both educators and laymen, theoretically believes in it. Not many people know what it is or what to do with it, but it is nevertheless widely regarded as "a good thing." The vague notion is that we can find out through some procedure (scientific or otherwise) what we are accomplishing with all these federal dollars spent on education.

Let me say first of all that I thoroughly support the idea of responsible evaluation of any program—and the more energy (which is to say money) that goes into it, the more I think it deserves disciplined study. But having said this, let me add two or three additional points. Evaluation of educational endeavors usually seeks to prove whether a given effort has produced a desirable change in a school or college or among a group of students. We need to remember that the two most difficult entities to change (with the possible exception of churches) are educational institutions and people. Each has a momentum of its own based on its past. The processes of change are necessarily slow, and they are difficult to describe and to assess quantitatively.

The President's request that the Elementary and Secondary Education Act be renewed for four years by the last Congress—rather than for a shorter period—seemed to me particularly appealing because I foresaw the possibility that some useful (even though preliminary) evaluative information might be developed by the time the Act came before Congress again. Instead it was renewed for only two years. We shall start testimony on its further renewal in the winter of 1968. Evaluative information which will provide that testimony with reliability will have to be in the hands of researchers for analysis by a year from now at the latest. It is possible that changes in schools or in children over such a short time span may become evident through intense and careful study. But they are unlikely to present a clear basis for public policy decisions for the future.

There is an understandable tendency in the federal government to want quick evaluation of new endeavors. The appropriation process is a yearly cycle, and the committees of Congress, the Bureau of the Budget, and the Office of Education itself cannot proceed with rational planning for future expenditure if there is no evidence of the effect of current programs. The political officials of the government must go before the people for re-election on two-, four-, or six-year cycles. These officials have supported or opposed education bills or appropriations, and when they talk with their constituents they quite properly want to know how the programs are going. Such demands for objective evidence about new programs are reasonable and necessary, but we need to keep in mind that they can force us into quick and superficial judgments about efforts which require time to mature if they are to produce change.

Looking ahead to the further development of the federal role in education, one broad position which has several implications is clear: The federal government, through the Congress and the President, and with substantial agreement from both political parties, has decided to use education as a major tool in solving some of the most urgent problems of the society and the economy, while at the same time helping individual citizens to find rewarding personal lives. A corollary of this position is that we have decided to emphasize building into each person the capacity to support himself, express his citizenship, and solve his problems. To strengthen education so that it can accomplish these ends for all citizens does not mean that Washington should usurp control over our schools or our universities. It does mean, however, that there must be mutual understanding between federal officials and those who do operate and control education, so that a number of critical problems of common concern may be identified and answered effectively. My list of those problems is neither complete nor arranged by priorities, but it includes at least some matters on which many educators agree:

1. In many communities and states, tax resources for the support of high-quality education at both the school and college levels are inadequate. Ways must be found by which the federal government can sensibly help to bridge the financial gap which creates the quality gap.

2. Inequality of educational opportunity is a problem for a large proportion of our citizens and even more of a problem for our racial and cultural minorities. The federal government must make adequate resources available to educational authorities to help them establish equal opportunities in education for all Americans. In addition, the government has an obligation to see that the rights of American citizens as defined by Congress and the courts are as well protected in the schools as elsewhere.

3. The professional and subprofessional manpower to serve education is not available in many places. Local and state educational agencies must be enabled to receive federal support and planning resources in this problem area, since it crosses state boundaries.

4. The growing proportion of Americans seeking education beyond high school or re-education during adult years points to the possibility of greater federal assistance to higher education. Programs which will help new as well as established institutions are called for.

5. The forward planning, research, and development capacities of education need strengthening. The federal government can sponsor research and development activities, but much of the planning for change must be done at the state level. One answer may lie in additional federal programs to help the states do this job better.

Anyone surveying the educational scene from Washington runs the risk of reaching the superficial conclusion that more federal money is the solution to just about any problem. Clearly it is not. Local and state leadership, jealously guarded university independence, and growing financial efforts from the private sector—each of these is necessary if our schools and colleges are to serve us as well as they should.

The touchstone of success for American education lies in marrying these independent traditions with the new and growing necessary federal contribution.

DISCUSSION QUESTIONS

1. Should federal aid to education be given in the form of lump-sum, general aid, to avoid the possibility of federal control?
2. Do the new educational structures set up by the Office of Education (the Job Corps and Head Start, for example) constitute viable alternatives to the present school model?
3. Mr. Howe states that the solution to our educational problems is not to be found simply in more federal money; state and local leadership and private monies are needed too. What is your prediction for federal intervention in education in the future and its effect upon state and local involvement?

EDNA LONIGAN

Federal Aid to Education

In the last session, Congress rejected two major programs for Federal "aid" to education—the Democratic proposal for general subsidies and the Republican compromise which was limited—at the start—to subsidies for school construction only.

Now the struggle has moved to the Congressional districts. The "educationists" want a more docile Congress. They will fight to re-elect the Members who voted with the education lobby, and to defeat those who dared to vote against their wishes.

They know the next session of Congress may decide the issue for all time. They know that once a bill for Federal assistance passes Congress, it is never rescinded but rather grows and grows like a banyan tree.

One curious aspect of the voting on education aid in Congress is that Members of Congress from the states which would have received the largest grants above their share of taxes were against the bills. The states which would have paid the largest amounts in taxes were most aggressive in support of the bills. Why?

The United States Chamber of Commerce has prepared a table, from United States Office of Education figures, listing the costs and benefits to each state of Federal funds for education. In 10 states the margin of Federal payments over taxes would exceed $2 million a year apiece. They are Virginia, North Carolina, South Carolina, Georgia, Alabama, Mississippi, Louisiana, Arkansas, Texas, and Tennessee. In these states 87 out of their 88 Representatives in Congress voted against the Federal funds for schools.

On the other hand, 17 states would have paid most of the bill for new Federal expenditures for schools, but 15 out of 17 of them voted for Federal aid. Only Ohio and Florida voted to hold down new expenditures.

One key to this curious lineup of votes is what might be called the "legislative interlock." Bills for Federal welfare spending in the states grant multiple powers. Some of these powers can be discovered by reading the bill at hand. Some can be discovered only by reading the fine print in quite separable bills in many diverse fields.

Legislative proposals for area redevelopment, community facilities, sewage control, juvenile delinquency, and revival of the Civilian Conservation Corps, all have these interlocking provisions. For example, area redevelopment bills amended the urban renewal acts, so that housing appropriations could be used for industrial construction as well as residential. Also, the

Reprinted from *Human Events,* Vol. XVII, No. 41 (October 13, 1960), with permission of the publisher.

dangerous provision for "back door financing," by which some Federal agencies print bonds and "sell" them to the Treasury, was ostensibly taken out of the bill, but it was, in fact, left in, because the Area Redevelopment Agency could use funds from urban renewal appropriations, which can still be raised by "back door" borrowing.

Earlier drafts of the area redevelopment bills openly permitted the Federal Government to move workers from their own communities to other cities or states for "retraining." But this would permit the Federal Government—as some of the earlier witnesses frankly admitted—to move Negroes from the South to other states. The idea was that whites and Negroes ought to be relocated until every community had a "fair share" of Negroes. This is like the ruling of the New York City Board of Education which compelled white children to go to schools distant from their homes so every school and classroom could have a "proper" mixture of Negro and white children.

Federal funds for school construction make it possible for the executive branch to rule that no money be paid to states unless their schools are forcibly integrated, according to the planners' new doctrines of "Constitutionality," and law enforcement with the use of Federal troops.

It is true that Representative Adam Clayton Powell tried to put such a provision into the legislative draft and was opposed by its supporters on the ground that it would kill the bill.

Does that mean that the planners in the executive branch do not intend to use school subsidies to enforce segregation or keep any other promise, to get mass votes? Not at all. It is simpler to impose reforms by executive ruling than by legislative consensus, and there is virtually no appeal from directives of the executive branch. Why put it in the law?

The states which stood up against the trend to Federal aid for schools were those in which the mass pressure groups, like CIO-PAC and NEA—are not strong. The states which voted—against their own self-interest—to subsidize the taxpayers of 33 other states, are those in which the mass pressure groups, which lead the fight for centralization, are strongest.

Now the appeal has been transferred from the old Congress to the new one. Every effort will be made to defeat the "reactionaries." We shall hear more of the little tots who have no seats in the classroom. The truth is that state and local boards of education have built new classrooms for ten million students and replaced obsolete classrooms seating another four million. The war-stimulated increase in population passed its peak in 1955, and the picture is getting constantly brighter, because local school construction remains high.

The real issue is this—Federal funds mean Federal control. The centralizers intend to control American education and American children. City fathers and boards of education are to be tempted by "aid" for school construction. Teachers will hear the siren promise of higher salaries. Administrators will be promised more funds for administration and services.

Of course nothing is said about the tax bite which will be necessary to pay for all this—when the bills are rendered.

The NEA and their friends will say they do not want Federal control. But no Federal official may pay out Federal money unless he knows the money will be used for the purposes stated in the law. With Federal money go the Federal auditor, the Federal advisor committee, the Federal requirement for "approved plans" before a penny is allotted, and the skill of the Federal bureaucrats in conveying to state and local officials how foolish it is to bite the hand that feeds you. People who say Federal "aid" will not mean Federal control are either not very honest or not very bright.

The "educationists" have told us frankly what the trouble is. We have in this country some 20,000 local boards of education, under citizen control, the fruit of our deep-rooted belief that government, where necessary, should be as close to the people as possible. But it is difficult business for the educationists in Washington to control 20,000 citizen groups scattered over the whole United States. Such independent bodies can delay, obstruct, or openly oppose plans to make all our schools into one monolithic system managed by control panels, with push-buttons hidden deep in the Federal bureaucracy.

Myron W. Leiberman, in "The Future of Public Education," has frankly explained why 20,000 boards of education are anathema to the planners. School boards cater to parents and taxpayers. You know, of course, if you have been reading educational literature, that the influence of parents and taxpayers over American children and their schooling must be ended.

Once the camel's nose is in the tent, we can predict the rest. Ten to fifteen billion a year, higher teachers' salaries, higher expenses for buildings, services, overhead. The 20,000 school systems will turn to Washington, first for money, then for "standards." The educationists will know how to coordinate them into one monolithic system. They will feel the irresistible pull to identical content, professional standards, buildings, supervision.

How will the protesting parent, the dissenting teacher, or the local parent, express his disagreement? He won't. That is the point. Federal "aid" is Federal politicalization of education, but a politicalization in which only the opinions of the "managers" will be heard. The notion that dissent is a healthy safeguard will pass from memory. The 20,000 local boards of education will probably be kept as exhibits of "democracy," but they will be shorn of their only strength, the power of the purse.

Do we want a monolithic educational system in the United States, even if it is a good one? Do we want a monolithic system following the blueprints of the NEA, the AFL-CIO, and their allies, with left-wing doctrinaire "intellectuals" at the control panels? The fight is the same whether it is waged over relief, social insurance, health, farm aid, or education. Only the simple-minded can believe Federal "aid" to education will be "different."

Behind the curious division in Congress over Federal subsidies for schools, we can see, then, the hardening of the lines between the collectivists who already occupy so many of the positions of power in American life and the Constitutionalists who believe in local self-government, self-help, and the power to dissent from orders from Washington.

The states which voted against Federal school grants, though they would have gained millions of dollars a year, were voting against the forces bringing all our local agencies into the Federal monolith with its simple control panels at the center.

The states which voted for Federal aid, though they would pay for the subsidies for 33 other states, voted to carry us further along the road to the Federal monolith in which education and all the other responsibilities of states and local governments are collectivized.

Each of the separate welfare programs has its own mass pressure groups to urge its cause. But in the contests for Congress, all these groups interlock, in the congressional districts, to elect their friends and to punish their enemies.

The NEA, the CIO-PAC, the ADA, and the rest, will work as one coordinated whole. They will bring all their influence to bear on the ballot box. Will conservatives work as hard to defend Constitutional government and to reward the men who have defended it for them?

DISCUSSION QUESTIONS

1. Do you agree with Lonigan that "People who say Federal 'aid' will not mean Federal control are either not very honest or not very bright"?
2. Does federal aid result inevitably in "politicalization of education," as Lonigan charges?
3. Are independent local school boards sounding boards for the resolution of disagreement and dissent for parent and for teacher, as Lonigan states?
4. Is it possible to have, at the same time, local control of education and equalization of educational opportunity?

Ohio Town Flunks Economy, Shuts Schools

Versailles, Ohio (AP)—Versailles schools stood closed and empty yesterday, silent symbols of conflict between better education and higher taxes.

"I don't like it a bit but I guess there's nothing we can do about it," said Larry Willhelm, a pharmacist, to sum up the feeling in this western Ohio farming community of 2,200 after the school board suspended classes be-

Reprinted from *Newsday,* February 1, 1967, with permission of the copyright owner, Associated Press Newsfeatures.

cause it was broke. It is the first time in 10 years an Ohio district has taken such a step.

The board plans to reopen schools for its 1,600 students Feb. 27 and run them until June 30, operating on income from a new tax payment. That will leave the schools with a debt to start next year and leave unresolved the dilemma of getting more money or cutting back educational programs, said School Superintendent E. A. Stoner. Voters twice rejected a five-mill tax levy that school officials said would have produced $75,000 to keep the schools operating normally. It was beaten 1,095 to 919 Jan. 17 after a vigorous campaign of support and little organized opposition.

Under Ohio law, it cannot be voted on again until November, although some legislators are trying to speed through a change to permit Versailles and districts in similar straits to vote in May. Ohio law requires periodic voter approval of property taxes which pay all local costs of schools.

"I'm not against schools," said Roy Pease, who faced a $225 a year boost in the levy, "but property tax just isn't fair." Ross Ward, another opponent, agreed: "I'm for good schools, but I want the tax base broadened. The public is getting sick."

"All the (92) seniors are upset," said Peg Barga, 17-year-old cheerleader and homecoming queen. Stoner predicts most of his 68 teachers will stick out the extra vacation, although some are looking for other jobs. But he hesitates to say how many may be back next year. Stoner also says unless more revenue is found "there will come a period in the next school year when this same thing will occur . . . unless drastic cutbacks are made." Even cuts, he said, would not make up the $61,000 deficit the district will have at the end of this year.

DISCUSSION QUESTIONS

1. Evaluate the plight of Versailles in terms of the local school board as a model of community organization for the financing and control of education.
2. What alternative would you suggest to solve Versailles's financial disaster?
3. Do the claims of proponents of decentralization of large city school systems run counter to the Versailles experience? What lessons could Versailles teach New York City?

FRED M. HECHINGER

The Problem Is To Separate Aid from Control

Three years ago, the Educational Policies Commission, the ideological voice of the National Education Association and the American Association of School Administrators, dropped a bombshell when it urged educators to throw their support behind "categorical" Federal aid to education. These powerful organizations had always demanded general aid—money which the states and local school districts could spend as they wished—and had rejected Federal subsidies with "categorical" strings attached, such as the requirement that funds be used to aid the disadvantaged or to improve science instruction.

Last week, during the annual convention of the N.E.A. in Minneapolis, the commission returned to its pre-1964 stand. It denounced categorical aid as a form of Federal control and urged that Washington henceforth strengthen the public schools with dollars to be used as the states see fit.

The 1964 reversal was born of political realism. President Kennedy's efforts to enact general aid had turned into a fiasco, as had 40 years of similar efforts. The combination of the Roman Catholic parochial school supporters' threat to torpedo such public-schools-only aid and Southern opposition to any move that might increase the Federal role and press for desegregation seemed unbeatable.

MANY VICTORIES

On the other hand, categorical aid had a history of triumphs. It has long supported vocational education, school transportation and lunches, created the land-grant colleges and provided the G. I. Bill of Rights. During the Eisenhower Administration, the National Defense Education Act of 1958 (N.D.E.A.) was as categorical a measure as anyone could devise. It reacted to the first Soviet Sputnik by trying to put American mathematics, science and foreign languages in orbit.

Though expedient, the 1964 line was never popular with school administrators who are trying hard to remain the power base of the N.E.A. Last week the commission, perhaps submitting to that power, said: "Categorical grants have been accepted by the educational community as a means of getting a flow of Federal funds established." And so, it went on, the time is ripe "to increase reliance" on general aid.

The flow referred to was the Elementary and Secondary Education Act of

1965 which provides aid in such categories as the support of disadvantaged children, remedial instruction, after-school centers, school libraries and teaching materials. That flow is now estimated at about $3-billion annually.

Perhaps the commission's desire to get back to aid-without-strings was fanned by the recent battle in Congress over just this issue. Representative Albert H. Quie of Minnesota, as a spokesman for the Republican attack on President Johnson's categorical aid legislation, called for $3-billion in direct grants to the states, with most of the categorical qualifications removed. The proposals, however, were defeated, although some of the existing Federal prerogatives were modified.

What are some of the major controversies tackled in the commission's policy statement, "Federal Financial Relationships to Education"?

The commission charged that "special-purpose Federal aid . . . is in itself a form of Federal control of education." It cited the N.D.E.A. as "an indirect but nevertheless powerful influence . . . upon what is taught; how it is taught; and the priority of resources, time, and money allocated to it."

Those who reject this view say that the professional educational leadership, over a considerable period of time, failed to establish priorities attuned to the needs of the nation. For example, those who hold this view recall that educators virtually struck foreign language study from the list of essential academic subjects and permitted a majority of students, including highly gifted ones, to leave school without instruction in physics.

FAILURE SEEN

The commission said "state and local educational authorities tend to view such [categorical] aid as a conglomeration of projects rather than as fundamental parts of a coherent educational program." It warned that this destroys the "essential unity of the educational enterprise, to the detriment of the educational program and the individual child."

Those who oppose this view reply that the Federal Government sensed an emergency exactly because the local and state experts had failed to evolve coherent programs. Far from working to the detriment of the individual child, this argument goes, the biggest item of the 1965 aid measure was aimed specifically at the individual child in the slums who had been ignored by the "essential unity of the educational enterprise." They suggest that special aid for a difficult school in the slums does, in fact, offer some of the benefits of general aid by freeing regular funds for the normal support of local schools.

Moreover, Secretary of H.E.W., John W. Gardner, in criticizing the commission's statement, charged that the anti-urban sentiments of the state capitols force the cities to rely on special aid from Washington.

The commission, while calling the enforcement of civil rights legislation "desirable and necessary," said categorical aid has had "limited success in reducing the problems of school desegregation."

The other side says that the combination of such aid with the desegregation guidelines has been responsible for most of the desegregation in the South.

Possibly the most serious flaw of local and state controlled American education in the past has been its leadership's failure to oppose, moderate and eliminate prejudice and inequality of opportunity. Much of the need for categorical aid is the direct result of that failure.

. . . .

Perhaps the most convincing argument against categorical aid put forth by the commission is that it too often comes only sporadically and therefore adds uncertainty to local school budgets. An objection even more basic is the fuzzy language which has created considerable legal doubt whether some of the funds now going to children who attend parochial schools are not in reality a subsidy of church-related institutions—and this in violation of the Constitution.

The extent of the controversy involved in the Policy Commission's reverse was underlined by a rare statement of dissent. Dr. John H. Fischer, president of Teachers College, Columbia University, and former school superintendent of Baltimore (where he insisted on school desegregation before the advent of categorical aid), agreed that some present categorical programs "are less than perfect." But he added: "The commission's position would be more tenable if one might safely assume that as the 50 states pursue their own interests the national interest will automatically be served. Long experience, to say nothing of recent events, will not support that assumption. . . ."

In fiscal terms, what does the commission propose? It seems to support a phasing out—though not a drastic elimination—of categorical aid, while general aid would be provided either through no-strings Federal grants-in-aid to the states or through tax-sharing, i.e. the return of a certain percentage of Federal income taxes to the states.

The Policies Commission said last week: "Indeed, there is good reason to believe that most local school systems, if not arbitrarily constrained, are both responsive and responsible to the public's quest for the best in education."

In reality, large segments of the public pointing to past educational history, deny that. They—along with many educational dissenters—have called in the Federal Government as a policy-influencing partner for just that reason.

The commission warns of the political intrusions by the Federal Government, while admitting that many state education authorities are weak. Yet the chief state education officers in 22 states continue to be politically elected and thus to be more political than the Federal authorities.

Ideally, Federal aid should come to the schools with as few Federal strings attached as possible. The road to that ideal will have to be paved with growing confidence that the public school leadership has its eyes on national goals as well as on local needs. Only such a program among state education authorities can confine Washington's role—sometimes excessive and ill-considered—to that of a balancing, mediating and guiding force. Perhaps this is when the Policy Commission could best play its part.

DISCUSSION QUESTIONS

1. Do you favor general or specific federal aid to education?
2. Do you see federal control as the big issue in the aid controversy?

CHAPTER 7 *Control of Education*

From the beginnings of mass public education in the United States, control has resided in local boards of education. The concept of local control seems to be uniquely American, growing out of the rural, Jacksonian democracy of the first half of the nineteenth century. The arrangement was fortuitous; the Constitution did not provide for a federal system of education so that it was quite natural for the states, under the states' rights doctrine, to move into the vacuum.

Massachusetts, led by Horace Mann, offered an outstanding example of the capacity of the state to influence and to direct education. But state departments, in general, have been cast in an advisory and regulatory role. They have too often been understaffed, underfinanced and politically oriented. Their ineffectuality has allowed local school boards practical autonomy. Traditionally, control has been one step away from the local citizen.

Prior to Sputnik (1957), there was very little contact between the federal educational authority and state and local levels. The Office of Education gathered statistics on the state of American schools and published resource materials. The Commissioner of Education was Washington's unknown man, and the position was considered a major step on the road to oblivion.

The federal role in education has changed radically since Sputnik. Education, formerly a branch of the Federal Security Agency, has grown to cabinet status, in the new Department of Health, Education and Welfare. Federal aid to education has become massive and pervasive; Washington has moved into virtually every school building in the land.

Proponents of local control have reacted to the federal presence with alarm. The issue of aid to education is seen as the desire for control of education. The dollar sign and dominance are directly associated.

The power and authority of local boards of education are under fire from two other sources, increasingly militant teachers and sometimes even more militant parents. Teachers, unified in power blocs and stimulated by the competition between rival organizations, have moved beyond routine union matters to demand a voice in shaping school policy. Militant black parents, lacking representation on large city school boards and faced with their children's educational failure, are demanding complete control of their local schools.

On the college level, students have disrupted and immobilized entire campuses in their insistence upon a redistribution of responsibility and control.

The locus of control must be resolved once more. An active and persuasive federal authority, a growing and broadening base of teacher power, aroused and vehement parents and radical students have created a revolutionary process for America's schools. Tomorrow's schools will be different from today's.

RUDOLF STEINER | *The Threefold Commonwealth*

Modern man has evolved a spiritual life, which is to a very great degree dependent on state institutions and on economic forces. The human being is brought whilst still a child under the education and instruction of the state; and he can be educated only in the way permitted by the industrial and economic conditions of the environment from which he springs.

It might easily be supposed that this would ensure a person's being well qualified for the conditions of life at the present day, for the state must possess every opportunity of arranging the whole system of education and instruction (which constitutes the essential part of public spiritual life) in the best interests of the human community. It might well be supposed too, that the way to make a person the best possible member of the human community is to educate him in accordance with the economic opportunities of the environment from which he comes, and then pass him on, thus educated, to fill one of the openings that these opportunities afford him.—It devolves upon this book,—an unpopular task to-day,—to show that the chaotic condition of our public life comes from the spiritual life's dependence on the State and on industrial economy—and to show further that one part of the burning social question is the emancipation of spiritual life from this dependence.

This involves attacking very widespread errors. That the State should take over the whole system of education has long been regarded as a beneficial step in human progress; and persons of a socialistic turn of mind find it difficult to conceive of anything else than that society should educate the individual to its service according to its own standards.

People are loathe to recognise, what nevertheless, in this field, it is absolutely necessary should be recognised; namely, that in the process of man's historic evolution a thing, that at an earlier period was all right, may at a later period become all wrong. In order that a new age might come about in human affairs, it was necessary that the whole system of education, and with it public spiritual life, should be removed from those circles that had exclusive possession of it all through the middle ages and entrusted to the State. But to continue to maintain this state of things is a grave social mistake.

This is what the first part of the book is intended to show. The spiritual life has matured to freedom within the framework of the state; but it cannot rightly enjoy and exercise this freedom unless it is granted complete self-government. The whole character assumed by the spiritual life requires that

Reprinted from Rudolf Steiner, *The Threefold Commonwealth* (New York: Anthroposophic Press, Inc., 1922), pp. xviii–xxix, with permission of the publisher.

it should form a completely independent branch of the body social. The educational and teaching system, lying as it does at the root of all spiritual life, must be put under the management of those people who are educating and teaching; and none of the influences at work in state or industry should have any say or interference in this management. No teacher should spend more time on teaching than will allow of his also being a manager in his own sphere of activity. And in the way that he himself conducts the teaching and education, so too he will conduct the management. Nobody will issue instructions, who is not at the same time actively engaged in teaching and educating. No parliament has any voice in it,—nor any individual, who once on a time may have taught, but is no longer personally teaching. The experience learnt at first hand in actual teaching passes direct into the management.—In such a system, practical knowledge and efficiency must, of course, tell in the very highest possible degree.

It may no doubt be objected, that even under such a selfgoverning spiritual life, things will not be quite perfect. But then, in real life, that is not to be looked for. All one can aim at is the best that is possible. With each child of man there are new abilities growing up, and these will really be passed on into the life of the community, when the care of developing them rests entirely with people who can judge and decide on spiritual grounds alone. How far a particular child should be brought on in one direction or another, can only be judged in a spiritual community that is quite free and detached. What steps should be taken to ensure their decision having its "rights," this too is a matter only to be determined by a free spiritual community. From such a community the State and the economic life can receive the forces they need, and which they cannot get of themselves when they fashion spiritual life from their own points of view.

It follows from the whole tenor of the following pages, that the directors of the free spiritual life will have charge also of the arrangements and course of teaching in those institutes also—which are specially directed to the service of the State or of the economic world—Law-schools, Trades-schools, Agricultural and Industrial Colleges, would all take their form from the free spiritual life. Many prejudices are bound to be aroused when the principles stated in this book are pursued to these, their right consequences. But from what do such prejudices proceed? The anti-social spirit in them becomes evident, when one recognises, that at bottom they proceed from an unconscious persuasion, that people connected with education must necessarily be unpractical persons, remote from life,—not the sort of people whom one could for a moment expect to institute arrangements that would be of any real use for the practical departments of life, and that all such arrangements must be instituted by the people actively engaged in practical life, whilst the educators must work on the lines laid down for them.

In thinking like this, people do not see, that the educators need to fix their lines of work themselves, from the smallest things up to the biggest, that it is when they cannot do so that they grow unpractical and remote from life. And then you may give them any principle to work on, laid down by apparently the most practical persons, and yet their education will not turn out people really practically equipped for life. Our anti-social conditions are brought about, because people are turned out into social life not educated to feel socially. People with social feelings can only come from a mode of education that is directed and carried on by persons who themselves feel socially. The *social* question will never be touched, until the education question and the question of the spiritual life are treated as a vital part of it. An anti-social spirit is created not merely by economic institutions, but through the attitude of the human beings within these institutions being an anti-social one. And it is anti-social to have the young brought up and taught by persons who themselves are made strangers to real life by having their lines of work and the substance of their work laid down for them from outside.

The State establishes law-schools. And it requires that the substance of the jurisprudence taught in these law-schools should be the same as the State has fixed for its own constitution and administration, from its own points of view. When the law-schools proceed wholly from a free spiritual life, this free spiritual life itself will supply the substance of the jurisprudence taught in them. The State will wait to take its mandate from the spiritual life. It will be fertilised by the reception of living ideas, such as can issue only from a spiritual life that is free.

But the human-beings, growing up to life, are within the spiritual domain, and will go forth with views of their own to put into practice. The education given by people who are strangers to life, inside educational institutes planned by mere practicians,—this is not an education that can be realised in practice. The only teaching that can find practical realisation comes from teachers who understand life and its practice from a point of view of their own. In this book an attempt is made to give at least a sketch of the way in which a free spiritual organisation will shape its details of working.

In Utopian minds, the book will rouse all manner of questions. Artists and other spiritual workers will anxiously ask whether genius will find itself better off in the free spiritual life than in the one at present provided by the State and the economic powers? In putting such questions, however, they must please to remember that the book is in no respect intended to be Utopian. Hence it never lays down a hard and fast theory. This must be so and so, or so and so.

Its aim is to promote the formation of such forms of human social life, as, from their joint working shall lead to desirable conditions. And anyone who judges life from experience, and not from theoretic prejudice, will say to himself "When there is a free spiritual community, whose dealings with life are guided by its own lights, then anyone who is creating out of his own free genius will have a prospect of his creations being duly appreciated."

The "social question" is not a thing that has cropped up at this particular point in the life of man, which can be solved straight away by a handful of people, or by parliaments, and [which] once solved, will remain solved. It is an integral part of our new civilised life; and it has come to stay. It will have to be solved afresh for each moment of the world's historic evolution. For man's life has entered with this new age upon a phase, when what starts by being a social institution turns ever and again into something *anti*-social, which has each time continually to be overcome afresh. Just as an organic body, when it has once been fed and satisfied, passes after a while into a state of hunger again, so the body social passes from one state of order again into disorder. There is no more a panacea for keeping social conditions in good order, than there is a food that will satisfy the body for ever and always. Men can however enter into forms of community, which, through their joint action in actual life, will bring man's existence constantly back into the social path. And one of these forms of community is the self-governing spiritual branch of the body social.

All the experiences of the present time make it plain that what is socially needed is, for the spiritual life *free self-administration,* and for the economic life *associative labour.* Industrial economy in modern human life is made up of the production of commodities, circulation of commodities and consumption of commodities. These are the processes for satisfying human wants; and human beings and their activities are involved in these processes. Each has his own part-interest in them; each must take such a share in them as he is able. What any individual actually needs, only he himself alone can know and feel. As to what he himself should perform, this will be judged by him according to his measure of insight into the mutual life of the whole. It was not always so; nor is it so to-day all the world over; but in the main it is so amongst the at-present civilised portion of the Earth's inhabitants. Economic evolution has kept widening its circles in the course of mankind's evolution. Household economy, once self-contained, has developed into town economy, and this again into State economy. To-day we stand before World economy. No doubt, in the New much still lingers on of the Old; and much that existed in the Old was already a forecast of the New. But the above evolutionary order is the one that has become paramount in certain relations of life, and the destinies of mankind are conditioned by it.

DISCUSSION QUESTIONS

1. Are the spiritual—and necessarily human—values Steiner speaks for missing in our schools today?
2. Are these the legitimate concern of the schools?

3. Must the schools be turned over to those who are educating and teaching, if we are to achieve meaningful values?
4. Steiner's position includes self-selection of schools by parents. Does this provide a balance to the power he allocates to teachers?

MELDRIM THOMSON, Jr.

Federal Control of Schools: Myth or Fact

The true purpose of this bill [The Elementary and Secondary Education Act of 1965] is to authorize general aid without regard to need, and the clear intent is to radically change our historic structure of education by a dramatic shift of power to the Federal level.

In terms of our structure of educational control, to say nothing of public policy, this progression of Federal influence in the sciences to Federal influence in the social sciences is a quantum leap toward a centralized, standardized, uniform national school system.

From Minority Views on Elementary and Secondary Education Act of 1965, House Report No. 143, 89th Congress, 1st Session.

IF

If you believe that local control of your schools is vital to an independent and vibrant educational system;

If you wonder whether there is another side to the story of Federal control of our schools, other than the one of innocence and rich gifts told by the professional educator;

And, if you oppose Federal scheming for the minds of your children;

Then you might find that a few minutes spent in reading this pamphlet could alert you to some unbelievable truths about the dangers confronting your local school.

FEDERAL CONTROL OF SCHOOLS

Danger ahead

Few voters in New Hampshire realize the speed with which Federal controls are invading their schools. The invasion is not confined to public

Reprinted with permission of the author, Meldrim Thomson, Jr., as privately circulated by him.

schools; a snare of controls awaits the unwary private school lured by the bait of Federal aid. Even fewer persons recognize the revolutionary changes in policy structure of which these controls are but the outward manifestations.

Fortunately, for those who believe that one of the supporting pillars of our Republic rests on the bedrock of local control of public schools, a fresh breeze of independence is blowing out of the north country.[1]

From Colebrook southward voters in six school districts had, as of January 1, 1966, rejected more than $30,000 in Federal funds for fear of Federal control.[2] Since very little has been written or said about the entrapments behind these Federal gifts, most of these rejections were prompted by an inherent fear on the part of the voter of Federal controls.

So lethargic has been the voter interest that in some school districts in New Hampshire these so-called entitlements have been accepted by voters where school board members constituted a majority of the persons voting.

The passage on April 11, 1965, of the Elementary and Secondary Education Act of 1965, Public Law 89–10, signalled a dramatic shift of power to the Federal level of our historic concept of local control of education.[3]

This Act was described in Congress as full of loopholes. "It presents a virtual bulldozer for Federal bureaucracy to overrun our long-established policy regarding local control of our schools."[4]

Even one Congressman who voted for P.L. 89–10 expressed, with many witnesses, a real concern over the possibility that this Act might be administered in an unconstitutional manner in some local programs.[5]

Under this Act vast power has been placed in the Office of Education in the Department of Health, Education and Welfare. There are $1.06 billion available to implement the Act. Of this huge sum $2.5 million are allocated to New Hampshire for the current fiscal year. That is about equivalent to the state aid our school districts receive in one year. And out of this $2.5 million more than $100,000 will be used to administer the program in our state.

Jubilant bureaucrats in the Office of Education were recently reported as saying their office now has a life of its own. "It has billions to disburse, and the commissioner is in charge. The Federal commitment can not help but get bigger."[6]

With this enormous fund it should be easy to shackle Federal controls on

---

1 *The New Hampshire Sunday News,* January 2, 1966. The arguments used by those opposed to accepting Federal school funds were described as "typical New England arguments" by Commissioner of Education, Paul E. Farnum.

2 *Ibid.*

3 Minority Views, House Report No. 143, 89th Congress, 1st Session.

4 Congressman Ashbrook, *Congressional Record,* March 26, 1965, p. 5918. "Its pitfalls will trouble educators, boards of education, and, indeed, communities for years to come."

5 Congressman Scheuer, House Report No. 143, *ibid.,* p. 80.

6 *National Observer,* December 27, 1965.

local schools, reasons the Washington bureaucrat. Thus, money becomes the weaponry in the battle to shift control over our public schools to Washington.

Expanding federal controls

THE ISSUE. Like the forked tongue of a snake, the issue is twofold. Is the Federal government really reaching into our communities to run our schools; and if so, would Federal control be good or bad for us?

The issue under Title III of the Act is "between (1) our historic pattern of local public education controlled locally under state law and (2) the establishment of a separate public education system financed and administered by a Federal agency."[7]

Recently an official of our State Department of Education was quoted as saying "There's no particular measure of control" under Title I of the Elementary and Secondary Education Act of 1965.[8]

School boards that have been in touch with the offices of their school superintendents know that all through the recent fall months their superintendents experienced a very real measure of control in the long hours of tedious labor exacted to prepare the mountain of forms required under Title I of the Act.

We can understand the position of the professional educator even if we do not sympathize with it. "Unfortunately, all too many educators take the position that as long as some money is being spent, they are for it and will accept it regardless of any erosive effect it may have on the future of education."[9]

CONTROLS UNDER PRIOR ACTS. We have accepted Federal funds under such prior Federal acts as the National School Lunch Act, the National Defense Education Act, and various vocational education acts. Because of this fact, educators are prone to equate Public Law 89–10 as just another grant of Federal funds to our schools.

Inevitably, whenever Federal funds were given to schools, the money carries with it controls. In the beginning controls were gentle, subtle and quiescent. Under these earlier acts the threat of control was ever present, but gloved; and so we lived with it while large and less palatable doses of control were quietly being prepared for us. The stinger was there but generally sheathed. Occasionally, a school district was stung.

Our Department of Education has admitted that even under the National School Lunch Program there was a little red tape or control.[10]

---

[7] House Report No. 143, *ibid.*, p. 76.

[8] The *Valley News*, December 29, 1965.

[9] Congressman Ashbrook, *ibid.*

[10] "We are confident that few Federal programs have as little 'red tape' or 'controls' as this program exercises for the benefits received." Letter to all New Hampshire School Board Chairmen, dated December 22, 1965.

Department of Education officials, with Federal funds available to implement the vo-ag program, recently indicated to the Orford School Board that about three thousand dollars would not be forthcoming this year, because among other things, the vo-ag curriculum was not changed as directed.[11]

BATTLE PLAN FOR THE BIG GRAB. The shadow that we see clearly today often portends the substance of the reality of tomorrow. So it was with a 56-page booklet entitled "A Federal Education Agency for the Future," issued in 1961 by the Department of Health, Education and Welfare.[12] This was the Federal blueprint for control of our local schools. This plan for the big grab of our schools stressed Federal participation and control in formulating educational policies. It urged Federal review of teacher preparation, curriculum and textbooks. It even proposed to have the Office of Education implement international educational projects in cooperation with UNESCO in the United Nations.

One important new role which the Washington educational bureaucrats planned to add to the Office of Education was designated in the 56-page report as "extensive involvement in formulation of national policy."

According to this battle plan, the Office of Education "must also prepare itself to assume larger responsibilities in carrying out Federal policy through the administration of operating programs. It must assume a new role, speaking within the Federal government for the long-term interests of education. And it must render assistance in the development of public educational policy."

This revealing report stated that "curriculum will have to undergo continual reshaping and upgrading, and new techniques and tools of instruction will have to be developed"; also, "teacher preparation, textbooks, and the curriculum in the subject fields must be improved in the decade ahead."

Judged by their own words, these Federal educators are ambitious men. In the area of international education, their report provided that, "the responsibilities of the Federal government in this effort are marked. Not only is it the constitutional responsibility of the Federal government to conduct the foreign affairs of the nation: it is almost equally evident that national observers are especially well qualified to assess the international deficiencies of our domestic educational system."

Certainly enough has been said in the Office of Education's own blueprint about the future role of that power-hungry agency to demonstrate conclusively that Federal aid without controls is a myth.

If there is any lingering doubt that Federal control of our public schools is just around the corner of Capitol Hill, then bear constantly in mind this

---

[11] Letter September 21, 1965, from New Hampshire Division Vocational-Technical Education.

[12] *Congressional Record,* July 18, 1961.

ominous warning from the report: "The Committee foresees an extension of the active Federal role in education."

THE RUTHLESS GRAB. It took the Federal educators only four years to implement their grandiose battle plan. In 1965 it was made effective, in large measure, by Public Law 89–10, and particularly by Title I of that Act.

Seldom has a law been so ruthlessly steamrolled through the Congress.

When Public Law 89–10 was before the House for consideration it was pushed through quickly by the raw power of the majority. One Congressman stated, "I have seen debate cut off with no opportunity to present views on vital amendments. In one instance the Chairman of the Education and Labor Committee moved that debate close in 5 minutes. He then took the entire 5 minutes himself!

"On one occasion he even flouted custom and refused to allow the minority leader to speak for an additional 5 minutes. On one occasion, he moved to close debate before it had even started, but fortunately the long-standing rules of the House required at least one speaker address himself to the matter before the motion could be made.

"It is only appropriate that these tactics brought the American people a bill so badly drafted and so tied together by sealing wax that no amendment could be accepted regardless of merit, lest the political support for the bill by various groups who put the coalition together be withdrawn."[13]

IN BATTLE ARRAY. The high command in the camp of the Federal educators has been expanded and strengthened.

Harold Howe II, described as an "eager innovator" was recently made U.S. Commissioner of Education. The former commissioner, Francis Keppel, was promoted to Assistant Secretary for education in the Department of Health, Education and Welfare. With the Secretary of the Department, John W. Gardner, a specialist in education, this "triumvirate provides the strongest educational leadership ever exerted from Washington—for the political battles that lie ahead."[14]

Thus, equipped with some of the best command talent in the nation, loaded with three billions of taxpayers' dollars, and with a battle plan designed to take over the operation of our local schools, the Federal educators have begun the fight in thousands of school yards all over the country. Initially, the battle will be waged through the exercise of Federal controls funneled through state agencies.

SOME EXAMPLES OF CONTROLS. To qualify for an entitlement, that is to say, Federal monies, a school board makes application through the State Department of Education for a "basic grant or a special incentive grant"

---

[13] Congressman Ashbrook, *Congressional Record,* March 26, 1965, p. 5918.
[14] *National Observer, ibid.*

under Title I of the Act. It must make several determinations, under section 205 of the Act, which, in the language of the statute, must be "consistent with such basic criteria as the Commissioner may establish." It would be difficult to imagine any better language to effectuate controls than that used in the statute.

"At first reading, this bill appears to leave approval of local programs to the State education agency, where the power belongs. However, there is inserted (hidden, almost) a power in the U.S. Commissioner of Education to require that such approval be consistent with basic criteria formulated by him. This effectively robs the State agency, or the local schools for that matter, of any real authority to shape the programs. This centralization of power in the U.S. Office of Education runs throughout the bill."[15]

There are eight determinations a school board must make under section 205 of Public Law 89–10. Citation of two of these should be sufficient to illustrate the type of controls the Act establishes.

Under par. (5) of section 205, a school board must find "that effective procedures, including provision for appropriate objective measurements of educational achievement, will be adopted for evaluating at least annually the effectiveness of the programs."

And under par. (8) a school board must determine that "effective procedures will be adopted for acquiring and disseminating to teachers and administrators significant information derived from educational research, demonstration, and similar projects, and for adopting, where appropriate, *promising educational practices* developed through such projects."[16]

Under paragraph (5) we open the school door to the administration of all kinds of tests on the nod of a Federal educator. These could include the obnoxious personality questionnaires in which the pupil must check out such prying statements as—

My father is a tyrant.
I wonder if I am normal in my sexual development.

Pupils in grades 4 through 7 could be required to take one of the so-called Wishing Well tests in which they check off such statements as—

I wish my parents did things that would make me feel more love toward them.

Under paragraph (8) we throw open our schools to the wildest forms of pedagogical experimentation. Conceivably, we could be required to give sex education, instructions in how to overthrow the United States Government, or a course in some Chinese dialect if the Federal educator found them to be "promising educational practices."

These possibilities may sound far fetched. But it has been said that under Title II of the Act, "if a text used in a single school district should depict

[15] House Report No. 143, *ibid.*
[16] Italics supplied.

one racial or national group as inferior, or leave the clear inference that a President or other public figure was a traitor, or covertly adopt a Marxist interpretation of history, Federal funds could be used to supply that text to every child in the State."[17]

CONTROLS IN ACTION. According to the administrator of the Title I program in New Hampshire, "Washington is not doing anything but allocating the funds and providing the mechanics of how they are administered to the districts."[18]

This sounds quite innocent. No evidence of control here; but does this statement square with the facts?

Following complaints last fall of racial discrimination in the schools of Chicago, $30 million in Federal funds were summarily withheld on orders from Washington. Later the funds were released upon direction from the White House.[19]

Last November Dr. Carl Hansen, superintendent of schools in Washington, D.C., admitted that controls did exist. He said, "despite soothing assurances that local schools are to remain fully independent in their management of Federal funds, the evidence is that controls are being imposed even at the early stages of the new programs."[20]

Vanishing local school powers

For decades the strength of our nation was taprooted in the soil of local institutions. On the anvil of local public forums, with the issue at cherry heat, were hammered out the decisions that fashioned our nation's greatness.

Through their locally elected school trustees, New Hampshire voters control the education and thus the destiny of their children. They have the last word in such vital areas as hiring teachers, approving curriculum, purchasing textbooks, and determining discipline.[21]

Curriculum and textbooks are the arteries to our educational system. Expose these to the Federal educators and the transfusion to a centralized, national school system will be swift and certain.

We have seen by their own battle plan published in 1961 that Federal educators would gain control over curriculum and textbooks. We have noted that the Office of Education is equipped with superior talent in the struggle to establish supremacy over local schools. And we have observed that the supply depots of the Federal educators are bursting with taxpayers' dollars with which to assert their ascendancy.

If our state laws on education can be circumvented through the administration of Public Law 89–10, and they can be; and if our voters and their

[17] House Report No. 143, *ibid.*, p. 74.
[18] *New Hampshire Sunday News, ibid.*
[19] *U.S. News & World Report,* Oct. 18, 1965.
[20] *U.S. News & World Report,* Nov. 8, 1965.
[21] N.H. RSA sections 189: 10, 189: 15, 189: 16, 189: 39.

representative school board members lose control over curriculum and textbooks, then local authority will be reduced to a caretaking role of the schoolhouses. Centralization will then be complete, and possibly some computer monster in Washington will even issue the report cards to our children.

Late is the hour

The hour is late, but not too late! You can reverse the onward sweep of Federal control over our schools.

If your school district has not yet voted to accept current Federal funds under Title I of Public Law 89–10, you can work to decisively reject these funds. A strong demonstration at the grass-root level that local voters want no part of Federal control, would show our representatives in Congress, more emphatically than words or letters, that we do not want our tax dollars spent on further appropriations under Public Law 89–10. Instead, let us keep these dollars at home and controls on Washington.

Unless amended, Public Law 89–10 will remain effective until 1968. To keep it operative, Congress will have to appropriate new funds each year. If your school district is one of many which accepted Federal funds under this Act, possibly because voters were unaware that control did accompany the funds, then you will have an opportunity to vote against accepting this aid at your next annual school district meeting. To avoid special school district meetings, convened by court order, school boards in New Hampshire will probably include a Federal aid item under Public Law 89–10 in their 1966–67 school budget.

If you are alarmed about Federal control of your school, then by all means attend your next school district meeting and vote against accepting Federal funds under the Elementary and Secondary Education Act of 1965.

DISCUSSION QUESTIONS

1. Should local school districts refuse federal aid for fear of federal control?
2. If poor districts reject federal aid, where will they get the financing to meet their needs? Are the alternatives offered either federal control or inadequate education for children?
3. Must control inevitably follow after dollars? Is federal control necessarily invidious? Is local control necessarily good?

MYRON LIEBERMAN

Local Control of Education

One of the most important educational trends in the next few decades is likely to be the decline of local control of education. Such a development is long overdue. Local control of education has clearly outlived its usefulness on the American scene. Practically, it must give way to a system of educational controls in which local communities play ceremonial rather than policy-making roles. *Intellectually,* it is already a corpse. At least, I propose to treat it as such in this book. The proper way to treat a corpse is to conduct an autopsy upon it and then bury it promptly. Having done this, we can better understand the rationale for the school system which will emerge from the present chaos in education.

An autopsy of local control reveals several reasons for its demise. In the first place, mobility and interdependence have completely undermined the notion that local communities ought to have a free hand in educating their children. Second, national survival now requires educational policies and programs which are not subject to local veto. Third, it is becoming increasingly clear that local control cannot in practice be reconciled with the ideals of a democratic society. Finally, local control is a major cause of the dull parochialism and attenuated totalitarianism that characterizes public education in operation.

Let us analyze these reasons briefly. In order to do so, consider carefully the following question: *Who* should decide whether the children in a given community should be required to learn to read and write?

Some persons would undoubtedly argue that parents should have the right to raise their children as illiterates if they wish to do so. Most people would probably feel that the public ought to have the right of final decision in this matter. Still, there are many publics: local, state, regional, national, international, and even publics which are not defined geographically. Which of these publics should be authorized to have the last word in the matter?

Until a short time ago, every state had a compulsory education law. These laws took the power to decide our hypothetical question out of the hands of parents and local communities. Recently, however, some states have passed standby legislation which would enable them to abolish compulsory education in order to avoid racial integration in their public schools. States cannot be prevented by the federal government from abolishing public

Reprinted from Myron Lieberman, *The Future of Public Education* (Chicago: University of Chicago Press, 1960), pp. 34–50, with permission of the publisher and author.

education. There is no way that the federal government can force a state legislature or local community to appropriate money to operate public schools. But what about our basic question—should the decision as to whether children shall learn to read and write be properly regarded as one for local communities or even state governments to make?

The reasons why the power to make this decision was taken away from parents and later from local communities will help us to answer this question. One reason was based upon the concept of fair play for the individual child. There was growing acceptance of the belief that a child's chances in life should not depend upon whether his parents or his local community were willing and able to educate him.

Should a child's chances depend upon whether he lives in a state which is willing to educate him? Certainly not as long as we adhere to the concept of an open society, one in which the individual's chances are not determined by fortuitous factors. As far as the individual child is concerned, the extent to which his state government is willing to provide him with an education is as much a fortuitous matter as the socioeconomic status of his parents or the educational values of his local community.

Consider the problem from a social standpoint instead of an individual one. We are an extremely mobile people. Most of us eventually move away from the community in which we received our education. In the year ending in April, 1958, 30,800,000 Americans changed their residence. Over 11,000,000 moved from one county to another; about half this number moved to a different state. Thus, on the average, every American moves to a different state two times during his life. Under these circumstances, does it make sense to insist that the citizens of one state have no right to insist upon literacy for the children of other states? Today, we plead for federal aid to education in order to equalize opportunities between states. Tomorrow, we could hardly contend that the federal government must stand by idly while a state legislature compounded the inequity by depriving children of an education altogether.[1]

As an abstract proposition, it has always been clear that it is undemocratic to permit educational opportunity to be determined by circumstances of race, geographical location, or economic status. It has also been clear that our national welfare was dependent upon the extent to which individual talents were able to flourish, regardless of their social, economic, racial, or geographical origins. Neither the ideal of equality of opportunity nor the fact of our interdependence is new. What is new is the urgency of these

[1] My argument treats control of education by the states as local control of education. Fundamentally, this identification is sound although people do not now think of control at the state level as local control. It is only a matter of time before they do so, and then the control of education at the state level will go the way of control at the parental and community levels. In point of time, the decline of community control over broad educational policy will precede the decline of state control over it, but the same forces that undermine the one will eventually undermine the other.

things. Proposals for federal aid to education in order to equalize educational opportunities between states have been ignored by Congress for generations. The same proposals, advanced as a counterpoise to Russian scientific progress, are now regarded as insufficient by panic-stricken congressmen who never supported them on equalitarian grounds.

Some idea of the bankruptcy of local control of education may be seen in the statistics concerning selective service registrants disqualified for failure to pass mental tests. In 1956 the lowest rate of rejection for failure was in Montana, where 2.5 per cent of the registrants failed these tests. The highest rate was in Mississippi, where 44.9 per cent of the registrants failed the tests. In ten states, fewer than one out of every twenty registrants failed to pass; in eleven other states, one or more out of every four registrants failed to pass.[2]

The vast differences among the states in the rate of disqualification are not due solely to the differences in the quality of their school systems. A registrant educated in Montana might take his selective service tests in Mississippi or vice versa. The statistics on rejection include the failures to pass because of inherited mental deficiency, and there are other causes for such failure over which the schools have no control. Nevertheless, the differences between the states cannot be explained solely by noneducational causes. Because some states and communities provide a decent minimum education for only a small minority of their children, we must, in all states, draft persons who, for family or occupational reasons, ought not to be in the armed services at all. This is only a small part of the exorbitant price we are paying for local control of education. The intellectual smog that has obscured our grasp of this fact is being cleared away once and for all by such dramatic events as the riots in Little Rock and the Russian conquests of space.

LOCAL CONTROL AND TOTALITARIAN CONTROL

The prevailing point of view is that anything but local control of education, with perhaps a few concessions made to control at the state level, would be a step toward totalitarianism. This view is profoundly mistaken. Our present system of local control is far more conducive to totalitarianism than a national system of schools would be. I know that this statement is not acceptable to the overwhelming majority of the American people, including the teachers, but I am willing to stand on it.

The assertion that our educational system tends toward totalitarianism seems absurd on its face. A totalitarian system is one which develops a massive uniformity of outlook. It is based upon a policy of intellectual protection for a point of view that cannot stand the test of free discussion. We have a multitude of schools of all denominations or no denomination at

---

2 NEA Research Division, *Research Bulletin,* XXXVI, No. 1 (February, 1958), 29.

all. Among the teachers and students in our public schools, there are adherents to every major political, economic, and religious point of view. What could be further from totalitarianism than this?

In most states the purposes and the content of education are left to local school boards to determine. Undoubtedly, there are some constitutional limits to the purposes for which communities may operate public schools. However, these limits have never been spelled out, and there is great latitude in what a community might require of its schools. Since the purposes of education are set forth locally, the predominant groups in the community tend to establish purposes which accord with their particular religious, political, economic, or social points of view. As a practical matter, therefore, local control results in the same kind of intellectual protectionism that characterizes schools in totalitarian countries.

The basic problem is not that communities define the purpose of education to be the acceptance of the Protestant faith or unswerving devotion to the single tax or the inculcation of the tenets of the Democratic party. Some communities have not blinked at adopting purposes as sectarian as these, but this is not where the problem lies. Even where a community accepts the most liberal educational purposes for its public schools, its interpretation of what intermediate objectives and what educational programs fulfil these purposes may have the same stultifying effect as outright adherence to a sectarian purpose. Every pressure group is for the general welfare, but each has its own version of what measures do in fact promote the general welfare. Similarly, every pressure group is for a liberal or a democratic education, but has a special version of what intermediate objectives and what educational programs lead to this result.

What is crucial is that, at the local level, it is relatively easy for a preponderant group to enforce a policy of intellectual protectionism for its sacred cows. Thus the white majorities in Southern communities exclude instruction that is critical of racial segregation. Communities in which fundamentalist sects predominate exclude instruction critical of evolution. Some communities have prohibited the study of the United Nations or of UNESCO. Ours is a heterogeneous country, but in most communities the predominant racial, religious, economic, or political groups are able to veto whatever in the school program displeases them.

Looking at our system as a whole and seeing the existence of public schools teaching diverse doctrines, one might infer that our schools are free. We do not readily recognize the totalitarianism implicit in our situation because not all schools protect the same dogmas. Nonetheless, a diversity of schools based upon intellectual protectionism for different dogmas does not constitute a "democratic school system." At least, it does not do so if "democratic" refers to the education actually provided in these schools instead of to the legal structure which encourages a variety of one-sided programs.

The diversity of our undemocratic schools is not the only factor which maintains the fiction that we have a democratic school system. No matter how successful a group may be in excluding certain facts and ideas from the public schools, television, radio, and other mass media are almost certain to expose students to these facts and ideas. The power structure of American society is such that no single group is able to enforce or to indoctrinate its dogmas on the population as a whole. People look at this situation and say "Our schools have kept us free." They should say "Our freedoms have survived our schools."

THE MYTHOLOGY OF LOCAL CONTROL

Many persons believe that public education was not made a federal responsibility in the Constitution because the founding fathers feared the potentialities for dictatorship in a federal school system. Actually, education was not included as a federal function in the Constitution because the idea of free public education had not even occurred to the founding fathers. At the time of the American Revolution, the concept of universal public education was receiving attention for the first time and then only from a few frontier thinkers. Our decentralized school system was not an inspired stroke of genius but a historical accident, resulting from the fact that the ideal of free public education for all became widely accepted only long after the American Revolution.

Our schools have never been an important foundation of our free society. Our freedom is partly due to a separation of powers which enables us to transact public business reasonably well while avoiding excessive subjection to government officials. Perhaps for this reason we tend to regard the diffusion of power over our schools as an essential element of our free society. But adherence to the general principle that we must avoid excessive concentration of power does not automatically justify every separation or diffusion of it. Everything depends upon the circumstances—what powers are involved, who is to wield them, and so on. It is preposterous to think that merely because their political genius was expressed through a constitution embodying a remarkably successful separation of powers, the founding fathers would align themselves today with the supporters of local control of education.

People are seldom aware of the non-public character of public education. They tend to regard it as a legal concept and to neglect it as an educational concept. However, the ideal of public education means more than having some governmental unit—local, state, or federal—provide the funds to operate schools. Public education has a referent in the quality of education as well as in its financial basis. The qualitative referent is an education in which the search for truth is carried on regardless of what empires topple, interests collapse, or heads roll. Without this, public education is a delusion, as dangerous as the notion that mere government ownership of the means of production will automatically result in their operation for the public welfare instead of for private interests. The socialization of a service at any level of government is no automatic guarantee that the service will be performed in the public interest. The "new class" should have ended all of our illusions on this score.

Public schools, then, are not necessarily infused with a public spirit. Likewise, the fact that a school is privately controlled does not mean that its program is necessarily sectarian in character. The program of some privately controlled institutions such as Harvard is more free of parochial limitations than the programs in most publicly controlled institutions. In short, we cannot assume anything about the educational program of a school merely from a knowledge of whether the school is publicly or privately controlled.[3] Nor can we infer that the educational program of a school is undemocratic merely because the school is locally controlled or that it is democratic merely because the schools are part of a national system. The relationship between the legal status of a school and the quality of its educational program is never one of strict logical implication.

The system of legal controls under which schools operate is only one factor which serves to shape their educational programs. However, it is an extremely important factor. Because a national system of controls is more likely to broaden the purposes of education and to preserve the professional autonomy of teachers, it is much more likely to provide a truly liberal education than a multitude of totalitarian systems under local control. It is a striking fact that in England, which has a national system of education, the teachers are on record as being opposed to local control of education precisely because they fear that it would undermine their professional autonomy.[4] Meanwhile, teachers in the United States, who lack any substantial measure of professional autonomy, continue to act as if local control must be maintained inviolate lest academic freedom (which they do not possess) be imperiled.

The decentralization of our schools is often justified by an appeal to the experimental nature of this situation. We supposedly have fifty state school

[3] The notion that private education per se is superior to public education is assiduously cultivated by private school interests at all levels. It is a myth insofar as it pretends to be a generalization or even a statement of probable tendency. This myth results in outright tragedy at the elementary and secondary levels if parents assume that exorbitant fees automatically purchase educational advantages not available in the public schools.

[4] Educational leaders in England are very outspoken in their view that any trend toward giving local boards of education increased control over the financing of education would be a threat to the freedom of the teaching profession. See Sir Ronald Gould, "The Teaching Profession," *The Concept of Professional Status* (London: College of Preceptors, 1957), p. 42.

systems, each of which is free to try something different from the others. Each state has delegated considerable power to local school boards, which supposedly multiplies the experimental possibilities. This is thought to make for progress, since each state and each system is not only free to try something new but is free to benefit from the experience of other systems.

There is no doubt that some change for the better occurs in this way. Nevertheless, such enormous decentralization cannot be justified on the grounds that the different school systems constitute a vast pool of educational experimentation. The different schools do not constitute experiments except in the loosest sense of the word. They do not operate under conditions carefully controlled for purposes of analysis and comparison. They just operate.

Much of the experience of different systems is valuable only on the premise that education should be a state or local responsibility. A school board may indeed be interested in how another community put over a school bond campaign. But if funds came from the federal government, the experience of this or that school system in raising money would be academic.

The truth is that local control of education has obstructed rather than facilitated educational research. By and large, only large urban systems allocate funds to research. Even in these cases, the research is generally limited to problems that are of local concern. Very few school systems support any research that is even theoretically of more than local interest.

Educational research is supposed to be a function of our universities, but they also have a tendency to concentrate on local problems. Thus a university will make a study of population trends in a nearby community which desires to know where to build its new schools. Few universities devote any substantial effort to research on teaching and learning which would be of universal interest.

Educators have not learned from the development of industrial research. In industry, most research is conducted by corporations with a monopoly or near monopoly of the market for a particular product. These firms can support research intended to have a national impact because they stand to benefit from it. On the other hand, little research is conducted from private funds on products whose ownership is diffused. For example, individual farmers are generally unwilling to support research from their private funds because they would be adding substantially to their own cost of operation, while the results of the research would be immediately available to all farmers whether they had contributed to it or not.

We have much the same problem in education. Why should a particular school system support research which is for everyone's benefit? If we do not expect an individual farmer to support basic agricultural research from his own funds, neither should we expect him to support an educational research program in his local schools from local funds. The federal government supports basic research in agriculture because of the clearly evident futility of waiting for the small operator to do so. The same policy can and should be followed in education.

The U.S. Office of Education, a branch of the Department of Health, Education, and Welfare, has conducted research on certain administrative problems for many years. However, it was not granted funds for research in the art and science of teaching until 1956. In that year, $3,000,000 was made available by Congress for grants in various fields of education. The National Defense Education Act passed by Congress in August, 1958, included an appropriation of $18,000,000 over a four-year period for research on the educational use of radio, television, and audiovisual aids. It is likely that larger amounts for educational research will be appropriated by Congress in the future. But as long as education is primarily a state and local responsibility, educational research will never receive the support it ought to have. Local communities and state governments will never adequately subsidize research which is clearly universal in application.

How much money ought to be spent on educational research? Public education is a $15,000,000,000 enterprise [1960]. Enlightened practice in large-scale industry and government is to spend 3 to 6 per cent of the total budget for research. In education, this would call for an expenditure of from $450,000,000 to $900,000,000 annually. In fact, it is unlikely that the country is spending more than $25,000,000 a year from all sources for educational research.

The suggestion that it is realistic to think in terms of a twentyfold increase in expenditures for educational research will be considered a pipe dream by most educators. Nevertheless, such an increase would still leave expenditures for educational research at a conservative level even if we are now spending only $25,000,000 annually for this purpose. Those who blanch at my proposal should remember that we are currently spending well over $300,000,000 annually for medical research. A report submitted to the Secretary of Health, Education, and Welfare in the summer of 1958 by a distinguished advisory committee of medical educators and research executives calls for increasing our expenditures for medical research to the point where the nation will be spending a billion dollars a year for such research by 1970. Foundations which are currently supporting educational research might well support studies and action programs designed to develop more adequate sources of funds on a national basis. It does not take such studies, however, to realize that educational research has been neglected under our system of local control of education.

In this connection, it is interesting to note that one of the most persistent and most pathetic arguments against a national school system is that such a system would not permit experimentation in the schools. The assumption seems to be that centralized administration is necessarily non-experimental or that it necessarily insists upon uniformity down to every detail. Actually, several federal departments which have centralized administration also subsidize programs of research which dwarf anything we have ever seen in education. The departments of Defense and Agriculture illustrate the possibilities.

If the present structure of American education is not conducive to the support of research, it is well designed to obstruct the utilization of it. On this subject, we need only to compare the lag between the discovery and the application of knowledge in education and the lag in other professions.

In the legal profession, important developments such as Supreme Court decisions are taken into account by all lawyers within a very short period of time. When the Bureau of Internal Revenue makes a ruling which affects a substantial number of tax returns, the accountants generally absorb it within a matter of months. Everyone is familiar with the short period of time between the discovery of an effective polio vaccine and its use by doctors everywhere. In education, however, the lags between discovery and practice are scandalous. These lags are reflected in what is taught as well as in how teachers teach their subjects.[5]

The average person is little aware how long it takes for important new knowledge to be reflected in the public school curriculum. The diffusion of teacher education and of the curriculum is so great that it often takes decades before teachers realize the need to add or delete a subject or to make radical changes in the content of an accepted subject. Even after this hurdle has been passed, tens of thousands of school boards must be persuaded that these changes are desirable. "Go ye therefore and persuade all those who are affected by the decision"—thus reads the Word in textbooks on school administration. The Curriculum Committee of the PTA, the school board, the parents, the students—all must have a voice in a decision which affects them. An infinite number of banana peels lie between the professional decision to modify the curriculum and actual practice in the school.

THE BREAKDOWN OF LOCAL SUPPORT FOR PUBLIC EDUCATION

The case against local control of education becomes more compelling when we consider the practical problems involved in introducing basic changes that require heavy expenditures. In recent years, our high schools have been severely criticized for their real or alleged neglect of science. For the sake of argument, suppose that we required every high-school student who has the ability to do college work to take three years of physics during

[5] The need for drastic revision in the mathematics and physics curriculum of the public schools is discussed in Howard F. Fehr, "The Mathematics Curriculum for the High School of the Future," *Teachers College Record,* LIX (February, 1958), 258–67, and the articles on the Physical Science Study Committee in *Science Teacher,* XXIV (November, 1957), 316–29; and *Harvard Educational Review,* XXIX (Winter, 1959), 1–36.

his high-school career. At this point, consider only the practical problems involved in implementing this recommendation. How would we get from the status quo to a situation in which all these high-school students take three years of physics? Regardless of whether this particular change is desirable, consider its implementation solely from the standpoint of the difficulties of making any basic curriculum reforms under the present system.

There are over 21,000 high schools across the country. In 1956, only 12,000 of these schools offered one full year's work in physics. As late as 1954, 50 per cent of all schools having tenth-grade pupils did not offer physics at all. These were usually the smaller schools, but it is interesting to note that only one-fourth of all high-school students in 1954 took as much as one full year of physics before graduation. We are thus confronted by thousands of school boards which have seen fit to offer one year's work or none at all in physics.[6] Each board must now be persuaded, one by one, to make drastic changes in its curriculum. Since it is unlikely that the additional work in physics will simply be added to the present curriculum, each board must make its own decision about what subjects shall be reduced or eliminated. Each board must decide what to do with the teachers in subjects to be eliminated.

Even assuming that most school boards could be convinced that more work in physics is desirable, can they be persuaded to implement such a change? If a school is to offer three years of physics instead of one or none, extensive remodeling would almost invariably be required. There would have to be substantial expenditures for new laboratory equipment and supplies. Just how substantial these would have to be is evident from a survey made in March, 1957, by the NEA's Research Division, which covered the needs for instructional equipment in high-school science and mathematics classes. More than half the schools responding to the inquiry from the Research Division reported that they did not even have direct electric current in their physics laboratory. Less than 15 per cent of the schools reporting had a calculator available for mathematics courses. Only one school in five had a graph board in every mathematics classroom; about two out of every five did not have a graph board in any mathematics classroom. The report indicated that 57 cents was the average per pupil expenditure for supplies and consumable equipment in science classrooms.[7]

Before most high schools could offer three years of physics, local school boards would have to adopt salary schedules much more attractive than the prevailing ones. Even though physics is now offered for only one year in the

---

[6] I do not mean to suggest that there is one school board for each high school. Actually, the number of school districts is over twice as large as the number of high schools, even though many districts include more than one high school.

[7] NEA Legislative Commission, *The Hidden Need: Basic Instructional Equipment for Schools* (Washington, D.C.: National Education Association, nd.). See also n. 8 below.

majority of schools which offer it at all, there is already a large and growing shortage of physics teachers.[8] It would be pleasant to think that school boards which have heretofore balked at making minimal expenditures for physics instruction will suddenly be inspired to vote the necessary taxes for an adequate program. Unfortunately, the odds are overwhelmingly against such a development.

Under our present system of financing education, the states and local communities supply over 95 per cent of the funds for public education. Our nation spent a total of $14,827,550,000 for public education in 1957–58. Of this total, about 3 per cent came from federal sources, 40.8 per cent from the state governments, and 56.2 per cent from local sources. On a state-by-state basis, there are wide variations in the relative amounts supplied by local, state, and federal sources. In Alaska, 14.7 per cent of the total expenditures for public education came from the federal government, whereas only 0.5 per cent of the total spent in New Jersey were from this source. Also in 1957–58, Delaware raised 88.2 per cent of its school revenues at the state level and 10.3 per cent at the local level. At the other extreme, Nebraska raised 6.9 per cent of its school revenues from state sources and 89.5 per cent from local sources.[9]

In general, the trend has been for local sources to provide a decreasing percentage of the total expenditures for public education. Expenditures by the state governments tend to constitute a much larger percentage of the total, while the percentage from federal sources has been increasing but at a much slower rate than that coming from the state governments. There are several reasons why this structure is not working and can never be made to work.

In the first place, some states have four to five times as much taxable wealth, on the average, as other states. The differences between school districts are even greater; some school districts have several hundred times as much taxable wealth as others. Ability to support education has also been studied in terms of what educators call "personal income payments per pupil enrolled," that is, the total income received by the residents of a state divided by the number of pupils enrolled in its public schools. In 1956–57, "personal income payments per pupil enrolled" amounted to $17,432 in Delaware and $3,754 in Mississippi. Needless to say, there were even greater differences between the richest and the poorest school districts.

For many years, authorities on school finance have pointed out that the

---

[8] The National Defense Education Act passed by Congress on August 23, 1958, provided an appropriation of $300,000,000 over a four-year period for science equipment. It will be interesting to see how long it takes for Congress to recognize the futility of waiting for local school boards to institute salary schedules high enough to attract reasonably competent science and mathematics teachers.

[9] Data from Research Division, *Estimates of School Statistics* (Washington, D.C.: National Education Association, 1959).

poorest states and school districts usually devote a higher proportion of their resources to education than do the wealthier ones. Theoretically, one might argue that this is not very significant because all states and school districts should be making a greater effort to support education. However, this argument overlooks many important considerations relating to our tax structure.

One such consideration is the competitive aspect of state and local taxation. In New York City, there is a concentration of high incomes unequaled anywhere in the country. Nearly 20 per cent of all internal revenue is collected in New York State. Thus it would appear that New York City, which is permitted to levy an income tax but does not [it does now], and New York State, which does levy an income tax, could easily have the very best schools in the nation. The difficulty is, however, that many high-income persons and corporations would move if tax rates were raised substantially. This is why it is often fallacious to criticize states and communities for not raising taxes; if they did so, they would lose people and businesses to areas less concerned about education. The need for, and justice of, federal taxation for education would thus remain even if there were substantial equality in wealth and revenues among all states and school districts. The fact that a federal tax cannot be evaded at the expense of children in a particular school district is one of the most compelling reasons why we must move toward an educational system financed by the federal government.

Still another factor makes it very unlikely that an adequate educational system could be financed without massive federal support. School districts have been forced to raise most of their funds (54 per cent in 1953–54) by means of the property tax. Unlike most other taxes, property taxes must usually be submitted to popular vote. As is usual in this type of situation, the people who are badly hurt by a substantial tax increase are more effective politically than the diffuse majority which benefits from the increase. The result is that an increasing number of bond issues for school funds are being defeated in communities sympathetic to public education. Here is some indication of the rising (and often justified) tide of resentment against such discriminatory taxation.

The need for federal support of public education, if not for a federal system, is also related to the way in which the federal government supports non-educational activities. In the new highway program, for example, the federal government will spend $9.00 for every dollar appropriated by the state governments. Obviously, this will result in a bigger share of the state dollar being spent on highways. And, in general, states are tending to appropriate funds for projects which will receive substantial support from the federal government. Thus the only way that education can compete for funds, even at the state level, is for the federal government to assume a much larger share of the educational budget.

DISCUSSION QUESTIONS

1. Is local control of education as inadequate, stultifying, and undemocratic as Lieberman charges? Do you agree with his thesis that our freedoms have survived in spite of our schools?
2. What dogmas were given intellectual protection in the schools you attended? What, in your experience, contradicts Lieberman's description of the narrow parochialism of the public schools? Would American teachers have greater professional autonomy under a federal system of education?
3. Does local control of education give little attention to educational research and stifle the utilization of it, as Lieberman states?
4. Do you accept as inevitable federal financing of education and a national system of schools? Would you oppose these vigorously?

PRESTON R. WILCOX

The Controversy over I.S. 201

I.S. 201—located between 127th Street and 128th Street and between Park and Madison Avenues in New York City—is scheduled to open in the Fall [of 1966]. The initials before the numeral mean that it is destined to be an "intermediate school," which is to say, it will serve children from the 5th through the 8th grade in accordance with the Board of Education's 4-4-4 plan for reorganizing the grade structure of the school system. Almost from the moment the Board announced its intention to build I.S. 201 on this site, the school has been the center of considerable controversy. Local community organizations such as Associated Community Teams (ACT), United Block Association (UBA), Massive Economic Neighborhood Development (MEND), Community Association of East Harlem Triangle, Inc., HARYOU-ACT, and others have all voiced various degrees and kinds of protest to the opening of the school as currently planned. Built on stilts, with no windows facing onto the streets—its design has been viewed by some in the neighborhood as a symbol of the city's attitude to this impoverished area, the windowless facade standing for an averted eye. Other local spokesmen have pointed to the fact that the choice of this site for all intents and purposes guarantees that the school be segregated. In reply, the Board has conceded that I.S. 201 will have a student population of 50 percent Negro and 50 percent Puerto Rican, but Board spokesmen have asserted that there is no way around this unfortunate circumstance if the neighborhood is to have a new school at all.

Reprinted from *The Urban Review,* Vol. I, No. 3 (June 1966), pp. 12–17, with permission of the publisher, the Center for Urban Education.

Late in April, the local school board for District Four (in which I.S. 201 falls) held an open meeting in the auditorium of James Fenimore Cooper Junior High School on Madison Avenue and 120th Street. Present at the meeting to listen to Parent Association representatives from almost every school in the District were Mayor John Lindsay, School Superintendent Bernard Donovan, and District Superintendent Daniel Schrieber. The attitude of the audience toward these leaders was distinctly hostile; speaker after speaker rose to demand action redressing their grievances against the public educational system of the city. More than one speaker referred to I.S. 201 as if its construction constituted a deliberate slap in the face of the community's pride and expectations. Superintendent Donovan defended the present plans for the school with firmness and vigor, saying that I.S. 201 would be provided with the best personnel and resources the Board could offer. From the remarks made following his presentations, however, it was clear that most of the local residents in the auditorium were not persuaded.

Criticism of I.S. 201 voiced at the meeting seemed rather diffuse, with one speaker addressing the problem of segregation, another the problem of educational quality, another the "bad faith" of the Board. Several flyers being circulated among the audience reflected these concerns. But one longer paper seemed to touch on a problem which was all too evident at the meeting itself: the quite impersonal but real antagonism between these community representatives and the leaders of the school system.

The author of the paper was Preston R. Wilcox, an Assistant Professor (of community organization) at the Columbia School of Social Work.

ONE VIEW AND A PROPOSAL BY PRESTON R. WILCOX

In this paper, I am going to set aside for the moment the issue of I.S. 201's segregated status and concentrate instead on what I see as an opportunity presented by the opening of this school to experiment with a new approach to relations between the community and the public educational system. This approach should not be construed as resignation in the face of continued school segregation, or as an acceptance of the "neighborhood school" as this is commonly regarded by opponents of integration. But if one believes that a segregated white school can be a "good" school, then one must believe that a segregated Negro and Puerto Rican school, like I.S. 201, can also be a "good" school. We must be concerned with those who are left behind and who will be left behind even if the best conceivable school desegregation program should be implemented. And behind my concern lies the conviction that one can be black (or white or Puerto Rican), reside and attend school in an enforced ghetto, and still be successfully educated to the limits of his potentialities.

I begin with the fact that the present public educational system is not training the vast majority of youth in the ghetto to anything like the limits of their potentialities.

If it is true that the public school system can do no more than it is already doing, then the communities of the poor must be prepared to act for themselves. The residents of the ghetto must seize the opportunity to assume a leadership role in the education of their own children, just as they must become involved in the direction of all programs set up to serve their needs. In this they claim only a chance to exercise, for better or worse, the same right which is exercised by some of those outside the ghetto. What this means is that "a community presence" be established at a high level of educational administration, and that an instrumentality be developed which would assure minority group parents of direct access to the channels of informed opinion and power.

In what follows, I am proposing a fundamental restructuring of the relations between school and community based on a radical redistribution of power. I am thinking of I.S. 201 and the population it will serve, but the relevance of what I propose to other schools and other communities should be readily apparent.

I suggest that a School-Community Committee be established at this school. It would be composed of individuals with close ties to, and knowledge of, the community. These individuals would be parents, local leaders and professionals in educational or social science fields who would be drawn from the community or outside it, if necessary. The Committee would be selected by parents of children enrolled in the school since these parents have already been alerted to their opportunity by the many neighborhood organizations in the area.

The first task of the School-Community Committee would be to screen and interview candidates for the position of principal. This may seem an extreme proposal, but it is essential if there is to be any cooperation between the school and the community. Moreover it is based on the fact that principals in the New York public school system have far more power and independence vis-à-vis the Board than is generally realized, or than they generally take advantage of. As such men as Edward Gottlieb and Elliot Schapiro have positively shown, the psychological stance of the principal toward his pupils and their backgrounds is a critical factor in his performance as an educator. A principal prepared to exploit his position for the benefit of his students is an inestimable asset to the community; such a man is the sine qua non of this experimental program. That the principal should be accountable to the parents of his students will be a new, and probably disagreeable experience for most men who have held this post in the New York system. But the man best suited for the role proposed here would be one whose devotion to education did not depend on his isolation from the community. Instead of being committed to the elimination in his pupils of all that he feels is repulsive in their backgrounds and values, this principal would be committed to utilizing these values as a resource for education.

Apart from selecting and supportively guiding the principal, the Committee would have extensive review functions. It would have access to all reports sent by school administrators to the District Supervisor and the Board of Education, and it would be empowered to hold open meetings to which parents and teachers would be invited to present their suggestions or complaints. Additionally, it would have the responsibility of providing a continuous review of the curriculum to ensure that it remains relevant to the needs and experience of the students and that it be sufficiently demanding to bring out their best possible performance.

Among the most important operational duties of the Committee would be the supervision and administration of all after-school and weekend programs held at the school. These activities should be directed on the one hand toward the students and on the other, toward adult members of the community. For the student, the Committee would operate remedial and enrichment programs in the school. Outside, it would take systematic responsibility for engaging the children in meaningful and effective community projects such as housing surveys, block cleanups, tutorial programs for younger children, publication of block newsletters, etc. The purpose of this effort, of course, would be to help the students adopt a positive stance toward their own communities and to stimulate them to employ their own intellectual resources outside the classroom as well as within. Students should also be assisted by the Committee in making career choices.

Reaching out to the adults, the Committee would first seek legal incorporation and work out procedures for annual elections to guarantee both continuity and representativeness. Then, as aspects of a thorough parent education and information program, the Committee would issue regular written reports to all community institutions and organizations, parents and other interested individuals, with regard to school enrollment, reading and mathematics levels of achievement, teacher turnover rates, curriculum content, and so on. In this way, parents will be enabled to measure the effectiveness of the educational program, and to better evaluate teacher performance. To relate the community to the school simply as an available, useful structure, the Committee might well sponsor a wide range of social events to be held there. The Committee should also concern itself with those larger issues such as police brutality and public safety, and the operations of the Welfare system, which impinge so critically on the lives of school children in the ghetto.

To provide a continuous link between the school staff and the Committee, the latter would be required to hire a full-time "educational expeditor." I apologize for the awkwardness of the title but it points up what would be his two most important qualifications: professional experience in education and an ability to get things done. He would be responsible for meeting with teachers and other administrative staff to hear and follow upon their problems and proposals, and to do the same for parents. As a representative of the Committee, he would also be permitted to make visits to classrooms at specified times, and to the homes of students. He would seek to involve local organizations in the affairs of the school and, as a means of meshing school and community even further, he would be in charge of training of local residents as "foster teachers." The latter would be recruited by the School-Community Committee to serve as advisors to specific classes in the school. They would be required to make home visitations, referrals for public and private welfare services, and to be involved in the after-school program.

There are a number of historical precedents for this scheme. One of them is very close to home, in Harlem. Leonard Covello, for whom, it is said, Fiorello LaGuardia built Benjamin Franklin High School on 116th St. and Roosevelt Drive, was one of the earliest advocates of the community-centered school. Before World War II, East Harlem was predominantly Italian and Covello was concerned lest a ruthless drive to "Americanize" the children of immigrants destroy "a great wealth of cultural resources" and, by an implicit process of invidious comparison, perpetuate in the minority population long-lasting feelings of inferiority. The school, therefore, should be sympathetically responsive to the customs and values of the community it serves. "In the concept of the community-centered school," he wrote in 1939, "we have, it seems to me, the ultimate objective of all education because it deals with the child in connection with his social background and in relation to all forces, disruptive as well as constructive, that contribute to his education."

More recently, in the Bannekar District of St. Louis, Assistant Superintendent Samuel Shepherd, Jr., has applied some of Covello's ideas to a school district which is 95 per cent Negro in both pupil and teacher personnel. While Shepherd believes unequivocally in the educational value of school integration, he refuses to regard its continued postponement as an excuse for educational failure. By reaching toward the community's pride, he has effectively convinced parents, teachers and students that they do not have to be white to be a success.

Closer, operationally, to the experiment I am advocating, is the program of the Child Development Group in Mississippi. There, parents and local leaders among the black poor have been trained by northern teachers and curriculum specialists to operate and set policy for their own Head Start program in eighty-four different locations. Their success in obtaining new funds from Washington, in addition to the attacks they have sustained from Senator Stennis, testify to their achievement.

In the light of the Mississippi experience, it might be asked why I do not propose that the people of the ghetto set up privately funded schools outside the public educational system. After all, in Jackson Heights, members of the

Parents and Taxpayers Association have founded a recently accredited school in response to what they consider an evil of the present system. But whose public school system is this? If it belongs to the public, there should be no necessity for communities to set up parallel systems. Rather, the question is how can we alter the relationship between the administrators of the existing system and the people in such a way as to bring the services offered more clearly into line with what is desired by the clientele?

The experimental program I have outlined should go far toward answering this question. It rests on a hypothesis which many people will greet with skepticism and hostility: that a community can organize effectively around the process of educating its children and that it has the capacity to intervene directly in that process. Yet this hypothesis has been proven correct in other communities in the country, although I am not prepared to argue that it has been with invariably happy results. In New York City we do not elect our school officials and indeed the educational system has for so long been perceived as being "above" politics that its administrators are today alternately baffled and enraged to discover that they are squarely in the middle of it.

In the viewpoint of the ghetto, the problem is stated in terms of a fact: the present system has failed, and is failing, in its task of enabling minority group youth to seize the opportunities America holds out to its other citizens. Of course the fault is not entirely the system's. But what this experimental program offers is the possibility that, in at least one school in one community, the school administrators and teachers will be made accountable to the community, and the community made obligated to them, *in such a way that responsibility for successes and failures is shared.* In the process, one can expect the school in the ghetto to become what schools in more privileged areas already are, a reflection of local interests and resources, instead of a subtle rejection of them. For the operating philosophy of the existing system is too often manifested in a conscious or unconscious belittling of the values and life styles of much of its clientele. By granting that clientele access to the direction of the school, a vicious circle of blame and rejection may be broken. For the students at the school this should mean a significant change in the current pattern of rewards and punishments. Instead of approval being attached almost exclusively to matters of comportment and dress, rewards may come to be derived from one's obligation to his peers and community. We must find a better balance between scholarship and citizenship. Able to bring what is of value to him into the classroom, he may find there the courage to build on it. For the parents (and as many of them as possible should be enlisted in the program) an active participation in positions of influence in the school should help to bring about a change in their positions in the larger community.

Thus, beside all else, the School-Community Committee represents an effort to activate parents in the ghetto to assume a kind of responsibility which the dominant society has failed to exercise and from which they stand to gain the most, the education of their own children. This effort will be wrought with controversy and conflict, but it must be made.

DISCUSSION QUESTIONS

1. Is it the school's obligation to give to its clientele what it wants? What responsibility does the school have to the group it serves?
2. Can schools function in a partnership where ". . . the school administrators and teachers will be made accountable to the community and the community made obligated to them. . ."?
3. To what extent are the schools serving as a whipping boy for the anger and frustration of the black community? To what extent is criticism justified?
4. What effect will community involvement have in helping solve the problems of the ghetto schools?

THE PROGRESSIVE LABOR PARTY EDUCATION COMMITTEE*

We Must Rule the School

What kind of life is ahead for our boys and girls who go to public school in New York?

Our boys and girls are on a slow boat to nowhere. There are a few good teachers and good classes, but these are for the middle-class children—mostly white. The working-class children get such bad schooling that they can hardly even read.

Even the Board of No Education says that most of our boys and girls are years behind. The end of the line for them will be a low-pay job, or maybe no job, or learning to kill other working people in Vietnam.

Now, why is this? Can we do anything about it?

Every school system in history has been the front man for the ruling power of the country. The schools aim to train people to serve the rulers' interests.

The New York City Board of No-Education is no different. This Board represents those who control this society: the ruling class. It "educates"

* The Progressive Labor Party asks that its present position be emphasized: that it is demanding "a better curriculum, smaller class sizes, more and better teachers, better lunches, crossing guards [and] for [its] children to be able to read. . ." Community control, the Party states, is a phrase used to divert parents from their goals, since "there can never be real community control under U.S. capitalism . . ."

people to fill the economic needs of our ruling class. Today they need a small group of intellectuals to teach, service and act as "spokesmen" for the people; a group of scientists and technicians to organize industry; a large mass of working people to run that industry; and a large group of unemployed unskilled workers to serve as "competition" for the employed labor force.

The rich ruling class** wants *service*. They want unthinking workers who will be forced to work in low-pay jobs. They want soldiers. They don't want to give our boys and girls good schooling—they want them to have just enough to put them in a bad job or the army. And the rich ruling class doesn't want to spend money on schooling the working class—they would rather spend billions on the army and police who keep working-class people down, here and around the world.

Of course, they have some good jobs which need better schooling. They want to give these jobs to "their own kind." The good public schooling goes to people whom the ruling class can trust to keep their robbery system going smoothly. These are the middle-class families—mostly white, plus a few other educated mis-leaders who will help to sell out and oppress their own people.

So let's look at the New York "school problem," the way the ruling class looks at it. All of a sudden it makes some sense. The middle-class parts of the city have the better schools. Manhattan and the south Bronx and the Brooklyn ghettos—all the sections where working-class people are crowded in—have the worst, most overcrowded schools. *These boys and girls just aren't taught.*

For instance, at P.S. 176, at 12th Avenue and 68th Street in Brooklyn, which is a white working-class neighborhood, the ethnic breakdown is:

Black	Puerto Rican	White
5.2%	1.5%	93.4%

The reading level for the 6th grade, as given out by the Board of Education, is 6.2; the level should be 6.8.

At P.S. 68 at 127th Street between 7th Avenue and Lenox Avenue in Manhattan, the ethnic breakdown is:

Black	Puerto Rican	White
96.9%	3.1%	0.0%

The reading level for the 6th grade is 4.9.

At P.S. 81 at Riverdale Avenue and 255th Street, a white upper-middle-class school, the ethnic breakdown is:

** We use the term "ruling class" here to describe the group of bankers, bosses and landlords who own the large industrial plants, factories and farms, and buildings. They actually determine who will be president, governor, mayor, police chief, judge, etc. This class of rich people that run this country are the exact opposite of us and are our enemy and as long as they run the country we will never be free!

Black	Puerto Rican	White
1.7%	2.6%	95.7%

The reading level for the 6th grade is 9.4.

These figures show that while the worst schools are in Harlem, the white working-class is not being taught either, and the children who are being taught by the Board are those who live in upper-middle-class areas like Riverdale.

Most upper-class children, of course, never go to public school. In case a middle-class family sends a child to public school, they have the "track" system. That means that inside these jail-houses that they call "schools" there are a few good classes—and if you come from a middle-class home, you will be "tracked" into these classes. That is, inside the public school system they have "private schools" for the middle class.

But if you are working-class Black or Puerto Rican, *You will not be educated.* If they educated you, would you work for the low pay they want to give you? Would you fight their wars when you could go to college instead? They know you wouldn't. That's why they don't improve the schools.

FIGHT FOR CHANGE

This book will try to show just what changes we need in our schools. But it won't do you any good to say "That sounds good. I'll send a copy of this book to the Mayor and the Board of Education." The Mayor and the Board of No-Education belong to the ruling class.

Working people will get what they need only by fighting for it. We have to get the parents and students together, join hands with any sincere teachers who really put the children's needs first, and say to the government:

We know you need this kind of school system to keep the country going the way you want it. But *we want* our boys and girls to grow up and be proud of their own people and ready to look any man in the eye. And any schools there are going to be, we're going to make you run them our way.

We want our youth to know enough to be able to do anything they want—maybe even reading and writing and planning about how to change the whole U.S. imperialist system so that our people don't get cheated all their life. We know that you rulers are afraid that workers—especially Black and Puerto Rican workers—will learn how to organize and fight harder for their own people. That is why you won't teach the real history—the fighting working-class history, the fighting Afro-American history, the fighting Hispanic-American history—in public schools today.

But there is no tomorrow for these old schools, because we are going to fight until we win our right to a full and proud education.

DISCUSSION QUESTIONS

1. Is there a "conspiracy" to deprive the poor of the kind of education that would break down social and economic barriers? Who are the "conspirators"?
2. Do the reading scores cited buttress the "conspiracy" argument? How do you explain these scores?
3. Are middle-class children "tracked" into good classes? Are poor children "tracked" into inferior classes?

TOM HAYDEN | *"Two, Three, Many Columbias"*

The goal written on the university walls was "Create two, three, many Columbias"; it meant expand the strike so that the U.S. must either change or send its troops to occupy American campuses.

At this point the goal seems realistic; an explosive mix is present on dozens of campuses where demands for attention to student views are being disregarded by university administrators.

The American student movement has continued to swell for nearly a decade: during the semi-peace of the early '60s as well as during Vietnam; during the token liberalism of John Kennedy as well as during the bankrupt racism of Lyndon Johnson. Students have responded most directly to the black movement of the '60s: from Mississippi Summer to the Free Speech Movement; from "Black Power" to "Student Power"; from the seizure of Howard University to the seizure of Hamilton Hall. As the racial crisis deepens so will the campus crisis. But the student protest is not just an offshoot of the black protest—it is based on authentic opposition to the middle-class world of manipulation, channeling and careerism. The students are in opposition to the fundamental institutions of society.

The students' protest constantly escalates by building on its achievements and legends. The issues being considered by seventeen-year-old freshmen at Columbia University would not have been within the imagination of most "veteran" student activists five years ago.

Columbia opened a new tactical stage in the resistance movement which began last fall: from the overnight occupation of buildings to permanent occupation; from mill-ins to the creation of revolutionary committees; from symbolic civil disobedience to barricaded resistance. Not only are these tactics already being duplicated on other campuses, but they are sure to be surpassed by even more militant tactics. In the future it is conceivable that

---

Reprinted from *Ramparts,* June 15, 1968, p. 40, with permission of the publisher.

students will threaten destruction of buildings as a last deterrent to police attacks. Many of the tactics learned can also be applied in smaller hit-and-run operations between strikes: raids on the offices of professors doing weapons research could win substantial support among students while making the university more blatantly repressive.

In the buildings occupied at Columbia, the students created what they called a "new society" or "liberated area" or "commune," a society in which decent values would be lived out even though university officials might cut short the communes through use of police. The students had fun, they sang and danced and wisecracked, but there was continual tension. There was no question of their constant awareness of the seriousness of their acts. Though there were a few violent arguments about tactics, the discourse was more in the form of endless meetings convened to explore the outside political situation, defense tactics, maintenance and morale problems within the group. Debating and then determining what leaders should do were alternatives to the remote and authoritarian decision-making of Columbia's trustees.

The Columbia strike represented more than a new tactical movement, however. There was a political message as well. The striking students were not holding onto a narrow conception of students as a privileged class asking for inclusion in the university as it now exists. This kind of demand could easily be met by administrators by opening minor opportunities for "student rights" while cracking down on campus radicals. The Columbia students were instead taking an internationalist and revolutionary view of themselves in opposition to the imperialism of the very institutions in which they have been groomed and educated. They did not even want to be included in the decision-making circles of the military-industrial complex that runs Columbia: *they want to be included only if their inclusion is a step toward transforming the university.* They want a new and independent university standing against the mainstream of American society, or they want no university at all. They are, in Fidel Castro's words, "guerrillas in the field of culture."

How many other schools can be considered ripe for such confrontations? The question is hard to answer, but it is clear that the demands of black students for cultural recognition rather than paternalistic tolerance, and radical white students' awareness of the sinister para-military activities carried on in secret by the faculty on many campuses, are hardly confined to Columbia. Columbia's problem is the American problem in miniature—the inability to provide answers to widespread social needs and the use of the military to protect the authorities against the people. This process can only lead to greater unity in the movement.

Support from outside the university communities can be counted on in many large cities. A crisis is foreseeable that would be too massive for police to handle. It can happen; whether or not it will be necessary is a question which only time will answer. What is certain is that we are moving toward power—the power to stop the machine if it cannot be made to serve humane ends.

American educators are fond of telling their students that barricades are part of the romantic past, that social change today can only come about through the processes of negotiation. But the students at Columbia discovered that barricades are only the beginning of what they call "bringing the war home."

DISCUSSION QUESTIONS

1. Do you agree with Hayden's characterization of the social order as one of ". . . manipulation, channeling, and careerism"?
2. Is Hayden performing a valuable social service in demanding the reformation of what he sees as a sterile and corrupt society?
3. Is he justified in his radical attempts ". . . to stop the machine if it cannot be made to serve humane ends"?

EDITORIAL | *The Siege of Columbia*

The important thing is to pull yourself up by your own hair; to turn yourself inside out and see the world with fresh eyes.

Peter Weiss, "Marat/Sade"

The outside world did not understand Columbia, nor did most commentators evidence any intention of trying. At the height of the crisis a New York Times' editorial expressed the very political theology against which the students were rebelling in the first place:

Convinced of the purity of their own motives and the rottenness of "the system," today's campus militants seek to impose their views upon the universities they attend and upon the societies in which they live, even if this means ignoring or violating the rights of others or preventing universities from going about their normal educational and research activities. In some countries and some situations such tactics and anger are understandable. . . .

But in the United States, Britain and other democratic countries there is no such justification. Here the right of peaceful demonstration is guaran-

Reprinted from *Ramparts,* June 15, 1968, p. 39, with permission of the publisher.

teed and real; here there are abundant opportunities for voicing dissident views and for bringing pressures to bear on public and private lawmakers; . . .

In society, as in physics, actions tend to produce reactions. . . . Fascism of the left raises the specter of fascism of the right, and either or both would bury freedom.

If the student radicals of Morningside Heights contemptuously rejected the liberal perorations of the Times, it wasn't as if they weren't familiar with their logic. They simply had had it. They had read David Truman's elitist theory of the pluralist society in their political science classes. And they saw what those theories meant in reality through the behavior of Dean Truman himself.

It was not a "fascism of the left" that the students were trying to counterpose to all that garbage, but rather a more radical and ultimately more appealing notion of what the obligations of democratic citizenship are than the one the Times entertained. The students knew that the distinction which the Times made between democratic societies and totalitarian societies obfuscated more than it clarified; their experience of months of frustration with the Columbia administration in futilely attempting to exercise dissent through the traditional "channels" only validated and allowed to proceed unimpaired a system which they knew to be rigged and oppressive behind the facade of its legalism. Finally, they came to understand that the civility and tolerance that was asked of them in the face of moral evil really meant that the established oppressive practices would continue to exist; the administration could easily put up with verbal protest.

Instead of remaining civil, the students became intransigently intolerant, rude, even downright nasty. But the result was not the constriction of freedom which the New York Times prophesied. On the contrary, the deliberate act of disruption actually led to a widening of the scope of freedom. When the ordinary processes of the university had come grinding to a halt, real alternatives to the established policies could be discussed for the first time as rational projects.

Columbia was no revolution because those who created it could never really hope to take power. The importance of the Columbia upheaval lies not in any concrete institutional changes that may eventually be achieved on that campus (although such a resolution is obviously important for the students and faculty who took part), but rather in its total educational impact.

Many, students and faculty alike, became radicalized by the rebellion. Some became more conservative, more committed to the status quo of the institution. Thus the atmosphere was polarized. It may well be that this polarization is the most valuable result of such crises, since the old reasonableness is no more than a cover, permitting education to be a vacuous thing that is meaningless in people's lives. In such university situations, everybody "does his thing," including professors who work on germ warfare next to others who spend their time doing humanistic research. After a crisis the university is divided into camps, each of which is stimulated to try to make its knowledge and its view of the world meaningful.

All of this is purgative and ultimately much healthier than the false sense of routine and reason which serves to obscure an enormous amount of banality. Thus, by disrupting the orderly process the veil has been lifted; the institution has been observed to have *real* interests, and one can determine for oneself whether one wishes to support those interests.

Since the end of World War II, American students had blithely accepted the advice of their teachers and made appropriate adjustments to a suffocating society. Their professors, of course, had surrendered first; many of them were ex-radicals and reformers who had given up the dream of radical change in order to celebrate the society because it was successful in delivering material goods. All of this was done in the name of "realism" and scientific objectivity and was heralded by Columbia professor of sociology Daniel Bell as the "End of Ideology," a phrase that for the radical students became an epitaph for an age.

DISCUSSION QUESTIONS

1. Was it necessary for the students to entirely disrupt the functioning of the university before ". . . real alternatives to the established policies could be discussed for the first time as rational projects"?
2. What are the purposes of a university?
3. What is the place of students in the university schema?
4. Might the student "revolt" be thought of as a return to the American tradition of political thought and action?

JOHN FISCHER

To: Mrs. J. Willoughby Carson
From: The Dean of Students

I fully sympathize with your distress about Junior's arrest and imprisonment, and I am glad to tell you that his injuries are not serious. When he bit one of the arresting officers and kicked the other in the groin, they regrettably lost their tempers; but I am informed that the stitches in his

---

Reprinted from *Harper's Magazine*, "The Easy Chair," July 1968, pp. 16, 20, with permission of the author.

scalp will not show, and that a reasonable amount of bridgework will make his mouth practically as good as new.

His formal education will be interrupted, of course, during the six months he will be spending at hard labor on the state prison farm, but I think you will agree with me that the time will not be wasted. We should regard his present experience as an important—indeed, an essential—part of his education.

When Junior arrived at the university he was a typical product of the child-rearing theories popular about twenty years ago among upper-middle-class parents of your generation. That is, he was brought up on the principle that the natural impulses of the child should never, under any circumstances, be frustrated. Consequently he was accustomed to getting anything he asked for; and he soon learned that if gratification wasn't forthcoming, a tantrum would produce it instantly.

"Compromise" was a concept he had never encountered, and when it was explained to him that it involved accommodating his own desires to the needs of other people, he immediately denounced it as evil. We find this a commonplace reaction among our more violent young radicals. They tend to equate "compromise" with "sellout," and to conclude that any institution which works by reconciling the interests of different people and pressure groups must be inherently corrupt. Naturally, too, they tend to regard anyone who disagrees with them as not only stupid, but wicked. This is doubly true of any older person in a position of authority who does not grant all their demands forthwith. In their eyes he is a father-figure who does not behave in the proper—*i.e.,* permissive—fatherly pattern.

We can readily understand, therefore, the behavior of Junior and his fellow members of Students for a Democratic Society when the Trustees refused to resign and to hand over the university endowment to the SDS Revolutionary Action Committee. Their first reaction was one of stunned disbelief. They next decided that such a corrupt and unresponsive institution had to be destroyed—or, in their terminology, "disrupted." In accordance with the tactics they had learned from infancy, they then threw a tantrum in the Board of Trustees meeting room. The subsequent events you already know.

It may comfort you to look at the matter in this light: at some point Junior had to learn that he will not be living in a permissive world—that the universe does not run on Spockian principles. He also was bound to meet somebody, sooner or later, who responds to disruption by disrupting right back.

Since he had to get busted someday, you may feel that the sooner it happened the better. Scalp wounds do heal more quickly at an early age. Of course it might have been better—or at least less painful—if he had learned these unavoidable lessons as a two-year-old; but it's too late for you to think about that now.

DISCUSSION QUESTIONS

1. Compare the Dean of Students' view of the Columbia University affair with Tom Hayden's.
2. Would you seek the Dean of Students' advice with an important personal problem of your own?

CASTLE W. FREEMAN, Jr.

The Psychology of Revolt: How It Felt at Columbia

On the afternoon and evening of November 22, 1963, word of John F. Kennedy's assassination spread across the country from Dallas and visited all Americans, of whatever opinion, with the feeling of something like apocalypse. However different individuals may have reacted to the news, there must have been at first the general impression that things were falling apart before their eyes, that the familiar standards and forms to which they had become accustomed were shattered, and that—for better or for worse—nothing could ever be the same again. It is appropriate to go to the chaos which followed President Kennedy's death for an image of the emotional environment created by the disorders at Columbia University in April and May. For, when we who are presently at the university try to understand our feelings about these events now, we are often reminded of what we felt then.

The most obtrusive fact about the demonstrations at Columbia was that they did away utterly with routine activity in and around the university. It was this complete upset of normal procedure at all levels that accounted for much of the mood surrounding the upheavals.

Everywhere were symptoms of the unnatural and the disorderly. Discarded leaflets, position papers, and fliers littered the quadrangles and lawns of the university, making it resemble the site of a vaguely sinister picnic. The haranguing noise of bullhorns echoed over the usually quiet campus. The unusual presence and behavior of the news media helped create an atmosphere of the extraordinary. Americans have come to associate abnormally extended news programing with disaster. And WKCR, the Columbia college radio station, pre-empted its routine offerings of music and conversation for continuous coverage of the demonstrations. Camera crews from television networks and news photographers worked busily everywhere.

Reprinted from *College & University Business,* Vol. XLIV, No. 6 (June 1968), pp. 54–56, with permission of the publisher. (The author was a senior at Columbia in April, 1968.)

More conspicuous than these, however, was the presence of the New York City police, quiet men armed with nightsticks and sometimes with revolvers, who marched about the campus in large numbers, two abreast.

Disorder—the disruption of routine—creates by itself a foreboding sense of disquiet. From the beginning of the crisis at Columbia on April 23, the atmosphere of the campus was one of profound malaise. Wednesday the 24th was overcast, and restless crowds of spectators moved from one occupied building to another in the way that livestock moves uneasily beneath troubled clouds. Their mood was generally grave and apprehensive. "What is going on *here?*" somebody asked. "Nothing good," somebody answered.

In contrast to the tension of those who observed them, the demonstrations themselves seemed to proceed in a kind of carnival atmosphere which evidently thrived on the prevailing disorder. On the night of Tuesday, April 23, access to Hamilton Hall was available to anyone who wanted to join the fun. The scene inside was festive. The demonstrators who occupied the building had run bright ribbons around the moldings in the lobby and filled the air with balloons. The stern bronze busts of Columbia notables of the past wore paper hats. Posters of Stokely Carmichael, Che Guevara, and Lenin had been taped to the walls, but they gave the place more an air of irreverent frivolity than of activist determination. A band had set up in a corner, and the room was loud with music and noisy activity. One spectator wondered at the gaiety of the proceedings. "Of course we're gay tonight," a sitter-in told him. "If you read about Castro and Guevara, look at the pictures of them in the Sierra Maestra, or of the October revolutionaries in Russia, they all look happy. They are making the revolution, and so are we. We *should* be gay."

But the gaiety always seemed a lie, imposed upon a situation which was obviously anything but merry. On the first morning of the strike, a group of pickets walked in single file before Hamilton Hall, quietly singing. One of them played a recorder. The tranquility of his music, like the ebullience of the demonstrations before their violent climax, seemed a misrepresentation of reality and served to increase the uneasiness which the situation properly implied.

With the overthrow of the customary routine and the breakdown of conventional patterns of activity, this situation remained in constant flux. A responsible history of the Columbia demonstrations will have to proceed by the half-hour and the hour rather than by the day and the week; the character of the entire affair evolved with baffling rapidity. Pressure groups, spokesmen and positions proliferated endlessly, to the confusion of everyone. The radical changes in the nature of the situation, and the speed with which they occurred, elicited wildly inconsistent responses from many people. During the occupation of the buildings, one student sat at dinner in the John Jay Hall dining rooms and loudly proclaimed that "the cops ought to come in and kick those sons of bitches out of there, I don't care who gets hurt. They can't get away with this. The cops ought to smash them." Less than two days later, they did just that. And on the morning after the police action, this same student was to be seen wearing an appalled expression and a black armband symbolizing outrage at the conduct of the police the night before.

His own self-contradiction reflected a sequence of events which contradicted itself at every turn.

Responding to the flux and flow of events, many people who had formerly taken no active part in the affairs of the campus leapt eagerly at executive responsibility and authority, or at least at its semblance. They acted to be busy at all costs, and they were constantly placing or receiving telephone messages, going somewhere. They were involved, and their activity was frenetic. Students compared notes on how little sleep they had gotten in the last two, three, four days and nights. Discussion groups and discussion leaders—armed with "Roberts Rules of Order"—sprang up everywhere, only to bog down in heated debate over parliamentary procedure, punctuated by impatient demands for relevance and an end to nit-picking rules about motions and seconds and who has the floor.

Certainly it was easier and more satisfying to act in this way than it was to try to think clearly about what was going on. We are taught to think through a situation in an orderly fashion bringing reason to bear on whatever in that situation cannot be doubted, and hence drawing out conclusions, usually ignoring our emotional responses to the problem as not susceptible of reasoned settlement. When we succeed in this, it is because what emotions we have happen not to conflict with our more intellectual values. Thinking about the situation at Columbia, conflict between feeling and belief was and is unavoidable. Many who tried to reach conclusions about the issues at stake ended in quandary. This is probably inevitable when anyone who is not committed to it tries to justify radical civil disobedience to himself.

"SDS has no right to use the tactics they are using," one student said. "They have no right to trample on the rights of others to enter the buildings they are occupying. I know this. But SDS feels that, although they have no *right,* they do have a *duty* to act as they are. And I can understand how you can have a duty to do something without having any right to do it. I can't get any further."

Many students sympathized with the causes of the demonstrators but felt outraged by their methods. Frequently, what offended was not so much that the demonstrators' tactics were morally or politically objectionable, as that they were in bad taste, importunate, rude. It was as though the real crime of the demonstrators was that they were in violation of the rule that gentlemen never make spectacles of themselves. Despite the irrelevance of this conviction, it was often impossible to get around. In this way emotional response impeded the process of rational opinion-forming and led to nagging, inconclusive ambivalence toward the situation at hand.

When events become excessively confused and disorderly, they may easily degenerate into low comedy and farce. During the demonstrations people holding various positions identified themselves by wearing armbands of various colors. It reached the point where one person could wear five differently colored armbands without obvious inconsistency, and some did.

Wearers of blue armbands proclaimed their desire, on a nonpartisan basis, for all parties to comport themselves nonviolently at all cost. One student encountered difficulty in distributing these armbands through a crowd. When he offered one to a girl, she was reluctant to accept it because the blue of the armband was the same shade as that of certain buttons which read "ABOLISH SDS!" Another student refused a similar armband because he had heard that blue signified membership in an underground cadre of SDS sympathizers.

In the course of the demonstrations, the expression "ad hoc" entered the language to stay, and nobody who was at Columbia this spring is likely to forget the occasions of its use and overuse. There were ad hoc committees for this, ad hoc coalitions for that, ad hoc petitions, even an ad hoc theater group. "If I hear anybody say 'ad hoc' again," one student warned another, "I will hoc all over him."

On Sunday April 28, a group of students ("The Majority Coalition") who opposed both the ends and the means of the demonstrators formed a cordon around Low Library to interdict the passage of food supplies to the students inside. Students who sympathized with the occupiers then took up positions beyond the Majority Coalition's line and proceeded to throw fruit and sandwiches over the cordon through the windows of the building. Members of the Coalition responded by mounting on the backs of their colleagues and attempting to bat down the flying food with cafeteria trays. A spirited rivalry developed. When somebody successfully lobbed an orange through one of the windows, a British visitor to Columbia turned to his companion and observed "Columbia two, visitors naught." "Which are Columbia and which are the visitors?" the other asked. "Ah, that is the question, of course," the Briton replied.

If these anecdotes do not seem very funny it is probably because they are not. Whoever wanted a laugh at Columbia this spring had to look hard for it and had to take what humor he could get.

There was nothing funny about the angry encounters between student and student. The predominant fear was always the fear of violence; during the week of April 23 to 30, violence was very much in the air. On the night of Thursday, April 25, it was rumored that a party of militant blacks was moving on the campus from Harlem to confront the university at Hamilton Hall. With this news some students in the quadrangle fronting on that building quickly began working to pull the thin iron fence poles out of the ground. When he saw what they were doing, one student said, "I'm getting out of here. I'm getting clear out of the city."

Throughout the demonstrations, sporadic but bitter fistfighting incidents displayed the clumsy, flailing violence of those unused to violence of any kind. The awkward appearance of these encounters, however, did not make them any less ugly and frightening.

In shocking contrast to the inept violence between students was the terrible efficiency of the police operation of April 30. The scene on the campus that night was like a wild, half-believed dream, full of cries and figures running in the darkness. More frightening than the actions of the police was the panic of the crowds which stampeded over the lawns to escape injury. One student stood apart from a large crowd which had gathered around one of the buildings in the process of being evacuated. When the police moved into the crowd to clear a path for themselves, the crowd turned and began swelling towards him. "I ran like a madman to stay in front of them," he said later. "Finally, when they were nearly on top of me, I got down behind some steps. They ran right over me."

Before that night, the angry response of students to the situation at Columbia had been channeled into opposing factions. But on the morning after the police action, most of the anger on all sides converged into a consensus of outrage directed against the forces which had called in the police. The mood of the university community that morning was one of sullen bitterness. Students of all stripes were shocked and silent; they felt somehow betrayed, and they were fearful. One girl, who had never sympathized with those who had occupied the buildings, woke on Tuesday to hear radio reports of the adventure of the preceding night. "I listened until I had heard the whole thing," she remembered. "Then I walked into the washroom, waited over the bathtub for a second, and threw up again and again."

A WKCR reporter, who had sustained an attitude of detachment during seven days of on-the-scene reporting, lost all semblance of composure as he described the police operation around Fayerweather Hall. "I feel now that I don't want a degree from a university that can do this," he said on the air, barely able to control his voice. The central controller in the studios warned him against editorializing on the air and switched off his channel.

"Columbia is finished," a student cried as the police entered Mathematics Hall at 3 P.M. on Tuesday morning.

This was the feeling of many, that, whatever else was happening, for whatever reasons, they were witnessing the final falling apart of an institution. Certainly that diagnosis was hasty. Columbia University the institution will survive (or at least persist), although, given the drastic nature of the upheavals of those three weeks, it can only survive in an altered form. It would be premature at this point to predict the substantive nature of the alterations which will in time reveal themselves. It is the form that change will take which will be the significance of the Columbia demonstrations, and significance can only be ascribed retrospectively. "What really happened at Columbia," then, remains to be seen.

DISCUSSION QUESTIONS

1. How would you characterize Freeman's position on the Columbia disturbance?
2. Should the police have been brought on campus? Should they ever be called in by the administration?
3. What do you think would have been your position, were you a student at Columbia?
4. If Columbia University can continue only in an altered form, in your opinion what changes must take place?

CHAPTER 8 | *Looking at Teaching and Learning*

In surveying education today, what impresses most is how greatly change is needed and how slowly and haltingly it occurs.

Until Sputnik, America seemed secure in the advantage her educational system gave her over the rest of the world. Sputnik shocked the nation and upset the American educational establishment. One immediate reaction was the pooling of our mathematical and scientific talents in revising and strengthening these disciplines. Belatedly, the national feeling of emergency created a new, active role for the federal government in education in supporting the competition with the Soviets for world supremacy in technology.

Recent curriculum revision has responded to consideration of the method, structure, and process of the various disciplines. Along with this movement has come a reemphasis on the power, the economy, and the retentiveness of inductive learning, though it be called "the discovery process" or any other name.

Among the psychologists who have studied cognition, the Frenchman, Jean Piaget, is especially noteworthy for having returned learning and teaching to its proper focus on the object of all education, the child. Piaget's research is directed toward a startling insight, the child's view of his universe. His procedures and findings are filled with warmth and feeling and compel recognition of the commonality of childhood everywhere.

Americans have only recently begun to know and appreciate Piaget's work. The English, who have known it longer, have found in it the rationale for the remaking of their primary schools, to the point where one-third are Piagetian in outlook and function, one-third are affected by him, while the remainder continue in the traditional pattern.

American education has changed little in form and structure although there is increasing recognition of the need to individualize instruction and to break out of rigid organizational molds. One attempt to provide an alternative to the age-grade format, the nongraded school, has too often resulted in more efficient "tracking" rather than in the flexibility of movement and fluidity of grouping that would offer the child a genuinely individual program.

Programmed learning has been suggested as an answer to the problem of individualizing instruction and giving the teacher greater mobility. However, a model for learning based on stimulus, response, and selective reinforcement raises in many minds thorny questions concerning teachers, children, and the goals of education.

The mass media have entered into active competition with the schools as instruments for learning. The nonschool environment is saturated with them to the point where, jointly, they are coming to create an all-inclusive, wraparound presence of sight and sound. The schools of the twenty-first century must learn to utilize the media—both singly and in a variety of combinations—without being overwhelmed by them.

The lack of responsiveness of the schools to change can only be fully comprehended when one views the society of which they are a part, a society so chaotic, so violently agitated, in such flux that the old established roles are no longer identifiable. What does it mean to be a teacher, a student, a parent? What is a school? What is education? What does it mean to be a human being?

To be armed for today with what McLuhan calls a rear-view mirror mentality is to attack space projectiles with peashooters. To fail to see things whole is to court doom. The revolution we confront is a revolution of rising expectations, born of an affluent society, with television as the midwife. The crisis arises out of denial of what is most deeply human, of decency, integrity, wholeness, manhood—a crisis brought about by man's inhumanity to man. It is remediable only by a return to humanness. Weston LaBarre speaks of "The Human Animal," and Desmond Morris of "The Naked Ape"; both remind us of man's origins and his limitations when acting in animality.

Education is the means whereby children learn their humanness; it is necessarily an interaction suffused with sentiment. Education begins when the child asks, "Am I loved?" It ends when the answer is, "No."

ROBERT T. SIDWELL

Cooling Down the Classroom: Some Educational Implications of the McLuhan Thesis

When Nietzsche's Zarathustra announced the death of God, the people continued to laugh and dance. Concluding that his inauguration of the period *post mortem Dei* was somewhat premature, the prophet retired once more to his mountain. Nietzsche (and his alter ego, Zarathustra) was, as he somewhere wryly conceded, born posthumously. Our modern seer, Marshall McLuhan, on the other hand, announced the death of the mechanical technology and was awarded the Albert Schweitzer professorship of a $100,000 chair in the humanities at Fordham University. "The times," as Bob Dylan sings "they are a-changin'."

Søren Kierkegaard describes a scene wherein a clown is called upon to announce a fire in a theater. He was greeted with laughter and applause (the melancholy Dane suggested that such would probably be the popular reaction to the end of the world). Laughter and applause have, by and large, been the reaction to Professor McLuhan's revolutionary thesis (in addition to outright bewilderment), possibly because he too tends to play the clown at times. In our admiration, amusement (or bewilderment), however, let us not lose sight of the fact that the McLuhan thesis *is* a revolutionary document, particularly for the educational profession.

Unlike Marx and Engels, McLuhan does not call for a revolution; he in fact describes one that is to a large degree a *fait accompli.* McLuhan's description is of a technological revolution, the replacement of the mechanical age by the electronic age. This is the content of the revolution, and, as such, is scarcely very exciting news to anyone over the age of twenty. The McLuhan thesis, however, does not rest on this obvious transformation from mechanical media to electronic media. The new medium of electric technology, suggests McLuhan, treated formally, is itself (like any medium) a "message" quite divorced from the sum of its contents. As a matter of fact, a preoccupation with the content of any medium or process is, from McLuhan's perspective, to ignore the message of that medium *qua* medium. As he has so catchingly phrased it, "the medium is the message."

McLuhan's contention that not content but the medium itself is the message is predicated upon his belief that "any technology creates a totally new human environment."[1] It, in fact, introduces a change of scale, or pace,

---

Reprinted from *The Educational Forum,* Vol. XXXII, No. 3 (March 1968), pp. 351–358, with permission of Kappa Delta Pi, an Honor Society in Education, owners of the copyright.

[1] Marshall McLuhan, *Understanding Media: The Extensions of Man* (New York: McGraw-Hill, 1966), p. vi. (Cited hereafter as McLuhan, *Understanding*).

or pattern into human affairs.[2] The real "message" of any medium, then, is to be found in those changes in perceptual patterns or sensual ratios that it, *qua* medium, engenders. That such changes *are* made, says McLuhan, is due to the fact that technological media represent an extention (or amputation) of some human faculty—psychic or physical.[3] Thus, the wheel is an extension of the foot, the book an extension of the eye, clothing an extension of the skin, etc. Furthermore, ". . . such extension demands new ratios or new equilibriums among the other organs and extensions of the body."[4] One cannot avoid these adjustments or accommodations. Media alter the environment and evoke in us, willy-nilly, ". . . unique ratios of sense perceptions. The extension of any one sense alters the way we think or act—the way we perceive the world. When these ratios change, men change."[5]

Although we cannot avoid these changes, we can, since McLuhan, be intelligently aware of them and of their implications.

"There is absolutely no inevitability as long as there is a willingness to contemplate what is happening."[6] As Father John Culkin notes, "Such influence [of media] are deterministic only if ignored."[7]

McLuhan's contention of an intimate relationship between technological process and modes of societal perceptions and sensual ratios has been shared by a number of other thinkers, usually in less explosive terms and with a more peripheral emphasis. Husserl, for example, noted that

> The scientific abstraction from concreteness, the quantification of qualities which yield exactness as well as universal validity, involve a specific concrete experience of the *Lebenswelt*—a specific mode of seeing the world.[8]

To put this into McLuhan's terminology, the "specific concrete experience" is provided by the technological media of that world, and the "specific mode of seeing the world" is the "message" of the media.

Herbert Marcuse has provided a similar analysis of the "message" of the science of Galileo, when he observed it ". . . is the science of methodical, systematic anticipation and projection. . . . that which experiences, comprehends, and shapes the world in terms of calculable, predictable relationships among exactly identifiable units."[9]

In reducing matter to quantifiable qualities, Marcuse suggests, science (Galilean) provided a new mode of seeing the world. This new perceptual

---

2 *Ibid.*, p. 8.

3 McLuhan and Quentin Fiore, *The Medium is the Massage* (New York: Bantam Books, 1967), p. 26. (Cited hereafter as McLuhan and Fiore, *Massage*).

4 *Ibid.*, p. 45.

5 *Ibid.*, p. 41.

6 *Ibid.*, p. 25.

7 John M. Culkin, S.J., "A Schoolman's Guide to Marshall McLuhan," *Saturday Review*, March 18, 1967, p. 51.

8 Herbert Marcuse, *One-Dimensional Man* (Boston: Beacon Press, 1966), p. 164.

9 *Ibid.*

framework tended to relate men to one another "in accordance with quantifiable qualities. . . ."[10]

McLuhan himself has devoted a considerable number of words to a description of the "message" of the media of the past age—the highly literate and mechanized age. The revolutionary impact of the McLuhan approach lies in his assertion that that is a *past* age. To glimpse some of the significant implications of the McLuhan thesis for education, it is necessary to look briefly at *The Gutenberg Galaxy*, which was ". . . intended to trace the ways in which the *forms* of experience and of mental outlook and expression have been modified, first by the phonetic alphabet and then by printing."[11]

Pre-alphabet man was predominately an auditory creature—the ear was the dominant sensory organ. He lived in "acoustic" space—undifferentiated, intuitive, total. His medium of communication was speech, and its "message" was a specific patterning of perception and sensual ratios. In this (auditory) patterning, action and reaction were simultaneous and demanded a total involvement. McLuhan's term for this modality of life is "mythic," by which he means a ". . . mode of simultaneous awareness of a complex group of causes and effects."[12] The mythic dimension that characterized pre-alphabetical life has been maintained in literate cultures (as the Chinese) which uses a nonphonetic (ideographic) script that ". . . enables them to retain a rich store of inclusive perception in depth of experience. . . . For the ideogram is an inclusive *gestalt,* not an analytic dissociation of senses and function like phonetic writing [as such, it] . . . invests each ideogram with a total intuition of being and reason that allows only a small role to visual sequence as a mark of mental effort and organization."[13]

That pre-alphabetical man's perceptual patterns *were* radically different has been eloquently demonstrated by S. Giedion's studies of spatial conception in prehistoric art. He concludes that:

> The distinguishing mark of the space perception of primeval art is the complete independence and freedom of its vision. . . . In our sense there is no above and no below, no clear distinction of separateness from an intermingling, and also, certainly, no rules of proportional size. . . . All is within the continual present, the perpetual interflow of today, yesterday, and tomorrow.[14]

Dorothy Lee has concluded that "The given as undifferentiated content is implicit in the nominal categories of the Wintu. . . . To the Wintu, the

---

[10] *Ibid.,* p. 157.
[11] Marshall McLuhan, *The Gutenberg Galaxy* (Toronto: University of Toronto Press, 1962), p. 1. (Cited hereafter as McLuhan, *Gutenberg*).
[12] McLuhan and Fiore, *Massage,* p. 114.
[13] McLuhan, *Understanding,* pp. 84–85.
[14] S. Giedion, "Space Conception in Prehistoric Art," in Edmund Carpenter and Marshall McLuhan, eds., *Explorations in Communication* (Boston: Beacon Press, 1960), pp. 85–86. (Cited hereafter as Carpenter and McLuhan, *Explorations*).

given is not a series of particulars . . . the given is unpartitioned mass. . . ."[15] Again, with regard to Malinowski's well-studied Trobrianders:

> Events and objects are self-contained points in another respect; there is a series of beings, but no becoming. There is no temporal connection between objects. . . . There is no arrangement of activities or events into means and ends, no causal or teleologic relationships. What we consider a causal relationship in a sequence of connected events is to the Trobriander an ingredient of a patterned whole.[16]

This totality of tribalistic involvement without differentiation of pre-alphabetical man (as reflected in his art and language) is the basis of the *Gemeinschaft* (community) so well delineated by Toennies—an organic rather than a mechanical formation.[17]

Then came the phonetic alphabet—its message, as McLuhan has so well shown, was devastating to the all-at-once-ness organicity of pre-alphabetical man's world.

> The alphabet is a construct of fragmented bits and parts which have no semantic meaning in themselves, and which must be strung together in a line, bead-like, and in prescribed order. Its use fostered and encouraged the habit of perceiving all environment in visual and spatial terms—particularly in terms of a space and of a time that are uniform, c,o,n,t,i,n,u,o,u,s and c-o-n-n-e-c-t-e-d.[18]

Man became linear, his activities fragmented, his thoughts sequential and departmentalized. From an undifferentiated all-at-one-ness, the phonetic alphabet encouraged a perceptual awareness of a sequential one-at-a-time-ness. Man became individualized (de-tribalized)—an individual and unrelated atom at large in sharply differentiated visual space.

> Phonetic culture endows men with the means of repressing their feelings and emotions when engaged in action. To act without reacting, without involvement, is the peculiar advantage of western literate man.[19]

The integral wholeness of pre-alphabetical man's world underwent a radical departmentalization—his sensual, emotional, imaginative facets were delineated and disassociated from the "whole," while he himself was individualized, detribalized and specialized.

Such a world view is the *sine qua non* of applied knowledge and technology. Printing, McLuhan notes, is merely an extension and intensification of the visual orientation. David Riesman noted that "Print may be said to mark the epoch of the middle class—the time-attentive, the future oriented,

---

15 Dorothy Lee, "Linguistic Reflections of Wintu Thought" in Carpenter and McLuhan, *Explorations*, pp. 12–13.

16 Lee, "Lineal and Nonlineal Codifications of Reality," in *ibid.*, p. 141.

17 Ferdinand Toennies, *Gemeinschaft und Gesellschaft*, quoted in Talcott Parsons, Edward Shils, Kaspar D. Naegle, Jesse R. Pitts (eds.), *Theories of Society* (New York: Free Press, 1961), 2 Vols., I, 192.

18 McLuhan and Fiore, *Massage*, p. 44.

19 McLuhan, *Understanding*, p. 86.

the mobile. . . . If oral communication keeps people together, print is the isolating medium par excellence."[20] Many a wife may have shared this feeling while staring at the back of her husband's morning paper at the breakfast table.

The supreme quality of print, McLuhan feels, is the simple fact of its repeatability—it is "a ditto device."

This fragmenting process of mechanized handicraft produced the "division of labor." Noting the detribalizing effects of this fragmented and linear perceptual pattern, Marx ". . . interpreted the division of labor as the social expression of self-alienation."[21] It would be interesting to hear what that dedicated rebel would have made of a recent newspaper item headed "Ten Specialists Required to Reset Phone Button."[22]

Another item in this same edition serves to demonstrate what may well be the epitome of a visually dominated sensorium. Dr. Edward E. Burns, of Texas A&M, is therein credited with the statement that "People eat with their eyes." SEE what I mean?

The education of typographic man has been a faithful reflection of the "message" of his media—it too has been linear, fragmented, non-participatory and sequential. Even the fragmented learning space (classroom) reflects this bias.

> Print meant the possibility of uniform texts, grammars and lexicon visually present to as many as asked for them. The classroom, as we know it, was entirely the by-product of print.[23]

The typographic extension of man brought in, among other things, universal literacy and education—homogenized and uniform. So much is past history. Enter the age of electric technology and *its* unique message.

If all media are extensions of some human faculty, then electric circuitry is the penultimate extension of man—an extension of his central nervous system. As such, its message is totality, not fragmentation; a cluster configuration rather than the sequential, linear configuration of print. Electric circuitry is SPEED, the acceleration of information. "At the high speeds of electric communication, purely visual means of apprehending the world are no longer possible; they are just too slow to be relevant or effective."[24] The electric world demands an involvement of the total sensorium for its apprehension. Meaning is altered by acceleration, and the totality of electric simultaneity demands a totality of perception which sounds the death-knell

---

20 David Riesman, "The Oral and Written Tradition," in Carpenter and McLuhan, *Explorations,* pp. 113–114.

21 Robert C. Tucker, *Philosophy and Myth in Karl Marx* (New York: Cambridge University Press, 1961), p. 185.

22 *The New York Times,* March 29, 1967.

23 Marshall McLuhan, "The Effect of the Printed Book on Language," in Carpenter and McLuhan, *Explorations,* p. 129.

24 McLuhan and Fiore, *Massage,* p. 63.

for fragmented, serial, one-at-a-time-ness. It is a world of all-at-once-ness. The electric extension of the central nervous system constitutes, as Father Culkin has aptly put it, ". . . a single instantaneous and coexistant field of experience."[25] As such, the media demand an involvement and participation in depth of the whole being, a mythic dimension. Segmented, individualistic typographic man is being "retribalized" by his media; the atomistic *Gesellschaft* of visual space is being "massaged" by the media into an organic, universal *Gemeinschaft.* A glance at some of the strange (to a typographic perception) goings-on among the students at our higher institutions of learning reveals, if nothing else, the mythic demands of the electric age student for involvement, participation, organic role. The attraction of such participatory activities as the Peace Corps, Civil Rights, etc., are precisely their mythic qualities—an organic *rôle* rather than a linear *position.*

The church has its *aggiornamento* (up-dating) movement—an attempt to establish new (organic) relationships between the fragmented two cities of Augustine—a realization of the demand for the restoration of a mythic dimension in religion. The transcendent God of the fragmented typographic world has surely died; the electric world demands immanentism not transcendent aloofness. "If anything characterizes the modern temper," writes theologian Gabriel Vahanian, "it is a radical immanentism."[26]

Easter Sunday, 1967. A group of some 10,000 young people gather in New York's Central Park for a "Be-In." "We wanted it to be an active celebration of being alive, of having that experience in the park," says Mr. James Fouratt, one of the organizers. "People in New York don't look at each other, don't see each other, don't talk to each other."[27]

Mexico City officials report that the Sunday afternoon band concerts became amazingly popular since jazz numbers were added to the traditional fare. The unprecedented crowds were "humming, clapping and shouting."[28] They were involved and participating because jazz is, in McLuhanese, a "cool" medium (one that is of low definition and demands participation or completion by the audience). The electronic age is cool, as illustrated by the TV screen which presents the audience with some three million "dots" of which only a few dozen are selected by the participant to form his visual image. As a product of these cool media of participation, the electronic age learner is a new breed of cat; he is involved and oriented to involve himself in depth, to live mythically. When this new learner is put into a linear, fragmented school environment (the creation of the typographic media) of low participation and high definition (as is print—a "hot" medium) —enter one big educational problem.

---

25 Culkin, *op. cit.,* p. 70.
26 Gabriel Vahanian, *The Death of God* (New York: George Braziller, 1961), p. 188.
27 *The New York Times,* March 27, 1967.
28 *Ibid.*

The youth of today live mythically and in depth. But they encounter instruction in situations organized by means of classified information—subjects are unrelated, they are visually conceived in terms of a blueprint. . . . The student finds no means of involvement for himself and cannot discover how the educational scheme relates to his mythic world of electronically processed data and experience that his clear and direct responses report.[29]

The implications of the McLuhan thesis are enormous for the educational profession (and threatening for linear educators). The student of the electric world is a participant in discovery and not the passive recipient of neatly pre-packaged linear learning. The linear, analytic, and irrelevantly fragmented bits of information make increasingly less sense to the products of the electronic media. "Young people are looking for a formula for putting on the universe—*participation mystique*. They do not look for detached patterns—for ways of relating themselves to the world, *à la* nineteenth century."[30]

Actually, McLuhan suggests, the T.V. child in a social and educational world that is visually oriented is an "underprivileged cripple."[31]

Apparently one reason why Johnny can't read is that he tries to apply the set of perceptual patterns of his cool electronic media (involvement in depth of *all* senses) to a hot (print) medium which demands an isolated and extended *visual* sensuality rather than a unified sensorium. This seems much like attempting precise target shooting with a shotgun.

How then are we to cool off the classroom in order to get in phase with our media?

Education, it would appear, in order to reflect the message of the electronic media, must begin to dismantle its linear organization pattern on all fronts. It would have to become more "formal" and synthesizing, and less analytic and instructional.

In our time John Dewey worked to restore education to its primitive, pre-print phase. He wanted to get the student out of the passive role of consumer of pre-packaged learning. In fact, Dewey in reacting against passive print culture was surf-boarding along on the new electronic age.[32]

If, in fact, our school audiences have been massaged by their media to take a participatory rôle in the learning process, all is not as dark and linear in the educational world as it might seem. As Father Culkin has observed, the current educational innovations display an interesting similarity—a break with the linear, print-oriented pattern: team teaching, audio-lingual language training, multi-media learning situations, seminars (cool and participatory as opposed to hot, passive lectures), individualized learning

---

[29] McLuhan and Fiore, *Massage*, p. 100.
[30] *Ibid.*, p. 114.
[31] McLuhan, *Understanding*, p. 332.
[32] McLuhan, *Gutenberg*, p. 144.

(learning responsibility shifting from teacher to student).[33] The mythic (not mystic) East would certainly appear to be a topic of increased interest to educators attempting to totalize learning; the teacher who introduces Haiku poetry and the Zen koan to the elementary grades might be surprised at what the electric age learner can do with these forms of mythic experience.

Clearly, the message is involvement, not "scholarly" detachment; synthesis of knowledge and experience, not fragmented analysis; wholeness and convergence, not sequential linearity. From a position of a curricular luxury, the arts ". . . now become a dynamic way of tuning up the sensorium and of providing fresh ways of looking at familiar things."[34] "The arts," of course, include non-western as well as western sources. The "empty" spaces in classical Chinese painting, for example, should prove quite comfortable to the young products of the participatory electronic media (although their teacher may feel a linear annoyance at the "incompleteness" of the undifferentiated aesthetic continuum). In terms of educational theory, the multi-disciplinary and cross-cultural emphases of such theorists as Theodore Brameld are very much in phase with the totality of electronics.

It is regrettably true that in the sharply linear groves of Academe, the pre-electrical perceptual pattern that resulted in fragmentation of knowledge, has been virtually reified in academic departmentalization. This (arbitrary) pattern of segmentation has acquired all of the sacrosanct qualities of an immutable natural law, a "ghostly objectivity" to borrow the apt phrase of Georg Lukács. That the reality is "ghostly" and merely the hypostatized human delineation is painfully obvious to the students of the electric age, who constantly complain that course x bears absolutely no relationship to the activities in courses y and z (and none seem to bear much relationship to their increasingly mythic *Lebenswelt*).

If the McLuhan thesis is indeed the message (commercial?) on the screen ("handwriting on the wall" seems too downright typographical to apply to McLuhan), the educational implications are clear enough. The electronic age pupil requires an educational environment that does not ask him to consume a carefully weighed bundle of pre-digested and pre-packaged knowledge, that allows him a maximum participation in discovery, that will relate and synthesize rather than linearly f/r/a/g/m/e/n/t knowledge. Not "rite words in rote order," but the unified all-at-once totality of instant automation.

"Paradoxically," McLuhan claims, "automation makes liberal education mandatory."[35] Should education persist in moving into the future looking steadfastly to the rear, continue the present fragmented unrelatedness of its

---

[33] Culkin, *op. cit.*, p. 72.
[34] *Ibid.*
[35] McLuhan, *Understanding*, p. 357.

curricular offerings, it will insure a future citizenry wholly alienated from the cybernetic world in which they will be living. "Control over change would seem to consist in moving not with it but ahead of it. Anticipation gives the power to deflect and control force."[36] Such anticipation may be seen in, for example, the new three-year college (tentatively named "Bensalem") which was to open its doors at Fordham University in July, 1967. Perhaps this experimental college will be the archetype of future experiments in providing student participation in matters of curriculum.[37]

If education must be the "civil defense against media fallout," it must become aware of the message of the media—the depth and interrelation of the new world of electronic organization.

Perhaps the best understanding of the message of the electronic media for education is presented in the advertisements for the Berlitz Language Schools—"total immersion."

DISCUSSION QUESTIONS

1. How can the schools help man to become "whole" if they accept McLuhan's premises?
2. Which of his educational ideas do you find most stimulating and provocative?
3. With which do you disagree?

B. F. SKINNER | *Teaching Machines*

There are more people in the world than ever before, and a far greater part of them want an education. The demand cannot be met simply by building more schools and training more teachers. Education must become more efficient. To this end curricula must be revised and simplified, and textbooks and classroom techniques improved. In any other field a demand for increased production would have led at once to the invention of laborsaving capital equipment. Education has reached this stage very late, possibly through a misconception of its task. Thanks to the advent of television, however, the so-called audio-visual aids are being re-examined. Film projectors, television sets, phonographs, and tape recorders are finding their way into American schools and colleges.

Reprinted from B. F. Skinner, *The Technology of Teaching* (New York: Appleton-Century-Crofts, 1968), pp. 29–39, with permission of the publisher. Revised and edited by author from *Science*, October 1958.

[36] *Ibid.*, p. 199.

[37] *The New York Times*, April 6, 1967.

Audio-visual aids supplement and may even supplant lectures, demonstrations, and textbooks. In doing so they serve one function of the teacher: they present material to the student and, when successful, make it so clear and interesting that the student learns. There is another function to which they contribute little or nothing. It is best seen in the productive interchange between teacher and student in the small classroom or tutorial situation. Much of that interchange has already been sacrificed in modern education in order to teach large numbers of students. There is a real danger that it will be wholly obscured if use of equipment designed simply to *present* material becomes widespread. The student is becoming more and more a mere passive receiver of instruction.

Another kind of capital equipment will encourage the student to take an active role in the instructional process. The possibility was recognized in the 1920's, when Sidney L. Pressey designed several machines for the automatic testing of intelligence and information . . . In using the device the student refers to a numbered item in a multiple-choice test. He presses the button corresponding to his first choice of answer. If he is right, the device moves on to the next item; if he is wrong, the error is tallied, and he must continue to make choices until he is right.[1] Such machines, Pressey pointed out, could not only test and score, they could *teach*. When an examination is corrected and returned after a delay of many hours or days, the student's behavior is not appreciably modified. The immediate report supplied by a self-scoring device, however, can have an important instructional effect. Pressey also pointed out that such machines would increase efficiency in another way. Even in a small classroom the teacher usually knows that he is moving too slowly for some students and too fast for others. Those who could go faster are penalized, and those who should go slower are poorly taught and unnecessarily punished by criticism and failure. Machine instruction would permit each student to proceed at his own rate.

The "industrial revolution in education" which Pressey envisioned stubbornly refused to come about. In 1932 he expressed his disappointment.

> The problems of invention are relatively simple. With a little money and engineering resource, a great deal could easily be done. The writer has found from bitter experience that one person alone can accomplish relatively little and he is regretfully dropping further work on these problems. But he hopes that enough may have been done to stimulate other workers, that this fascinating field may be developed.

Pressey's machines succumbed in part to cultural inertia; the world of education was not ready for them. But they also had limitations which probably contributed to their failure. Pressey was working against a background of psychological theory which had not come to grips with the

[1] The Navy's "Self-Rater" is a larger version if Pressey's machine. The items are printed on code-punched plastic cards fed by the machine. The time required to answer is taken into account in scoring.

learning process. The study of human learning was dominated by the "memory drum" and similar devices originally designed to study forgetting. Rate of learning was observed, but little was done to change it. Why the subject of such an experiment bothered to learn at all was of little interest. Frequency and recency theories of learning and principles of massed and spaced practice concerned the conditions under which responses were remembered.

Pressey's machines were designed against this theoretical background. As versions of the memory drum, they were primarily testing devices. They were to be used after some amount of learning had already taken place elsewhere. By confirming correct responses and by weakening responses which should not have been acquired, a self-testing machine does, indeed, teach; but it is not designed primarily for that purpose. Nevertheless, Pressey seems to have been the first to emphasize the importance of immediate feedback in education and to propose a system in which each student could move at his own pace. He saw the need for capital equipment in realizing these objectives. Above all he conceived of a machine which (in contrast with the audio-visual aids which were beginning to be developed) permitted the student to play an active role.

OTHER KINDS OF TEACHING MACHINES

The learning process is now much better understood. Much of what we know has come from studying the behavior of lower organisms, but the results hold surprisingly well for human subjects. The emphasis in this research has not been on proving or disproving theories but on discovering and controlling the variables of which learning is a function. This practical orientation has paid off, for a surprising degree of control has been achieved. By arranging appropriate contingencies of reinforcement, specific forms of behavior can be set up and brought under the control of specific classes of stimuli. The resulting behavior can be maintained in strength for long periods of time. A technology based on this work has already been put to use in neurology, pharmacology, nutrition, psychophysics, psychiatry, and elsewhere.

The analysis is also relevant to education. A student is "taught" in the sense that he is induced to engage in new forms of behavior and in specific forms upon specific occasions. It is not merely a matter of teaching him *what* to do; we are as much concerned with the probability that appropriate behavior will, indeed, appear at the proper time—an issue which would be classed traditionally under motivation. In education the behavior to be shaped and maintained is usually verbal, and it is to be brought under the control of both verbal and nonverbal stimuli. Fortunately, the special problems raised by verbal behavior can be submitted to a similar analysis.

If our current knowledge of the acquisition and maintenance of verbal behavior is to be applied to education, some sort of teaching machine is needed. Contingencies of reinforcement which change the behavior of lower organisms often cannot be arranged by hand; rather elaborate apparatus is needed. The human organism requires even more subtle instrumentation. An appropriate teaching machine will have several important features. The student must *compose* his response rather than select it from a set of alternatives, as in a multiple-choice self-rater. One reason for this is that we want him to recall rather than recognize—to make a response as well as see that it is right. Another reason is that effective multiple-choice material must contain plausible wrong responses, which are out of place in the delicate process of "shaping" behavior because they strengthen unwanted forms.[2] Although it is much easier to build a machine to score multiple-choice answers than to evaluate a composed response, the technical advantage is outweighed by these and other considerations.

A second requirement of a minimal teaching machine also distinguishes it from earlier versions. In acquiring complex behavior the student must pass through a carefully designed sequence of steps, often of considerable length. Each step must be so small that it can always be taken, yet in taking it the student moves somewhat closer to fully competent behavior. The machine must make sure that these steps are taken in a carefully prescribed order.

---

[2] "Those who have written multiple-choice tests know how much time, energy, and ingenuity are needed to construct plausible wrong answers. (They must be plausible or the test will be of little value.) In a multiple-choice *test*, they may do no harm, since a student who has already learned the right answer may reject wrong answers with ease and possibly with no undesirable side-effects. The student who is *learning*, however, can scarcely avoid trouble. Traces of erroneous responses survive in spite of the correction of errors or the confirmation of a right answer. In multiple-choice material designed to teach literary appreciation, for example, the student is asked to consider three or four plausible paraphrases of a passage in a poem and to identify the most acceptable. But as the student reads and considers inacceptable paraphrases, the very processes the poet used to get an effect are at work to destroy it. Neither the vigorous correction of wrong choices nor the confirmation of a right choice will free the student of the verbal and nonverbal associations thus generated.

Scientific subjects offer more specific examples. Consider an item such as the following, which might be part of a course in high school physics:

As the pressure of a gas increases, volume decreases. This is because:

(a) the space between the molecules grows smaller
(b) the molecules are flattened
(c) etc. . . .

Unless the student is as industrious and as ingenious as the multiple-choice programmer, it will probably not have occurred to him that molecules may be flattened as a gas is compressed. If he chooses item (b) and is corrected by the machine, we may say that he 'has learned that it is wrong,' but this does not mean that the sentence will never occur to him again. And if he is unlucky enough to select the right answer first, his reading of the plausible but erroneous answer will be corrected only 'by implication'—an equally vague and presumably less effective process. In either case, he may later find himself recalling that 'somewhere he has read that molecules are flattened when a gas is compressed.' And, of course, somewhere he has."

Several machines with the required characteristics have been built and tested. Sets of separate presentations or "frames" of visual material are stored on disks, cards, or tapes. One frame is presented at a time, adjacent frames being out of sight. . . . For more advanced students—from junior high school, say, through college—such a machine is unnecessarily rigid in specifying form of response. Fortunately, such students may be asked to compare their responses with printed material revealed by the machine. . . . The student inserts the disk and closes the machine. He cannot proceed until the machine has been locked, and once he has begun, the machine cannot be unlocked. All but a corner of one frame is visible through a window. The student writes his response on a paper strip exposed through a second opening. By lifting a lever on the front of the machine, he moves what he has written under a transparent cover and uncovers the correct response in the remaining corner of the frame. If the two responses correspond, he moves the lever horizontally. This movement punches a hole in the paper opposite his response, recording the fact that he called it correct, and alters the machine so that the frame will not appear again when the student works around the disk a second time. Whether the response was correct or not, a second frame appears when the lever is returned to its starting position. The student proceeds in this way until he has responded to all frames. He then works around the disk a second time, but only those frames appear to which he has not correctly responded. When the disk revolves without stopping, the assignment is finished. (The student is asked to repeat each frame until a correct response is made to allow for the fact that, in telling him that a response is wrong, such a machine tells him what is right.)

When the machine was designed, the power of programming had not yet been fully appreciated. It was assumed that the student would make many mistakes and would need to see many frames a second time. (The machine was, in fact, designed to require *two* correct responses to each frame if necessary.) As programming improved, a second chance became less important. A simpler machine was devised which had other advantages: a set of frames was not limited by the number of spaces on a disk, frames were larger, and so on. . . . The material is stored on fan-folded paper tapes, and the student writes on a separate strip. He sees printed material in the large window at the left and writes his response on the uncovered strip at the right. By moving a slider he then covers the response he has written with a transparent mask and uncovers additional material in the larger opening. This may tell him that his response is wrong without telling him what is right. For example, it may list a few of the commonest errors, one of which may be his response. He makes a second response if necessary on a newly uncovered portion of the paper strip. This is covered by a further operation of the machine, which uncovers the correct response. He records an error by punching a hole alongside his response, leaving a record for the instructor and operating a counter which becomes visible at the end of the set. The student may record the number of mistakes he has made and perhaps compare it with a par score.

The machine itself, of course, does not teach. It simply brings the student into contact with the person who composed the material it presents. It is a laborsaving device because it can bring one programmer into contact with an indefinite number of students. This may suggest mass production, but the effect upon each student is surprisingly like that of a private tutor. The comparison holds in several respects. (1) There is a constant interchange between program and student. Unlike lectures, textbooks, and the usual audio-visual aids, the machine induces sustained activity. The student is always alert and busy. (2) Like a good tutor, the machine insists that a given point be thoroughly understood, either frame by frame or set by set, before the student moves on. Lectures, textbooks, and their mechanized equivalents, on the other hand, proceed without making sure that the student understands and easily leave him behind. (3) Like a good tutor the machine presents just that material for which the student is ready. It asks him to take only that step which he is at the moment best equipped and most likely to take. (4) Like a skillful tutor the machine helps the student to come up with the right answer. It does this in part through the orderly construction of the program and in part with such techniques as hinting, prompting, and suggesting, derived from an analysis of verbal behavior . . . Lastly, of course, the machine, like the private tutor, reinforces the student for every correct response, using this immediate feedback not only to shape his behavior most efficiently but to maintain it in strength in a manner which the layman would describe as "holding the student's interest."

DISCUSSION QUESTIONS

1. What are the alternatives Skinner proposes for the act of teaching? How does his conception of the role of the teacher compare with yours?
2. What are the strengths and limitations of a teaching model built upon a pattern of stimulus, response, and selective reinforcement?
3. Evaluate programmed teaching as a way of "individualizing" instruction.
4. Rogers sees the need for infusing the means of education with the values we ascribe to the goals. How does programmed learning meet this test?

HARRY S. BROUDY

Socrates and the Teaching Machine

In the November, 1962, issue of *American Psychologist* one reads the following:

> What conclusions can be drawn from this simple demonstration? It would perhaps not be unfair to say that Socrates had the beginnings of an effective program. He began with that which was within the behavioral repertoire and moved in small steps to a response which was not simply rote memorized, but understood. But not quite so. For in the *Meno* one cannot really determine whether such understanding took place. And the programed adaptation (Socrates' program) seems hardly to have been particularly effective with our college students. By casting his sequence into programing format we were able to determine whether such understanding occurred and, through feedback, at what juncture communications broke down. . . .
> It is clear that programed instruction is similar to the Socratic dialogue, but in its differences lies the potential for widespread and enduring changes in the educational enterprise.[1]

That such a passage should appear in a current scientific journal is a tantalizing invitation to make a host of observations, but I shall confine myself to some of the implications of the belief of the author and others that programed instruction is "similar" to the Socratic dialogue.

Now the most striking ingredient of the Socratic dialogues is supposed to be Socrates. He was not noted as a mathematics teacher and we shall see that even in the *Meno* the geometry lesson was used only as an illustrative episode. Socrates thought of himself and others thought of him primarily as an inquirer into human virtue, as one profoundly concerned with the state of his own soul and that of his pupil's soul.

Although Socrates would have appreciated being told that he had "the beginnings of an effective program" which, with a little modern help, could be made into a really effective program, it still seems odd that Socrates should have been picked as typical of the teacher whose pedagogy resembled programed instruction. Presumably such a Socratic program would also include the Socratic irony. And the program, one supposes, would replicate Socrates as the *agent provocateur* who vexed his fellow citizens into such extreme measures of retaliation.

Drawing a parallel between the Socratic dialogue and programed instruction arouses mixed feelings. On the one hand, we recognize that Socrates' performance in the mathematics episode of the *Meno* can be simulated, and once simulated, it can be extended and possibly improved. On the other

---

Reprinted from *Phi Delta Kappan,* Vol. XLIV, No. 6 (March 1963), pp. 243–246, with permission of the publisher.

[1] Ira S. Cohen, "Programed Learning and Socratic Dialogue," p. 775.

hand, there lurks a conviction that what was simulated in the program was the least significant aspect of Socrates' teaching. This ambivalence, I believe, still characterizes the attitudes of educators toward automated instruction.[2] It is toward the understanding of this ambivalence that this essay is hopefully directed.

Machines are contrivances that extend the power of man's muscles (rakes, hoes, hammers, vehicles, levers, etc.), or his senses (microscopes, eyeglasses, hearing aids, radar, sonoscopes, etc.), or his brain, especially that part of it held to be responsible for sorting and relating experience (computers of all sorts). We also have machines that take the place of hearts, lungs, and kidneys; one cannot rule out the possibility of other artificial bodily organs.

These artifacts need not look like the organs or structures whose functions they mimic. Indeed, if we ever fabricate a machine that performs like a brain, we are likely to conclude that the brain really resembles the machine or that it ought to. Thus, if a machine teaches the Pythagorean theorem better than did Socrates, then the modern Socrates would do well to imitate the machine. Technology forces us to analyze minutely the operations we wish to simulate and successful simulation provides us with norms for the improvement of the "natural" processes that served as models for imitation.

MAN: A HAND TO OPERATE ARTIFICIAL HANDS?

Machines augment *actually* the muscles, organs, senses, or brain only of the individual who has access to the machines, but *potentially* they are the great "body" of the body politic. The notion of a group body and group mind is not so fantastic once it is recognized that technology through machines creates a collective power that can do the sort of things an individual body does but on a much vaster scale. One can even produce machines by machine. But, as Karl Marx clearly saw, the greater the growth of collective productive power, the more alienated the individual becomes from the tools of production. Compared to the power of machinery his own body and brain are miniscule. He becomes a "hand" that is hired to operate the huge artificial hands created by industrial technology.

Do we have here at least part of the reason for the ambivalence of educators toward the teaching machine? On the one hand, it represents a rich promise of increased social power and efficiency. We are overcome by admiration for its inventors. But then we realize that the mechanization of teaching renders it detachable from the person of any individual teacher. The teacher is thus made an interchangeable part which, if not dispensable, is nevertheless substitutable.

Further, we know only too well that machine power, if massive enough, acquires a career of its own. What has set out as an adjunct to teaching may

2 In what follows I shall not, unless the context requires it, distinguish among programed instruction, automated instruction, and teaching machines.

end up as the master whom the live teacher must obey. This we may call the Frankenstein effect.

The natural defense against the machine has been, accordingly, to argue that there are some instructional tasks that the machine cannot perform, e.g., training for creativity, or discovery, teaching abstruse subject matter, forming attitudes, and other subtle school outcomes.

I have elsewhere[3] tried to indicate that such a defense is little more than whistling in the dark. In principle, any process that can be objectified can be broken down into steps and programed for instruction. If one can specify what is to be done so that someone else can understand the description, the process can be replicated. If the steps can be translated into physical stimuli and responses, the process can be mechanized. To the extent that the teaching-learning act can be objectified, replicated, and spatialized, it can be methodized and mechanized.

It follows that only what cannot be thus objectified blocks precise replication and mechanization. What might this be? Obviously it is the inner side of experience whose texture is made up of colors, sounds, odors, flavors, pain, pleasure, images, emotions and affective tones endlessly varied and without names. We operate on the belief that the human bodies we daily encounter also have such an inner side to them, but there is no way to objectify for public scrutiny any individual's subjectivity. This ghost differentiates the human "machine" from all other machines.

Our success in replicating human experience is most notable when the "feel" of experience can be ignored. A good house thermostat can do its work without being aware of feeling cold or hot; a camera can simulate the work of the human eye without being aware that it is seeing; the computer can predict election results without being proud of its accomplishments. A teaching machine can run through a course of first-rate instruction without knowing that it is teaching and with only "materials" fatigue.

It is, of course, nothing against the machine that it has no consciousness. If it did, we could no longer treat it as a machine. A boiler that "felt" the heat it generated as "pain" would command our pity and would result in the immediate establishment of a society for the prevention of cruelty to boilers.

HUMAN BEHAVIOR AND QUALITATIVE FEEDBACK

However, whether we can mechanize human experience depends heavily on the degree to which we can ignore subjectivity in the human being and not whether we can ignore it in the machine. And it so happens, for better or worse, that human behavior is largely controlled by qualitative feedback, viz., perceptual clues, interpretive categorial systems, imagery, associational

[3] "Teaching Machines: Threats and Promise," *Educational Theory* 12:3 (July, 1962), p. 151–56.

patterns of retrieval, hopes, aspirations, ideals, and above all by the signals of pleasure and pain. While to some extent we can verbalize these, while we can make shrewd guesses about the inner experience of others, in the last analysis they are directly inspectable, if at all, only by the mind they constitute. Each individual is a unique qualitative version of a generic sense of beauty, rightness, harmony, and fittingness; so is every teacher and every pupil, but only if they are human and alive.

The qualities of the inner life, however, are more than controls. They are ends in themselves, intrinsic values, for the sake of which we undergo great toil and trouble. In themselves they are less the means to life than the source of its meaning.

All of which means that the teaching transaction is mechanizable only insofar as the qualitative aspect of that transaction can safely be ignored or dealt with mechanically. And there are many aspects of instruction in which this is possible. Learning to apprehend logical patterns, concept attainment, even of a quite subtle sort, the perfection of verbal and motor skills, are examples of such transactions. However important the feelings of the learner are with respect to boredom, levels of aspiration, readiness, and the reinforcement patterns, they do not require that the machine have comparable feelings. One can build into the program and the machine the tactics that take account of boredom, novelty, reinforcement, and so on.

It is not hard to imagine a machine that by judicious awards of lollipops to the learner every time he judged a sample of Beethoven to be superior to be-bop, and electric shocks whenever the contrary choice was made, could shape the taste of a generation far more efficiently than our schools have been able to do—by analogous methods, one may add. One can *train* the preferences of persons as well as of pigeons. Externally, conditioned taste and educated taste may be indistinguishable; the difference lies in the internal quality of the experience.

A TRAVESTY ON THE TEACHING TRANSACTION

There is, however, a difference between a machine that computes with extraordinary rapidity and one that conditions the pupil to thrill at Beethoven. It matters little how the machine feels while calculating, but somehow that the machine shall not even hear the music it is conditioning the pupil to like seems a travesty on the teaching transaction. We expect the Beethoven teacher to use the same sort of qualitative cues as does the pupil. In a way, the teaching machine that conditions us to like Beethoven seems more repugnant than the phonograph that plays Beethoven. The phonograph at least does not pose as a partner in appreciation. But, it may be objected, what if the machine programed to reinforce positive responses to Beethoven does not "hear" or "like" Beethoven samples? Must a physician feel the pain of his patient in order to alleviate it?

We must admit that the human teacher, if he is to differ significantly from a machine, has to make a unique and irreplaceable contribution to the teaching act. When and only when such a contribution is made, does "who" the teacher is becomes part of "what" is being taught. But to make a unique and irreplaceable contribution a teacher cannot be a personality stereotype.

PERSONALITY NOT A COMPONENT OF CONTENT

Lest this intrusion of the "who" into the "what" be misconstrued, we should ask how this takes place without distorting the content of instruction. Clearly, Socrates as a person ought not to distort mathematics. If his personality enters the situation at all, it is as a component of the mathematics *lesson* rather than of the subject of mathematics.

In the segment of the *Meno* dealing with the slave boy's venture into mathematics, the teacher's identity is unimportant. However, the real pupil in this dialogue is not the slave boy; it is Meno himself, the wealthy, well-born, self-assured Thessalian. The theme of the dialogue is not mathematics *per se*, but rather the paradox: If virtue is knowledge, and therefore is teachable, why, then, are there no teachers of virtue? To the lesson represented by the dialogue as a whole, the identity of the teacher is not indifferent; hence programing the *Meno* as a whole might present quite a different kettle of fish from that of programing the mathematics bit.

Why this identity is important may be brought out by noting some of the characteristics of Socrates' teaching style.

In many of the early dialogues Socrates' opening gambit was to provoke the pupil by forcing him to admit that his knowledge was neither his nor knowledge. The pupil was really harboring opinions and conventions that betrayed their logical fragility in the very first rounds of inquiry. The dialogue was more like a logical inquisition than a conversation. Socrates' irony only added to the victim's discomfiture. Anyone who has used this questioning in class—even with graduate students—knows the havoc it spreads among the egos.

Next, Socrates leads the pupil to acquiesce in turning the world upside down. That all forms of virtue are essentially one; that the most real things in the world are forms and not physical objects; that death is a deliverance rather than a curse; that learning is a kind of recollection—these are radical inversions of common sense and profoundly disturbing to the pupil.

The soul, having been cleansed and shaken out by this self-examination, is now ready to undertake the search for the archetypes of the good, the true, and the beautiful. Roughly, the process is an ascent from imprecise sense impressions, through clarified sense perception, more or less warranted opinion and belief, scientific understanding, and finally to the comprehension by reason of the scheme of things entire. This is the Idea of the Good or that system of ends which gives meaning to the universe and its human inhabitants. Thus the slave boy runs through common sense notions and errors about numbers until he gets an insight into necessary truth. In doing so he illustrates the Socratic doctrine that cognition is recognition.

SOCRATES WAS INTERESTED IN VALUE EDUCATION

It seems clear that the type of educational outcome sought by Socrates is neither a motor skill nor a verbal skill. It is not a body of empirically verified concepts or even a theory about such concepts. Socrates was primarily interested in what we would call value education, in norms, and in evaluational maps.

It is characteristic of this kind of outcome that it involves a kind of seduction or capture of the pupil by a mode of human existence that displays vividly its human import and possibility. Images of perfection are apparently irresistible; hence value teaching succeeds when knowledge, ideals, and values are vividly and dramatically embodied in an individual object. This object can be a real person, or it can be a fictitious character in literature, history, philosophy.

Willy-nilly, the classroom teacher operates as a value model, even when not explicitly engaged in value education. Pupils "learn" the teacher whatever else they learn or fail to learn. How replaceable a classroom teacher is depends therefore on what is being learned of him.

Occasionally great personalities become the "teachers" of mankind precisely because their lives enact the drama of existence with almost irresistible charm and power. Great religions are distinguished not so much by their doctrine as by the lives of their founders. These lives are regarded as witnesses that the divine had made ingress into the human enterprise and endowed it with transcendent meaning. What would Christianity be without the life of Christ; Buddhism without the life of Buddha, Judaism without the lives of Abraham, Isaac, Jacob, and Moses? At a considerably lower level, we note that the students of Pestalozzi carried away in their notebooks everything about his schools except the fact that he was Papa Pestalozzi.

But most of us in the teaching business are not individuals of his caliber and thus, if we are seriously engaged in value education, have to direct our pupils to the works of art, literature, history, and philosophy where the Great Teachers are on display.

But displayed how? Certainly not merely as a body of knowledge or as a cluster of skills. They are, rather, invitations to see the world and ourselves *as* something we literally are not. The world as a dramatic spectacle, as a web of meaning, as a logical net and a cosmological design, man as a significant item in the total scene, what are these but the great metaphors of human experience? They display vividly the import of facts; they themselves are facts only in a very special sense of that word. Teaching at this level is an incitement to imaginative reconstruction of experience, but the "truths" of the imagination are not necessarily the truths of logic and science.

We are closer than ever before to appreciating the profound difference between the content of a discipline and the content of a lesson in that discipline. Perhaps we are also nearer to realizing that the content of a value lesson has to include the persons of teacher and pupil in a way that a skill lesson or a purely cognitive lesson does not. That we swing between enthusiasm and anxiety about the prospects of automated instruction reflects, I believe, these insights into the teaching task. However, it may also be a symptom of dismay at how far the technical and scientific components of schooling have pushed the value outcomes into the periphery of educational concern.

DISCUSSION QUESTIONS

1. Are there qualities in the classroom which are ends in themselves and which cannot be duplicated in a teaching machine? Defend your answer.
2. Has the "person" of any teacher affected or enriched your life in a way that a teaching machine could not duplicate?
3. Compare Broudy's concept of education with Skinner's. Are the two mutually antagonistic or irreconcilable?

DAVID ELKIND

Giant in the Nursery—Jean Piaget

In February, 1967, Jean Piaget, the Swiss psychologist, arrived at Clark University in Worcester, Mass., to deliver the Heinz Werner Memorial Lectures. The lectures were to be given in the evening, and before the first one a small dinner party was arranged in honor of Piaget and was attended by colleagues, former students and friends. I was invited because of my long advocacy of Piaget's work and because I had spent a year (1964–65) at his Institute for Educational Science in Geneva. Piaget had changed very little since I had last seen him, but he did appear tired and mildly apprehensive.

Although Piaget has lectured all over the world, this particular occasion had special significance. Almost 60 years before, in 1909, another famous European, Sigmund Freud, also lectured at Clark University. Piaget was certainly aware of the historical parallel. He was, moreover, going to speak to a huge American audience in French and, despite the offices of his remarkable translator, Eleanor Duckworth, he must have had some reservations about how it would go.

Piaget's apprehension was apparent during the dinner. For one who is usually a lively and charming dinner companion, he was surprisingly quiet and unresponsive. About half way through the meal there was a small disturbance. The room in which the dinner was held was at a garden level and two boys suddenly appeared at the windows and began tapping at them. The inclination of most of us, I think, was to shoo them away. Before we had a chance to do that, however, Piaget had turned to face the children. He smiled up at the lads, hunched his shoulders and gave them a slight wave with his hand. They hunched their shoulders and smiled in return, gave a slight wave and disappeared. After a moment, Piaget turned back to the table and began telling stories and entering into animated conversation.

Although I am sure his lecture would have been a success in any case and that the standing ovation he received would have occurred without the little incident, I nonetheless like to think that the encounter with the boys did much to restore his vigor and good humor.

It is Piaget's genius for empathy with children, together with true intellectual genius, that has made him the outstanding child psychologist in the world today and one destined to stand beside Freud with respect to his contributions to psychology, education and related disciplines. Just as Freud's discoveries of unconscious motivation, infantile sexuality and the stages of psychosexual growth changed our ways of thinking about human personality, so Piaget's discoveries of children's implicit philosophies, the construction of reality by the infant and the stages of mental development have altered our ways of thinking about human intelligence.

The man behind these discoveries is an arresting figure. He is tall and somewhat portly, and his stooped walk, bulky suits and crown of long white hair give him the appearance of a thrice-magnified Einstein. (When he was at the Institute for Advanced Study at Princeton in 1953, a friend of his wife rushed to a window one day and exclaimed, "Look, Einstein!" Madame Piaget looked and replied, "No, just my Piaget.") Piaget's personal trademarks are his meerschaum pipes (now burned deep amber), his navy blue beret and his bicycle.

Meeting Piaget is a memorable experience. Although Piaget has an abundance of Old-World charm and graciousness, he seems to emanate an aura of intellectual presence not unlike the aura of personality presence conveyed by a great actor. While as a psychologist I am unable to explain how this sense of presence is communicated, I am nevertheless convinced that everyone who meets Piaget experiences it. While talking to me, for example, he was able to divine in my remarks and questions a significance and depth of which I was entirely unaware and certainly hadn't intended. Evidently one characteristic of genius is to search for relevance in the apparently commonplace and frivolous.

Piaget's is a superbly disciplined life. He arises early each morning, sometimes as early as 4 A.M., and writes four or more publishable pages on square sheets of white paper in an even, small hand. Later in the morning he may teach classes and attend meetings. His afternoons include long walks during which he thinks about the problems he is currently confronting. He says, "I always like to think on a problem before reading about it." In the evenings, he reads and retires early. Even on his international trips, Piaget keeps to this schedule.

Each summer, as soon as classes are over, Piaget gathers up the research findings that have been collected by his assistants during the year and departs for the Alps, where he takes up solitary residence in a room in an abandoned farmhouse. The whereabouts of this retreat is as closely guarded as the names of depositors in numbered Swiss bank accounts; only Piaget's family, his longtime colleague Bärbel Inhelder and a trusted secretary know where he is. During the summer Piaget takes walks, meditates, writes *and* writes. Then, when the leaves begin to turn, he descends from the mountains with the several books and articles he has written on his "vacation."

Although Piaget, now in his 72d year, has been carrying his works down from the mountains for almost 50 summers (he has published more than 30 books and hundreds of articles), it is only within the past decade that his writings have come to be fully appreciated in America. This was due, in part, to the fact that until fairly recently only a few of his books had been translated into English. In addition, American psychology and education were simply not ready for Piaget until the fifties. Now the ideas that Piaget has been advocating for more than 30 years are regarded as exceedingly innovative and even as avant-garde.

His work falls into three more or less distinct periods within each of which he covered an enormous amount of psychological territory and developed a multitude of insights. (Like most creative men, Piaget is hard put to it to say when a particular idea came to him. If he ever came suddenly upon an idea which sent him shouting through the halls, he has never admitted to it.)

During the first period (roughly 1922–29), Piaget explored the extent and depth of children's spontaneous ideas about the physical world and about their own mental processes. He happened upon this line of inquiry while working in Alfred Binet's laboratory school in Paris where he arrived, still seeking a direction for his talents, a year after receiving his doctorate in biological science at the University of Lausanne. It was in the course of some routine intelligence testing that Piaget became interested in what lay behind children's correct, and particularly their incorrect, answers. To clarify the origins of these answers he began to interview the children in the open-ended manner he had learned while serving a brief interneship at Bleuler's psychiatric clinic in Zurich. This semiclinical interview procedure, aimed at revealing the processes by which a child arrives at a particular reply to a test question, has become a trademark of Piagetian research investigation.

What Piaget found with this method of inquiry was that children not only reasoned differently from adults but also that they had quite different world-views, literally different philosophies. This led Piaget to attend to those childish remarks and questions which most adults find amusing or nonsensical. Just as Freud used seemingly accidental slips of the tongue and pen as evidence for unconscious motivations, so Piaget has employed the "cute" sayings of children to demonstrate the existence of ideas quite foreign to the adult mind.

Piaget had read in the recollections of a deaf mute (recorded by William James) that as a child he had regarded the sun and moon as gods and believed they followed him about. Piaget sought to verify this recollection by interviewing children on the subject, and he found that many youngsters do believe that the sun and moon follow them when they are out for a walk. Similar remarks Piaget either overheard or was told about led to a large number of investigations which revealed, among many similar findings, that young children believe that anything which moves is alive, that the names of objects reside in the objects themselves and that dreams come in through the window at night.

Such beliefs, Piaget pointed out in an early article entitled "Children's Philosophies," are not unrelated to but rather derive from an implicit animism and artificialism with many parallels to primitive and Greek philosophies. In the child's view, objects like stones and clouds are imbued with motives, intentions and feelings, while mental events such as dreams and thoughts are endowed with corporality and force. Children also believe that everything has a purpose and that everything in the world is made by and for man. (My 5-year-old son asked me why we have snow and answered his own question by saying, "It is for children to play in.")

The child's animism and artificialism help to explain his famous and often unanswerable "why" questions. It is because children believe that everything has a purpose that they ask, "Why is grass green?" and "Why do the stars shine?" The parent who attempts to answer such questions with a physical explanation has missed the point.

In addition to disclosing the existence of children's philosophies during this first period, Piaget also found the clue to the egocentrism of childhood. In observing young children at play at the *Maison des Petits,* the modified Montessori school associated with the Institute of Educational Science in Geneva, Piaget noted a peculiar lack of social orientation which was also present in their conversation and in their approaches to certain intellectual tasks. A child would make up a new word ("stocks" for socks and stockings) and just assume that everyone knew what he was talking about as if this were the conventional name for the objects he had in mind. Likewise, Piaget noted that when two nursery school children were at play they often spoke *at* rather than *to* one another and were frequently chattering on about two quite different and unrelated topics. Piaget observed, moreover, that when he stood a child of 5 years opposite him, the child who could tell his own right and left nevertheless insisted that Piaget's right and left hands were directly opposite his own.

In Piaget's view, all of these behaviors can be explained by the young child's inability to put himself in another person's position and to take that person's point of view. Unlike the egocentric adult, who can take another person's point of view but does not, the egocentric child does not take another person's viewpoint because he cannot. This conception of childish egocentrism has produced a fundamental alteration in our evaluation of the preschool child's behavior. We now appreciate that it is intellectual immaturity and not moral perversity which makes, for example, a young child continue to pester his mother after she has told him she has a headache and wishes to be left alone. The preschool child is simply unable to put himself in his mother's position and see things from her point of view.

The second period of Piaget's investigations began when, in 1929, he sought to trace the origins of the child's spontaneous mental growth to the behavior of infants; in this case, his own three children, Jaqueline, Lucienne and Laurent. Piaget kept very detailed records of their behavior and of their performance on a series of ingenious tasks which he invented and presented to them. The books resulting from these investigations, "The Origins of Intelligence in Children," "Play, Dreams and Imitation in Children" and "The Construction of Reality in the Child" are now generally regarded as classics in the field and have been one of the major forces behind the scurry of research activity in the area of infant behavior now current both in America and abroad. The publication of these books in the middle and late nineteen-thirties marked the end of the second phase of Piaget's work.

Some of the most telling observations Piaget made during this period had to do with what he called the *conservation of the object* (using the word conservation to convey the idea of permanence). To the older child and to the adult, the existence of objects and persons who are not immediately present is taken as self-evident. The child at school knows that while he is working at his desk his mother is simultaneously at home and his father is at work. This is not the case for the young infant playing in his crib, for whom out of sight is literally out of mind. Piaget observed that when an infant 4 or 5 months old is playing with a toy which subsequently rolls out of sight (behind another toy) but is still within reach, the infant ceases to look for it. The infant behaves as if the toy had not only disappeared but as if it had gone entirely out of existence.

This helps to explain the pleasure infants take in the game of peek-a-boo. If the infant believed that the object existed when it was not seen, he would not be surprised and delighted at its re-emergence and there would be no point to the game. It is only during the second year of life, when children begin to represent objects mentally, that they seek after toys that have disappeared from view. Only then do they attribute an independent existence to objects which are not present to their senses.

The third and major phase of Piaget's endeavors began about 1940 and continues until the present day. During this period Piaget has studied the development in children and adolescents of those mental abilities which gradually enable the child to construct a world-view which is in conformance with reality as seen by adults. He has, at the same time, been concerned with how children acquire the adult versions of various concepts such as number, quantity and speed. Piaget and his colleagues have amassed, in the last 28 years, an astounding amount of information about the thinking of children and adolescents which is only now beginning to be used by psychologists and educators.

Two discoveries made during this last period are of particular importance because they were so unexpected and because of their relevance for education. It is perhaps fair to say that education tends to focus upon the static aspects of reality rather than upon its dynamic transformations. The child is taught how and what things are but not the conditions under which they change or remain the same. And yet the child is constantly confronted with change and alteration. His view of the world alters as he grows in height and perceptual acuity. And the world changes. Seasons come and go, trees gain and lose their foliage, snow falls and melts. People change, too. They may change over brief time periods in mood and over long periods in weight and hair coloration or fullness. The child receives a static education while living amidst a world in transition.

Piaget's investigations since 1940 have focused upon how the child copes with change, how he comes to distinguish between the permanent and the transient and between appearance and reality. An incident that probably played a part in initiating this line of investigation occurred during Piaget's short-lived flirtation with the automobile. (When his children were young, Piaget learned to drive and bought a car, but he gave it up for his beloved bicycle after a couple of years.) He took his son for a drive and Laurent asked the name of the mountain they were passing. The mountain was the Salève, the crocodile-shaped mass that dominates the city of Geneva. Laurent was in fact familiar with the mountain and its name because he could see it from his garden, although from a different perspective. Laurent's question brought home to Piaget the fact that a child has difficulty in dealing with the results of transformations whether they are brought about by an alteration in the object itself or by the child's movement with respect to the object.

The methods Piaget used to study how the child comes to deal with transformations are ingenuously simple and can be used by any interested parent or teacher. These methods all have to do with testing the child's abilities to discover that a quantity remains the same across a change in its appearance. In other words, that the quantity is conserved.

To give just one illustration from among hundreds, a child is shown two identical drinking glasses filled equally full with orangeade and he is asked to say whether there is the "same to drink" in the two glasses. After the child says that this is the case, the orangeade from one glass is poured into another which is taller and thinner so that the orangeade now reaches a higher level. Then the child is asked to say whether there is the same amount to drink in the two differently shaped glasses. Before the age of 6 or 7, most children say that the tall, narrow glass has more orangeade. The young child cannot deal with the transformation and bases his judgment on the static features of the orangeade, namely the levels.

How does the older child arrive at the notion that the amounts of orangeade in the two differently shaped glasses is the same? The answer, according to Piaget, is that he discovers the equality with the aid of reason. If the child judges only on the basis of appearances he cannot solve the problem. When he compares the two glasses with respect to width he must conclude that the wide glass has more while if he compares them with respect to the level of the orangeade he must conclude that the tall glass has more. There is then no way, on the basis of appearance, that he can solve the problem. If, on the other hand, the child reasons that there was the same in the two glasses before and that nothing was added or taken away during the pouring, he concludes that both glasses still have the same drink although this does not appear to be true.

On the basis of this and many similar findings, Piaget argues that much of our knowledge about reality comes to us not from without like the wail of a siren but rather from within by the force of our own logic.

It is hard to overemphasize the importance of this fact, because it is so often forgotten, particularly in education. For those who are not philosophically inclined, it appears that our knowledge of things comes about rather directly as if our mind simply copied the forms, colors and textures of things. From this point of view the mind acts as a sort of mirror which is limited to reflecting the reality which is presented to it.

The portrait painter does not merely copy what he sees, he interprets his subject. Before even commencing the portrait, the artist learns a great deal about the individual subject and does not limit himself to studying the face alone. Into the portrait goes not only what the artist sees but also what he knows about his subject. A good portrait is larger than life because it carries much more information than could ever be conveyed by a mirror image.

In forming his spontaneous conception of the world, therefore, the child does more than reflect what is presented to his senses. His image of reality is in fact a portrait or reconstruction of the world and not a simple copy of it. It is only by reasoning about the information which the child receives from the external world that he is able to overcome the transient nature of sense experience and arrive at that awareness of permanence within apparent change that is the mark of adult thought. The importance of reason in the child's spontaneous construction of his world is thus one of the major discoveries of Piaget's third period.

The second major discovery of this time has to do with the nature of the elementary school child's reasoning ability. Long before there was anything like a discipline of child psychology, the age of 6 to 7 was recognized as *the age of reason.* It was also assumed, however, that once the child attained the age of reason, there were no longer any substantial differences between his reasoning abilities and those of adolescents and adults. What Piaget discovered is that this is in fact not the case. While the elementary school child is indeed able to reason, his reasoning ability is limited in a very important respect—he can reason about things but not about verbal propositions.

If a child of 8 or 9 is shown a series of three blocks, ABC, which differ in size, then he can tell by looking at them, and without comparing them directly, that if A is greater than B and B greater than C, then A is greater than C. When the same child is given this problem, "Helen is taller than Mary and Mary is taller than Jane, who is the tallest of the three?" the result is quite different. He cannot solve it despite the fact that it repeats in words the problem with the blocks. Adolescents and adults, however, encounter no difficulty with this problem because they can reason about verbal propositions as well as about things.

This discovery that children think differently from adults even after attaining the age of reason has educational implications which are only now beginning to be applied. Robert Karplus, the physicist who heads the Science Curriculum Improvement Study at Berkeley has pointed out that most teachers use verbal propositions in teaching elementary school children. At least some of their instruction is thus destined to go over the heads of their pupils. Karplus and his co-workers are now attempting to train teachers to instruct children at a verbal level which is appropriate to their level of mental ability.

An example of the effects of the failure to take into account the difference between the reasoning abilities of children and adults comes from the New Math experiment. In building materials for the New Math, it was hoped that the construction of a new language would facilitate instruction of set concepts. This new language has been less than successful and the originators of the New Math are currently attempting to devise a physical model to convey the New Math concepts. It is likely that the new language created to teach the set concepts failed because it was geared to the logic of adults rather than to the reasoning of children. Attention to the research on children's thinking carried out during Piaget's third period might have helped to avoid some of the difficulties of the "New Math" program.

In the course of these many years of research into children's thinking, Piaget has elaborated a general theory of intellectual development which, in its scope and comprehensiveness, rivals Freud's theory of personality development. Piaget proposes that intelligence—adaptive thinking and action—develops in a sequence of stages that is related to age. Each stage sees the elaboration of new mental abilities which set the limits and determine the character of what can be learned during that period. (Piaget finds incomprehensible Harvard psychologist Jerome Bruner's famous hypothesis to the effect that "any subject can be taught effectively in some intellectually honest form to any child at any stage of development.") Although Piaget believes that the order in which the stages appear holds true for all children, he also believes that the ages at which the stages evolve will depend upon the native endowment of the child and upon the quality of the physical and social environment in which he is reared. In a very real sense, then, Piaget's is both a nature *and* a nurture theory.

The first stage in the development of intelligence (usually 0–2 years) Piaget calls the sensory-motor period and it is concerned with the evolution of those abilities necessary to construct and reconstruct objects. To illustrate, Piaget observed that when he held a cigarette case in front of his daughter Jaqueline (who was 8 months old at the time) and then dropped it, she did not follow the trajectory of the case but continued looking at his hand. Even at 8 months (Lucienne and Laurent succeeded in following the object at about 5 months but had been exposed to more experiments than Jaqueline) she was not able to reconstruct the path of the object which she had seen dropped in front of her.

Toward the end of this period, however, Jaqueline was even able to reconstruct the position of objects which had undergone hidden displacement. When she was 19 months old, Piaget placed a coin in his hand and then placed his hand under a coverlet where he dropped the coin before removing his hand. Jaqueline first looked in his hand and then immediately lifted the coverlet and found the coin. This reconstruction was accomplished with the aid of an elementary form of reasoning. The coin was in the hand, the hand was under the coverlet, the coin was not in the hand so the coin is under the coverlet. Such reasoning, it must be said, is accomplished without the aid of language and by means of mental images.

The second stage (usually 2–7 years), which Piaget calls the preoperational stage bears witness to the elaboration of the symbolic function, those abilities which have to do with representing things. The presence of these new abilities is shown by the gradual acquisition of language, the first indications of dreams and night terrors, the advent of symbolic play (two sticks at right angles are an airplane) and the first attempts at drawing and graphic representation.

At the beginning of this stage the child tends to identify words and symbols with the objects they are intended to represent. He is upset if someone tramps on a stone which he has designated as a turtle. And he believes that names are as much a part of objects as their color and form.

(The child at this point is like the old gentleman who, when asked why noodles are called noodles, replied that "they are white like noodles, soft like noodles and taste like noodles so we call them noodles.")

By the end of this period the child can clearly distinguish between words and symbols and what they represent. He now recognizes that names are arbitrary designations. The child's discovery of the arbitrariness of names is often manifested in the "name calling" so prevalent during the early school years.

At the next stage (usually 7–11 years) the child acquires what Piaget calls concrete operations, internalized actions that permit the child to do "in his head" what before he would have had to accomplish through real actions. Concrete operations enable the child to think about things. To illustrate, in one study Piaget presented 5-, 6- and 7-year-old children with six sticks in a row and asked them to take the same number of sticks from a pile on the table. The young children solved the problem by placing their sticks beneath the sample and matching the sticks one by one. The older children merely picked up the six sticks and held them in their hands. The older children had counted the sticks mentally and hence felt no need to actually match them with the sticks in the row. It should be said that even the youngest children were able to count to six, so that this was not a factor in their performance.

Concrete operations also enable children to deal with the relations among classes of things. In another study Piaget presented 5-, 6- and 7-year-old children with a box containing 20 white and seven brown wooden beads. Each child was first asked if there were more white or more brown beads and all were able to say that there were more white than brown beads. Then Piaget asked, "Are there more white or more wooden beads?" The young children could not fathom the question and replied that "there are more white than brown beads." For such children classes are not regarded as abstractions but are thought of as concrete places. (I once asked a pre-operational child if he could be a Protestant and an American at the same time, to which he replied, "No," and then as an afterthought, "only if you move.")

When a child thought of a bead in the white "place" he could not think of it as being in the wooden "place" since objects cannot be in two places at once. He could only compare the white with the brown "places." The older children, who had attained concrete operations, encountered no difficulty with the task and readily replied that "there are more wooden than white beads because all of the beads are wooden and only some are white." By the end of the concrete operational period, children are remarkably adept at doing thought problems and at combining and dividing class concepts.

During the last stage (usually 12–15 years) there gradually emerge what Piaget calls formal operations and which, in effect, permit adolescents to think about their thoughts, to construct ideals and to reason realistically about the future. Formal operations also enable young people to reason about contrary-to-fact propositions. If, for example, a child is asked to assume that coal is white he is likely to reply, "But coal is black," whereas the adolescent can accept the contrary-to-fact assumption and reason from it.

Formal operational thought also makes possible the understanding of metaphor. It is for this reason that political and other satirical cartoons are not understood until adolescence. The child's inability to understand metaphor helps to explain why books such as "Alice in Wonderland" and "Gulliver's Travels" are enjoyed at different levels during childhood than in adolescence and adulthood, when their social significance can be understood.

No new mental systems emerge after the formal operations, which are the common coin of adult thought. After adolescence, mental growth takes the form—it is hoped—of a gradual increase in wisdom.

This capsule summary of Piaget's theory of intellectual development would not be complete without some words about Piaget's position with respect to language and thought. Piaget regards thought and language as different but closely related systems. Language, to a much greater extent than thought, is determined by particular forms of environmental stimulation. Inner-city Negro children, who tend to be retarded in language development, are much less retarded with respect to the ages at which they attain concrete operations. Indeed, not only inner-city children but children in bush Africa, Hong Kong and Appalachia all attain concrete operations at about the same age as middle-class children in Geneva and Boston.

Likewise, attempts to teach children concrete operations have been almost uniformly unsuccessful. This does not mean that these operations are independent of the environment but only that their development takes time and can be nourished by a much wider variety of environmental nutriments than is true for the growth of language, which is dependent upon much more specific forms of stimulation.

Language is, then, deceptive with respect to thought. Teachers of middle-class children are often misled, by the verbal facility of these youngsters, into believing that they understand more than they actually comprehend. (My 5-year-old asked me what my true identity was and as I tried to recover my composure he explained that Clark Kent was Superman's true identity.) At the other end, the teachers of inner-city children are often fooled by the language handicaps of these children into thinking that they have much lower mental ability than they actually possess. It is appropriate, therefore, that preschool programs for the disadvantaged should focus upon training these children in language and perception rather than upon trying to teach them concrete operations.

The impact which the foregoing Piagetian discoveries and conceptions is having upon education and child psychology has come as something of a shock to a good many educators and psychological research in America which relies heavily upon statistics, electronics and computers, Piaget's studies of children's thinking seem hardly a step beyond the pre-scientific baby biographies kept by such men as Charles Darwin and Bronson Alcott. Indeed, in many of Piaget's research papers he supports his conclusions simply with illustrative examples of how children at different age levels respond to his tasks.

Many of Piaget's critics have focused upon his apparently casual methodology and have argued that while Piaget has arrived at some original ideas about children's thinking, his research lacks scientific rigor. It is likely that few, if any, of Piaget's research reports would have been accepted for publication in American psychological journals.

Other critics have taken somewhat the opposite tack. Jerome Bruner, who has done so much to bring Piaget to the attention of American social scientists, acknowledges the fruitfulness of Piaget's methods, modifications of which he has employed in his own investigations. But he argues against Piaget's theoretical interpretations. Bruner believes that Piaget has "missed the heart" of the problem of change and permanence or conservation in children's thinking. In the case of the orangeade poured into a different-sized container, Bruner argues that it is not reason, or mental operations, but some "internalized verbal formula that shields him [the child] from the overpowering appearance of the visual displays." Bruner seems to believe that the syntactical rules of language rather than logic can account for the child's discovery that a quantity remains unchanged despite alterations in its appearance.

Piaget is willing to answer his critics but only when he feels that the criticism is responsible and informed. With respect to his methods, their casualness is only apparent. Before they set out collecting data, his students are given a year of training in the art of interviewing children. They learn to ask questions without suggesting the answers and to test, by counter-suggestion, the strength of the child's conviction. Many of Piaget's studies have now been repeated with more rigorous procedures by other investigators all over the world and the results have been remarkably consistent with Piaget's findings. Attempts are currently under way to build a new intelligence scale on the basis of the Piaget tests, many of which are already in widespread use as evaluative procedures in education.

When it comes to criticisms of his theoretical views, Piaget is remarkably open and does not claim to be infallible. He frequently invites scholars who are in genuine disagreement with him to come to Geneva for a year so that the differences can be discussed and studied in depth. He has no desire to form a cult and says, in fact, "To the extent that there are Piagetians, to that extent have I failed." Piaget's lack of dogmatism is illustrated in his response to Bruner:

Bruner does say that I "missed the heart" of the conservation problem, a problem I have been working on for the last 30 years. He is right, of course, but that does not mean that he himself has understood it in a much shorter time . . . Adults, just like children, need time to reach the right ideas . . . This is the great mystery of development, which is irreducible to an accumulation of isolated learning acquisitions. Even psychology cannot be learned or constructed in a short time.

(Despite his disclaimer, Piaget has offered a comprehensive theory of how the child arrives at conservation and this theory has received much research support.)

Piaget would probably agree with those who are critical about premature applications of his work to education. He finds particularly disturbing the efforts by some American educators to accelerate children intellectually. When he was giving his other 1967 lectures, in New York, he remarked:

If we accept the fact that there are stages of development, another question arises which I call "the American question," and I am asked it every time I come here. If there are stages that children reach at given norms of ages can we accelerate the stages? Do we have to go through each one of these stages, or can't we speed it up a bit? Well, surely, the answer is yes . . . but how far can we speed them up? . . . I have a hypothesis which I am so far incapable of proving: probably the organization of operations has an optimal time . . . For example, we know that it takes 9 to 12 months before babies develop the notion that an object is still there even when a screen is placed in front of it. Now kittens go through the same sub-stages but they do it in three months—so they're six months ahead of the babies. Is this an advantage or isn't it?

We can certainly see our answer in one sense. The kitten is not going to go much further. The child has taken longer, but he is capable of going further so it seems to me that the nine months were not for nothing . . . It is probably possible to accelerate, but maximal acceleration is not desirable. There seems to be an optimal time. What this optimal time is will surely depend upon each individual and on the subject matter. We still need a great deal of research to know what the optimal time would be.

Piaget's stance against using his findings as a justification for accelerating children intellectually recalls a remark made by Freud when he was asked whatever became of those bright, aggressive shoeshine boys one encounters in city streets. Freud's reply was, "They become cobblers." In Piaget's terms they get to a certain point earlier but they don't go as far. And the New York educator Eliot Shapiro has pointed out that one of the Negro child's problems is that he is forced to grow up and take responsibility too soon and doesn't have time to be a child.

Despite some premature and erroneous applications of his thinking to education, Piaget has had an over-all effect much more positive than negative. His findings about children's understanding of scientific and mathematical concepts are being used as guidelines for new curricula in these subjects. And his tests are being more and more widely used to evaluate educational outcomes. Perhaps the most significant and widespread positive effect that Piaget has had upon education is in the changed attitudes on the part of teachers who have been exposed to his thinking. After becoming acquainted with Piaget's work, teachers can never again see children in quite the same way as they had before. Once teachers begin to look at children from the Piagetian perspective they can also appreciate his views with regard to the aims of education.

"The principal goal of education," he once said, "is to create men who are capable of doing new things, not simply of repeating what other generations have done—men who are creative, inventive and discoverers. The second goal of education is to form minds which can be critical, can verify, and not accept everything they are offered. The great danger today is of slogans, collective opinions, ready-made trends of thought. We have to be able to resist individually, to criticize, to distinguish between what is proven and what is not. So we need pupils who are active, who learn early to find out by themselves, partly by their own spontaneous activity and partly through materials we set up for them; who learn early to tell what is verifiable and what is simply the first idea to come to them."

At the beginning of his eighth decade, Jean Piaget is as busy as ever. A new book of his on memory will be published soon and another on the mental functions in the preschool child is in preparation. The International Center for Genetic Epistemology, which Piaget founded in 1955 with a grant from the Rockefeller Foundation, continues to draw scholars from around the world who wish to explore with Piaget the origin of scientific concepts. As Professor of Experimental Psychology at the University of Geneva, Piaget also continues to teach courses and conduct seminars.

And his students still continue to collect the data which at the end of the school year Piaget will take with him up to the mountains. The methods employed by his students today are not markedly different from those which were used by their predecessors decades ago. While there are occasional statistics, there are still no electronics or computers. In an age of moon shots and automation, the remarkable discoveries of Jean Piaget are evidence that in the realm of scientific achievement, technological sophistication is still no substitute for creative genius.

DISCUSSION QUESTIONS

1. Compare Piaget's learning theory with Skinner's.
2. What major changes in American education would we be forced to make, were we to adopt Piaget's theories on how children grow and learn?
3. How, in your eyes, does Piaget's personal outlook on children affect his experimental style?
4. Do you agree with Elkind that teachers, after exposure to Piaget, cannot approach children as they had before? Why have they changed?

THE CENTRAL ADVISORY COUNCIL FOR EDUCATION (The Plowden Committee)

Children and Their Primary Schools

A school is not merely a teaching shop, it must transmit values and attitudes. It is a community in which children learn to live first and foremost as children and not as future adults. In family life children learn to live with people of all ages. The school sets out deliberately to devise the right environment for children, to allow them to be themselves and to develop in the way and at the pace appropriate to them. It tries to equalise opportunities and to compensate for handicaps. It lays special stress on individual discovery, on first hand experience and on opportunities for creative work. It insists that knowledge does not fall into neatly separate compartments and that work and play are not opposite but complementary. A child brought up in such an atmosphere at all stages of his education has some hope of becoming a balanced and mature adult and of being able to live in, to contribute to, and to look critically at the society of which he forms a part. Not all primary schools correspond to this picture, but it does represent a general and quickening trend.

Some people, while conceding that children are happier under the modern regime and perhaps more versatile, question whether they are being fitted to grapple with the world which they will enter when they leave school. This view is worth examining because it is quite widely held, but we think it rests on a misconception. It isolates the long term objective, that of living in and serving society, and regards education as being at all stages recognisably and specifically a preparation for this. It fails to understand that the best preparation for being a happy and useful man or woman is to live fully as a child. Finally, it assumes, quite wrongly, that the older virtues, as they are usually called, of neatness, accuracy, care and perseverance, and the sheer knowledge which is an essential of being educated, will decline. These are genuine virtues and an education which does not foster them is faulty.

Society is right to expect that importance will be attached to these virtues in all schools. Children need them and need knowledge, if they are to gain satisfaction from their education. What we repudiate is the view that they were automatically fostered by the old kind of elementary education. Patently they were not, for enormous numbers of the products of that education do not possess them. Still more we repudiate the fear that the modern primary approach leads to their neglect. On the contrary it can,

Reprinted from A Report of the Central Advisory Council for Education (Lady Plowden, Chairman), *Children and Their Primary Schools,* Vol. I (London: Her Majesty's Stationery Office, 1967), pp. 187–202, with permission of the Controller of the Office.

and, when properly understood, does lay a much firmer foundation for their development and it is more in the interests of the children. But those interests are complex. Children need to be themselves, to live with other children and with grown ups, to learn from their environment, to enjoy the present, to get ready for the future, to create and to love, to learn to face adversity, to behave responsibly, in a word, to be human beings. Decisions about the influences and situations that ought to be contrived to these ends must be left to individual schools, teachers and parents. What must be ensured is that the decisions taken in schools spring from the best available knowledge and are not simply dictated by habit or convention.

Children learning in school

TOWARDS FREEDOM OF CURRICULUM. The ending, in 1898, of the system of payment by results, under which a proportion of teachers' salaries was dependent upon the results of an annual examination of pupils held by H.M. Inspectors, led to an increasing freedom for teachers to exercise their own judgment in matters of syllabus. In 1905 the Board of Education first issued a Handbook of Suggestions for the Consideration of Teachers, a title that itself indicated a change in outlook. The Elementary Code laid down some very broad requirements, but a large measure of choice was left to the individual school. In the preface to the 1918 edition of the Handbook occurs the following significant passage: "Neither the present volume nor any developments or amendments of it are designed to impose any regulations supplementary to those contained in the Code. The only uniformity of practice that the Board of Education desire to see in the teaching of public elementary schools is that each teacher shall think for himself, and work out for himself such methods of teaching as may use his powers to the best advantage and be best suited to the particular needs and conditions of the school. Uniformity in detail of practice (except in the mere routine of school management) is not desirable, even if it were attainable. But freedom implies a corresponding responsibility in its use." This passage was reprinted in the preface to the 1937 edition of the Handbook. In 1944 the Code, which had become increasingly permissive, finally disappeared, and in the 1944 Education Act the only statutory requirement that remained was that children should be educated according to "their age, ability and aptitude."

During the 46 years that elapsed between the abolition of payment by results and the abolition of the Code, the use made by teachers of their growing freedom varied considerably. The force of tradition and of the inherent conservatism of all teaching professions made for a slow rate of change. The requirements of selection examinations for grammar schools also exercised a strong influence towards uniformity. In the earlier part of the period, too, H.M. Inspectors, who for the previous thirty years had been examiners, were probably restraining influences on innovation, though as time went on they tended increasingly to be agents of experiment and change. A minority of teachers, particularly in the infant schools, responded eagerly to freedom. The infant schools themselves were influenced by ideas on nursery education partly because training for nursery work was often given in colleges which specialised in infant education.

A considerable body of liberal thinking on the education of children was available to teachers. Rousseau, Pestalozzi, Froebel, Whitehead, Dewey, Montessori and Rachel Macmillan, to mention only a few, had all written on lines that encouraged change and innovation. Yet it may be doubted whether the direct influence of these or of any other writers was great. It was rare to find teachers who had given much time to the study of educational theory, even in their training college days. Perhaps the strongest influence was that of Froebel, mediated through the Froebel training colleges which bore his name.

In some infant schools, a "blocked" time table began to take the place of a day fragmented into 15 or 20 minute periods, which was as long as little children could tolerate when most of the instruction was oral. It became quite common to give two periods each day to physical activity and, in the more enlightened schools, the distinction between physical education and play was blurred. In some schools, the "occupations," which owed their place in the curriculum to Froebel but were usually very different from what he had intended, were superseded by dramatic play and large scale construction. There was an increased tendency to allocate blocks of time to the three Rs and within these periods to provide . . . for group and individual work.

For children between the ages of 8 and 11, experiments were mainly in method, class organisation and use of materials. The curriculum, in the narrow sense of the subjects studied, remained almost unchanged. It included Scripture, English, arithmetic, history, geography, art, craft, music, nature study and physical training. It was rare, in the period 1898 to 1944, to find a primary school in which any of these subjects was omitted and any other included. But there was, especially after the publication of the Consultative Committee's 1931 Report, much variety of content and approach. English was beginning to involve a freer use of composition, and drama was making an appearance. The first signs of a change in the conception of mathematical learning were there for those who searched. The boundaries of history and geography were sometimes blurred and something called environmental studies—or social studies—which embraced them both, was beginning to be talked of. Art was already moving rapidly away from the dreary pencil drawing that had been universal. Craft was still limited and formal. A beginning was being made in the use of musical instruments. Nature study increasingly took place outside the classroom and physical education advanced greatly when the old conception of drill was swept away by the publication in 1933 of the Board of Education's new syllabus. Here and there schools were making a much more radical approach to education than this would indicate. The freedom was genuine, even if it was seized a little gingerly.

During the war, when there was a growing consciousness of social problems, much thought was given to the hitherto largely neglected report of 1931 and to the writings of educationalists such as Susan Isaacs. Despite overcrowding and large classes, many post-war primary schools did much to enlarge children's experience and involve them more actively in the learning process—the main themes of the 1931 Report. This was a period when a great many descriptive books, of considerable practical help to teachers, were being written about both infant and junior schools, and, for the first time, a sizeable number of junior schools, backed by H.M. Inspectors and local inspectors, began to work on lines similar to those already common in infant schools. For a brief time "activity" and child-centred education became dangerously fashionable and misunderstandings on the part of the camp followers endangered the progress made by the pioneers. The misunderstandings were never as widespread in the schools as might have been supposed by reading the press, and certainly did not outweigh the gains which were especially notable in the English subjects. Then as now, the schools which continued on traditional lines to emphasise instruction exceeded the number of those which erred by excess of innovation. In any case, correctives came in an emphasis on quality in the learning experiences provided for children, and on the positive function of the teacher.

Among the many influences which have eased the task of the teachers wishing to experiment have been the new school buildings, in which a third of primary school children are housed, more generous equipment allowances, and increased in-service training.

Recently, there have been changes in the curriculum which must be attributed to influences sufficiently distinct from those just mentioned to require separate treatment. A second language, in almost every case French, has been introduced in a substantial number of primary schools. The teaching of mathematics is undergoing a radical change and a wider field of science is replacing nature study. . . . All that need be said here is that these changes seem to be taking place unusually rapidly, often because of the in-service training which has been encouraged and sometimes planned by the Department in concert with other bodies.

Looked at from any point of view, the changes that have taken place between 1898 and the fifties and sixties have been striking, but they have been largely unco-ordinated, except perhaps by in-service training. It was argued that the establishment of some central organisation could accelerate the process of change, and co-ordinate and evaluate whatever changes were taking place. Such thoughts as these led to the setting up in 1964 of the Schools Council for the Curriculum and Examinations.

The Council is a consortium of bodies concerned with education, the teachers' organisations, the local education authorities, the universities and colleges of education, the Department being one member among others. One of its main functions is to enlist teachers' help in curricular development. The Council's activities in the short time they have been established have been principally concerned with secondary education, save for their interest in the Nuffield primary school projects in French, science and mathematics. The Council have a great number of subject sub-committees as well as steering committees concerned with the different stages of education, including one for primary education.

RESEARCH ON CHILDREN'S LEARNING. Towards the end of the nineteenth century, research began to supplement general observation of children's methods of learning, though even now it would be difficult to find many teachers who could relate what they are doing in the classroom to any particular piece of research. Here, as in other fields, the pace has recently quickened. Many teachers, for example, are following research on various methods of teaching children to read. More fundamentally, an encouraging number of teachers are beginning to concern themselves with theories of learning. By their practical work in the classroom, teachers have perhaps as much to contribute to psychology as the psychologists to educational practice.

Research into the ways in which children learn has produced, broadly, two interpretations of the learning process. One, which is still dominant in the United States, and is associated with the names of Thorndike, Hull, Pavlov and Skinner among others, is essentially behaviourist. It is concerned with simple and complex operant conditioning, the place of reinforcement in learning, habit formation and the measurement of various kinds of stimulus-response behaviour. Much of the more recent work derives from animal studies and its main relevance is to motor learning, though some work has been done on the learning of information, concepts and skills by children and adults. It does not offer very much direct help to teachers since, for the most part, the motives and sequence of children's learning are too complicated for analysis in terms of simple models. A recent review of programmed learning suggests that even simple segments of learning do not always conform closely to models of learning theory such as Skinner's. It is in a whole situation with a history behind it that a child or adult learns. Success in using a machine may be due as much to relaxation from anxiety or to a feeling of self-importance as to the small steps used in linear programming on the Skinner system. Most teachers of young children have seen the value of a gradual build-up of vocabulary in the teaching of reading. But they have also had evidence of the rapid strides that children can make when a particular book holds such interest for them that they are determined to read it quickly.

Some of the experiments of the behaviourists confirm that prolonged periods of routine practice in, for example, computation or handwriting reduce rather than improve accuracy. This is a lesson which is particularly relevant to schools working on traditional lines.

A second school of research, which is dominant in Great Britain and apparently gaining ground in the United States, is associated with the names of Baldwin, Isaacs, Luria, Bruner, and in particular Jean Piaget. This school is interested in discovering the ground plan of the growth of intellectual powers and the order in which they are acquired. One of its most important conclusions is that the great majority of primary school children can only learn efficiently from concrete situations, as lived or described. From these situations, children acquire concepts in every area of the curriculum. According to Piaget, all learning calls for organisation of material or of behaviour on the part of the learner, and the learner has to adapt himself and is altered in the process. Learning takes place through a continuous process of interaction between the learner and his environment, which results in the building up of consistent and stable patterns of behaviour, physical and mental. Each new experience reorganises, however slightly, the structure of the mind and contributes to the child's world picture.

Piaget's thought, which influenced the 1931 Report and our own, is not easy to understand. It is almost impossible to express in other than technical terms. Although he is not primarily an educationalist, his work has important implications for teachers. His observations of the sequence in the development of children's concepts are being tested on samples of children in many countries and these tests are tending to confirm his main findings. Much more investigation is needed on the extent to which the school environment and the guidance and teaching provided by teachers can accelerate children's progress. The effect of social expectations on the way children learn also calls for study. Nevertheless Piaget's explanations appear to most educationalists in this country to fit the observed facts of children's learning more satisfactorily than any other. It is in accord with previous research by genetic psychologists and with what is generally regarded as the most effective primary school practice, as it has been worked out empirically. The main implications of that practice are described in the following paragraphs and, where relevant, reference is made to the support given them by the Piagetian school of thought.

ASPECTS OF CHILDREN'S LEARNING. Play is the central activity in all nursery schools and in many infant schools. This sometimes leads to accusations that children are wasting their time in school: they should be "working." But this distinction between work and play is false, possibly throughout life, certainly in the primary school. Its essence lies in past notions of what is done in school hours (work) and what is done out of school (play). We know now that play—in the sense of "messing about" either with material objects or with other children, and of creating fantasies—is vital to children's learning and therefore vital in school. Adults who criticise teachers for allowing children to play are unaware that play is the principal means of learning in early childhood. It is the way through which children reconcile their inner lives with external reality. In play, children gradually develop concepts of causal relationships, the power to discriminate, to make judgements, to analyse and synthesise, to imagine and to formulate. Children become absorbed in their play and the satisfaction of bringing it to a satisfactory conclusion fixes habits of concentration which can be transferred to other learning.

From infancy, children investigate the material world. Their interest is not wholly scientific but arises from a desire to control or use the things about them. Pleasure in "being a cause" seems to permeate children's earliest contact with materials. To destroy and construct involves learning the properties of things and in this way children can build up concepts of weight, height, size, volume and texture.

Primitive materials such as sand, water, clay and wood attract young children and evoke concentration and inventiveness. Children are also stimulated by natural or manufactured materials of many shapes, colours and textures. Their imagination seizes on particular facets of objects and leads them to invent as well as to create. All kinds of causal connections are discovered, illustrated and used. Children also use objects as symbols for things, feelings and experiences, for which they may lack words. A small girl may use a piece of material in slightly different ways to make herself into a bride, a queen or a nurse. When teachers enter into the play activity of children, they can help by watching the connections and relationships which children are making and by introducing, almost incidentally, the words for the concepts and feelings that are being expressed. Some symbolism is unconscious and may be the means by which children come to terms with actions or thoughts which are not acceptable to adults or are too frightening for the children themselves. In play are the roots of drama, expressive movement and art. In this way too children learn to understand other people. The earliest play of this kind probably emerges from play with materials. A child playing with a toy aeroplane can be seen to take the role of both the aeroplane and the pilot apparently simultaneously. All the important people of his world figure in this play: he imitates, he becomes, he symbolises. He works off aggression or compensates himself for lack of love by "being" one or other of the people who impinge on his life. By acting as he conceives they do, he tries to understand them. Since children tend to have inflexible roles thrust on them by adults, they need opportunities to explore different roles and to make a freer choice of their own. Early exploration of the actions, motives and feelings of themselves and of others is likely to be an important factor in the ability to form right relationships, which in its turn seems to be a crucial element in mental health. The difficulties of blind and deaf children whose play is restricted show how much play enriches the lives of ordinary children. Adults can help children in this form of play, and in their social development, by references to the thoughts, feelings and needs of other people. Through stories told to them, children enter into different ways of behaving and of looking at the world, and play new parts.

Just as adults relive experience in thought or words, so children play over and over the important happenings of their lives. The repetition is usually selective. Children who re-enact a painful scene repeatedly are not doing it to preserve the pain but to make it bearable and understandable. They incorporate those parts of the difficult situation which are endurable and add others as their courage and confidence grows. This is one of the ways in which they bring under control the feelings of frustration which must be experienced by those who are dependent on the will and love of adults. This kind of play can preserve self esteem by reducing unpleasant experiences to size, and reinforce confidence by dwelling on success.

Much of children's play is "cultural" play as opposed to the "natural" play of animals which mainly practices physical and survival skills. It often needs adult participation so that cultural facts and their significance can be communicated to children. The introduction into the classroom of objects for hospital play provides opportunities for coming to terms with one of the most common fears. Similarly the arrival of a new baby in the family, the death of someone important to the child, the invention of space rockets or new weapons may all call for the provision of materials for dramatic play which will help children to give expression to their feelings as a preliminary to understanding and controlling them. Sensitivity and observation are called for rather than intervention from the teacher. The knowledge of children gained from "active" observation is invaluable to teachers. It gives common ground for conversation and exchange of ideas which it is among the most important duties of teachers to initiate and foster.

A child's play at any given moment contains many elements. The layers of meaning may include a highly conscious organisation of the environment, exploration of physical and social relationships and an expression of the deepest levels of fantasy. Wide ranging and satisfying play is a means of learning, a powerful stimulus to learning, and a way to free learning from distortion by the emotions. Several writers have recently emphasised the importance of a period of play and exploration in new learning as, for example, in mathematics and science. Adults as well as children approach new learning in this way.

The child is the agent in his own learning. This was the message of the often quoted comment from the 1931 Report: "The curriculum is to be thought of in terms of activity and experience rather than of knowledge to be acquired and facts to be stored." Read in isolation, the passage has sometimes been taken to imply that children could not learn from imaginative experience and that activity and experience did not lead to the acquisition of knowledge. The context makes it plain that the actual implication is almost the opposite of this. It is that activity and experience, both physical and mental, are often the best means of gaining knowledge and acquiring facts. This is more generally recognised today but still needs to be said. We certainly would not wish to undervalue knowledge and facts, but facts are best retained when they are used and understood, when right attitudes to learning are created, when children learn to learn. Instruction in many primary schools continues to bewilder children because it outruns their experience. Even in infant schools, where innovation has gone furthest, time is sometimes wasted in teaching written "sums" before children are able to understand what they are doing. The N.C.D.S. Survey . . . shows that 17 per cent of children start doing sums in infant schools before the age of five and a half.

The intense interest shown by young children in the world about them, their powers of concentration on whatever is occupying their attention, or serving their immediate purposes, are apparent to both teachers and parents. Skills of reading and writing or the techniques used in art and craft can best be taught when the need for them is evident to children. A child who has no immediate incentive for learning to read is unlikely to succeed because of warnings about the disadvantages of illiteracy in adult life. There is, therefore, good reason for allowing young children to choose within a carefully prepared environment in which choices and interest are supported by their teachers, who will have in mind the potentialities for further learning. Piaget's observations support the belief that children have a natural urge to explore and discover, that they find pleasure in satisfying it and that it is therefore self-perpetuating. When children are learning new patterns of behaviour or new concepts, they tend both to practise them spontaneously and to seek out relevant experience, as can be seen from the way they acquire skills in movement. It takes much longer than teachers have previously realised for children to master through experience new concepts or new levels of complex concepts. When understanding has been achieved, consolidation should follow. At this stage children profit from various types of practice devised by their teachers, and from direct instruction.

Children will of course vary in the degree of interest that they show and their urge to learn will be strengthened or weakened . . . by the attitudes of parents, teachers and others with whom they identify themselves. Apathy may result when parents show no interest, clamp down on children's curiosity and enterprise, tell them constantly not to touch and do not answer their questions. Children can also learn to be passive from a teacher who allows them little scope in managing their own affairs and in learning. A teacher who relies only on instruction, who forestalls children's questions or who answers them too quickly, instead of asking the further questions which will set children on the way to their own solution, will disincline children to learn. A new teacher with time and patience can usually help children who have learnt from their teachers to be too dependent. Those who have been deprived at home need more than that. Their self-confidence can only be restored by affection, stability and order. They must have special attention from adults who can discover, by observing their responses, what experiences awaken interest, and can seize on them to reinforce the desire to learn.

External incentives such as marks and stars, and other rewards and punishments, influence children's learning mainly by evoking or representing parents' or teachers' approval. Although children vary temperamentally in their response to rewards and punishments, positive incentives are generally more effective than punishment, and neither is as damaging as neglect. But the children who most need the incentive of good marks are least likely to gain them, even when, as in many primary schools, they are given for effort rather than for achievement. In any case, one of the main educational tasks of the primary school is to build on and strengthen children's intrinsic interest in learning and lead them to learn for themselves rather than from fear of disapproval or desire for praise.

Learning is a continuous process from birth. The teacher's task is to provide an environment and opportunities which are sufficiently challenging for children and yet not so difficult as to be outside their reach. There has to be the right mixture of the familiar and the novel, the right match to the stage of learning the child has reached. If the material is too familiar or the learning skills too easy, children will become inattentive and bored. If too great maturity is demanded of them, they fall back on half remembered formulae and become concerned only to give the reply the teacher wants. Children can think and form concepts, so long as they work at their own level, and are not made to feel that they are failures.

Teachers must rely both on their general knowledge of child development and on detailed observation of individual children for matching their demands to children's stages of development. This concept of "readiness" was first applied to reading. It has sometimes been thought of in too negative a way. Children can . . . be led to want to read, provided that they are sufficiently mature. Learning can be undertaken too late as well as too early. Piaget's work can help teachers in diagnosing children's readiness in mathematics, and gives some pointers as to how it can be encouraged.

At every stage of learning children need rich and varied materials and situations, though the pace at which they should be introduced may vary according to the children. If children are limited in materials, they tend to solve problems in isolation and fail to see their relevance to other similar situations. This stands out particularly clearly in young children's learning of mathematics. Similarly, children need to accumulate much experience of human behaviour before they can develop moral concepts. If teachers or parents are inconsistent in their attitudes or contradict by their behaviour what they preach, it becomes difficult for children to develop stable and mature concepts. Verbal explanation, in advance of understanding based on experience, may be an obstacle to learning, and children's knowledge of the right words may conceal from teachers their lack of understanding. Yet it is inevitable that children will pick up words which outstrip their understanding. Discussion with other children and with adults is one of the principal ways in which children check their concepts against those of others and build up an objective view of reality. There is every justification for the conversation which is a characteristic feature of the contemporary primary school. One of the most important responsibilities of teachers is to help children to see order and pattern in experience, and to extend their ideas by analogies and by the provision of suitable vocabulary. Rigid division of the curriculum into subjects tends to interrupt children's trains of thought and of interest and to hinder them from realising the common elements in problem solving. These are among the many reasons why some work, at least, should cut across subject divisions at all stages in the primary school.

SOME PRACTICAL IMPLICATIONS: THE TIME TABLE. These beliefs about how children learn have practical implications for the time table and the curriculum. One idea now widespread is embodied in the expression "free day" and another, associated with it, is the "integrated curriculum." The strongest influence making for the free day has been the conviction of some teachers and other educationalists that it is through play that young children learn. Nursery schools began by devoting half an hour to free play. This is still done by many kindergartens which we visited abroad. Now the whole day is spent on various forms of play, though groups of children may break away to enjoy stories or music with an adult. Infant schools usually give at least an hour a day to play, though it may be called by many different names. If teachers encourage overlap between what is done in periods of self-chosen activity and in the times allocated, for example, to reading and to writing, a good learning situation will probably result. Children who are not yet ready to read can go on playing and building up vocabulary while other children are reading. Play can lead naturally to reading and writing associated with it. Children do not flit from activity to activity in their anxiety to make use of materials not available at other times of the day. Some infant schools are now confident enough in the value of self-chosen activity to give the whole day to it, except for times which are used for stories, poetry, movement, and music—and even these may be voluntary, particularly for the younger children. The tendency is spreading in junior schools. Children may plan when to do work assigned to them and also have time in which to follow personal or group interests of their own choice. In a few infant and junior schools the day is still divided into a succession of short periods. In the great majority, we are glad to say, there are longer periods and these can be adjusted at the teacher's discretion.

These changes represent a revolution from the type of time table implied by the forms completed by schools for local education authorities until quite recently. Heads were expected to show exactly what each class was doing during every minute of the week and to provide a summary showing the total number of minutes to be spent on each subject. In extreme cases, the curriculum was divided into spelling, dictation, grammar, exercises, composition, recitation, reading, handwriting, tables and mental arithmetic. It is obvious that this arrangement was not suited to what was known of the nature of children, of the classification of subject matter, or of the art of teaching. Children's interest varies in length according to personality, age and circumstances, and it is folly either to interrupt it when it is intense, or to flog it when it has declined. The teacher can best judge when to make a change and the moment of change may not be the same for each child in the class. In many schools, as we have said, children plan much of their work. Yet the teacher must constantly ensure a balance within the day or week both for the class and for individuals. He must see that time is profitably spent and give guidance on its use. In the last resort, the teacher's relationship with his pupils, his openness to their suggestions and their trust in him are far more important than the nominal degree of freedom in the time table.

FLEXIBILITY IN THE CURRICULUM. The extent to which subject matter ought to be classified and the headings under which the classification is made will vary with the age of the children, with the demands made by the structure of the subject matter which is being studied, and with the circumstances of the school. Any practice which predetermines the pattern and imposes it upon all is to be condemned. Some teachers find it helpful in maintaining a balance in individual and class work to think in terms of broad areas of the curriculum such as language, science and mathematics, environmental study and the expressive arts. No pattern can be perfect since many subjects fall into one category or another according to the aspect which is being studied. For young children, the broadest of divisions is suitable. For children from 9 to 12, more subject divisions can be expected, though experience in secondary schools has shown that teaching of rigidly defined subjects, often by specialist teachers, is far from suitable for the oldest children who will be in the middle schools. This is one of our reasons for suggesting a change in the age of transfer to secondary education.

There is little place for the type of scheme which sets down exactly what ground should be covered and what skill should be acquired by each class in the school. Yet to put nothing in its place may be to leave some teachers prisoners of tradition and to make difficulties for newcomers to a staff who are left to pick up, little by little, the ethos of a school. The best solution seems to be to provide brief schemes for the school as a whole: outlines of aims in various areas of the curriculum, the sequence of development which can be expected in children and the methods through which work can be soundly based and progress accelerated. It is also useful to have a record of experiences, topics, books, poems and music which have been found to succeed with children of different ages, and for attention to be drawn to notable experimental work. In good schools, schemes are often subject to a process of accretion which may make them so long that few teachers have time to read them. It is better for them to be sifted and revised, for matter to be dropped as well as added. Individual members of staff, with such help as the head and others can give, will need to plan in more detail the work of their particular classes. Often it will develop in an unexpected direction. A brief report on the topics, literature and so forth which have absorbed children during the course of the year will be necessary for teachers who take them later in their school career.

The idea of flexibility has found expression in a number of practices, all of them designed to make good use of the interest and curiosity of children, to minimise the notion of subject matter being rigidly compartmental, and to allow the teacher to adopt a consultative, guiding, stimulating role rather than a purely didactic one. The oldest of these methods is the "project." Some topic, such as "transport" is chosen, ideally by the children, but frequently by the teacher. The topic cuts across the boundaries of subjects and is treated as its nature requires without reference to subjects as such. At its best the method leads to the use of books of reference, to individual work and to active participation in learning. Unfortunately it is no guarantee of this and the appearance of text books of projects, which achieved at one time considerable popularity, is proof of how completely a good idea can be misunderstood.

A variation on the project, originally associated with the infant school but often better suited to older children, is "the centre of interest." It begins with a topic which is of such inherent interest and variety as to make it possible and reasonable to make much of the work of the class revolve round it for a period of a week, a month or a term or even longer. Experience has shown that it is artificial to try to link most of the work of a class to one centre of interest. It has become more common to have several interests —topic is now the usual word—going at once. Much of the work may be individual, falling under broad subject headings. One topic for the time being can involve both group and class interest, and may splinter off into all kinds of individual work.

When a class of seven year olds notice the birds that come to the bird table outside the classroom window, they may decide, after discussion with their teacher, to make their own aviary. They will set to with a will, and paint the birds in flight, make models of them in clay or papier mâché, write stories and poems about them and look up reference books to find out more about their habits. Children are not assimilating inert ideas but are wholly involved in thinking, feeling and doing. The slow and the bright share a common experience and each takes from it what he can at his own level. There is no attempt to put reading and writing into separate compartments; both serve a wider purpose, and artificial barriers do not fragment the learning experience. A top junior class became interested in the problem of measuring the area of an awkwardly shaped field at the back of the school. The problem stimulated much learning about surveying and triangles. From surveying, interest passed to navigation; for the more difficult aspects of the work, co-operation between members of staff as well as pupils was needed. For one boy, the work on navigation took the form of a story of encounters of pirate ships and men-of-war, and involved a great deal of calculation, history, geography and English. Integration is not only a question of allowing time for interests which do not fit under subject headings; it is as much a matter of seeing the different dimensions of subject work and of using the forms of observation and communication which are most suitable to a given sequence of learning.

USE OF THE ENVIRONMENT. Another effective way of integrating the curriculum is to relate it through the use of the environment to the boundless curiosity which children have about the world about them. When teachers talk about "first-hand experience" what they often have in mind is the exploration of the physical environment of the school, though the expression of course includes other kinds of experiences as well. Whereas once the teacher brought autumn leaves into the classroom and talked about the seasons and their characteristics, now he will take the children out to see for themselves. Rural schools can be overwhelmed by the variety of material on their doorsteps. Crops and pastures, wild flowers and weeds, farm animals, wild creatures of every kind, roads and footpaths, verges, hedges, ditches, streams, woods, the weather, the season, the stars, all provide starting points for curiosity, discussion, observation, recording and enquiry, at every level from that of the five year old to that of the 12 year old and beyond. Much of this material is also available to the newer urban schools though their sites are often laid out too formally to be suitable for children's play or for interesting studies. The most difficult problem of all is not so much that of the older urban school, despite its often restricted site, as that of the school on the large housing estate. But the weather and the stars are available to all; so are the occupations of fathers which offer a way of enlisting co-operation and interest in their children's education as well as an approach to local industry.

Teachers in town schools can make use of railways and other transport systems, and the local shops and factories, all of which can provide suitable material. Building sites are almost ubiquitous and can provide an approach to geography, mathematics and science. We have heard of children doing "traffic counts," discovering from shop keepers the source of their goods and even, in one case, exploring unofficially the sewage system of their area. Museums, geared to children's interests, may also be within reach and are becoming ready to let children handle as well as look, and to lend to schools some of the surplus stock which is otherwise often stored away in basements. It may be well to look a little at this approach as it can work out in a favourable environment. A group of H.M.Is. working in a division in which some particularly good work is to be found, write as follows:—

The newer methods start with the direct impact of the environment on the child and the child's individual response to it. The results are unpredictable, but extremely worth while. The teacher has to be prepared to follow up the personal interests of the children who, either singly, or in groups, follow divergent paths of discovery. Books of reference, maps, enquiries of local officials, museums, archives, elderly residents in the area are all called upon to give the information needed to complete the picture that the child is seeking to construct. When this enthusiasm is unleashed in a class, the time table may even be dispensed with, as the resulting occupations may easily cover mathematics, geology, astronomy, history, navigation, religious instruction, literature, art and craft. The teacher needs perception to appreciate the value that can be gained from this method of working, and he needs also energy to keep up with the children's demands.

Another possibility is to take children out of their own environment into a contrasting one, either for the day or for a longer period. This of course applies as much to rural children visiting towns as to urban children visiting the countryside. Such visits, carefully prepared for and not just sight-seeing, are generally used as the culmination of an interest or interests. They would often serve better as starting points. For day visits, when the school situation makes it possible, those places are best which are near enough for children to visit and to revisit, individually, in groups or as a class when new questions arise. There is then a strong incentive for them to look closely at the objects which have made a further visit necessary.

In one northern city a school, well situated in a park on the outskirts of the city, is being used for a fortnight at a time by children from the central slum areas. The school has a small resident staff and is well equipped. Since the visiting children's own teachers accompany them, they can be taught in small groups of 15. During the summer months the school day is extended into the evening so that the children, who are conveyed by buses, can gain the maximum from their experiences.

Authorities can help schools, as some indeed do, by providing hutted camps and other residential centres which do much for children socially as well as educationally. Useful experiments have also been tried in linking country and urban schools and arranging for exchange visits. Expeditions too far afield are to be avoided, as they are generally speaking pure sight-seeing tours. We have considerable doubts about overseas expeditions for primary school children.

A third possibility, which is open to all schools, is to make the school environment itself as rich as possible. Nearly all children are interested in living forms, whether they be animal or plants. Some acquaintance with them is an essential part of being educated. To care for living creatures offers an emotional outlet to some children and demands discipline from all. However rich the locality, emphasis must always be put on the school itself, which is an environment contrived for children's learning.

DISCOVERY. A word which has fairly recently come into use in educational circles is "discovery." It includes many of the ideas so far discussed and is a useful shorthand description. It has the disadvantage of comprehensiveness that it can be loosely interpreted and misunderstood. We have more to say about the value of discovery in the section on science. The sense of personal discovery influences the intensity of a child's experience, the vividness of his memory and the probability of effective transfer of learning. At the same time it is true that trivial ideas and inefficient methods may be "discovered." Furthermore, time does not allow children to find their way by discovery to all that they have to learn. In this matter, as in all education, the teacher is responsible for encouraging children in enquiries which lead to discovery and for asking leading questions.

Free and sometimes indiscriminate use of words such as discovery has led some critics to the view that English primary education needs to be more firmly based on closely argued educational theory. Nevertheless great advances appear to have been made without such theory, and research has still a long way to go before it can make a marked contribution. At many points even so fruitful an approach is that of Piaget needs further verification. What is immediately needed is that teachers should bring to bear on their day to day problems astringent intellectual scrutiny. Yet all good teachers must work intuitively and be sensitive to the emotive and imaginative needs of their children. Teaching is an art and, as long as that with all its implications is firmly grasped, it will not be harmed by intellectual stiffening.

EVALUATION OF CHILDREN'S PROGRESS. We have considered whether we can lay down standards that should be achieved by the end of the primary school but concluded that it is not possible to describe a standard of attainment that should be reached by all or most children. Any set standard would seriously limit the bright child and be impossibly high for the dull. What could be achieved in one school might be impossible in another. We have suggested in Chapter 11 that, with the ending of selection examinations, teachers—and parents—will need some yardstick of the progress of their children in relation to what is achieved elsewhere. Without it teachers may be tempted to go on teaching and testing in much the same way as they did before. We therefore envisage that some use will continue to be made of objective tests within schools. Such tests can be helpful—and their norms can serve as a basis of comparison—as long as they are used with insight and discrimination, and teachers do not assume that only what is measurable is valuable. . . . Primary schools should hear regularly from the secondary schools to which they contribute how their pupils compare over a period with children from other schools. One of the principal functions of H.M. Inspectors is to help teachers to know what to expect from children in the circumstances of their neighbourhood and to advise teachers on standards in aspects of the curriculum where objective measurement is not practicable.

We have already suggested that surveys of the quality of primary schools should be made by H.M. Inspectorate at regular intervals. We also think that there should be recurring national surveys of attainment similar to that undertaken in reading by the Department of Education, and those carried out by the N.F.E.R. in reading and mathematics.

In this chapter . . . we describe how children learn and make broad suggestions for the curriculum and organisation of primary schools. Our views derive from evidence given to us and our own observations of good practice in the schools. At some points research supports strongly our emphasis on active learning. But many problems remain unresolved and we have, therefore, recommended further enquiry into child development and the results of new methods. We endorse the trend towards individual and active learning and "learning by acquaintance," and should like many more schools to be more deeply influenced by it. Yet we certainly do not deny the value of "learning by description" or the need for practice of skills and consolidation of knowledge. This part of our Report should be read in conjunction with Part IV where we discuss the teacher's responsibility for ensuring that what children learn is worth learning. At the extremes of the ability range, as we have said in other chapters, there will always be children who need special help. Not enough is known about how far, apart from variations in ability, children differ, according to temperament in the way they learn. Even as children differ so do teachers. They must select those of our suggestions which their knowledge and skill enable them to put into practice in the circumstances of their schools.

DISCUSSION QUESTIONS

1. Of what value are the findings of the Plowden Committee to American educators?
2. Is there anything in the British philosophy and experience that might not be acceptable or applicable to American education?
3. Do you agree with the report that ". . . the best preparation for life is to live fully as a child"?
4. The British seek to give their teachers freedom and professional leeway and cherish educational nonconformity. Compare the American educational establishment's relationship to its teachers with that of the British.

EARL S. JOHNSON | *Secondary Education*

The concern that sets our task is this: What good may come from inquiry into the manifold ways of mankind, pursued through comparative cultural studies? How may students come to know better the diverse peoples with whom they share space on a shrinking globe and, in the light of the fruits of such exploration, come to know themselves better because they see themselves in the "mirror of man"?

Such a concern seeks an understanding of mankind, the "universal subject," rather than strange and exotic individuals. It is bespoken in Ernst Cassirer's observation that "humanity is not to be explained by man but man by humanity" and in Goethe's belief that "man knows himself only in mankind." It is, albeit with a sense of guilt, in Cain's immortal question; it is the essence of the Golden Rule found, variously stated, in all the great religions. It is the theme of John Donne's "for whom the bell tolls" and of Whitman's "Song of Myself," which is also the song of all other selves. It is what Martin Buber seeks to understand, in its largest dimension, in the relations of "I" and "Thou"; and George H. Mead's view of the origin of the self is grounded on it.

Thus, it is clear that the process by which students may know mankind is reciprocal: they must know "the other one" and they must know the image that "the other one" has of them. And, to make the matter both more precise and more difficult, each must know how he knows "the other one," that is, by what uses of the mind and from what social, moral, and technological conditions and perspectives.

Robert Burns' words come to mind—and the moral of them, too:

> Oh wad some power the giftie gie us
> To see oursels as others see us!
> It wad frae monie a blunder free us,
> An' foolish notion.

If it be assumed that the concept of mankind is now taken account of in the curriculum of our secondary school, the reply is "Perhaps," if the humanities are thought to be the area, but a qualified "No" if the social studies in their present status are thought to be the vehicle for its study. Nevertheless, we shall consider the concept as the concern of the humane *and* the social studies, without, however, suggesting that they have or ought

Reprinted from Robert Ulich (ed.), *Education and the Idea of Mankind* (New York: Harcourt, Brace & World, Inc., 1964), pp. 120–126, by permission of the publisher.

to have sole proprietorship of it. On the contrary, if the concept of mankind were elaborated in its widest meaning, each of the three great fields of knowledge—the humanities, the social studies, and the natural sciences—through their course surrogates in the secondary school, would have much to contribute. One might look forward to the day when the sciences, the humanities, and the social studies achieve a genuine and exciting unity of labor in syntheses of various kinds effected through the concept of mankind.

A knowledge of "culture," as the anthropologist understands it, must, of course, provide the substantive ground for the study of mankind through all studies. In the social studies, as they are generally taught, the phenomenon of culture, so conceived, is either little known or is interpreted chiefly to refer either to "polite manners" or the achievements of various elites in the fine arts. Such interpretations have some, although a narrow, validity, but are a far cry from Clark Wissler's view of culture as "the whole round of life."

In the more traditional secondary school textbooks in United States history—whose major concern is with economic, political, and still to a large degree military matters—one usually finds a chapter or two that undertakes a rapid and necessarily shallow survey of what are called "cultural achievements." Chief attention under this heading is given to education, reform movements, and advances in the arts, letters, and sciences. Thus the term "culture" is conceived to refer to only a part of the "whole round of life," something a little more sturdy than a mere decoration but still far less comprehensive than culture viewed as the very warp and woof of a society.[1]

The situation in the secondary school is, however, brighter when account is taken of the work done by such scholars as Robert Redfield, Margaret Mead, Dorothy Lee, Lawrence Frank, Sol Tax, George Spindler, Theodore Brameld, and Solon Kimball. They have done much to encourage introduction of anthropological concepts into secondary school studies. Outstanding among courses in cultural anthropology is the one that Mr. Jack Ellison, of the Francis W. Parker school in Chicago, organized and has taught for ten years or more.[2]

The course in world history that is characteristically required in the

---

1 See Edward Sapir, "Culture: Genuine and Spurious," *American Journal of Sociology,* Vol. 29 (1924), for a comprehensive treatment of culture: ". . . as any socially inherited element in man's life; as a conventional idea of refinement, and as the general attitudes and views of life that give a particular people its distinctive place in the world."

2 Noteworthy contributions to the journal literature in this connection are the following: Robert Redfield, "The Study of Culture in General Education," *Social Education,* Vol. XI (October 1947); Alex Weingrod, "Anthropology and the Social Studies," *Social Education,* Vol. XX (January 1956); and Jack L. Ellison, "Anthropology Brings Human Nature into the Classroom," *Social Education,* Vol. XXIV, (November 1960). See also George D. Spindler, ed., *Education and Anthropology* (Stanford: Stanford University Press, 1955), and a forthcoming report by the American Council of Learned Societies on the role of anthropology (and many other of the traditional disciplines, social and natural) in secondary education.

sophomore year warrants special comment. Courses under this rubric usually undertake to treat with man's experience in the framework of nation-states, which are taken as units of the great civilizations. Some of the texts open with a chapter on prehistoric man, usually referred to as "early man." The dominant pattern and theme of such courses, at least as revealed in representative textbooks, is the story of "human progress"—as the account is usually styled. Their final concern is usually to impress students with twentieth-century man's debt to all that has gone before and to which he is now legatee.

It is the view of an increasing number of historians and specialists in secondary school social studies that such courses presume a fund and quality of historical knowledge that is so extravagant as to be unattainable even by teachers; only by remote inference do they provide a world perspective on man-in-society; they are committed, perforce, more to coverage of factual knowledge than to mastering the meaning of the great social changes that are the substance of man's history. Nor do they illuminate the concept of mankind, because they do not examine societies in frames of reference that reveal the common, recurrent, and pervasive aspects of the life of peoples.[3]

Before we offer our approach to the study of mankind we believe that some definitions and interpretations of the concept of "culture" are in order.

Edward B. Tylor, one of the patriarchs of cultural anthropology, understood culture to be "that whole complex which includes knowledge, belief, art, morals, law, custom and any other capabilities and habits acquired by men as members of society."[4] To the late Professor Alfred Kroeber it is that for which man "has a propensity," which suggests that it is coterminous with mankind. Bronislaw Malinowski understands culture to be "that full context of all man's activities . . . the vast instrumentality through which man achieves his ends, both as an animal who has to eat, rest and reproduce, and as a spiritual being who desires to extend his horizon to produce works of art and develop systems of faith."[5]

Malinowski's term, "the vast instrumentality," is uniquely appropriate to our purpose—to show that culture is the great middle principle through which all that man has made that lies outside him, as well as all that which lies within him—methods of thought, technical skills, ideas, and ideals—is related and gives meaning to his self and to his relation with his fellows.

---

[3] See Stanley N. Miller, "The World Cultures Course," *Social Education,* Vol. XXVI (February 1962); and four papers on various aspects of the problems related to world-history courses in *Social Education,* Vol. XXIV (April 1960). An excellent high school text in world history, written by Professor L. S. Stavrianos, of Northwestern University, provides a constant schema for comparative study of nations and civilizations.

[4] Edward B. Tylor, *Primitive Culture* (New York: Brentano, 1874), p. 1.

[5] Bronislaw Malinowski, "The Scientific Approach to the Study of Man," in Ruth Anshen, ed., *Science and Man* (New York: Harcourt, Brace & World, Inc., 1942), p. 207.

Not even Rousseau's "natural man" escaped the impact of his culture, so conceived.

But there is a quality in the phenomenon of culture that these terse and almost epigrammatic definitions hardly convey. For that quality we turn to the late Professor Clyde Kluckhohn:

> A culture is not merely a congeries of customs. . . . The way of life that is handed down as the social heritage of every people does more than supply a set of skills for making a living and a set of blueprints for human relations. Each different way of life makes its own assumptions about the ends and purposes of human existence, about ways by which knowledge may be obtained, about the organization of the pigeonholes in which each sense datum is filed, about what human beings have a right to expect from each other and the gods, about what is 'good' and 'right' or 'better' and 'worse,' about what constitutes fulfillment or frustration. Some of these assumptions are made explicit in the lore of the folk; others are tacit premises which the observer must infer from finding consistent trends in word and deed. The unstated assumptions (in particular) are ordinarily taken for granted as an ineradicable part of human nature and naive participants in one culture find it hard to understand what normal persons could possibly conceive life in other terms. In other words, many cultural premises and categories are nonrational and defensive attitudes related to them may be decidedly irrational.[6]

What Professor Kluckhohn implies ought now to be made explicit: every culture is a system *sui generis.* This fact may well give to comparative cultural study its most interesting and likewise its most enigmatic and troublesome character. Even so, high school students ought to learn that every culture is like every other, and every one is also unlike every other. Each is a "patterned selectivity," manifesting certain universal forms that tend, in content, to be unique to particular histories and traditions.

At the cost of some simplification, we would refer these common aspects of all cultures to mankind's biological, physiological, psychological, and rational equipment and mechanism, and to the fact that everywhere man confronts recurrent and common situations. The latter we are disposed to think of as universal exigencies of human existence. Thus it is that the more apparent universals in the cultures that man has elaborated are not identities in their behavioral *content* but in their *forms.*

Through studies of how these processes work, both independently (if they ever do!) and interdependently in a variety of cultures, students may get an understanding of how cultures are alike and how they are unalike, respecting both the forms and the content that such processes manifest. Thus they may develop some identity, even kinship, with mankind: historic with prehistoric; advanced with primitive; complex with simple; and preliterate with literate.

Our first concern is with patterns or frames of reference that will serve

---

[6] Clyde Kluckhohn, "Common Humanity and Diverse Cultures," in David Lerner, ed., *The Human Meaning of the Social Sciences* (New York: Meridian Books, 1959), pp. 247–48.

adequately to discipline and direct comparative cultural studies so that the concept of mankind may be discovered and revealed.

DISCUSSION QUESTIONS

1. What are the chief purposes of American secondary education today?
2. How well are our high-school youths prepared by their education for citizenship in the national and international communities?
3. How relevant to the problems facing the world today is an understanding of the concept of "culture"?
4. What firsthand experiences in the study of other cultures would you suggest for our present secondary students?

HAROLD TAYLOR — *The Need for Radical Reform*

One of the astonishing facts about the otherwise unastonishing White House Conference on Education of 1965 was its neglect of the problem of teacher education. All the subject got was an almost unreadable paper that rehearsed once more the conventions of Mr. Conant's thinking and ended with a curious summary of hypothetical issues, along with a two-hour panel discussion session that yielded some of the least surprising conclusions ever reported to the plenary session of any conference or to any occupant of the White House.

If one wishes to think of the conference itself as a reflection of the present situation in public rhetoric and private thinking about education in America, the place assigned to teacher education at the conference was about what it is everywhere else. That is to say, it is put off to one side and dealt with perfunctorily, as if its major questions had all been answered by a call for more academic preparation, better practice-teaching, and a less inhibiting system of accreditation. The direct link between the education of teachers and the going concerns of every sector in American society from the poor and the deprived to the intellectually and financially well-to-do, the direct connection to the major political and social issues of contemporary world society, the direct responsibility for the quality and scope of America's cultural and moral life, have all been missed or ignored.

In short, the education of teachers has been separated from the major intellectual and social forces of contemporary history. It is conceived to be

---

Reprinted from *Saturday Review,* November 20, 1965, pp. 75, 76, 92, 93, with permission of author and publisher.

the acquisition of a skill, a skill in assembling authorized information, distributing it to children and young adults, and testing their ability to receive it and reassemble it.

In fact, it is nothing of the kind. The role of the teacher in any society lies at the heart of its intellectual and social life, and it is through the teacher that each generation comes to terms with its heritage, produces new knowledge, and learns to deal with change. Provided, that is, that the teacher has been well enough educated to act as the transforming element.

The education of teachers is at the nerve center of the whole educational system, and if it fails to function there, the system fails. When we talk about equality of opportunity for all American children we are really talking about an equal chance for every child to be taught by a teacher who understands him, takes his limitations and strengths into account, and has command over a body of knowledge relevant to his teaching and to his place in contemporary society. When we talk about educating the gifted, we are really talking about people who are gifted enough to teach the gifted. When we talk about educational failures and weaknesses we are really talking about failures and weaknesses in teachers and teaching, if teaching is defined as the means through which those who are taught are enabled to learn.

Why, in the face of these facts, which are at the very least self-evident, has the education of teachers never received the attention its massive importance demands?

Mainly, I think, because the public concept of education itself has been too narrow for the large dimension of the task to which it has been assigned. The task is to sustain the spiritual force of a democratic ethos and, at the same time, to create the conditions out of which the millions of children and adults of an expanding society can each make a contribution to the creation of great art, great discovery, great works, great science, and a great society. In a democracy, the welfare of the society rests on its educational system.

But the concept of education held in the public mind and reflected in the practices of the schools is that of a formal training in academic subjects leading toward the achievement of a favorable position in society. Higher education thus becomes a higher form of the same kind of training, leading to a higher position in society. Lower education, or vocational training, is for those whose abilities do not reach to the expert use of language and abstractions, or skill in the academic disciplines, and who will normally occupy a lower place in the society. Those who fit neither vocational nor academic education are left without anything. They drop out, it is said. In reality they are left out.

What is missing in the concept is the idea of education as a liberation of oneself into new levels of intellect and emotion, education as a means of achieving new capacities and insights, which can then become part of the stream of contributions made by the human race in the development of societies and civilizations. The concept contains no call to lend oneself to great enterprises, to become *useful* in the larger sense.

Consequently, the idea of teaching and of the education of teachers has been narrowly conceived to fit a narrow concept, and the teacher is less an intellectual or cultural leader than an agent of social service. He prepares himself, not to serve as an example of man thinking or of man bringing ideas into life, but as man transmitting a curriculum. It follows that his education as a teacher need consist of nothing more than a knowledge of the material in the curriculum which he has learned how to transmit to pupils by studying methods of transmittal and practicing them in a classroom with practice-children.

The education of teachers, or teacher-training, to use its name, is therefore of no great consequence in the public mind. The teacher is a person who is certified as a practitioner of cultural transmission. It is not necessary for his employment that he be a scholar with an intellectual life of his own, nor is it necessary that the people who administer the schools be scholars or even teachers. They are cultural entrepreneurs, responsible to the parents and the community for seeing to it that the cultural transmission occurs properly and that the children become qualified for entry into further education and entry into a congenial place in society.

We will never achieve the goals we seek in education until we alter these concepts and turn again to the truth about teaching, that it is a creative art, a healing art, that it demands for its true accomplishment the qualities of character and intellect that can be gained only by those who are moved to reach out toward them. The beginning point and the secret of the whole undertaking lies in the sense of fulfilment that comes to the one who is able to make an honest act of commitment to a vocation in the true sense of that word, the kind of commitment the poet, the dancer, the painter, the sculptor, the doctor makes when he decides that this is what he must do and what he must be. Once a commitment has been made, the image of oneself as a dancer, a doctor, a scientist, an architect, a teacher, begins to take effect as a goal toward which each separate effort day by day in preparation makes its own contribution. One sets out to become what has been imagined, and the discipline of becoming is then undergone willingly and gladly, in the way the violinist lends himself to the demands of his instrument. The problem with so much of undergraduate education, for the general student and for the teacher, is that it is not undertaken for a purpose; it is not infused with energy by an act of commitment to prepare oneself for carrying out a task of known significance.

It is the sense of commitment to a useful purpose that sustains the Peace Corps volunteer, both in his act of volunteering and his preparation for Peace Corps service. The volunteer is asked to give himself, in whatever his capacity, to the world's task of improving the lot of mankind. His two years of service are a contribution to the sum total of human welfare, and his self-assignment for low pay in difficult conditions is like that of the civil rights worker who leaves his career in college or elsewhere to teach and to work with the Negro in the South. To begin the reformation of teacher education it is necessary to return to the roots of the matter, in the restoration of teaching to its place among vocations.

Until now, we have never mounted a full national attack on the problem of educating teachers, using large resources in money and intellect, no matter what proclamations have been made about the crucial role of education in the national welfare. The universities have left it to the teachers' colleges, the teachers' colleges have now begun to model themselves on the universities and to seek the respectability of not being colleges for teachers. In doing so they have usually given up the idea of teaching as a vocation in favor of the idea of the teacher as a man who has met university requirements. Nor have we ever called upon American youth to take up teaching as a vocation in which all their talents can be used to the full in the cause of American society. We can no longer afford our negligence. The urgency of the present situation demands head-on action, on a large scale.

When I speak of the present situation, I begin with the proposition that the radical social changes of the postwar years have far outrun the ability of the educational system to keep up with them. It is of course true that there is always an organic connection between changes in society that force new demands upon education, which, in turn, by the character of its response, transforms the demands into a series of further changes within the society. If the demands are for more scientists and technologists, who are then produced by the educational system, the mere existence of an expanded body of scientific talent produces new possibilities for change within the society. Except in general terms, certain of the changes can neither be predicted nor controlled; the process of change has a life of its own and throws off events and phenomena that cannot be stopped and that simply must be dealt with.

In the early Fifties, who would have predicted with any confidence that in the middle of the Sixties the major world issue facing America would be the problem of a war in Vietnam and the major domestic question would be a rapidly developing social revolution inspired by the Negro protest movement? Who would have predicted that the major legislation racing through the 1965 Congress would be an extraordinarily far-reaching series of measures having to do with civil rights and education, or that a Southern President whose career had included high school teaching would put education at the top of the national agenda?

Yet the function of education is to anticipate and to give directions to changes that are occurring day by day within world society and its local counterparts, not simply to confirm those changes. The circumstances of contemporary American society are now making extreme demands that the educational system is not ready to meet—demands for an education of quality for those who have until now been deprived of it, demands for the reconstruction of society from top to bottom in order to bring the fruits of an expanding economy in a post-industrial era to all American citizens. The dimensions of the reconstruction reach from establishment of equality in economic and social opportunity to the enrichment of the cultural and esthetic life of all citizens.

When we look for the sources of new ideas in education to meet these needs, we find them more often among the energetic and concerned activists of government, busy with new plans and new legislation, and among the activist college students, than we do in the ranks of the educators. In fact, few people outside government have come to understand the enormous power for educational and social change that lies in the new federal legislation. It is jammed with educational provisions, not merely in the clauses of the Elementary and Secondary School Act, but in the Community Action program of the Civil Rights Bill, the Economic Opportunity Act with its Job Training Centers, the Domestic Service Corps, VISTA, Head Start, the Peace Corps.

Although it has never been fully described, there is a social and educational philosophy implicit in the legislation that holds the seeds of a powerful new educational movement. The Anti-Poverty Program and the Peace Corps movement are a call to public service; the funds provided by the legislation are merely the catalyst for voluntary effort. A power for action through this legislation lies in the deep strain of voluntarism and individualism in American life out of which have come the thousands of voluntary organizations to deal with everything from protecting animals and children to directing American foreign policy. It also lies in the progressive tradition of social thinking that has its roots in Emerson, Horace Mann, John Dewey and others—the idea of participatory democracy, indigenous leadership, activism, pluralism, experimentalism, with the test of an idea to be found in the way it works in practice.

It is this power that must now be used in joining the forces of social change in a frontal attack on the problem of educating teachers. We have already seen the power at work in the student movement in civil rights through which dozens of new programs in education, both for teachers and for children, have emerged in the Freedom Schools established by students and in the adult education programs that they have organized as part of voter-registration projects. The students from the North, the West, and the Midwest who in these past three years have volunteered for service in the rural South and in the slums of big cities found themselves immediately faced with all the problems of education as soon as they joined the movement. In one sense the student movement became one vast program in teacher education, in which the student volunteers were forced to educate themselves, to invent their own teaching methods, write their own mimeographed texts, organize their own classes, create their own curricula, and motivate their students while surrounded by a hostile and potentially dangerous white community.

As they joined forces with the young Southern Negroes whose education had either been interrupted or had never begun, the white college students began to see ways in which college study, if it were made relevant to actual conditions within American and world society, could become an essential component in the development of political awareness and social action. Knowledge was seen as something necessary to the achievement of broad social goals. In some cases the students developed new work-study programs and proposals for their own education that were accepted by colleges and universities on their return there; in other cases they called upon faculty members in schools of education and universities for special help in teaching courses and seminars on the spot to the Southern students, Negro and white.

In a comparable way, the experience of the Peace Corps volunteer abroad could be classified as a program in teacher education through which he learns to use his wits to find the ways of being useful to the community he serves. He may not be teaching a school subject, although in many cases he is thrust into service as an English or science teacher whether he has been prepared for it or not, but whatever he does abroad is an aspect of the task of teachers—to help a community to help itself.

We have here the concept and the elements for a radical reform in the education of the American teacher. The reform starts with an exact reversal of the philosophy dominant in present programs. That is to say, rather than thinking of the number of courses, credits, and subjects necessary to certify a teacher, we set aside all formal requirements and start from the beginning with the question of what is to be done to enhance the personal and intellectual growth of the person who is learning to be a teacher.

One of the first things we would then do is invite all those students who have done volunteer service in the rural and urban slums to come into the schools of education and the universities to work out fresh and interesting programs of study and experience through which they could prepare to become members of the teaching profession. A general invitation would be made to all other interested youths to join in a national recruitment of teachers backed by state and federal scholarships.

For those interested in social science or literature or biology or sculpture, arrangements would be made for work in depth in the field of their concern, regardless of whether or not they intended to teach in it. Each student would be asked to work out a tentative study plan for his first two years, identifying the areas of study he proposes for his own education and the reasons he has chosen them. Each would be asked to suggest an appropriate program of field work for himself, either in a nonresident term or year devoted to the civil rights movements, Vista, counseling, or elsewhere in government or private social welfare programs. Each would be asked to choose one of the creative arts in which to engage himself for a time, to suggest possibilities for foreign travel, work, and study of the kind developed through the Experiment in International Living.

Direct relations would be established between federal and state agencies responsible for various parts of the Anti-poverty program and social welfare legislation, to discover how students preparing to become teachers could work directly in the programs as part of their curriculum. Other arrangements would be made with the Peace Corps for a variety of programs similar to the five-year Peace Corps curriculum at Western Michigan University, which includes two years of overseas duty as part of the degree requirements. Direct arrangements would be made with slum schools in all the major cities for the placement of teams of student-teachers who would serve the teachers and children there as tutors, assistants, apprentices, and recreation leaders for three to six months at a time.

In other words, starting from a base in a concern for the total development of each teacher, the university or school of education would work with him to put together an individual program of experience and study that placed a major responsibility on the student himself for choice and decision about the content of his own education. His preparation might take four years or five, depending on the length of time that seemed appropriate for the various stretches of work and study. His experience in preparation would naturally include direct work with children in subjects that he had mastered at a respectable intellectual level.

But that kind of experience could start even before college, when the teacher-candidate was in high school, through tutoring assignments in nearby elementary schools after hours, or through experience in leading seminars, discussions, and tutorials in the high school, provided his talents had developed sufficiently in that direction. He would also be given the chance to teach his peers in his university classes as well as to share in the development of new courses in collaboration with the faculty, using materials from his own research and field work experience. It would be an education in which everyone taught everyone else, since, in a reformed program of teacher education, the major part of the instruction would be through student-run seminars, tutorials, independent study, and discussion. How else could a teacher learn what it means to teach?

Students of foreign language and of foreign cultures would travel abroad for their field periods, and new international centers would be started on a number of campuses to which would be invited foreign students and foreign teachers in large numbers for the express purpose of joining in the teacher-preparation programs. Foreign and American students would work in teams, preparing, in the case of Latin American students for example, to work together for voluntary service in Latin America and in the United States. Soviet and Eastern European students could be invited to attend the international centers to act as teaching assistants in foreign languages and literature, and to prepare for volunteer service both here and at home.

The first step toward the larger support of teacher education has already been taken by President Johnson in legislation proposed for recruiting experienced teachers for work in deprived areas, for financing experimental projects in teacher education, and for financing the education of teachers through national and state fellowships. If the invitation from Congress and the President to experiment in teacher education were taken up by the colleges and universities, and a national program of reform of the present system were to begin through such experiments, a large-scale attack on the problem would then find its support in the power of the social changes now moving through the world of the poor and the deprived. The intention of the President and his Administration is very clear. The President aims to develop the pent-up resources of the American people through a continually expanding program of education, and what we have seen this last year is just a beginning. Educational expansion can go only as far as the teachers can take it.

What becomes of what has been so highly regarded as the major problem of the education of teachers, the problem of their certification? It slips back into its rightful place as a technical matter connected with record-keeping. There is no reason why students preparing to become teachers should not enjoy serious and sustained work in the history, psychology, and philosophy of education, and learn something about its methods by work-study programs and practice-teaching in Venezuela, Iran, Bakersfield, or Selma. There is no reason why responsible universities and colleges cannot bestow the correct number of credits on their students for work in these fields when it satisfies the requirements of honesty, integrity, intellectual achievement, and educational experience. There is no reason why we cannot begin again, with bigger conceptions than we have ever had in our history, the historical task of raising the level of democratic society by raising the level of its education.

DISCUSSION QUESTIONS

1. Taylor argues that "The role of the teacher in any society lies at the heart of its intellectual and social life." From this premise, who shall be the teachers in our schools? How shall they be recruited? How rewarded?
2. To what extent is our narrow and constricted view of teaching an outcome of our vision of the role of education in the social order?
3. How can teacher education become the "personal and intellectual growth of the person who is learning to be a teacher" instead of the present acquisition of courses and credits?
4. Evaluate Taylor's design for the preparation of teachers.

CARL R. ROGERS

The Interpersonal Relationship in the Facilitation of Learning

. . . It is in fact nothing short of a miracle that the modern methods of instruction have not yet entirely strangled the holy curiosity of inquiry; for this delicate little plant, aside from stimulation, stands mainly in need of freedom; without this it goes to wrack and ruin without fail.

Albert Einstein

I wish to begin this paper with a statement which may seem surprising to some and perhaps offensive to others. It is simply this: Teaching, in my estimation, is a vastly overrated function.

Having made such a statement, I scurry to the dictionary to see if I really mean what I say. Teaching means "to instruct." Personally I am not much interested in instructing another. "To impart knowledge or skill." My reaction is, why not be more efficient, using a book or programmed learning? "To make to know." Here my hackles rise. I have no wish to *make* anyone know something. "To show, guide, direct." As I see it, too many people have been shown, guided, directed. So I come to the conclusion that I *do* mean what I said. Teaching is, for me, a relatively unimportant and vastly overvalued activity.

But there is more in my attitude than this. I have a negative reaction to teaching. Why? I think it is because it raises all the wrong questions. As soon as we focus on teaching, the question arises, what shall we teach? What, from our superior vantage point, does the other person need to know? This raises the ridiculous question of coverage. What shall the course cover? (Here I am acutely aware of the fact that "to cover" means both "to take in" and "to conceal from view," and I believe that most courses admirably achieve both these aims.) This notion of coverage is based on the assumption that what is taught is what is learned; what is presented is what is assimilated. I know of no assumption so obviously untrue. One does not need research to provide evidence that this is false. One needs only to talk with a few students.

But I ask myself, "Am I so prejudiced against teaching that I find no situation in which it is worthwhile?" I immediately think of my experience in Australia only a few months ago. I became much interested in the

Reprinted from Robert R. Leeper (ed.), *Humanizing Education: The Person in the Process,* (Washington, D.C.: Association for Supervision and Curriculum Development, 1967), pp. 1–18, with permission of publisher and author.

Australian aborigine. Here is a group which for more than 20,000 years has managed to live and exist in a desolate environment in which a modern man would perish within a few days. The secret of his survival has been teaching. He has passed on to the young every shred of knowledge about how to find water, about how to track game, about how to kill the kangaroo, about how to find his way through the trackless desert. Such knowledge is conveyed to the young as being *the* way to behave, and any innovation is frowned upon. It is clear that teaching has provided him the way to survive in a hostile and relatively unchanging environment.

Now I am closer to the nub of the question which excites me. Teaching and the imparting of knowledge make sense in an unchanging environment. This is why it has been an unquestioned function for centuries. But if there is one truth about modern man, it is that he lives in an environment which is *continually changing.* The one thing I can be sure of is that the physics which is taught to the present day student will be outdated in a decade. The teaching in psychology will certainly be out of date in 20 years. The so-called "facts of history" depend very largely upon the current mood and temper of the culture. Chemistry, biology, genetics, sociology, are in such flux that a firm statement made today will almost certainly be modified by the time the student gets around to using the knowledge.

We are, in my view, faced with an entirely new situation in education where the goal of education, if we are to survive, is the *facilitation of change and learning.* The only man who is educated is the man who has learned how to learn; the man who has learned how to adapt and change; the man who has realized that no knowledge is secure, that only the process of *seeking* knowledge gives a basis for security. Changingness, a reliance on *process* rather than upon static knowledge, is the only thing that makes any sense as a goal for education in the modern world.

So now with some relief I turn to an activity, a purpose, which really warms me—the *facilitation of learning.* When I have been able to transform a group—and here I mean all the members of a group, myself included—into a community of *learners,* then the excitement has been almost beyond belief. To free curiosity; to permit individuals to go charging off in new directions dictated by their own interests; to unleash curiosity; to open everything to questioning and exploration; to recognize that everything is in process of change—here is an experience I can never forget. I cannot always achieve it in groups with which I am associated but when it is partially or largely achieved then it becomes a never-to-be-forgotten group experience. Out of such a context arise true students, real learners, creative scientists and scholars and practitioners, the kind of individuals who can live in a delicate but ever-changing balance between what is presently known and the flowing, moving, altering, problems and facts of the future.

Here then is a goal to which I can give myself wholeheartedly. I see the facilitation of learning as the aim of education, the way in which we might develop the learning man, the way in which we can learn to live as individuals in process. I see the facilitation of learning as the function which may hold constructive, tentative, changing, process answers to some of the deepest perplexities which beset man today.

But do we know how to achieve this new goal in education, or is it a will-of-the-wisp which sometimes occurs, sometimes fails to occur, and thus offers little real hope? My answer is that we possess a very considerable knowledge of the conditions which encourage self-initiated, significant, experiential, "gut-level" learning by the whole person. We do not frequently see these conditions put into effect because they mean a real revolution in our approach to education and revolutions are not for the timid. But we do find examples of this revolution in action.

We know—and I will briefly describe some of the evidence—that the initiation of such learning rests not upon the teaching skills of the leader, not upon his scholarly knowledge of the field, not upon his curricular planning, not upon his use of audio-visual aids, not upon the programmed learning he utilizes, not upon his lectures and presentations, not upon an abundance of books, though each of these might at one time or another be utilized as an important resource. No, the facilitation of significant learning rests upon certain attitudinal qualities which exist in the personal *relationship* between the facilitator and the learner.

We came upon such findings first in the field of psychotherapy, but increasingly there is evidence which shows that these findings apply in the classroom as well. We find it easier to think that the intensive relationship between therapist and client might possess these qualities, but we are also finding that they may exist in the countless interpersonal interactions (as many as 1,000 per day, as Jackson [1966] has shown) between the teacher and his pupils.

What are these qualities, these attitudes, which facilitate learning? Let me describe them very briefly, drawing illustrations from the teaching field.

REALNESS IN THE FACILITATOR OF LEARNING

Perhaps the most basic of these essential attitudes is realness or genuineness. When the facilitator is a real person, being what he is, entering into a relationship with the learner without presenting a front or a facade, he is much more likely to be effective. This means that the feelings which he is experiencing are available to him, available to his awareness, that he is able to live these feelings, be them, and able to communicate them if appropriate. It means that he comes into a direct personal encounter with the learner, meeting him on a person-to-person basis. It means that he is *being* himself, not denying himself.

Seen from this point of view it is suggested that the teacher can be a real person in his relationship with his students. He can be enthusiastic, he can be bored, he can be interested in students, he can be angry, he can be sensitive and sympathetic. Because he accepts these feelings as his own he has no need to impose them on his students. He can like or dislike a student product without implying that it is objectively good or bad or that the student is good or bad. He is simply expressing a feeling for the product, a feeling which exists within himself. Thus, he is a person to his students, not a faceless embodiment of a curricular requirement nor a sterile tube through which knowledge is passed from one generation to the next.

It is obvious that this attitudinal set, found to be effective in psychotherapy, is sharply in contrast with the tendency of most teachers to show themselves to their pupils simply as roles. It is quite customary for teachers rather consciously to put on the mask, the role, the facade, of being a teacher, and to wear this facade all day removing it only when they have left the school at night.

But not all teachers are like this. Take Sylvia Ashton-Warner, who took resistant, supposedly slow-learning primary school Maori children in New Zealand, and let them develop their own reading vocabulary. Each child could request one word—whatever word he wished—each day, and she would print it on a card and give it to him. "Kiss," "ghost," "bomb," "tiger," "fight," "love," "daddy"—these are samples. Soon they were building sentences, which they could also keep. "He'll get a licking." "Pussy's frightened." The children simply never forgot these self-initiated learnings. Yet it is not my purpose to tell you of her methods. I want instead to give you a glimpse of her attitude, of the passionate realness which must have been as evident to her tiny pupils as to her readers. An editor asked her some questions and she responded: " 'A few cool facts' you asked me for. . . . I don't know that there's a cool fact in me, or anything else cool for that matter, on this particular subject. I've got only hot long facts on the matter of Creative Teaching, scorching both the page and me" (Ashton-Warner, 1963, p. 26).

Here is no sterile facade. Here is a vital *person,* with convictions, with feelings. It is her transparent realness which was, I am sure, one of the elements that made her an exciting facilitator of learning. She does not fit into some neat educational formula. She *is,* and students grow by being in contact with someone who really *is.*

Take another very different person, Barbara Shiel, also doing exciting work facilitating learning in sixth graders.[1] She gave them a great deal of responsible freedom, and I will mention some of the reactions of her students later. But here is an example of the way she shared herself with her pupils—not just sharing feelings of sweetness and light, but anger and

---

[1] For a more extended account of Miss Shiel's initial attempts, see Rogers, 1966a. Her later experience is described in Shiel, 1966.

frustration. She had made art materials freely available, and students often used these in creative ways, but the room frequently looked like a picture of chaos. Here is her report of her feelings and what she did with them.

I find it (still) maddening to live with the mess—with a capital M! No one seems to care except me. Finally, one day I told the children . . . that I am a neat, orderly person by nature and that the mess was driving me to distraction. Did they have a solution? It was suggested they could have volunteers to clean up. . . . I said it didn't seem fair to me to have the same people clean up all the time for others—but it *would* solve it for me. "Well, some people *like* to clean," they replied. So that's the way it is (Shiel, 1966).

I hope this example puts some lively meaning into the phrases I used earlier, that the facilitator "is able to live these feelings, be them, and able to communicate them if appropriate." I have chosen an example of negative feelings, because I think it is more difficult for most of us to visualize what this would mean. In this instance, Misss Shiel is taking the risk of being transparent in her angry frustrations about the mess. And what happens? The same thing which, in my experience, nearly always happens. These young people accept and respect her feelings, take them into account, and work out a novel solution which none of us, I believe, would have suggested in advance. Miss Shiel wisely comments, "I used to get upset and feel guilty when I became angry—I finally realized the children could accept *my* feelings, too. And it is important for them to know when they've 'pushed me.' I have limits, too" (Shiel, 1966).

Just to show that positive feelings, when they are real, are equally effective, let me quote briefly a college student's reaction, in a different course. ". . . Your sense of humor in the class was cheering; we all felt relaxed because you showed us your human self, not a mechanical teacher image. I feel as if I have more understanding and faith in my teachers now. . . . I feel closer to the students too." Another says, ". . . You conducted the class on a personal level and therefore in my mind I was able to formulate a picture of you as a person and not as merely a walking textbook." Or another student in the same course,

. . . It wasn't as if there was a teacher in the class, but rather someone whom we could trust and identify as a "sharer." You were so perceptive and sensitive to our thoughts, and this made it all the more "authentic" for me. It was an "authentic" *experience,* not just a class (Bull, 1966).

I trust I am making it clear that to be real is not always easy, nor is it achieved all at once, but it is basic to the person who wants to become that revolutionary individual, a facilitator of learning.

PRIZING, ACCEPTANCE, TRUST

There is another attitude which stands out in those who are successful in facilitating learning. I have observed this attitude. I have experienced it.

Yet, it is hard to know what term to put to it so I shall use several. I think of it as prizing the learner, prizing his feelings, his opinions, his person. It is a caring for the learner, but a non-possessive caring. It is an acceptance of this other individual as a separate person, having worth in his own right. It is a basic trust—a belief that this other person is somehow fundamentally trustworthy.

Whether we call it prizing, acceptance, trust, or by some other term, it shows up in a variety of observable ways. The facilitator who has a considerable degree of this attitude can be fully acceptant of the fear and hesitation of the student as he approaches a new problem as well as acceptant of the pupil's satisfaction in achievement. Such a teacher can accept the student's occasional apathy, his erratic desires to explore byroads of knowledge, as well as his disciplined efforts to achieve major goals. He can accept personal feelings which both disturb and promote learning—rivalry with a sibling, hatred of authority, concern about personal adequacy. What we are describing is a prizing of the learner as an imperfect human being with many feelings, many potentialities. The facilitator's prizing or acceptance of the learner is an operational expression of his essential confidence and trust in the capacity of the human organism.

I would like to give some examples of this attitude from the classroom situation. Here any teacher statements would be properly suspect, since many of us would like to feel we hold such attitudes, and might have a biased perception of our qualities. But let me indicate how this attitude of prizing, of accepting, of trusting, appears to the student who is fortunate enough to experience it.

Here is a statement from a college student in a class with Morey Appell.

> Your way of being with us is a revelation to me. In your class I feel important, mature, and capable of doing things on my own. I want to think for myself and this need cannot be accomplished through textbooks and lectures alone, but through living. I think you see me as a person with real feelings and needs, an individual. What I say and do are significant expressions from me, and you recognize this (Appell, 1959).

One of Miss Shiel's sixth graders expresses much more briefly her misspelled appreciation of this attitude, "You are a wounderful teacher period!!!"

College students in a class with Dr. Patricia Bull describe not only these prizing, trusting attitudes, but the effect these have had on their other interactions.

> . . . I feel that I can say things to you that I can't say to other professors . . . Never before have I been so aware of the other students or their personalities. I have never had so much interaction in a college classroom with my classmates. The climate of the classroom has had a very profound effect on me . . . the free atmosphere for discussion affected me . . . the general atmosphere of a particular session affected me. There have been many times when I have carried the discussion out of the class with me and thought about it for a long time.

. . . I still feel close to you, as though there were some tacit understanding between us, almost a conspiracy. This adds to the in-class participation on my part because I feel that at least one person in the group will react, even when I am not sure of the others. It does not matter really whether your reaction is positive or negative, it just *is*. Thank you.

. . . I appreciate the respect and concern you have for others, including myself. . . . As a result of my experience in class, plus the influence of my readings, I sincerely believe that the student-centered teaching method does provide an ideal framework for learning; not just for the accumulation of facts, but more important, for learning about ourselves in relation to others. . . . When I think back to my shallow awareness in September compared to the depth of my insights now, I know that this course has offered me a learning experience of great value which I couldn't have acquired in any other way.

. . . Very few teachers would attempt this method because they would feel that they would lose the students' respect. On the contrary. You gained our respect, through your ability to speak to us on our level, instead of ten miles above us. With the complete lack of communication we see in this school, it was a wonderful experience to see people listening to each other and really communicating on an adult, intelligent level. More classes should afford us this experience (Bull, 1966).

As you might expect, college students are often suspicious that these seeming attitudes are phony. One of Dr. Bull's students writes:

. . . Rather than observe my classmates for the first few weeks, I concentrated my observations on you, Dr. Bull. I tried to figure out your motivations and purposes. I was convinced that you were a hypocrite. . . . I did change my opinion, however. You are not a hypocrite, by any means. . . . I do wish the course could continue. "Let each become all he is capable of being." . . . Perhaps my most disturbing question, which relates to this course is: When will we stop hiding things from ourselves and our contemporaries? (Bull, 1966).

I am sure these examples are more than enough to show that the facilitator who cares, who prizes, who trusts the learner, creates a climate for learning so different from the ordinary classroom that any resemblance is, as they say, "purely coincidental."

EMPATHIC UNDERSTANDING

A further element which establishes a climate for self-initiated, experiential learning is empathic understanding. When the teacher has the ability to understand the student's reactions from the inside, has a sensitive awareness of the way the process of education and learning seems *to the student,* then again the likelihood of significant learning is increased.

This kind of understanding is sharply different from the usual evaluative understanding, which follows the pattern of, "I understand what is wrong with you." When there is a sensitive empathy, however, the reaction in the learner follows something of this pattern, "At last someone understands how it feels and seems to be *me* without wanting to analyze me or judge me. Now I can blossom and grow and learn."

This attitude of standing in the other's shoes, of viewing the world through the student's eyes, is almost unheard of in the classroom. One could listen to thousands of ordinary classroom interactions without coming across one instance of clearly communicated, sensitively accurate, empathic understanding. But it has a tremendously releasing effect when it occurs.

Let me take an illustration from Virginia Axline, dealing with a second grade boy. Jay, age 7, has been aggressive, a trouble maker, slow of speech and learning. Because of his "cussing" he was taken to the principal, who paddled him, unknown to Miss Axline. During a free work period, he fashioned a man of clay, very carefully, down to a hat and a handkerchief in his pocket. "Who is that?" asked Miss Axline. "Dunno," replied Jay. "Maybe it is the principal. He has a handkerchief in his pocket like that." Jay glared at the clay figure. "Yes," he said. Then he began to tear the head off and looked up and smiled. Miss Axline said, "You sometimes feel like twisting his head off, don't you? You get so mad at him." Jay tore off one arm, another, then beat the figure to a pulp with his fists. Another boy, with the perception of the young, explained, "Jay is mad at Mr. X because he licked him this noon." "Then you must feel lots better now," Miss Axline commented. Jay grinned and began to rebuild Mr. X. (Adapted from Axline, 1944.)

The other examples I have cited also indicate how deeply appreciative students feel when they are simply *understood*—not evaluated, not judged, simply understood from their *own* point of view, not the teacher's. If any teacher set herself the task of endeavoring to make one non-evaluative, acceptant, empathic response per day to a pupil's demonstrated or verbalized feeling, I believe he would discover the potency of this currently almost nonexistent kind of understanding.

Let me wind up this portion of my remarks by saying that when a facilitator creates, even to a modest degree, a classroom climate characterized by such realness, prizing, and empathy, he discovers that he has inaugurated an educational revolution. Learning of a different quality, proceeding at a different pace, with a greater degree of pervasiveness, occurs. Feelings—positive and negative, confused—become a part of the classroom experience. Learning becomes life, and a very vital life at that. The student is on his way, sometimes excitedly, sometimes reluctantly, to becoming a learning, changing being.

THE EVIDENCE

Already I can hear the mutterings of some of my so-called "hard-headed" colleagues. "A very pretty picture—very touching. But these are all self reports." (As if there were any other type of expression! But that's another issue.) They ask, "Where is the evidence? How do you know?" I would like to turn to this evidence. It is not overwhelming, but it is consistent. It is not perfect, but it is suggestive.

First of all, in the field of psychotherapy, Barrett-Lennard (1962) developed an instrument whereby he could measure these attitudinal qualities: genuineness or congruence, prizing or positive regard, empathy or understanding. This instrument was given to both client and therapist, so that we have the perception of the relationship both by the therapist and by the client whom he is trying to help. To state some of the findings very briefly it may be said that those clients who eventually showed more therapeutic change as measured by various instruments, perceived *more* of these qualities in their relationship with the therapist than did those who eventually showed less change. It is also significant that this difference in perceived relationships was evident as early as the fifth interview, and predicted later change or lack of change in therapy. Furthermore, it was found that the *client's* perception of the relationship, his experience of it, was a better predictor of ultimate outcome than was the perception of the relationship by the therapist. Barrett-Lennard's original study has been amplified and generally confirmed by other studies.

So we may say, cautiously, and with qualifications which would be too cumbersome for the present paper, that if, in therapy, the client perceives his therapist as real and genuine, as one who likes, prizes, and empathically understands him, self-learning and therapeutic change are facilitated.

Now another thread of evidence, this time related more closely to education. Emmerling (1961) found that when high school teachers were asked to identify the problems they regarded as most urgent, they could be divided into two groups. Those who regarded their most serious problems, for example, as "Helping children think for themselves and be independent"; "Getting students to participate"; "Learning new ways of helping students develop their maximum potential"; "Helping students express individual needs and interests"; fell into what he called the "open" or "positively oriented" group. When Barrett-Lennard's Relationship Inventory was administered to the students of these teachers, it was found that they were perceived as significantly more real, more acceptant, more empathic than the other group of teachers whom I shall now describe.

The second category of teachers were those who tended to see their most urgent problems in negative terms, and in terms of student deficiencies and inabilities. For them the urgent problems were such as these: "Trying to teach children who don't even have the ability to follow directions"; "Teaching children who lack a desire to learn"; "Students who are not able to do the work required for their grade"; "Getting the children to listen." It probably will be no surprise that when the students of these teachers filled out the Relationship Inventory they saw their teachers as exhibiting relatively little of genuineness, of acceptance and trust, or of empathic understanding.

Hence we may say that the teacher whose orientation is toward releasing the student's potential exhibits a high degree of these attitudinal qualities which facilitate learning. The teacher whose orientation is toward the shortcomings of his students exhibits much less of these qualities.

A small pilot study by Bills (1961, 1966) extends the significance of these findings. A group of eight teachers was selected, four of them rated as adequate and effective by their superiors, and also showing this more positive orientation to their problems. The other four were rated as inadequate teachers and also had a more negative orientation to their problems, as described above. The students of these teachers were then asked to fill out the Barrett-Lennard Relationship Inventory, giving their perception of their teacher's relationship to them. This made the students very happy. Those who saw their relationship with the teacher as good were happy to describe this relationship. Those who had an unfavorable relationship were pleased to have, for the first time, an opportunity to specify the ways in which the relationship was unsatisfactory.

The more effective teachers were rated higher in every attitude measured by the Inventory: they were seen as more real, as having a higher level of regard for their students, were less conditional or judgmental in their attitudes, showed more empathic understanding. Without going into the details of the study it may be illuminating to mention that the total scores summing these attitudes vary sharply. For example, the relationships of a group of clients with their therapists, as perceived by the clients, received an average score of 108. The four most adequate high school teachers as seen by their students, received a score of 60. The four less adequate teachers received a score of 34. The lowest rated teacher received an average score of 2 from her students on the Relationship Inventory.

This small study certainly suggests that the teacher regarded as effective displays in her attitudes those qualities I have described as facilitative of learning, while the inadequate teacher shows little of these qualities.

Approaching the problem from a different angle, Schmuck (1963) has shown that in classrooms where pupils perceive their teachers as understanding them, there is likely to be a more diffuse liking structure among the pupils. This means that where the teacher is empathic, there are not a few students strongly liked and a few strongly disliked, but liking and affection are more evenly diffused throughout the group. In a later study he has shown that among students who are highly involved in their classroom peer group, "significant relationships exist between actual liking status on the one hand and utilization of abilities, attitude toward self, and attitude toward school on the other hand" (1966, p. 357–58). This seems to lend confirmation to the other evidence by indicating that in an understanding classroom climate every student tends to feel liked by all the others, to have a more positive attitude toward himself and toward school. If he is highly involved with his peer group (and this appears probable in such a classroom climate), he also tends to utilize his abilities more fully in his school achievement.

But you may still ask, does the student actually *learn* more where these attitudes are present? Here an interesting study of third graders by Aspy (1965) helps to round out the suggestive evidence. He worked in six third-grade classes. The teachers tape-recorded two full weeks of their interaction with their students in the periods devoted to the teaching of reading. These recordings were done two months apart so as to obtain an adequate sampling of the teacher's interactions with her pupils. Four-minute segments of these recordings were randomly selected for rating. Three raters, working independently and "blind," rated each segment for the degree of congruence or genuineness shown by the teacher, the degree of her prizing or unconditional positive regard, and the degree of her empathic understanding.

The Reading Achievement Tests (Stanford Achievement) were used as the criterion. Again, omitting some of the details of a carefully and rigorously controlled study, it may be said that the children in the three classes with the highest degree of the attitudes described above showed a significantly greater gain in reading achievement than those students in the three classes with a lesser degree of these qualities.

So we may say, with a certain degree of assurance, that the attitudes I have endeavored to describe are not only effective in facilitating a deeper learning and understanding of self in a relationship such as psychotherapy, but that these attitudes characterize teachers who are regarded as effective teachers, and that the students of these teachers learn more, even of a conventional curriculum, than do students of teachers who are lacking in these attitudes.

I am pleased that such evidence is accumulating. It may help to justify the revolution in education for which I am obviously hoping. But the most striking learnings of students exposed to such a climate are by no means restricted to greater achievement in the three R's. The significant learnings are the more personal ones—independence, self-initiated and responsible learning; release of creativity, a tendency to become more of a person. I can only illustrate this by picking, almost at random, statements from students whose teachers have endeavored to create a climate of trust, of prizing, of realness, of understanding, and above all, of freedom.

Again I must quote from Sylvia Ashton-Warner one of the central effects of such a climate.

> . . . The drive is no longer the teacher's, but the children's own. . . . The teacher is at last with the stream and not against it, the stream of children's inexorable creativeness (Ashton-Warner, p. 93).

If you need verification of this, listen to a few of Dr. Bull's sophomore students. The first two are mid-semester comments.

. . . This course is proving to be a vital and profound experience for me. . . . This unique learning situation is giving me a whole new conception of just what learning is. . . . I am experiencing a real growth in this atmosphere of constructive freedom. . . . The whole experience is very challenging. . . .

. . . I feel that the course has been of great value to me. . . . I'm glad to have had this experience because it has made me think. . . . I've never been so personally involved with a course before, especially *outside* the classroom. It's been frustrating, rewarding, enjoyable and tiring!

The other comments are from the end of the course.

. . . This course is not ending with the close of the semester for me, but continuing. . . . I don't know of any greater benefit which can be gained from a course than this desire for further knowledge. . . .

. . . I feel as though this type of class situation has stimulated me more in making me realize where my responsibilities lie, especially as far as doing required work on my own. I no longer feel as though a test date is the criterion for reading a book. I feel as though my future work will be done for what *I* will get out of it, not just for a test mark.

. . . I have enjoyed the experience of being in this course. I guess that any dissatisfaction I feel at this point is a disappointment in myself, for not having taken full advantage of the opportunities the course offered.

. . . I think that now I am acutely aware of the breakdown in communications that does exist in our society from seeing what happened in our class. . . . I've grown immensely. I know that I am a different person than I was when I came into that class. . . . It has done a great deal in helping me understand myself better. . . . Thank you for contributing to my growth.

. . . My idea of education has been to gain information from the teacher by attending lectures. The emphasis and focus were on the teacher. . . . One of the biggest changes that I experienced in this class was my outlook on education. Learning is something more than a grade on a report card. No one can measure what you have learned because it's a personal thing. I was very confused between learning and memorization. I could memorize very well, but I doubt if I ever learned as much as I could have. I believe my attitude toward learning has changed from a grade-centered outlook to a more personal one.

. . . I have learned a lot more about myself and adolescents in general. . . . I also gained more confidence in myself and my study habits by realizing that I could learn by myself without a teacher leading me by the hand. I have also learned a lot by listening to my classmates and evaluating their opinions and thoughts. . . . This course has proved to be a most meaningful and worthwhile experience. . . . (Bull, 1966).

If you wish to know what this type of course seems like to a sixth grader, let me give you a sampling of the reactions of Miss Shiel's youngsters, misspellings and all.

. . . I feel that I am learning self ability. I am learning not only school work but I am learning that you can learn on your own as well as someone can teach you.

. . . I have a little trouble in Social Studies finding things to do. I have a hard time working the exact amount of time. Sometimes I talk to much.

. . . My parents don't understand the program. My mother say's it will give me a responsibility and it will let me go at my own speed.

. . . I like this plan because thire is a lot of freedom. I also learn more this way than the other way you don't have to wate for others you can go at your on speed rate it also takes a lot of responsibility (Shiel, 1966).

Or let me take two more, from Dr. Appell's graduate class.

. . . I have been thinking about what happened through this experience. The only conclusion I come to is that if I try to measure what is going on, or what I was at the beginning, I have got to know what I was when I started—and I don't. . . . So many things I did and feel are just lost . . . scrambled up inside. . . . They don't seem to come out in a nice little pattern or organization I can say or write. . . . There are so many things left unsaid. I know I have only scratched the surface, I guess. I can feel so many things almost ready to come out . . . maybe that's enough. *It seems all kinds of things have so much more meaning now than ever before. . . .* This experience has had meaning, has done things to me and I am not sure how much or how far just yet. I think I am going to be a better me in the fall. *That's one thing I think I am sure of* (Appell, 1963).

. . . You follow no plan, yet I'm learning. Since the term began I seem to feel more alive, more real to myself. I enjoy being alone as well as with other people. My relationships with children and other adults are becoming more emotional and involved. Eating an orange last week, I peeled the skin off each separate orange section and liked it better with the transparent shell off. It was jucier and fresher tasting that way. I began to think, that's how I feel sometimes, without a transparent wall around me, really communicating my feelings. I feel that I'm growing, how much, I don't know. I'm thinking, considering, pondering and learning (Appell, 1959).

I can't read these student statements—6th grade, college, graduate level—without my eyes growing moist. Here are teachers, risking themselves, *being* themselves, *trusting* their students, adventuring into the existential unknown, taking the subjective leap. And what happens? Exciting, incredible *human* events. You can sense persons being created, learnings being initiated, future citizens rising to meet the challenge of unknown worlds. If only one teacher out of one hundred dared to risk, dared to be, dared to trust, dared to understand, we would have an infusion of a living spirit into education which would, in my estimation, be priceless.

I have heard scientists at leading schools of science, and scholars in leading universities, arguing that it is absurd to try to encourage all students to be creative—we need hosts of mediocre technicians and workers and if a few creative scientists and artists and leaders emerge, that will be enough. That may be enough for them. It may be enough to suit you. I want to go on record as saying it is *not* enough to suit me. When I realize the incredible potential in the ordinary student, I want to try to release it. We are working hard to release the incredible energy in the atom and the nucleus of the atom. If we do not devote equal energy—yes, and equal money—to the release of the potential of the individual person, then the enormous discrepancy between our level of physical energy resources and human energy resources will doom us to a deserved and universal destruction.

I'm sorry I can't be coolly scientific about this. The issue is too urgent. I can only be passionate in my statement that people count, that interpersonal relationships *are* important, that we know something about releasing human potential, that we could learn much more, and that unless we give strong positive attention to the human interpersonal side of our educational dilemma, our civilization is on its way down the drain. Better courses, better curricula, better coverage, better teaching machines, will never resolve our dilemma in a basic way. Only persons, acting like persons in their relationships with their students can even begin to make a dent on this most urgent problem of modern education.

I cannot, of course, stop here in a professional lecture. An academic lecture should be calm, factual, scholarly, critical, preferably devoid of any personal beliefs, completely devoid of passion. (This is one of the reasons I left university life, but that is a completely different story.) I cannot fully fulfill these requirements for a professional lecture, but let me at least try to state, somewhat more calmly and soberly, what I have said with such feeling and passion.

I have said that it is most unfortunate that educators and the public think about, and focus on, *teaching*. It leads them into a host of questions which are either irrelevant or absurd so far as real education is concerned.

I have said that if we focused on the facilitation of *learning*—how, why, and when the student learns, and how learning seems and feels from the inside, we might be on a much more profitable track.

I have said that we have some knowledge, and could gain more, about the conditions which facilitate learning, and that one of the most important of these conditions is the attitudinal quality of the interpersonal relationship between facilitator and learner. (There are other conditions, too, which I have tried to spell out elsewhere [Rogers, 1966b]).

Those attitudes which appear effective in promoting learning can be described. First of all is a transparent realness in the facilitator, a willingness to be a person, to be and to live the feelings and thoughts of the moment. When this realness includes a prizing, a caring, a trust and respect for the learner, the climate for learning is enhanced. When it includes a sensitive and accurate empathic listening, then indeed a freeing climate, stimulative of self-initiated learning and growth, exists.

I have tried to make plain that individuals who hold such attitudes, and are bold enough to act on them, do not simply modify classroom methods—they revolutionize them. They perform almost none of the functions of teachers. It is no longer accurate to call them teachers. They are catalyzers, facilitators, giving freedom and life and the opportunity to learn, to students.

I have brought in the cumulating research evidence which suggests that individuals who hold such attitudes are regarded as effective in the classroom; that the problems which concern them have to do with the release of potential, not the deficiencies of their students; that they seem to create classroom situations in which there are not admired children and disliked children, but in which affection and liking are a part of the life of every child; that in classrooms approaching such a psychological climate, children learn more of the conventional subjects.

But I have intentionally gone beyond the empirical findings to try to take you into the inner life of the student—elementary, college, and graduate—who is fortunate enough to live and learn in such an interpersonal relationship with a facilitator, in order to let you see what learning feels like when it is free, self-initiated and spontaneous. I have tried to indicate how it even changes the student-student relationship—making it more aware, more caring, more sensitive, as well as increasing the self-related learning of significant material.

Throughout my paper I have tried to indicate that if we are to have citizens who can live constructively in this kaleidoscopically changing world, we can *only* have them if we are willing for them to become self-starting, self-initiating learners. Finally, it has been my purpose to show that this kind of learner develops best, so far as we now know, in a growth-promoting, facilitative, relationship with a *person.*

REFERENCES

Appell, M. L. "Selected Student Reactions to Student-centered Courses." Mimeographed manuscript, 1959.

Appell, M. L. "Self-understanding for the Guidance Counselor." *Personnel and Guidance Journal* 42 (2) : 143–48; October 1963.

Ashton-Warner, S. *Teache*r. New York: Simon and Schuster, 1963.

Aspy, D. N. "A Study of Three Facilitative Conditions and Their Relationship to the Achievement of Third Grade Students." Unpublished Ed.D. dissertation, University of Kentucky, 1965.

Axline, Virginia M. "Morale on the School Front." *Journal of Educational Research* 38: 521–33; 1944.

Barrett-Lennard, G. T. "Dimensions of Therapist Response as Causal Factors in Therapeutic Change." *Psychological Monographs,* 76, 1962. (Whole No. 562.)

Bills, R. E. Personal correspondence, 1961, 1966.

Bull, Patricia. Student reactions, Fall 1965. State University College, Cortland, New York. Mimeographed manuscripts, 1966.

Emmerling, F. C. "A Study of the Relationships Between Personality Characteristics of Classroom Teachers and Pupil Perceptions." Unpublished Ph.D. dissertation, Auburn University, Auburn, Alabama. 1961.

Jackson, P. W. "The Student's World." University of Chicago. Mimeographed, 1966.

Rogers, C. R. "To Facilitate Learning." In: Malcolm Provus, editor. NEA Handbook for Teachers, *Innovations for Time To Teach.* Washington, D.C.: Department of Classroom Teachers, NEA, 1966a.

Rogers, C. R. "The Facilitation of Significant Learning." In: L. Siegel, editor. *Contemporary Theories of Instruction.* San Francisco. California: Chandler Publishing Co., 1966b.

Schmuck, R. "Some Aspects of Classroom Social Climate." *Psychology in the Schools* 3: 59–65; 1966.

Schmuck, R. "Some Relationships of Peer Liking Patterns in the Classroom to Pupil Attitudes and Achievement." *The School Review* 71: 337–59; 1963.

Shiel, Barbara J. "Evaluation: A Self-directed Curriculum, 1965." Mimeographed, 1966.

DISCUSSION QUESTIONS

1. Compare Rogers' views on the facilitation of learning with those of Skinner and of Taylor.
2. How do your own learning experiences bear out Rogers' exegesis?
3. Has every child in our schools the right to ask that his teachers respect him, his language, his "style," his background?
4. What changes would be mandated upon our teacher-education institutions were they to become "Rogerian" in outlook and practice?

69707172738 7654321